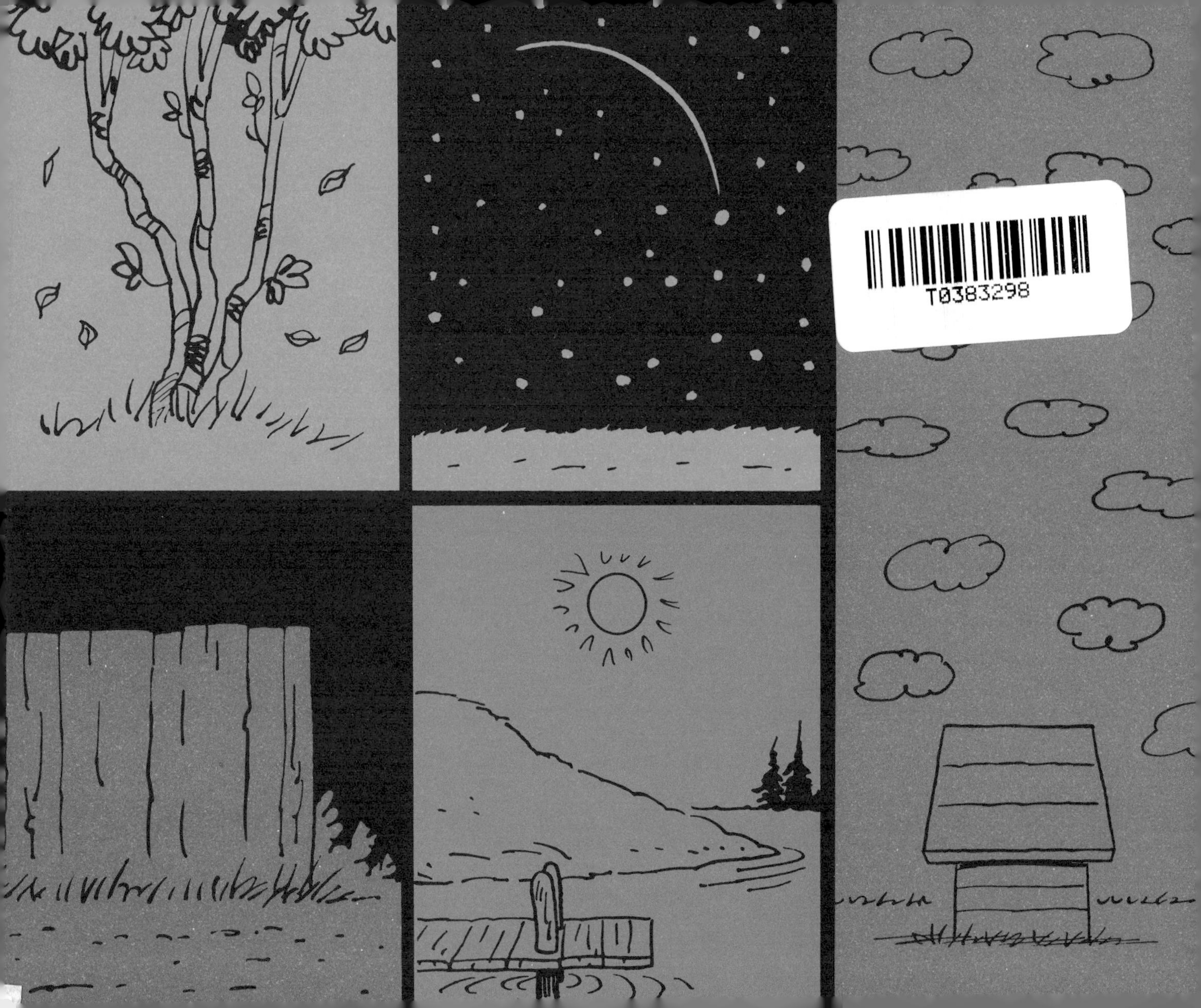

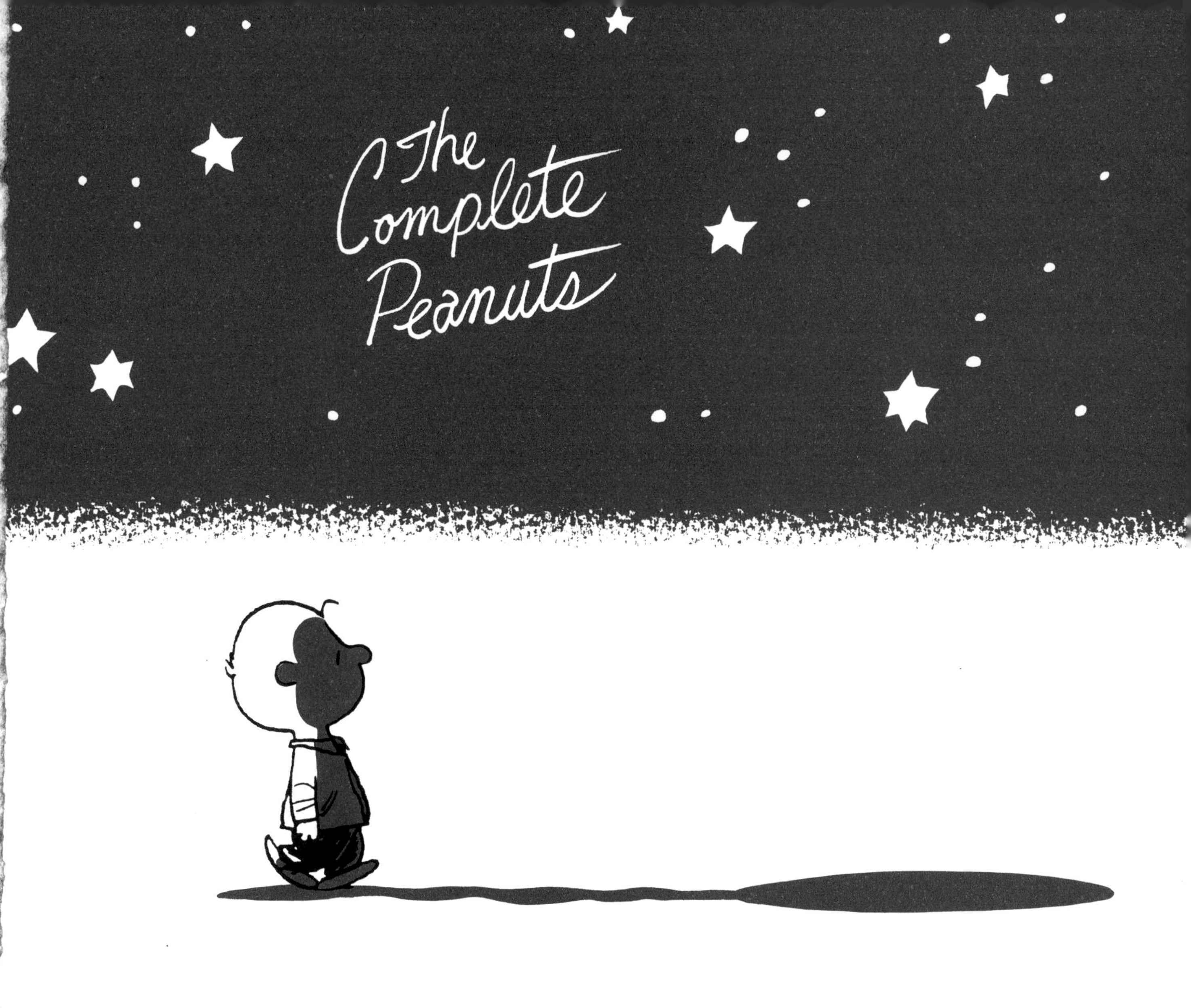
The Complete Peanuts

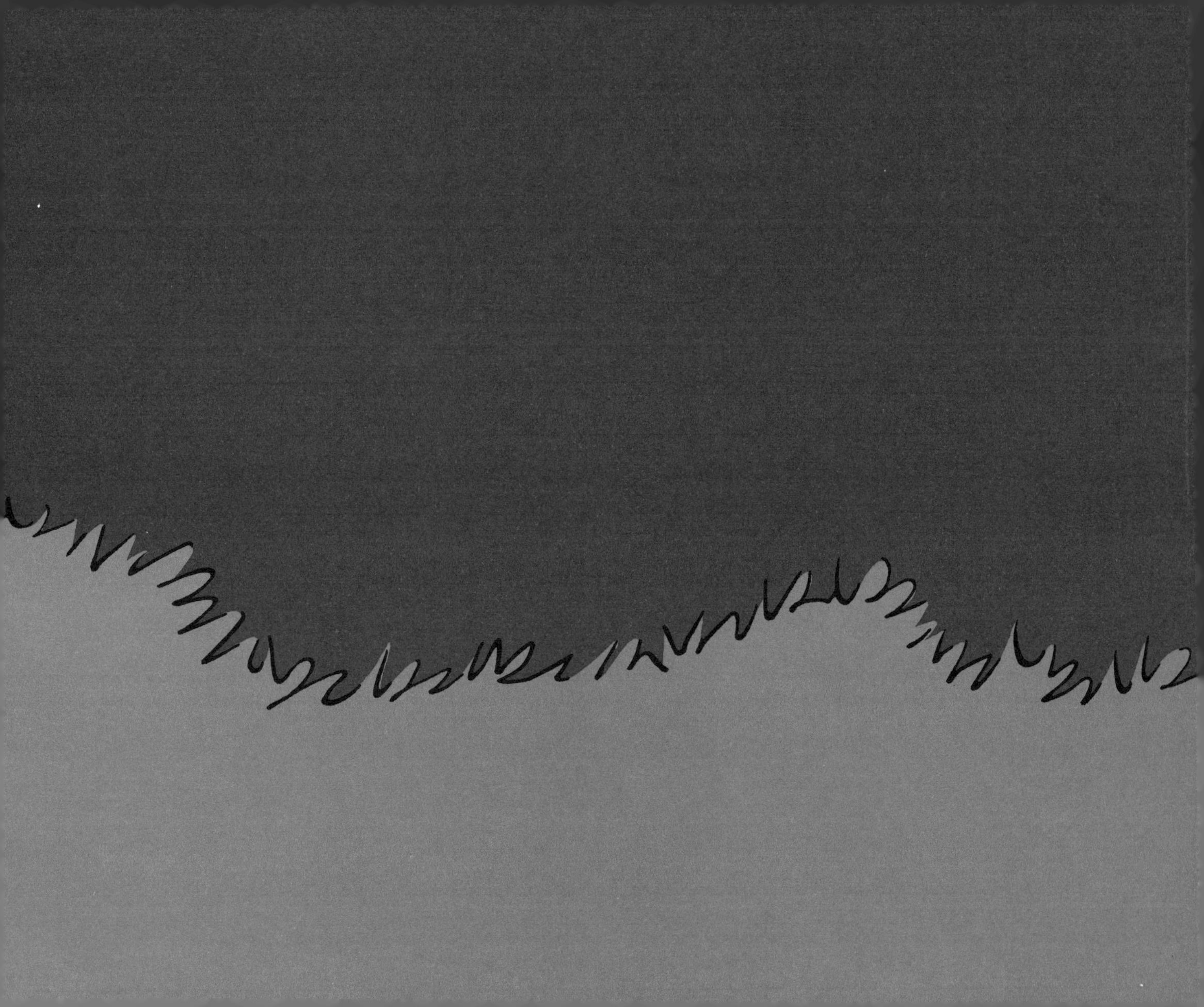

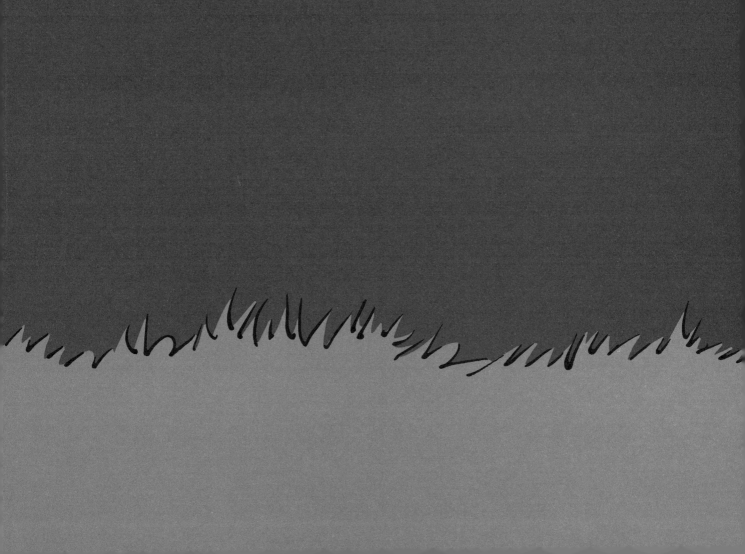

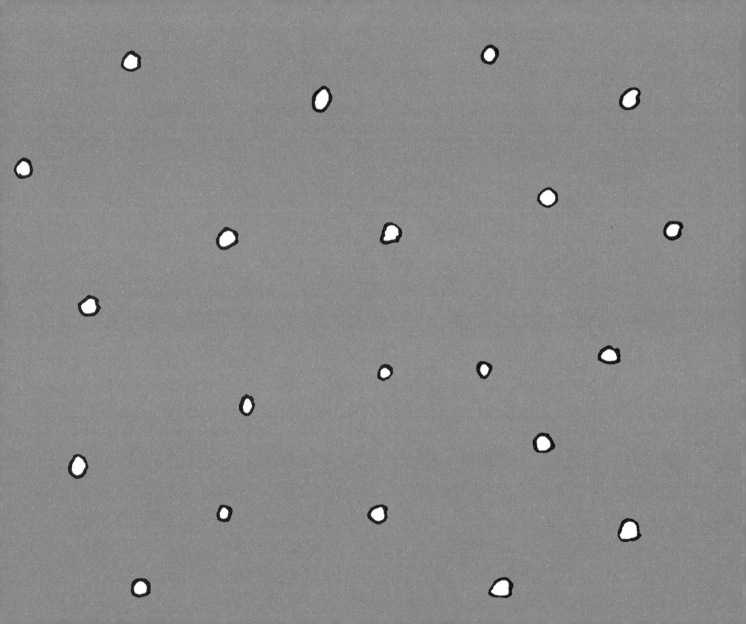

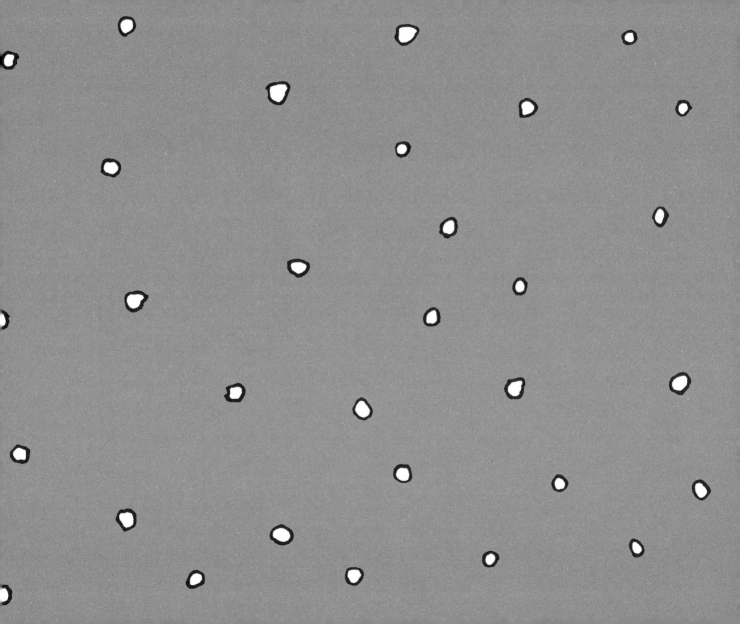

THE COMPLETE PEANUTS
by Charles M. Schulz

Editor: Gary Groth
Designer: Seth
Production Manager: Kim Thompson
Production, assembly and restoration: Paul Baresh
Archival and production assistance: Marcie Lee, Stephanie Hayes and Alexa Koenings
Index compiled by Ben Neusius and Kim Thompson
Publishers: Gary Groth & Kim Thompson

Special thanks to Jeannie Schulz, without whom this project would not have come to fruition.
Thanks to Charles M. Schulz Creative Associates, especially Paige Braddock and Kim Towner.
Thanks for special support from United Media.

First published in America in 2009 by Fantagraphics Books, 7563 Lake City Way, Seattle, WA 98115, USA

First published in Great Britain in 2012 by Canongate Books Ltd, 14 High Street, Edinburgh, EH1 1TE

4

British Library Cataloguing-in-Publication Data
A catalogue record for this book is available on request from the British Library

ISBN 978 0 85786 407 9
Printed and bound in Malaysia

www.canongate.co.uk

CHARLES M. SCHULZ

THE COMPLETE PEANUTS

1971 TO 1972

"LET'S GET BACK TO THOSE
CHILDHOOD PROBLEMS.."

CANONGATE BOOKS

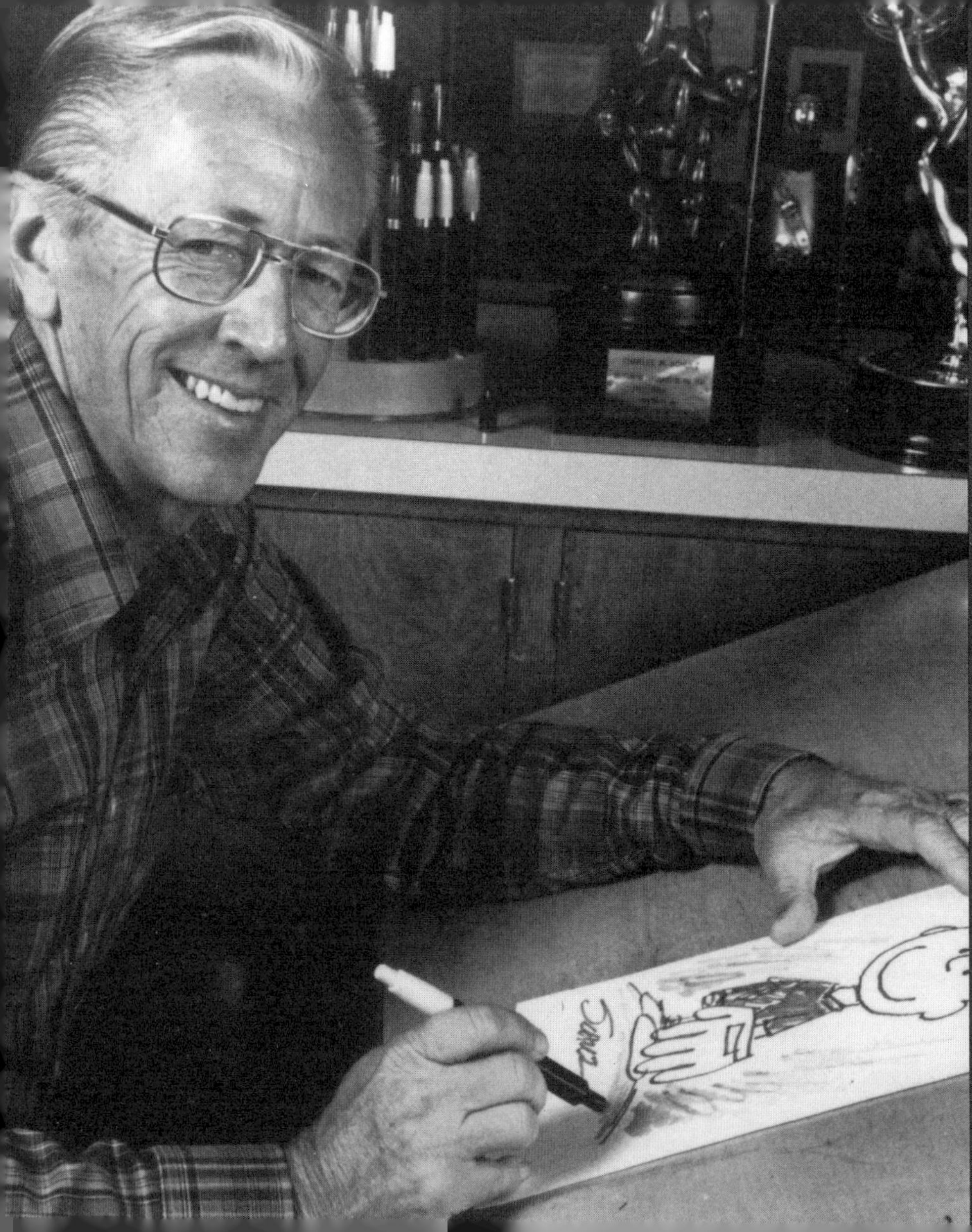

Charles M. Schulz at his drawing board at 1 Snoopy Place, circa 1975. Courtesy of the Schulz Family.

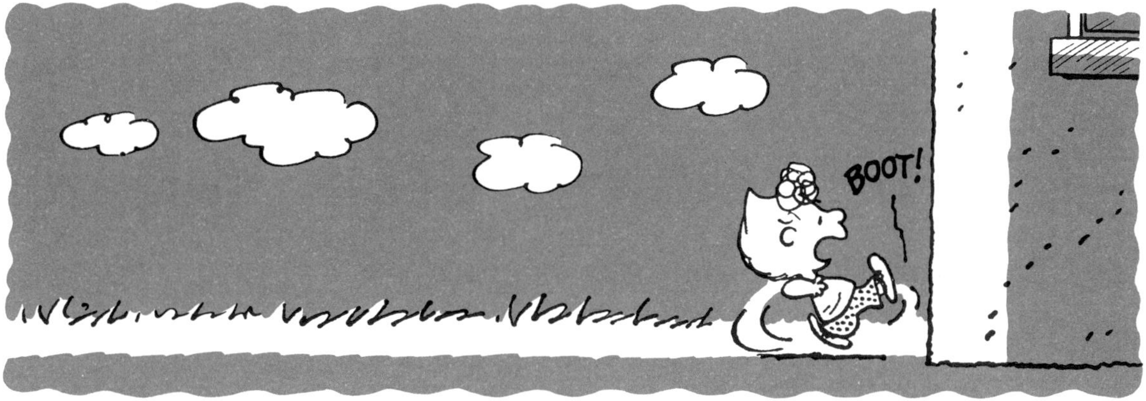
BOOT!

FOREWORD by KRISTIN CHENOWETH

The pint-sized (four feet eleven inches) dynamo Kristin Chenoweth swept the Tony, Drama Desk and Outer Critics Circle Awards with her turbocharged portrayal of Sally Brown in the 1998-1999 revival of the musical You're a Good Man, Charlie Brown. *(The notoriously hard to please drama critic John Simon called her performance "perfection.")*

*Since then she has split her exploding career among the roles of recording artist (two solo CDs), film and television actress (*The West Wing, Pushing Daisies*), and stage actress, including a Tony-nominated run as the original Glinda in* Wicked— *but she maintains a special fondness for her role as Charlie Brown's little sister.*

Ms. Chenoweth took time out from her busy schedule to answer questions about You're a Good Man, Charlie Brown, Peanuts, *and Charles Schulz.*

(To see her perform Sally's signature song "My New Philosophy" go to YouTube and search, using the words "Chenoweth" and "Philosophy." The soundtrack album is also available.)

How did you get the role of Sally in You're a Good Man, Charlie Brown*?*

I had been offered a role in *Annie Get Your Gun* with Bernadette Peters. I then got the appointment to audition for *Charlie Brown*. The director, Michael Mayer, cast me and the rest is history.

Did you read Peanuts *as a child or young girl, and did you feel any special kinship to Sally?*

I was lucky to play Sally because she was my favorite character. I was a little sister myself, so I could relate to being the youngest. I also thought she was the funniest because she had the most adult sense of humor, which, coming out of that little body, is pretty funny.

The consensus was certainly that your Sally pretty much stole the show in that version of the play.

Sally could not have been a breakthrough character without the rest of the characters being so strong. Her relationship with Snoopy was especially important. We can thank Charles Schulz for all of that. I also adored the Sally wig that Paul Huntley made. She had these crazy loose curls that unraveled when she did!

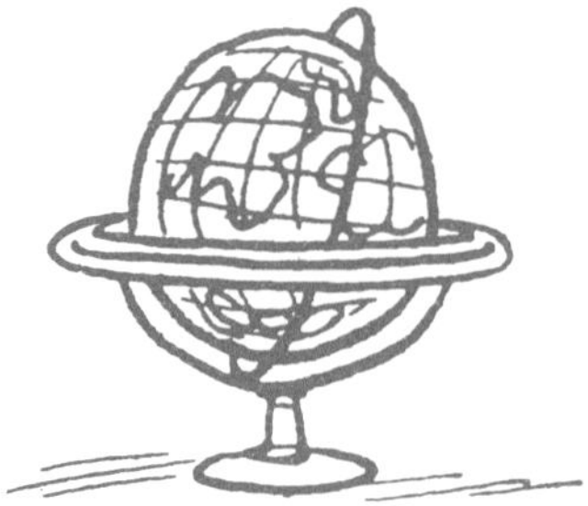

Even though they were introduced as babies in the early days of the strip, characters like Schroeder, Lucy and Linus all quickly "grew up" to the point where they were implicitly close in age to the "older" characters (Linus doesn't act any younger than Charlie Brown, for instance); Sally is unique — at least until Rerun came along — in that she remained younger (both smaller and in terms of her personality) than the rest. How did this affect your portrayal of Sally?

Because I was a little sister myself and I was much smaller than everybody else, I knew exactly how she felt. Trying to keep up with the big kids, but falling short and being frustrated about it. That's what made her so fun to play. Her frustration about it. It's funny that the person she most related to was the dog.

Can you draw any lines or comparisons between Sally and other characters you've played, such as Cunegonde (in Candide*) or Glinda? Is there a "type" of character you're attracted to or are being cast as?*

I've been lucky enough in my career, to not necessarily be type cast. I find it lucky that I get to play Lily in the movie musical *Annie*, then turn around and play Marian in *The Music Man*. All the characters I've chosen to play in film, television, and theatre are very different.

That's true. We thought you might specialize in extroverts, but Marian the Librarian sinks that theory. Do you think, based on the strips (and the show), Schulz had a good insight into girls and women?

Yes! I also loved his sophisticated sense of humor.

What does Sally see in Linus, do you think? How hurt is she at his rejection? (Actually, of all the Peanuts *characters suffering from unrequited love, she seems to take it the most in stride — if not outright denial.)*

I don't think there's a girl alive who doesn't know the pain of rejection.

Aside from Linus and Snoopy, Sally's most important relationship is obviously with her brother Charlie Brown. How do you, as the person who played Sally, think she sees her brother? She seems to be both solicitous of his (relatively) greater wisdom and dismissive of it, with a combination of irritation and fondness. But maybe that's every younger sibling in a nutshell?

I think that when you're a young sibling you really don't want to believe everything your older siblings say, but deep down you know you should. You also really trust them. When I was a little girl my brother had me put a stick in my mouth and wanted to try to use a whip to get it out... Because I trusted him so much I willingly put the stick in my mouth. My mom caught us just in time to stop the fiasco.

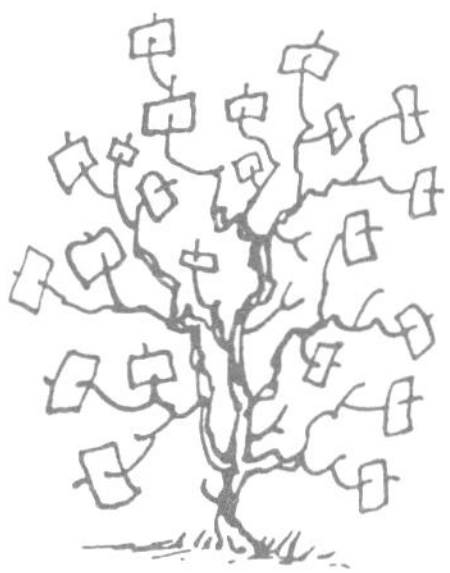

What's your favorite line (or lines) of Sally's from the play?

She comes out very sadly dragging her jump rope. Charlie Brown says, "Sally, what's wrong?" Sally replies, "I was jumping rope. Everything was fine. And then suddenly everything seemed so futile." The adults in the crowd loved that one.

Is there any other comics or cartoon character you could ever imagine playing?

Betty Boop.

We can totally see that. Did you ever get to meet Charles Schulz?

I never had the fortune of meeting Charles face to face; however, when I was nominated for the Tony, and later when I won, he sent me flowers and told me I was born to play Sally.

You were one of a few people who sang at Charles Schulz's memorial service. Was that an emotional experience?

Singing at Charles Schulz's memorial was incredibly emotional because an American treasure had passed away. Seeing people like Billie Jean King was amazing. Charles Schulz would've been pleased.

How do you place Peanuts *in your own history, both personal and in terms of your career?*

Peanuts will always remain special to me. Doing *Charlie Brown* on Broadway was one of the happiest times of my life.

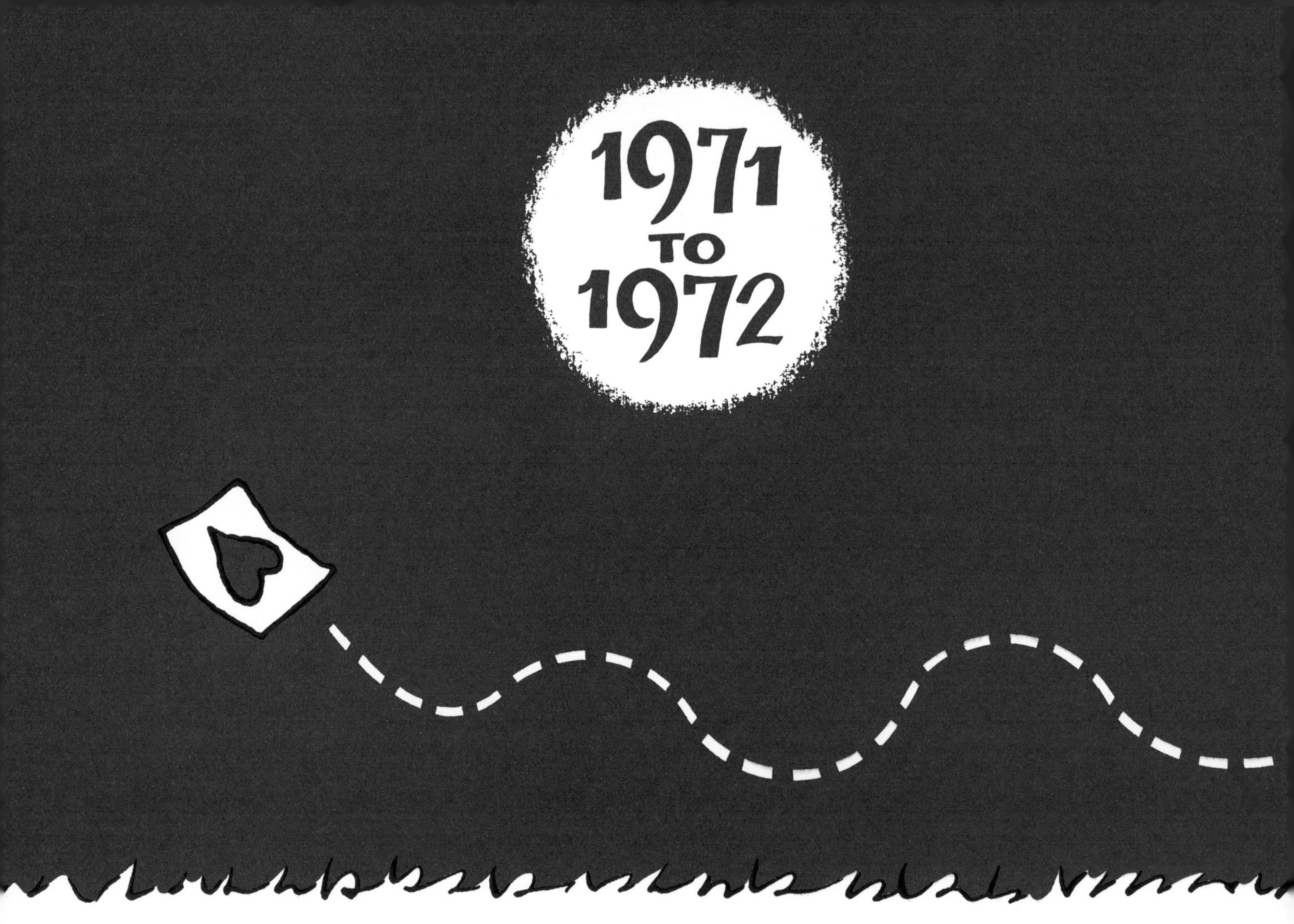
1971
TO
1972

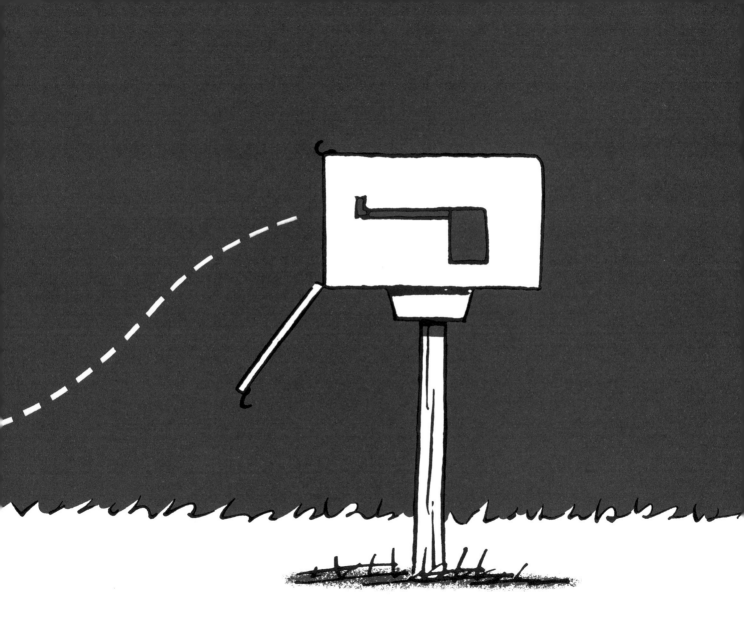

THIS IS OUR "HAPPY NEW YEAR" DANCE..
IT SYMBOLIZES OUR BEST WISHES FOR A WONDERFUL YEAR TO ALL CREATURES...
EXCEPT CATS!
HEE HEE HEE HEE!
SCHULZ

ASK YOUR "BEAGLE-BOARD" WHAT THIS NEW YEAR HOLDS FOR ME..
OH, BEAGLE-BOARD, SPEAK THY TRUTHS! SPEAK! SPEAK!
AAUGH!
UNFORTUNATELY, THE BEAGLE-BOARD NEVER LIES...
SCHULZ

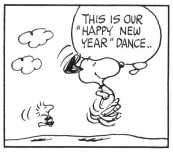

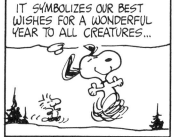

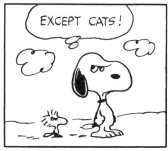

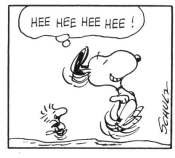

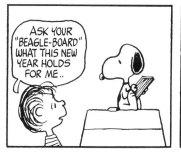

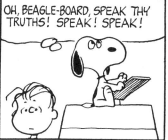

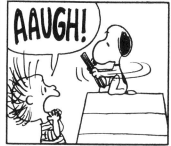

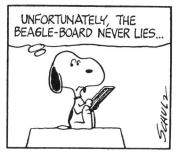

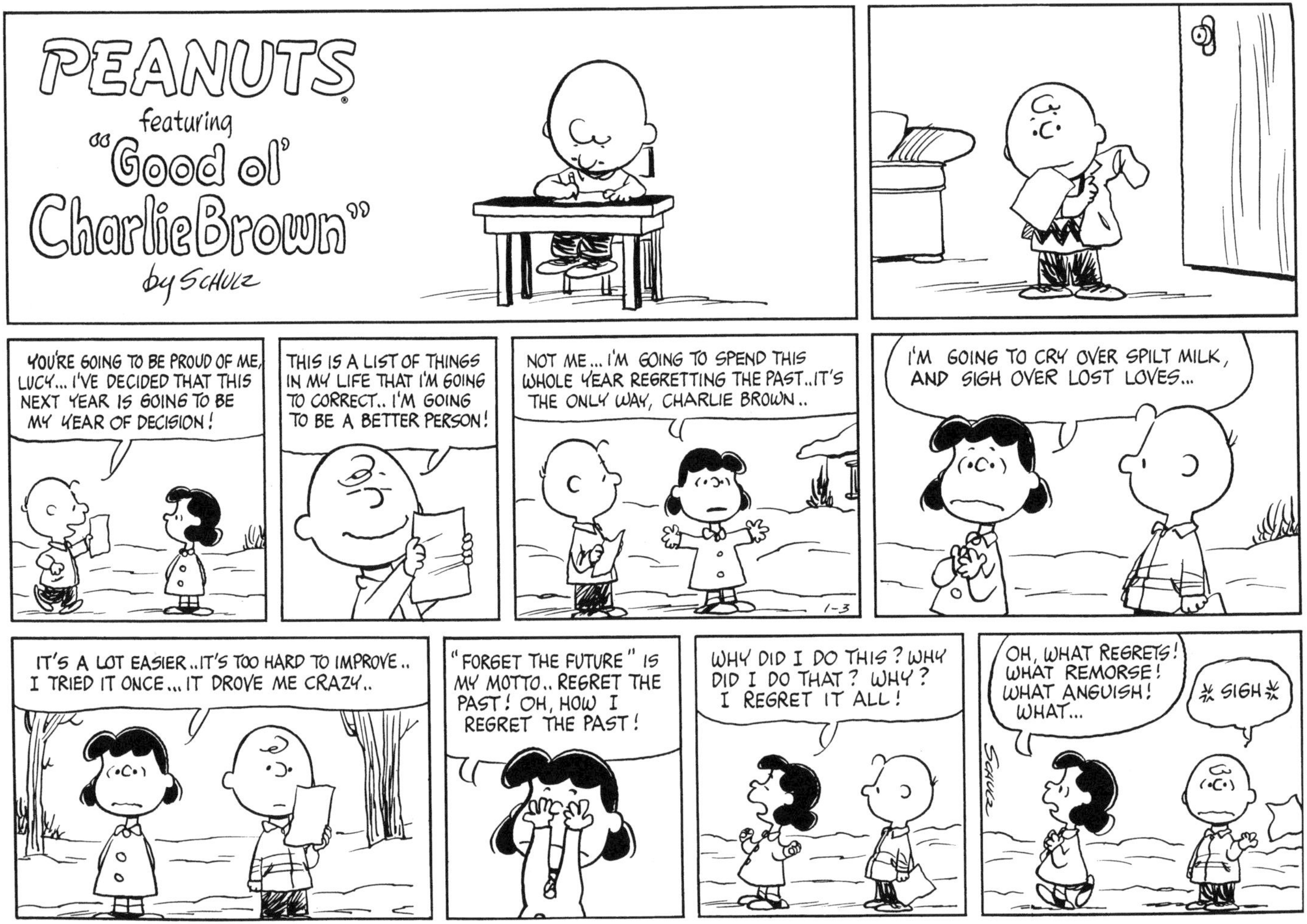
PEANUTS
featuring
"Good ol' CharlieBrown"
by SCHULZ
YOU'RE GOING TO BE PROUD OF ME, LUCY... I'VE DECIDED THAT THIS NEXT YEAR IS GOING TO BE MY YEAR OF DECISION!
THIS IS A LIST OF THINGS IN MY LIFE THAT I'M GOING TO CORRECT.. I'M GOING TO BE A BETTER PERSON!
NOT ME... I'M GOING TO SPEND THIS WHOLE YEAR REGRETTING THE PAST..IT'S THE ONLY WAY, CHARLIE BROWN..
1-3
I'M GOING TO CRY OVER SPILT MILK, AND SIGH OVER LOST LOVES...
IT'S A LOT EASIER..IT'S TOO HARD TO IMPROVE.. I TRIED IT ONCE... IT DROVE ME CRAZY..
"FORGET THE FUTURE" IS MY MOTTO.. REGRET THE PAST! OH, HOW I REGRET THE PAST!
WHY DID I DO THIS? WHY DID I DO THAT? WHY? I REGRET IT ALL!
SCHULZ
OH, WHAT REGRETS! WHAT REMORSE! WHAT ANGUISH! WHAT...
SIGH

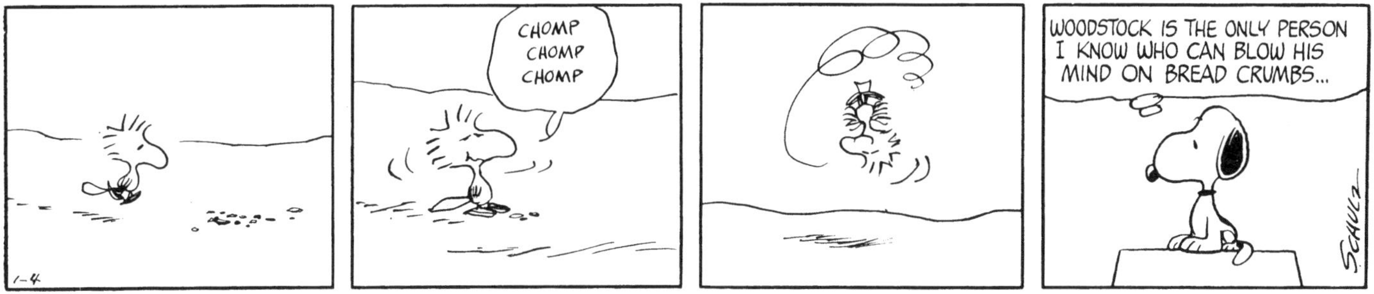
1-4
CHOMP
CHOMP
CHOMP
WOODSTOCK IS THE ONLY PERSON I KNOW WHO CAN BLOW HIS MIND ON BREAD CRUMBS...

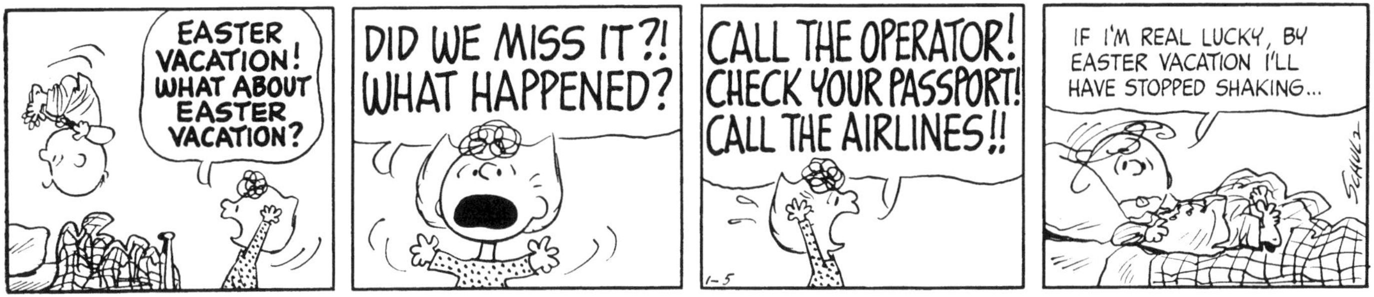
EASTER VACATION! WHAT ABOUT EASTER VACATION?
DID WE MISS IT?! WHAT HAPPENED?
CALL THE OPERATOR! CHECK YOUR PASSPORT! CALL THE AIRLINES!!
1-5
IF I'M REAL LUCKY, BY EASTER VACATION I'LL HAVE STOPPED SHAKING...

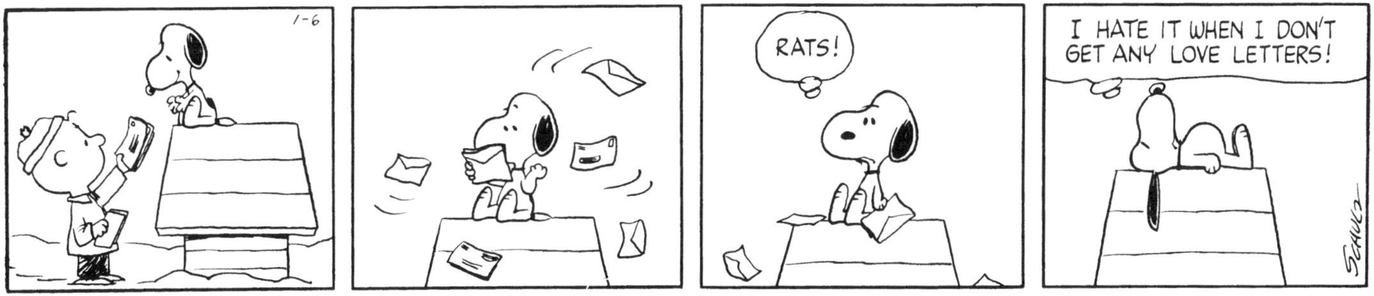
1-6
RATS!
I HATE IT WHEN I DON'T GET ANY LOVE LETTERS!

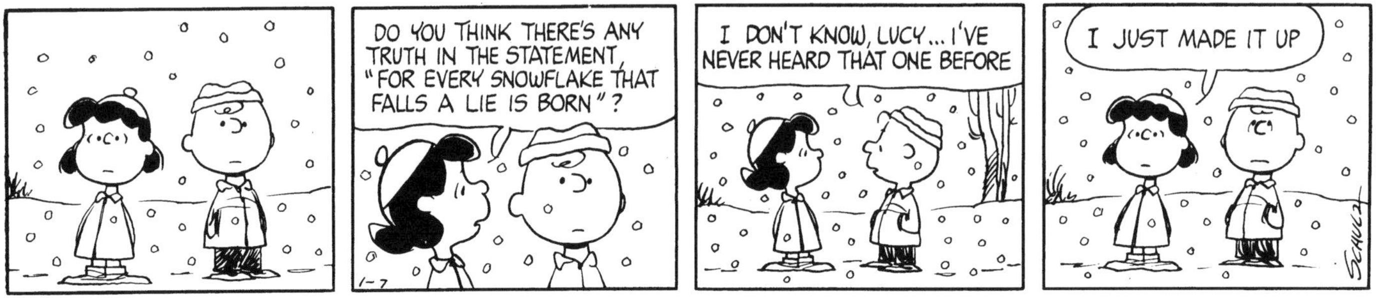
DO YOU THINK THERE'S ANY TRUTH IN THE STATEMENT, "FOR EVERY SNOWFLAKE THAT FALLS A LIE IS BORN"?
I DON'T KNOW, LUCY... I'VE NEVER HEARD THAT ONE BEFORE
I JUST MADE IT UP

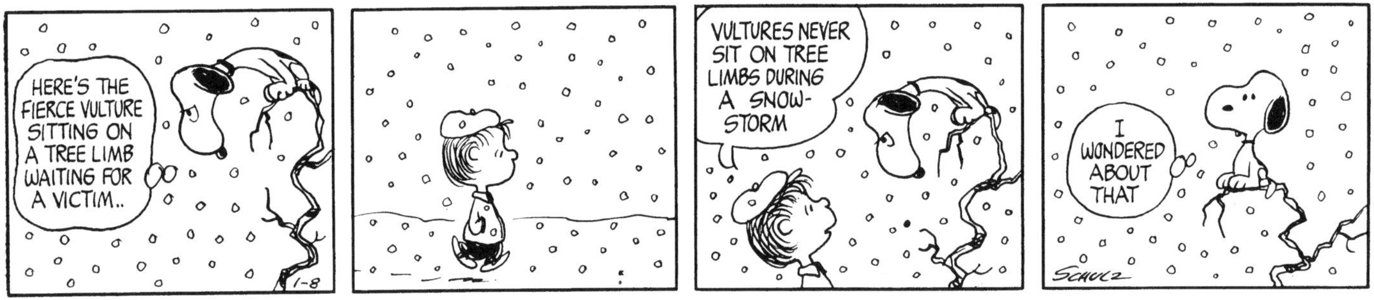
HERE'S THE FIERCE VULTURE SITTING ON A TREE LIMB WAITING FOR A VICTIM..
VULTURES NEVER SIT ON TREE LIMBS DURING A SNOW-STORM
I WONDERED ABOUT THAT

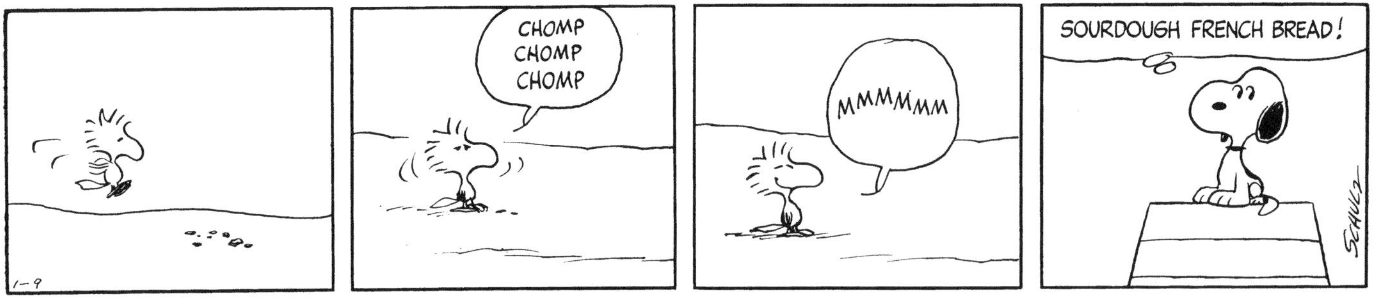
CHOMP CHOMP CHOMP
MMMMMM
SOURDOUGH FRENCH BREAD!

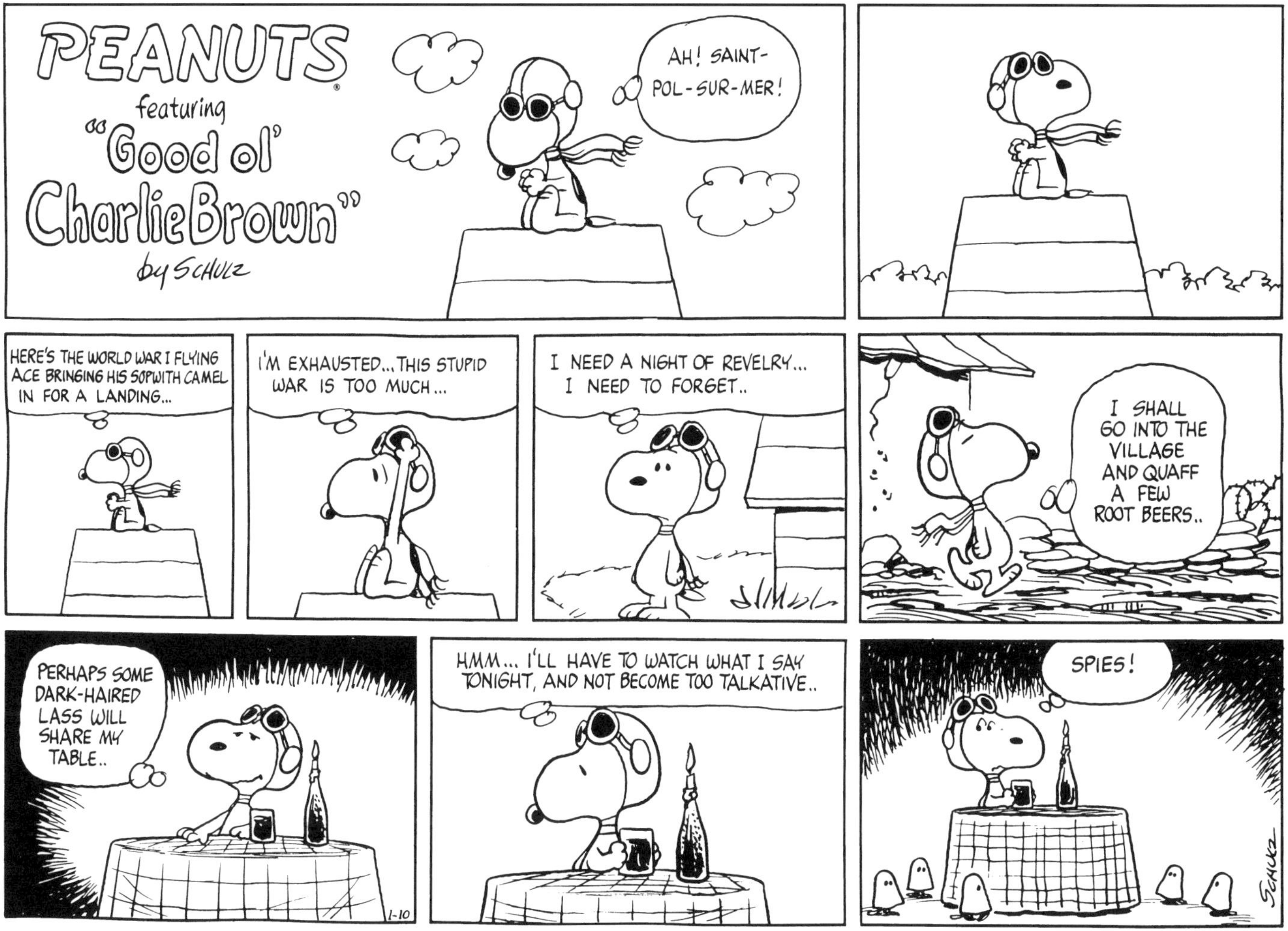
PEANUTS
featuring "Good ol' Charlie Brown"
by SCHULZ
AH! SAINT-POL-SUR-MER!
HERE'S THE WORLD WAR I FLYING ACE BRINGING HIS SOPWITH CAMEL IN FOR A LANDING...
I'M EXHAUSTED... THIS STUPID WAR IS TOO MUCH...
I NEED A NIGHT OF REVELRY... I NEED TO FORGET..
I SHALL GO INTO THE VILLAGE AND QUAFF A FEW ROOT BEERS..
PERHAPS SOME DARK-HAIRED LASS WILL SHARE MY TABLE..
1-10
HMM... I'LL HAVE TO WATCH WHAT I SAY TONIGHT, AND NOT BECOME TOO TALKATIVE..
SPIES!
SCHULZ

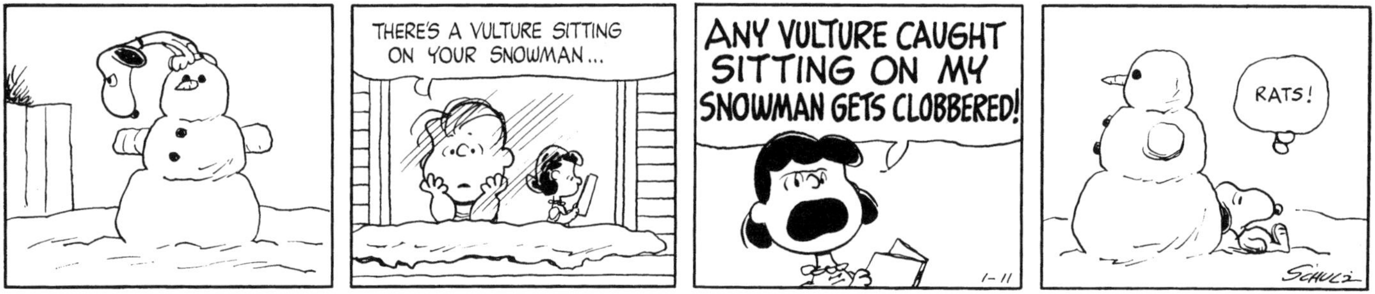
THERE'S A VULTURE SITTING ON YOUR SNOWMAN...
ANY VULTURE CAUGHT SITTING ON MY SNOWMAN GETS CLOBBERED!
1-11
RATS!
SCHULZ

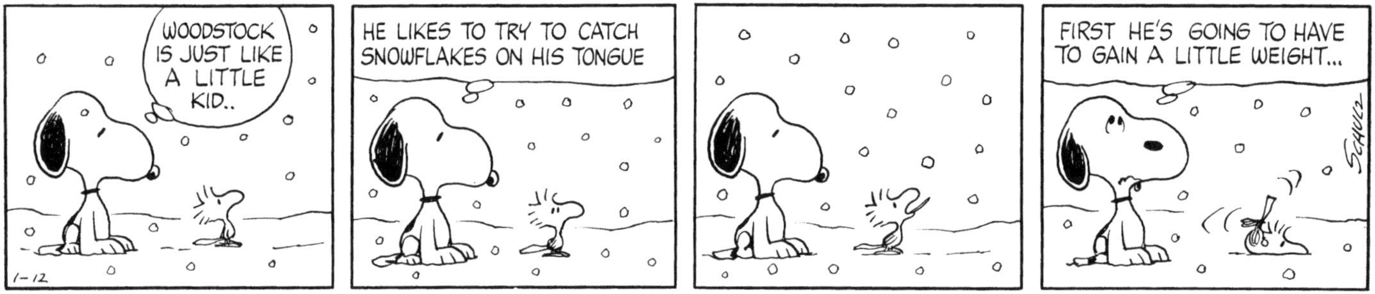
WOODSTOCK IS JUST LIKE A LITTLE KID..
1-12
HE LIKES TO TRY TO CATCH SNOWFLAKES ON HIS TONGUE
FIRST HE'S GOING TO HAVE TO GAIN A LITTLE WEIGHT...
SCHULZ

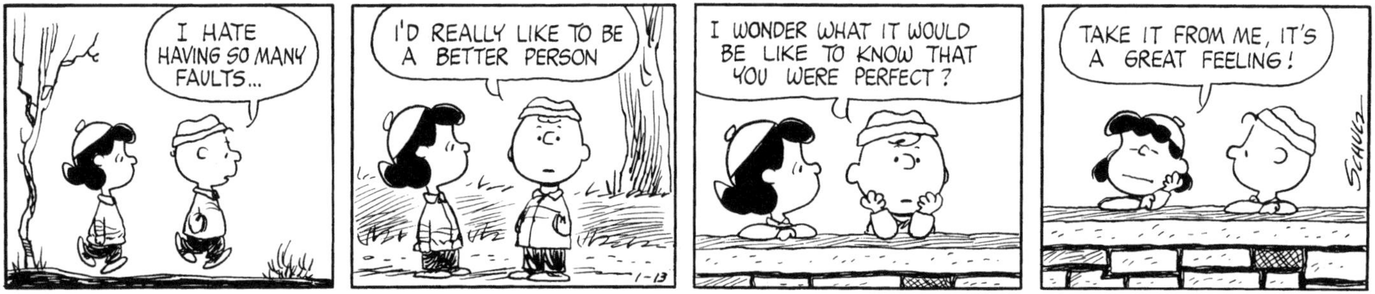
I HATE HAVING SO MANY FAULTS...
I'D REALLY LIKE TO BE A BETTER PERSON
1-13
I WONDER WHAT IT WOULD BE LIKE TO KNOW THAT YOU WERE PERFECT?
TAKE IT FROM ME, IT'S A GREAT FEELING!
SCHULZ

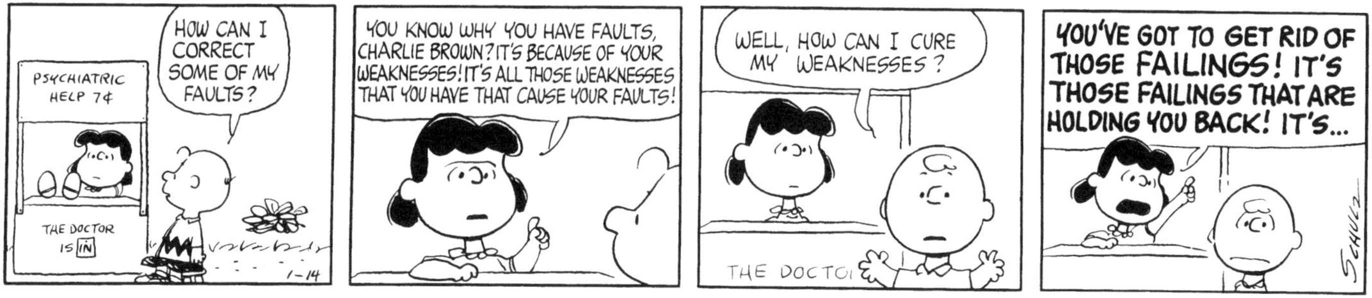
PSYCHIATRIC HELP 7¢
THE DOCTOR IS IN
HOW CAN I CORRECT SOME OF MY FAULTS?
1-14
YOU KNOW WHY YOU HAVE FAULTS, CHARLIE BROWN? IT'S BECAUSE OF YOUR WEAKNESSES! IT'S ALL THOSE WEAKNESSES THAT YOU HAVE THAT CAUSE YOUR FAULTS!
WELL, HOW CAN I CURE MY WEAKNESSES?
THE DOCTOI
YOU'VE GOT TO GET RID OF THOSE FAILINGS! IT'S THOSE FAILINGS THAT ARE HOLDING YOU BACK! IT'S...
SCHULZ

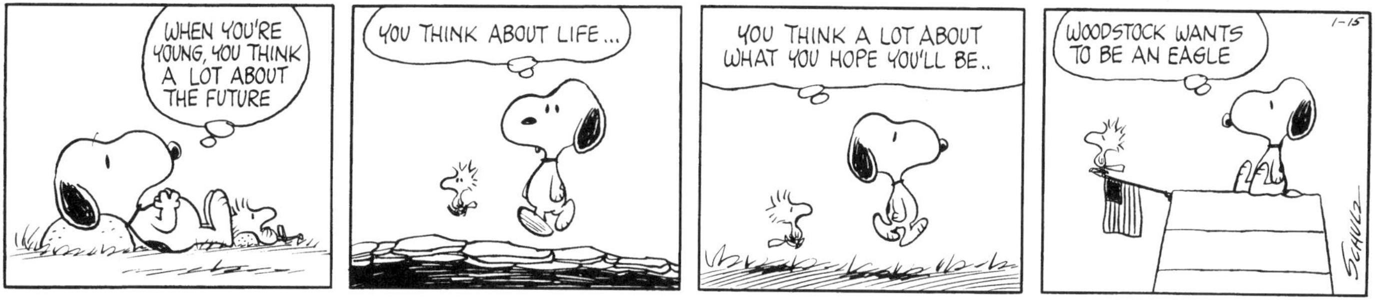
WHEN YOU'RE YOUNG, YOU THINK A LOT ABOUT THE FUTURE
YOU THINK ABOUT LIFE...
YOU THINK A LOT ABOUT WHAT YOU HOPE YOU'LL BE..
1-15
WOODSTOCK WANTS TO BE AN EAGLE
SCHULZ

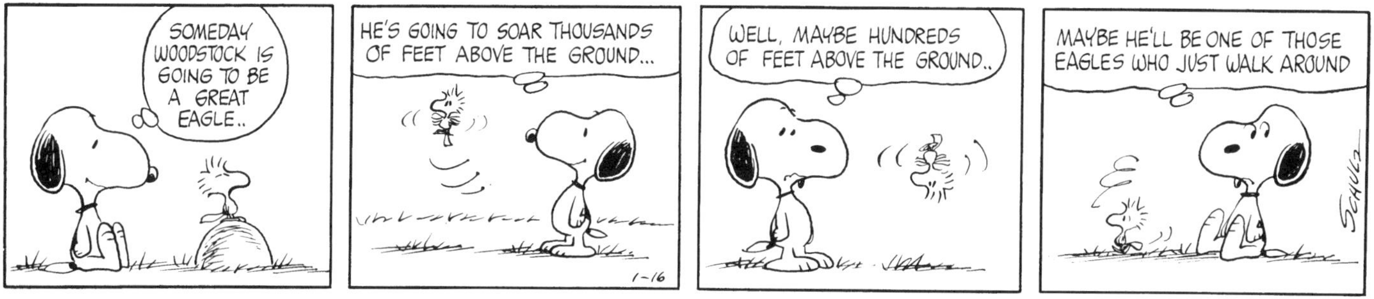
SOMEDAY WOODSTOCK IS GOING TO BE A GREAT EAGLE..
HE'S GOING TO SOAR THOUSANDS OF FEET ABOVE THE GROUND...
1-16
WELL, MAYBE HUNDREDS OF FEET ABOVE THE GROUND..
MAYBE HE'LL BE ONE OF THOSE EAGLES WHO JUST WALK AROUND
SCHULZ

PEANUTS featuring "Good ol' Charlie Brown" by Schulz

"The Cabin"

Chapter One

When he got up that morning, the sky was clear.

By now, however, it had turned gray. He shivered slightly.

Soon it began to snow.

At first, only a few feathers swirling in the wind.

Then heavy, wet flakes which quickly covered everything.

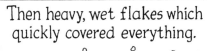

RATS!

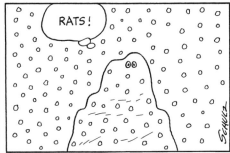

January

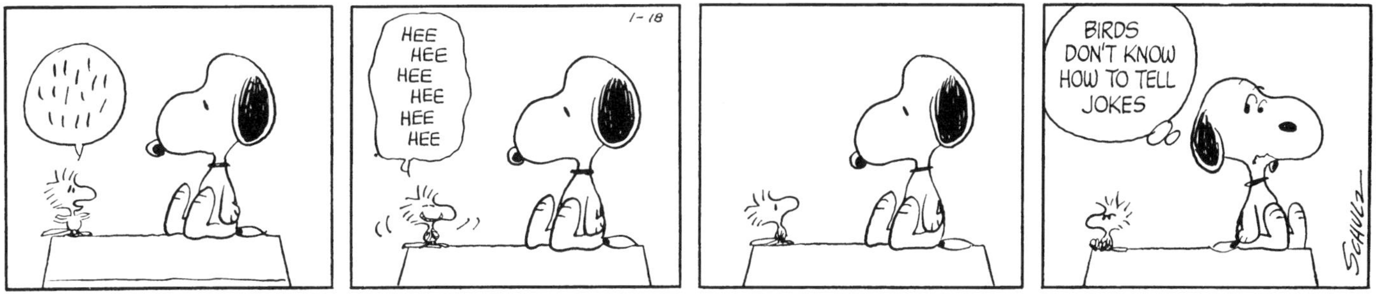
1-18
HEE HEE HEE HEE HEE HEE
BIRDS DON'T KNOW HOW TO TELL JOKES

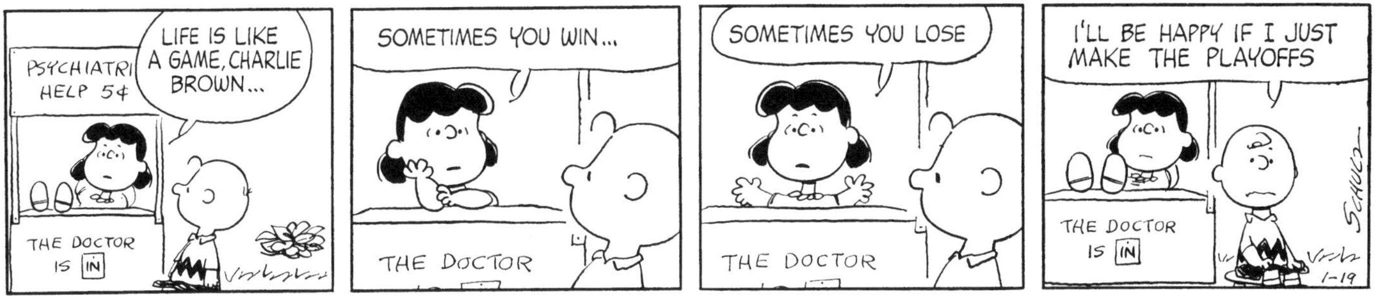
PSYCHIATRI HELP 5¢
LIFE IS LIKE A GAME, CHARLIE BROWN...
THE DOCTOR IS IN
SOMETIMES YOU WIN...
THE DOCTOR
SOMETIMES YOU LOSE
THE DOCTOR
I'LL BE HAPPY IF I JUST MAKE THE PLAYOFFS
THE DOCTOR IS IN
1-19

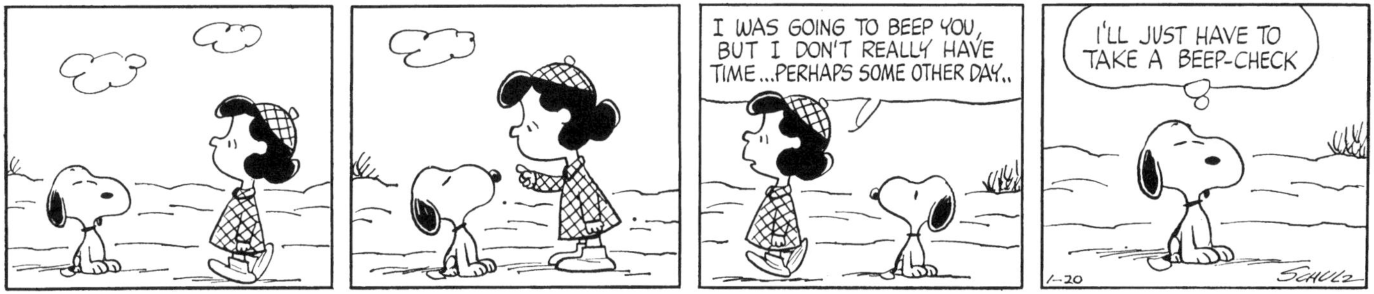
I WAS GOING TO BEEP YOU, BUT I DON'T REALLY HAVE TIME...PERHAPS SOME OTHER DAY..
I'LL JUST HAVE TO TAKE A BEEP-CHECK
1-20

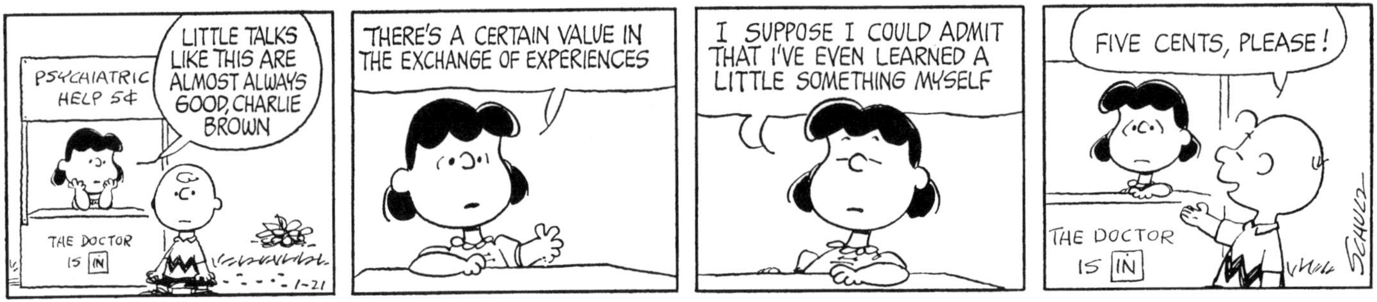
PSYCHIATRIC HELP 5¢
THE DOCTOR IS IN
LITTLE TALKS LIKE THIS ARE ALMOST ALWAYS GOOD, CHARLIE BROWN
1-21
THERE'S A CERTAIN VALUE IN THE EXCHANGE OF EXPERIENCES
I SUPPOSE I COULD ADMIT THAT I'VE EVEN LEARNED A LITTLE SOMETHING MYSELF
FIVE CENTS, PLEASE!
THE DOCTOR IS IN
SCHULZ

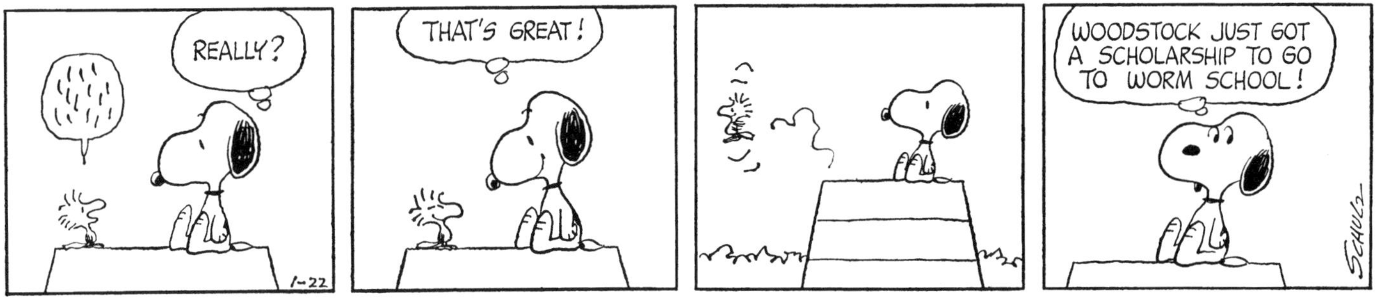
REALLY?
1-22
THAT'S GREAT!
WOODSTOCK JUST GOT A SCHOLARSHIP TO GO TO WORM SCHOOL!
SCHULZ

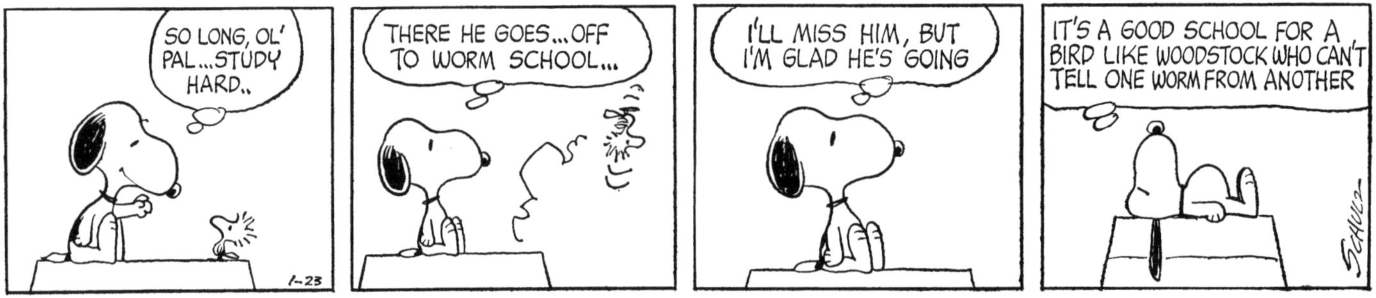
SO LONG, OL' PAL...STUDY HARD..
1-23
THERE HE GOES...OFF TO WORM SCHOOL...
I'LL MISS HIM, BUT I'M GLAD HE'S GOING
IT'S A GOOD SCHOOL FOR A BIRD LIKE WOODSTOCK WHO CAN'T TELL ONE WORM FROM ANOTHER
SCHULZ

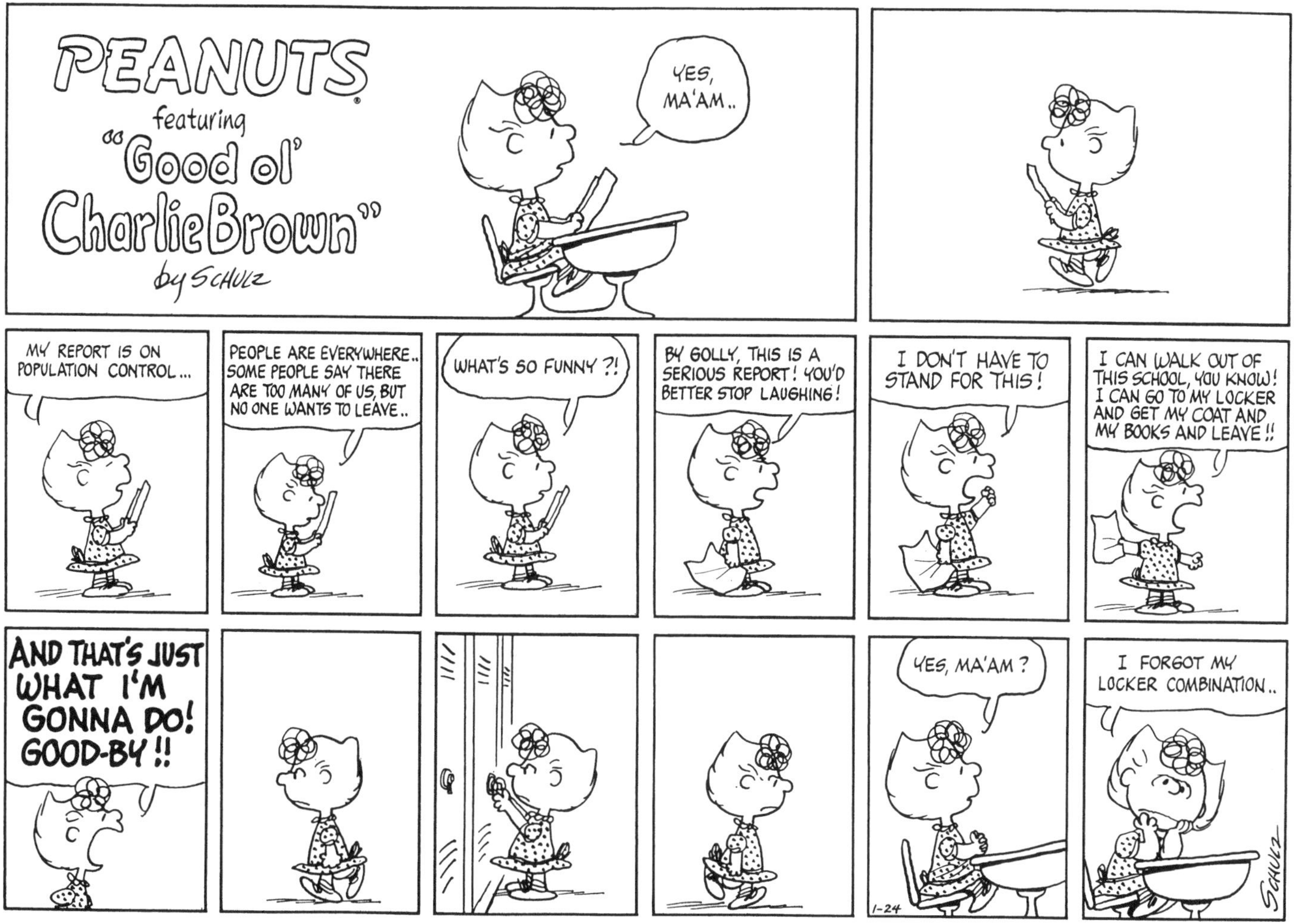
PEANUTS
featuring "Good ol' Charlie Brown"
by SCHULZ
YES, MA'AM..
MY REPORT IS ON POPULATION CONTROL...
PEOPLE ARE EVERYWHERE.. SOME PEOPLE SAY THERE ARE TOO MANY OF US, BUT NO ONE WANTS TO LEAVE..
WHAT'S SO FUNNY ?!
BY GOLLY, THIS IS A SERIOUS REPORT! YOU'D BETTER STOP LAUGHING!
I DON'T HAVE TO STAND FOR THIS!
I CAN WALK OUT OF THIS SCHOOL, YOU KNOW! I CAN GO TO MY LOCKER AND GET MY COAT AND MY BOOKS AND LEAVE!!
AND THAT'S JUST WHAT I'M GONNA DO! GOOD-BY!!
YES, MA'AM?
I FORGOT MY LOCKER COMBINATION..
1-24
SCHULZ

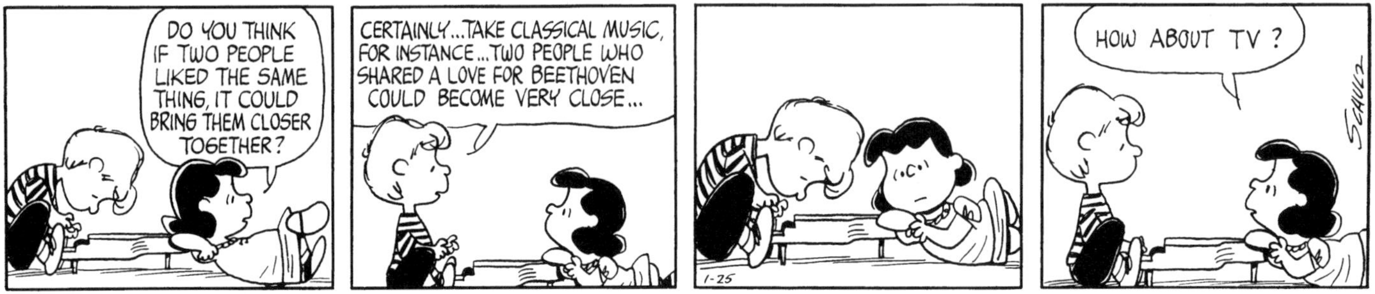
DO YOU THINK IF TWO PEOPLE LIKED THE SAME THING, IT COULD BRING THEM CLOSER TOGETHER?
CERTAINLY...TAKE CLASSICAL MUSIC, FOR INSTANCE...TWO PEOPLE WHO SHARED A LOVE FOR BEETHOVEN COULD BECOME VERY CLOSE...
HOW ABOUT TV ?

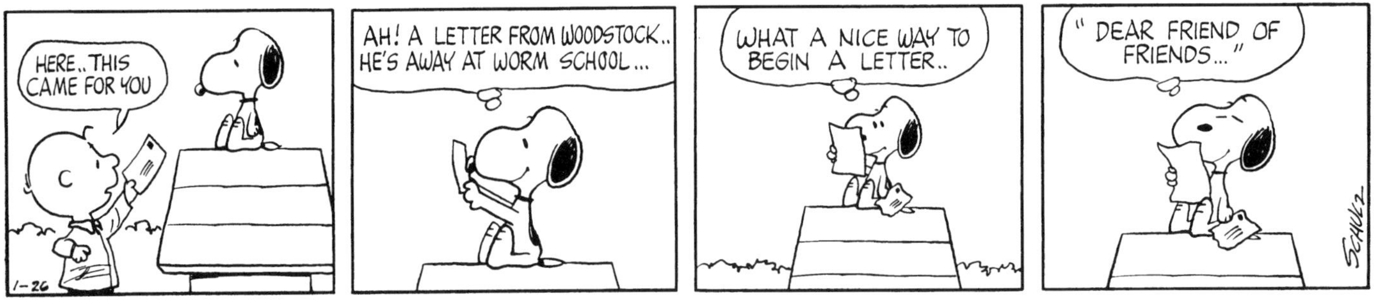
HERE..THIS CAME FOR YOU
AH! A LETTER FROM WOODSTOCK.. HE'S AWAY AT WORM SCHOOL...
WHAT A NICE WAY TO BEGIN A LETTER..
" DEAR FRIEND OF FRIENDS..."

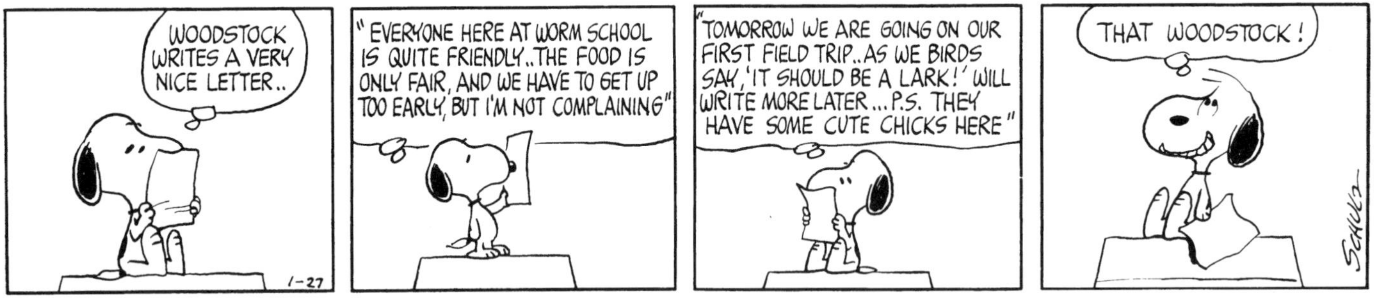
WOODSTOCK WRITES A VERY NICE LETTER..
" EVERYONE HERE AT WORM SCHOOL IS QUITE FRIENDLY..THE FOOD IS ONLY FAIR, AND WE HAVE TO GET UP TOO EARLY, BUT I'M NOT COMPLAINING"
"TOMORROW WE ARE GOING ON OUR FIRST FIELD TRIP..AS WE BIRDS SAY, 'IT SHOULD BE A LARK!' WILL WRITE MORE LATER... P.S. THEY HAVE SOME CUTE CHICKS HERE"
THAT WOODSTOCK!

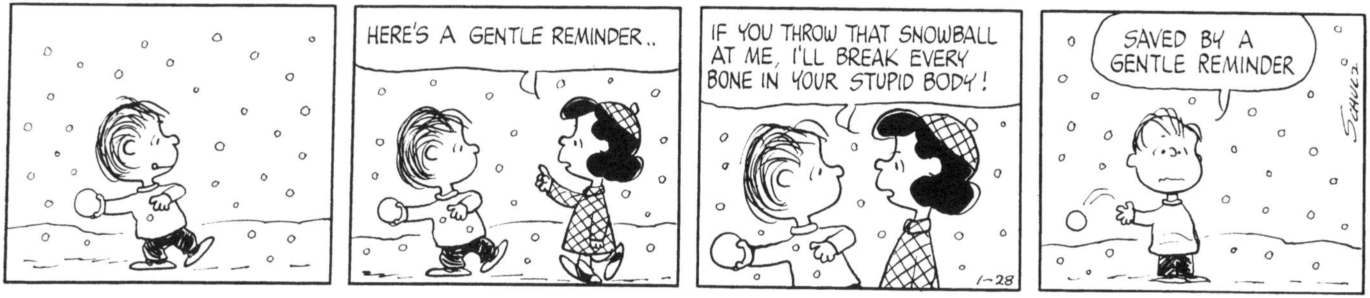

HERE'S A GENTLE REMINDER..
IF YOU THROW THAT SNOWBALL AT ME, I'LL BREAK EVERY BONE IN YOUR STUPID BODY!
1-28
SAVED BY A GENTLE REMINDER
SCHULZ

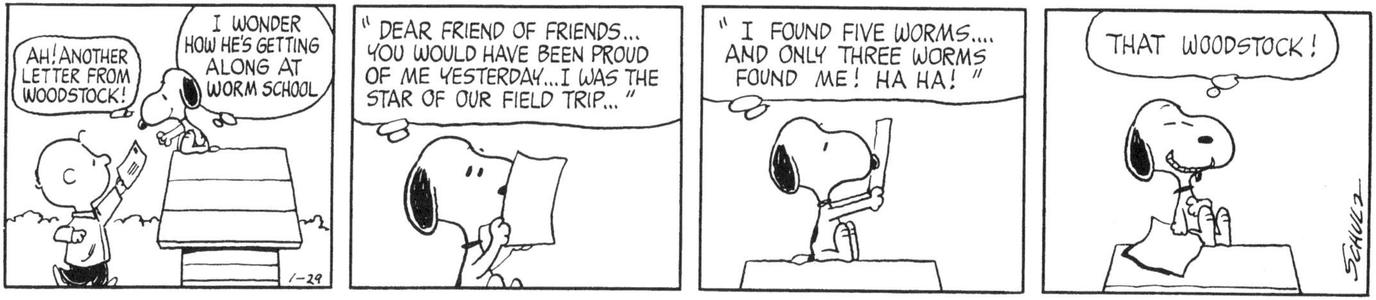

AH! ANOTHER LETTER FROM WOODSTOCK!
I WONDER HOW HE'S GETTING ALONG AT WORM SCHOOL
1-29
" DEAR FRIEND OF FRIENDS... YOU WOULD HAVE BEEN PROUD OF ME YESTERDAY...I WAS THE STAR OF OUR FIELD TRIP... "
" I FOUND FIVE WORMS.... AND ONLY THREE WORMS FOUND ME! HA HA! "
THAT WOODSTOCK!
SCHULZ

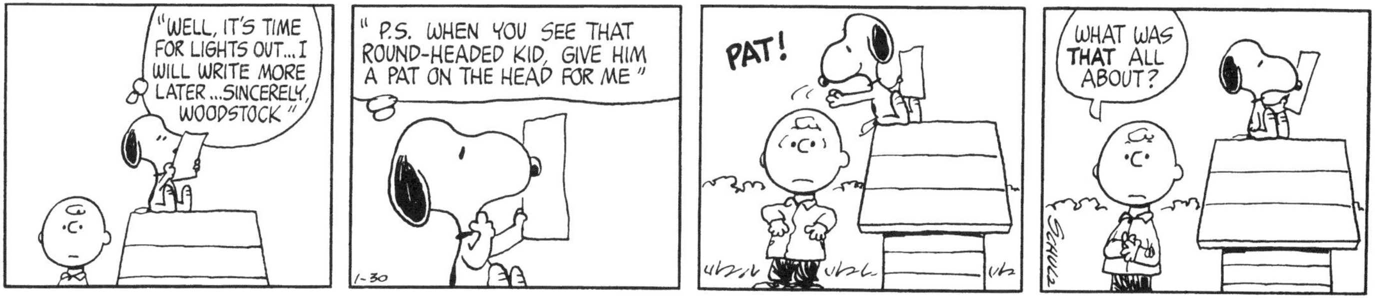

"WELL, IT'S TIME FOR LIGHTS OUT...I WILL WRITE MORE LATER...SINCERELY, WOODSTOCK "
" P.S. WHEN YOU SEE THAT ROUND-HEADED KID, GIVE HIM A PAT ON THE HEAD FOR ME "
1-30
PAT!
SCHULZ
WHAT WAS THAT ALL ABOUT?

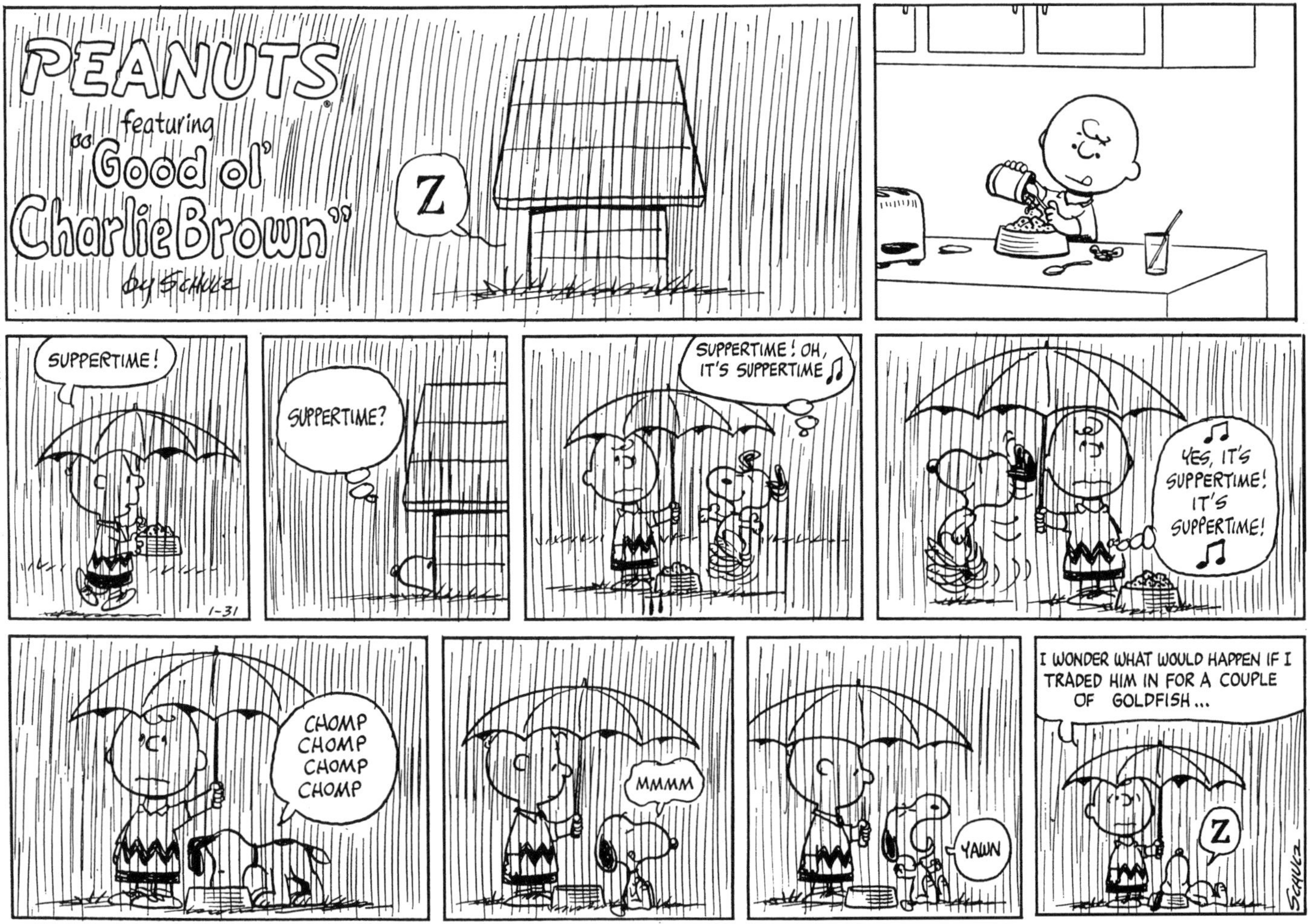
PEANUTS
featuring
"Good ol' Charlie Brown"
by Schulz
Z
SUPPERTIME!
1-31
SUPPERTIME?
SUPPERTIME! OH, IT'S SUPPERTIME
YES, IT'S SUPPERTIME! IT'S SUPPERTIME!
CHOMP CHOMP CHOMP CHOMP
MMMM
YAWN
I WONDER WHAT WOULD HAPPEN IF I TRADED HIM IN FOR A COUPLE OF GOLDFISH...
Z
SCHULZ

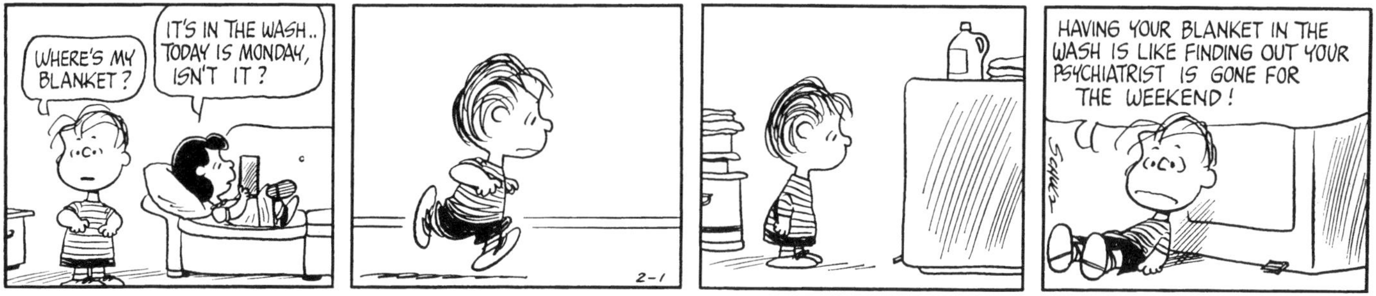
WHERE'S MY BLANKET?
IT'S IN THE WASH.. TODAY IS MONDAY, ISN'T IT?
2-1
HAVING YOUR BLANKET IN THE WASH IS LIKE FINDING OUT YOUR PSYCHIATRIST IS GONE FOR THE WEEKEND!
SCHULZ

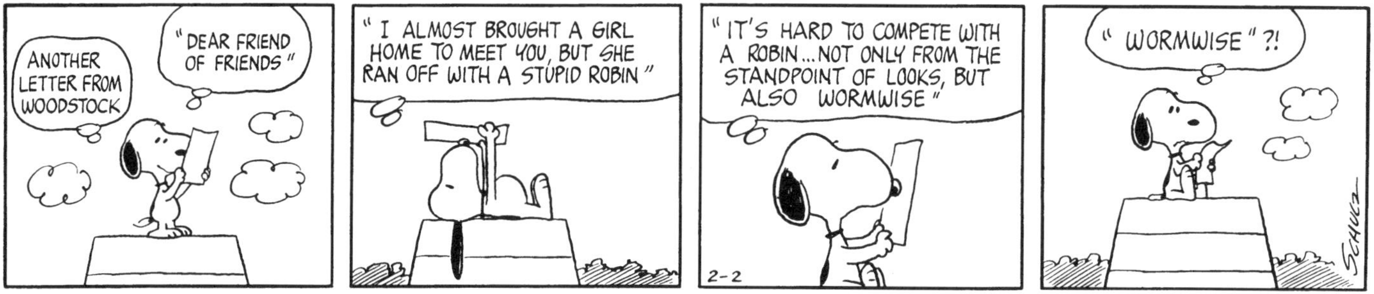
ANOTHER LETTER FROM WOODSTOCK
"DEAR FRIEND OF FRIENDS"
"I ALMOST BROUGHT A GIRL HOME TO MEET YOU, BUT SHE RAN OFF WITH A STUPID ROBIN"
"IT'S HARD TO COMPETE WITH A ROBIN...NOT ONLY FROM THE STANDPOINT OF LOOKS, BUT ALSO WORMWISE"
2-2
"WORMWISE"?!
SCHULZ

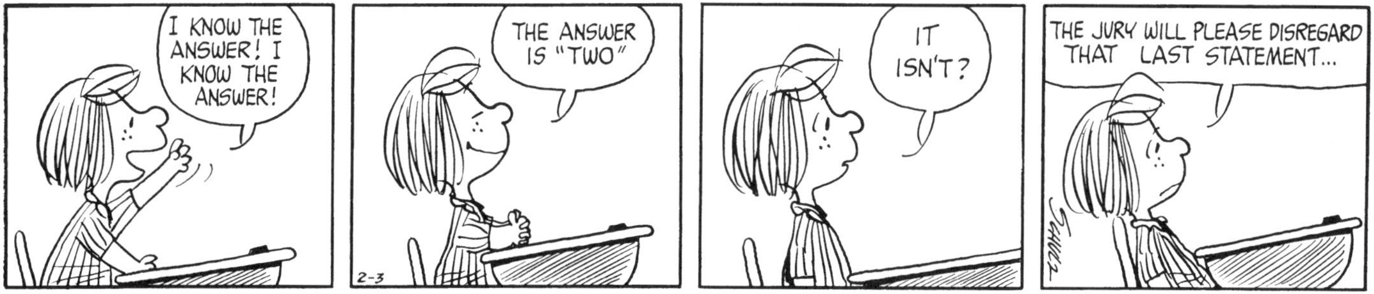
I KNOW THE ANSWER! I KNOW THE ANSWER!
THE ANSWER IS "TWO"
2-3
IT ISN'T?
THE JURY WILL PLEASE DISREGARD THAT LAST STATEMENT...
SCHULZ

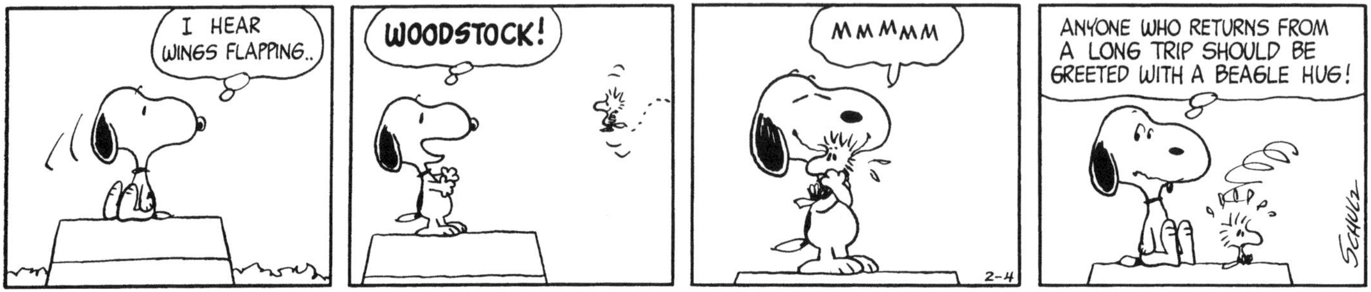
I HEAR WINGS FLAPPING..
WOODSTOCK!
MMMMM
2-4
ANYONE WHO RETURNS FROM A LONG TRIP SHOULD BE GREETED WITH A BEAGLE HUG!
SCHULZ

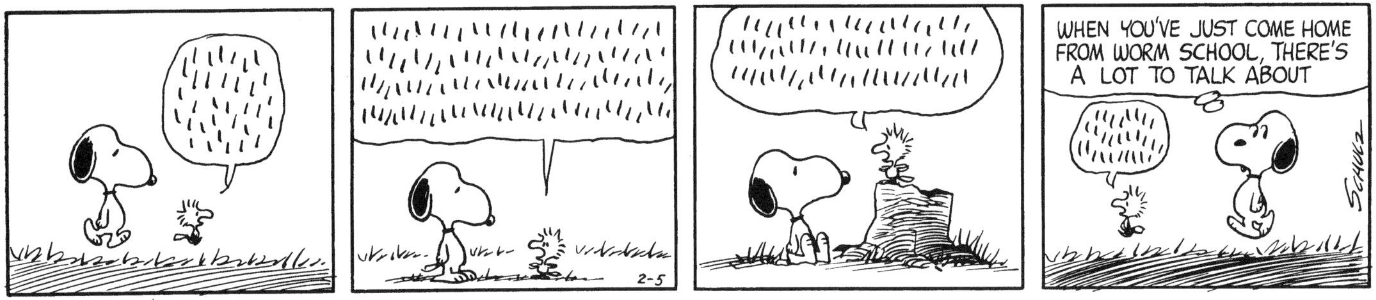
2-5
WHEN YOU'VE JUST COME HOME FROM WORM SCHOOL, THERE'S A LOT TO TALK ABOUT
SCHULZ

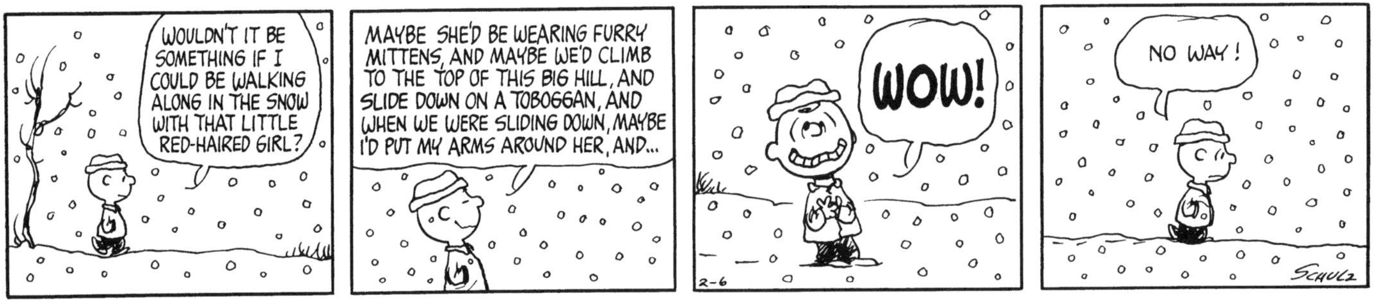
WOULDN'T IT BE SOMETHING IF I COULD BE WALKING ALONG IN THE SNOW WITH THAT LITTLE RED-HAIRED GIRL?
MAYBE SHE'D BE WEARING FURRY MITTENS, AND MAYBE WE'D CLIMB TO THE TOP OF THIS BIG HILL, AND SLIDE DOWN ON A TOBOGGAN, AND WHEN WE WERE SLIDING DOWN, MAYBE I'D PUT MY ARMS AROUND HER, AND...
WOW!
2-6
NO WAY!
SCHULZ

PEANUTS featuring "Good ol' CharlieBrown" by SCHULZ

NOW SHOWING

ONE, PLEASE

ONE, PLEASE

See this MOVIE WITH SOMEONE YOU LOVE

2-7

See th MOVIE W SOMEON YOU LO

Se MO SO YOU

FORGET IT!

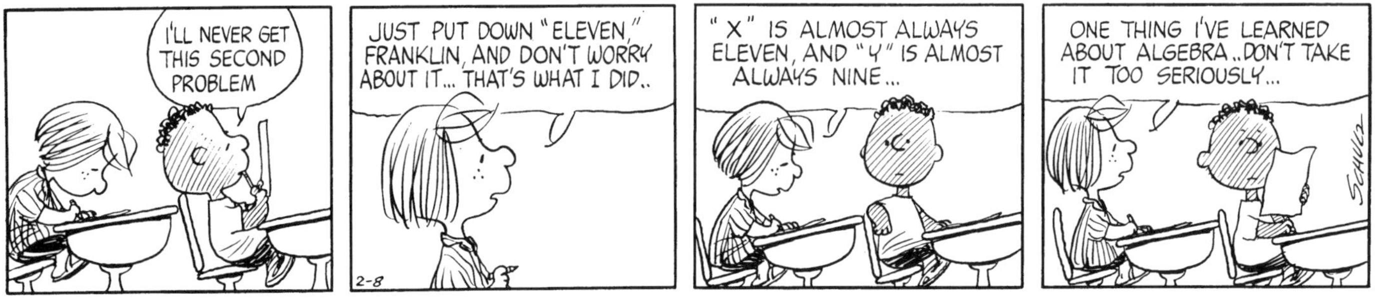
I'LL NEVER GET THIS SECOND PROBLEM
JUST PUT DOWN "ELEVEN," FRANKLIN, AND DON'T WORRY ABOUT IT... THAT'S WHAT I DID..
2-8
"X" IS ALMOST ALWAYS ELEVEN, AND "Y" IS ALMOST ALWAYS NINE...
ONE THING I'VE LEARNED ABOUT ALGEBRA..DON'T TAKE IT TOO SERIOUSLY...
SCHULZ

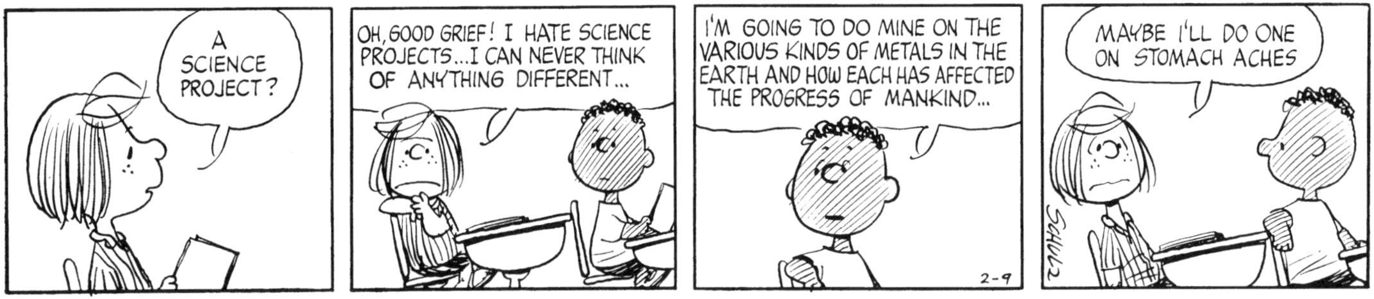
A SCIENCE PROJECT?
OH, GOOD GRIEF! I HATE SCIENCE PROJECTS...I CAN NEVER THINK OF ANYTHING DIFFERENT...
I'M GOING TO DO MINE ON THE VARIOUS KINDS OF METALS IN THE EARTH AND HOW EACH HAS AFFECTED THE PROGRESS OF MANKIND...
2-9
MAYBE I'LL DO ONE ON STOMACH ACHES
SCHULZ

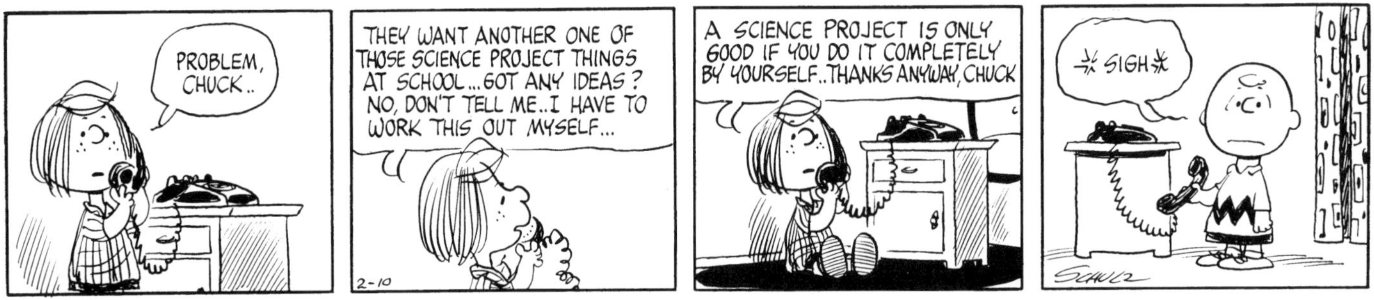
PROBLEM, CHUCK..
THEY WANT ANOTHER ONE OF THOSE SCIENCE PROJECT THINGS AT SCHOOL...GOT ANY IDEAS? NO, DON'T TELL ME..I HAVE TO WORK THIS OUT MYSELF...
2-10
A SCIENCE PROJECT IS ONLY GOOD IF YOU DO IT COMPLETELY BY YOURSELF..THANKS ANYWAY, CHUCK
SIGH
SCHULZ

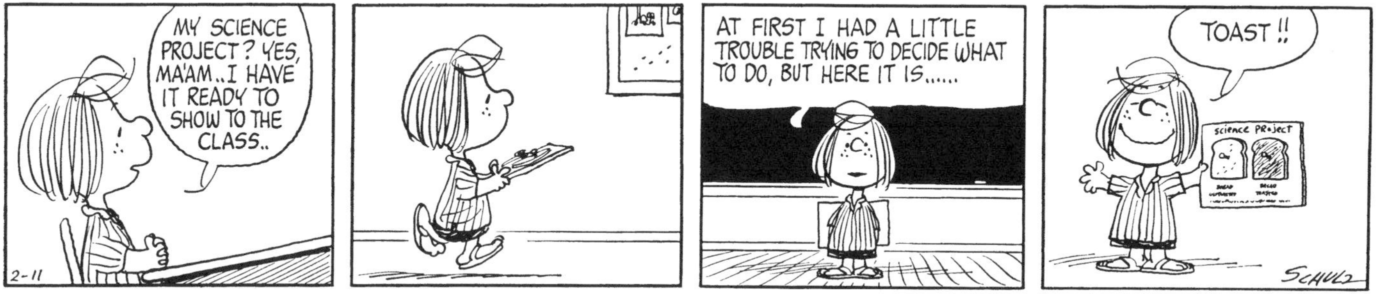
MY SCIENCE PROJECT? YES, MA'AM..I HAVE IT READY TO SHOW TO THE CLASS..
AT FIRST I HAD A LITTLE TROUBLE TRYING TO DECIDE WHAT TO DO, BUT HERE IT IS......
TOAST!!
science Project
SCHULZ

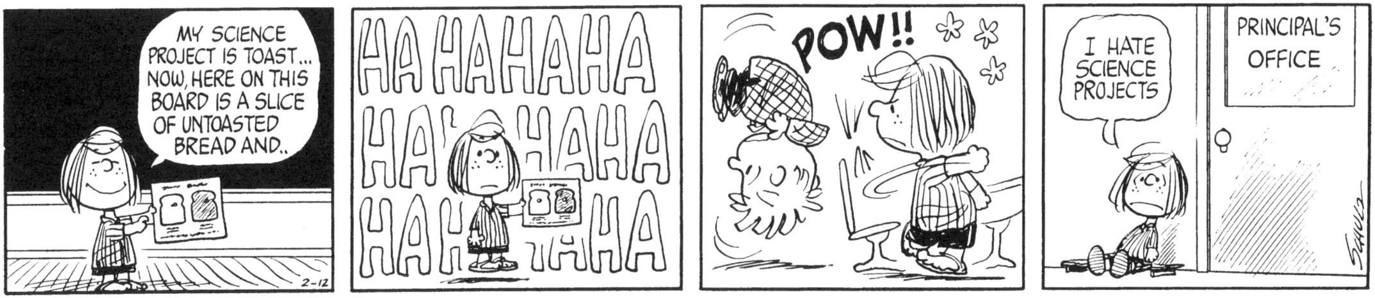
MY SCIENCE PROJECT IS TOAST... NOW, HERE ON THIS BOARD IS A SLICE OF UNTOASTED BREAD AND..
HA HAHAHAHA HA HAHA HA HAHA
POW!!
PRINCIPAL'S OFFICE
I HATE SCIENCE PROJECTS
SCHULZ

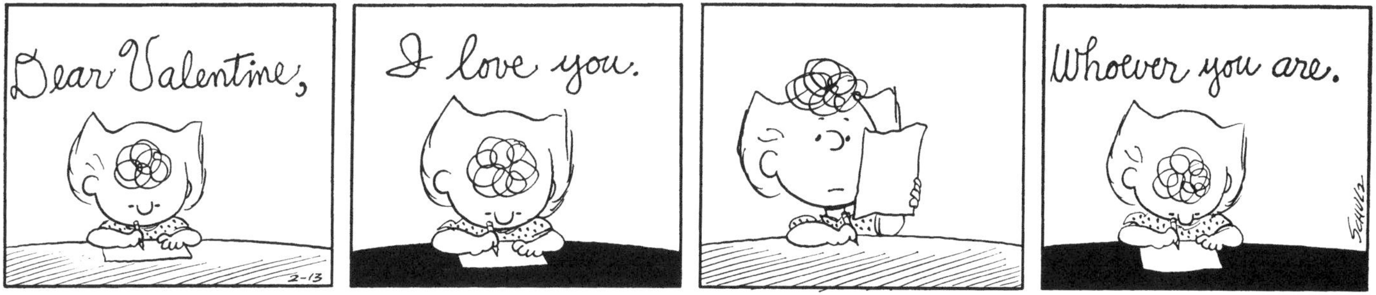
Dear Valentine,
I love you.
Whoever you are.
SCHULZ

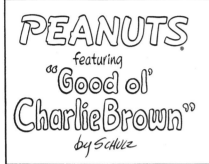

Peanuts featuring "Good ol' Charlie Brown" *by Schulz*

THERE'S OUR MAILBOX...WOULDN'T IT BE GREAT IF THERE WAS A VALENTINE IN THERE FOR ME FROM THAT LITTLE RED-HAIRED GIRL?

WOULDN'T IT BE GREAT IF IT WAS A REAL FANCY ONE WITH ALL SORTS OF HEARTS ALL OVER IT AND LACE AND EVERYTHING?

MAYBE IT WILL EVEN BE A SCENTED VALENTINE..IT WILL SMELL SORT OF LIKE VIOLETS OR A RARE PERFUME...

THIS IS SUNDAY, CHARLIE BROWN...THERE'S NO MAIL DELIVERY ON SUNDAY...

SIGH

2-14

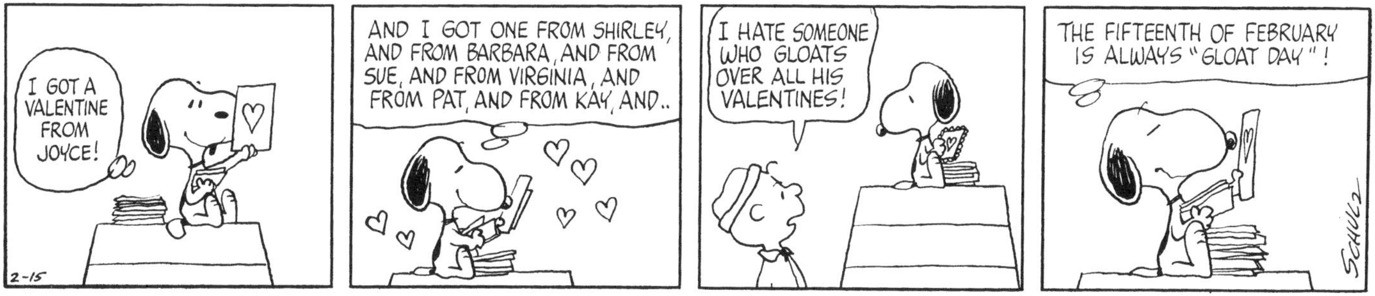
I GOT A VALENTINE FROM JOYCE!
AND I GOT ONE FROM SHIRLEY, AND FROM BARBARA, AND FROM SUE, AND FROM VIRGINIA, AND FROM PAT, AND FROM KAY, AND..
I HATE SOMEONE WHO GLOATS OVER ALL HIS VALENTINES!
THE FIFTEENTH OF FEBRUARY IS ALWAYS "GLOAT DAY"!
2-15
SCHULZ

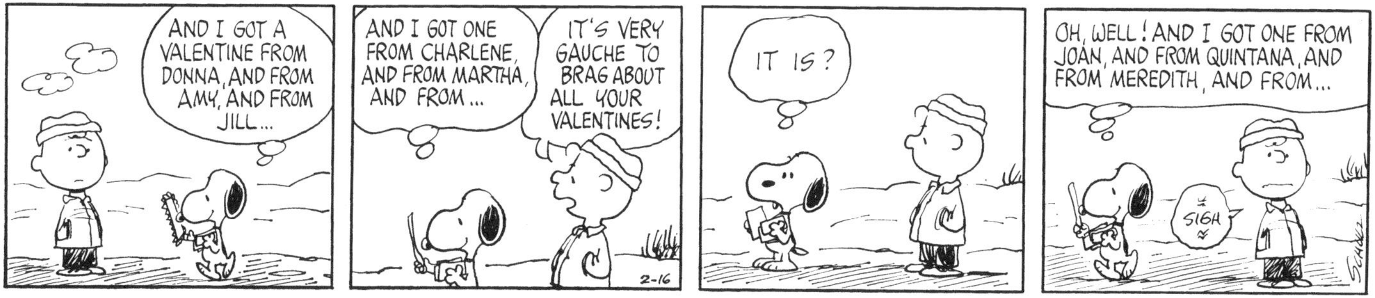
AND I GOT A VALENTINE FROM DONNA, AND FROM AMY, AND FROM JILL...
AND I GOT ONE FROM CHARLENE, AND FROM MARTHA, AND FROM...
IT'S VERY GAUCHE TO BRAG ABOUT ALL YOUR VALENTINES!
2-16
IT IS?
OH, WELL! AND I GOT ONE FROM JOAN, AND FROM QUINTANA, AND FROM MEREDITH, AND FROM...
SIGH
SCHULZ

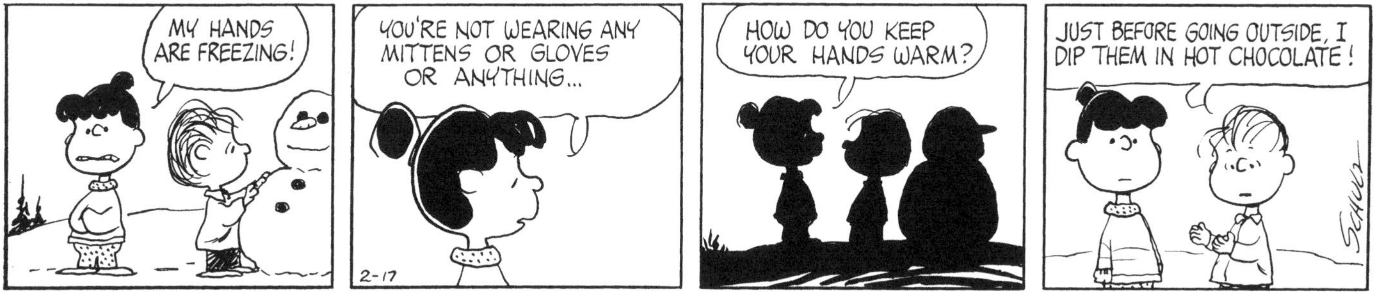
MY HANDS ARE FREEZING!
YOU'RE NOT WEARING ANY MITTENS OR GLOVES OR ANYTHING...
2-17
HOW DO YOU KEEP YOUR HANDS WARM?
JUST BEFORE GOING OUTSIDE, I DIP THEM IN HOT CHOCOLATE!
SCHULZ

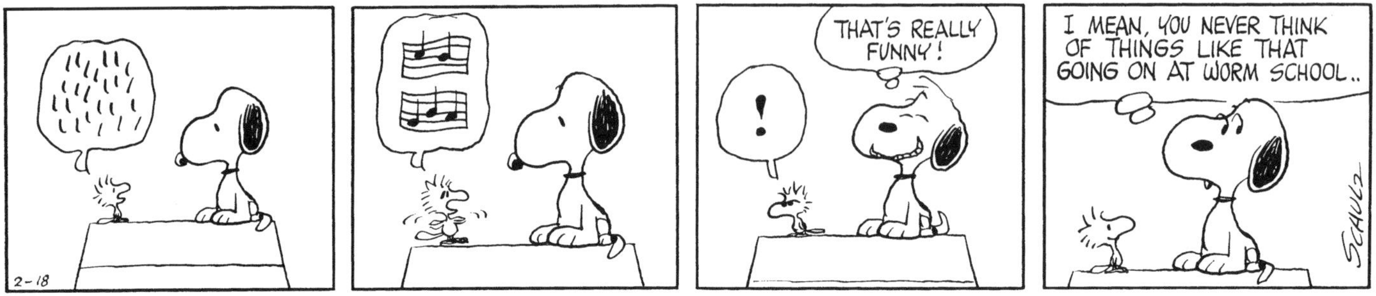
2-18
!
THAT'S REALLY FUNNY!
I MEAN, YOU NEVER THINK OF THINGS LIKE THAT GOING ON AT WORM SCHOOL..
SCHULZ

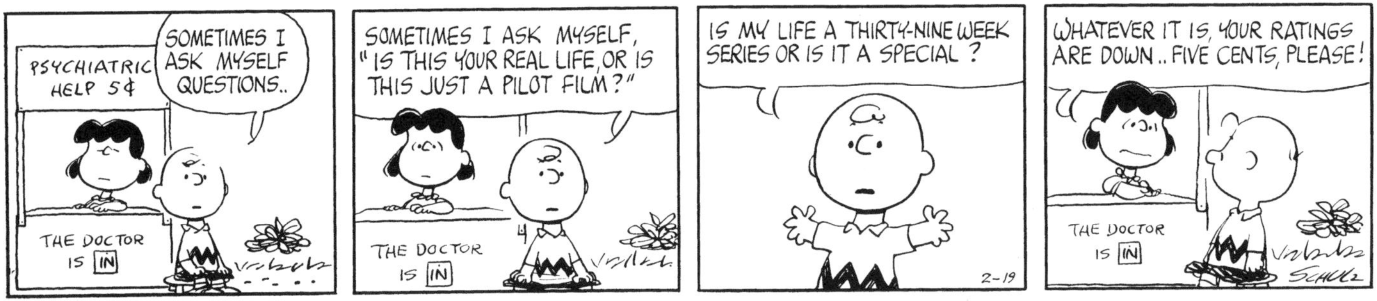
PSYCHIATRIC HELP 5¢
SOMETIMES I ASK MYSELF QUESTIONS..
THE DOCTOR IS IN
SOMETIMES I ASK MYSELF, "IS THIS YOUR REAL LIFE, OR IS THIS JUST A PILOT FILM?"
THE DOCTOR IS IN
IS MY LIFE A THIRTY-NINE WEEK SERIES OR IS IT A SPECIAL?
2-19
WHATEVER IT IS, YOUR RATINGS ARE DOWN.. FIVE CENTS, PLEASE!
THE DOCTOR IS IN
SCHULZ

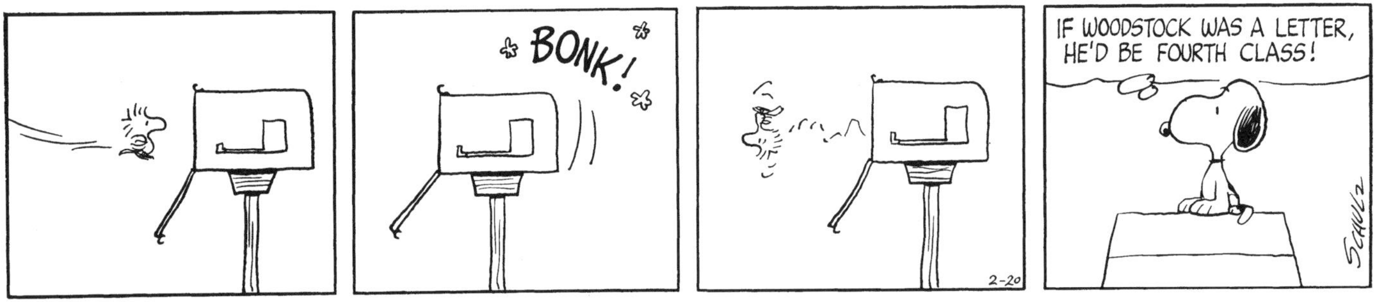
BONK!
2-20
IF WOODSTOCK WAS A LETTER, HE'D BE FOURTH CLASS!
SCHULZ

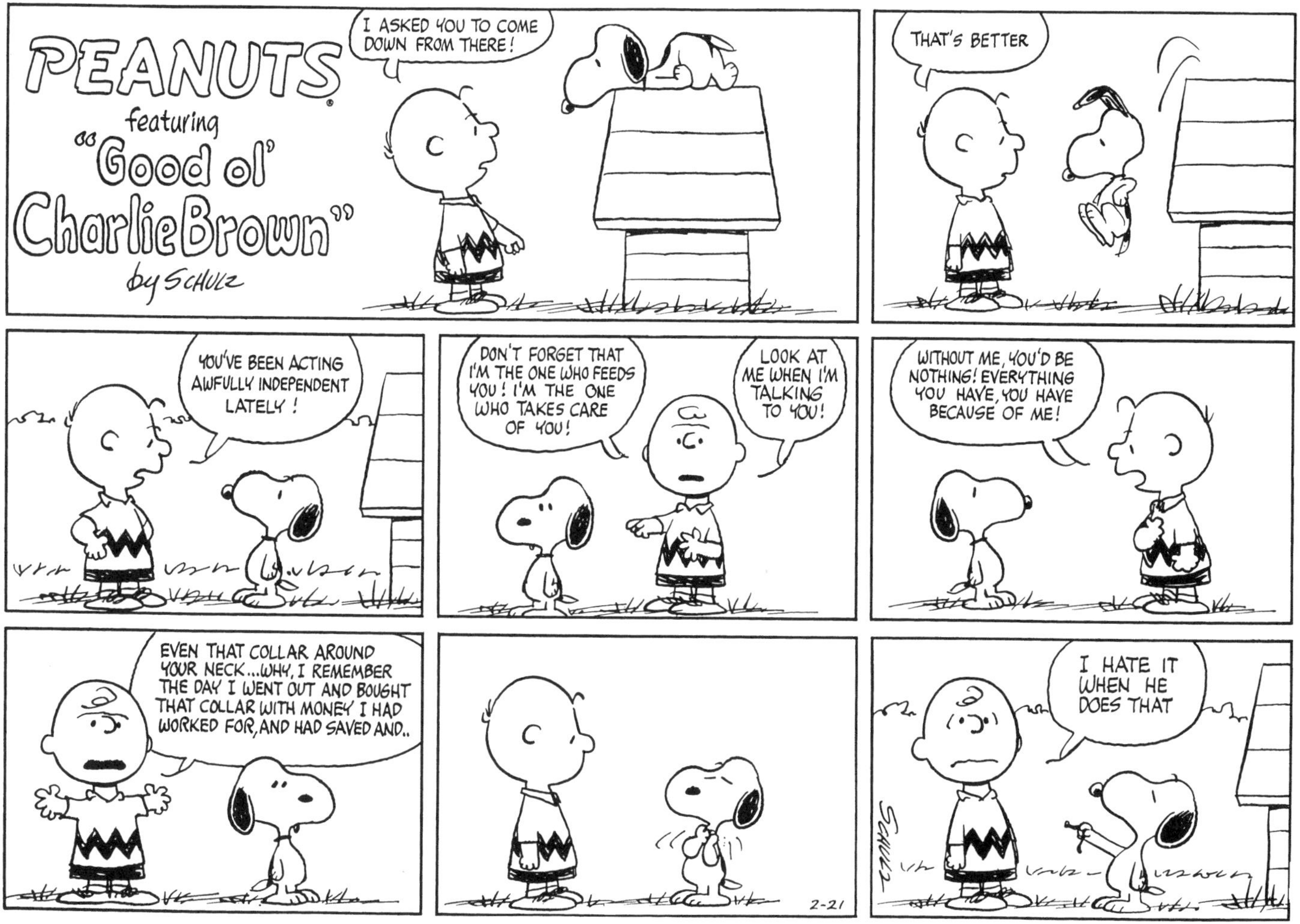
PEANUTS
featuring
"Good ol' Charlie Brown"
by SCHULZ
I ASKED YOU TO COME DOWN FROM THERE!
THAT'S BETTER
YOU'VE BEEN ACTING AWFULLY INDEPENDENT LATELY!
DON'T FORGET THAT I'M THE ONE WHO FEEDS YOU! I'M THE ONE WHO TAKES CARE OF YOU!
LOOK AT ME WHEN I'M TALKING TO YOU!
WITHOUT ME, YOU'D BE NOTHING! EVERYTHING YOU HAVE, YOU HAVE BECAUSE OF ME!
EVEN THAT COLLAR AROUND YOUR NECK...WHY, I REMEMBER THE DAY I WENT OUT AND BOUGHT THAT COLLAR WITH MONEY I HAD WORKED FOR, AND HAD SAVED AND..
2-21
I HATE IT WHEN HE DOES THAT
SCHULZ

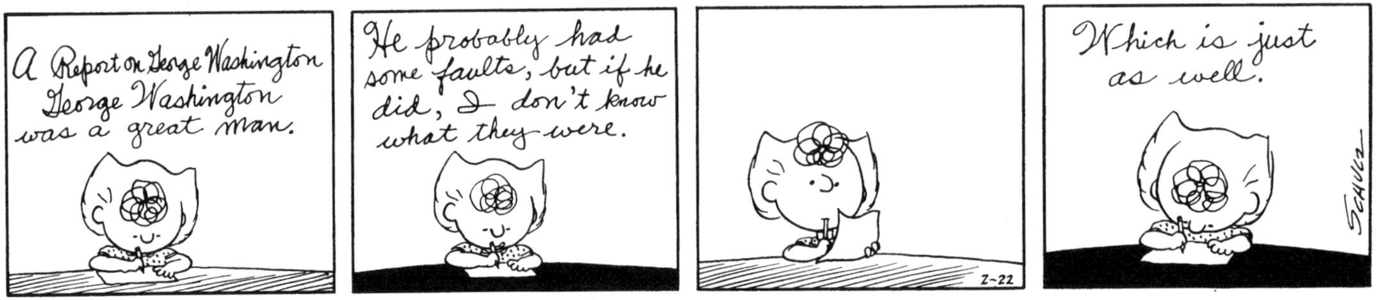
A Report on George Washington
George Washington was a great man.
He probably had some faults, but if he did, I don't know what they were.
Which is just as well.
2-22
SCHULZ

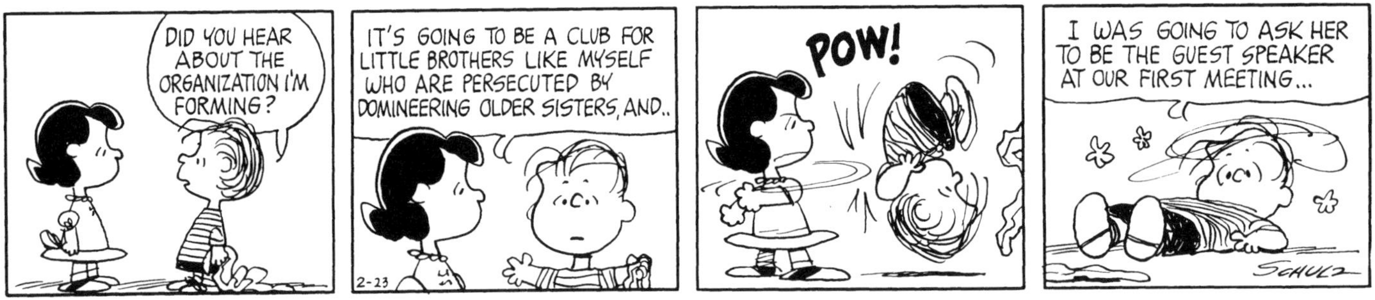
DID YOU HEAR ABOUT THE ORGANIZATION I'M FORMING?
IT'S GOING TO BE A CLUB FOR LITTLE BROTHERS LIKE MYSELF WHO ARE PERSECUTED BY DOMINEERING OLDER SISTERS, AND..
2-23
POW!
I WAS GOING TO ASK HER TO BE THE GUEST SPEAKER AT OUR FIRST MEETING...
SCHULZ

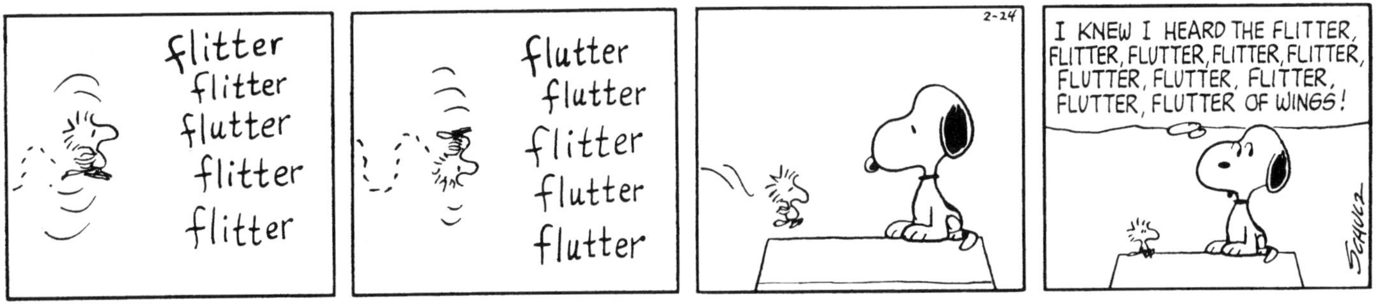
flitter
flitter
flutter
flitter
flitter
flutter
flutter
flitter
flutter
flutter
2-24
I KNEW I HEARD THE FLITTER, FLITTER, FLUTTER, FLITTER, FLITTER, FLUTTER, FLUTTER, FLITTER, FLUTTER, FLUTTER OF WINGS!
SCHULZ

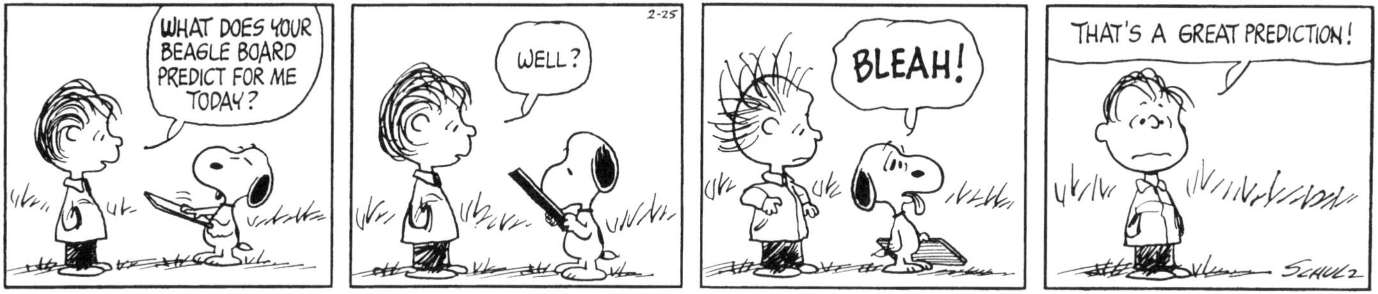
2-25
WHAT DOES YOUR BEAGLE BOARD PREDICT FOR ME TODAY?
WELL?
BLEAH!
THAT'S A GREAT PREDICTION!
SCHULZ

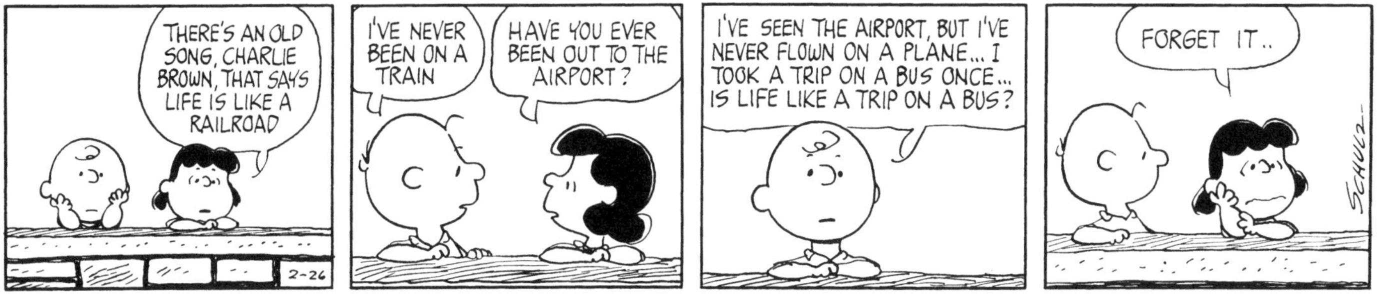
THERE'S AN OLD SONG, CHARLIE BROWN, THAT SAYS LIFE IS LIKE A RAILROAD
2-26
I'VE NEVER BEEN ON A TRAIN
HAVE YOU EVER BEEN OUT TO THE AIRPORT?
I'VE SEEN THE AIRPORT, BUT I'VE NEVER FLOWN ON A PLANE... I TOOK A TRIP ON A BUS ONCE... IS LIFE LIKE A TRIP ON A BUS?
FORGET IT..
SCHULZ

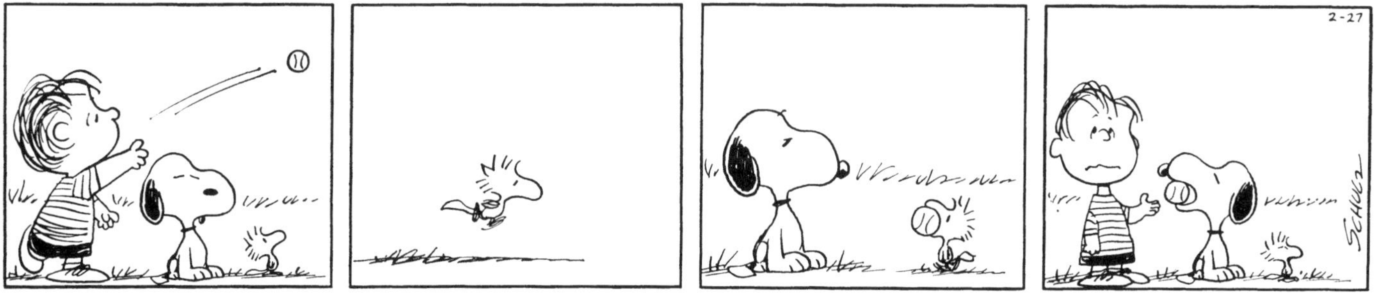
2-27
SCHULZ

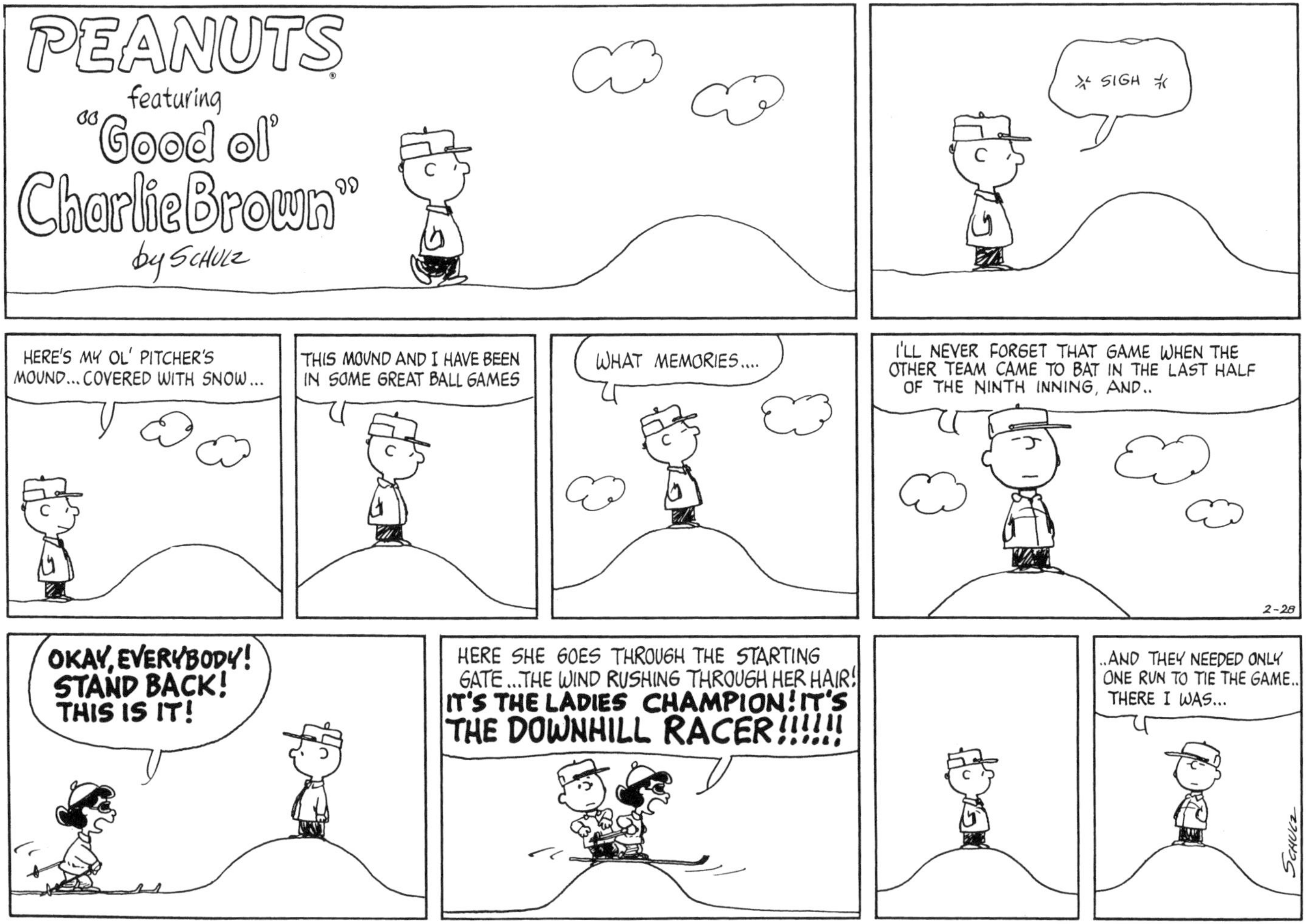
PEANUTS
featuring "Good ol' CharlieBrown"
by SCHULZ
SIGH
HERE'S MY OL' PITCHER'S MOUND... COVERED WITH SNOW...
THIS MOUND AND I HAVE BEEN IN SOME GREAT BALL GAMES
WHAT MEMORIES....
I'LL NEVER FORGET THAT GAME WHEN THE OTHER TEAM CAME TO BAT IN THE LAST HALF OF THE NINTH INNING, AND..
2-28
OKAY, EVERYBODY! STAND BACK! THIS IS IT!
HERE SHE GOES THROUGH THE STARTING GATE...THE WIND RUSHING THROUGH HER HAIR! IT'S THE LADIES CHAMPION! IT'S THE DOWNHILL RACER!!!!!!
..AND THEY NEEDED ONLY ONE RUN TO TIE THE GAME.. THERE I WAS...
SCHULZ

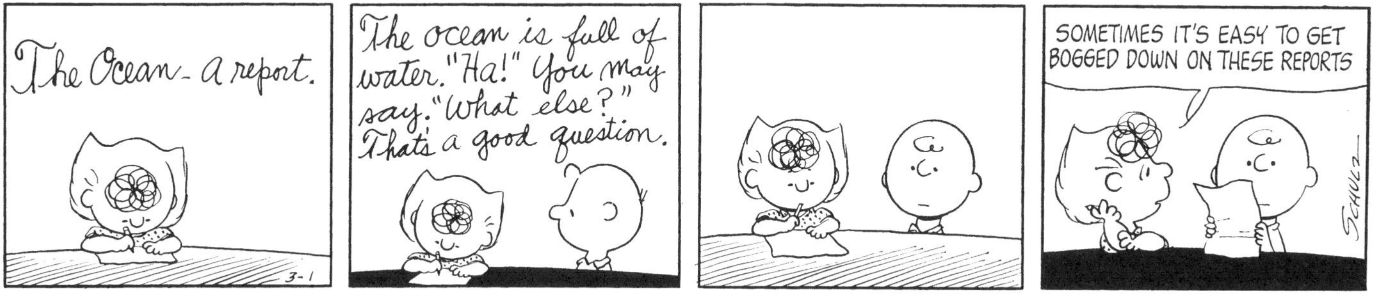

The Ocean - a report.
3-1
The ocean is full of water. "Ha!" You may say. "What else?" That's a good question.
SOMETIMES IT'S EASY TO GET BOGGED DOWN ON THESE REPORTS
SCHULZ

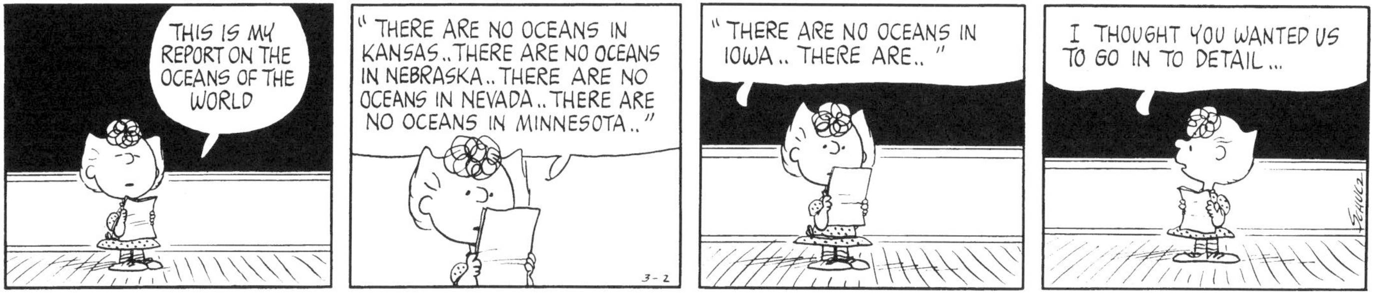

THIS IS MY REPORT ON THE OCEANS OF THE WORLD
" THERE ARE NO OCEANS IN KANSAS.. THERE ARE NO OCEANS IN NEBRASKA.. THERE ARE NO OCEANS IN NEVADA.. THERE ARE NO OCEANS IN MINNESOTA.. "
3-2
" THERE ARE NO OCEANS IN IOWA.. THERE ARE.. "
I THOUGHT YOU WANTED US TO GO IN TO DETAIL...
SCHULZ

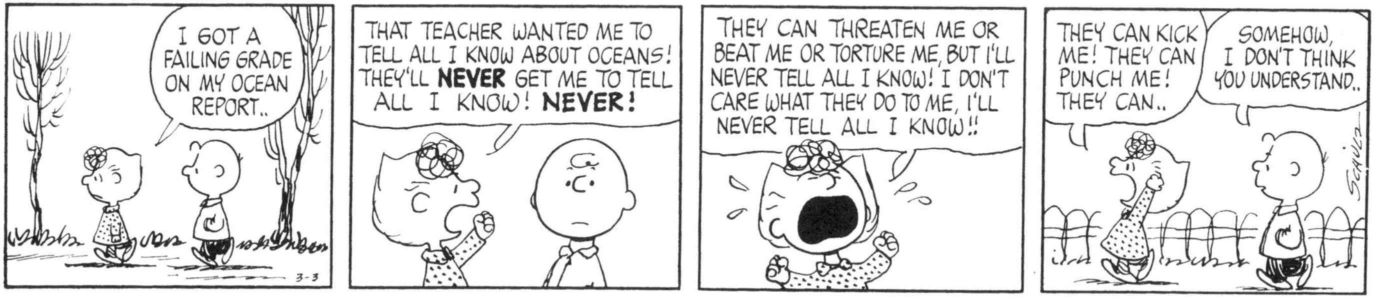

I GOT A FAILING GRADE ON MY OCEAN REPORT..
3-3
THAT TEACHER WANTED ME TO TELL ALL I KNOW ABOUT OCEANS! THEY'LL **NEVER** GET ME TO TELL ALL I KNOW! **NEVER!**
THEY CAN THREATEN ME OR BEAT ME OR TORTURE ME, BUT I'LL NEVER TELL ALL I KNOW! I DON'T CARE WHAT THEY DO TO ME, I'LL NEVER TELL ALL I KNOW!!
THEY CAN KICK ME! THEY CAN PUNCH ME! THEY CAN..
SOMEHOW, I DON'T THINK YOU UNDERSTAND..
SCHULZ

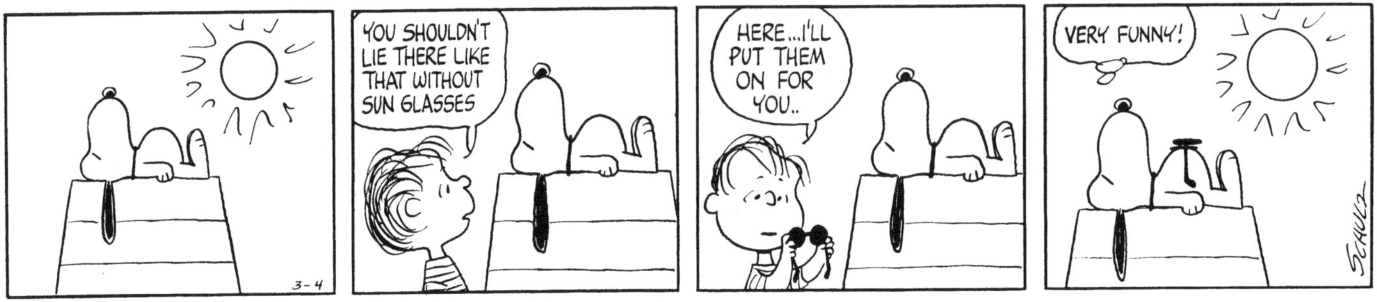
3-4
YOU SHOULDN'T LIE THERE LIKE THAT WITHOUT SUN GLASSES
HERE...I'LL PUT THEM ON FOR YOU..
VERY FUNNY!
SCHULZ

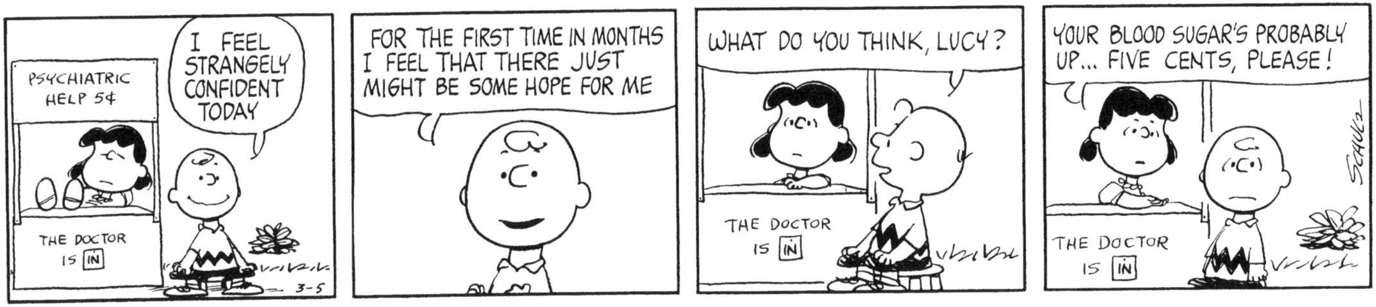
PSYCHIATRIC HELP 5¢
THE DOCTOR IS IN
I FEEL STRANGELY CONFIDENT TODAY
3-5
FOR THE FIRST TIME IN MONTHS I FEEL THAT THERE JUST MIGHT BE SOME HOPE FOR ME
WHAT DO YOU THINK, LUCY?
THE DOCTOR IS IN
YOUR BLOOD SUGAR'S PROBABLY UP... FIVE CENTS, PLEASE!
THE DOCTOR IS IN
SCHULZ

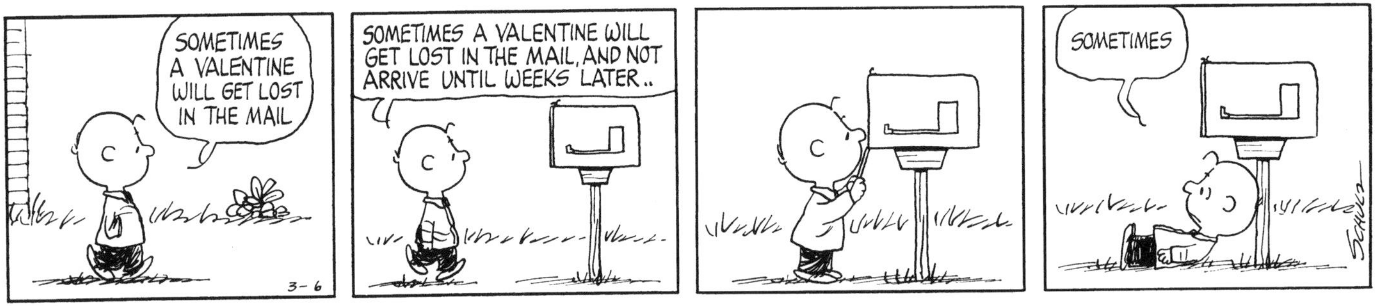
SOMETIMES A VALENTINE WILL GET LOST IN THE MAIL
3-6
SOMETIMES A VALENTINE WILL GET LOST IN THE MAIL, AND NOT ARRIVE UNTIL WEEKS LATER..
SOMETIMES
SCHULZ

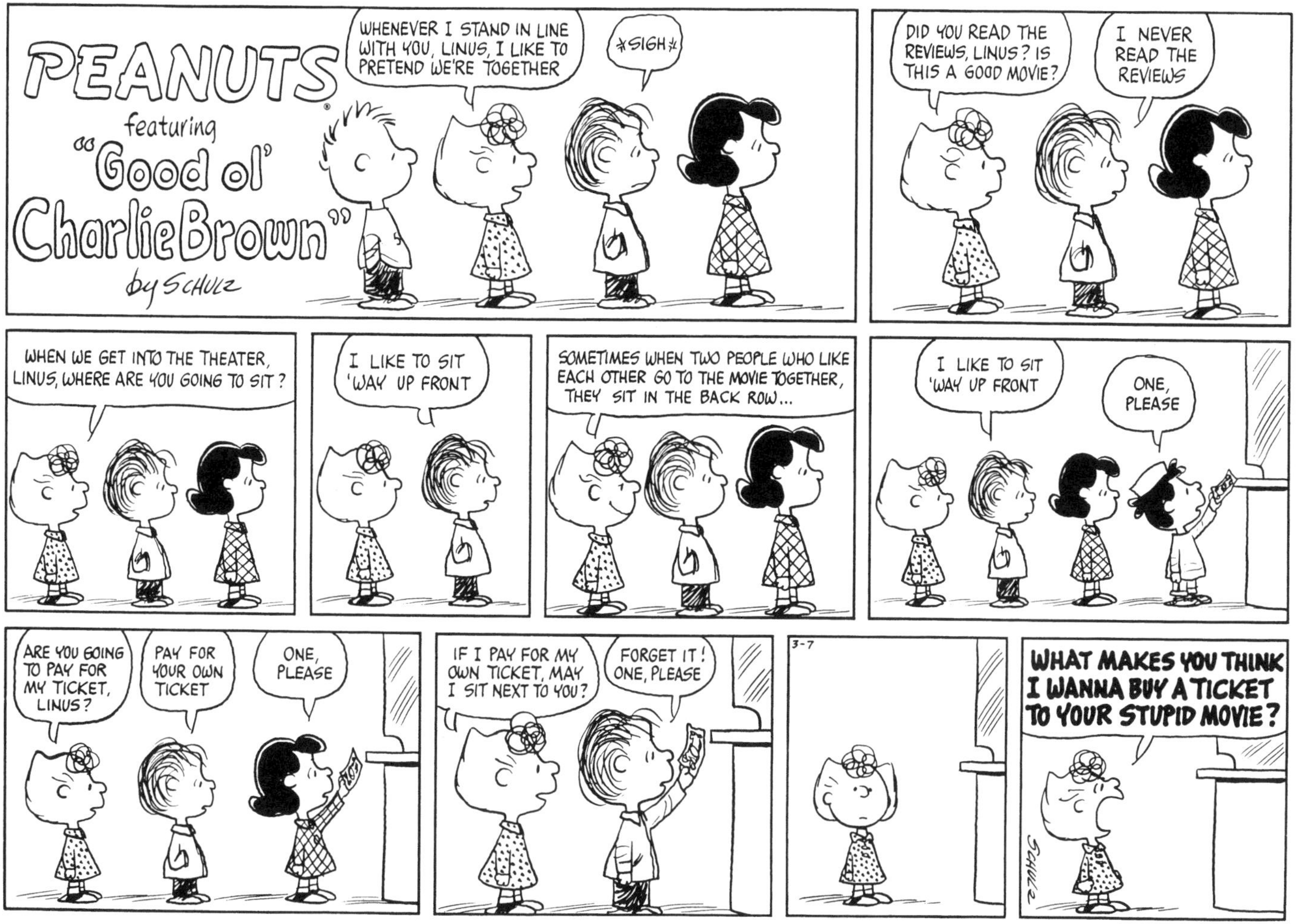
PEANUTS
featuring "Good ol' Charlie Brown"
by SCHULZ
WHENEVER I STAND IN LINE WITH YOU, LINUS, I LIKE TO PRETEND WE'RE TOGETHER
SIGH
DID YOU READ THE REVIEWS, LINUS? IS THIS A GOOD MOVIE?
I NEVER READ THE REVIEWS
WHEN WE GET INTO THE THEATER, LINUS, WHERE ARE YOU GOING TO SIT?
I LIKE TO SIT 'WAY UP FRONT
SOMETIMES WHEN TWO PEOPLE WHO LIKE EACH OTHER GO TO THE MOVIE TOGETHER, THEY SIT IN THE BACK ROW...
I LIKE TO SIT 'WAY UP FRONT
ONE, PLEASE
ARE YOU GOING TO PAY FOR MY TICKET, LINUS?
PAY FOR YOUR OWN TICKET
ONE, PLEASE
IF I PAY FOR MY OWN TICKET, MAY I SIT NEXT TO YOU?
FORGET IT! ONE, PLEASE
3-7
WHAT MAKES YOU THINK I WANNA BUY A TICKET TO YOUR STUPID MOVIE?
SCHULZ

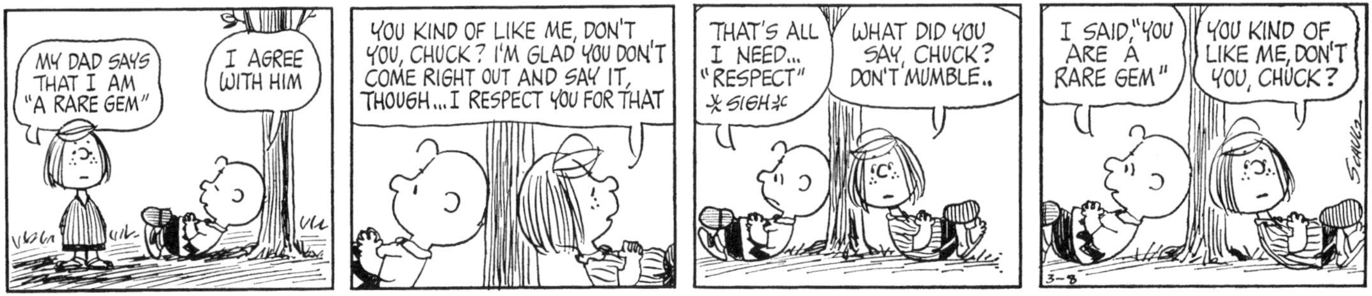

MY DAD SAYS THAT I AM "A RARE GEM"
I AGREE WITH HIM
YOU KIND OF LIKE ME, DON'T YOU, CHUCK? I'M GLAD YOU DON'T COME RIGHT OUT AND SAY IT, THOUGH...I RESPECT YOU FOR THAT
THAT'S ALL I NEED... "RESPECT" *SIGH*
WHAT DID YOU SAY, CHUCK? DON'T MUMBLE..
I SAID, "YOU ARE A RARE GEM"
YOU KIND OF LIKE ME, DON'T YOU, CHUCK?
SCHULZ
3-8

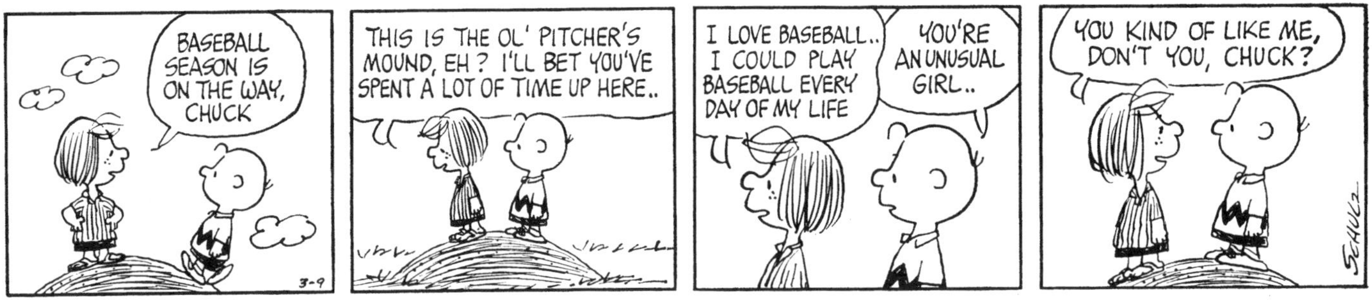

BASEBALL SEASON IS ON THE WAY, CHUCK
3-9
THIS IS THE OL' PITCHER'S MOUND, EH? I'LL BET YOU'VE SPENT A LOT OF TIME UP HERE..
I LOVE BASEBALL.. I COULD PLAY BASEBALL EVERY DAY OF MY LIFE
YOU'RE AN UNUSUAL GIRL..
YOU KIND OF LIKE ME, DON'T YOU, CHUCK?
SCHULZ

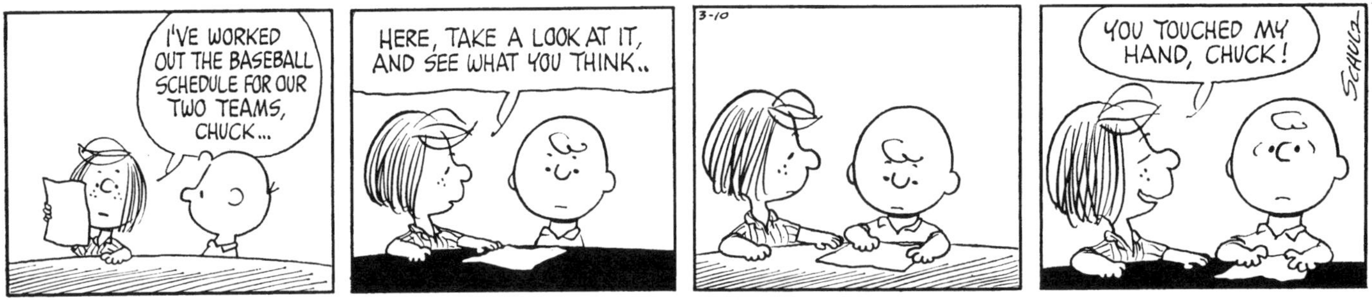

I'VE WORKED OUT THE BASEBALL SCHEDULE FOR OUR TWO TEAMS, CHUCK...
HERE, TAKE A LOOK AT IT, AND SEE WHAT YOU THINK..
3-10
YOU TOUCHED MY HAND, CHUCK!
SCHULZ

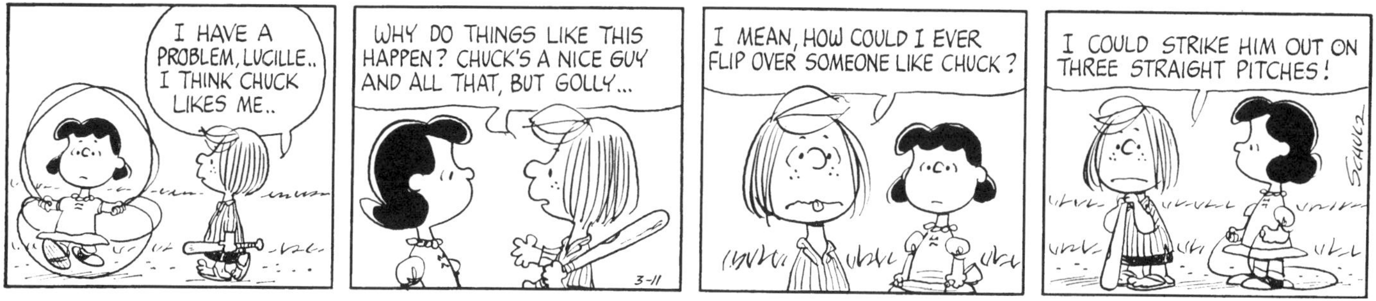
I HAVE A PROBLEM, LUCILLE.. I THINK CHUCK LIKES ME..
WHY DO THINGS LIKE THIS HAPPEN? CHUCK'S A NICE GUY AND ALL THAT, BUT GOLLY...
3-11
I MEAN, HOW COULD I EVER FLIP OVER SOMEONE LIKE CHUCK?
I COULD STRIKE HIM OUT ON THREE STRAIGHT PITCHES!
SCHULZ

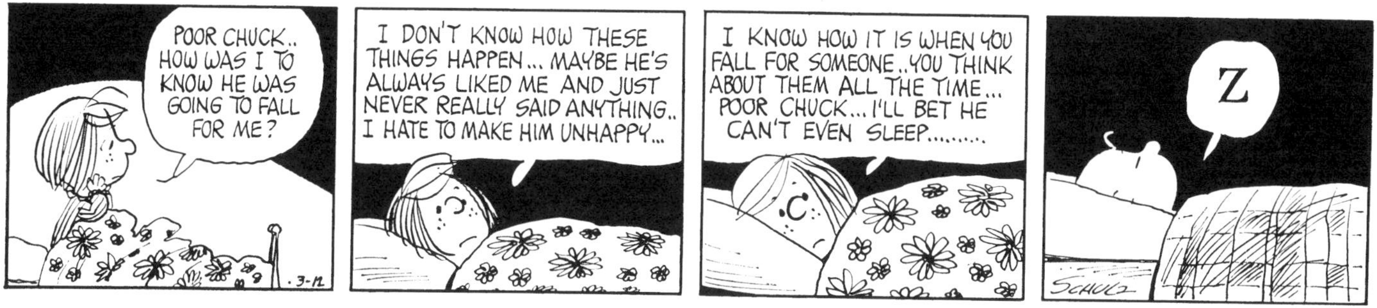
POOR CHUCK.. HOW WAS I TO KNOW HE WAS GOING TO FALL FOR ME?
3-12
I DON'T KNOW HOW THESE THINGS HAPPEN... MAYBE HE'S ALWAYS LIKED ME AND JUST NEVER REALLY SAID ANYTHING.. I HATE TO MAKE HIM UNHAPPY...
I KNOW HOW IT IS WHEN YOU FALL FOR SOMEONE..YOU THINK ABOUT THEM ALL THE TIME... POOR CHUCK... I'LL BET HE CAN'T EVEN SLEEP.........
Z
SCHULZ

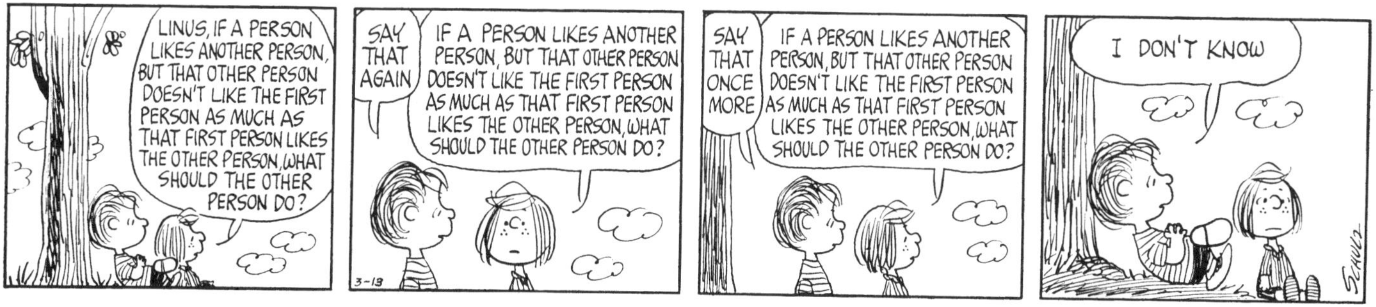
LINUS, IF A PERSON LIKES ANOTHER PERSON, BUT THAT OTHER PERSON DOESN'T LIKE THE FIRST PERSON AS MUCH AS THAT FIRST PERSON LIKES THE OTHER PERSON, WHAT SHOULD THE OTHER PERSON DO?
SAY THAT AGAIN
IF A PERSON LIKES ANOTHER PERSON, BUT THAT OTHER PERSON DOESN'T LIKE THE FIRST PERSON AS MUCH AS THAT FIRST PERSON LIKES THE OTHER PERSON, WHAT SHOULD THE OTHER PERSON DO?
3-13
SAY THAT ONCE MORE
IF A PERSON LIKES ANOTHER PERSON, BUT THAT OTHER PERSON DOESN'T LIKE THE FIRST PERSON AS MUCH AS THAT FIRST PERSON LIKES THE OTHER PERSON, WHAT SHOULD THE OTHER PERSON DO?
I DON'T KNOW
SCHULZ

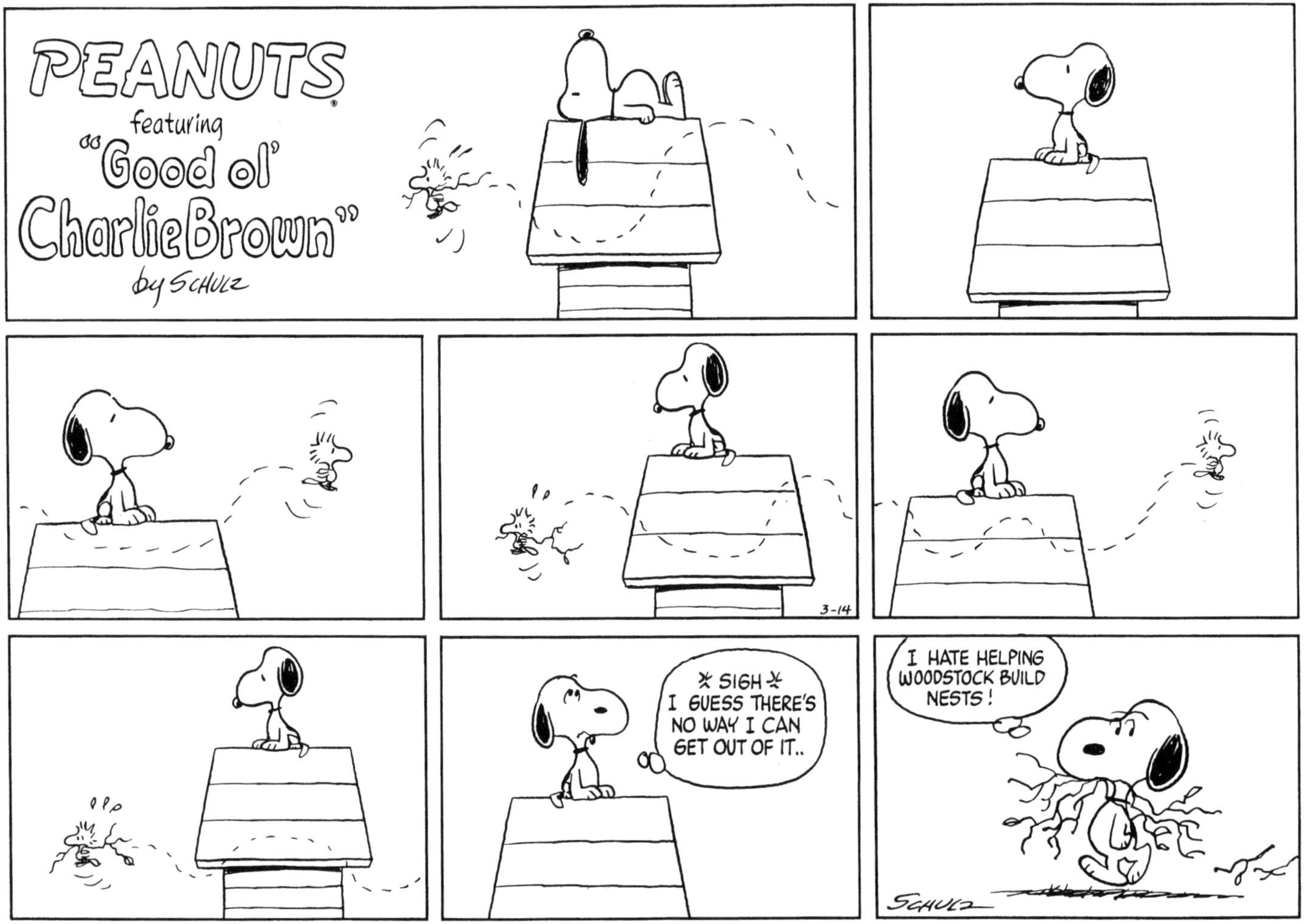
PEANUTS
featuring
"Good ol' Charlie Brown"
by SCHULZ
3-14
* SIGH *
I GUESS THERE'S NO WAY I CAN GET OUT OF IT..
I HATE HELPING WOODSTOCK BUILD NESTS!
SCHULZ

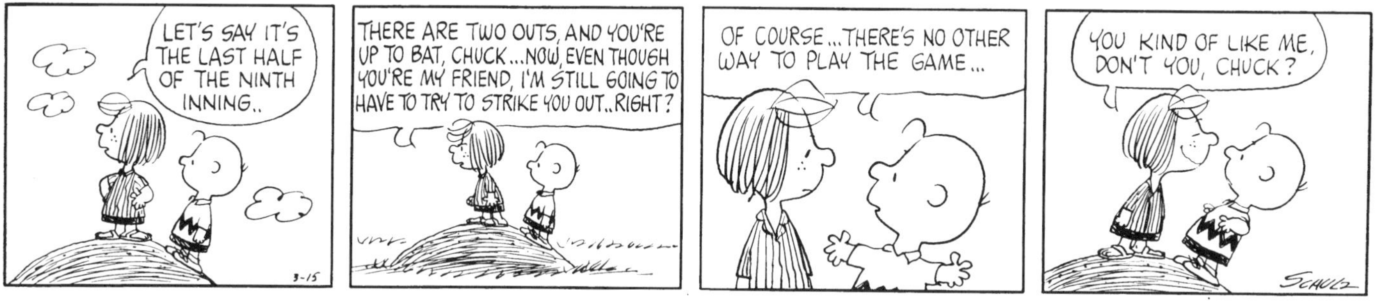
LET'S SAY IT'S THE LAST HALF OF THE NINTH INNING..
3-15
THERE ARE TWO OUTS, AND YOU'RE UP TO BAT, CHUCK...NOW, EVEN THOUGH YOU'RE MY FRIEND, I'M STILL GOING TO HAVE TO TRY TO STRIKE YOU OUT..RIGHT?
OF COURSE...THERE'S NO OTHER WAY TO PLAY THE GAME...
YOU KIND OF LIKE ME, DON'T YOU, CHUCK?
SCHULZ

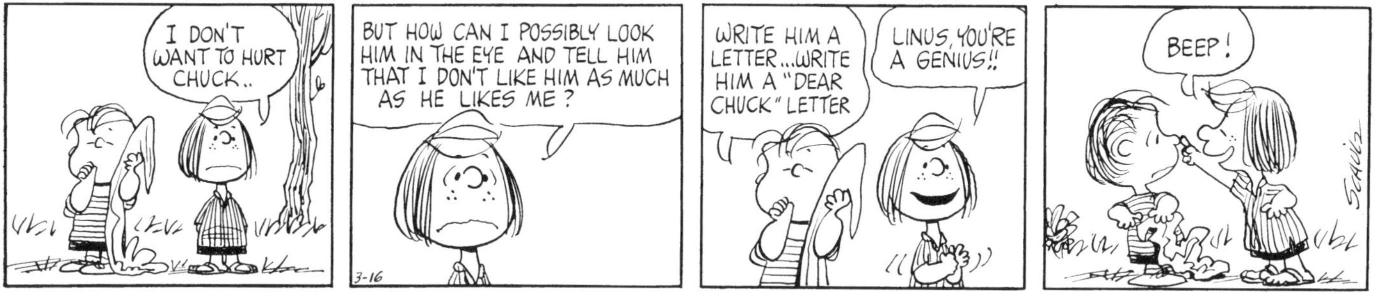
I DON'T WANT TO HURT CHUCK..
BUT HOW CAN I POSSIBLY LOOK HIM IN THE EYE AND TELL HIM THAT I DON'T LIKE HIM AS MUCH AS HE LIKES ME?
3-16
WRITE HIM A LETTER...WRITE HIM A "DEAR CHUCK" LETTER
LINUS, YOU'RE A GENIUS!!
BEEP!
SCHULZ

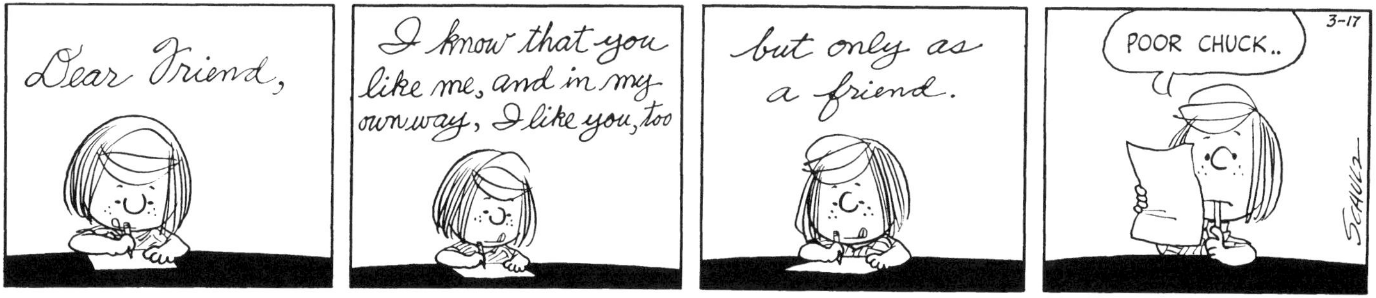
Dear Friend,
I know that you like me, and in my own way, I like you, too
but only as a friend.
3-17
POOR CHUCK..
SCHULZ

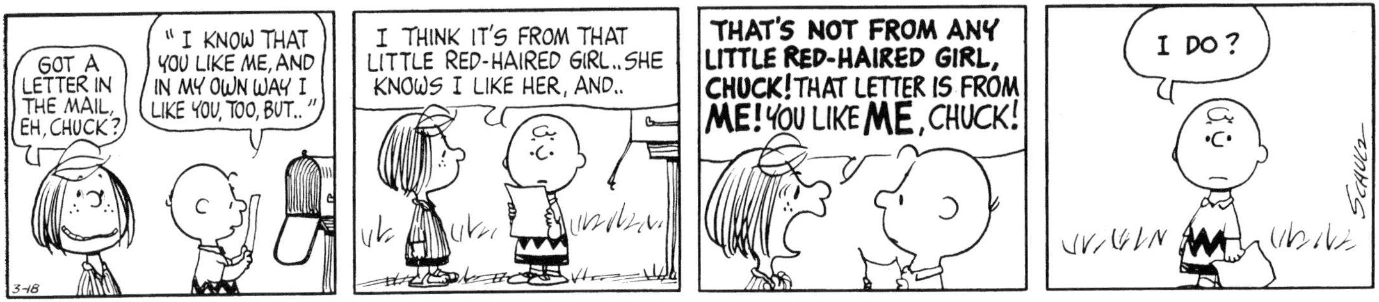
GOT A LETTER IN THE MAIL, EH, CHUCK?
" I KNOW THAT YOU LIKE ME, AND IN MY OWN WAY I LIKE YOU, TOO, BUT.. "
I THINK IT'S FROM THAT LITTLE RED-HAIRED GIRL.. SHE KNOWS I LIKE HER, AND..
THAT'S NOT FROM ANY LITTLE RED-HAIRED GIRL, CHUCK! THAT LETTER IS FROM ME! YOU LIKE ME, CHUCK!
I DO?
3-18
SCHULZ

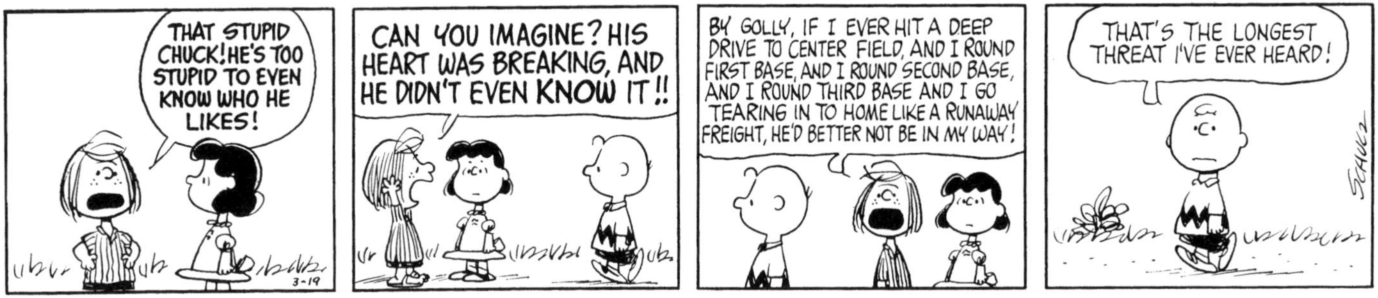
THAT STUPID CHUCK! HE'S TOO STUPID TO EVEN KNOW WHO HE LIKES!
CAN YOU IMAGINE? HIS HEART WAS BREAKING, AND HE DIDN'T EVEN KNOW IT!!
BY GOLLY, IF I EVER HIT A DEEP DRIVE TO CENTER FIELD, AND I ROUND FIRST BASE, AND I ROUND SECOND BASE, AND I ROUND THIRD BASE AND I GO TEARING IN TO HOME LIKE A RUNAWAY FREIGHT, HE'D BETTER NOT BE IN MY WAY!
THAT'S THE LONGEST THREAT I'VE EVER HEARD!
3-19
SCHULZ

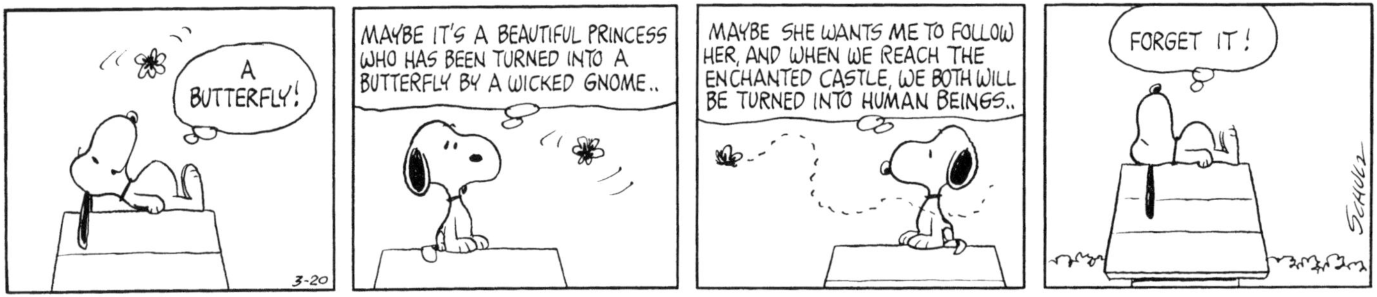
A BUTTERFLY!
MAYBE IT'S A BEAUTIFUL PRINCESS WHO HAS BEEN TURNED INTO A BUTTERFLY BY A WICKED GNOME..
MAYBE SHE WANTS ME TO FOLLOW HER, AND WHEN WE REACH THE ENCHANTED CASTLE, WE BOTH WILL BE TURNED INTO HUMAN BEINGS..
FORGET IT!
3-20
SCHULZ

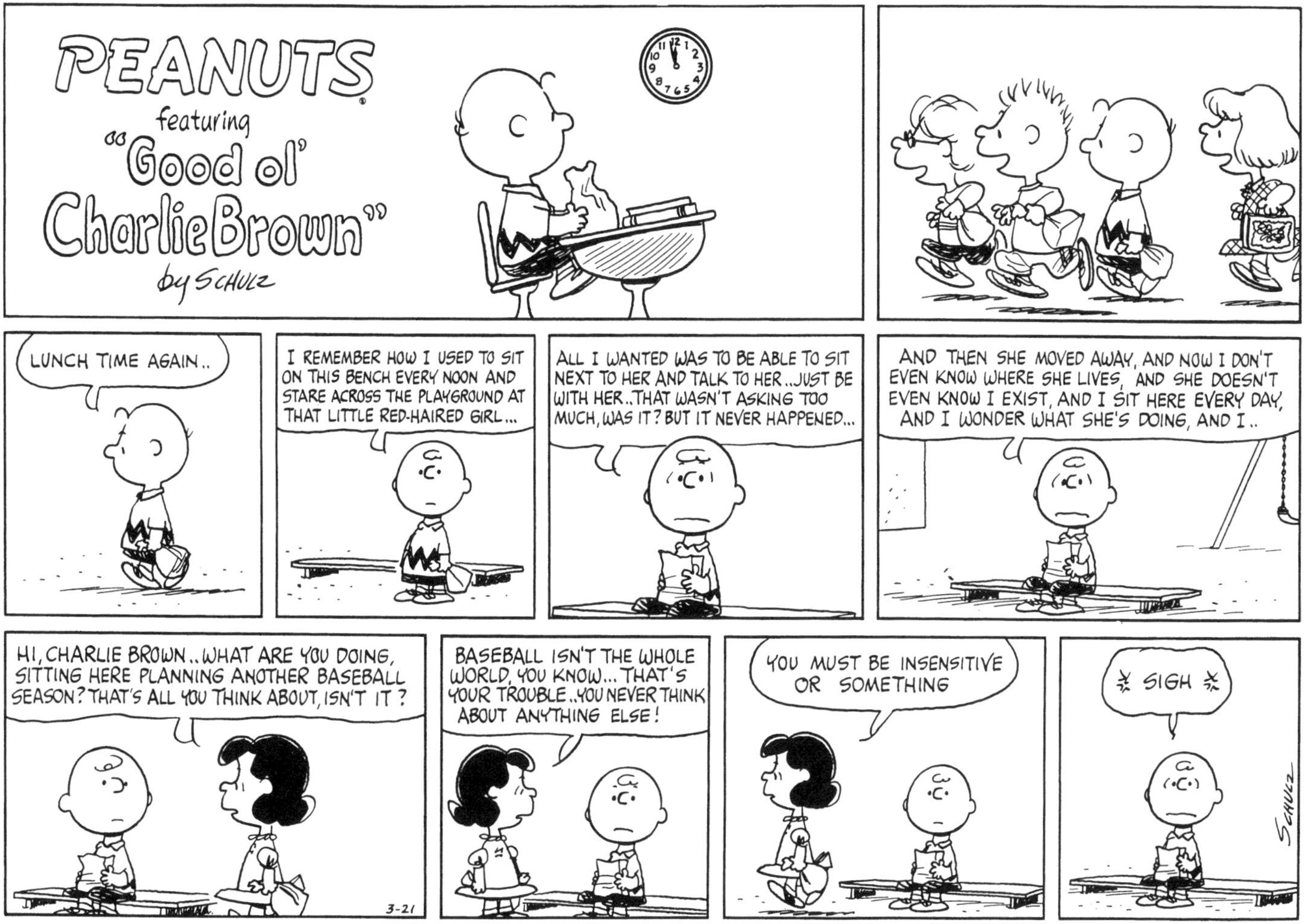
PEANUTS
featuring
"Good ol' CharlieBrown"
by SCHULZ
LUNCH TIME AGAIN..
I REMEMBER HOW I USED TO SIT ON THIS BENCH EVERY NOON AND STARE ACROSS THE PLAYGROUND AT THAT LITTLE RED-HAIRED GIRL...
ALL I WANTED WAS TO BE ABLE TO SIT NEXT TO HER AND TALK TO HER..JUST BE WITH HER..THAT WASN'T ASKING TOO MUCH, WAS IT? BUT IT NEVER HAPPENED...
AND THEN SHE MOVED AWAY, AND NOW I DON'T EVEN KNOW WHERE SHE LIVES, AND SHE DOESN'T EVEN KNOW I EXIST, AND I SIT HERE EVERY DAY, AND I WONDER WHAT SHE'S DOING, AND I..
HI, CHARLIE BROWN..WHAT ARE YOU DOING, SITTING HERE PLANNING ANOTHER BASEBALL SEASON? THAT'S ALL YOU THINK ABOUT, ISN'T IT?
3-21
BASEBALL ISN'T THE WHOLE WORLD, YOU KNOW... THAT'S YOUR TROUBLE..YOU NEVER THINK ABOUT ANYTHING ELSE!
YOU MUST BE INSENSITIVE OR SOMETHING
SIGH
SCHULZ

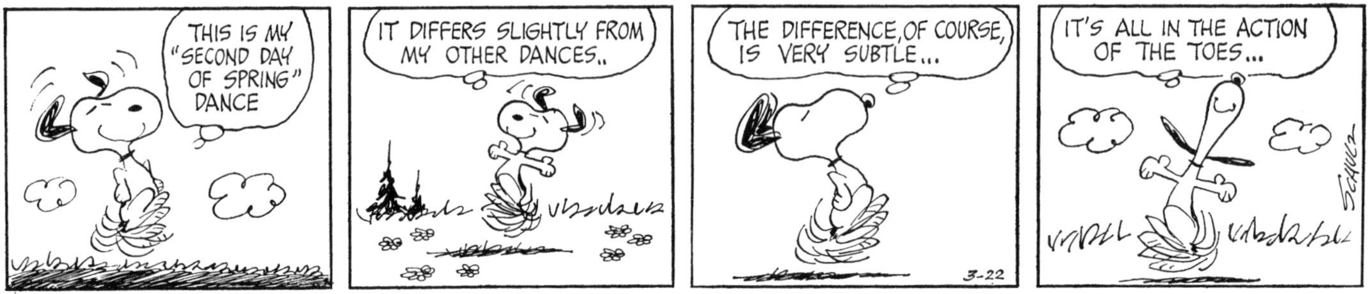
THIS IS MY "SECOND DAY OF SPRING" DANCE
IT DIFFERS SLIGHTLY FROM MY OTHER DANCES..
THE DIFFERENCE, OF COURSE, IS VERY SUBTLE...
IT'S ALL IN THE ACTION OF THE TOES...
3-22
SCHULZ

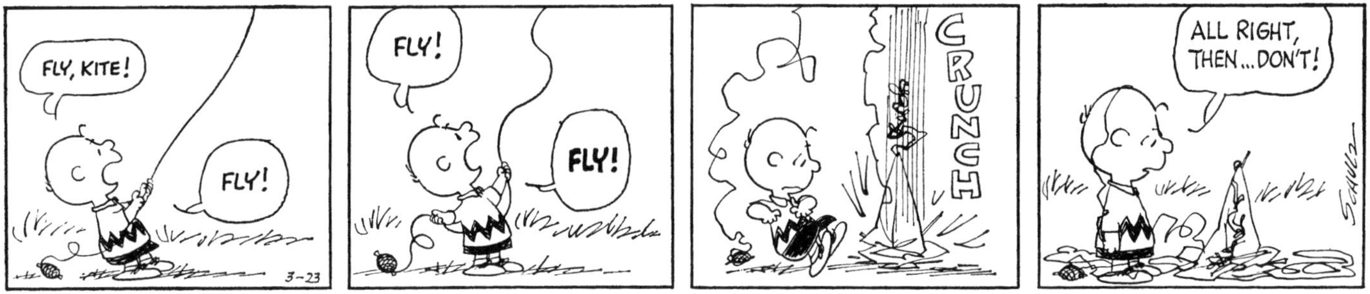
FLY, KITE!
FLY!
FLY!
FLY!
CRUNCH
ALL RIGHT, THEN...DON'T!
3-23
SCHULZ

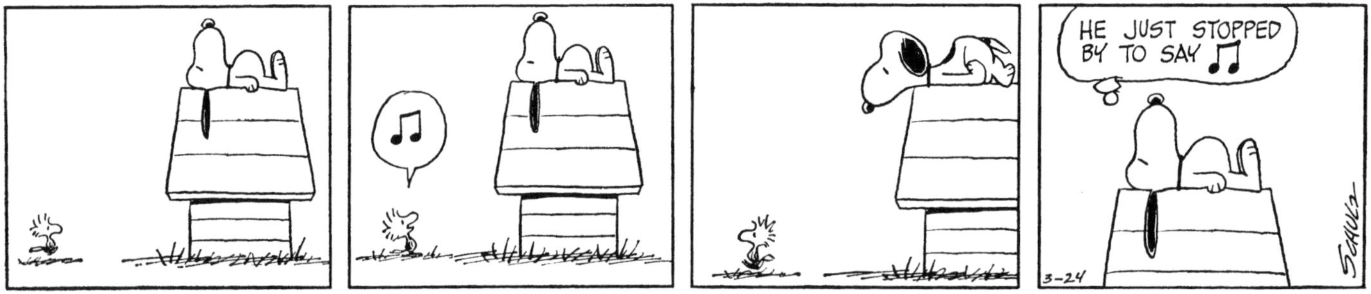
HE JUST STOPPED BY TO SAY
3-24
SCHULZ

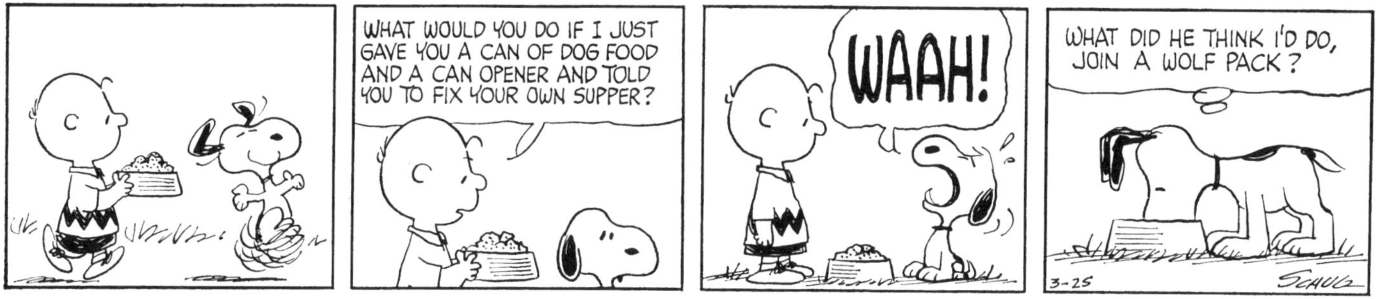
WHAT WOULD YOU DO IF I JUST GAVE YOU A CAN OF DOG FOOD AND A CAN OPENER AND TOLD YOU TO FIX YOUR OWN SUPPER?
WAAH!
WHAT DID HE THINK I'D DO, JOIN A WOLF PACK?
3-25
SCHULZ

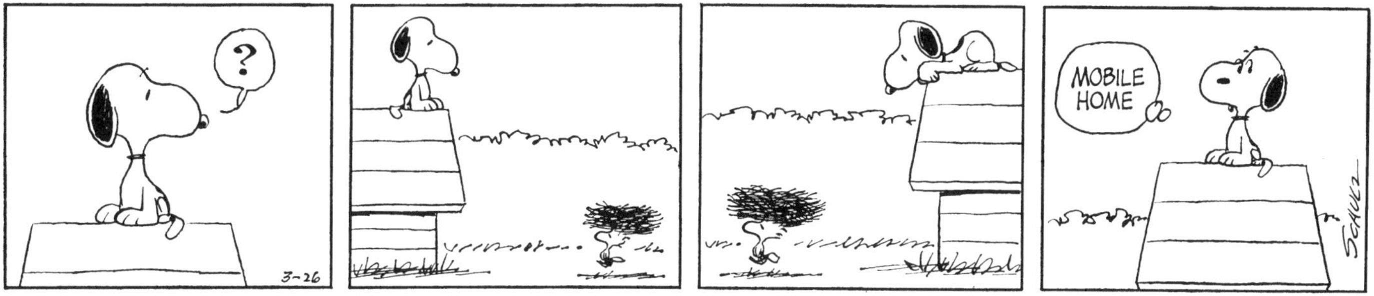
?
3-26
MOBILE HOME
SCHULZ

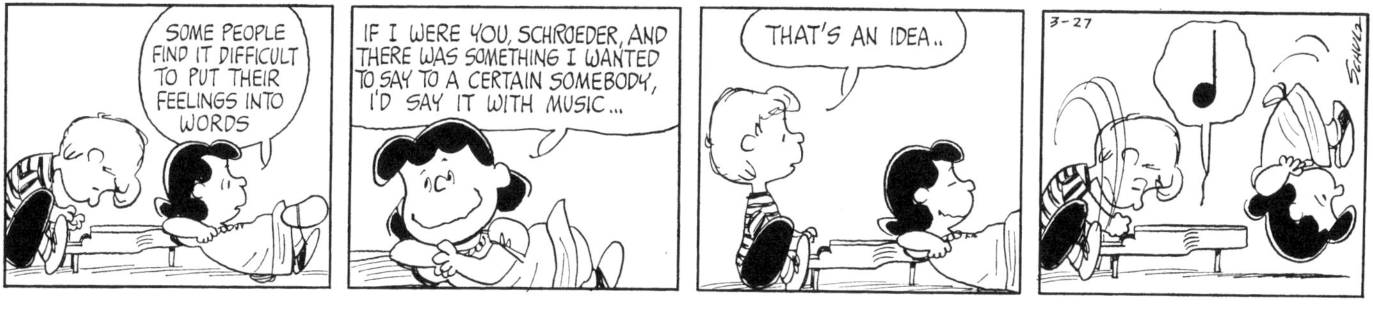
SOME PEOPLE FIND IT DIFFICULT TO PUT THEIR FEELINGS INTO WORDS
IF I WERE YOU, SCHROEDER, AND THERE WAS SOMETHING I WANTED TO SAY TO A CERTAIN SOMEBODY, I'D SAY IT WITH MUSIC...
THAT'S AN IDEA..
3-27
SCHULZ

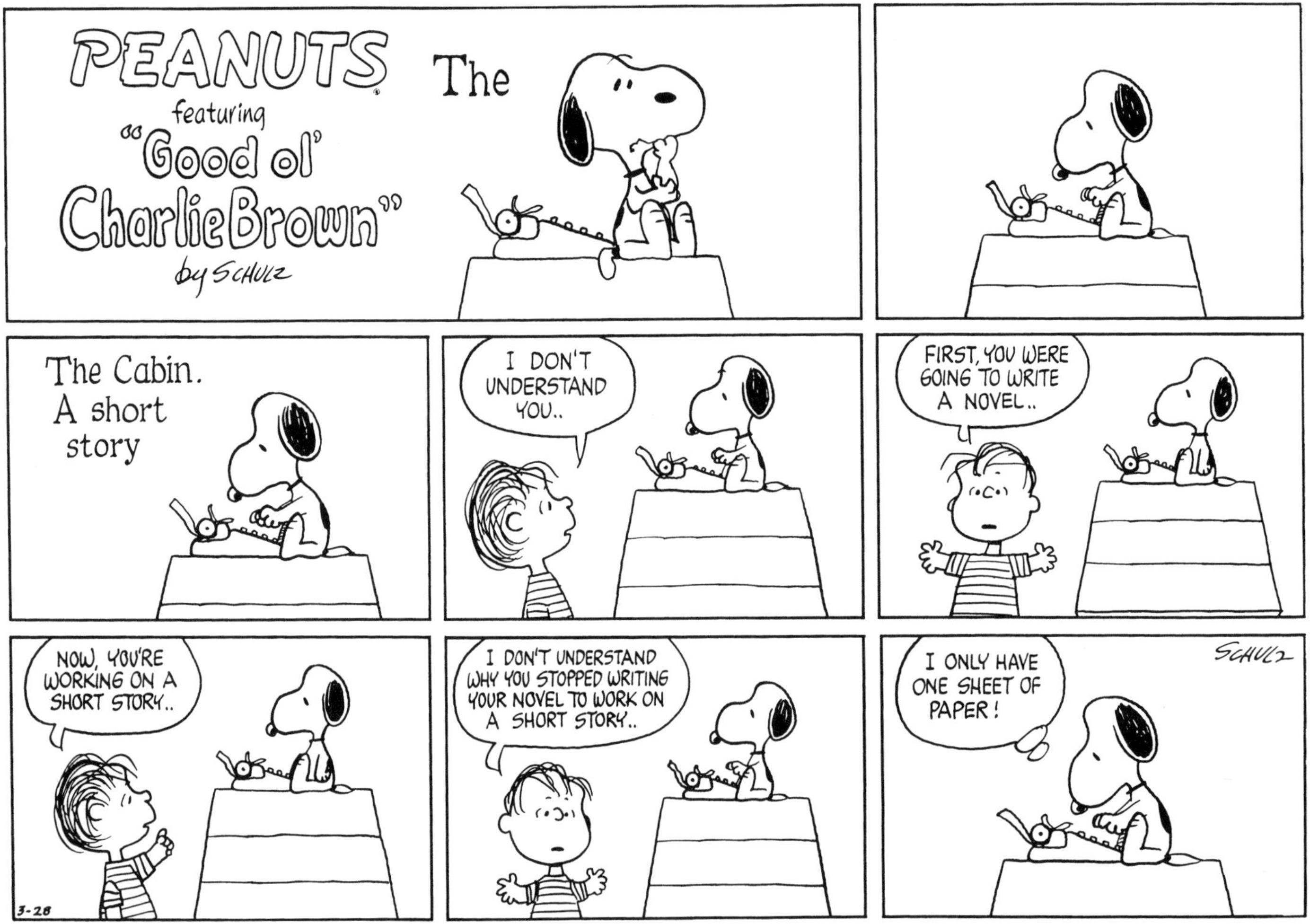
PEANUTS
featuring
"Good ol' Charlie Brown"
by SCHULZ
The
The Cabin.
A short
story
I DON'T UNDERSTAND YOU..
FIRST, YOU WERE GOING TO WRITE A NOVEL..
NOW, YOU'RE WORKING ON A SHORT STORY..
3-28
I DON'T UNDERSTAND WHY YOU STOPPED WRITING YOUR NOVEL TO WORK ON A SHORT STORY..
I ONLY HAVE ONE SHEET OF PAPER!
SCHULZ

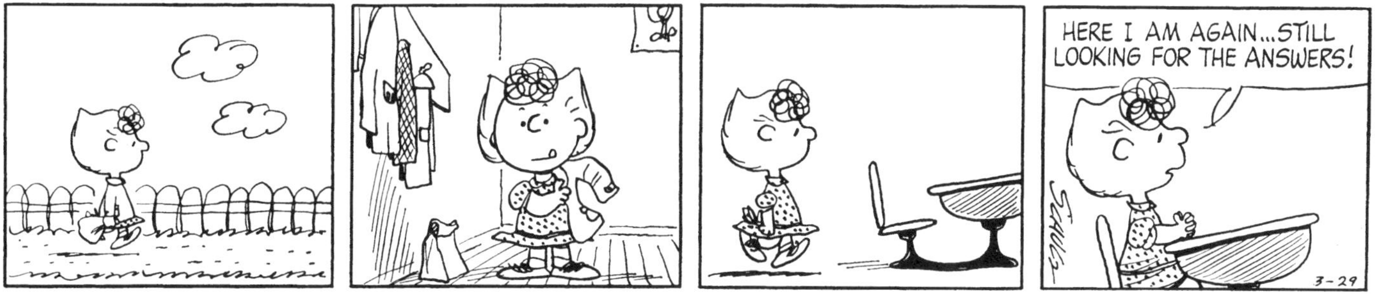
HERE I AM AGAIN...STILL LOOKING FOR THE ANSWERS!
3-29

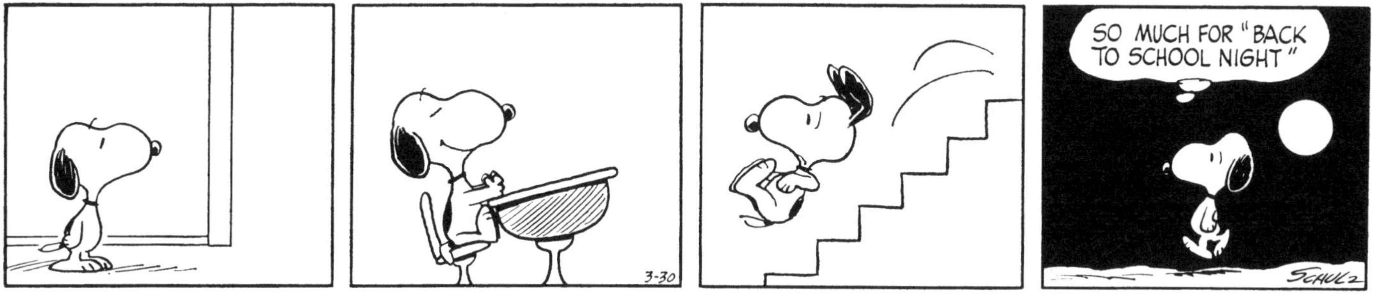
3-30
SO MUCH FOR "BACK TO SCHOOL NIGHT"

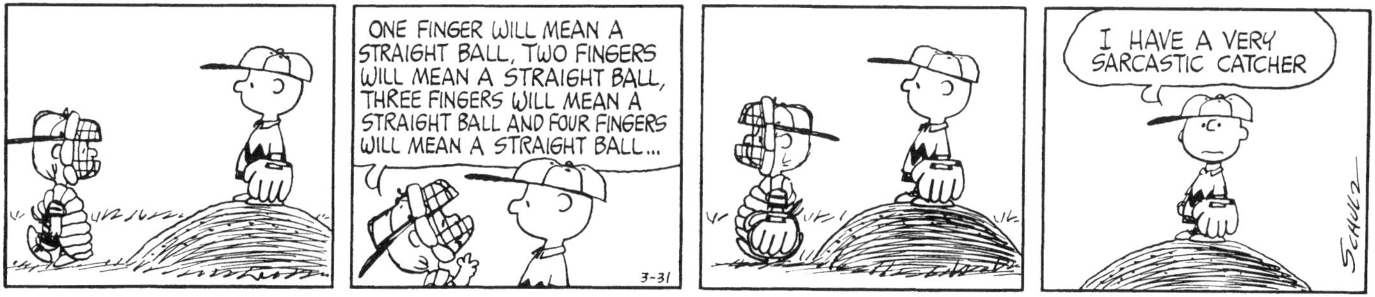
ONE FINGER WILL MEAN A STRAIGHT BALL, TWO FINGERS WILL MEAN A STRAIGHT BALL, THREE FINGERS WILL MEAN A STRAIGHT BALL AND FOUR FINGERS WILL MEAN A STRAIGHT BALL...
3-31
I HAVE A VERY SARCASTIC CATCHER

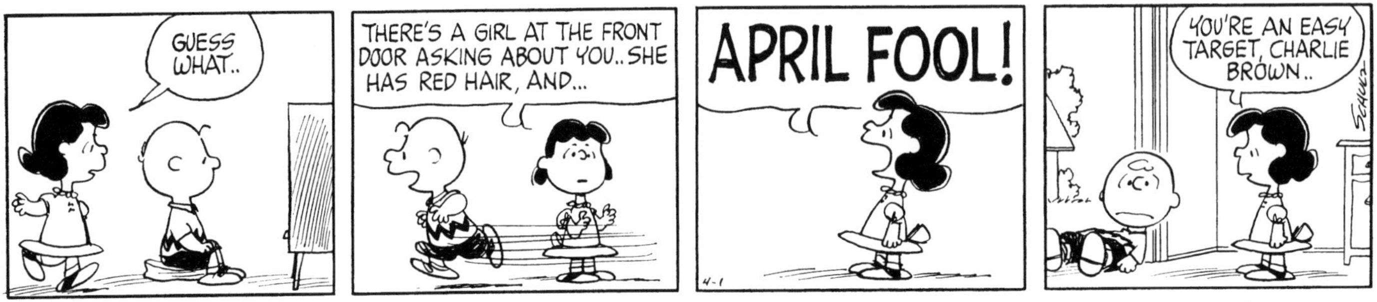
GUESS WHAT..
THERE'S A GIRL AT THE FRONT DOOR ASKING ABOUT YOU.. SHE HAS RED HAIR, AND...
APRIL FOOL!
YOU'RE AN EASY TARGET, CHARLIE BROWN..

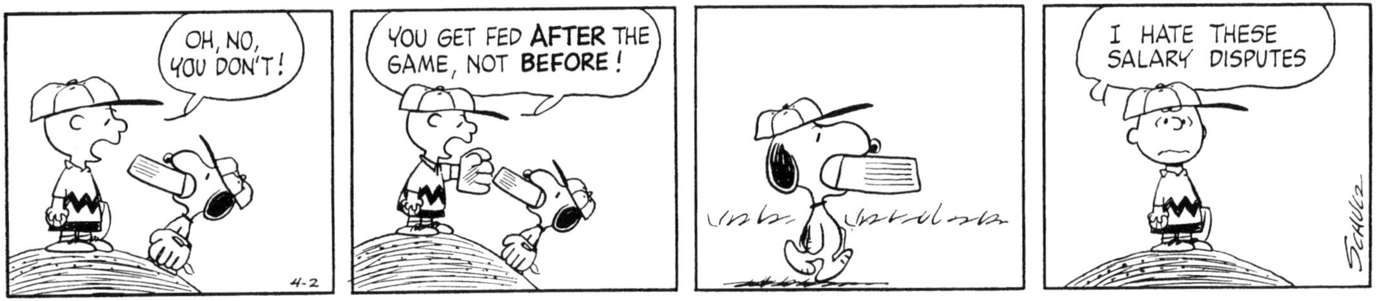
OH, NO, YOU DON'T!
YOU GET FED **AFTER** THE GAME, NOT **BEFORE**!
I HATE THESE SALARY DISPUTES

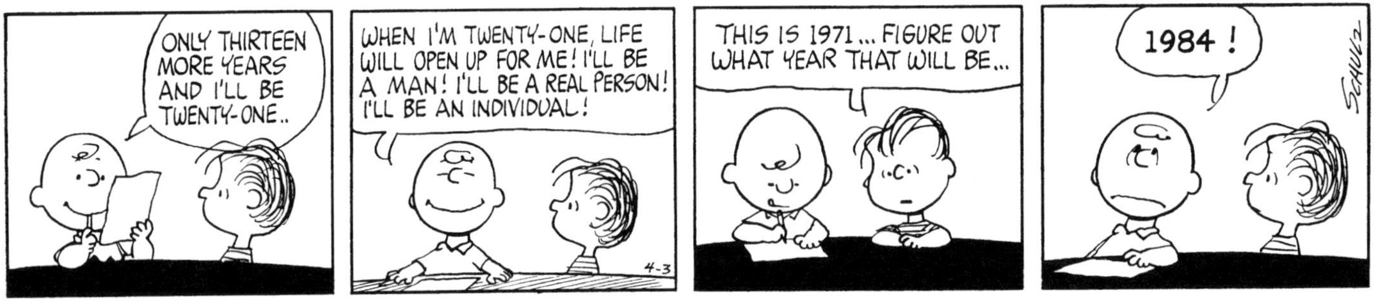
ONLY THIRTEEN MORE YEARS AND I'LL BE TWENTY-ONE..
WHEN I'M TWENTY-ONE, LIFE WILL OPEN UP FOR ME! I'LL BE A MAN! I'LL BE A REAL PERSON! I'LL BE AN INDIVIDUAL!
THIS IS 1971... FIGURE OUT WHAT YEAR THAT WILL BE...
1984!

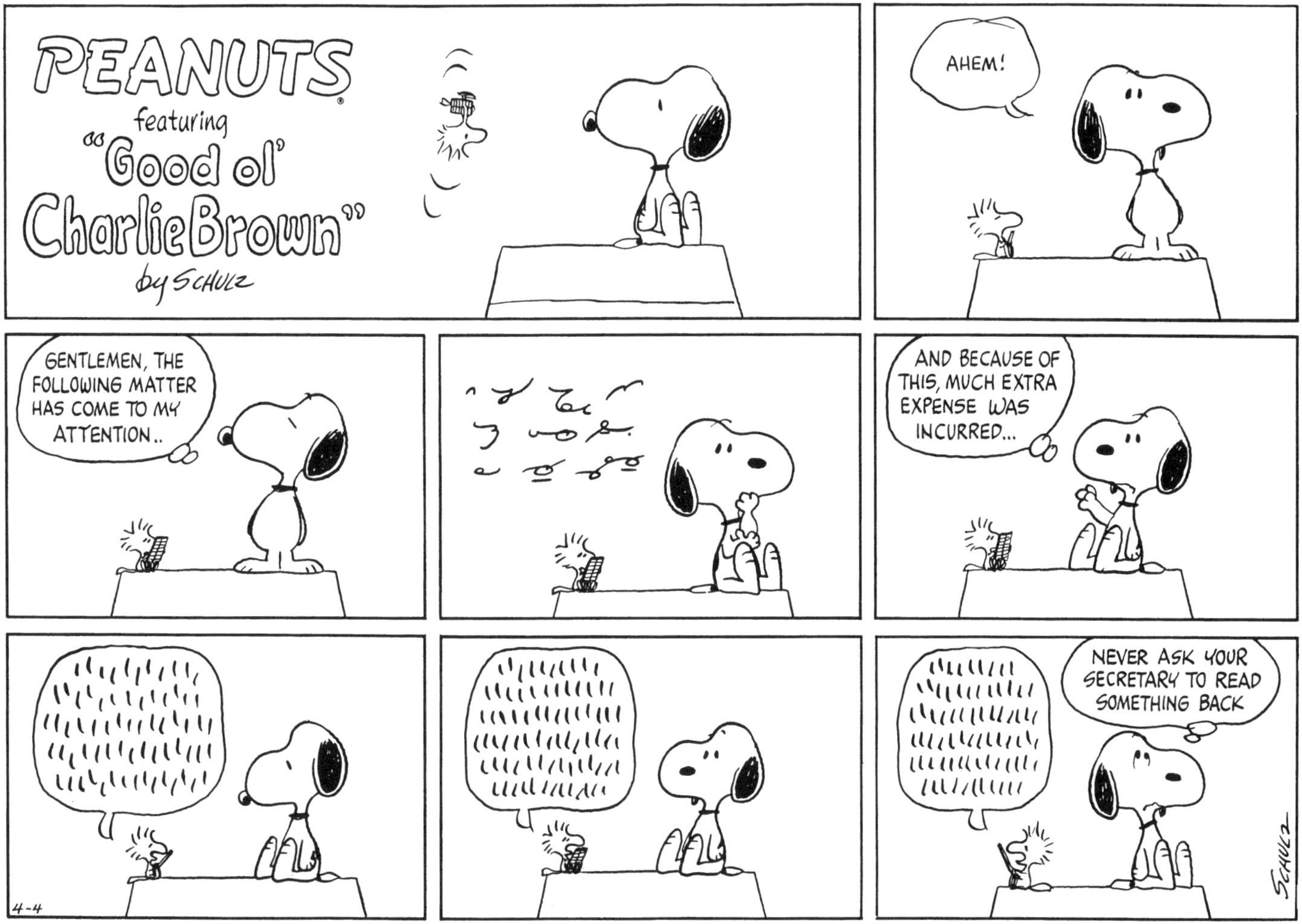
PEANUTS
featuring
"Good ol' Charlie Brown"
by SCHULZ
AHEM!
GENTLEMEN, THE FOLLOWING MATTER HAS COME TO MY ATTENTION..
AND BECAUSE OF THIS, MUCH EXTRA EXPENSE WAS INCURRED...
4-4
NEVER ASK YOUR SECRETARY TO READ SOMETHING BACK
SCHULZ

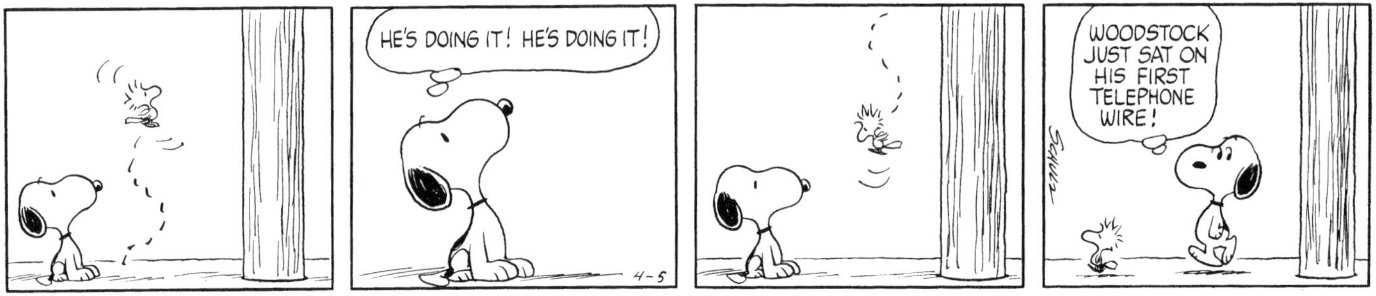
HE'S DOING IT! HE'S DOING IT!
4-5
WOODSTOCK JUST SAT ON HIS FIRST TELEPHONE WIRE!

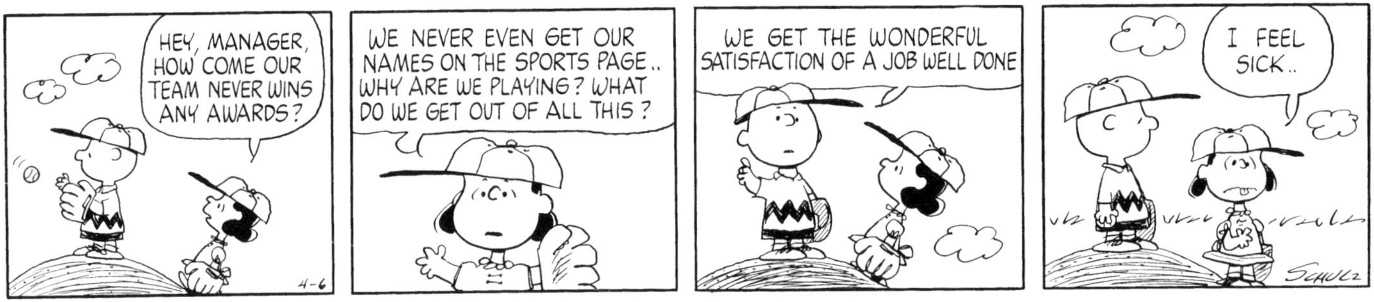
HEY, MANAGER, HOW COME OUR TEAM NEVER WINS ANY AWARDS?
4-6
WE NEVER EVEN GET OUR NAMES ON THE SPORTS PAGE.. WHY ARE WE PLAYING? WHAT DO WE GET OUT OF ALL THIS?
WE GET THE WONDERFUL SATISFACTION OF A JOB WELL DONE
I FEEL SICK..

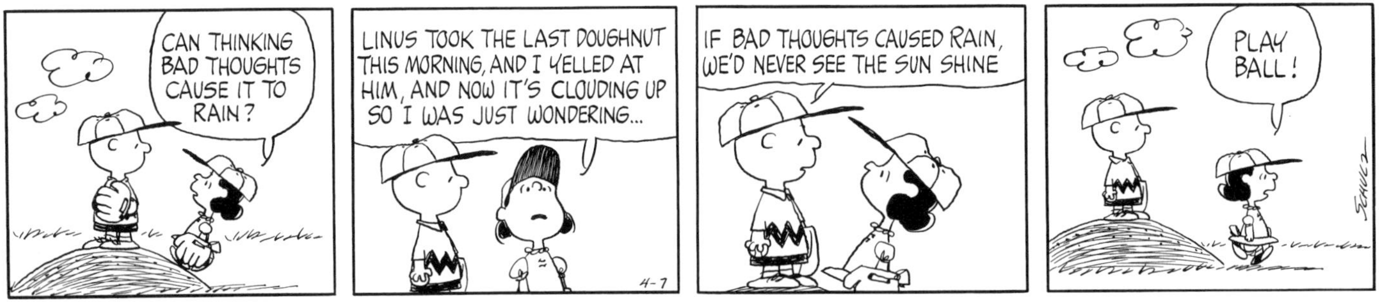
CAN THINKING BAD THOUGHTS CAUSE IT TO RAIN?
LINUS TOOK THE LAST DOUGHNUT THIS MORNING, AND I YELLED AT HIM, AND NOW IT'S CLOUDING UP SO I WAS JUST WONDERING...
4-7
IF BAD THOUGHTS CAUSED RAIN, WE'D NEVER SEE THE SUN SHINE
PLAY BALL!

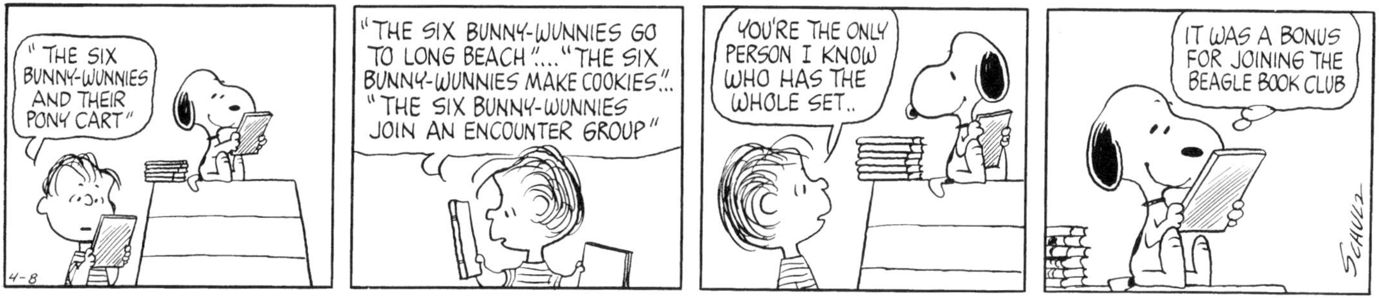
4-8
" THE SIX BUNNY-WUNNIES AND THEIR PONY CART "
" THE SIX BUNNY-WUNNIES GO TO LONG BEACH "... " THE SIX BUNNY-WUNNIES MAKE COOKIES "... " THE SIX BUNNY-WUNNIES JOIN AN ENCOUNTER GROUP "
YOU'RE THE ONLY PERSON I KNOW WHO HAS THE WHOLE SET..
IT WAS A BONUS FOR JOINING THE BEAGLE BOOK CLUB
SCHULZ

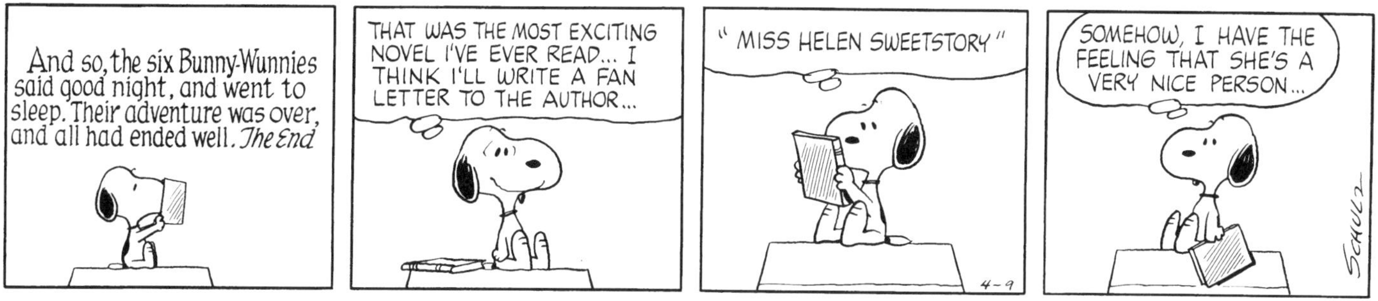
And so, the six Bunny-Wunnies said good night, and went to sleep. Their adventure was over, and all had ended well. The End
THAT WAS THE MOST EXCITING NOVEL I'VE EVER READ... I THINK I'LL WRITE A FAN LETTER TO THE AUTHOR...
" MISS HELEN SWEETSTORY "
4-9
SOMEHOW, I HAVE THE FEELING THAT SHE'S A VERY NICE PERSON...
SCHULZ

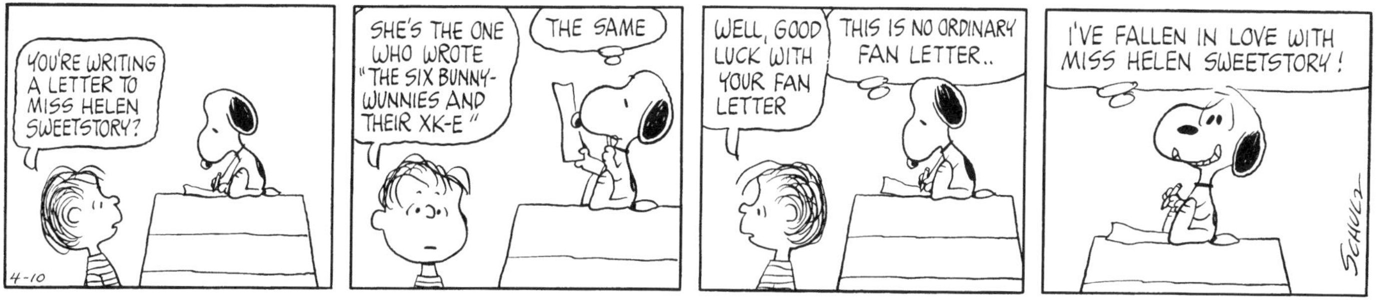
YOU'RE WRITING A LETTER TO MISS HELEN SWEETSTORY?
4-10
SHE'S THE ONE WHO WROTE " THE SIX BUNNY-WUNNIES AND THEIR XK-E "
THE SAME
WELL, GOOD LUCK WITH YOUR FAN LETTER
THIS IS NO ORDINARY FAN LETTER..
I'VE FALLEN IN LOVE WITH MISS HELEN SWEETSTORY!
SCHULZ

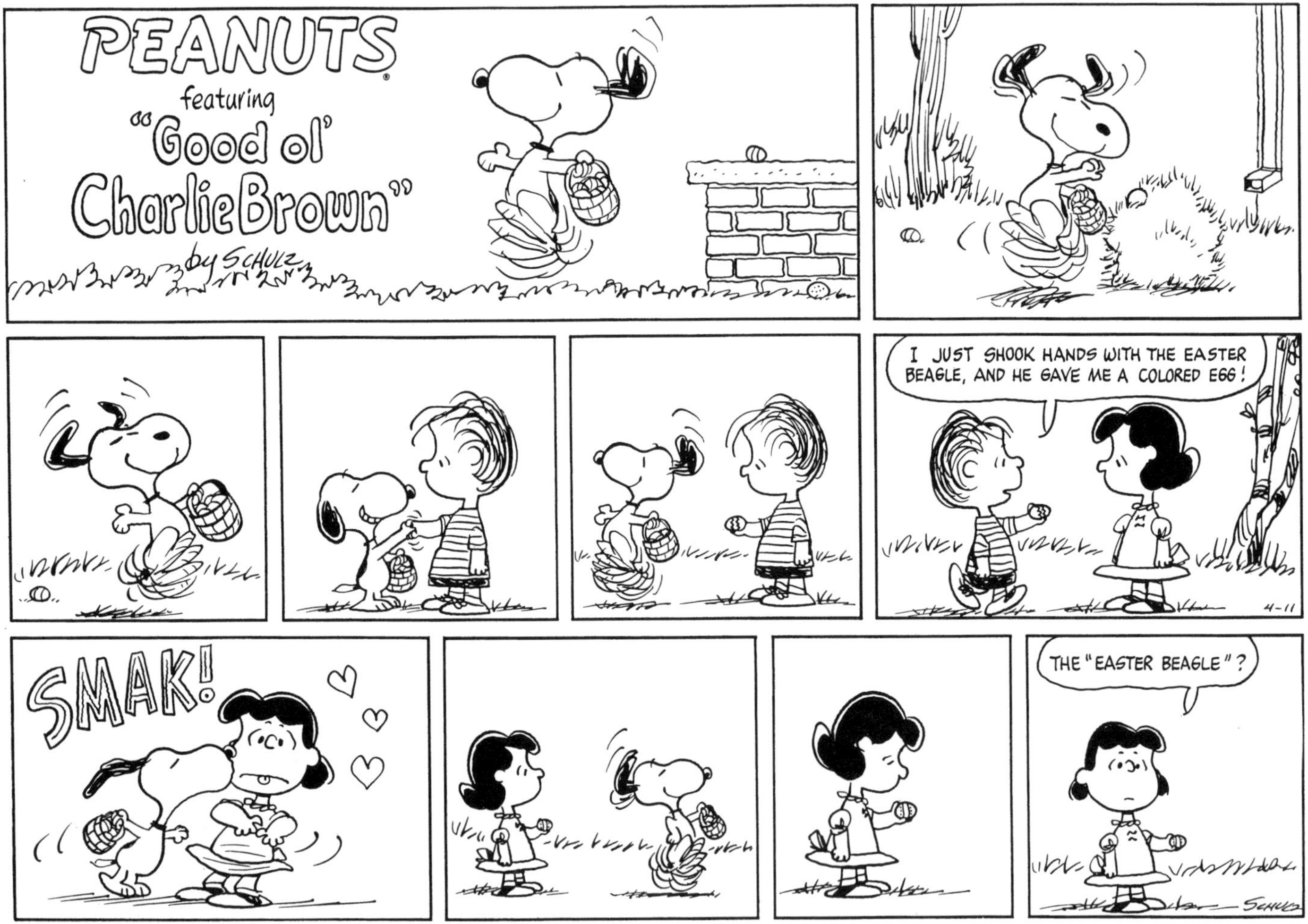
PEANUTS
featuring
"Good ol' Charlie Brown"
by SCHULZ
I JUST SHOOK HANDS WITH THE EASTER BEAGLE, AND HE GAVE ME A COLORED EGG!
4-11
SMAK!
THE "EASTER BEAGLE"?
SCHULZ

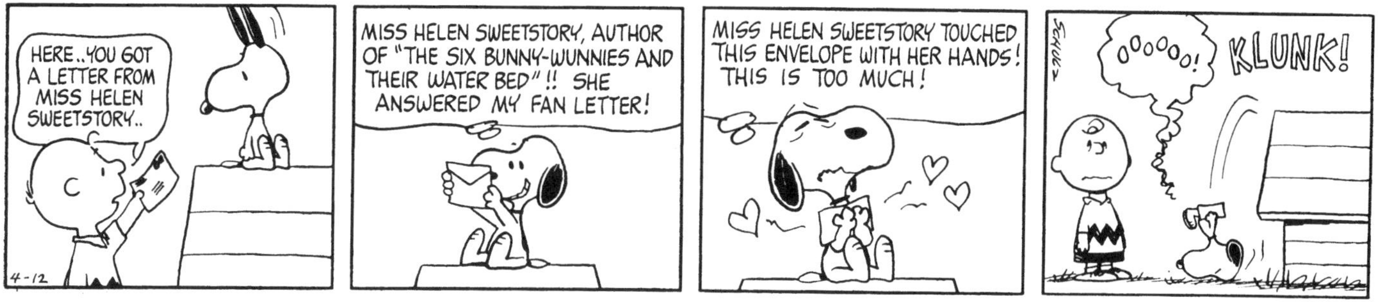
HERE..YOU GOT A LETTER FROM MISS HELEN SWEETSTORY..
MISS HELEN SWEETSTORY, AUTHOR OF "THE SIX BUNNY-WUNNIES AND THEIR WATER BED"!! SHE ANSWERED MY FAN LETTER!
MISS HELEN SWEETSTORY TOUCHED THIS ENVELOPE WITH HER HANDS! THIS IS TOO MUCH!
OOOOOO!
KLUNK!

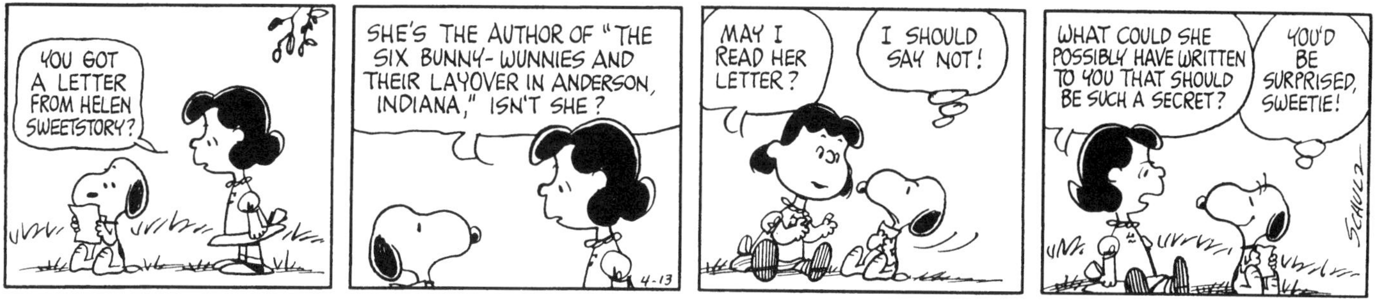
YOU GOT A LETTER FROM HELEN SWEETSTORY?
SHE'S THE AUTHOR OF "THE SIX BUNNY-WUNNIES AND THEIR LAYOVER IN ANDERSON, INDIANA," ISN'T SHE?
MAY I READ HER LETTER?
I SHOULD SAY NOT!
WHAT COULD SHE POSSIBLY HAVE WRITTEN TO YOU THAT SHOULD BE SUCH A SECRET?
YOU'D BE SURPRISED, SWEETIE!

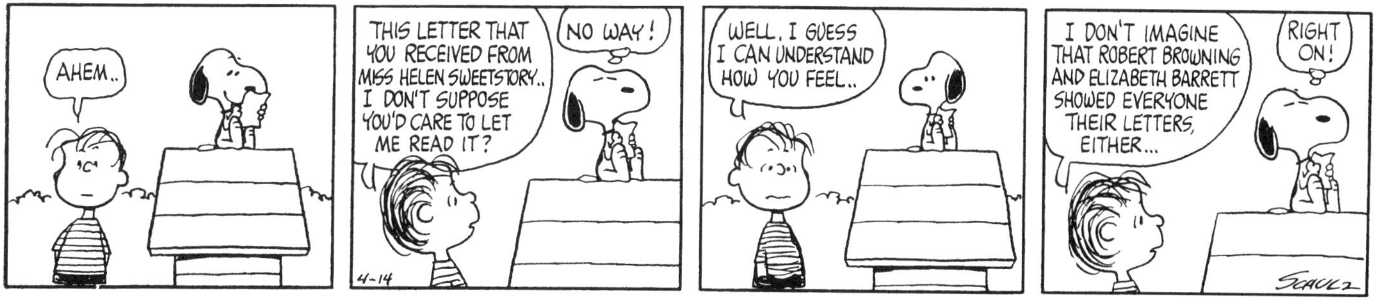
AHEM..
THIS LETTER THAT YOU RECEIVED FROM MISS HELEN SWEETSTORY.. I DON'T SUPPOSE YOU'D CARE TO LET ME READ IT?
NO WAY!
WELL, I GUESS I CAN UNDERSTAND HOW YOU FEEL..
I DON'T IMAGINE THAT ROBERT BROWNING AND ELIZABETH BARRETT SHOWED EVERYONE THEIR LETTERS, EITHER...
RIGHT ON!

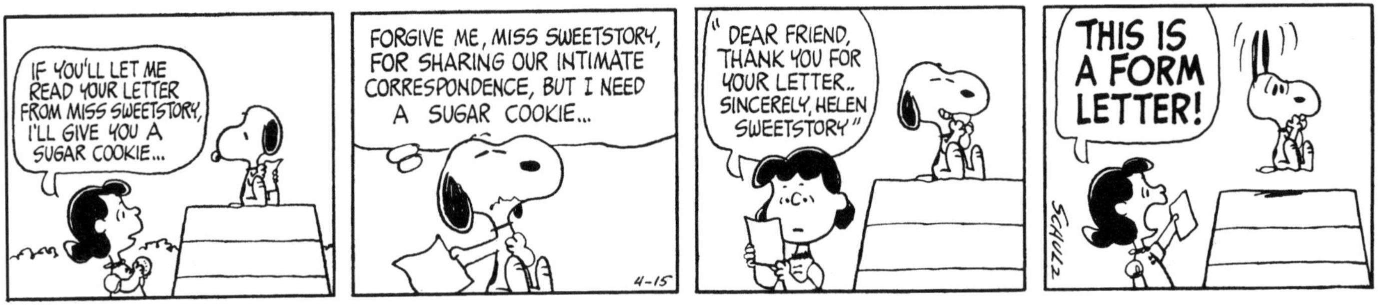
IF YOU'LL LET ME READ YOUR LETTER FROM MISS SWEETSTORY, I'LL GIVE YOU A SUGAR COOKIE...
FORGIVE ME, MISS SWEETSTORY, FOR SHARING OUR INTIMATE CORRESPONDENCE, BUT I NEED A SUGAR COOKIE...
4-15
"DEAR FRIEND, THANK YOU FOR YOUR LETTER.. SINCERELY, HELEN SWEETSTORY"
THIS IS A FORM LETTER!
SCHULZ

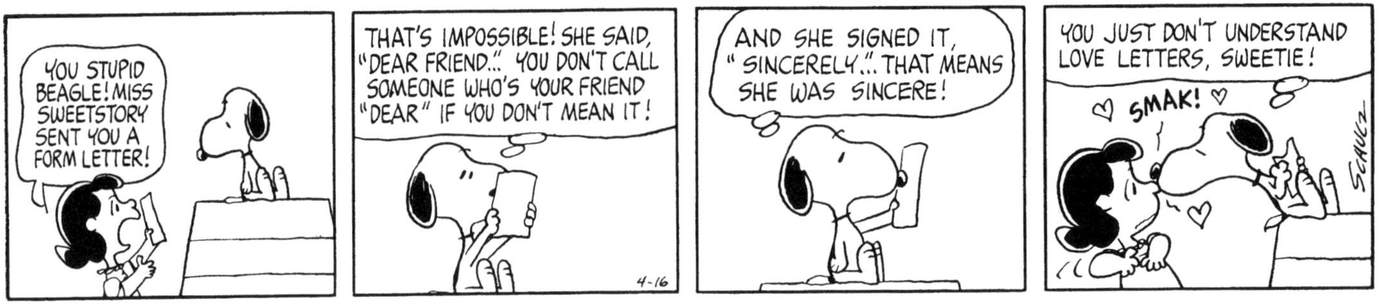
YOU STUPID BEAGLE! MISS SWEETSTORY SENT YOU A FORM LETTER!
THAT'S IMPOSSIBLE! SHE SAID, "DEAR FRIEND.." YOU DON'T CALL SOMEONE WHO'S YOUR FRIEND "DEAR" IF YOU DON'T MEAN IT!
4-16
AND SHE SIGNED IT, "SINCERELY.." THAT MEANS SHE WAS SINCERE!
YOU JUST DON'T UNDERSTAND LOVE LETTERS, SWEETIE!
SMAK!
SCHULZ

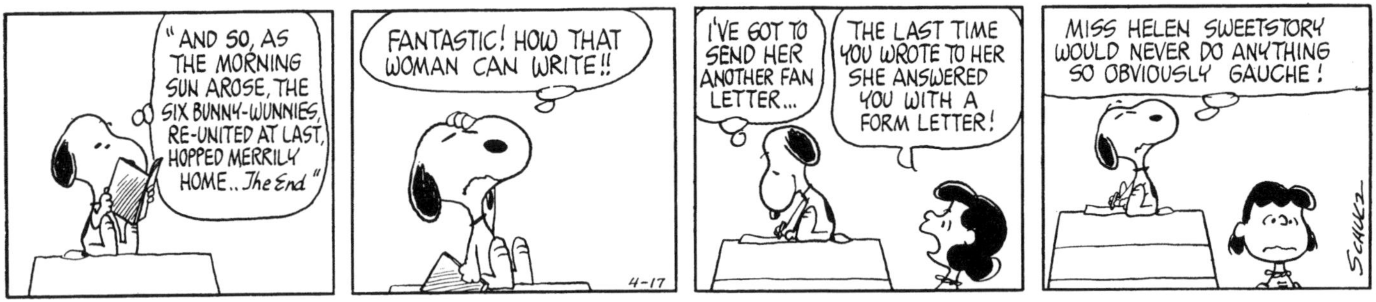
"AND SO, AS THE MORNING SUN AROSE, THE SIX BUNNY-WUNNIES, RE-UNITED AT LAST, HOPPED MERRILY HOME.. The End"
FANTASTIC! HOW THAT WOMAN CAN WRITE!!
4-17
I'VE GOT TO SEND HER ANOTHER FAN LETTER...
THE LAST TIME YOU WROTE TO HER SHE ANSWERED YOU WITH A FORM LETTER!
MISS HELEN SWEETSTORY WOULD NEVER DO ANYTHING SO OBVIOUSLY GAUCHE!
SCHULZ

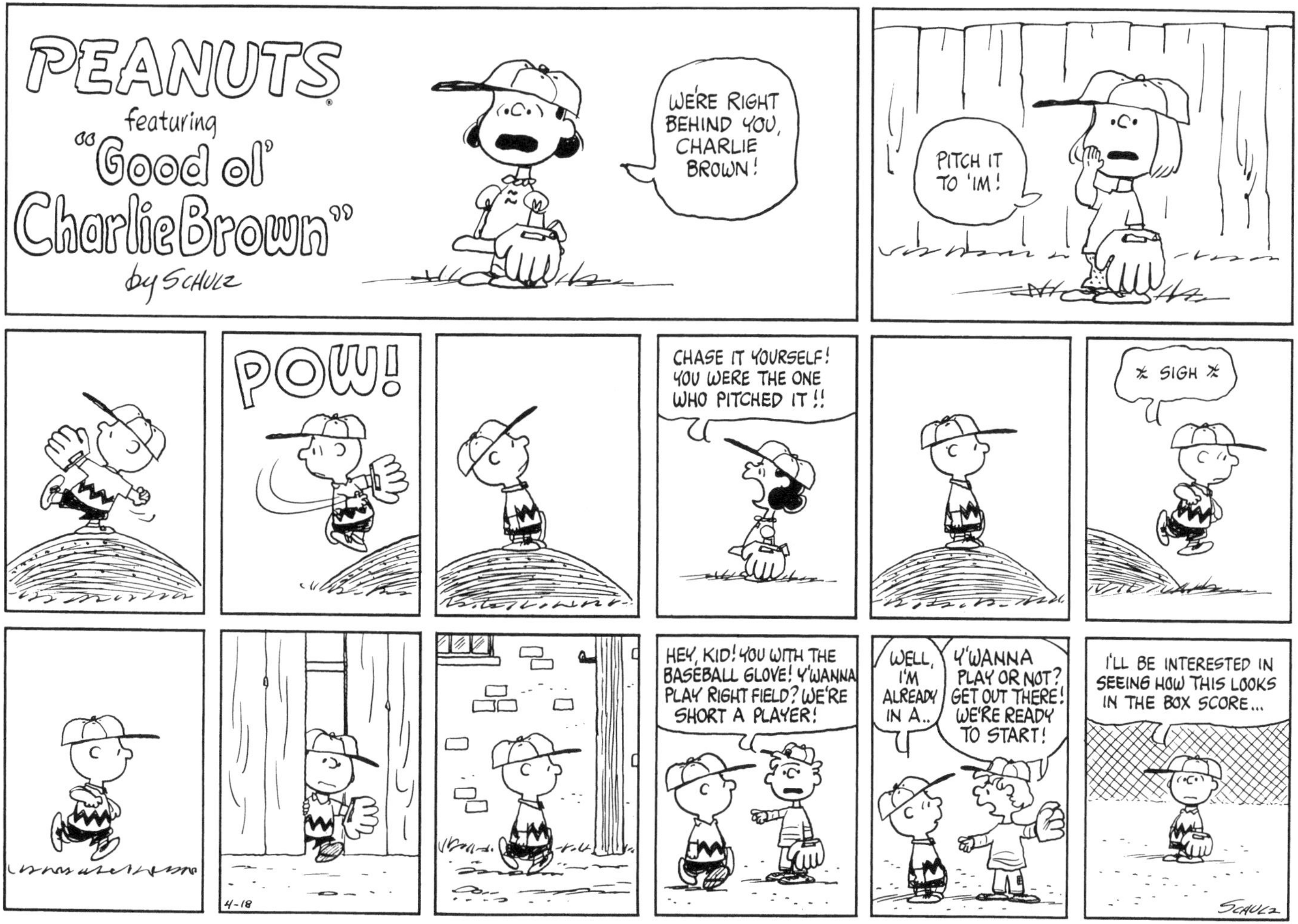
PEANUTS
featuring
"Good ol' Charlie Brown"
by SCHULZ
WE'RE RIGHT BEHIND YOU, CHARLIE BROWN!
PITCH IT TO 'IM!
POW!
CHASE IT YOURSELF! YOU WERE THE ONE WHO PITCHED IT!!
* SIGH *
4-18
HEY, KID! YOU WITH THE BASEBALL GLOVE! Y'WANNA PLAY RIGHT FIELD? WE'RE SHORT A PLAYER!
WELL, I'M ALREADY IN A..
Y'WANNA PLAY OR NOT? GET OUT THERE! WE'RE READY TO START!
I'LL BE INTERESTED IN SEEING HOW THIS LOOKS IN THE BOX SCORE...
SCHULZ

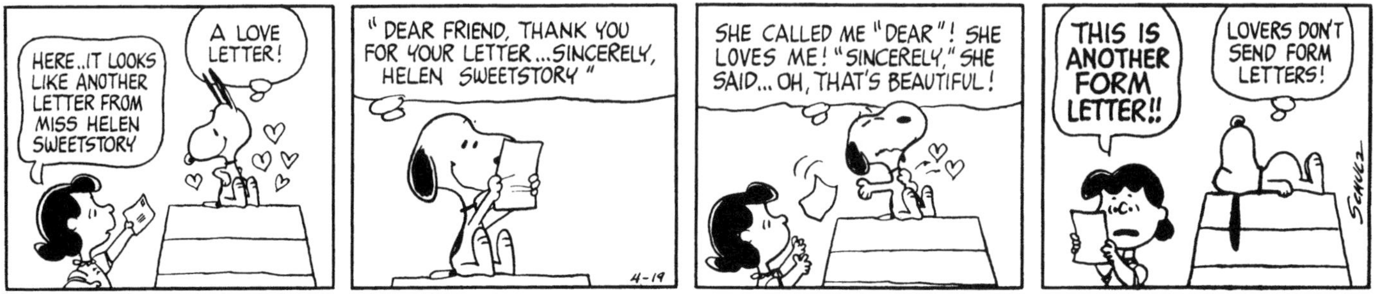
HERE..IT LOOKS LIKE ANOTHER LETTER FROM MISS HELEN SWEETSTORY
A LOVE LETTER!
"DEAR FRIEND, THANK YOU FOR YOUR LETTER...SINCERELY, HELEN SWEETSTORY"
4-19
SHE CALLED ME "DEAR"! SHE LOVES ME! "SINCERELY," SHE SAID... OH, THAT'S BEAUTIFUL!
THIS IS ANOTHER FORM LETTER!!
LOVERS DON'T SEND FORM LETTERS!
SCHULZ

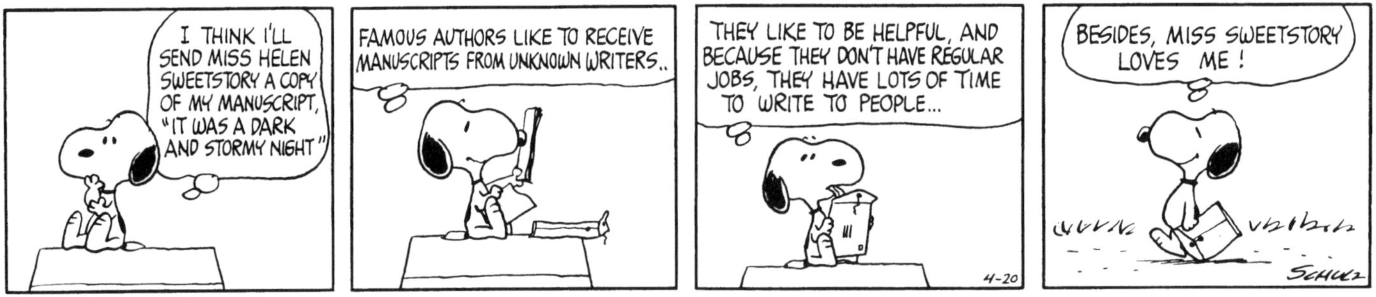
I THINK I'LL SEND MISS HELEN SWEETSTORY A COPY OF MY MANUSCRIPT, "IT WAS A DARK AND STORMY NIGHT"
FAMOUS AUTHORS LIKE TO RECEIVE MANUSCRIPTS FROM UNKNOWN WRITERS..
THEY LIKE TO BE HELPFUL, AND BECAUSE THEY DON'T HAVE REGULAR JOBS, THEY HAVE LOTS OF TIME TO WRITE TO PEOPLE...
4-20
BESIDES, MISS SWEETSTORY LOVES ME!
SCHULZ

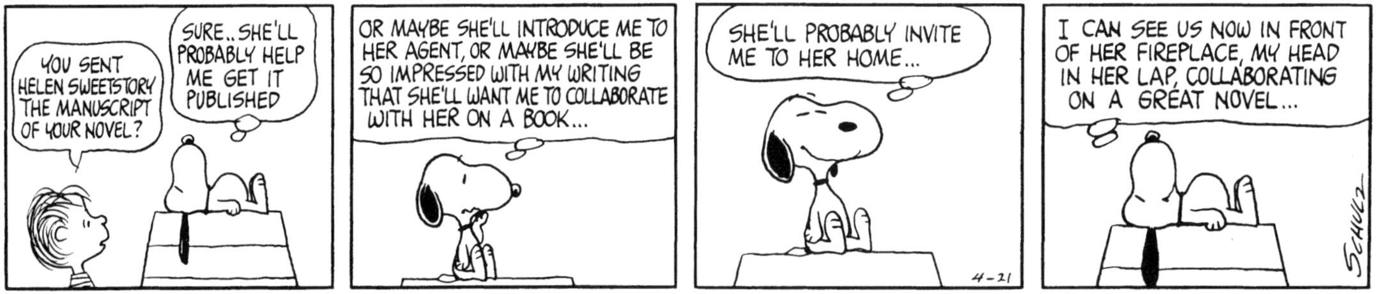
YOU SENT HELEN SWEETSTORY THE MANUSCRIPT OF YOUR NOVEL?
SURE..SHE'LL PROBABLY HELP ME GET IT PUBLISHED
OR MAYBE SHE'LL INTRODUCE ME TO HER AGENT, OR MAYBE SHE'LL BE SO IMPRESSED WITH MY WRITING THAT SHE'LL WANT ME TO COLLABORATE WITH HER ON A BOOK...
SHE'LL PROBABLY INVITE ME TO HER HOME...
4-21
I CAN SEE US NOW IN FRONT OF HER FIREPLACE, MY HEAD IN HER LAP, COLLABORATING ON A GREAT NOVEL...
SCHULZ

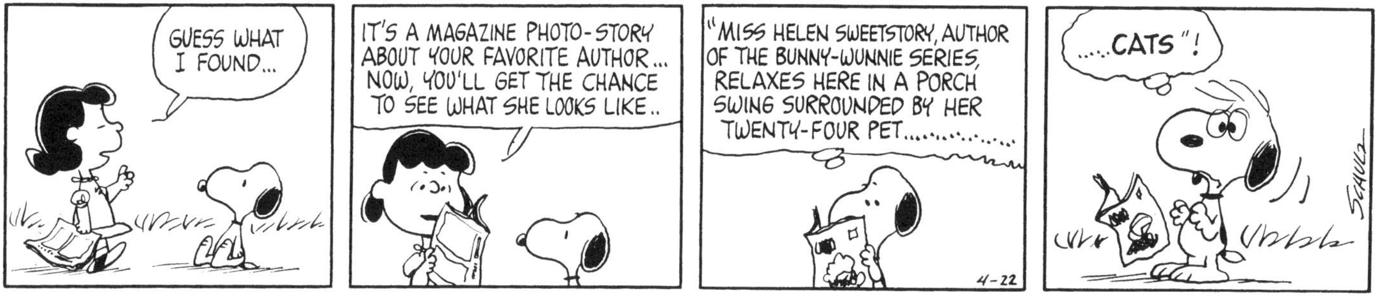
GUESS WHAT I FOUND...
IT'S A MAGAZINE PHOTO-STORY ABOUT YOUR FAVORITE AUTHOR... NOW, YOU'LL GET THE CHANCE TO SEE WHAT SHE LOOKS LIKE..
"MISS HELEN SWEETSTORY, AUTHOR OF THE BUNNY-WUNNIE SERIES, RELAXES HERE IN A PORCH SWING SURROUNDED BY HER TWENTY-FOUR PET.........
4-22
.....CATS"!
SCHULZ

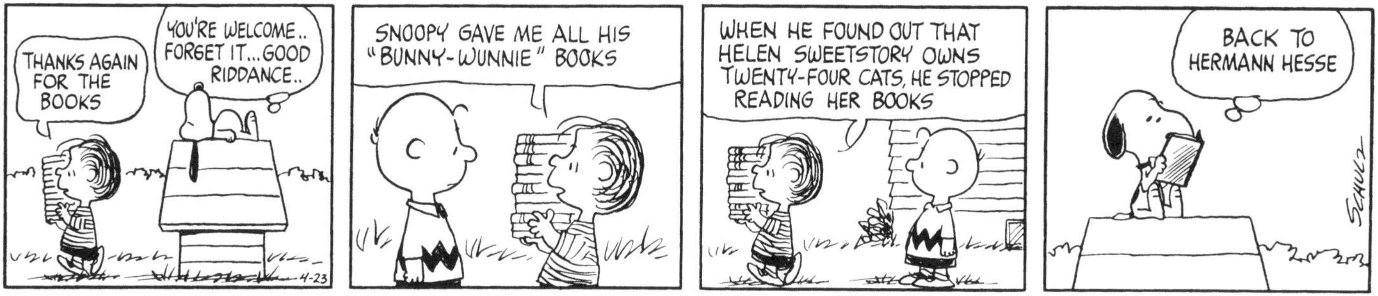
THANKS AGAIN FOR THE BOOKS
YOU'RE WELCOME.. FORGET IT...GOOD RIDDANCE..
4-23
SNOOPY GAVE ME ALL HIS "BUNNY-WUNNIE" BOOKS
WHEN HE FOUND OUT THAT HELEN SWEETSTORY OWNS TWENTY-FOUR CATS, HE STOPPED READING HER BOOKS
BACK TO HERMANN HESSE
SCHULZ

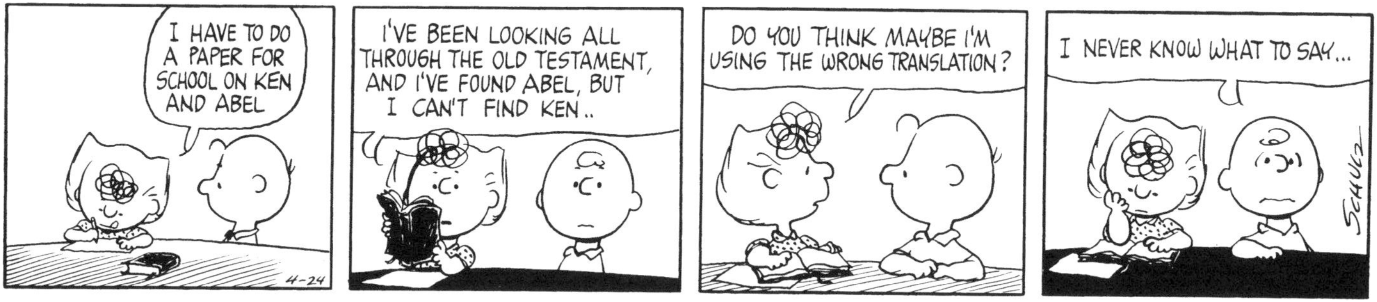
I HAVE TO DO A PAPER FOR SCHOOL ON KEN AND ABEL
4-24
I'VE BEEN LOOKING ALL THROUGH THE OLD TESTAMENT, AND I'VE FOUND ABEL, BUT I CAN'T FIND KEN..
DO YOU THINK MAYBE I'M USING THE WRONG TRANSLATION?
I NEVER KNOW WHAT TO SAY...
SCHULZ

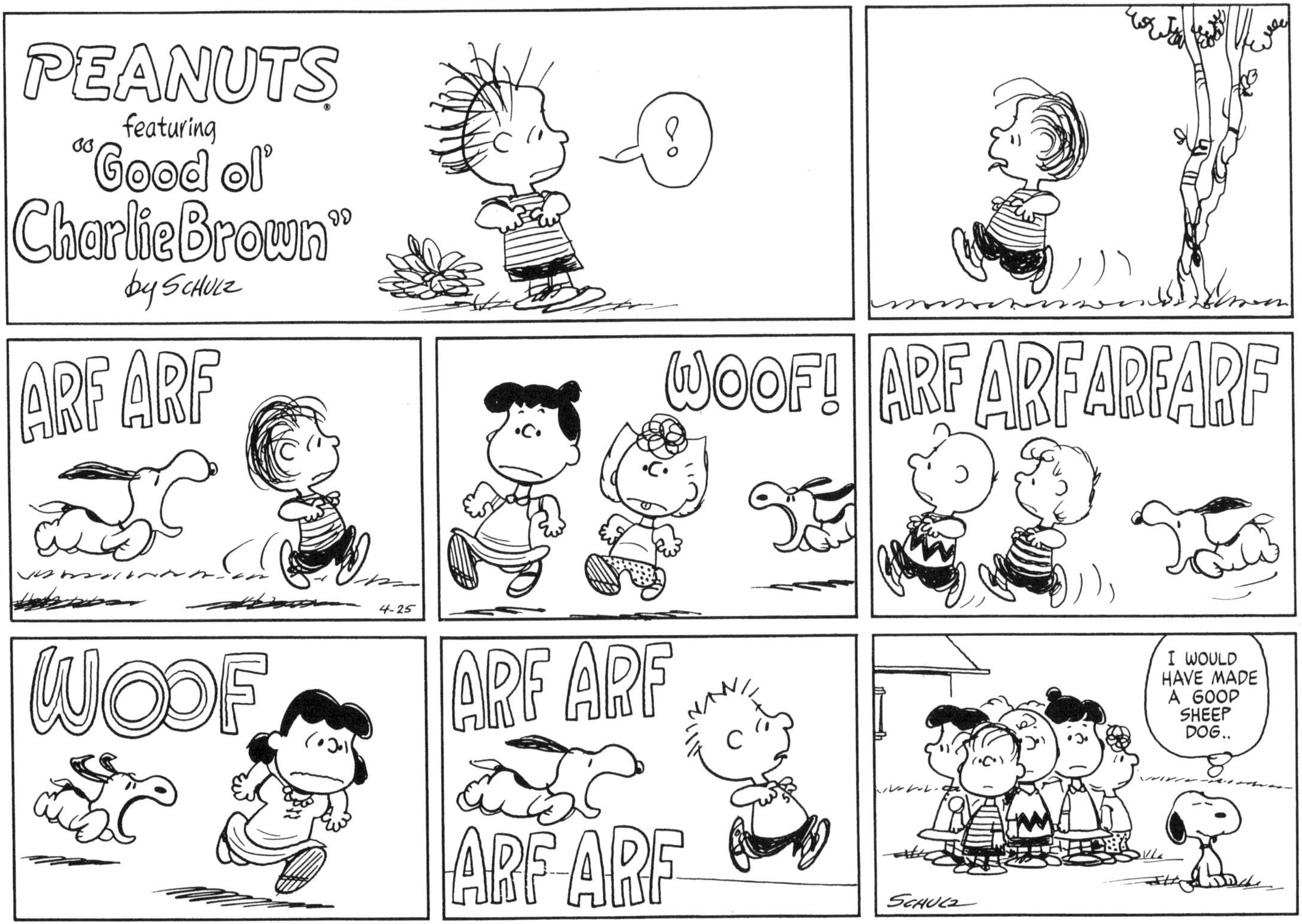
PEANUTS
featuring
"Good ol' Charlie Brown"
by SCHULZ
!
ARF ARF
4-25
WOOF!
ARF ARF ARF ARF
WOOF
ARF ARF
ARF ARF
I WOULD HAVE MADE A GOOD SHEEP DOG..
SCHULZ

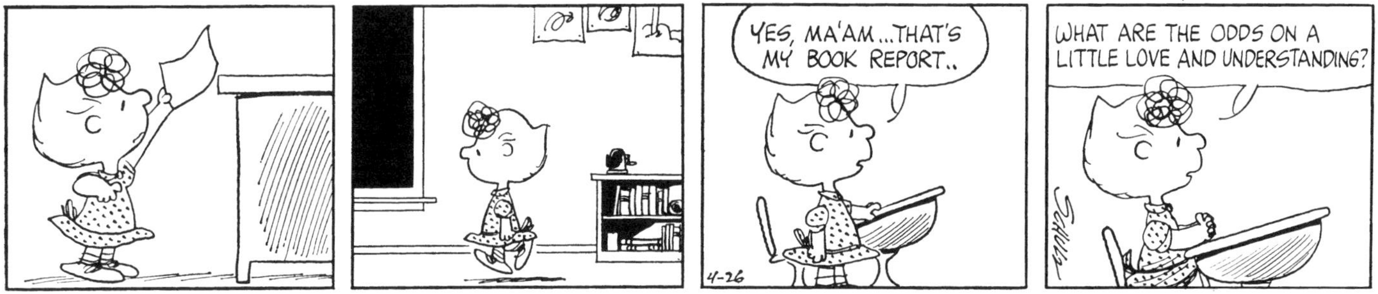
YES, MA'AM...THAT'S MY BOOK REPORT..
WHAT ARE THE ODDS ON A LITTLE LOVE AND UNDERSTANDING?
4-26

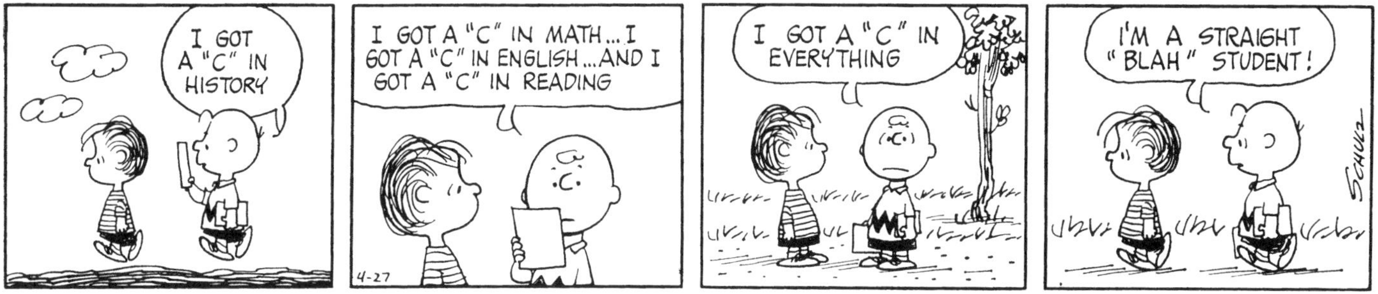
I GOT A "C" IN HISTORY
I GOT A "C" IN MATH...I GOT A "C" IN ENGLISH...AND I GOT A "C" IN READING
I GOT A "C" IN EVERYTHING
I'M A STRAIGHT "BLAH" STUDENT!
4-27

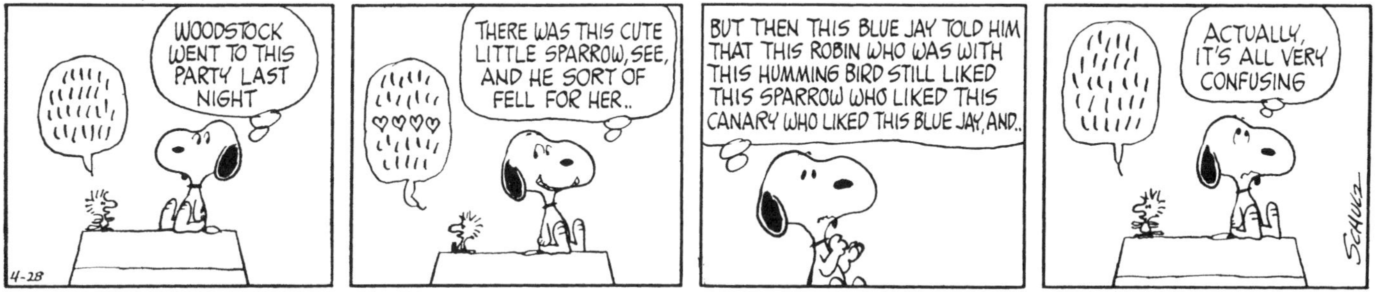
WOODSTOCK WENT TO THIS PARTY LAST NIGHT
THERE WAS THIS CUTE LITTLE SPARROW, SEE, AND HE SORT OF FELL FOR HER..
BUT THEN THIS BLUE JAY TOLD HIM THAT THIS ROBIN WHO WAS WITH THIS HUMMING BIRD STILL LIKED THIS SPARROW WHO LIKED THIS CANARY WHO LIKED THIS BLUE JAY, AND..
ACTUALLY, IT'S ALL VERY CONFUSING
4-28

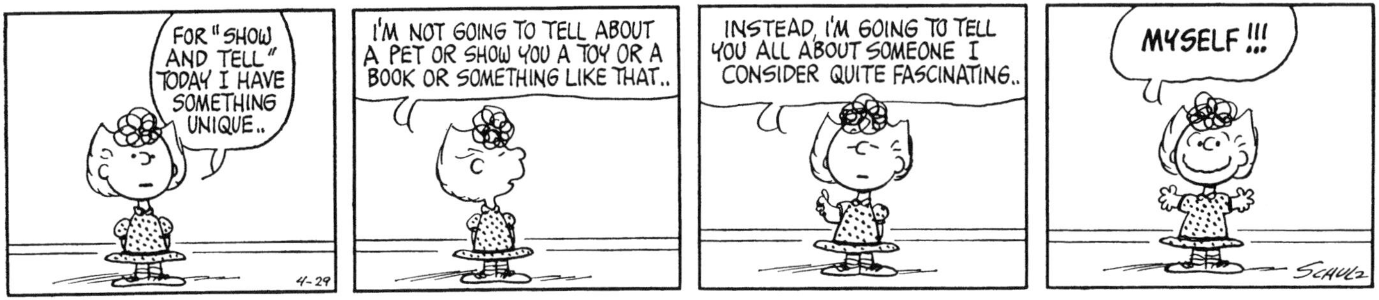
FOR "SHOW AND TELL" TODAY I HAVE SOMETHING UNIQUE..
I'M NOT GOING TO TELL ABOUT A PET OR SHOW YOU A TOY OR A BOOK OR SOMETHING LIKE THAT..
INSTEAD, I'M GOING TO TELL YOU ALL ABOUT SOMEONE I CONSIDER QUITE FASCINATING..
MYSELF!!!

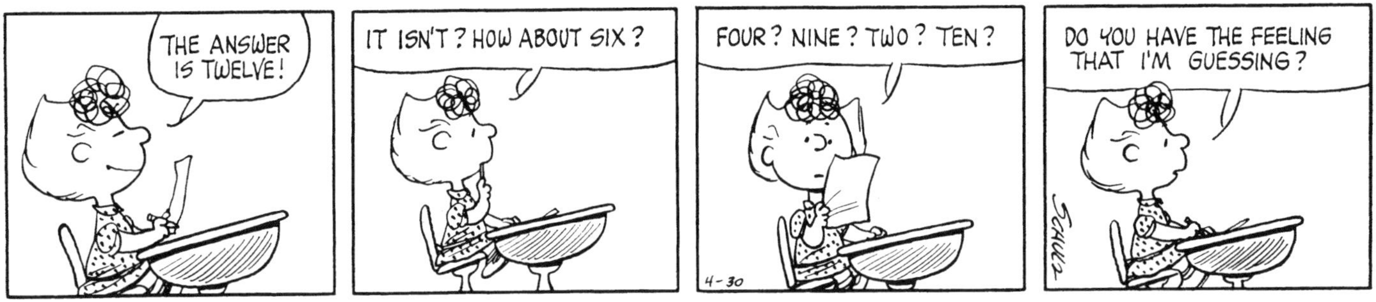
THE ANSWER IS TWELVE!
IT ISN'T? HOW ABOUT SIX?
FOUR? NINE? TWO? TEN?
DO YOU HAVE THE FEELING THAT I'M GUESSING?

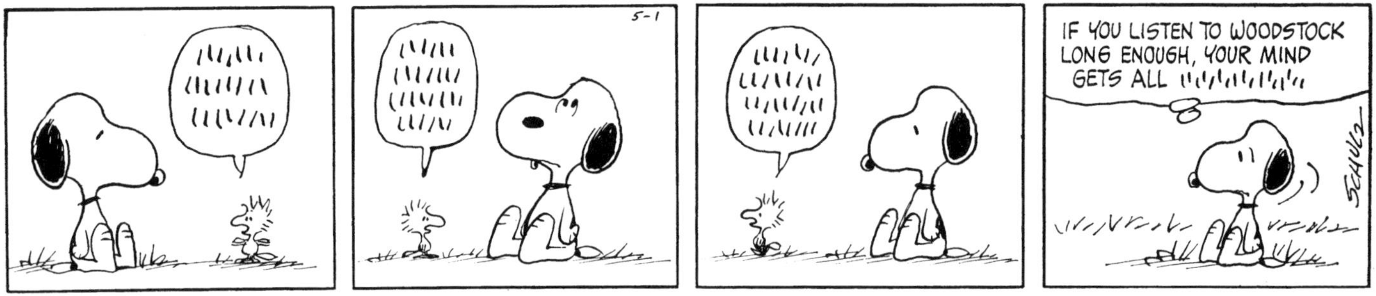
IF YOU LISTEN TO WOODSTOCK LONG ENOUGH, YOUR MIND GETS ALL

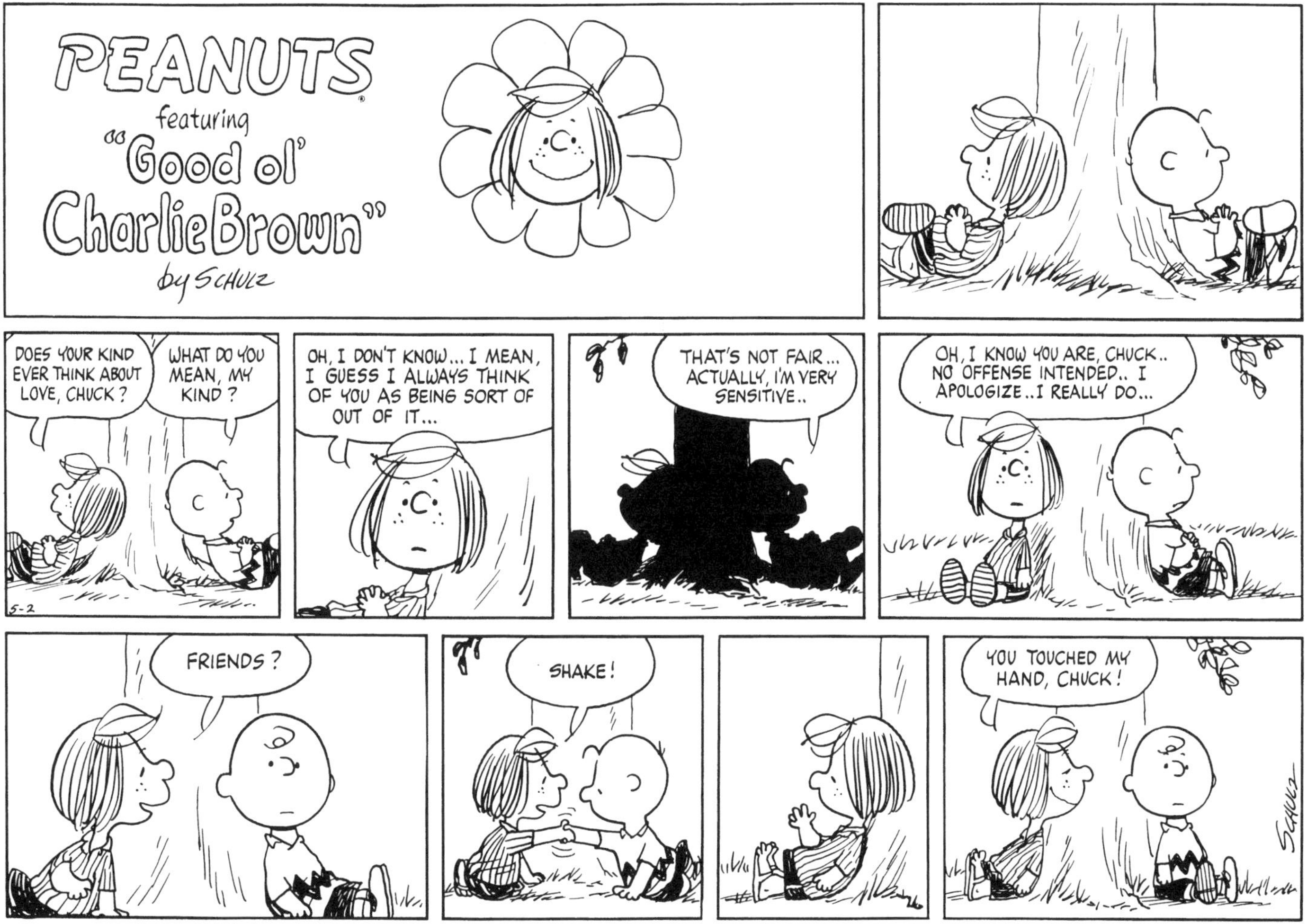
PEANUTS
featuring
"Good ol' CharlieBrown"
by SCHULZ
DOES YOUR KIND EVER THINK ABOUT LOVE, CHUCK?
WHAT DO YOU MEAN, MY KIND?
5-2
OH, I DON'T KNOW... I MEAN, I GUESS I ALWAYS THINK OF YOU AS BEING SORT OF OUT OF IT...
THAT'S NOT FAIR... ACTUALLY, I'M VERY SENSITIVE..
OH, I KNOW YOU ARE, CHUCK.. NO OFFENSE INTENDED.. I APOLOGIZE..I REALLY DO...
FRIENDS?
SHAKE!
YOU TOUCHED MY HAND, CHUCK!
SCHULZ

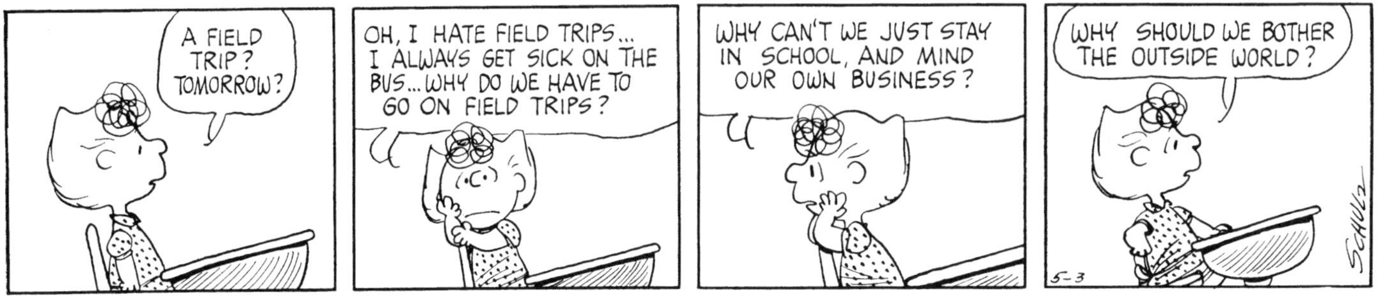
A FIELD TRIP? TOMORROW?
OH, I HATE FIELD TRIPS... I ALWAYS GET SICK ON THE BUS... WHY DO WE HAVE TO GO ON FIELD TRIPS?
WHY CAN'T WE JUST STAY IN SCHOOL, AND MIND OUR OWN BUSINESS?
WHY SHOULD WE BOTHER THE OUTSIDE WORLD?
SCHULZ
5-3

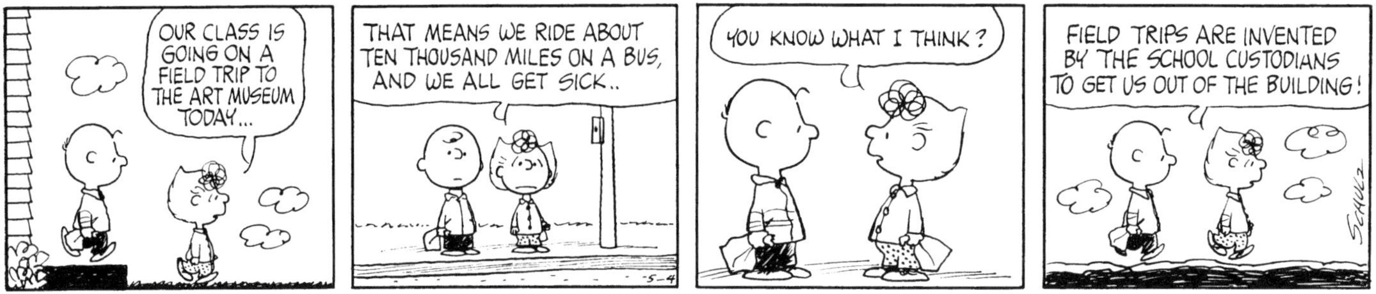
OUR CLASS IS GOING ON A FIELD TRIP TO THE ART MUSEUM TODAY...
THAT MEANS WE RIDE ABOUT TEN THOUSAND MILES ON A BUS, AND WE ALL GET SICK..
5-4
YOU KNOW WHAT I THINK?
FIELD TRIPS ARE INVENTED BY THE SCHOOL CUSTODIANS TO GET US OUT OF THE BUILDING!
SCHULZ

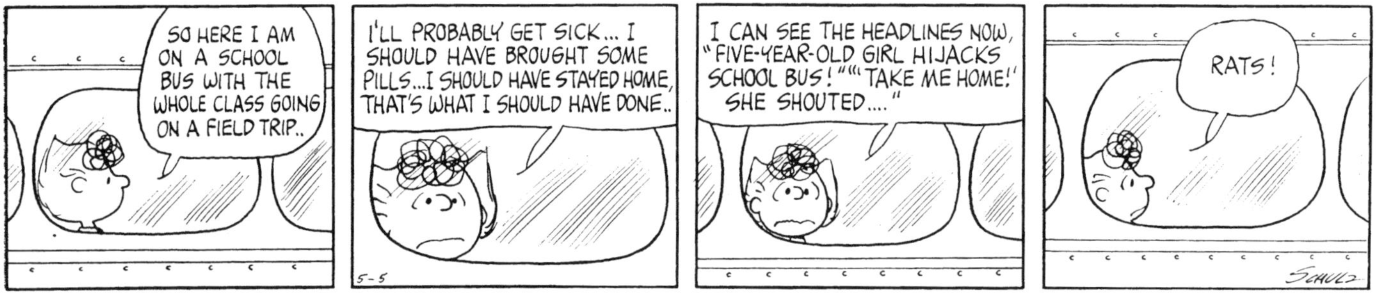
SO HERE I AM ON A SCHOOL BUS WITH THE WHOLE CLASS GOING ON A FIELD TRIP..
I'LL PROBABLY GET SICK... I SHOULD HAVE BROUGHT SOME PILLS...I SHOULD HAVE STAYED HOME, THAT'S WHAT I SHOULD HAVE DONE..
5-5
I CAN SEE THE HEADLINES NOW, "FIVE-YEAR-OLD GIRL HIJACKS SCHOOL BUS!" "'TAKE ME HOME!' SHE SHOUTED...."
RATS!
SCHULZ

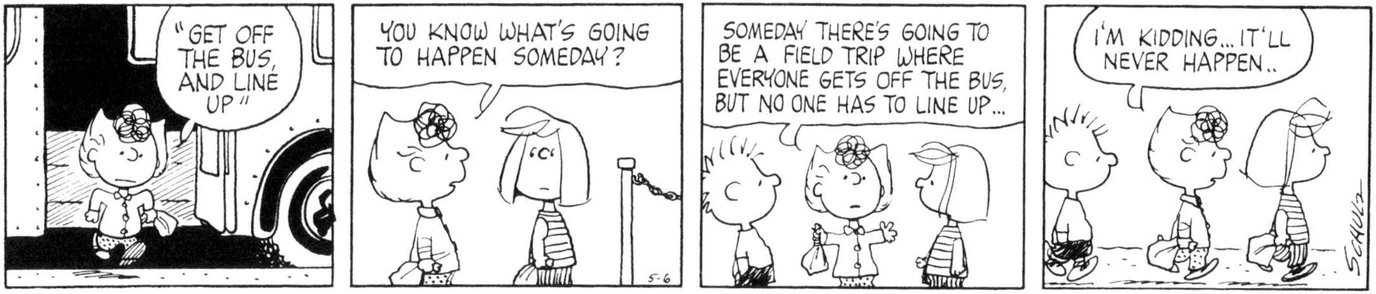
"GET OFF THE BUS, AND LINE UP"
YOU KNOW WHAT'S GOING TO HAPPEN SOMEDAY?
SOMEDAY THERE'S GOING TO BE A FIELD TRIP WHERE EVERYONE GETS OFF THE BUS, BUT NO ONE HAS TO LINE UP...
I'M KIDDING... IT'LL NEVER HAPPEN..

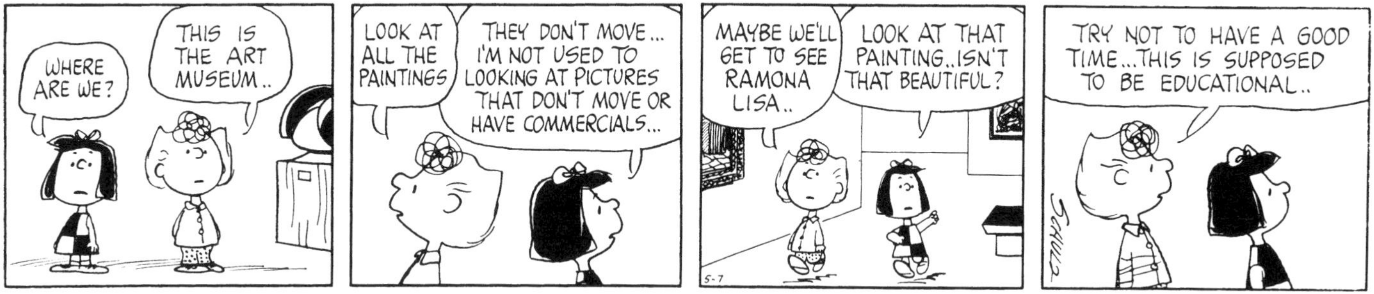
WHERE ARE WE?
THIS IS THE ART MUSEUM..
LOOK AT ALL THE PAINTINGS
THEY DON'T MOVE... I'M NOT USED TO LOOKING AT PICTURES THAT DON'T MOVE OR HAVE COMMERCIALS...
MAYBE WE'LL GET TO SEE RAMONA LISA..
LOOK AT THAT PAINTING..ISN'T THAT BEAUTIFUL?
TRY NOT TO HAVE A GOOD TIME...THIS IS SUPPOSED TO BE EDUCATIONAL..

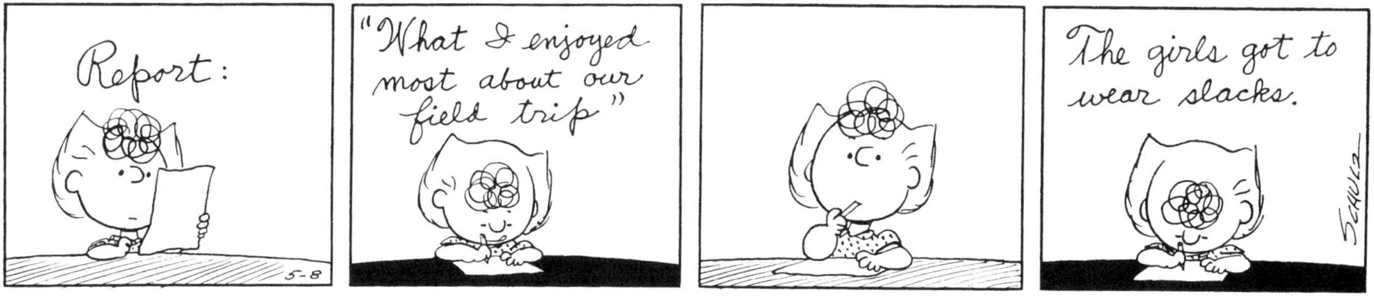
Report:
"What I enjoyed most about our field trip"
The girls got to wear slacks.

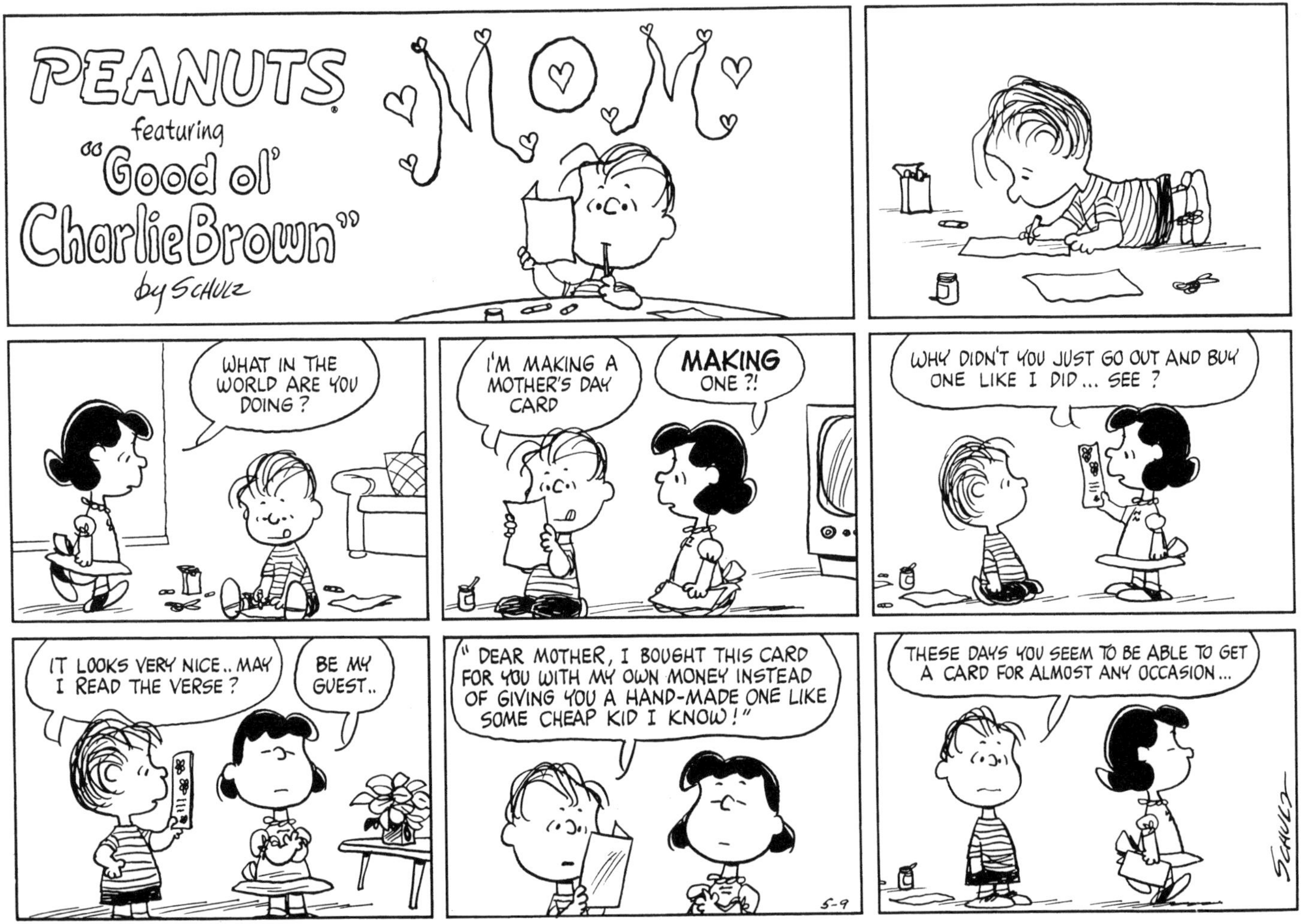
PEANUTS
featuring
"Good ol' Charlie Brown"
by SCHULZ
MOM
WHAT IN THE WORLD ARE YOU DOING?
I'M MAKING A MOTHER'S DAY CARD
MAKING ONE ?!
WHY DIDN'T YOU JUST GO OUT AND BUY ONE LIKE I DID... SEE ?
IT LOOKS VERY NICE.. MAY I READ THE VERSE ?
BE MY GUEST..
" DEAR MOTHER, I BOUGHT THIS CARD FOR YOU WITH MY OWN MONEY INSTEAD OF GIVING YOU A HAND-MADE ONE LIKE SOME CHEAP KID I KNOW!"
5-9
THESE DAYS YOU SEEM TO BE ABLE TO GET A CARD FOR ALMOST ANY OCCASION...
SCHULZ

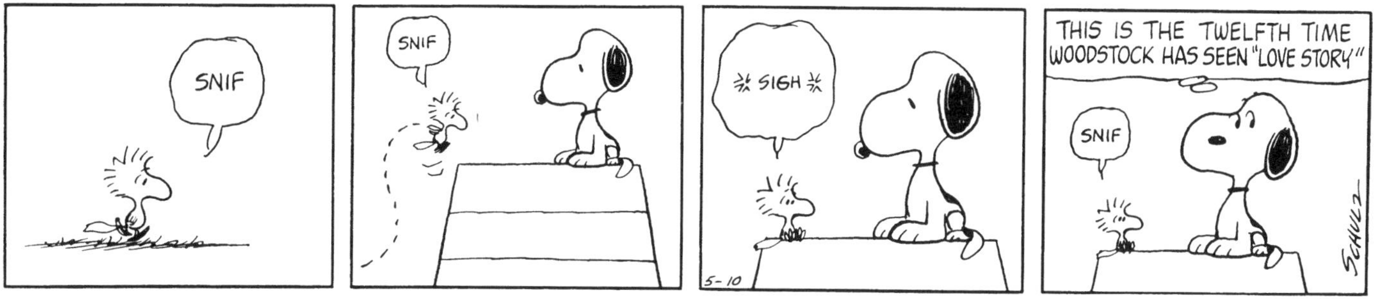
SNIF
SNIF
SIGH
THIS IS THE TWELFTH TIME WOODSTOCK HAS SEEN "LOVE STORY"
SNIF
5-10
SCHULZ

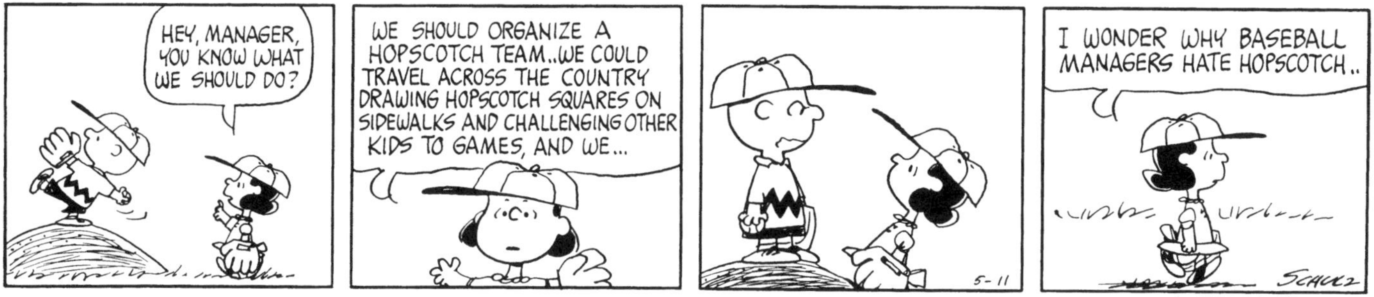
HEY, MANAGER, YOU KNOW WHAT WE SHOULD DO?
WE SHOULD ORGANIZE A HOPSCOTCH TEAM..WE COULD TRAVEL ACROSS THE COUNTRY DRAWING HOPSCOTCH SQUARES ON SIDEWALKS AND CHALLENGING OTHER KIDS TO GAMES, AND WE...
5-11
I WONDER WHY BASEBALL MANAGERS HATE HOPSCOTCH..
SCHULZ

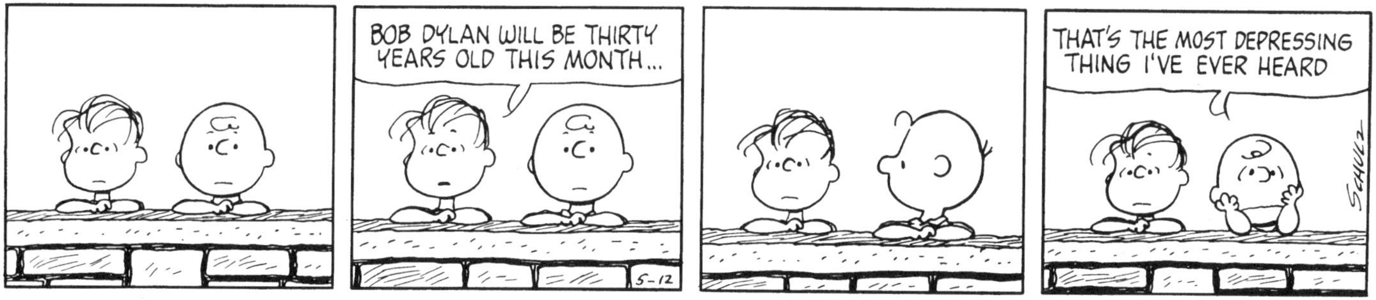
BOB DYLAN WILL BE THIRTY YEARS OLD THIS MONTH...
5-12
THAT'S THE MOST DEPRESSING THING I'VE EVER HEARD
SCHULZ

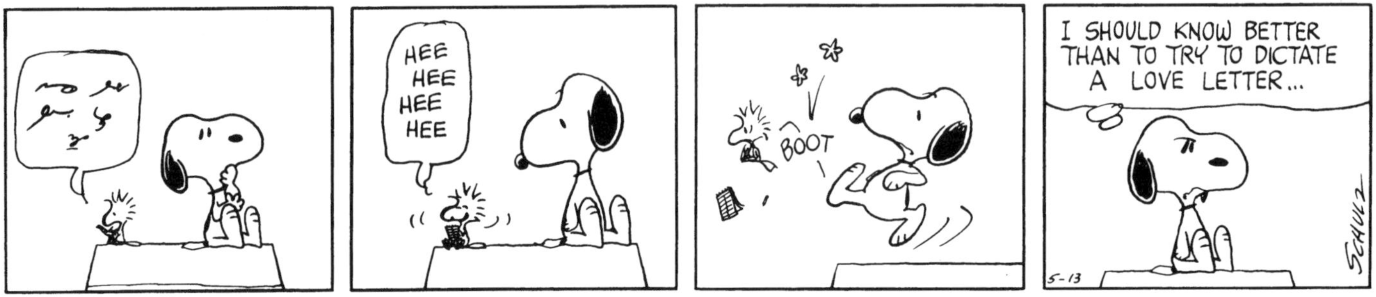
HEE
HEE
HEE
HEE
BOOT
I SHOULD KNOW BETTER THAN TO TRY TO DICTATE A LOVE LETTER...
5-13
SCHULZ

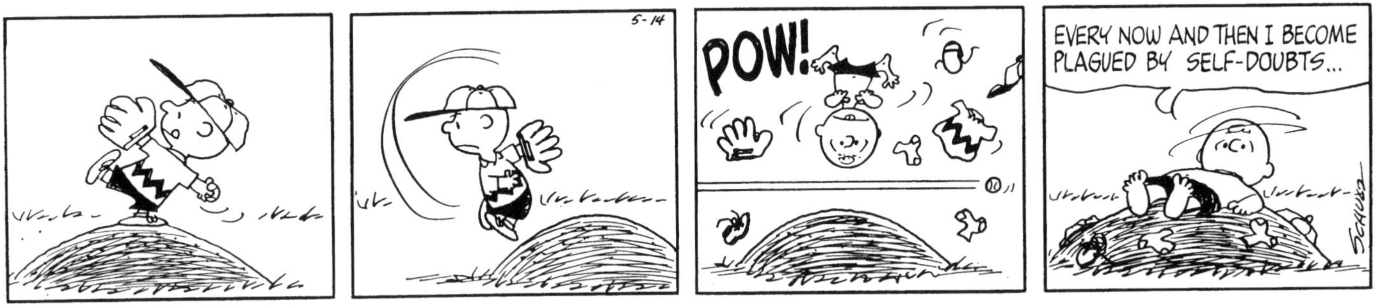
5-14
POW!
EVERY NOW AND THEN I BECOME PLAGUED BY SELF-DOUBTS...
SCHULZ

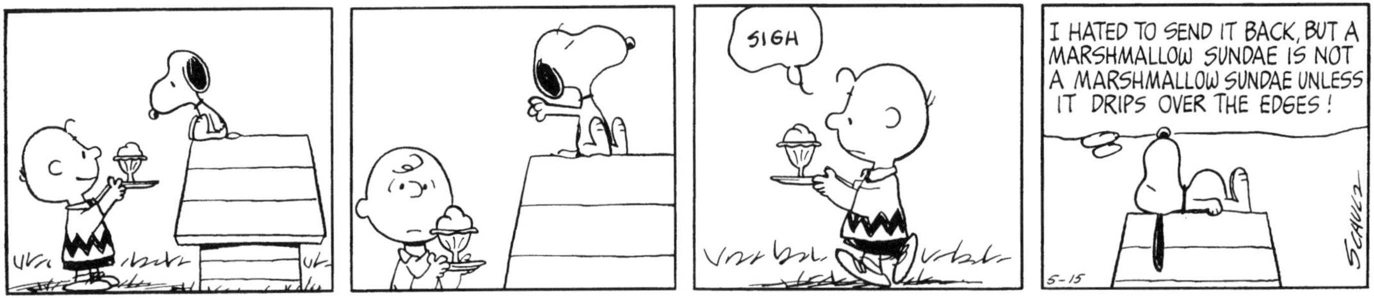
SIGH
I HATED TO SEND IT BACK, BUT A MARSHMALLOW SUNDAE IS NOT A MARSHMALLOW SUNDAE UNLESS IT DRIPS OVER THE EDGES!
5-15
SCHULZ

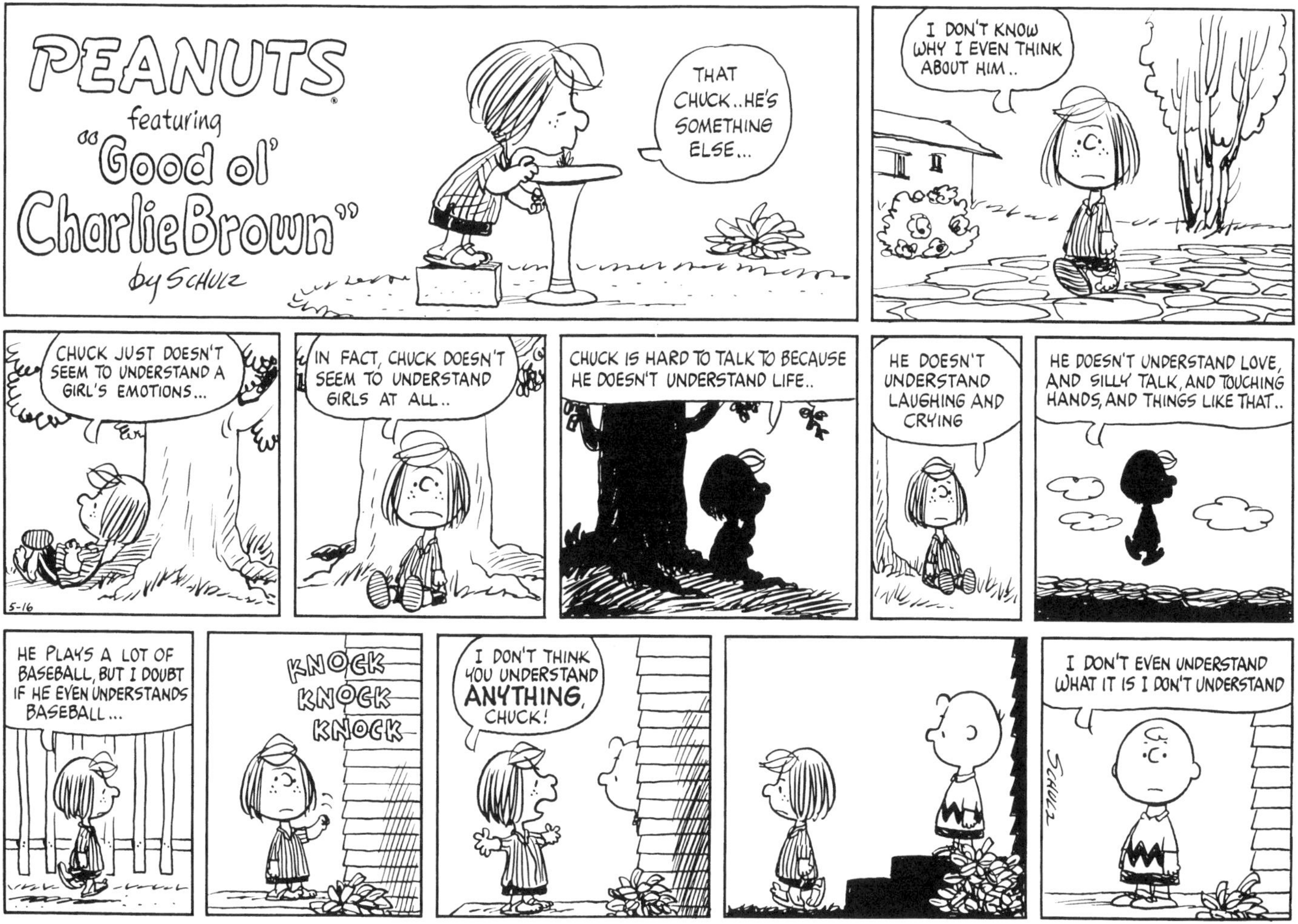
PEANUTS
featuring "Good ol' Charlie Brown"
by SCHULZ
THAT CHUCK..HE'S SOMETHING ELSE...
I DON'T KNOW WHY I EVEN THINK ABOUT HIM..
CHUCK JUST DOESN'T SEEM TO UNDERSTAND A GIRL'S EMOTIONS...
5-16
IN FACT, CHUCK DOESN'T SEEM TO UNDERSTAND GIRLS AT ALL..
CHUCK IS HARD TO TALK TO BECAUSE HE DOESN'T UNDERSTAND LIFE..
HE DOESN'T UNDERSTAND LAUGHING AND CRYING
HE DOESN'T UNDERSTAND LOVE, AND SILLY TALK, AND TOUCHING HANDS, AND THINGS LIKE THAT..
HE PLAYS A LOT OF BASEBALL, BUT I DOUBT IF HE EVEN UNDERSTANDS BASEBALL...
KNOCK KNOCK KNOCK
I DON'T THINK YOU UNDERSTAND ANYTHING, CHUCK!
I DON'T EVEN UNDERSTAND WHAT IT IS I DON'T UNDERSTAND
SCHULZ

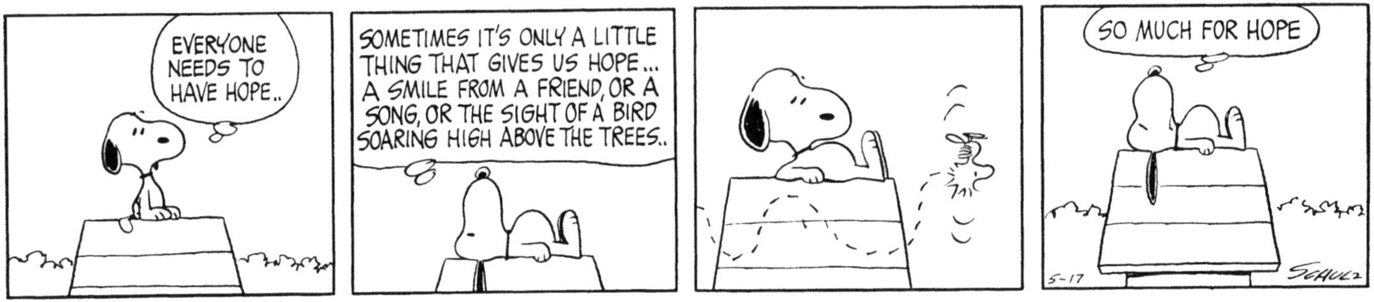
EVERYONE NEEDS TO HAVE HOPE..
SOMETIMES IT'S ONLY A LITTLE THING THAT GIVES US HOPE... A SMILE FROM A FRIEND, OR A SONG, OR THE SIGHT OF A BIRD SOARING HIGH ABOVE THE TREES..
SO MUCH FOR HOPE
5-17
SCHULZ

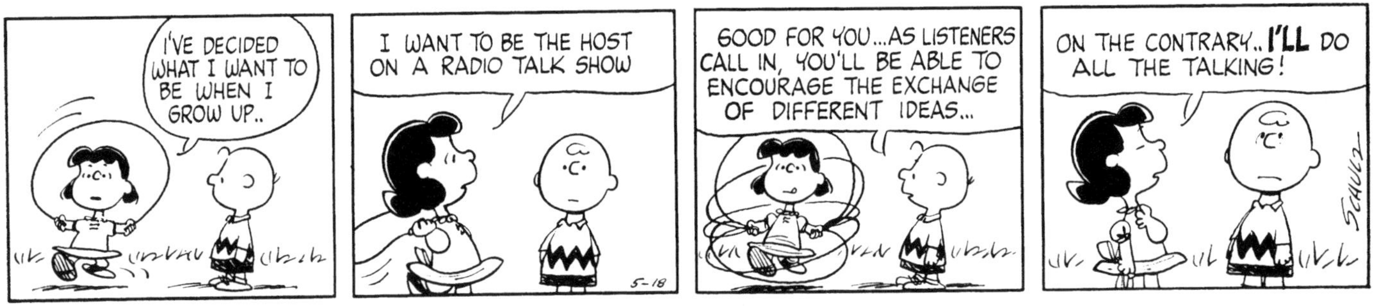
I'VE DECIDED WHAT I WANT TO BE WHEN I GROW UP..
I WANT TO BE THE HOST ON A RADIO TALK SHOW
5-18
GOOD FOR YOU...AS LISTENERS CALL IN, YOU'LL BE ABLE TO ENCOURAGE THE EXCHANGE OF DIFFERENT IDEAS...
ON THE CONTRARY.. I'LL DO ALL THE TALKING!
SCHULZ

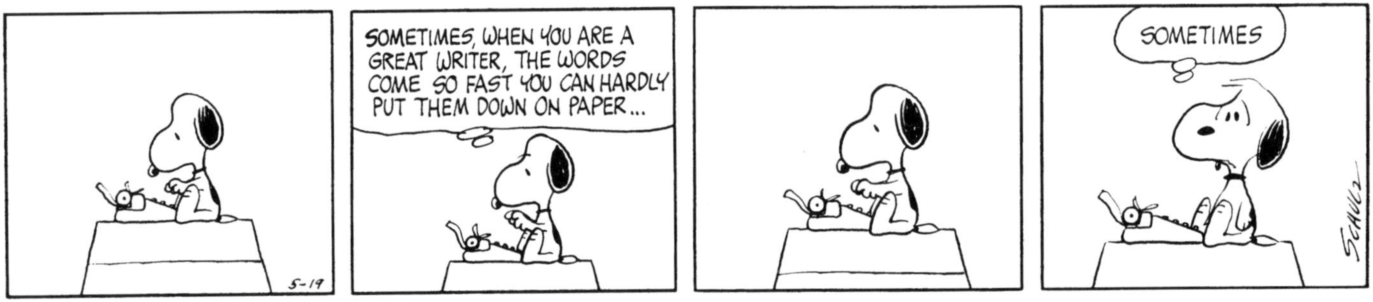
5-19
SOMETIMES, WHEN YOU ARE A GREAT WRITER, THE WORDS COME SO FAST YOU CAN HARDLY PUT THEM DOWN ON PAPER...
SOMETIMES
SCHULZ

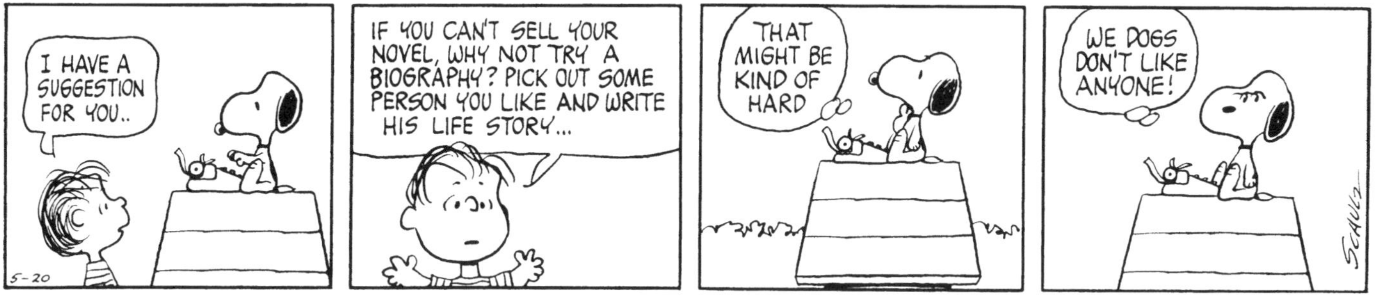
I HAVE A SUGGESTION FOR YOU..
IF YOU CAN'T SELL YOUR NOVEL, WHY NOT TRY A BIOGRAPHY? PICK OUT SOME PERSON YOU LIKE AND WRITE HIS LIFE STORY...
THAT MIGHT BE KIND OF HARD
WE DOGS DON'T LIKE ANYONE!
5-20
SCHULZ

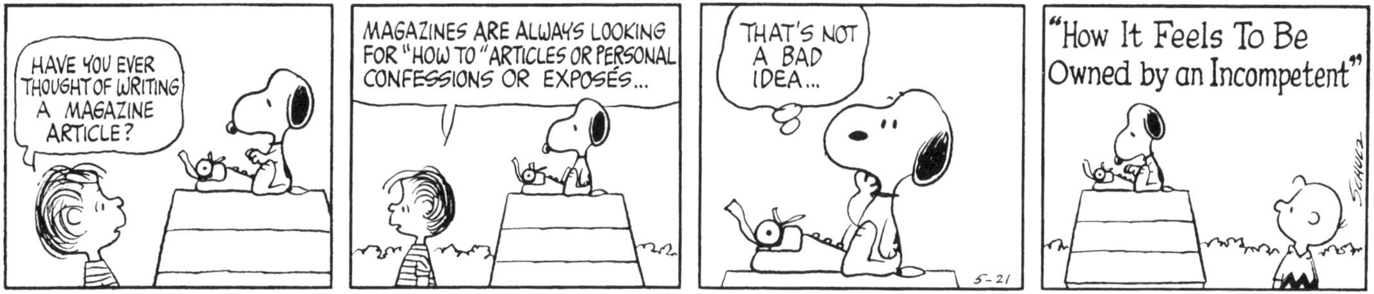
HAVE YOU EVER THOUGHT OF WRITING A MAGAZINE ARTICLE?
MAGAZINES ARE ALWAYS LOOKING FOR "HOW TO" ARTICLES OR PERSONAL CONFESSIONS OR EXPOSÉS...
THAT'S NOT A BAD IDEA...
5-21
"How It Feels To Be Owned by an Incompetent"
SCHULZ

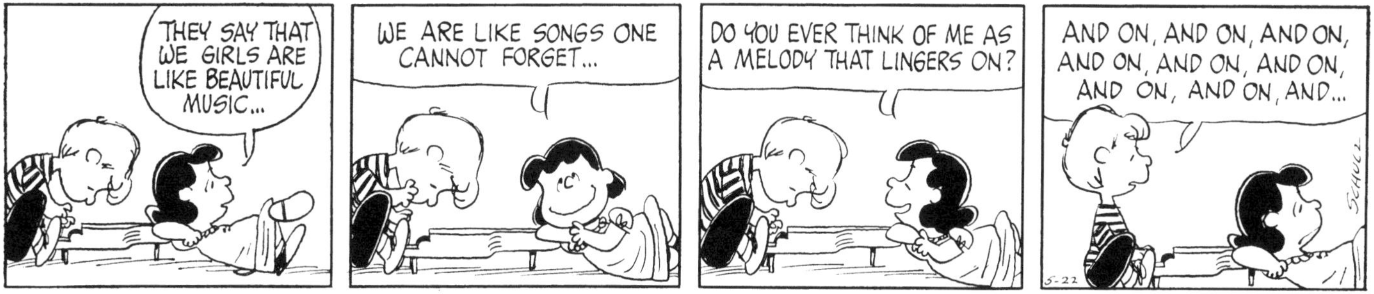
THEY SAY THAT WE GIRLS ARE LIKE BEAUTIFUL MUSIC...
WE ARE LIKE SONGS ONE CANNOT FORGET...
DO YOU EVER THINK OF ME AS A MELODY THAT LINGERS ON?
AND ON, AND ON, AND ON, AND ON, AND ON, AND ON, AND ON, AND ON, AND ON, AND...
5-22
SCHULZ

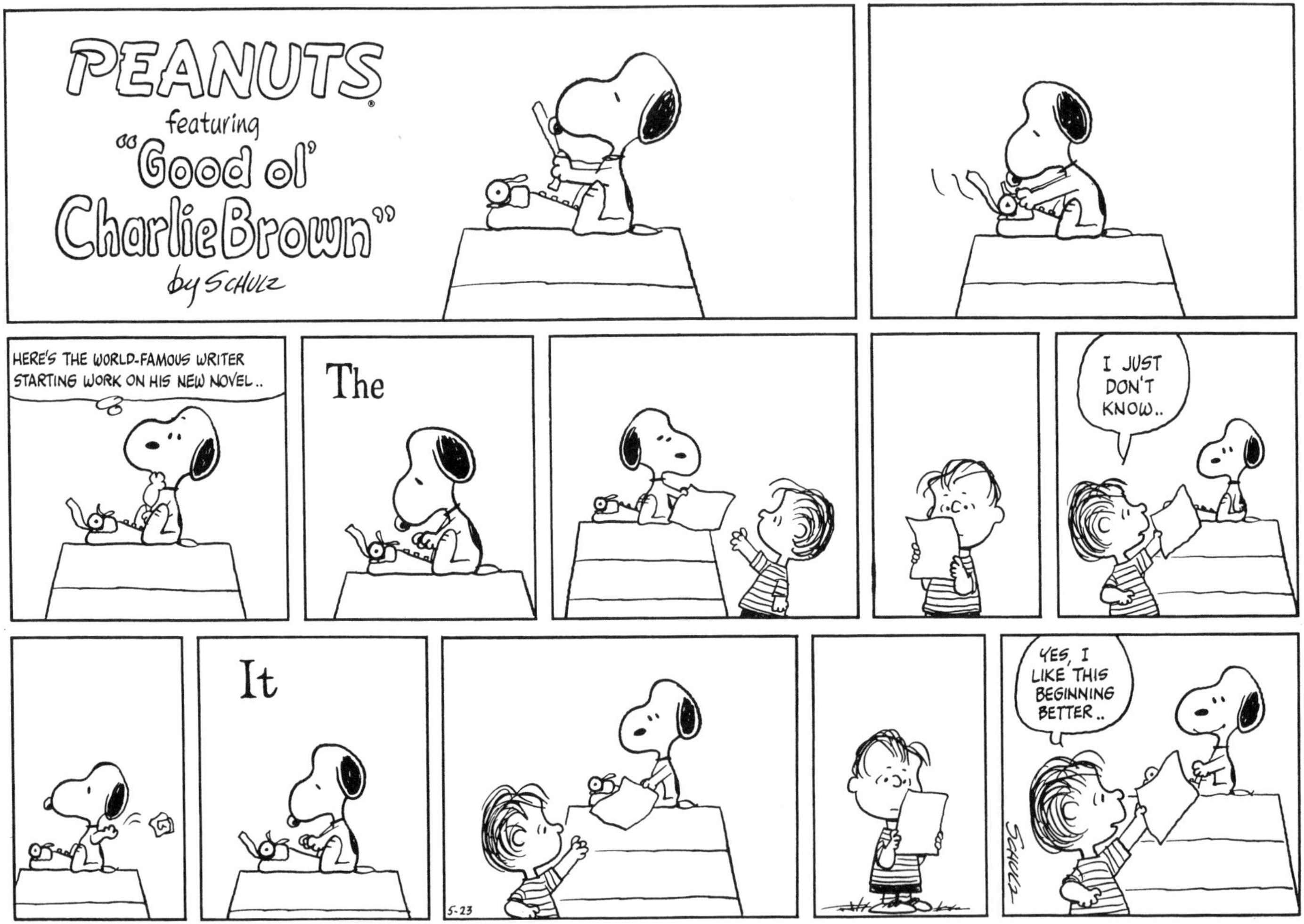
PEANUTS
featuring "Good ol' Charlie Brown"
by SCHULZ
HERE'S THE WORLD-FAMOUS WRITER STARTING WORK ON HIS NEW NOVEL..
The
I JUST DON'T KNOW..
It
5-23
YES, I LIKE THIS BEGINNING BETTER..
SCHULZ

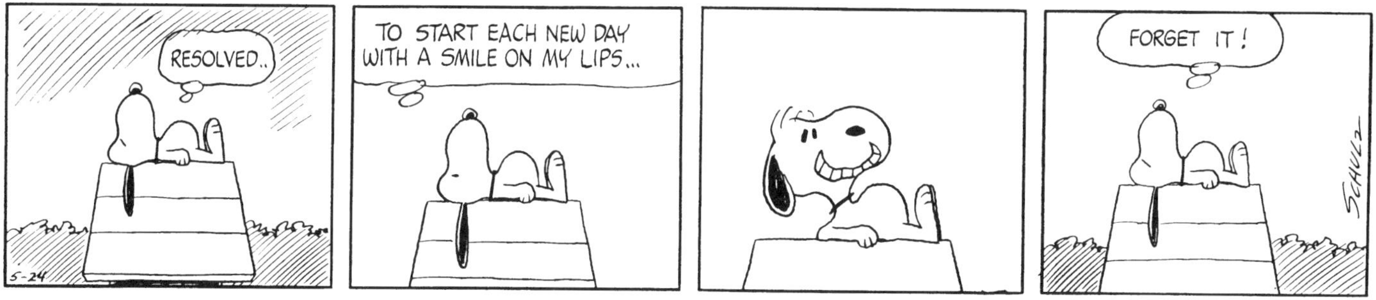
RESOLVED..
TO START EACH NEW DAY WITH A SMILE ON MY LIPS...
FORGET IT!
SCHULZ
5-24

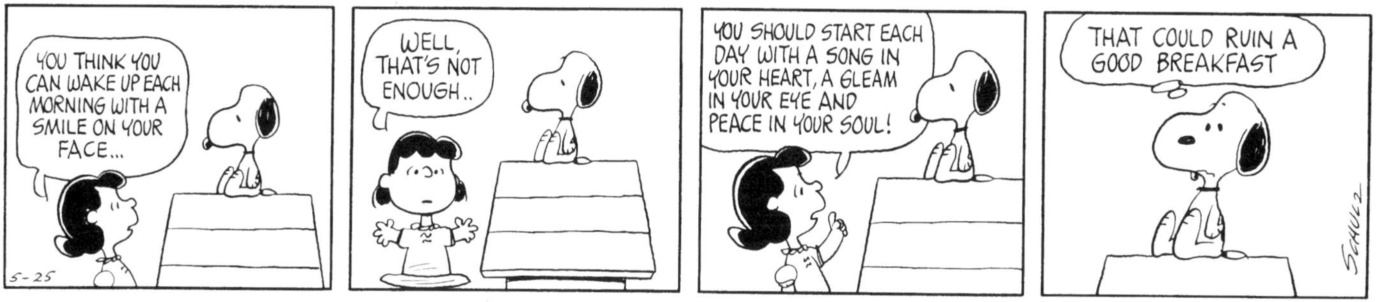
YOU THINK YOU CAN WAKE UP EACH MORNING WITH A SMILE ON YOUR FACE...
WELL, THAT'S NOT ENOUGH..
YOU SHOULD START EACH DAY WITH A SONG IN YOUR HEART, A GLEAM IN YOUR EYE AND PEACE IN YOUR SOUL!
THAT COULD RUIN A GOOD BREAKFAST
SCHULZ
5-25

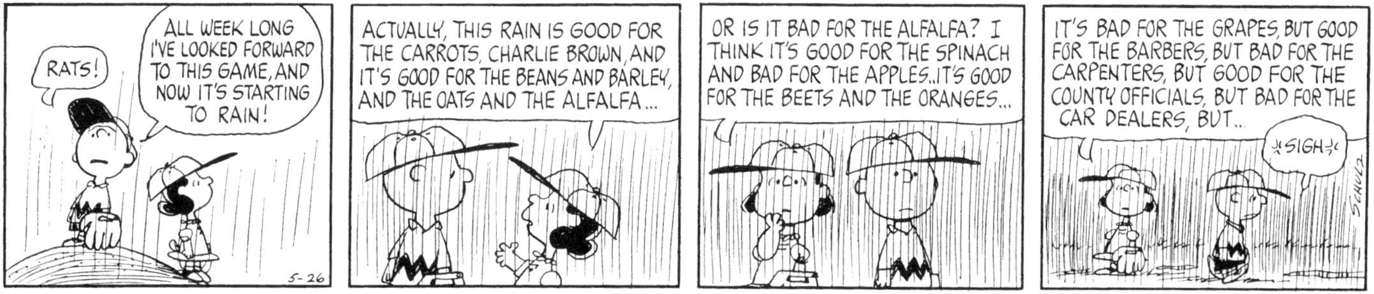
RATS!
ALL WEEK LONG I'VE LOOKED FORWARD TO THIS GAME, AND NOW IT'S STARTING TO RAIN!
ACTUALLY, THIS RAIN IS GOOD FOR THE CARROTS, CHARLIE BROWN, AND IT'S GOOD FOR THE BEANS AND BARLEY, AND THE OATS AND THE ALFALFA...
OR IS IT BAD FOR THE ALFALFA? I THINK IT'S GOOD FOR THE SPINACH AND BAD FOR THE APPLES..IT'S GOOD FOR THE BEETS AND THE ORANGES...
IT'S BAD FOR THE GRAPES, BUT GOOD FOR THE BARBERS, BUT BAD FOR THE CARPENTERS, BUT GOOD FOR THE COUNTY OFFICIALS, BUT BAD FOR THE CAR DEALERS, BUT...
SIGH
SCHULZ
5-26

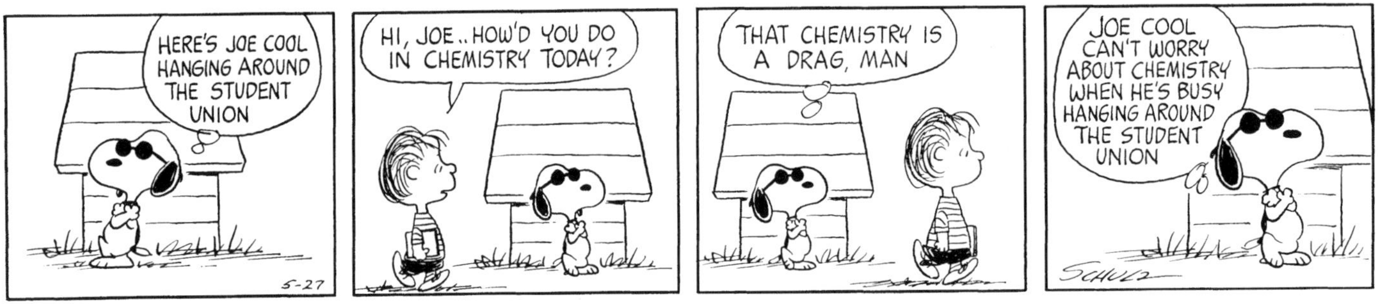
HERE'S JOE COOL HANGING AROUND THE STUDENT UNION
HI, JOE.. HOW'D YOU DO IN CHEMISTRY TODAY?
THAT CHEMISTRY IS A DRAG, MAN
JOE COOL CAN'T WORRY ABOUT CHEMISTRY WHEN HE'S BUSY HANGING AROUND THE STUDENT UNION
5-27
SCHULZ

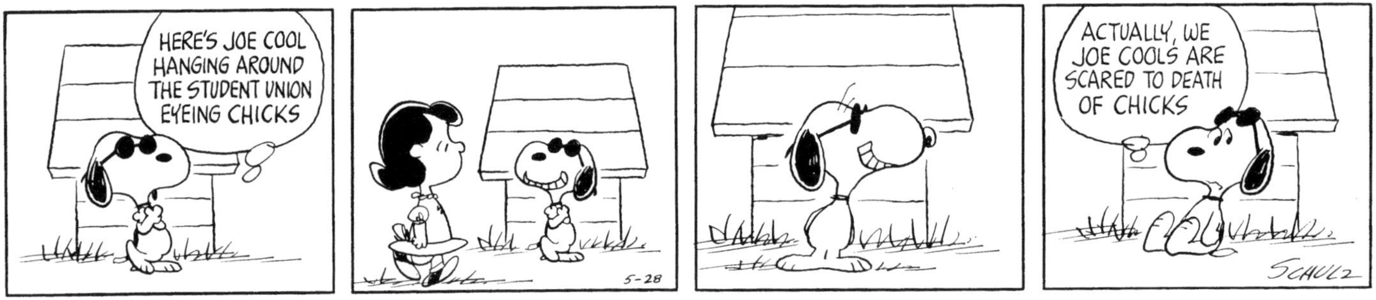
HERE'S JOE COOL HANGING AROUND THE STUDENT UNION EYEING CHICKS
ACTUALLY, WE JOE COOLS ARE SCARED TO DEATH OF CHICKS
5-28
SCHULZ

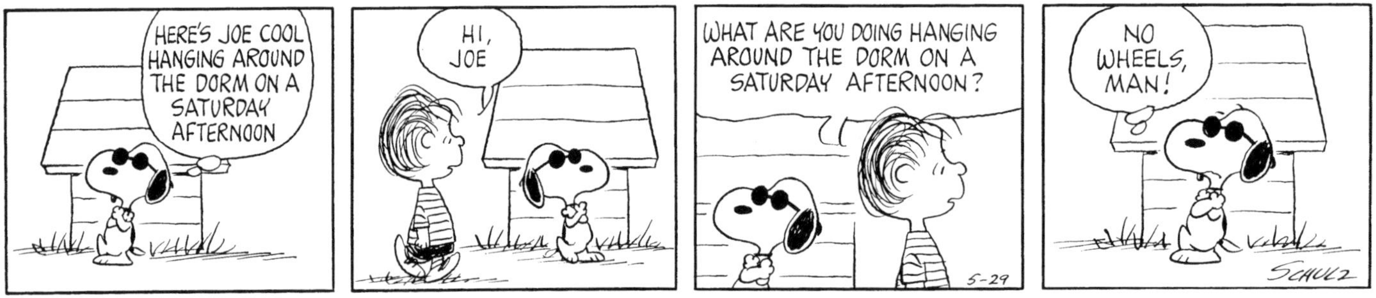
HERE'S JOE COOL HANGING AROUND THE DORM ON A SATURDAY AFTERNOON
HI, JOE
WHAT ARE YOU DOING HANGING AROUND THE DORM ON A SATURDAY AFTERNOON?
NO WHEELS, MAN!
5-29
SCHULZ

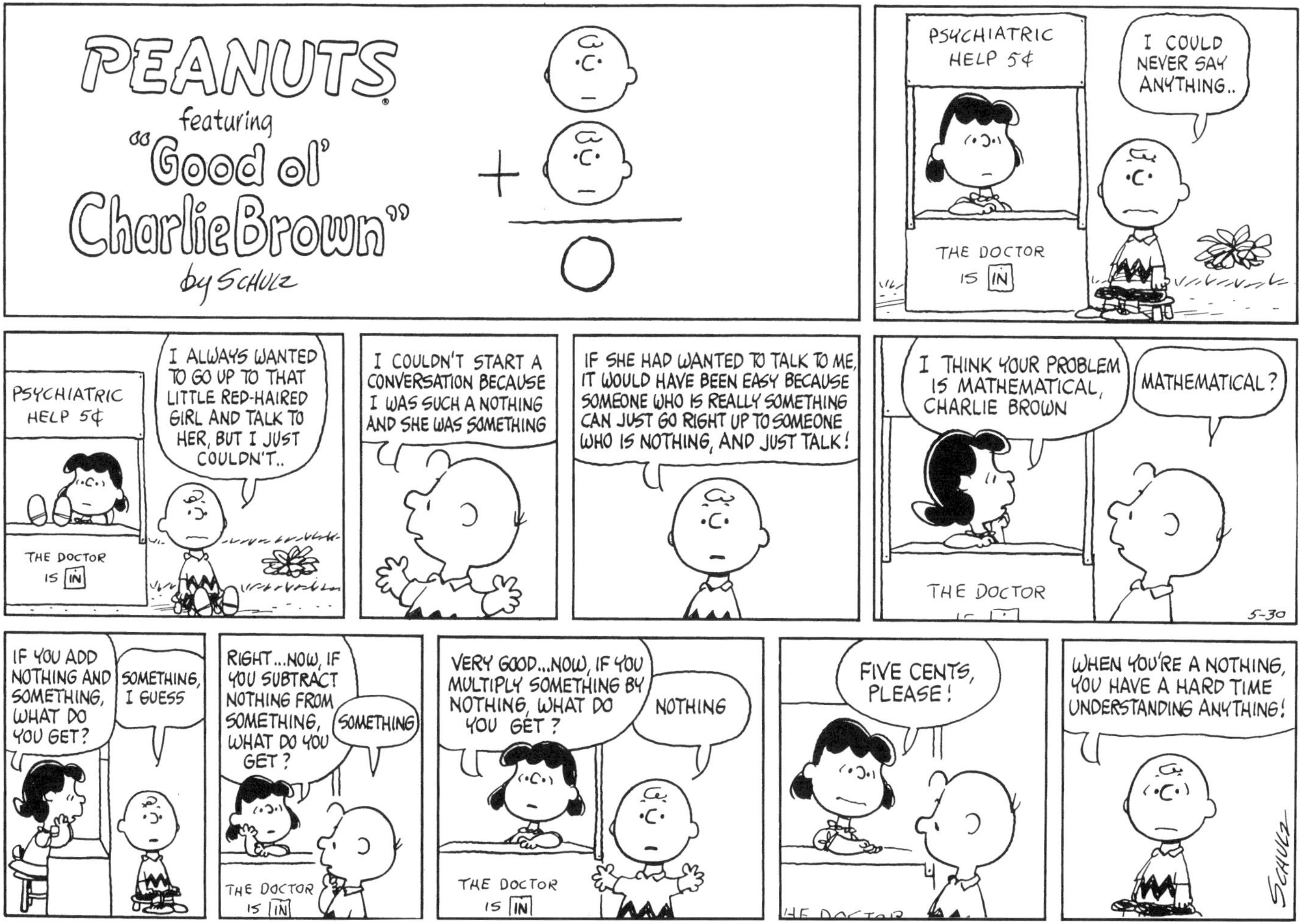

PEANUTS®
featuring "Good ol' Charlie Brown"
by SCHULZ
PSYCHIATRIC HELP 5¢
I COULD NEVER SAY ANYTHING..
THE DOCTOR IS IN
I ALWAYS WANTED TO GO UP TO THAT LITTLE RED-HAIRED GIRL AND TALK TO HER, BUT I JUST COULDN'T..
I COULDN'T START A CONVERSATION BECAUSE I WAS SUCH A NOTHING AND SHE WAS SOMETHING
IF SHE HAD WANTED TO TALK TO ME, IT WOULD HAVE BEEN EASY BECAUSE SOMEONE WHO IS REALLY SOMETHING CAN JUST GO RIGHT UP TO SOMEONE WHO IS NOTHING, AND JUST TALK!
I THINK YOUR PROBLEM IS MATHEMATICAL, CHARLIE BROWN
MATHEMATICAL?
THE DOCTOR
5-30
IF YOU ADD NOTHING AND SOMETHING, WHAT DO YOU GET?
SOMETHING, I GUESS
RIGHT...NOW, IF YOU SUBTRACT NOTHING FROM SOMETHING, WHAT DO YOU GET?
SOMETHING
VERY GOOD...NOW, IF YOU MULTIPLY SOMETHING BY NOTHING, WHAT DO YOU GET?
NOTHING
FIVE CENTS, PLEASE!
WHEN YOU'RE A NOTHING, YOU HAVE A HARD TIME UNDERSTANDING ANYTHING!
SCHULZ

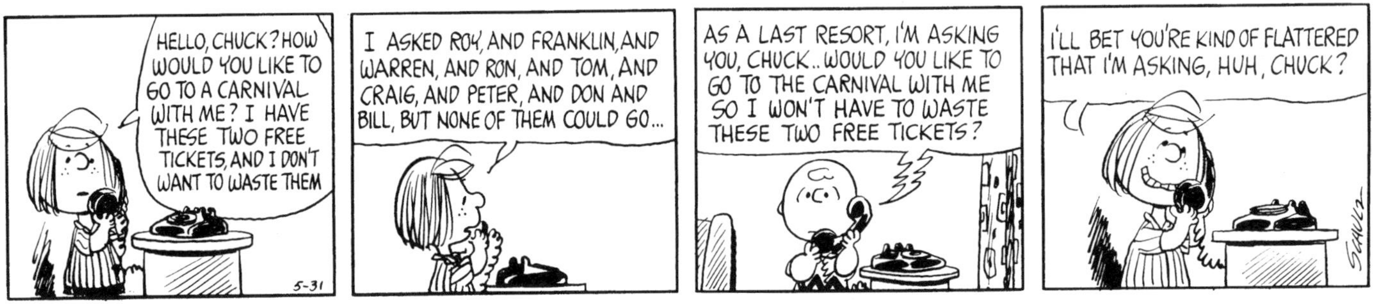
HELLO, CHUCK? HOW WOULD YOU LIKE TO GO TO A CARNIVAL WITH ME? I HAVE THESE TWO FREE TICKETS, AND I DON'T WANT TO WASTE THEM
5-31
I ASKED ROY, AND FRANKLIN, AND WARREN, AND RON, AND TOM, AND CRAIG, AND PETER, AND DON AND BILL, BUT NONE OF THEM COULD GO...
AS A LAST RESORT, I'M ASKING YOU, CHUCK.. WOULD YOU LIKE TO GO TO THE CARNIVAL WITH ME SO I WON'T HAVE TO WASTE THESE TWO FREE TICKETS?
I'LL BET YOU'RE KIND OF FLATTERED THAT I'M ASKING, HUH, CHUCK?
SCHULZ

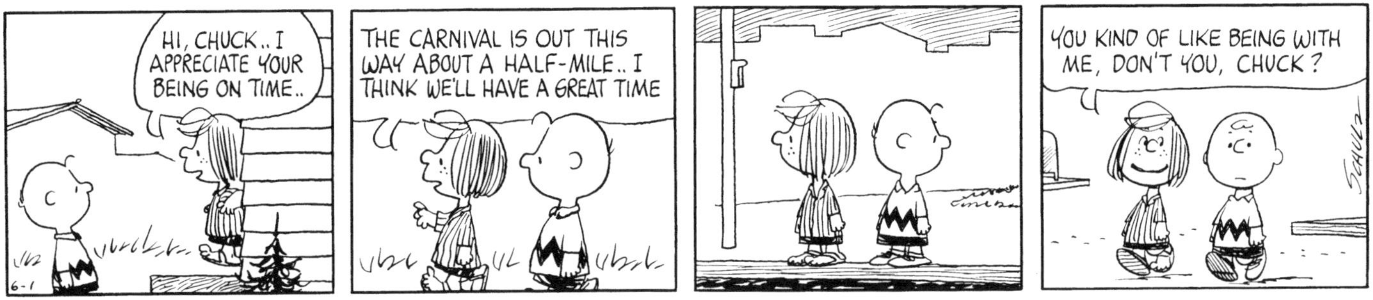
HI, CHUCK.. I APPRECIATE YOUR BEING ON TIME..
6-1
THE CARNIVAL IS OUT THIS WAY ABOUT A HALF-MILE.. I THINK WE'LL HAVE A GREAT TIME
YOU KIND OF LIKE BEING WITH ME, DON'T YOU, CHUCK?
SCHULZ

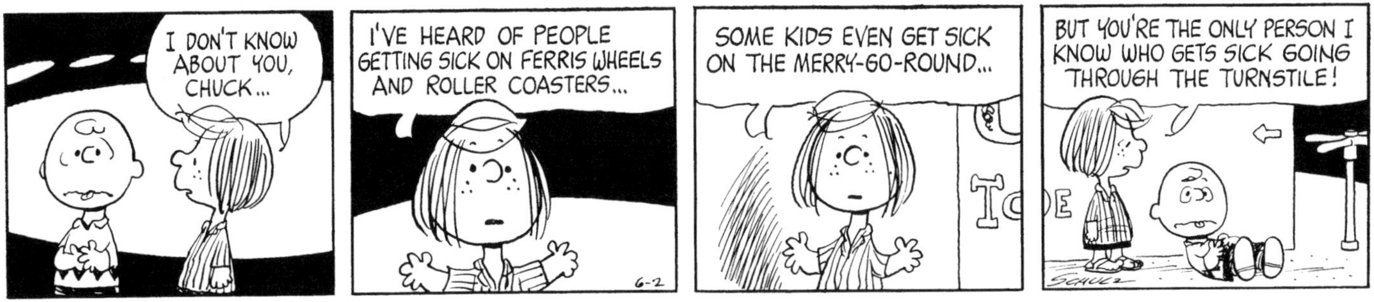
I DON'T KNOW ABOUT YOU, CHUCK...
I'VE HEARD OF PEOPLE GETTING SICK ON FERRIS WHEELS AND ROLLER COASTERS...
6-2
SOME KIDS EVEN GET SICK ON THE MERRY-GO-ROUND...
BUT YOU'RE THE ONLY PERSON I KNOW WHO GETS SICK GOING THROUGH THE TURNSTILE!
SCHULZ

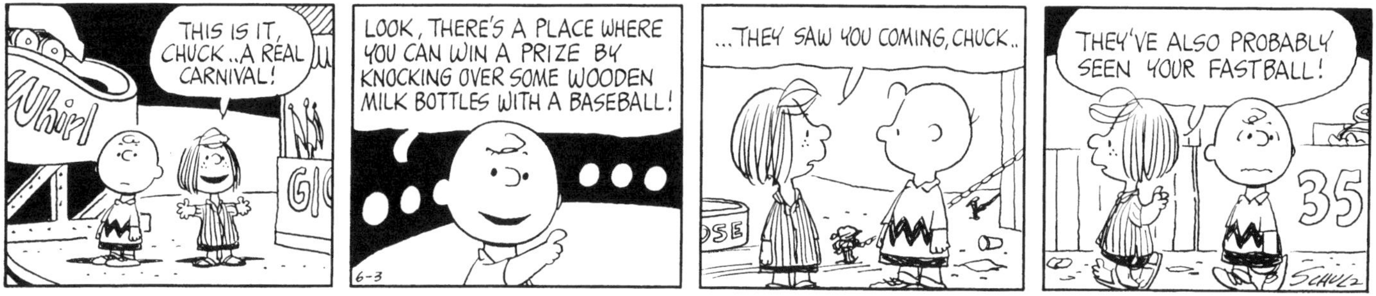
THIS IS IT, CHUCK..A REAL CARNIVAL!
LOOK, THERE'S A PLACE WHERE YOU CAN WIN A PRIZE BY KNOCKING OVER SOME WOODEN MILK BOTTLES WITH A BASEBALL!
6-3
...THEY SAW YOU COMING, CHUCK..
THEY'VE ALSO PROBABLY SEEN YOUR FASTBALL!
35
SCHULZ

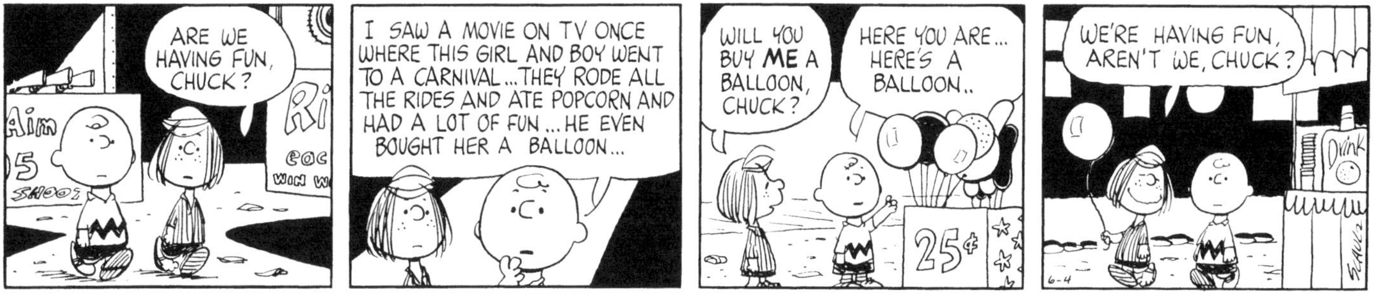
ARE WE HAVING FUN, CHUCK?
I SAW A MOVIE ON TV ONCE WHERE THIS GIRL AND BOY WENT TO A CARNIVAL...THEY RODE ALL THE RIDES AND ATE POPCORN AND HAD A LOT OF FUN...HE EVEN BOUGHT HER A BALLOON...
WILL YOU BUY **ME** A BALLOON, CHUCK?
HERE YOU ARE... HERE'S A BALLOON..
25¢
WE'RE HAVING FUN, AREN'T WE, CHUCK?
Drink
6-4
SCHULZ

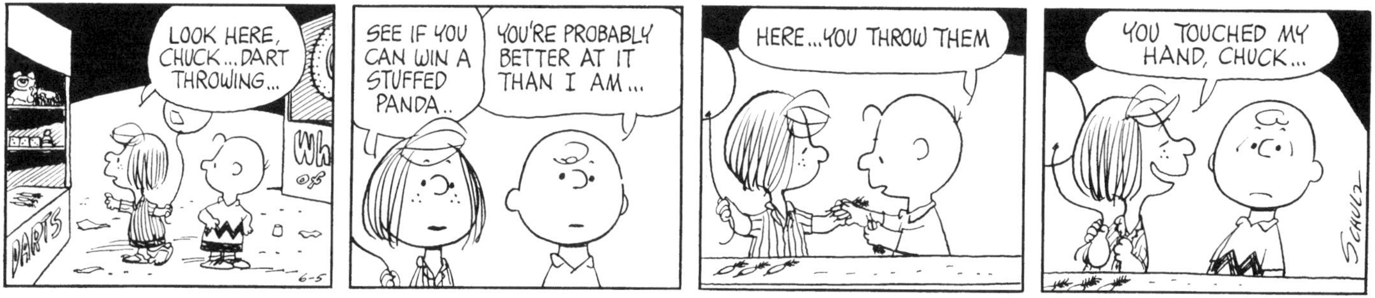
LOOK HERE, CHUCK...DART THROWING...
DARTS
6-5
SEE IF YOU CAN WIN A STUFFED PANDA..
YOU'RE PROBABLY BETTER AT IT THAN I AM...
HERE...YOU THROW THEM
YOU TOUCHED MY HAND, CHUCK...
SCHULZ

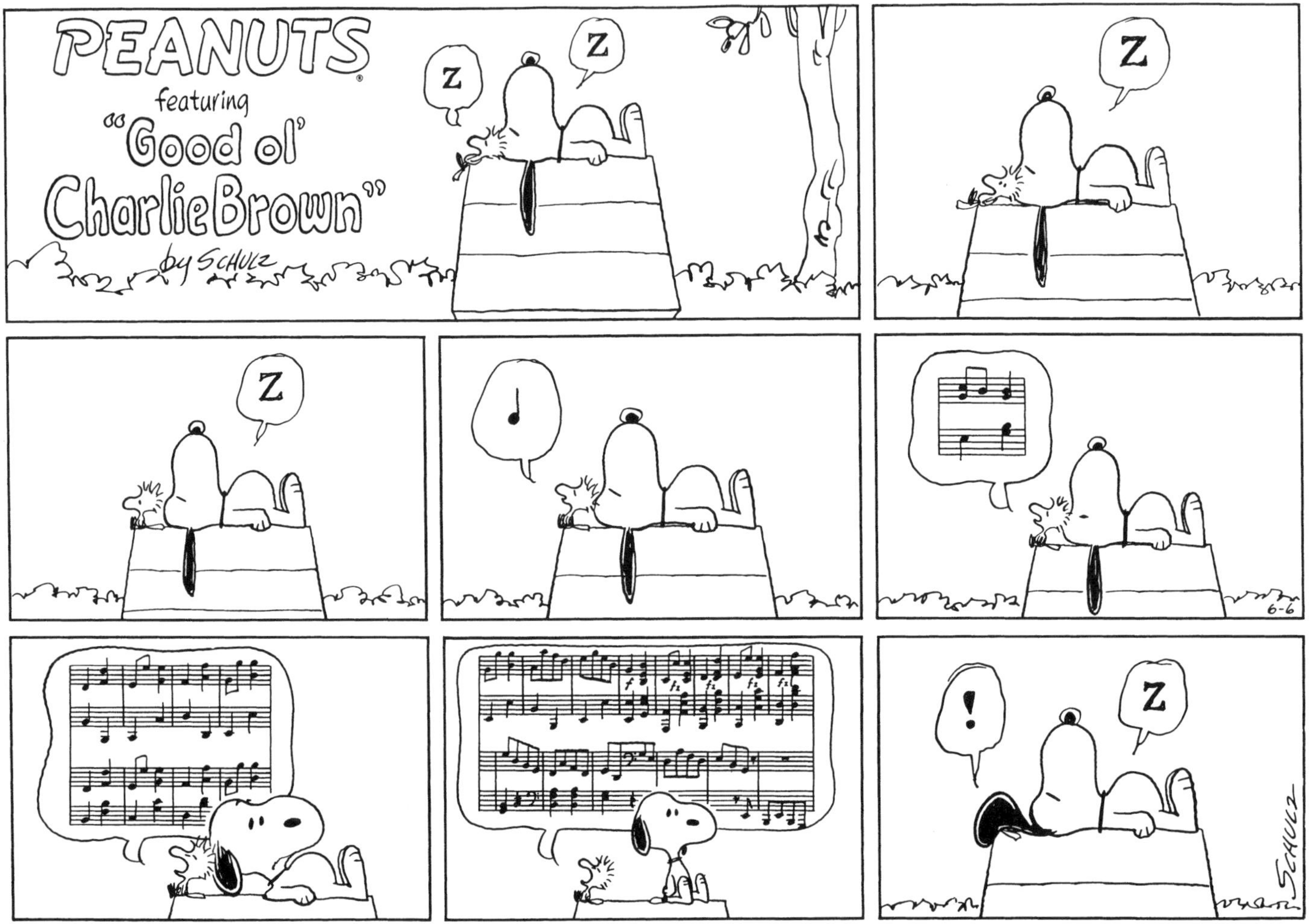
PEANUTS
featuring "Good ol' Charlie Brown"
by SCHULZ
Z
Z
Z
Z
!
Z
SCHULZ

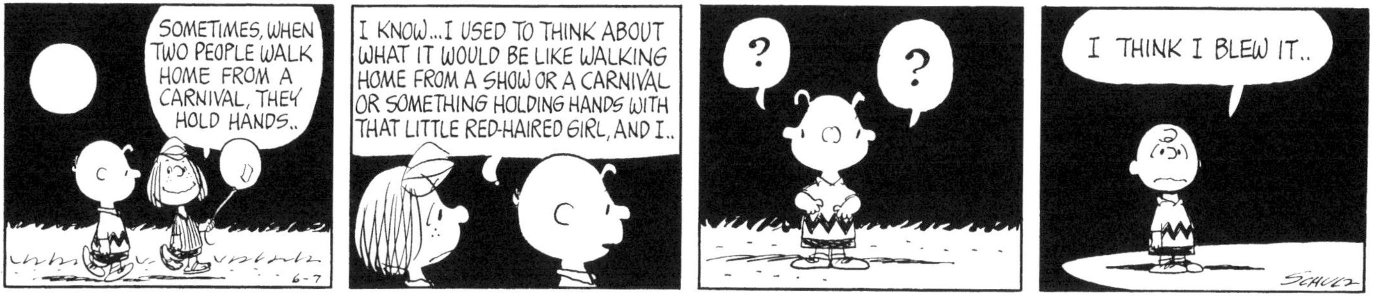
SOMETIMES, WHEN TWO PEOPLE WALK HOME FROM A CARNIVAL, THEY HOLD HANDS..
I KNOW...I USED TO THINK ABOUT WHAT IT WOULD BE LIKE WALKING HOME FROM A SHOW OR A CARNIVAL OR SOMETHING HOLDING HANDS WITH THAT LITTLE RED-HAIRED GIRL, AND I..
?
?
I THINK I BLEW IT..

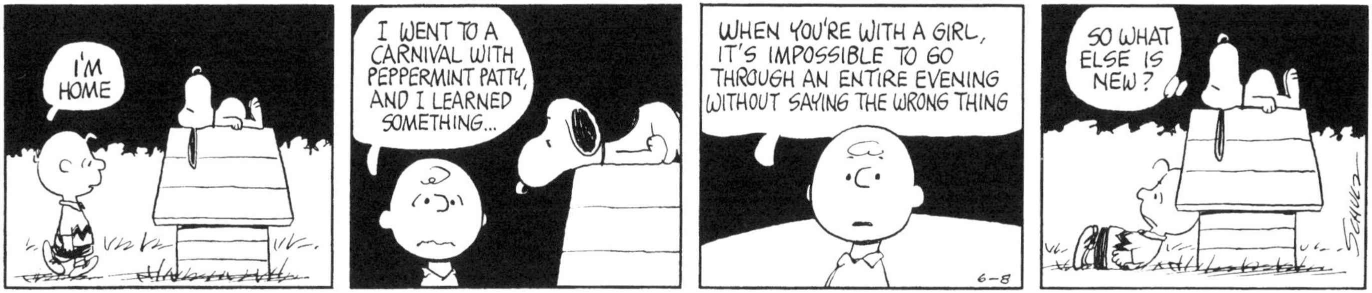
I'M HOME
I WENT TO A CARNIVAL WITH PEPPERMINT PATTY, AND I LEARNED SOMETHING...
WHEN YOU'RE WITH A GIRL, IT'S IMPOSSIBLE TO GO THROUGH AN ENTIRE EVENING WITHOUT SAYING THE WRONG THING
SO WHAT ELSE IS NEW?

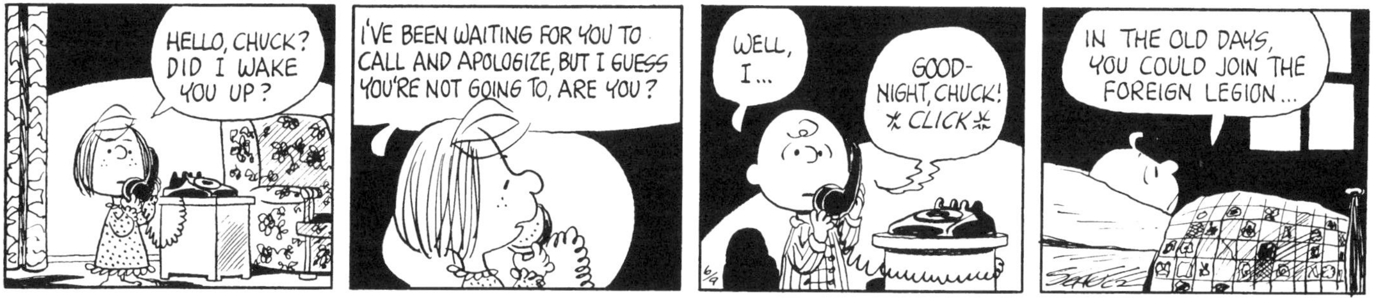
HELLO, CHUCK? DID I WAKE YOU UP?
I'VE BEEN WAITING FOR YOU TO CALL AND APOLOGIZE, BUT I GUESS YOU'RE NOT GOING TO, ARE YOU?
WELL, I...
GOOD-NIGHT, CHUCK! *CLICK*
IN THE OLD DAYS, YOU COULD JOIN THE FOREIGN LEGION...

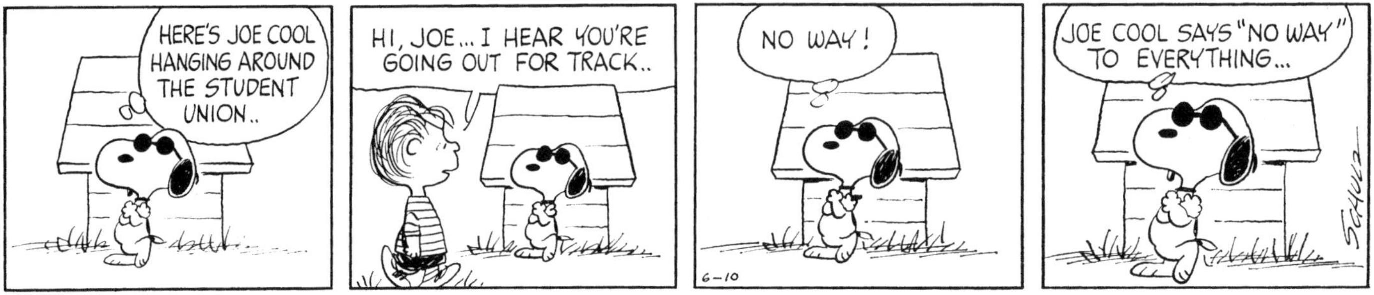
HERE'S JOE COOL HANGING AROUND THE STUDENT UNION..
HI, JOE... I HEAR YOU'RE GOING OUT FOR TRACK..
NO WAY!
6-10
JOE COOL SAYS "NO WAY" TO EVERYTHING...
SCHULZ

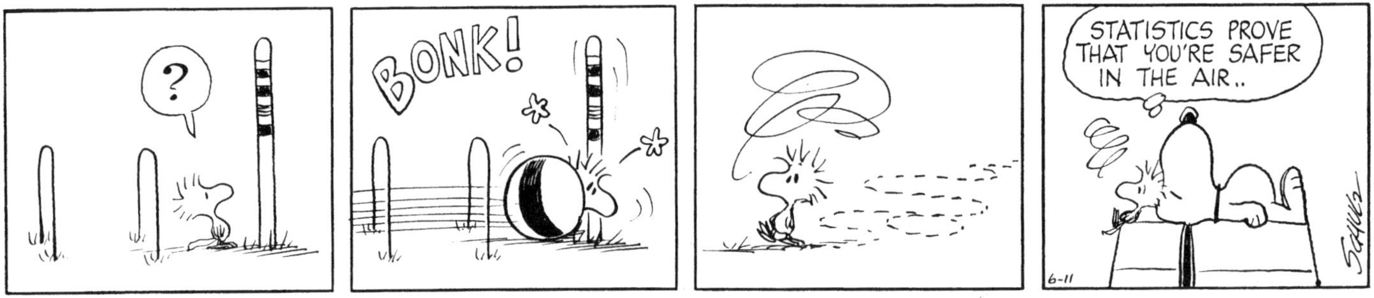
?
BONK!
STATISTICS PROVE THAT YOU'RE SAFER IN THE AIR..
6-11
SCHULZ

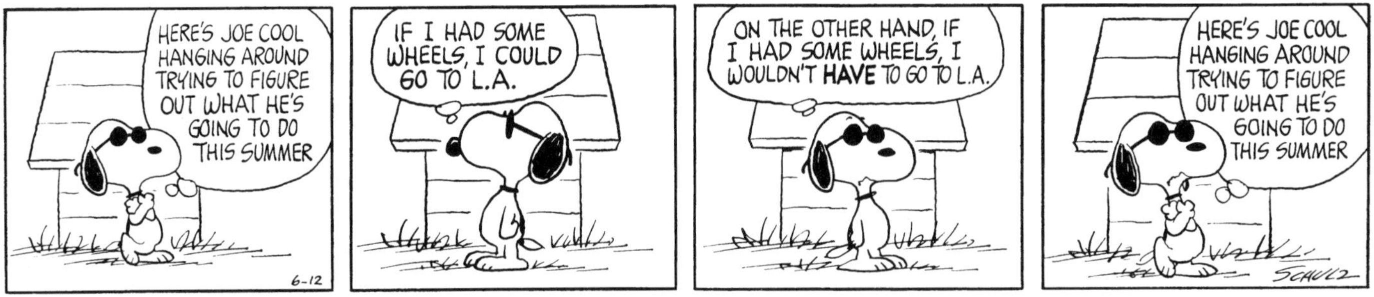
HERE'S JOE COOL HANGING AROUND TRYING TO FIGURE OUT WHAT HE'S GOING TO DO THIS SUMMER
6-12
IF I HAD SOME WHEELS, I COULD GO TO L.A.
ON THE OTHER HAND, IF I HAD SOME WHEELS, I WOULDN'T **HAVE** TO GO TO L.A.
HERE'S JOE COOL HANGING AROUND TRYING TO FIGURE OUT WHAT HE'S GOING TO DO THIS SUMMER
SCHULZ

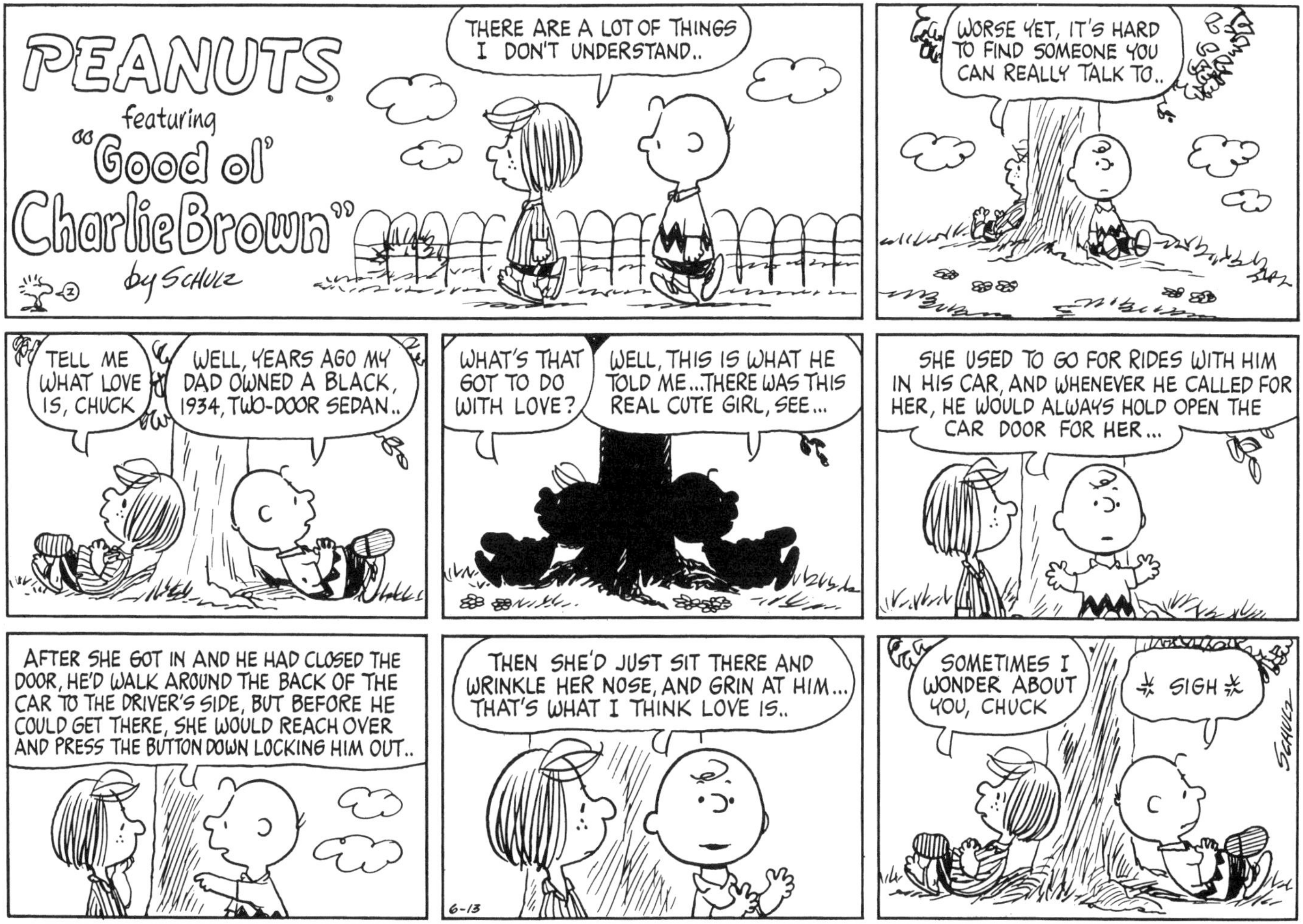
PEANUTS
featuring
"Good ol' Charlie Brown"
by SCHULZ
THERE ARE A LOT OF THINGS I DON'T UNDERSTAND..
WORSE YET, IT'S HARD TO FIND SOMEONE YOU CAN REALLY TALK TO..
TELL ME WHAT LOVE IS, CHUCK
WELL, YEARS AGO MY DAD OWNED A BLACK, 1934, TWO-DOOR SEDAN..
WHAT'S THAT GOT TO DO WITH LOVE?
WELL, THIS IS WHAT HE TOLD ME...THERE WAS THIS REAL CUTE GIRL, SEE...
SHE USED TO GO FOR RIDES WITH HIM IN HIS CAR, AND WHENEVER HE CALLED FOR HER, HE WOULD ALWAYS HOLD OPEN THE CAR DOOR FOR HER...
AFTER SHE GOT IN AND HE HAD CLOSED THE DOOR, HE'D WALK AROUND THE BACK OF THE CAR TO THE DRIVER'S SIDE, BUT BEFORE HE COULD GET THERE, SHE WOULD REACH OVER AND PRESS THE BUTTON DOWN LOCKING HIM OUT..
THEN SHE'D JUST SIT THERE AND WRINKLE HER NOSE, AND GRIN AT HIM... THAT'S WHAT I THINK LOVE IS..
6-13
SOMETIMES I WONDER ABOUT YOU, CHUCK
* SIGH *
SCHULZ

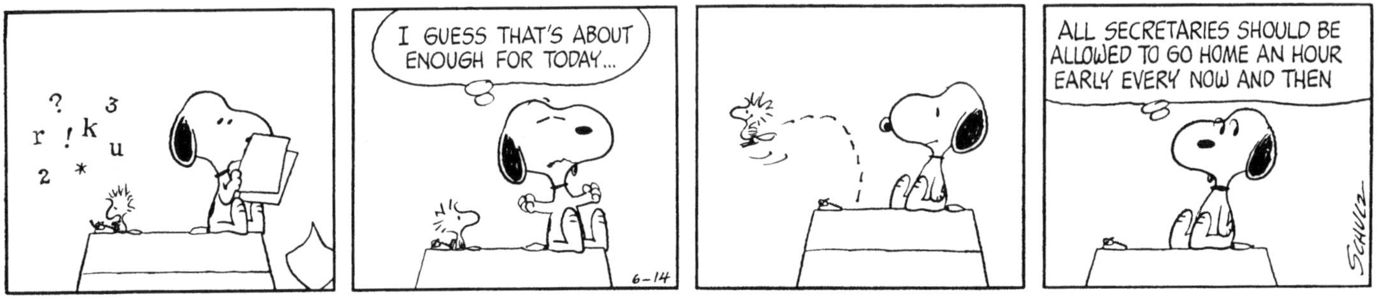
? 3
r ! k u
2 *
I GUESS THAT'S ABOUT ENOUGH FOR TODAY...
6-14
ALL SECRETARIES SHOULD BE ALLOWED TO GO HOME AN HOUR EARLY EVERY NOW AND THEN
SCHULZ

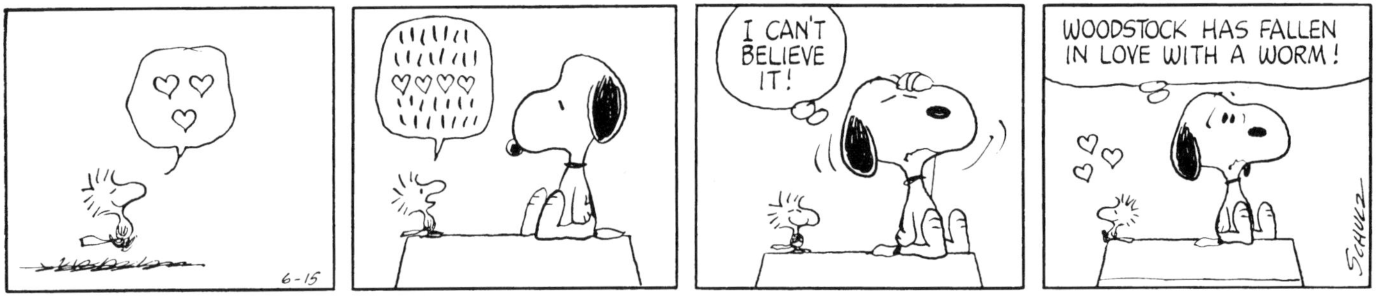
6-15
I CAN'T BELIEVE IT!
WOODSTOCK HAS FALLEN IN LOVE WITH A WORM!
SCHULZ

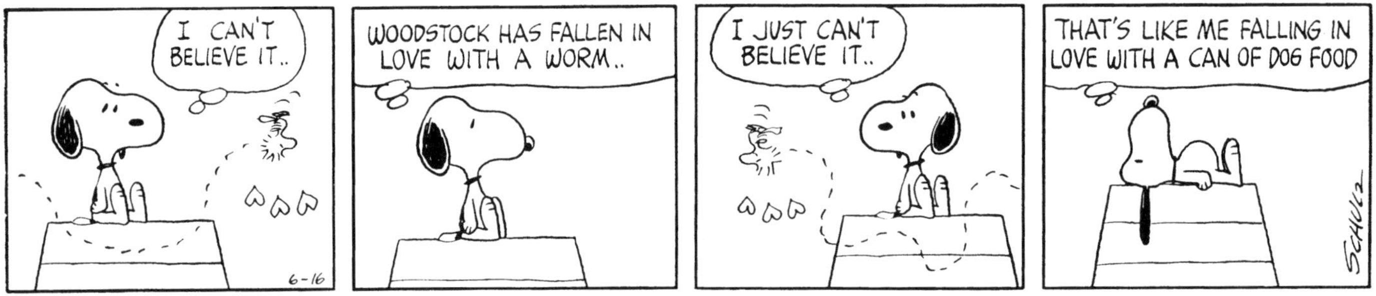
I CAN'T BELIEVE IT..
6-16
WOODSTOCK HAS FALLEN IN LOVE WITH A WORM..
I JUST CAN'T BELIEVE IT..
THAT'S LIKE ME FALLING IN LOVE WITH A CAN OF DOG FOOD
SCHULZ

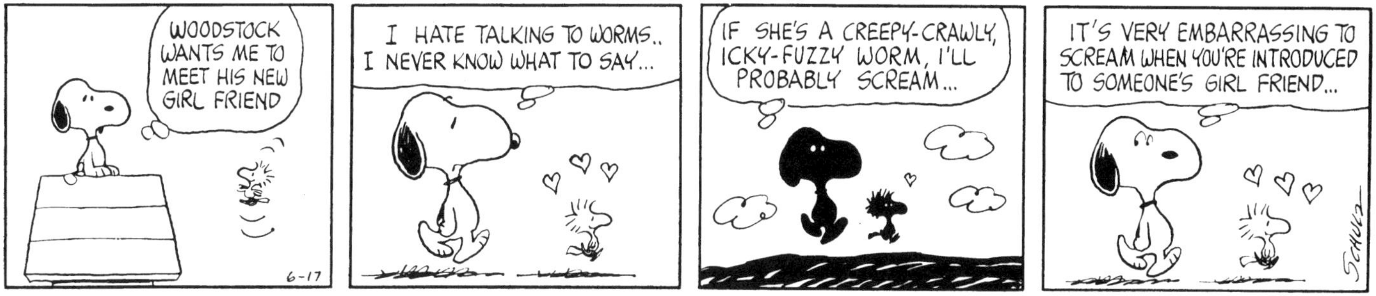
WOODSTOCK WANTS ME TO MEET HIS NEW GIRL FRIEND
6-17
I HATE TALKING TO WORMS.. I NEVER KNOW WHAT TO SAY...
IF SHE'S A CREEPY-CRAWLY, ICKY-FUZZY WORM, I'LL PROBABLY SCREAM...
IT'S VERY EMBARRASSING TO SCREAM WHEN YOU'RE INTRODUCED TO SOMEONE'S GIRL FRIEND...
SCHULZ

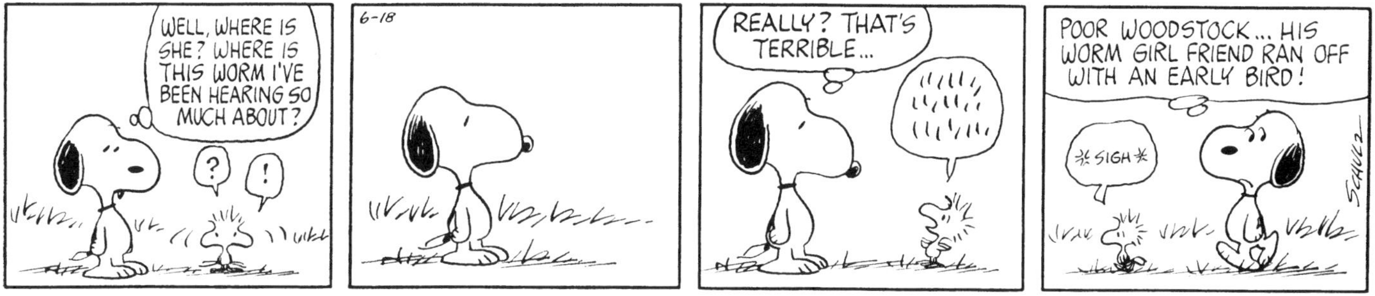
WELL, WHERE IS SHE? WHERE IS THIS WORM I'VE BEEN HEARING SO MUCH ABOUT?
?
!
6-18
REALLY? THAT'S TERRIBLE...
POOR WOODSTOCK... HIS WORM GIRL FRIEND RAN OFF WITH AN EARLY BIRD!
SIGH
SCHULZ

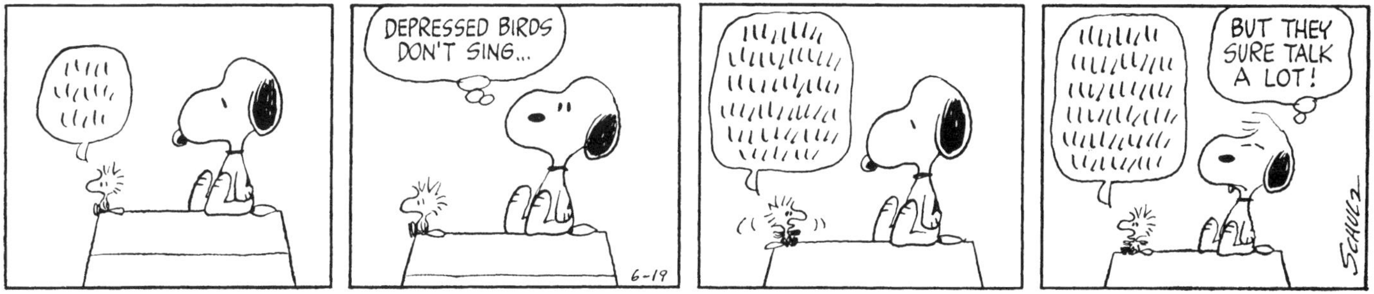
DEPRESSED BIRDS DON'T SING...
6-19
BUT THEY SURE TALK A LOT!
SCHULZ

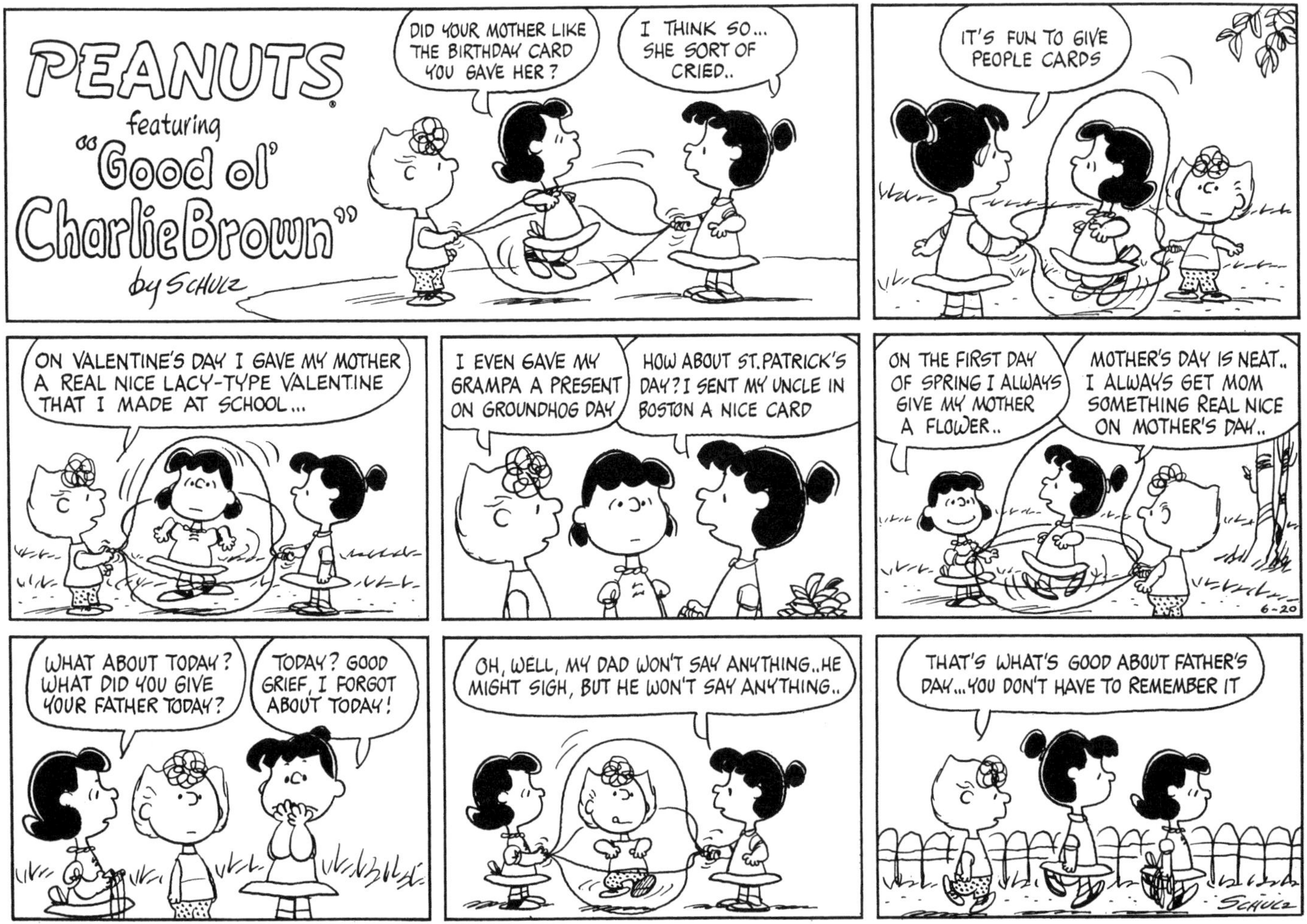
PEANUTS
featuring "Good ol' Charlie Brown"
by SCHULZ
DID YOUR MOTHER LIKE THE BIRTHDAY CARD YOU GAVE HER?
I THINK SO... SHE SORT OF CRIED..
IT'S FUN TO GIVE PEOPLE CARDS
ON VALENTINE'S DAY I GAVE MY MOTHER A REAL NICE LACY-TYPE VALENTINE THAT I MADE AT SCHOOL...
I EVEN GAVE MY GRAMPA A PRESENT ON GROUNDHOG DAY
HOW ABOUT ST. PATRICK'S DAY? I SENT MY UNCLE IN BOSTON A NICE CARD
ON THE FIRST DAY OF SPRING I ALWAYS GIVE MY MOTHER A FLOWER..
MOTHER'S DAY IS NEAT.. I ALWAYS GET MOM SOMETHING REAL NICE ON MOTHER'S DAY..
6-20
WHAT ABOUT TODAY? WHAT DID YOU GIVE YOUR FATHER TODAY?
TODAY? GOOD GRIEF, I FORGOT ABOUT TODAY!
OH, WELL, MY DAD WON'T SAY ANYTHING..HE MIGHT SIGH, BUT HE WON'T SAY ANYTHING..
THAT'S WHAT'S GOOD ABOUT FATHER'S DAY...YOU DON'T HAVE TO REMEMBER IT
SCHULZ

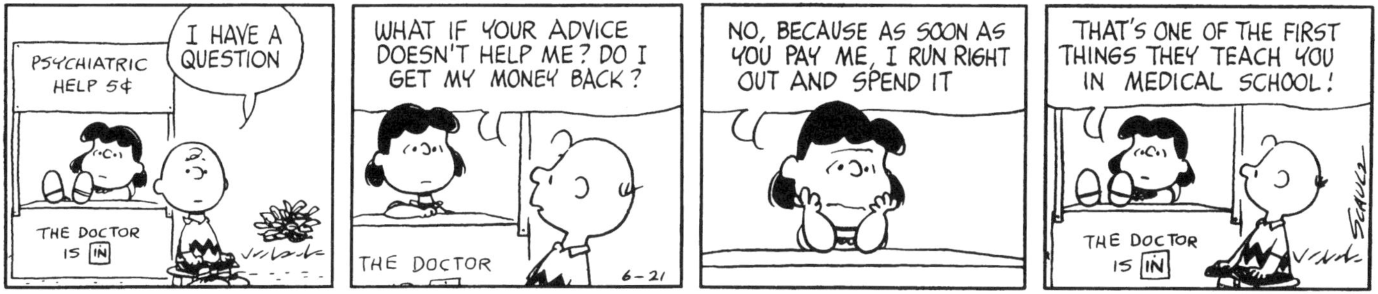
PSYCHIATRIC HELP 5¢
THE DOCTOR IS IN
I HAVE A QUESTION
WHAT IF YOUR ADVICE DOESN'T HELP ME? DO I GET MY MONEY BACK?
THE DOCTOR
6-21
NO, BECAUSE AS SOON AS YOU PAY ME, I RUN RIGHT OUT AND SPEND IT
THAT'S ONE OF THE FIRST THINGS THEY TEACH YOU IN MEDICAL SCHOOL!
THE DOCTOR IS IN
SCHULZ

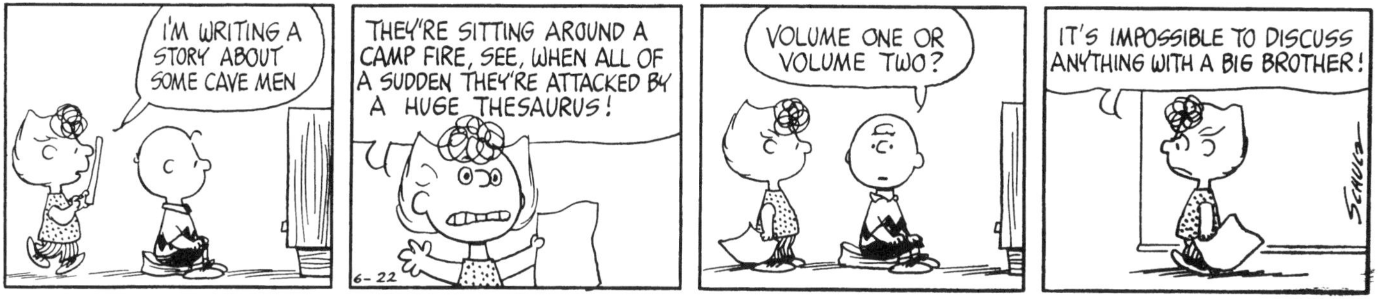
I'M WRITING A STORY ABOUT SOME CAVE MEN
THEY'RE SITTING AROUND A CAMP FIRE, SEE, WHEN ALL OF A SUDDEN THEY'RE ATTACKED BY A HUGE THESAURUS!
6-22
VOLUME ONE OR VOLUME TWO?
IT'S IMPOSSIBLE TO DISCUSS ANYTHING WITH A BIG BROTHER!
SCHULZ

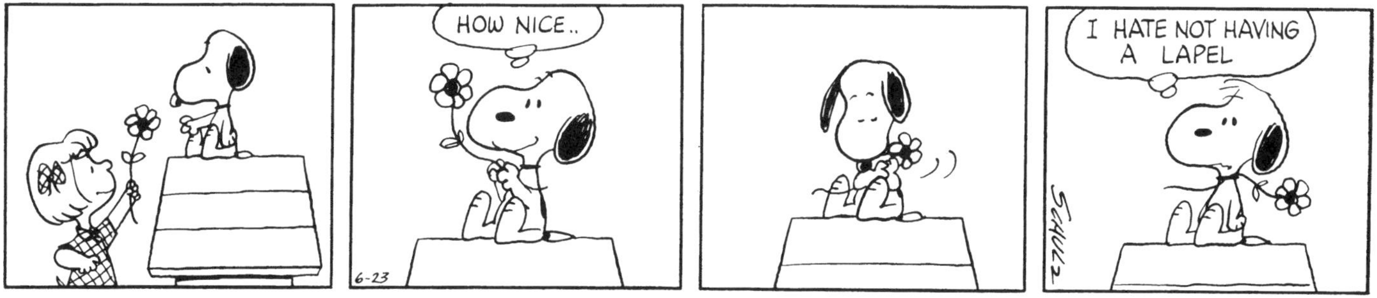
HOW NICE..
6-23
SCHULZ
I HATE NOT HAVING A LAPEL

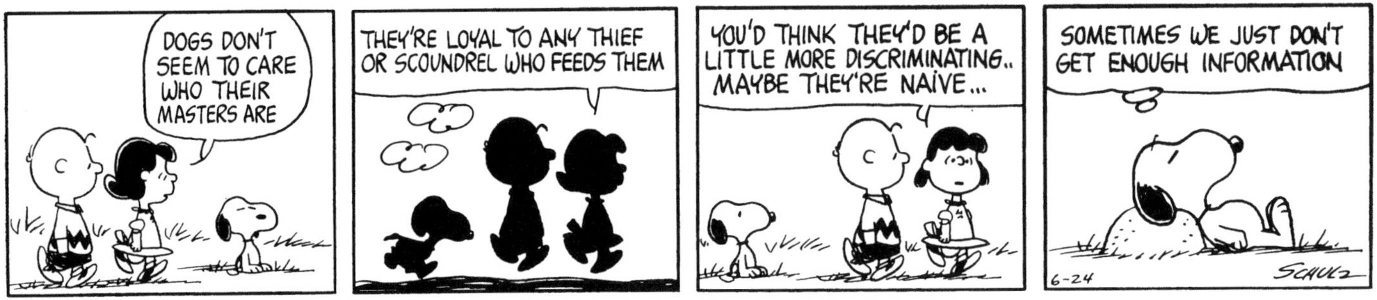
DOGS DON'T SEEM TO CARE WHO THEIR MASTERS ARE
THEY'RE LOYAL TO ANY THIEF OR SCOUNDREL WHO FEEDS THEM
YOU'D THINK THEY'D BE A LITTLE MORE DISCRIMINATING.. MAYBE THEY'RE NAIVE...
SOMETIMES WE JUST DON'T GET ENOUGH INFORMATION
6-24

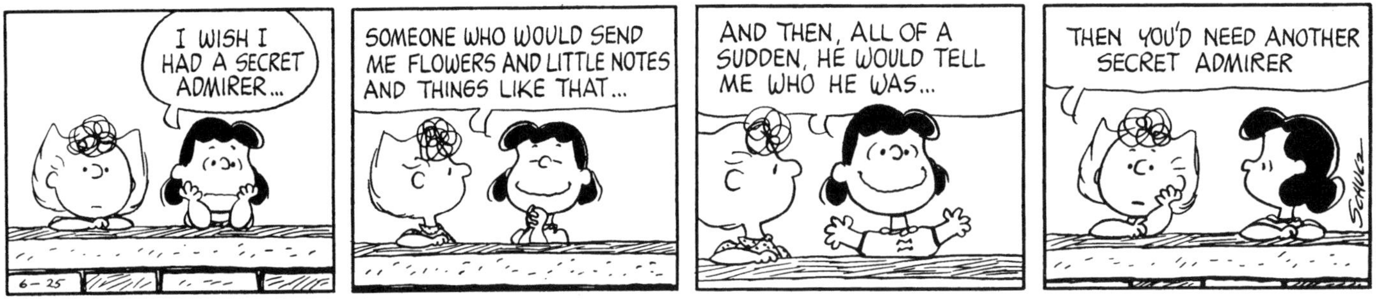
I WISH I HAD A SECRET ADMIRER...
SOMEONE WHO WOULD SEND ME FLOWERS AND LITTLE NOTES AND THINGS LIKE THAT...
AND THEN, ALL OF A SUDDEN, HE WOULD TELL ME WHO HE WAS...
THEN YOU'D NEED ANOTHER SECRET ADMIRER
6-25

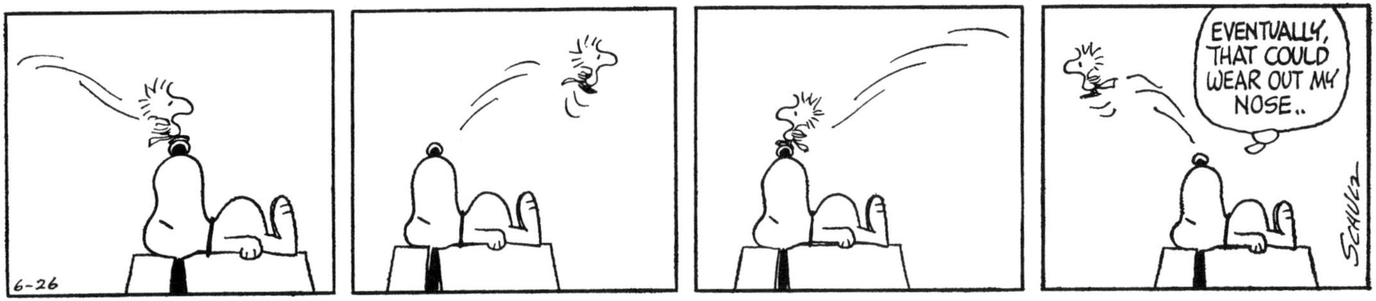
6-26
EVENTUALLY, THAT COULD WEAR OUT MY NOSE..

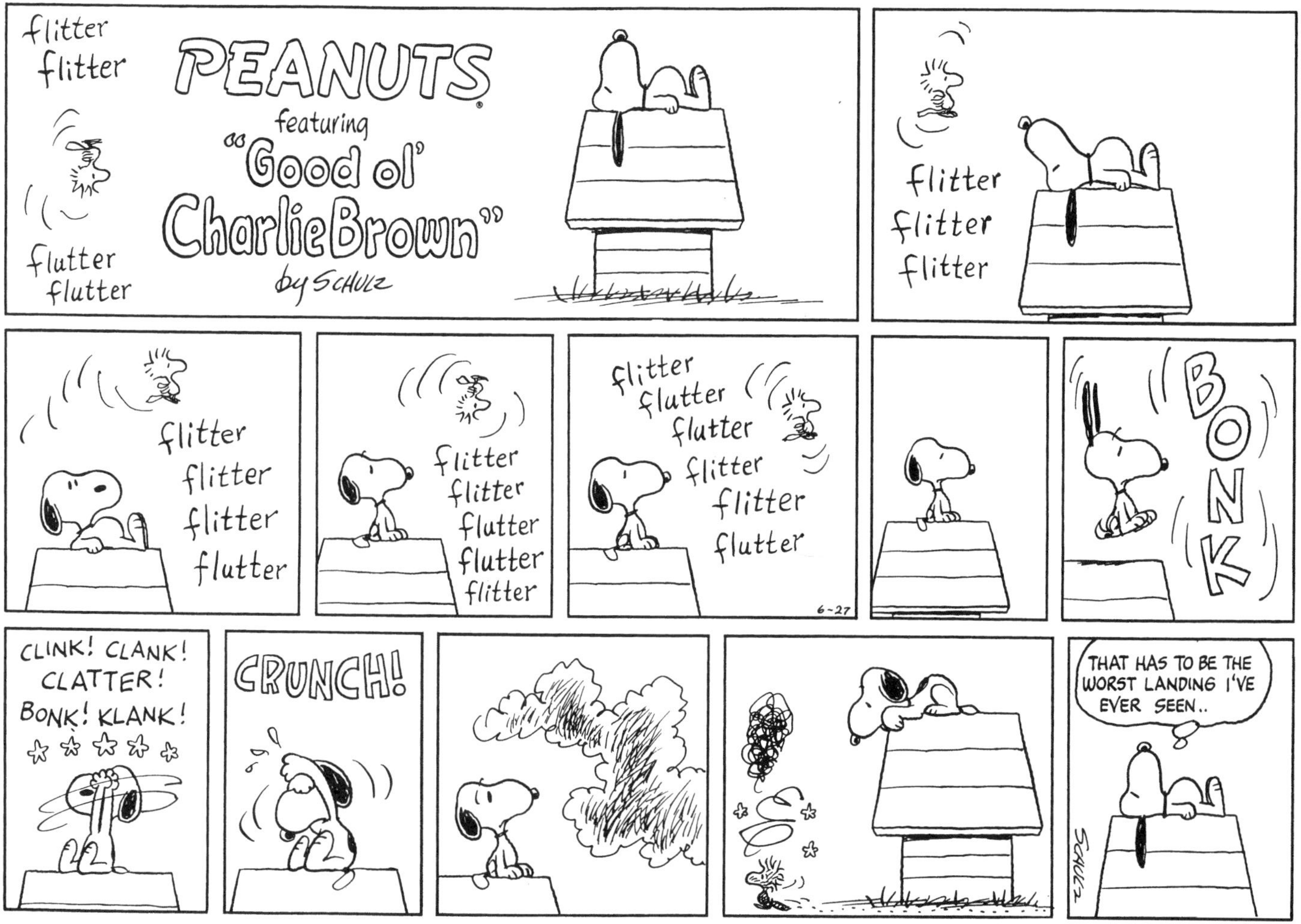
flitter flitter
PEANUTS
featuring
"Good ol' Charlie Brown"
by SCHULZ
flutter flutter
flitter flitter flitter
flitter flitter flitter flutter
flitter flitter flutter flutter flitter
flitter flutter flutter flitter flitter flutter
6-27
BONK
CLINK! CLANK! CLATTER! BONK! KLANK!
CRUNCH!
THAT HAS TO BE THE WORST LANDING I'VE EVER SEEN..

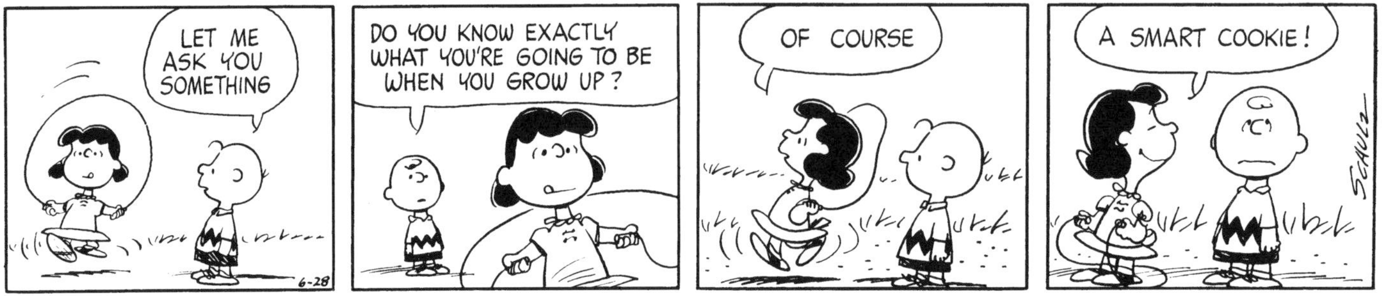
LET ME ASK YOU SOMETHING
6-28
DO YOU KNOW EXACTLY WHAT YOU'RE GOING TO BE WHEN YOU GROW UP?
OF COURSE
A SMART COOKIE!
SCHULZ

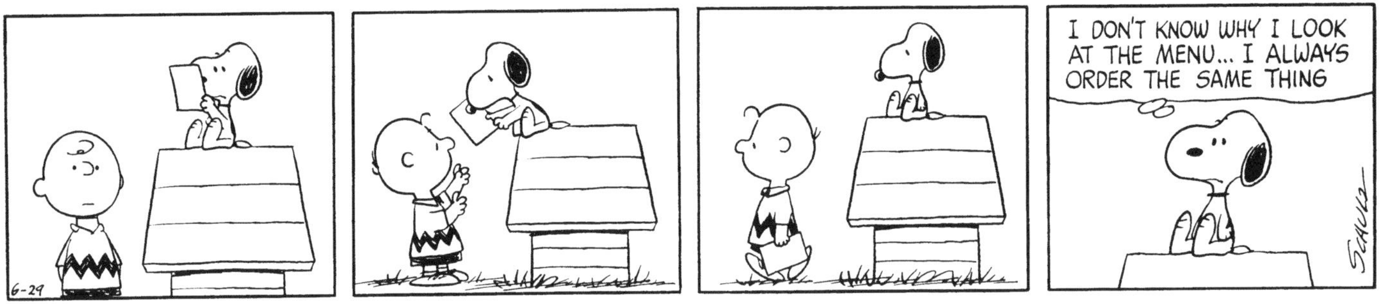
6-29
I DON'T KNOW WHY I LOOK AT THE MENU... I ALWAYS ORDER THE SAME THING
SCHULZ

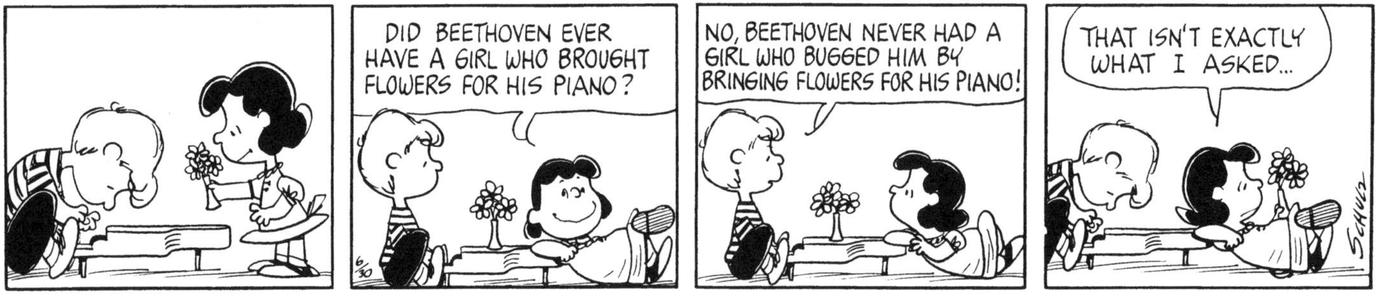
DID BEETHOVEN EVER HAVE A GIRL WHO BROUGHT FLOWERS FOR HIS PIANO?
6/30
NO, BEETHOVEN NEVER HAD A GIRL WHO BUGGED HIM BY BRINGING FLOWERS FOR HIS PIANO!
THAT ISN'T EXACTLY WHAT I ASKED...
SCHULZ

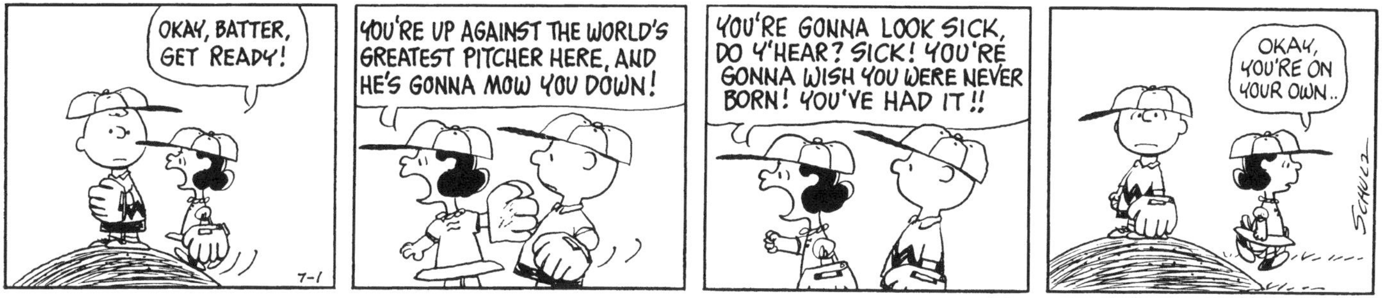
OKAY, BATTER, GET READY!
YOU'RE UP AGAINST THE WORLD'S GREATEST PITCHER HERE, AND HE'S GONNA MOW YOU DOWN!
YOU'RE GONNA LOOK SICK, DO Y'HEAR? SICK! YOU'RE GONNA WISH YOU WERE NEVER BORN! YOU'VE HAD IT!!
OKAY, YOU'RE ON YOUR OWN..
7-1
SCHULZ

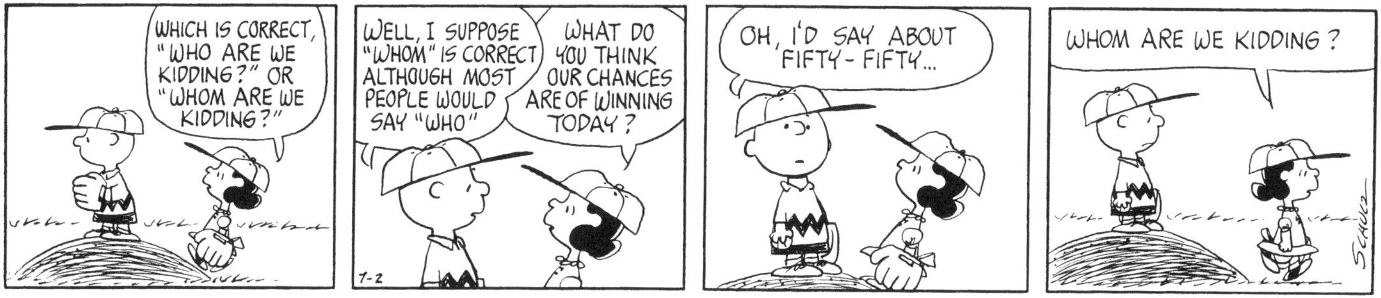
WHICH IS CORRECT, "WHO ARE WE KIDDING?" OR "WHOM ARE WE KIDDING?"
WELL, I SUPPOSE "WHOM" IS CORRECT ALTHOUGH MOST PEOPLE WOULD SAY "WHO"
WHAT DO YOU THINK OUR CHANCES ARE OF WINNING TODAY?
OH, I'D SAY ABOUT FIFTY-FIFTY...
WHOM ARE WE KIDDING?
7-2
SCHULZ

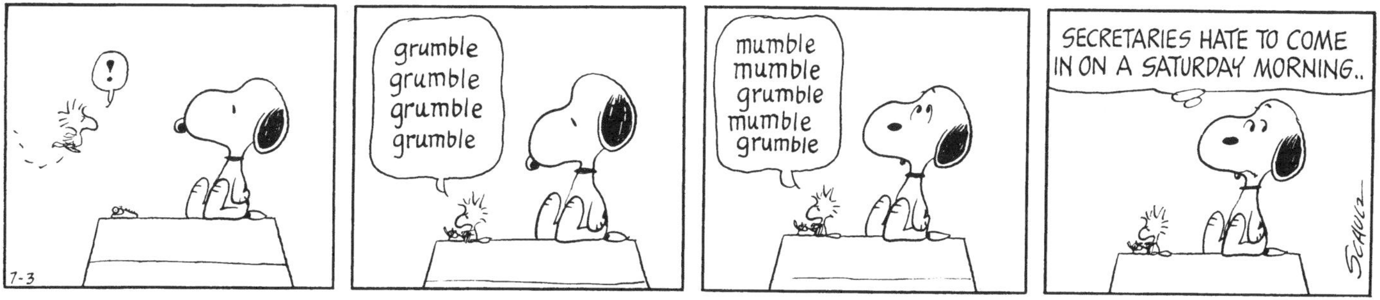
!
grumble grumble grumble grumble
mumble mumble grumble mumble grumble
SECRETARIES HATE TO COME IN ON A SATURDAY MORNING..
7-3
SCHULZ

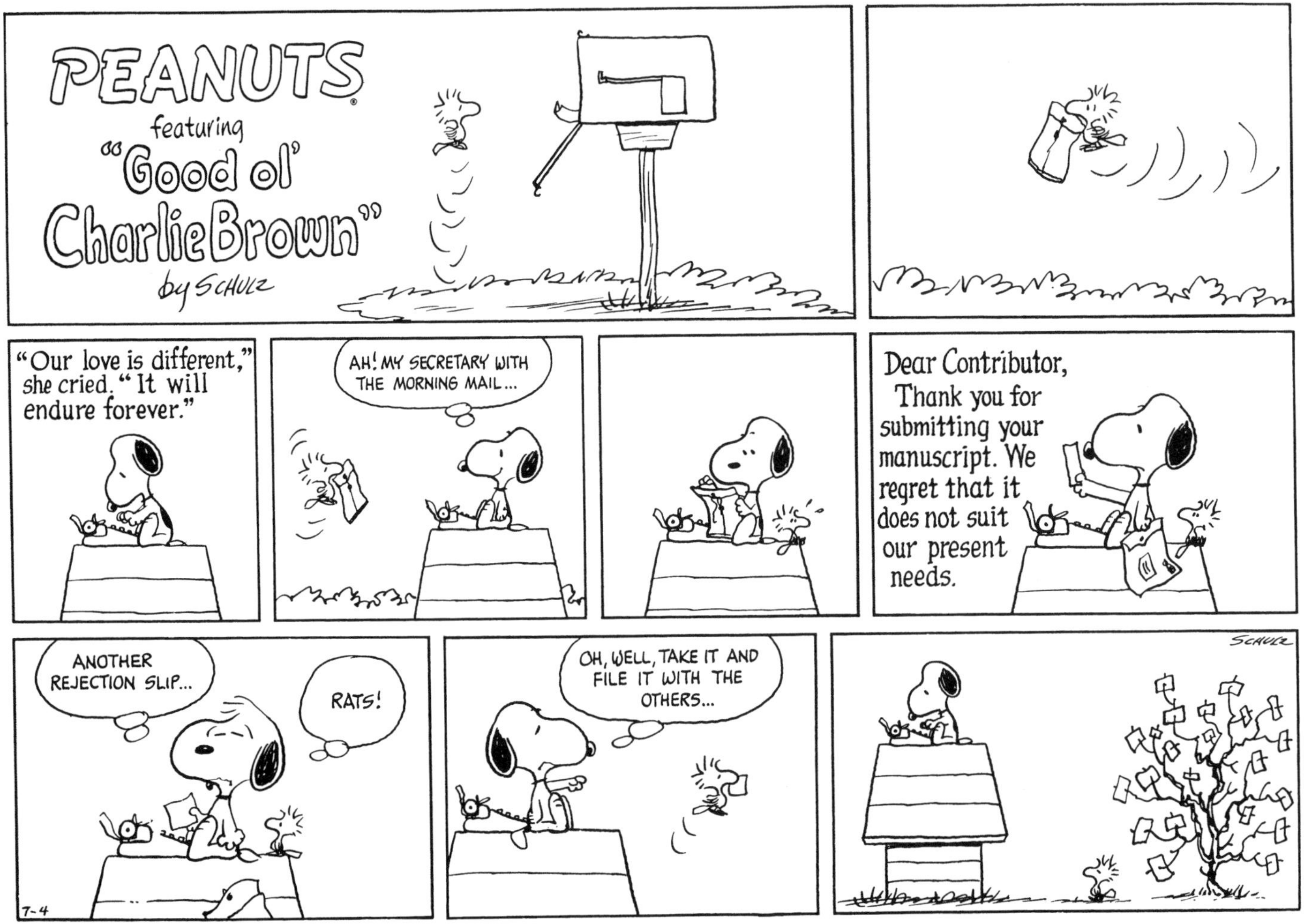
PEANUTS
featuring
"Good ol' CharlieBrown"
by SCHULZ
"Our love is different," she cried. "It will endure forever."
AH! MY SECRETARY WITH THE MORNING MAIL...
Dear Contributor,
Thank you for submitting your manuscript. We regret that it does not suit our present needs.
ANOTHER REJECTION SLIP...
RATS!
OH, WELL, TAKE IT AND FILE IT WITH THE OTHERS...
7-4
SCHULZ

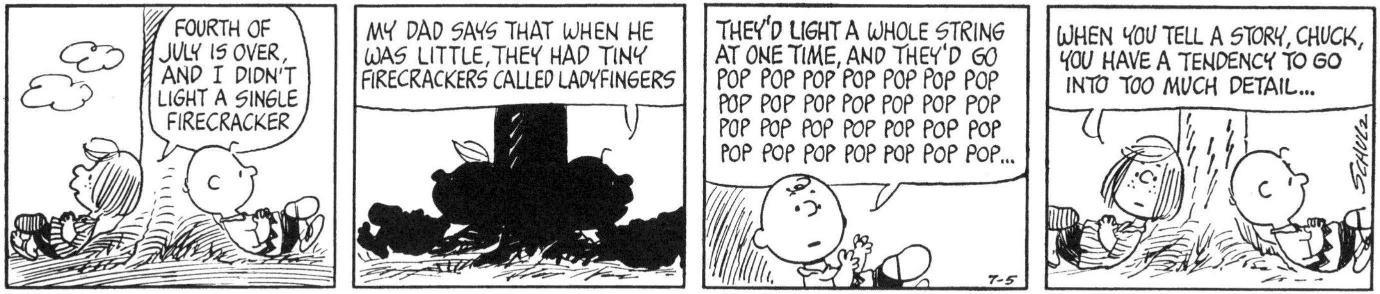
FOURTH OF JULY IS OVER, AND I DIDN'T LIGHT A SINGLE FIRECRACKER
MY DAD SAYS THAT WHEN HE WAS LITTLE, THEY HAD TINY FIRECRACKERS CALLED LADYFINGERS
THEY'D LIGHT A WHOLE STRING AT ONE TIME, AND THEY'D GO POP POP POP POP POP POP POP POP POP POP POP POP POP POP POP POP POP POP POP POP POP POP POP POP POP POP POP POP...
7-5
WHEN YOU TELL A STORY, CHUCK, YOU HAVE A TENDENCY TO GO INTO TOO MUCH DETAIL...
SCHULZ

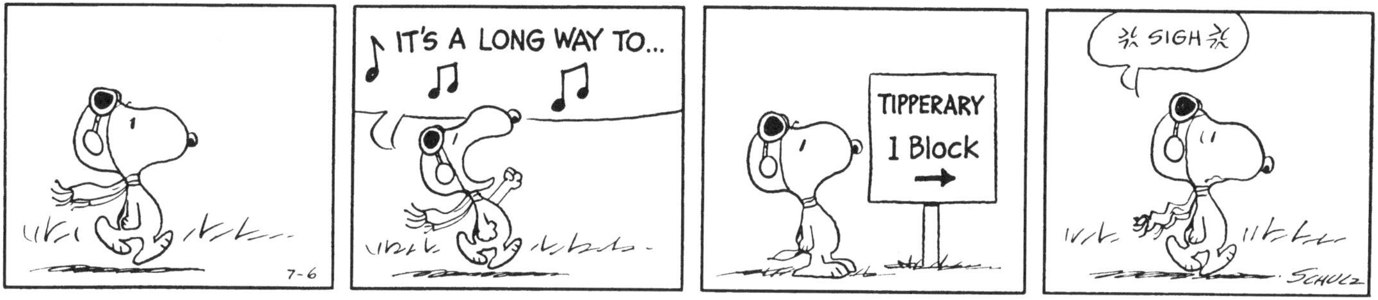
7-6
IT'S A LONG WAY TO...
TIPPERARY
1 Block
SIGH
SCHULZ

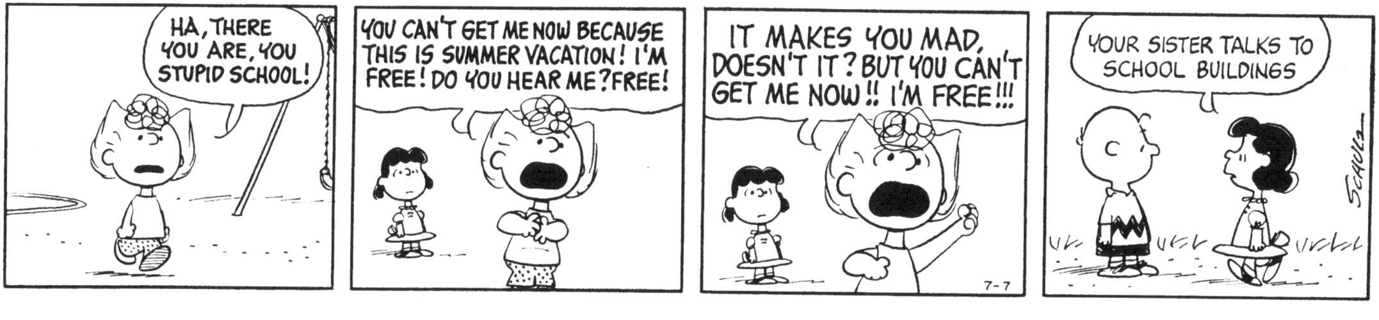
HA, THERE YOU ARE, YOU STUPID SCHOOL!
YOU CAN'T GET ME NOW BECAUSE THIS IS SUMMER VACATION! I'M FREE! DO YOU HEAR ME? FREE!
IT MAKES YOU MAD, DOESN'T IT? BUT YOU CAN'T GET ME NOW!! I'M FREE!!!
7-7
YOUR SISTER TALKS TO SCHOOL BUILDINGS
SCHULZ

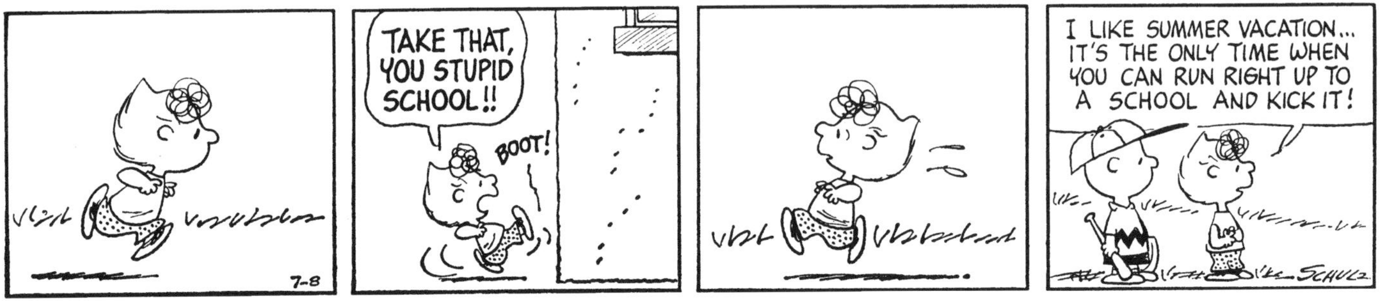
7-8
TAKE THAT, YOU STUPID SCHOOL!!
BOOT!
I LIKE SUMMER VACATION... IT'S THE ONLY TIME WHEN YOU CAN RUN RIGHT UP TO A SCHOOL AND KICK IT!
SCHULZ

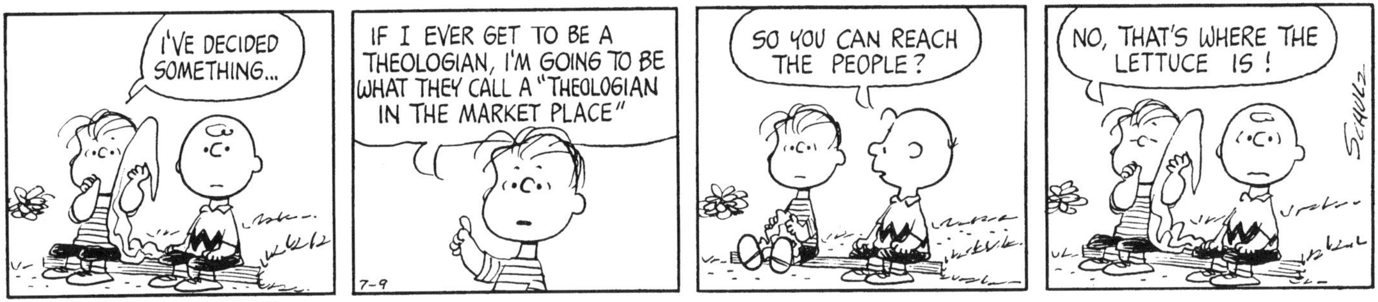
I'VE DECIDED SOMETHING...
IF I EVER GET TO BE A THEOLOGIAN, I'M GOING TO BE WHAT THEY CALL A "THEOLOGIAN IN THE MARKET PLACE"
7-9
SO YOU CAN REACH THE PEOPLE?
NO, THAT'S WHERE THE LETTUCE IS!
SCHULZ

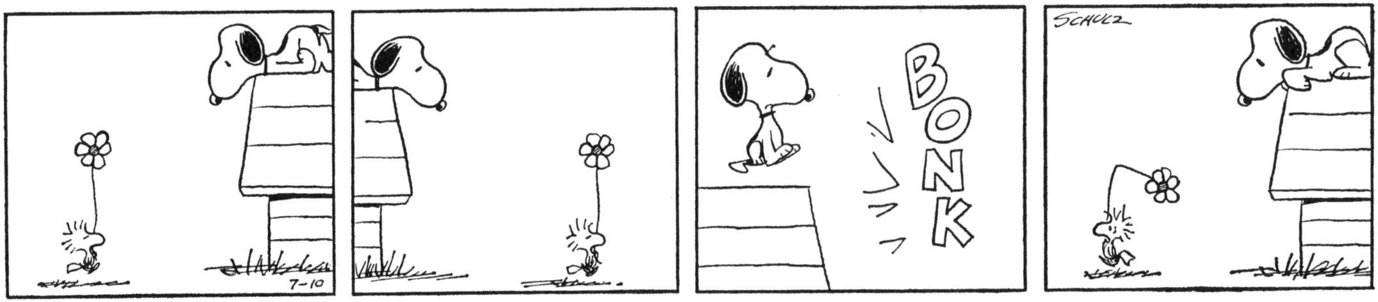
7-10
BONK
SCHULZ

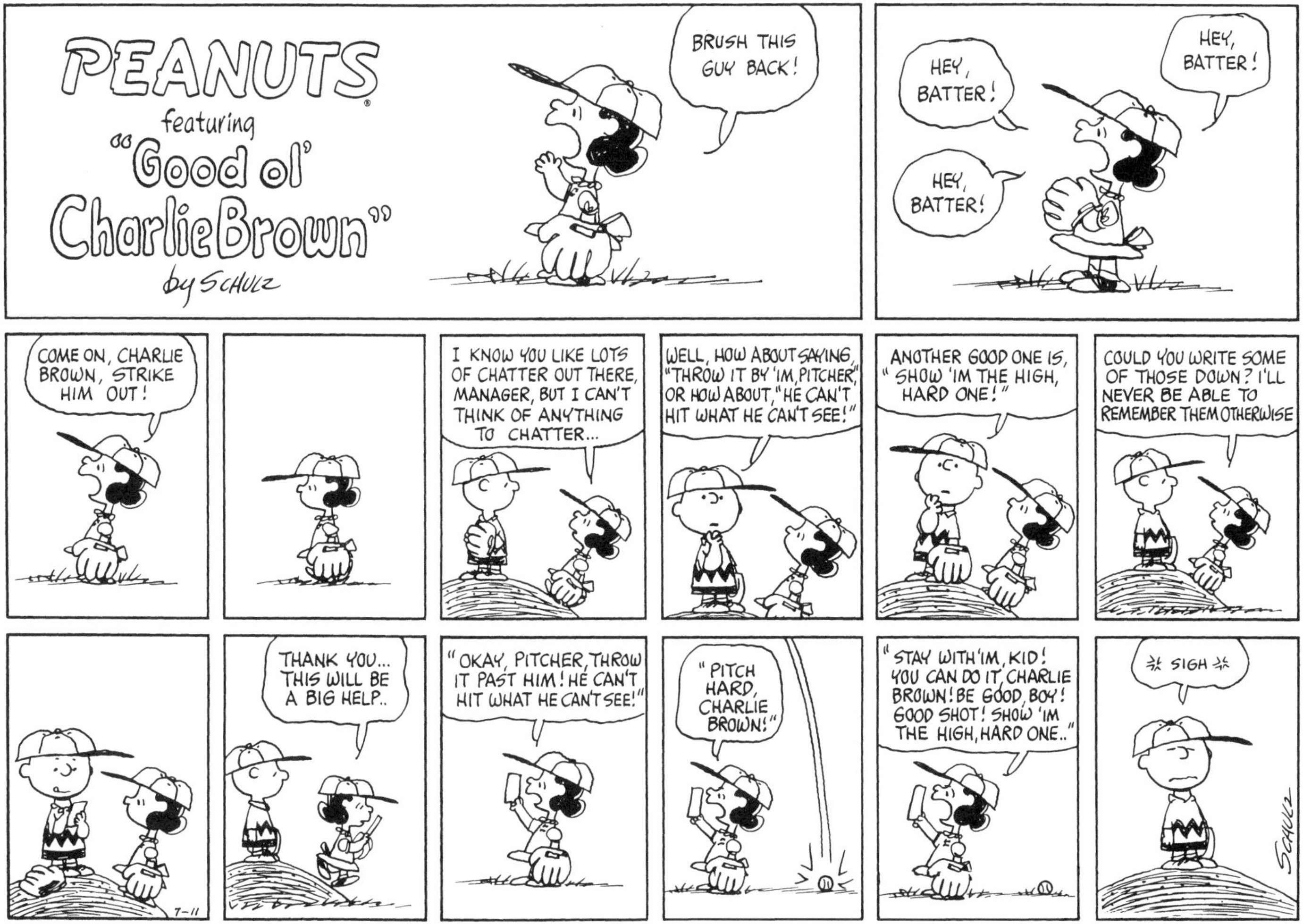
PEANUTS
featuring "Good ol' CharlieBrown"
by SCHULZ
BRUSH THIS GUY BACK!
HEY, BATTER!
HEY, BATTER!
HEY, BATTER!
COME ON, CHARLIE BROWN, STRIKE HIM OUT!
I KNOW YOU LIKE LOTS OF CHATTER OUT THERE, MANAGER, BUT I CAN'T THINK OF ANYTHING TO CHATTER...
WELL, HOW ABOUT SAYING, "THROW IT BY 'IM, PITCHER" OR HOW ABOUT, "HE CAN'T HIT WHAT HE CAN'T SEE!"
ANOTHER GOOD ONE IS, "SHOW 'IM THE HIGH, HARD ONE!"
COULD YOU WRITE SOME OF THOSE DOWN? I'LL NEVER BE ABLE TO REMEMBER THEM OTHERWISE
THANK YOU... THIS WILL BE A BIG HELP..
"OKAY, PITCHER, THROW IT PAST HIM! HE CAN'T HIT WHAT HE CAN'T SEE!"
"PITCH HARD, CHARLIE BROWN!"
"STAY WITH 'IM, KID! YOU CAN DO IT, CHARLIE BROWN! BE GOOD, BOY! GOOD SHOT! SHOW 'IM THE HIGH, HARD ONE.."
SIGH
SCHULZ

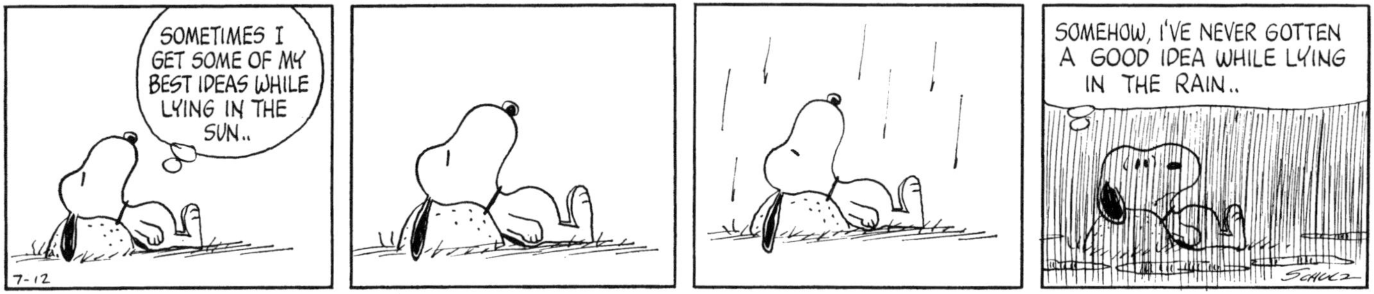
SOMETIMES I GET SOME OF MY BEST IDEAS WHILE LYING IN THE SUN..
SOMEHOW, I'VE NEVER GOTTEN A GOOD IDEA WHILE LYING IN THE RAIN..
7-12
SCHULZ

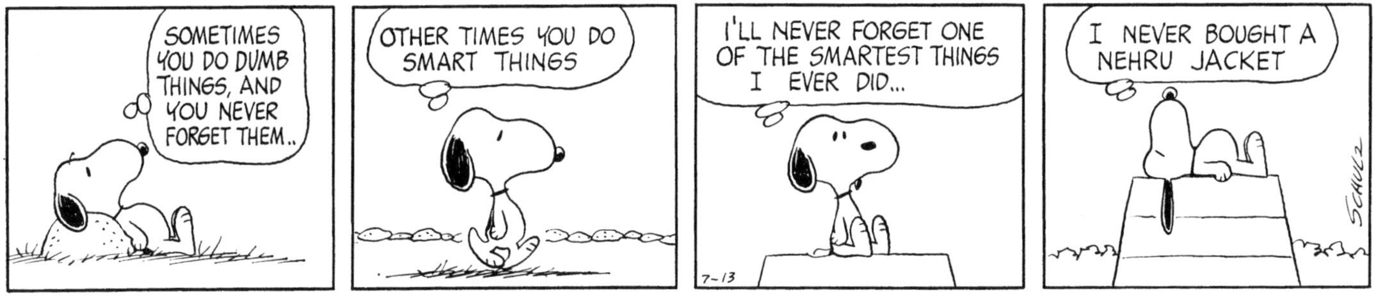
SOMETIMES YOU DO DUMB THINGS, AND YOU NEVER FORGET THEM..
OTHER TIMES YOU DO SMART THINGS
I'LL NEVER FORGET ONE OF THE SMARTEST THINGS I EVER DID...
I NEVER BOUGHT A NEHRU JACKET
7-13
SCHULZ

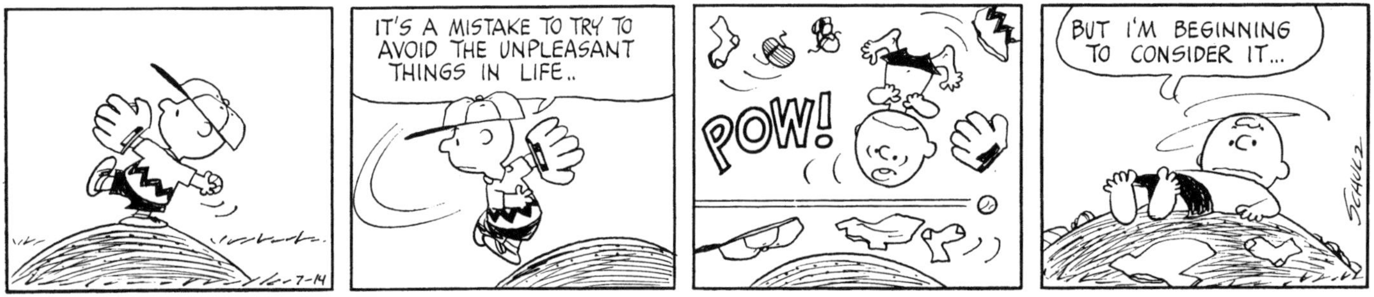
IT'S A MISTAKE TO TRY TO AVOID THE UNPLEASANT THINGS IN LIFE..
POW!
BUT I'M BEGINNING TO CONSIDER IT...
7-14
SCHULZ

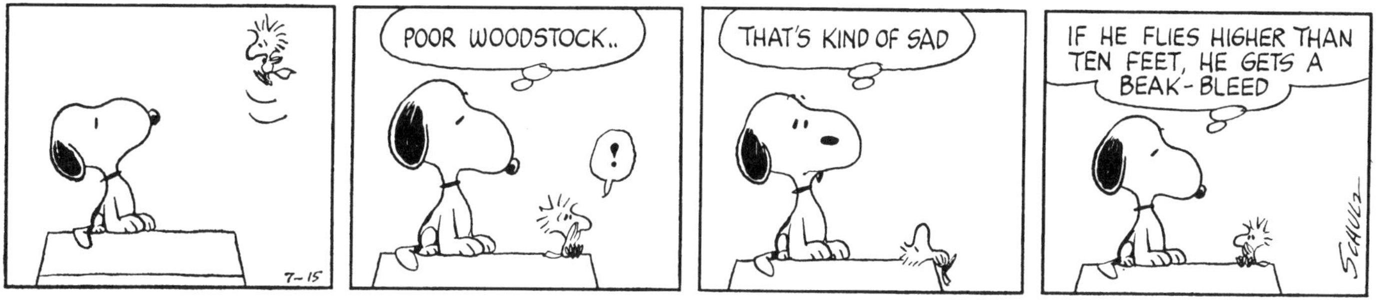
7-15
POOR WOODSTOCK..
!
THAT'S KIND OF SAD
IF HE FLIES HIGHER THAN TEN FEET, HE GETS A BEAK-BLEED
SCHULZ

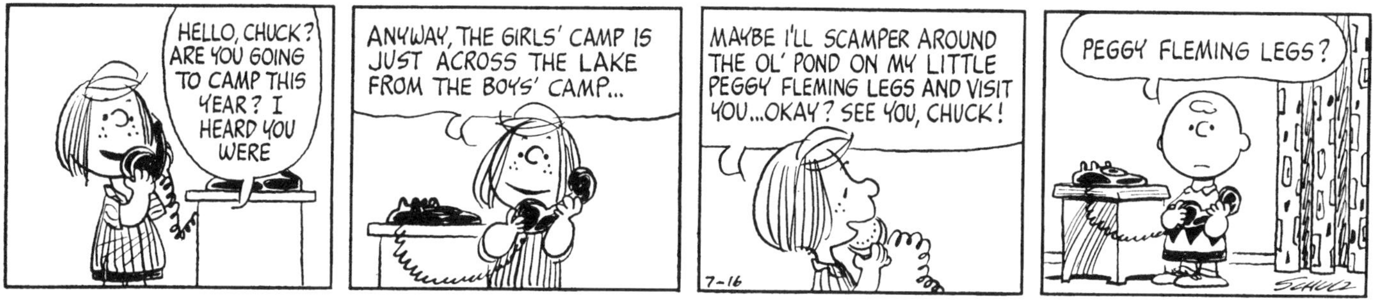
HELLO, CHUCK? ARE YOU GOING TO CAMP THIS YEAR? I HEARD YOU WERE
ANYWAY, THE GIRLS' CAMP IS JUST ACROSS THE LAKE FROM THE BOYS' CAMP...
MAYBE I'LL SCAMPER AROUND THE OL' POND ON MY LITTLE PEGGY FLEMING LEGS AND VISIT YOU...OKAY? SEE YOU, CHUCK!
7-16
PEGGY FLEMING LEGS?
SCHULZ

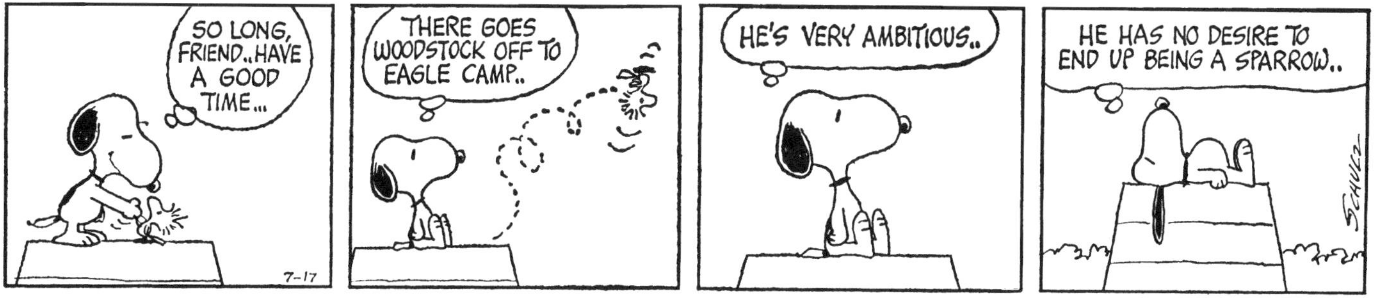
SO LONG, FRIEND..HAVE A GOOD TIME...
7-17
THERE GOES WOODSTOCK OFF TO EAGLE CAMP..
HE'S VERY AMBITIOUS..
HE HAS NO DESIRE TO END UP BEING A SPARROW..
SCHULZ

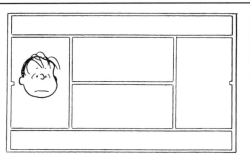

PEANUTS
featuring
"Good ol'
Charlie Brown"
by Schulz

I APPRECIATE YOUR TAKING ME ALONG TO PLAY TENNIS, LINUS...

THAT'S THE ONLY TROUBLE WITH TENNIS.. YOU CAN'T PLAY IT ALONE

MAYBE WE WON'T GET TO PLAY AT ALL... THE COURTS ARE ALL FULL...

THE COURTS ARE ALWAYS FULL WITH BIG KIDS, AND THEY NEVER LET YOU PLAY... I HATE BIG KIDS! THEY NEVER GIVE YOU A CHANCE!

THEY'LL PLAY ALL DAY...JUST YOU WATCH! THEY'LL HOG THE COURTS ALL DAY! THEY'LL NEVER QUIT...THEY'LL JUST KEEP ON PLAYING AND PLAYING, AND THEY'LL NEVER...

YOU BIG KIDS GET OFF THAT COURT RIGHT NOW, OR MY BOY FRIEND WILL CLOBBER YOU!!

7-18

THAT'S THE ONLY TROUBLE WITH TENNIS... YOU CAN'T PLAY IT ALONE

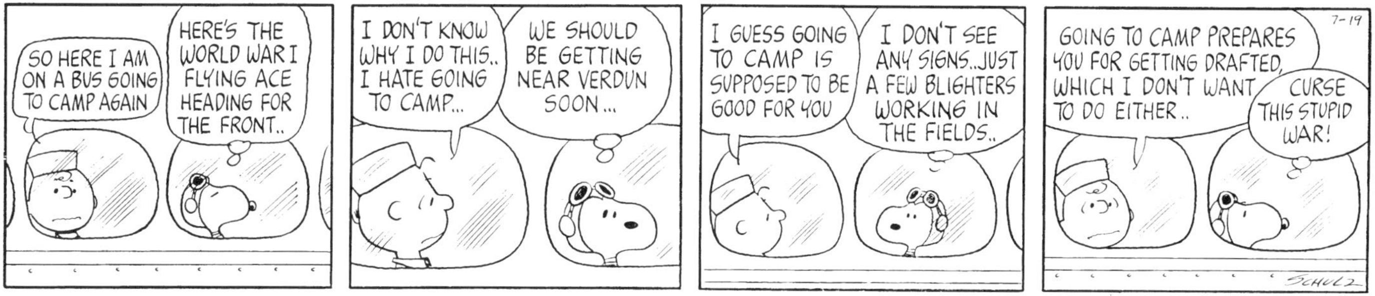
SO HERE I AM ON A BUS GOING TO CAMP AGAIN
HERE'S THE WORLD WAR I FLYING ACE HEADING FOR THE FRONT..
I DON'T KNOW WHY I DO THIS.. I HATE GOING TO CAMP...
WE SHOULD BE GETTING NEAR VERDUN SOON...
I GUESS GOING TO CAMP IS SUPPOSED TO BE GOOD FOR YOU
I DON'T SEE ANY SIGNS..JUST A FEW BLIGHTERS WORKING IN THE FIELDS..
GOING TO CAMP PREPARES YOU FOR GETTING DRAFTED, WHICH I DON'T WANT TO DO EITHER..
CURSE THIS STUPID WAR!

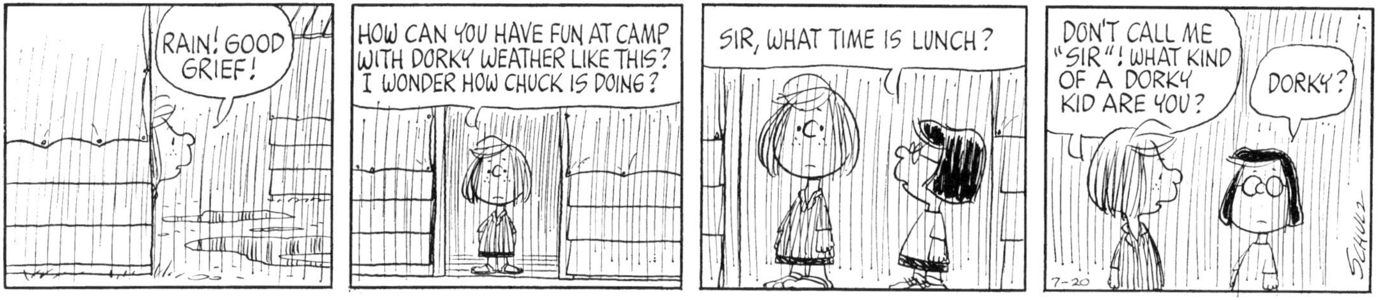
RAIN! GOOD GRIEF!
HOW CAN YOU HAVE FUN AT CAMP WITH DORKY WEATHER LIKE THIS? I WONDER HOW CHUCK IS DOING?
SIR, WHAT TIME IS LUNCH?
DON'T CALL ME "SIR"! WHAT KIND OF A DORKY KID ARE YOU?
DORKY?

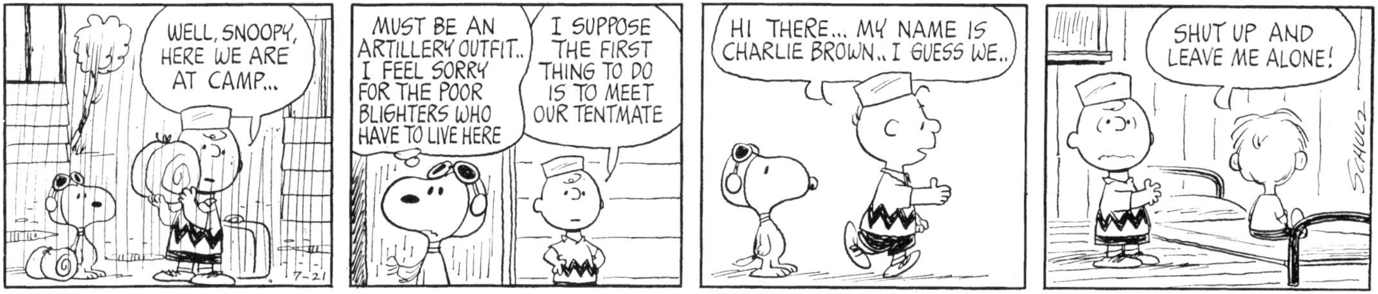
WELL, SNOOPY, HERE WE ARE AT CAMP...
MUST BE AN ARTILLERY OUTFIT.. I FEEL SORRY FOR THE POOR BLIGHTERS WHO HAVE TO LIVE HERE
I SUPPOSE THE FIRST THING TO DO IS TO MEET OUR TENTMATE
HI THERE... MY NAME IS CHARLIE BROWN.. I GUESS WE..
SHUT UP AND LEAVE ME ALONE!

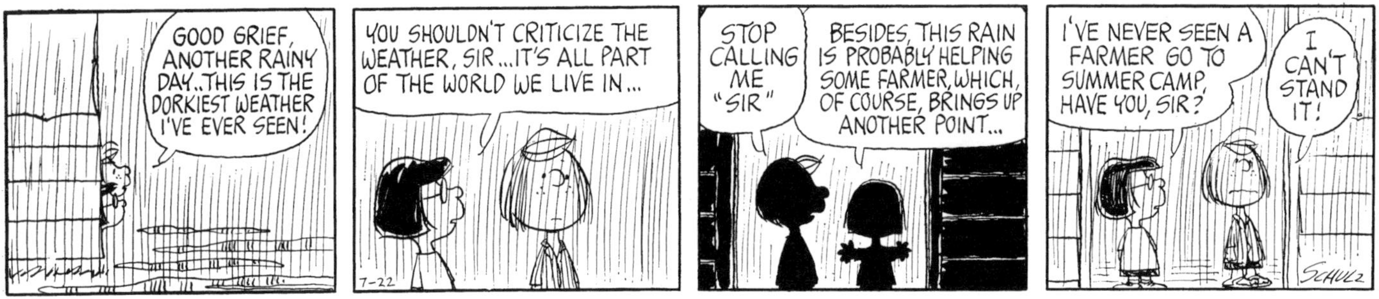
GOOD GRIEF, ANOTHER RAINY DAY..THIS IS THE DORKIEST WEATHER I'VE EVER SEEN!
YOU SHOULDN'T CRITICIZE THE WEATHER, SIR...IT'S ALL PART OF THE WORLD WE LIVE IN...
7-22
STOP CALLING ME "SIR"
BESIDES, THIS RAIN IS PROBABLY HELPING SOME FARMER, WHICH, OF COURSE, BRINGS UP ANOTHER POINT...
I'VE NEVER SEEN A FARMER GO TO SUMMER CAMP, HAVE YOU, SIR?
I CAN'T STAND IT!
SCHULZ

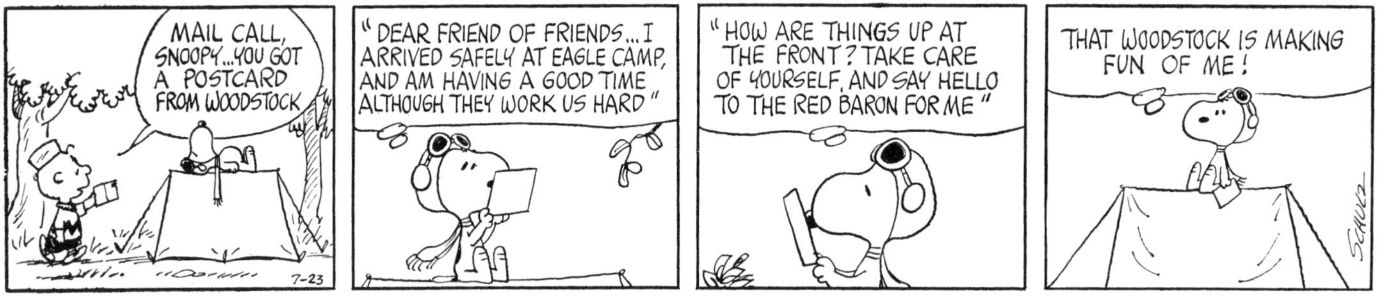
MAIL CALL, SNOOPY...YOU GOT A POSTCARD FROM WOODSTOCK
7-23
"DEAR FRIEND OF FRIENDS...I ARRIVED SAFELY AT EAGLE CAMP, AND AM HAVING A GOOD TIME ALTHOUGH THEY WORK US HARD"
"HOW ARE THINGS UP AT THE FRONT? TAKE CARE OF YOURSELF, AND SAY HELLO TO THE RED BARON FOR ME"
THAT WOODSTOCK IS MAKING FUN OF ME!
SCHULZ

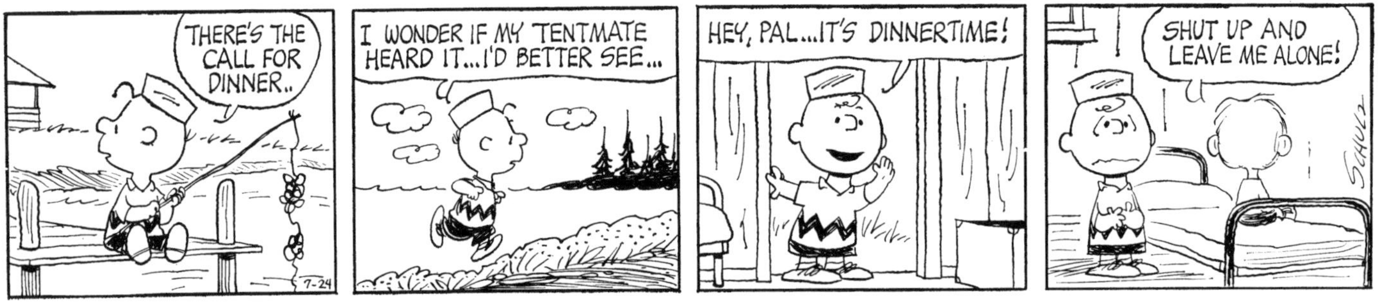
THERE'S THE CALL FOR DINNER..
7-24
I WONDER IF MY TENTMATE HEARD IT...I'D BETTER SEE...
HEY, PAL...IT'S DINNERTIME!
SHUT UP AND LEAVE ME ALONE!
SCHULZ

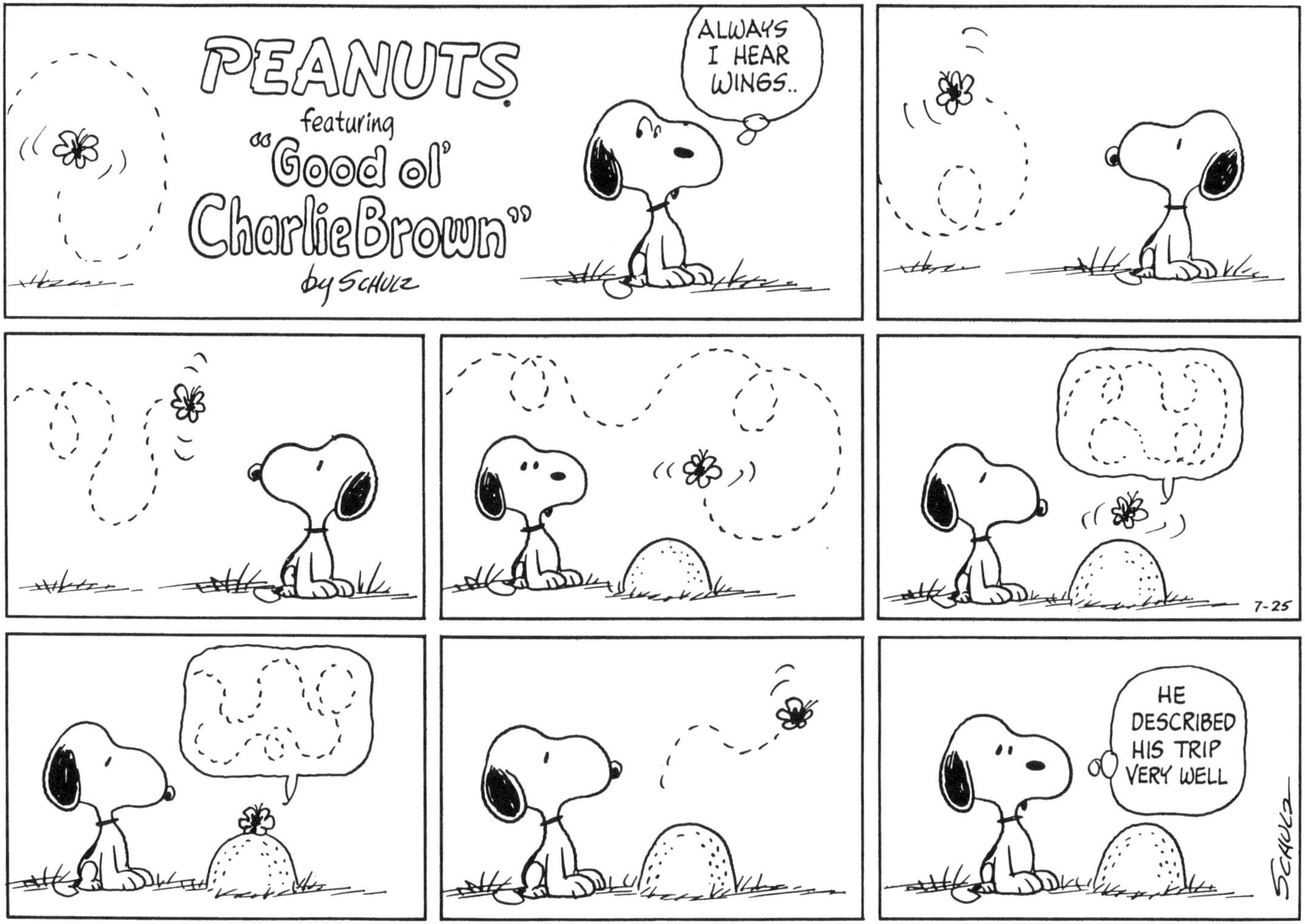
PEANUTS
featuring
"Good ol' CharlieBrown"
by SCHULZ
ALWAYS I HEAR WINGS..
7-25
HE DESCRIBED HIS TRIP VERY WELL
SCHULZ

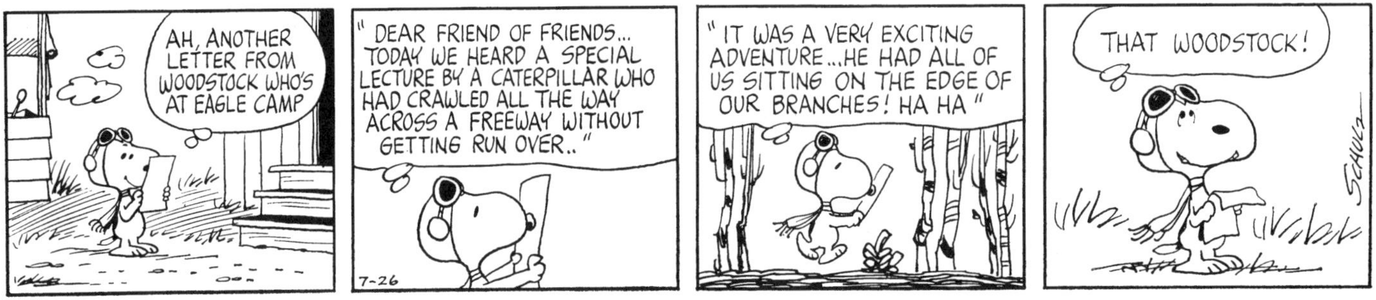
AH, ANOTHER LETTER FROM WOODSTOCK WHO'S AT EAGLE CAMP
" DEAR FRIEND OF FRIENDS... TODAY WE HEARD A SPECIAL LECTURE BY A CATERPILLAR WHO HAD CRAWLED ALL THE WAY ACROSS A FREEWAY WITHOUT GETTING RUN OVER.. "
7-26
" IT WAS A VERY EXCITING ADVENTURE...HE HAD ALL OF US SITTING ON THE EDGE OF OUR BRANCHES! HA HA "
THAT WOODSTOCK!
SCHULZ

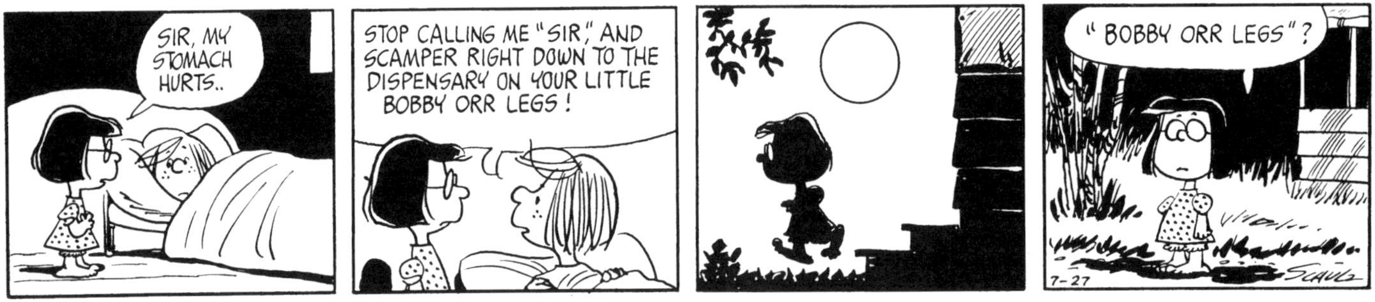
SIR, MY STOMACH HURTS..
STOP CALLING ME "SIR," AND SCAMPER RIGHT DOWN TO THE DISPENSARY ON YOUR LITTLE BOBBY ORR LEGS!
" BOBBY ORR LEGS " ?
7-27
SCHULZ

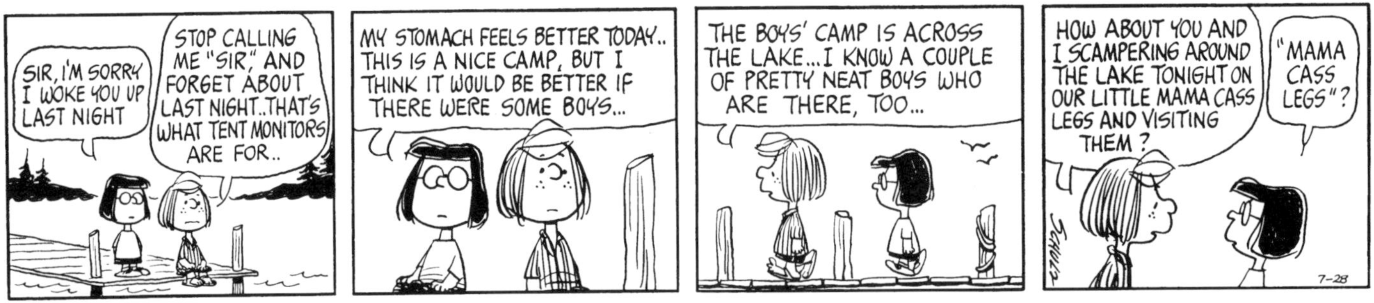
SIR, I'M SORRY I WOKE YOU UP LAST NIGHT
STOP CALLING ME "SIR," AND FORGET ABOUT LAST NIGHT..THAT'S WHAT TENT MONITORS ARE FOR..
MY STOMACH FEELS BETTER TODAY.. THIS IS A NICE CAMP, BUT I THINK IT WOULD BE BETTER IF THERE WERE SOME BOYS...
THE BOYS' CAMP IS ACROSS THE LAKE...I KNOW A COUPLE OF PRETTY NEAT BOYS WHO ARE THERE, TOO...
HOW ABOUT YOU AND I SCAMPERING AROUND THE LAKE TONIGHT ON OUR LITTLE MAMA CASS LEGS AND VISITING THEM ?
"MAMA CASS LEGS" ?
SCHULZ
7-28

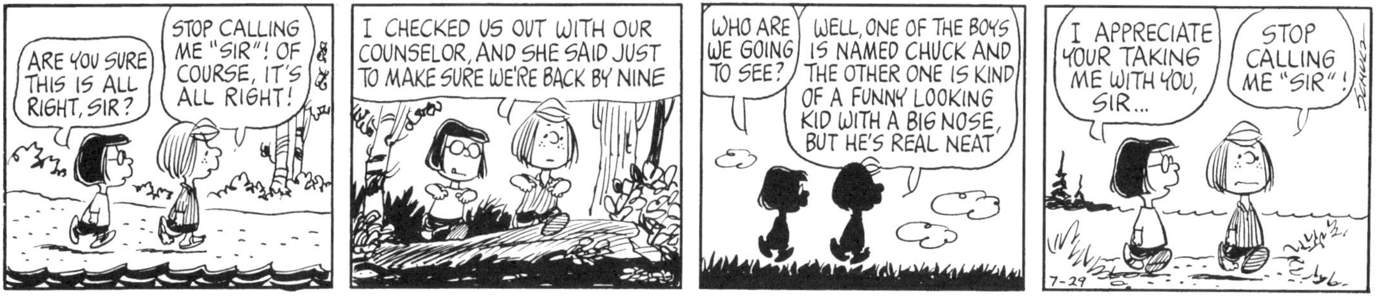
ARE YOU SURE THIS IS ALL RIGHT, SIR?
STOP CALLING ME "SIR"! OF COURSE, IT'S ALL RIGHT!
I CHECKED US OUT WITH OUR COUNSELOR, AND SHE SAID JUST TO MAKE SURE WE'RE BACK BY NINE
WHO ARE WE GOING TO SEE?
WELL, ONE OF THE BOYS IS NAMED CHUCK AND THE OTHER ONE IS KIND OF A FUNNY LOOKING KID WITH A BIG NOSE, BUT HE'S REAL NEAT
I APPRECIATE YOUR TAKING ME WITH YOU, SIR...
STOP CALLING ME "SIR"!
7-29

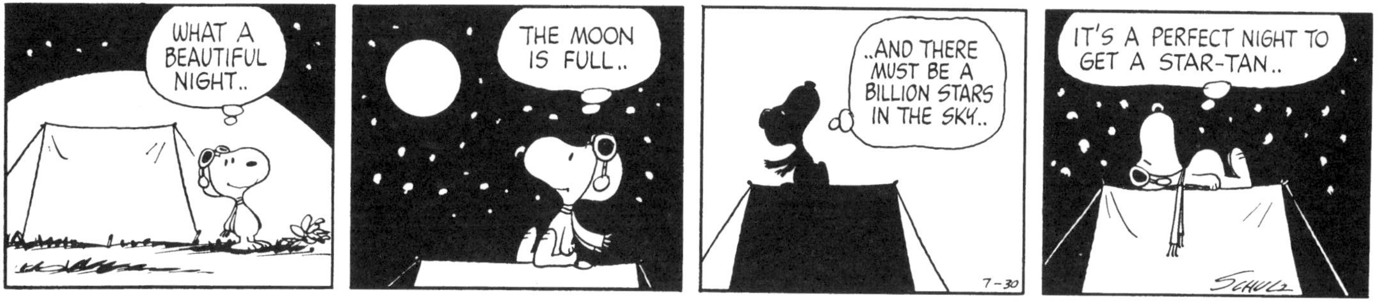
WHAT A BEAUTIFUL NIGHT..
THE MOON IS FULL..
..AND THERE MUST BE A BILLION STARS IN THE SKY..
IT'S A PERFECT NIGHT TO GET A STAR-TAN..
7-30

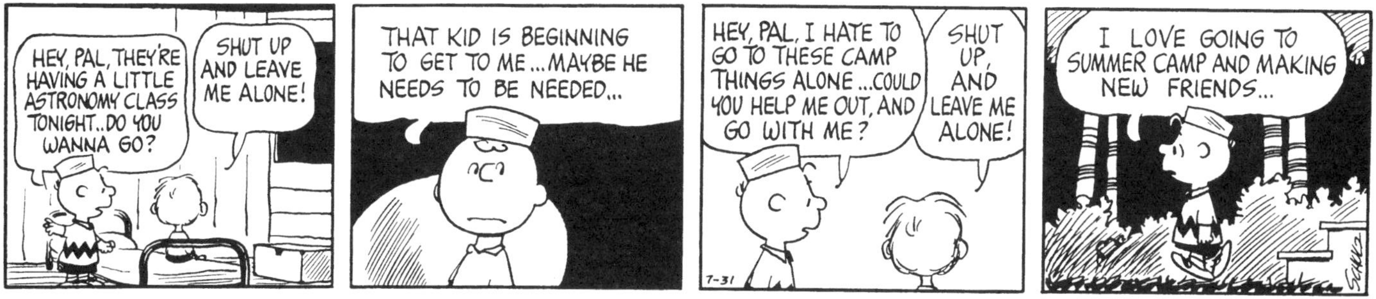
HEY, PAL, THEY'RE HAVING A LITTLE ASTRONOMY CLASS TONIGHT..DO YOU WANNA GO?
SHUT UP AND LEAVE ME ALONE!
THAT KID IS BEGINNING TO GET TO ME...MAYBE HE NEEDS TO BE NEEDED...
HEY, PAL, I HATE TO GO TO THESE CAMP THINGS ALONE...COULD YOU HELP ME OUT, AND GO WITH ME?
SHUT UP, AND LEAVE ME ALONE!
I LOVE GOING TO SUMMER CAMP AND MAKING NEW FRIENDS...
7-31

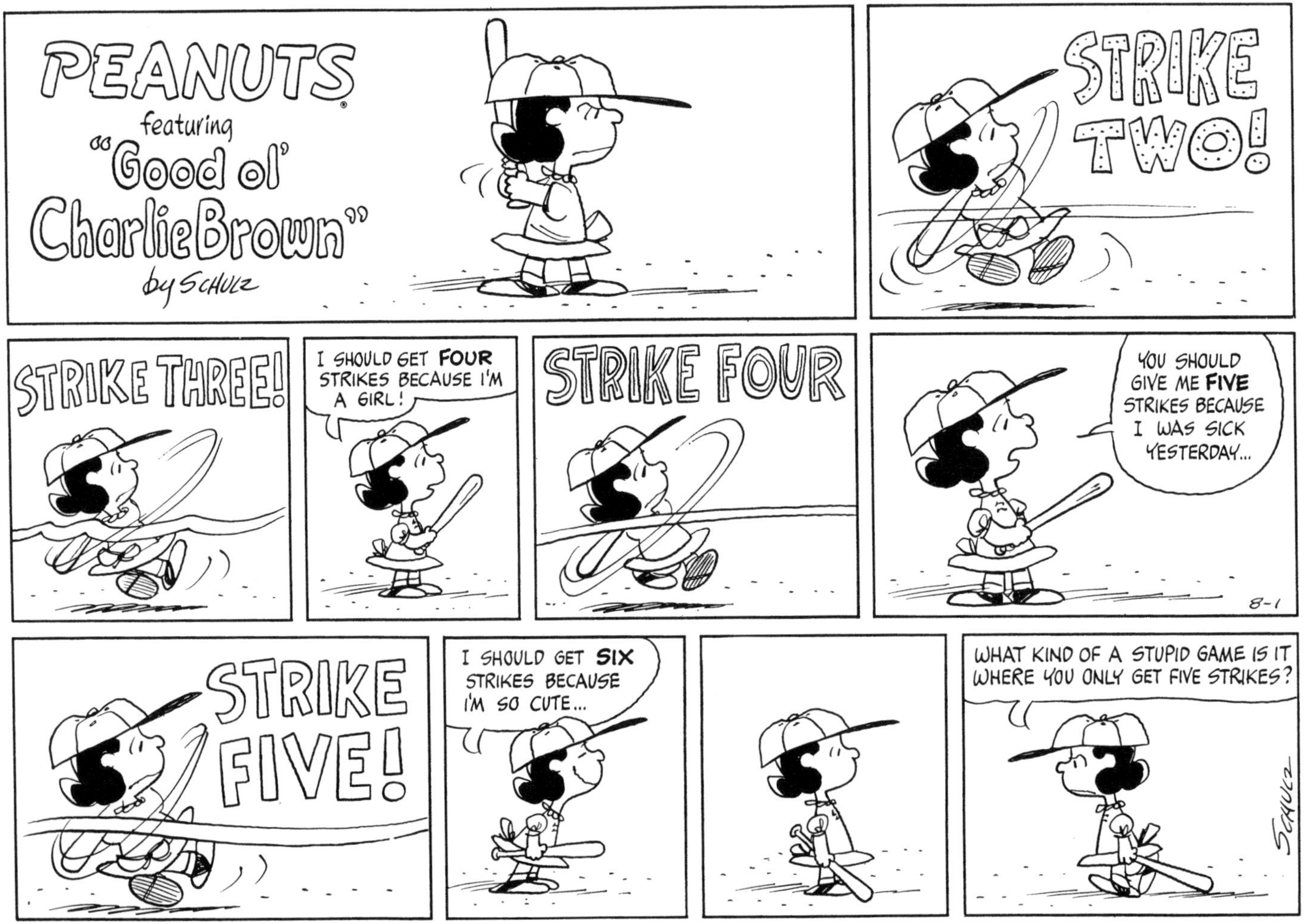
PEANUTS
featuring
"Good ol' Charlie Brown"
by SCHULZ
STRIKE TWO!
STRIKE THREE!
I SHOULD GET FOUR STRIKES BECAUSE I'M A GIRL!
STRIKE FOUR
YOU SHOULD GIVE ME FIVE STRIKES BECAUSE I WAS SICK YESTERDAY...
8-1
STRIKE FIVE!
I SHOULD GET SIX STRIKES BECAUSE I'M SO CUTE...
WHAT KIND OF A STUPID GAME IS IT WHERE YOU ONLY GET FIVE STRIKES?
SCHULZ

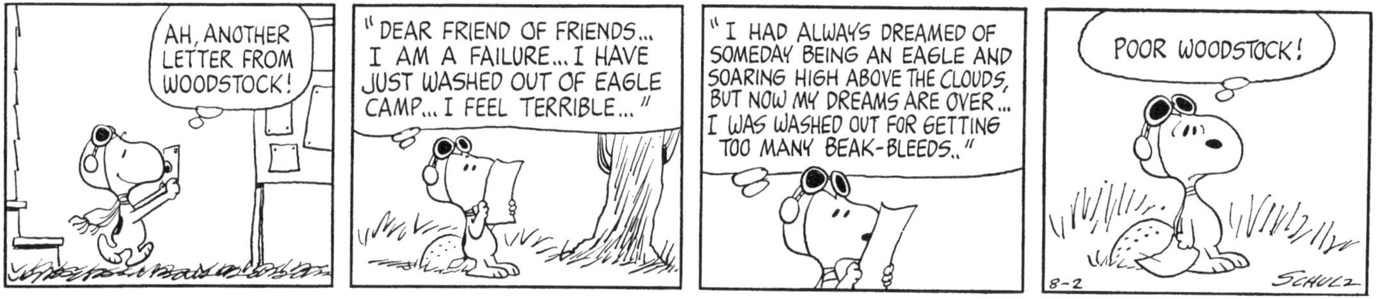
AH, ANOTHER LETTER FROM WOODSTOCK!
"DEAR FRIEND OF FRIENDS... I AM A FAILURE... I HAVE JUST WASHED OUT OF EAGLE CAMP... I FEEL TERRIBLE..."
"I HAD ALWAYS DREAMED OF SOMEDAY BEING AN EAGLE AND SOARING HIGH ABOVE THE CLOUDS, BUT NOW MY DREAMS ARE OVER... I WAS WASHED OUT FOR GETTING TOO MANY BEAK-BLEEDS.."
POOR WOODSTOCK!
8-2
SCHULZ

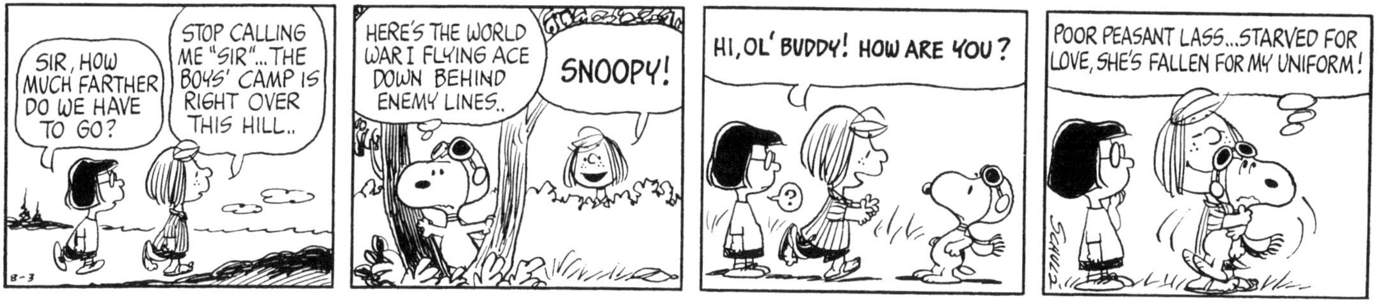
SIR, HOW MUCH FARTHER DO WE HAVE TO GO?
STOP CALLING ME "SIR"... THE BOYS' CAMP IS RIGHT OVER THIS HILL..
8-3
HERE'S THE WORLD WAR I FLYING ACE DOWN BEHIND ENEMY LINES..
SNOOPY!
HI, OL' BUDDY! HOW ARE YOU?
?
POOR PEASANT LASS...STARVED FOR LOVE, SHE'S FALLEN FOR MY UNIFORM!
SCHULZ

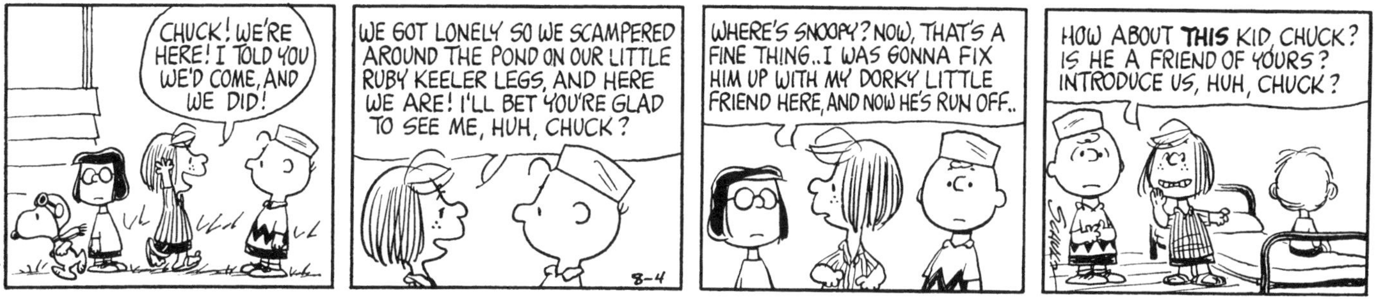
CHUCK! WE'RE HERE! I TOLD YOU WE'D COME, AND WE DID!
WE GOT LONELY SO WE SCAMPERED AROUND THE POND ON OUR LITTLE RUBY KEELER LEGS, AND HERE WE ARE! I'LL BET YOU'RE GLAD TO SEE ME, HUH, CHUCK?
8-4
WHERE'S SNOOPY? NOW, THAT'S A FINE THING..I WAS GONNA FIX HIM UP WITH MY DORKY LITTLE FRIEND HERE, AND NOW HE'S RUN OFF..
HOW ABOUT THIS KID, CHUCK? IS HE A FRIEND OF YOURS? INTRODUCE US, HUH, CHUCK?
SCHULZ

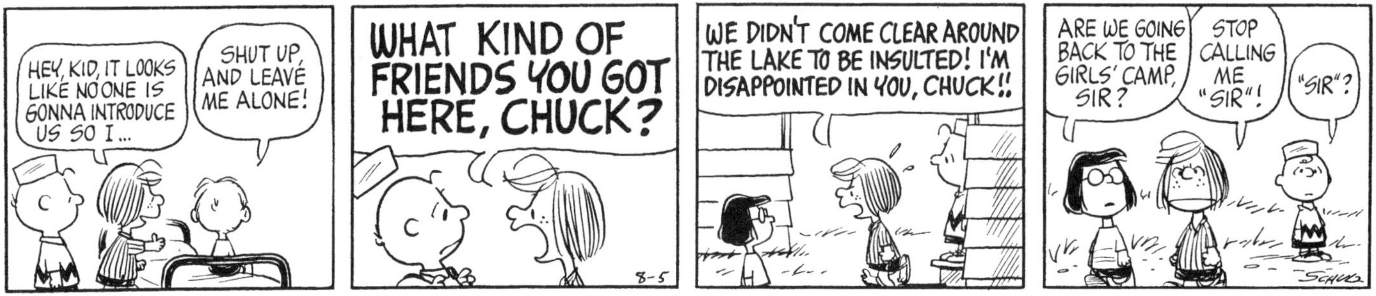
HEY, KID, IT LOOKS LIKE NO ONE IS GONNA INTRODUCE US SO I...
SHUT UP, AND LEAVE ME ALONE!
WHAT KIND OF FRIENDS YOU GOT HERE, CHUCK?
8-5
WE DIDN'T COME CLEAR AROUND THE LAKE TO BE INSULTED! I'M DISAPPOINTED IN YOU, CHUCK!!
ARE WE GOING BACK TO THE GIRLS' CAMP, SIR?
STOP CALLING ME "SIR"!
"SIR"?
SCHULZ

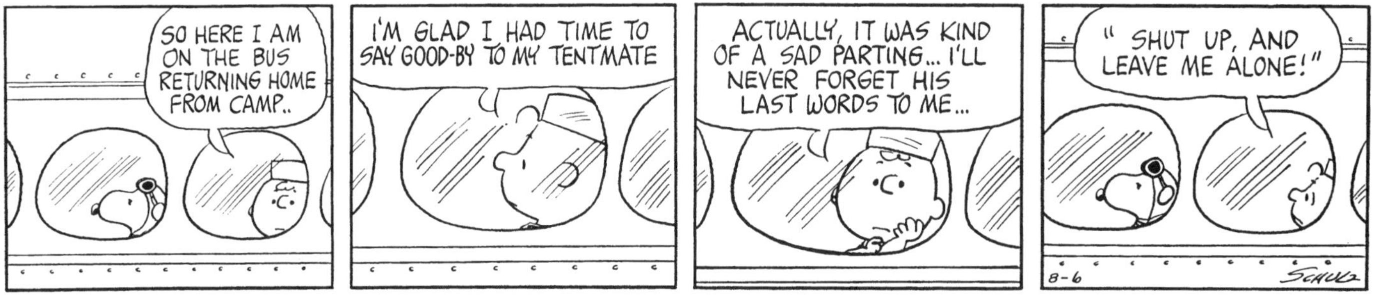
SO HERE I AM ON THE BUS RETURNING HOME FROM CAMP..
I'M GLAD I HAD TIME TO SAY GOOD-BY TO MY TENTMATE
ACTUALLY, IT WAS KIND OF A SAD PARTING... I'LL NEVER FORGET HIS LAST WORDS TO ME...
" SHUT UP, AND LEAVE ME ALONE!"
8-6
SCHULZ

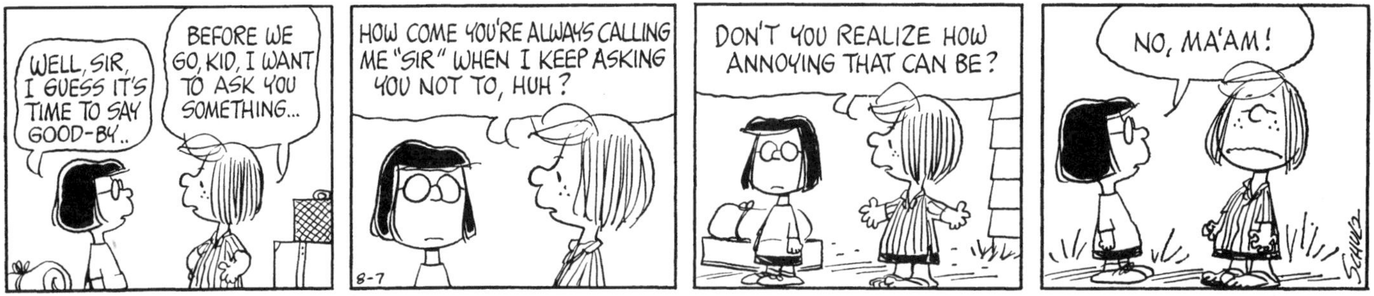
WELL, SIR, I GUESS IT'S TIME TO SAY GOOD-BY..
BEFORE WE GO, KID, I WANT TO ASK YOU SOMETHING...
HOW COME YOU'RE ALWAYS CALLING ME "SIR" WHEN I KEEP ASKING YOU NOT TO, HUH?
8-7
DON'T YOU REALIZE HOW ANNOYING THAT CAN BE?
NO, MA'AM!
SCHULZ

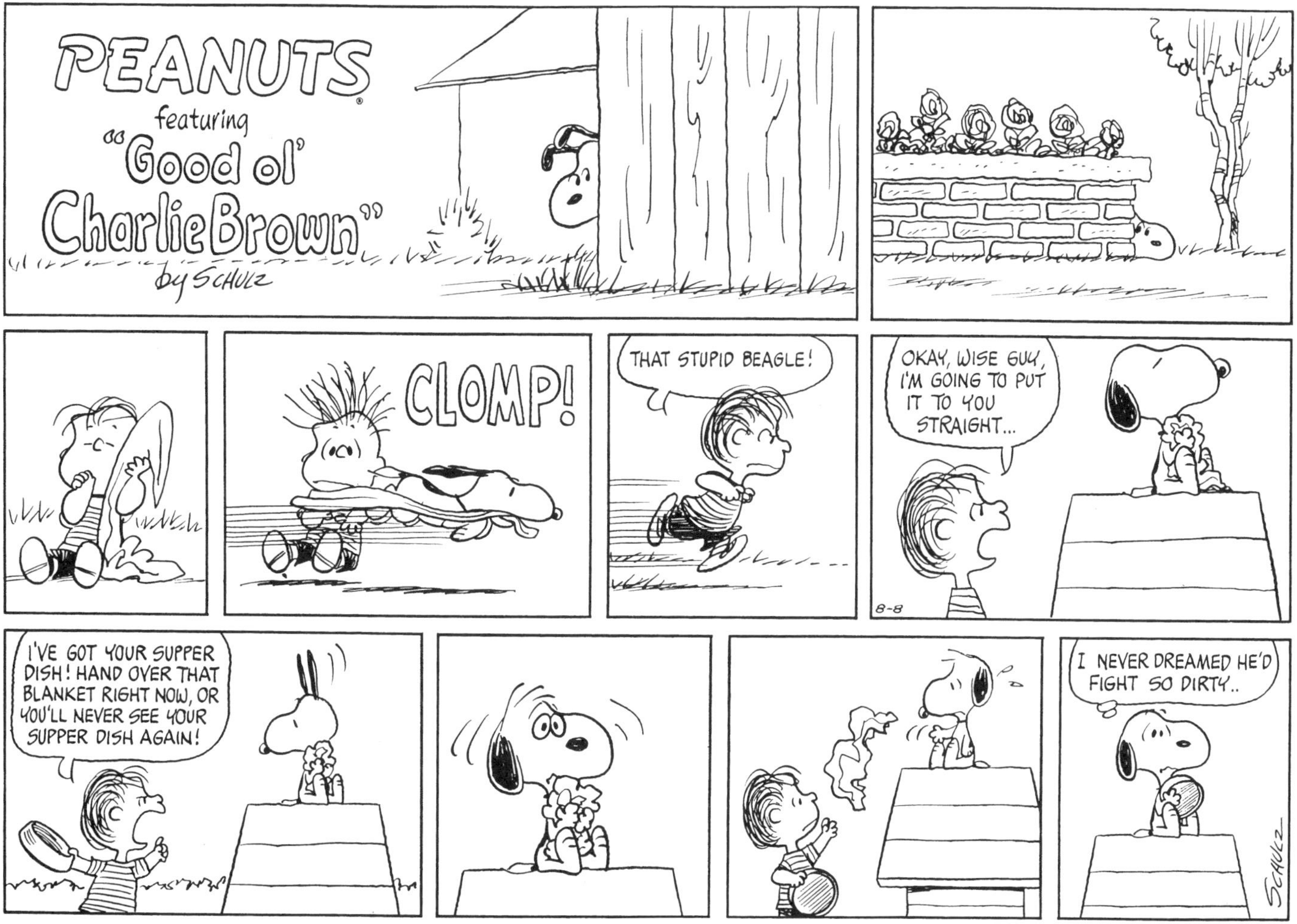
PEANUTS
featuring
"Good ol' Charlie Brown"
by SCHULZ
CLOMP!
THAT STUPID BEAGLE!
OKAY, WISE GUY, I'M GOING TO PUT IT TO YOU STRAIGHT...
8-8
I'VE GOT YOUR SUPPER DISH! HAND OVER THAT BLANKET RIGHT NOW, OR YOU'LL NEVER SEE YOUR SUPPER DISH AGAIN!
I NEVER DREAMED HE'D FIGHT SO DIRTY..
SCHULZ

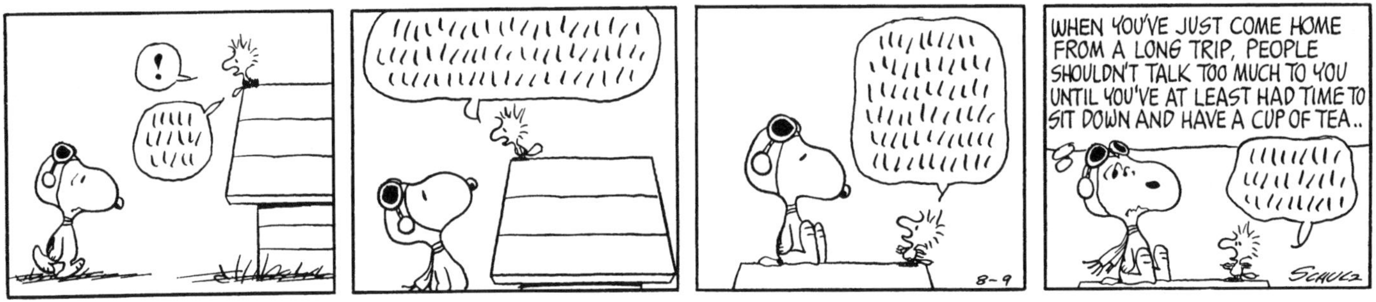
!
8-9
WHEN YOU'VE JUST COME HOME FROM A LONG TRIP, PEOPLE SHOULDN'T TALK TOO MUCH TO YOU UNTIL YOU'VE AT LEAST HAD TIME TO SIT DOWN AND HAVE A CUP OF TEA..
SCHULZ

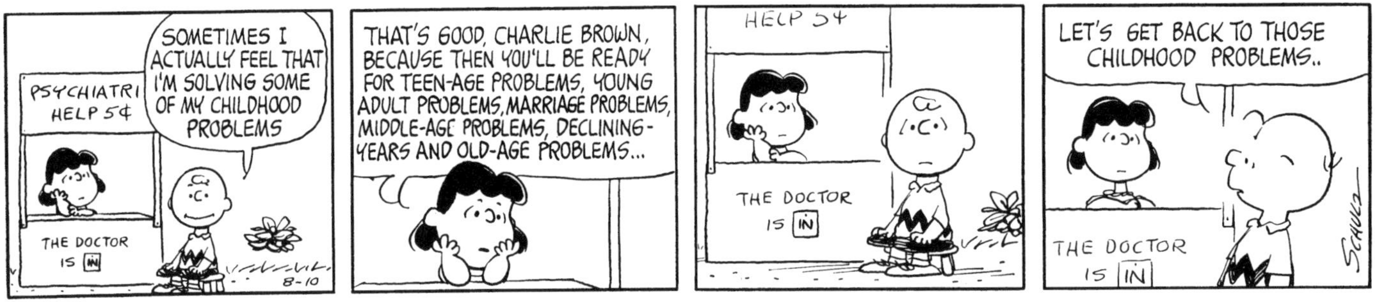
PSYCHIATRI HELP 5¢
THE DOCTOR IS IN
SOMETIMES I ACTUALLY FEEL THAT I'M SOLVING SOME OF MY CHILDHOOD PROBLEMS
8-10
THAT'S GOOD, CHARLIE BROWN, BECAUSE THEN YOU'LL BE READY FOR TEEN-AGE PROBLEMS, YOUNG ADULT PROBLEMS, MARRIAGE PROBLEMS, MIDDLE-AGE PROBLEMS, DECLINING-YEARS AND OLD-AGE PROBLEMS...
HELP 5¢
THE DOCTOR IS IN
LET'S GET BACK TO THOSE CHILDHOOD PROBLEMS..
THE DOCTOR IS IN
SCHULZ

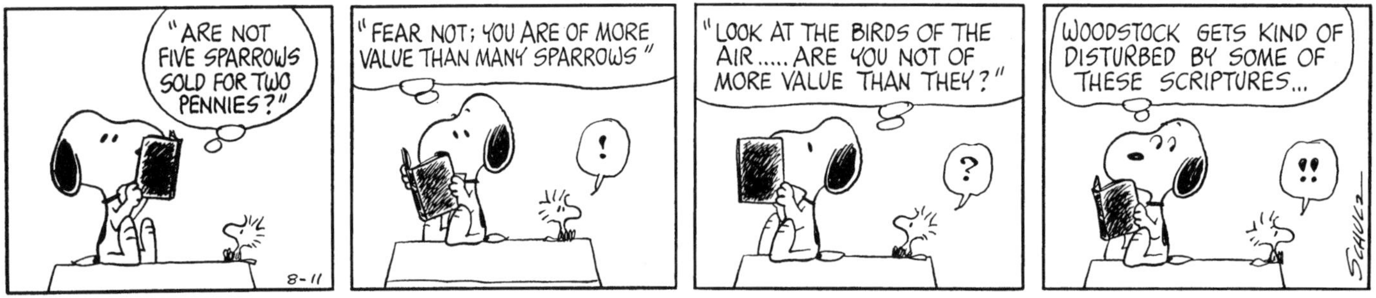
"ARE NOT FIVE SPARROWS SOLD FOR TWO PENNIES?"
8-11
"FEAR NOT; YOU ARE OF MORE VALUE THAN MANY SPARROWS"
!
"LOOK AT THE BIRDS OF THE AIR..... ARE YOU NOT OF MORE VALUE THAN THEY?"
?
WOODSTOCK GETS KIND OF DISTURBED BY SOME OF THESE SCRIPTURES...
!!
SCHULZ

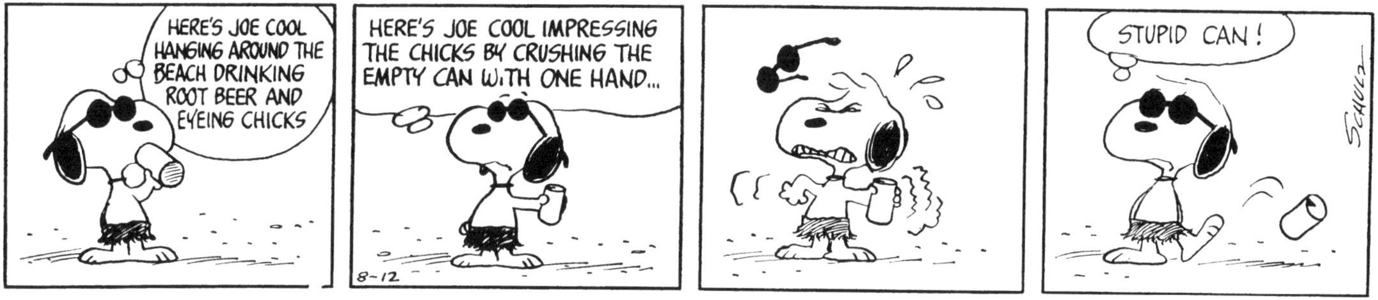
HERE'S JOE COOL HANGING AROUND THE BEACH DRINKING ROOT BEER AND EYEING CHICKS
HERE'S JOE COOL IMPRESSING THE CHICKS BY CRUSHING THE EMPTY CAN WITH ONE HAND...
STUPID CAN!

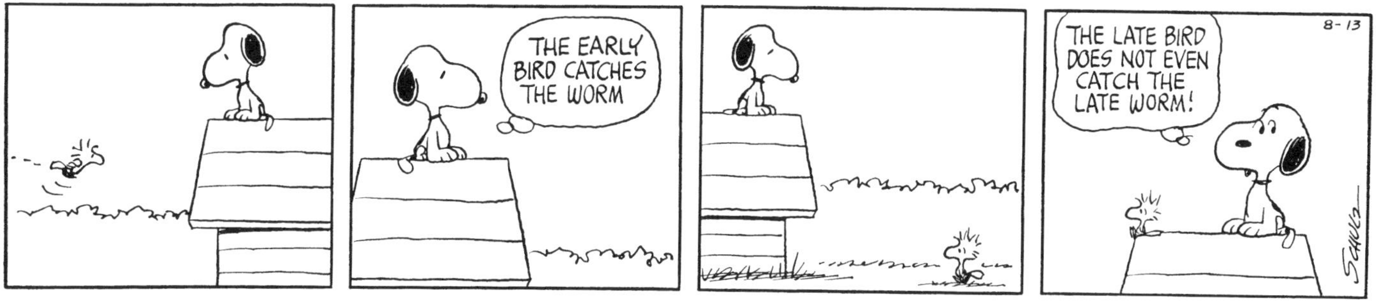
THE EARLY BIRD CATCHES THE WORM
THE LATE BIRD DOES NOT EVEN CATCH THE LATE WORM!

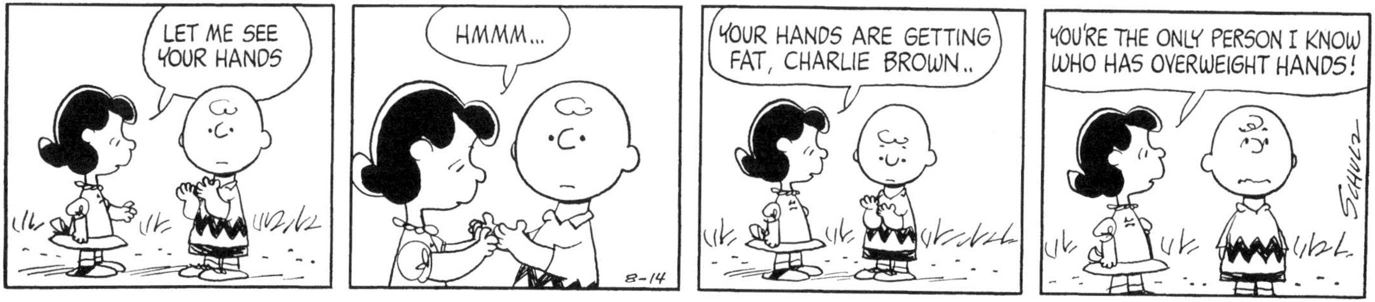
LET ME SEE YOUR HANDS
HMMM...
YOUR HANDS ARE GETTING FAT, CHARLIE BROWN..
YOU'RE THE ONLY PERSON I KNOW WHO HAS OVERWEIGHT HANDS!

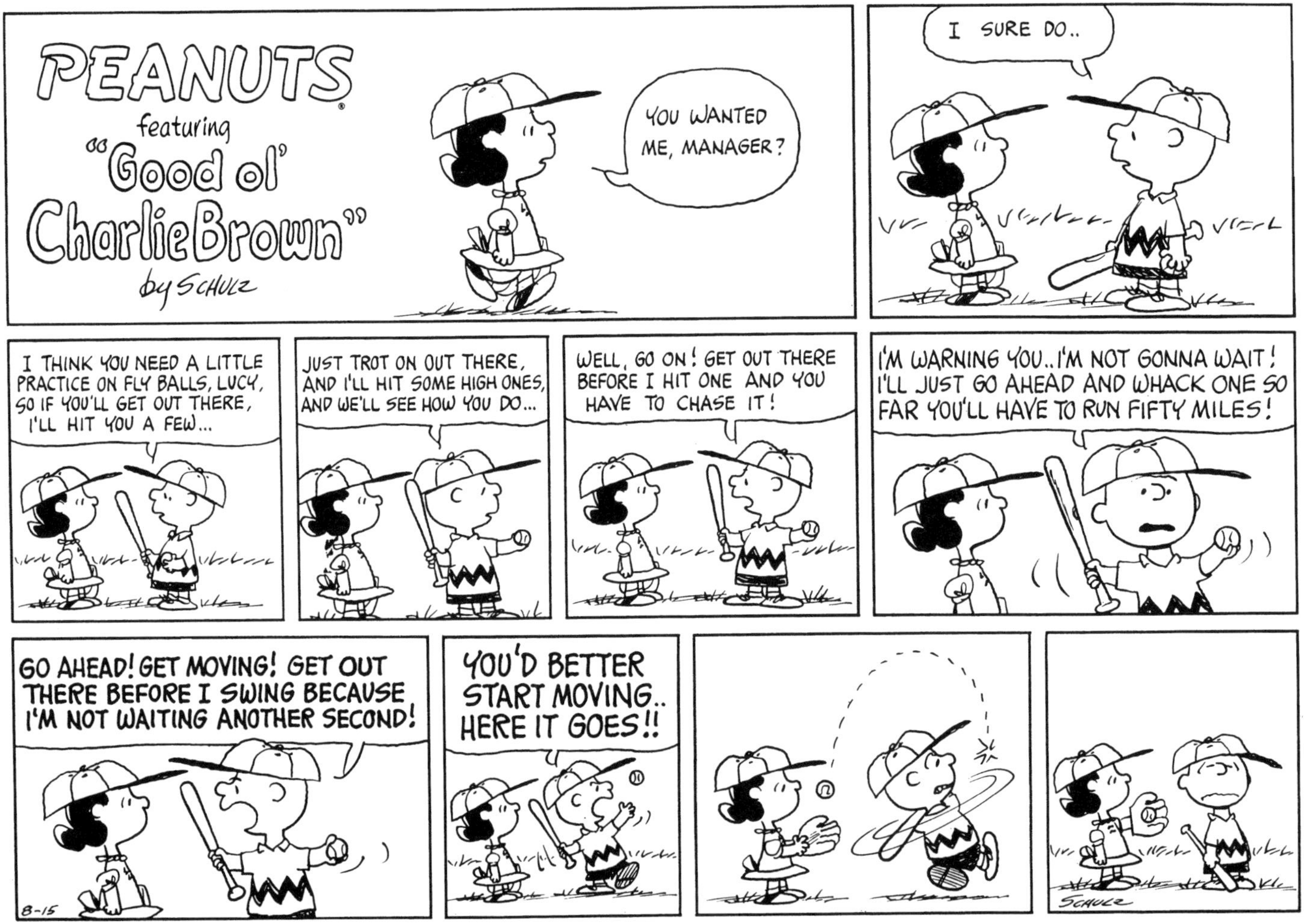
PEANUTS
featuring
"Good ol' Charlie Brown"
by SCHULZ
YOU WANTED ME, MANAGER?
I SURE DO..
I THINK YOU NEED A LITTLE PRACTICE ON FLY BALLS, LUCY, SO IF YOU'LL GET OUT THERE, I'LL HIT YOU A FEW...
JUST TROT ON OUT THERE, AND I'LL HIT SOME HIGH ONES, AND WE'LL SEE HOW YOU DO...
WELL, GO ON! GET OUT THERE BEFORE I HIT ONE AND YOU HAVE TO CHASE IT!
I'M WARNING YOU..I'M NOT GONNA WAIT! I'LL JUST GO AHEAD AND WHACK ONE SO FAR YOU'LL HAVE TO RUN FIFTY MILES!
GO AHEAD! GET MOVING! GET OUT THERE BEFORE I SWING BECAUSE I'M NOT WAITING ANOTHER SECOND!
8-15
YOU'D BETTER START MOVING.. HERE IT GOES!!
SCHULZ

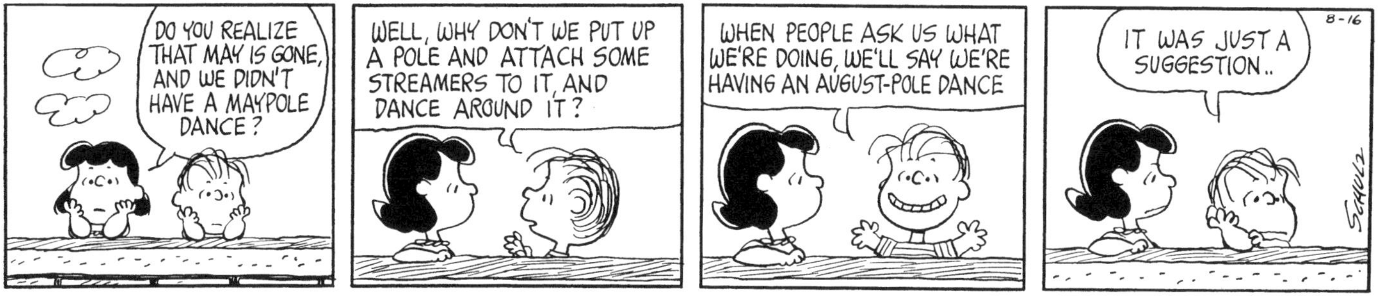
DO YOU REALIZE THAT MAY IS GONE, AND WE DIDN'T HAVE A MAYPOLE DANCE?
WELL, WHY DON'T WE PUT UP A POLE AND ATTACH SOME STREAMERS TO IT, AND DANCE AROUND IT?
WHEN PEOPLE ASK US WHAT WE'RE DOING, WE'LL SAY WE'RE HAVING AN AUGUST-POLE DANCE
8-16
IT WAS JUST A SUGGESTION..
SCHULZ

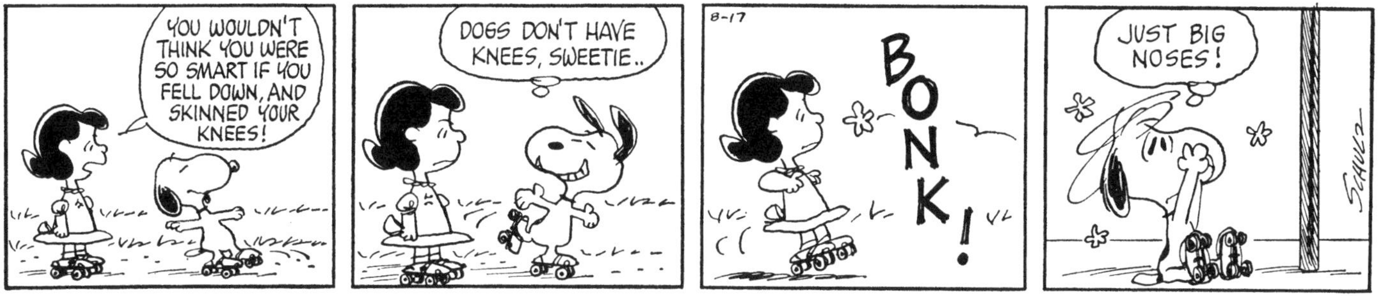
YOU WOULDN'T THINK YOU WERE SO SMART IF YOU FELL DOWN, AND SKINNED YOUR KNEES!
DOGS DON'T HAVE KNEES, SWEETIE..
8-17
BONK!
JUST BIG NOSES!
SCHULZ

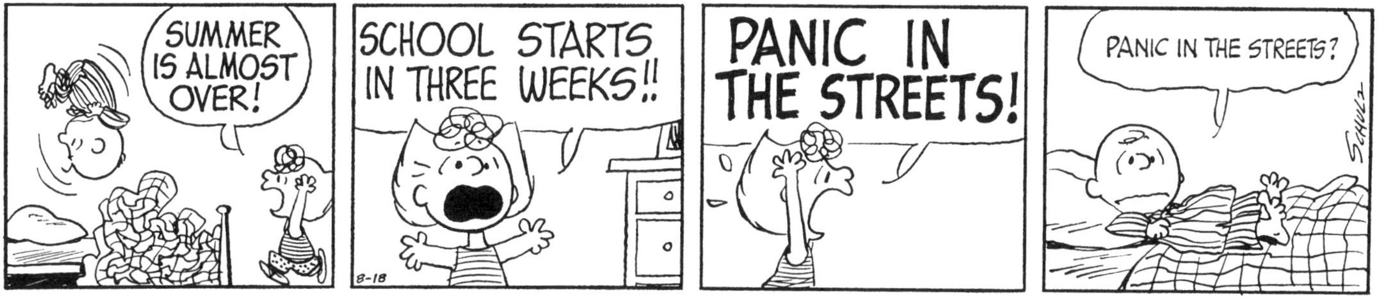
SUMMER IS ALMOST OVER!
SCHOOL STARTS IN THREE WEEKS!!
8-18
PANIC IN THE STREETS!
PANIC IN THE STREETS?
SCHULZ

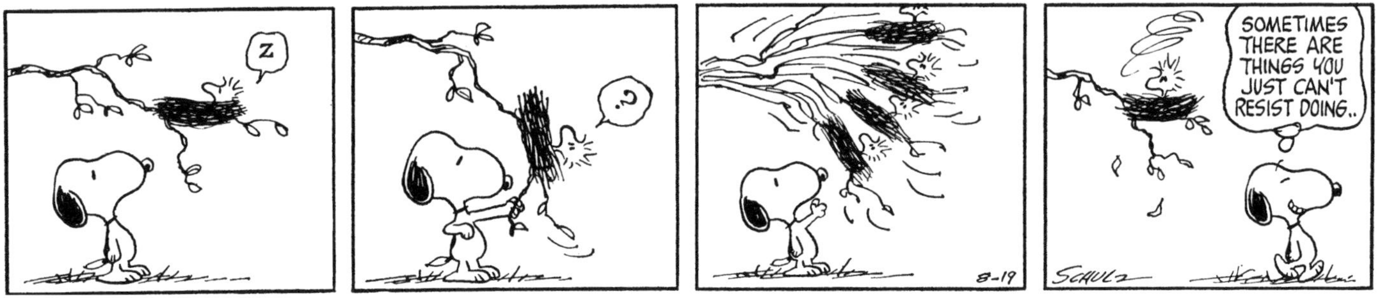
Z
?
8-19
SCHULZ
SOMETIMES THERE ARE THINGS YOU JUST CAN'T RESIST DOING..

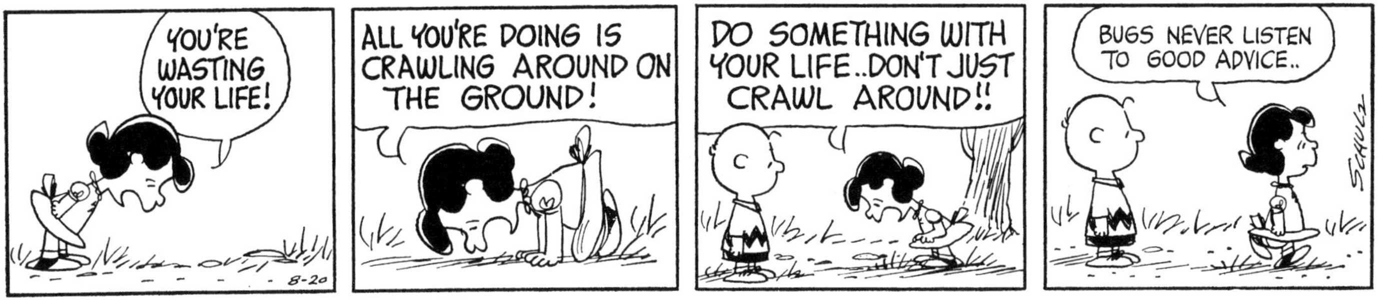
YOU'RE WASTING YOUR LIFE!
8-20
ALL YOU'RE DOING IS CRAWLING AROUND ON THE GROUND!
DO SOMETHING WITH YOUR LIFE..DON'T JUST CRAWL AROUND!!
BUGS NEVER LISTEN TO GOOD ADVICE..
SCHULZ

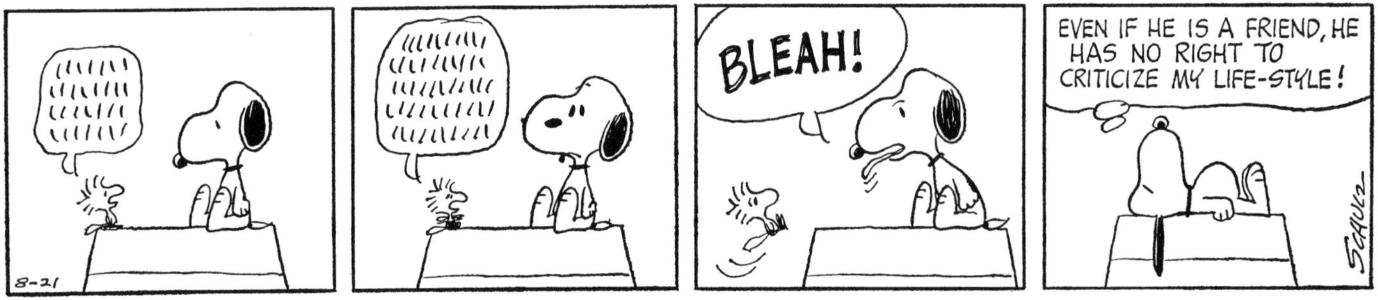
8-21
BLEAH!
EVEN IF HE IS A FRIEND, HE HAS NO RIGHT TO CRITICIZE MY LIFE-STYLE!
SCHULZ

PEANUTS
featuring
"Good ol' Charlie Brown"
by SCHULZ
YAWN
Z
WAP!
8-22
!
BOOT!
SCHULZ

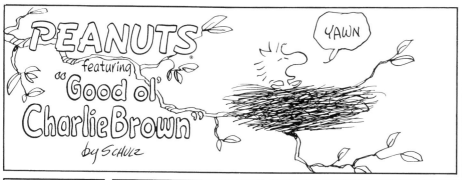

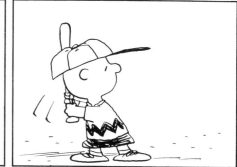

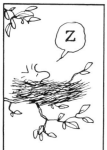

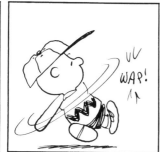

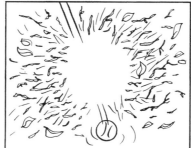

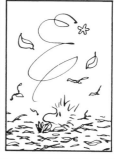

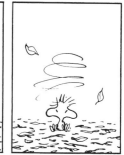

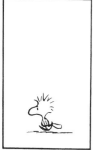

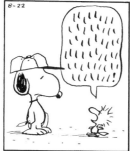

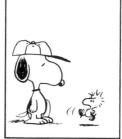

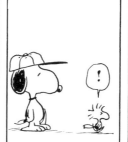

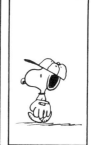

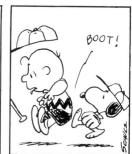

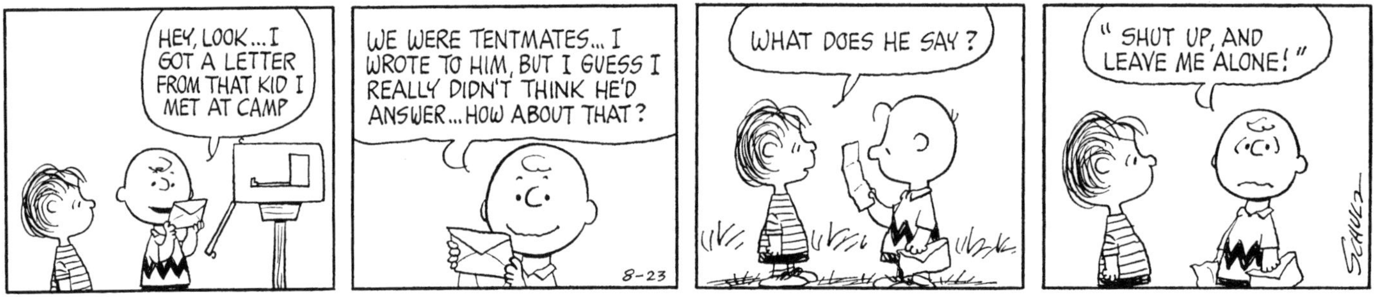
HEY, LOOK... I GOT A LETTER FROM THAT KID I MET AT CAMP
WE WERE TENTMATES... I WROTE TO HIM, BUT I GUESS I REALLY DIDN'T THINK HE'D ANSWER... HOW ABOUT THAT?
8-23
WHAT DOES HE SAY?
"SHUT UP, AND LEAVE ME ALONE!"
SCHULZ

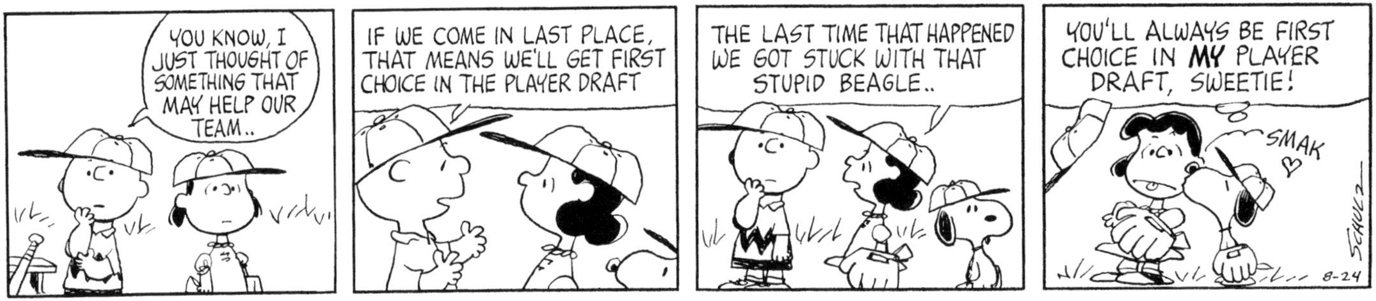
YOU KNOW, I JUST THOUGHT OF SOMETHING THAT MAY HELP OUR TEAM..
IF WE COME IN LAST PLACE, THAT MEANS WE'LL GET FIRST CHOICE IN THE PLAYER DRAFT
THE LAST TIME THAT HAPPENED WE GOT STUCK WITH THAT STUPID BEAGLE..
YOU'LL ALWAYS BE FIRST CHOICE IN **MY** PLAYER DRAFT, SWEETIE!
SMAK
SCHULZ
8-24

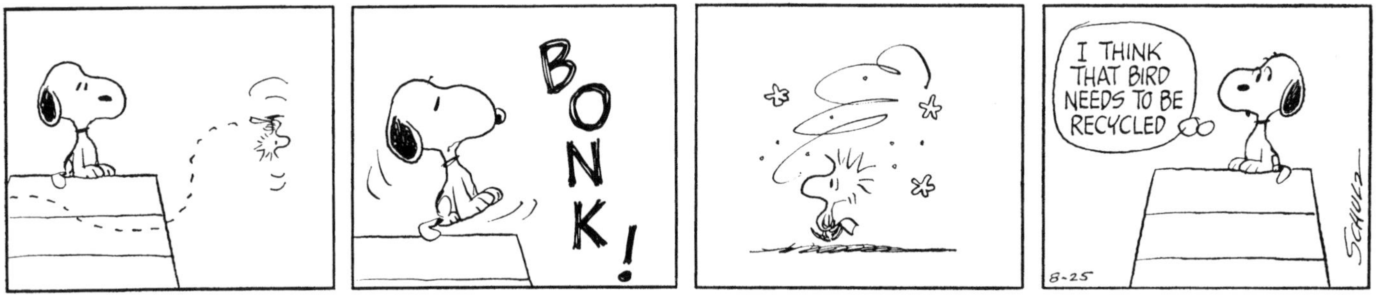
BONK!
I THINK THAT BIRD NEEDS TO BE RECYCLED
8-25
SCHULZ

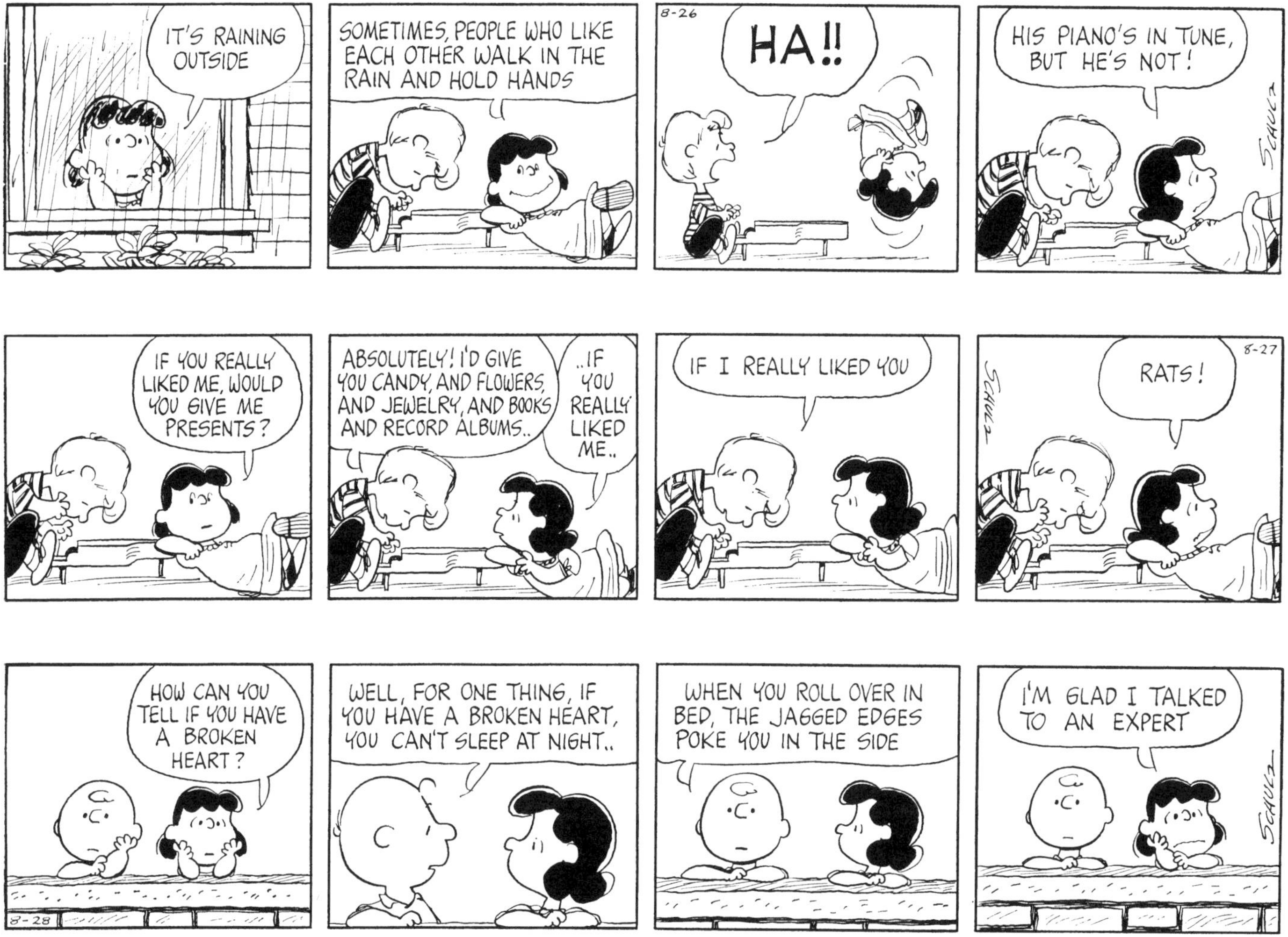
IT'S RAINING OUTSIDE
SOMETIMES, PEOPLE WHO LIKE EACH OTHER WALK IN THE RAIN AND HOLD HANDS
8-26
HA!!
HIS PIANO'S IN TUNE, BUT HE'S NOT!
SCHULZ
IF YOU REALLY LIKED ME, WOULD YOU GIVE ME PRESENTS?
ABSOLUTELY! I'D GIVE YOU CANDY, AND FLOWERS, AND JEWELRY, AND BOOKS AND RECORD ALBUMS..
..IF YOU REALLY LIKED ME..
IF I REALLY LIKED YOU
SCHULZ
8-27
RATS!
HOW CAN YOU TELL IF YOU HAVE A BROKEN HEART?
8-28
WELL, FOR ONE THING, IF YOU HAVE A BROKEN HEART, YOU CAN'T SLEEP AT NIGHT..
WHEN YOU ROLL OVER IN BED, THE JAGGED EDGES POKE YOU IN THE SIDE
I'M GLAD I TALKED TO AN EXPERT
SCHULZ

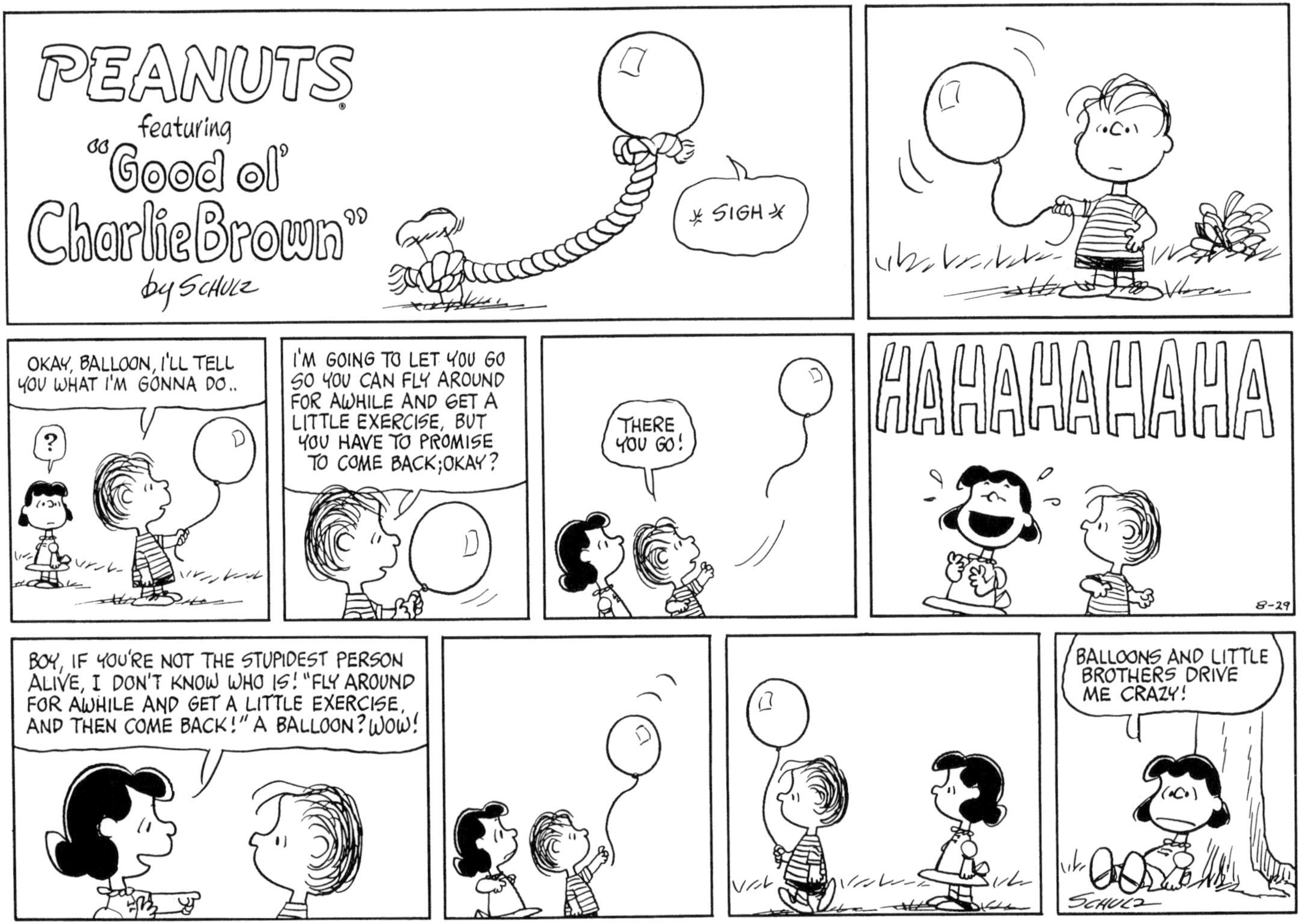
PEANUTS
featuring
"Good ol' Charlie Brown"
by SCHULZ
* SIGH *
OKAY, BALLOON, I'LL TELL YOU WHAT I'M GONNA DO..
?
I'M GOING TO LET YOU GO SO YOU CAN FLY AROUND FOR AWHILE AND GET A LITTLE EXERCISE, BUT YOU HAVE TO PROMISE TO COME BACK; OKAY?
THERE YOU GO!
HAHAHAHAHAHA
8-29
BOY, IF YOU'RE NOT THE STUPIDEST PERSON ALIVE, I DON'T KNOW WHO IS! "FLY AROUND FOR AWHILE AND GET A LITTLE EXERCISE, AND THEN COME BACK!" A BALLOON? WOW!
BALLOONS AND LITTLE BROTHERS DRIVE ME CRAZY!
SCHULZ

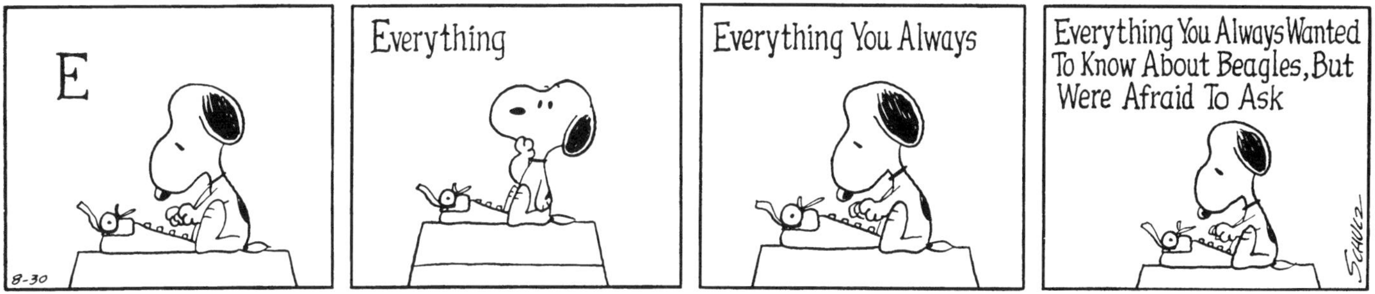
E
Everything
Everything You Always
Everything You Always Wanted To Know About Beagles, But Were Afraid To Ask
8-30
SCHULZ

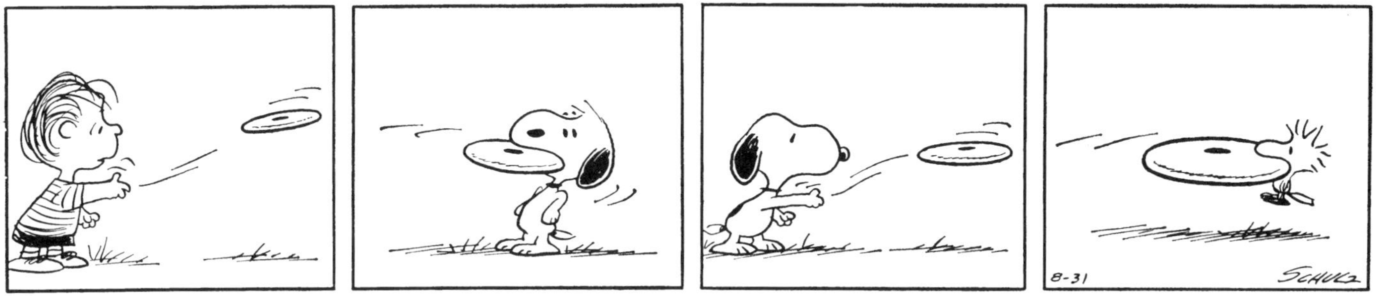
8-31
SCHULZ

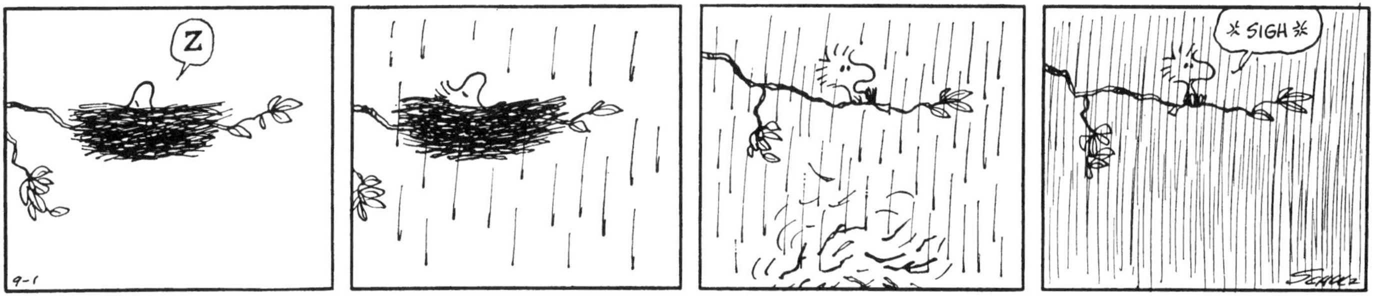
Z
* SIGH *
9-1
SCHULZ

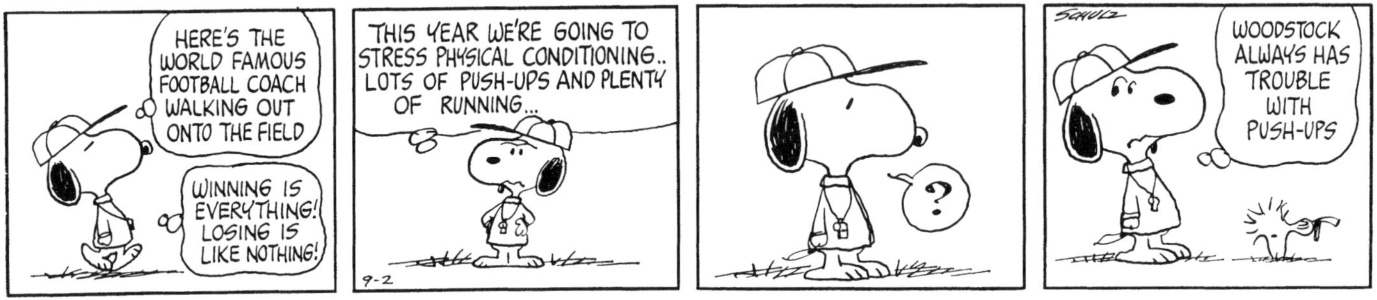
HERE'S THE WORLD FAMOUS FOOTBALL COACH WALKING OUT ONTO THE FIELD
WINNING IS EVERYTHING! LOSING IS LIKE NOTHING!
THIS YEAR WE'RE GOING TO STRESS PHYSICAL CONDITIONING.. LOTS OF PUSH-UPS AND PLENTY OF RUNNING...
9-2
?
SCHULZ
WOODSTOCK ALWAYS HAS TROUBLE WITH PUSH-UPS

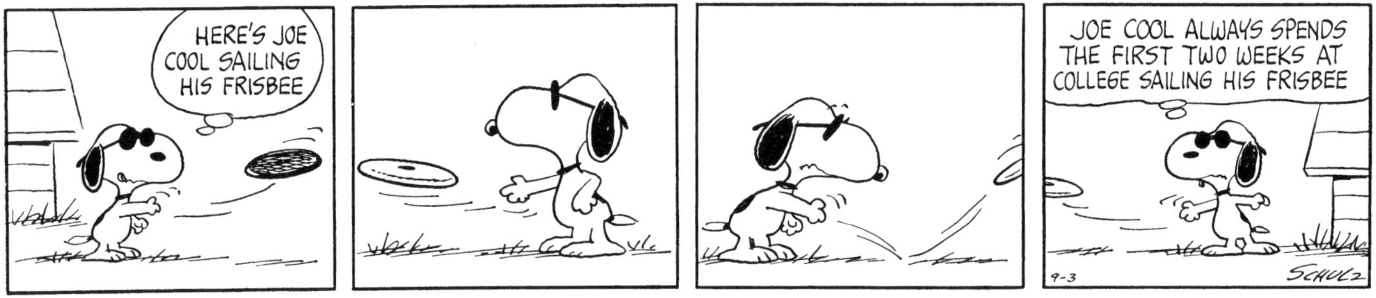
HERE'S JOE COOL SAILING HIS FRISBEE
JOE COOL ALWAYS SPENDS THE FIRST TWO WEEKS AT COLLEGE SAILING HIS FRISBEE
9-3
SCHULZ

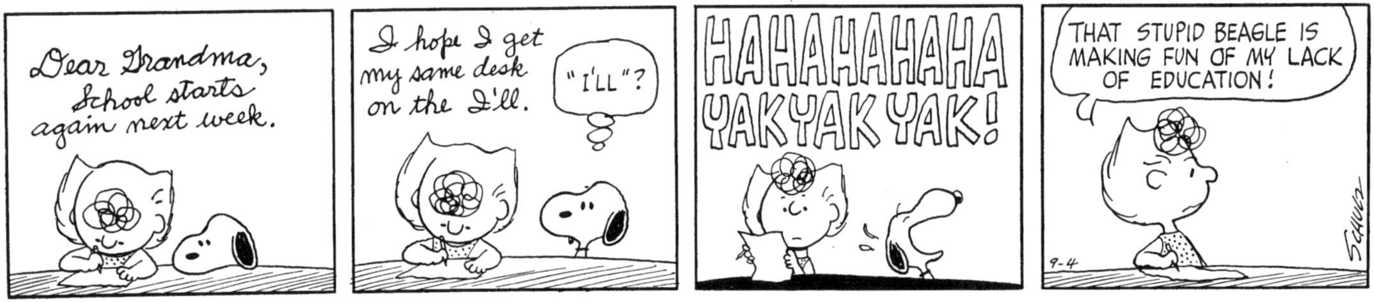
Dear Grandma, School starts again next week.
I hope I get my same desk on the I'll.
"I'LL"?
HAHAHAHAHA YAKYAKYAK!
THAT STUPID BEAGLE IS MAKING FUN OF MY LACK OF EDUCATION!
9-4
SCHULZ

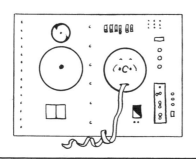

PEANUTS
featuring
"Good ol' CharlieBrown"
by SCHULZ

DID YOU KNOW THAT THERE ARE THREE BILLION, FOUR HUNDRED AND NINETEEN MILLION, FOUR HUNDRED AND TWENTY THOUSAND PEOPLE IN THE WORLD?

WELL, ACTUALLY, THAT FIGURE IS QUITE A BIT LOW..

JUST THE OTHER NIGHT I WAS LYING IN BED THINKING ABOUT THAT VERY THING...I CAME UP WITH A MUCH HIGHER FIGURE...

YOU SEE, THERE'S MARTHA, AND SAM, AND PAUL, AND GEORGE, AND JANE, AND GREG, AND FAITH, AND SUE, AND TOM, AND PEGGY, AND JERRY, AND BETTY, AND PETER, AND SHIRLEY...

AND THERE'S MARGE, AND BOB, AND KENNY, AND WARREN, AND LEE, AND BILL, AND DAVE, AND MOLLIE, AND SANDRA...

AND NINO, AND ELAINE, AND CURT, AND DONNA, AND NAOMI, AND RAYMOND, AND OTTO, AND KEVIN, AND AMY, AND JILL, AND MEREDITH, AND GARY, AND LOIS..

..THERE'S PAT, AND WALTER, AND IVAN, AND JANICE, AND ED, AND LILLIAN, AND FRANK, AND..

SHE'S THE ONLY PERSON I KNOW WHO CAN NAME ALL THE PEOPLE IN THE WORLD..

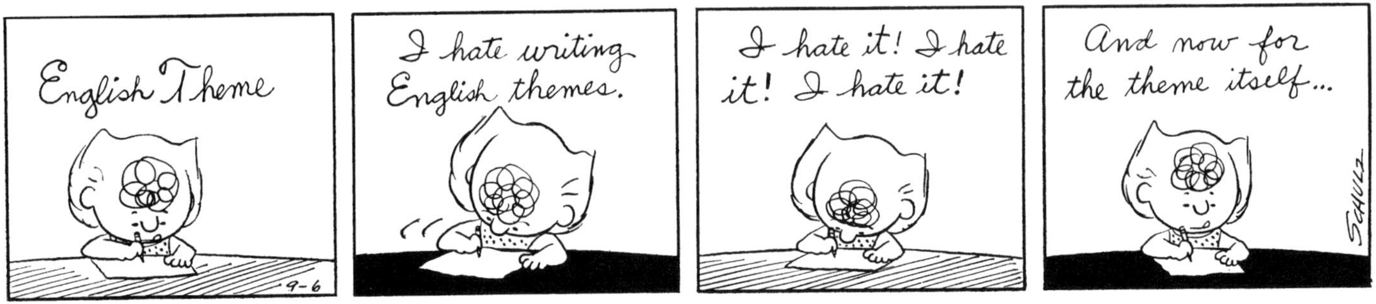
English Theme
I hate writing English themes.
I hate it! I hate it! I hate it!
And now for the theme itself...
9-6
SCHULZ

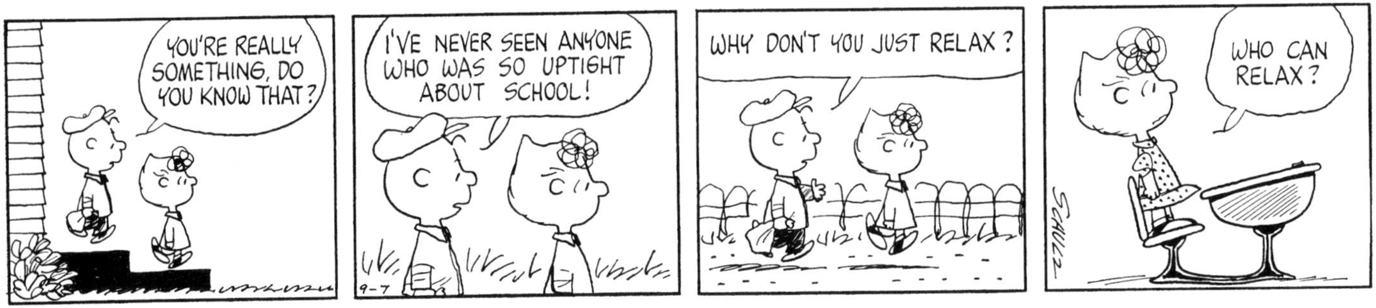
YOU'RE REALLY SOMETHING, DO YOU KNOW THAT?
I'VE NEVER SEEN ANYONE WHO WAS SO UPTIGHT ABOUT SCHOOL!
9-7
WHY DON'T YOU JUST RELAX?
WHO CAN RELAX?
SCHULZ

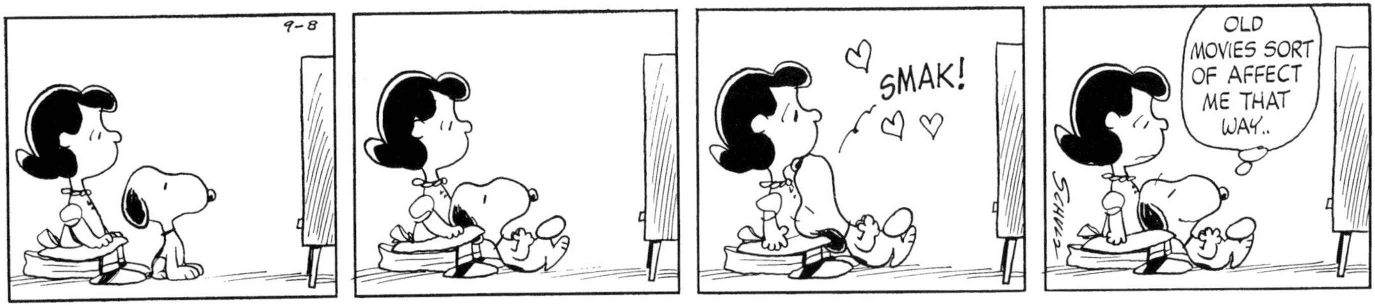
9-8
SMAK!
OLD MOVIES SORT OF AFFECT ME THAT WAY..
SCHULZ

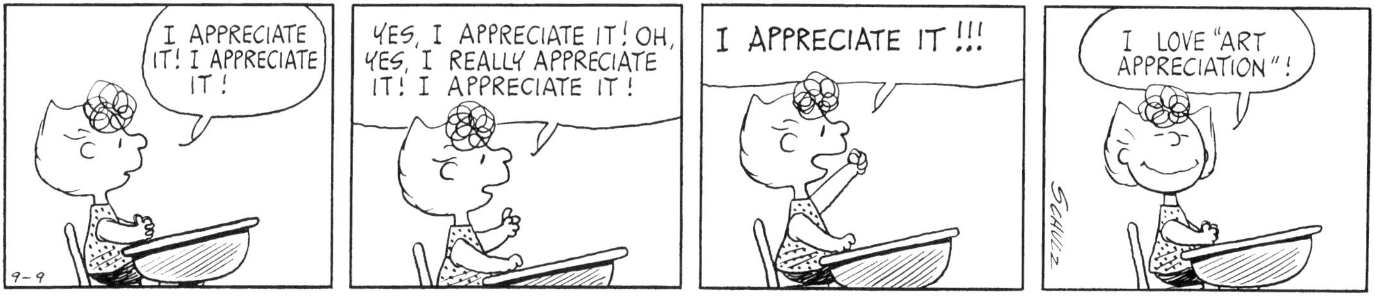
9-9
I APPRECIATE IT! I APPRECIATE IT!
YES, I APPRECIATE IT! OH, YES, I REALLY APPRECIATE IT! I APPRECIATE IT!
I APPRECIATE IT!!!
I LOVE "ART APPRECIATION"!
SCHULZ

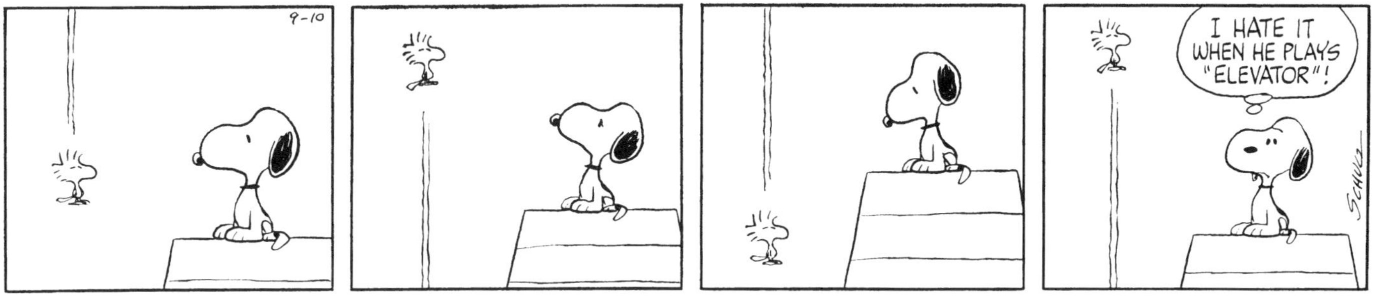
9-10
I HATE IT WHEN HE PLAYS "ELEVATOR"!
SCHULZ

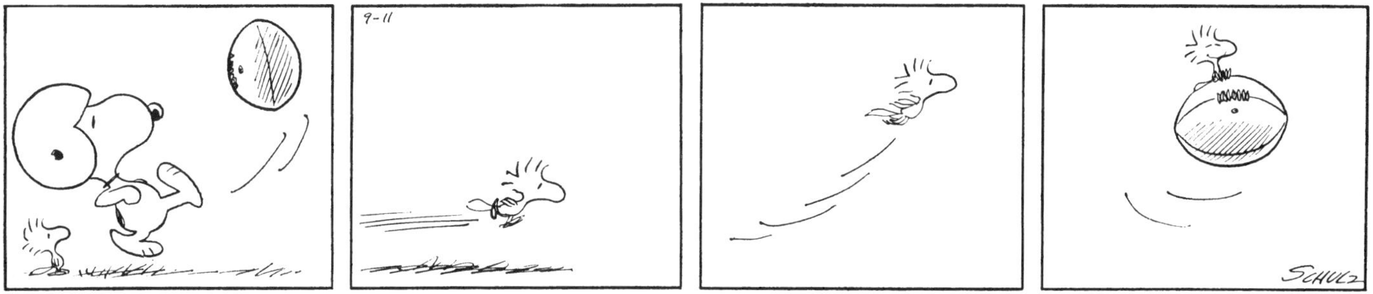
9-11
SCHULZ

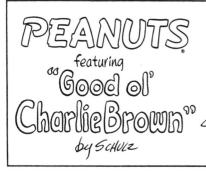

PEANUTS

featuring

"Good ol' CharlieBrown"

by SCHULZ

QUIET

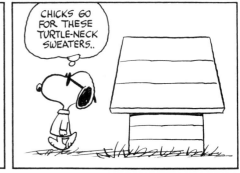

CHICKS GO
FOR THESE
TURTLE-NECK
SWEATERS..

HERE'S JOE COOL
HANGING AROUND THE
DORM ON A SUNDAY
AFTERNOON..

9-12

MAYBE I'LL GO
OVER TO THE
STUDENT UNION,
AND CHECK OUT
THE SCENE

HERE'S JOE COOL
HANGING AROUND THE
STUDENT UNION
LOOKING FOR ACTION..

I SEE THEY'RE SHOWING
"CITIZEN KANE" AGAIN...
I'VE ONLY SEEN IT
TWENTY-THREE TIMES..

MAYBE I'LL GO OVER
TO THE LIBRARY, AND
SEE WHO'S THERE

RATS..NO CHICKS!
MAYBE I SHOULD GO OVER
TO THE GYM AND SHOOT
A FEW BASKETS...

IF I HAD SOME
WHEELS, I'D CRUISE
AROUND FOR AWHILE..
MAYBE I SHOULD WALK
OVER, AND LOOK AT THE
GEOLOGICAL EXHIBIT...

I'VE GOTTA BE
KIDDING... LOOK AT
THOSE ROCKS AGAIN?
NO WAY!

THERE'S A GUY
WITH TWO CHICKS..
HOW DOES HE
DO IT?

THE LEAVES ARE
BEGINNING TO FALL..
THE SUN IS WARM, BUT
IT'S KIND OF CHILLY
IN THE SHADE

I WONDER WHAT'S
GOING ON AT HOME..
MAYBE I SHOULD GO
BACK TO THE DORM AND
WRITE SOME LETTERS...

✳SIGH✳ JOE COOL
HATES SUNDAY
AFTERNOONS...

SCHULZ

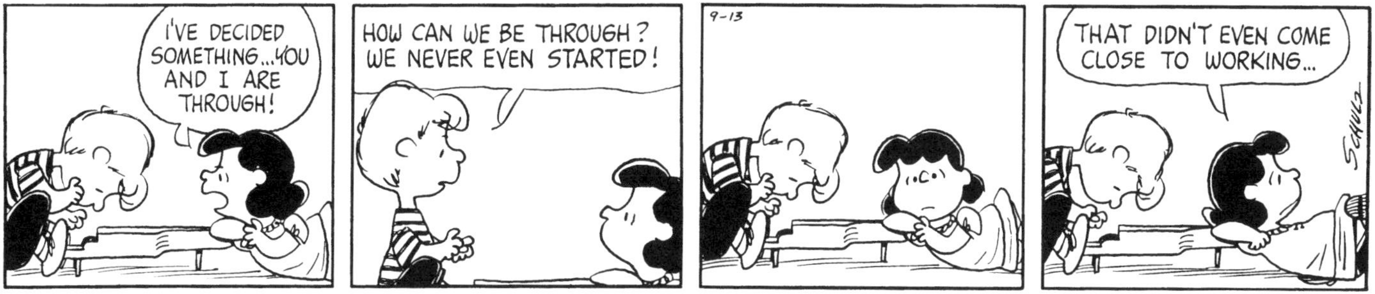
I'VE DECIDED SOMETHING...YOU AND I ARE THROUGH!
HOW CAN WE BE THROUGH? WE NEVER EVEN STARTED!
9-13
THAT DIDN'T EVEN COME CLOSE TO WORKING...
SCHULZ

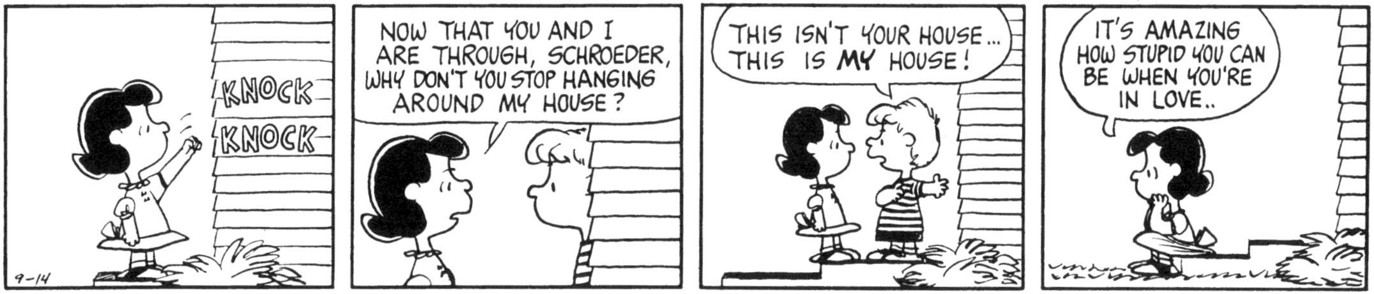
KNOCK
KNOCK
9-14
NOW THAT YOU AND I ARE THROUGH, SCHROEDER, WHY DON'T YOU STOP HANGING AROUND MY HOUSE?
THIS ISN'T YOUR HOUSE... THIS IS MY HOUSE!
IT'S AMAZING HOW STUPID YOU CAN BE WHEN YOU'RE IN LOVE..

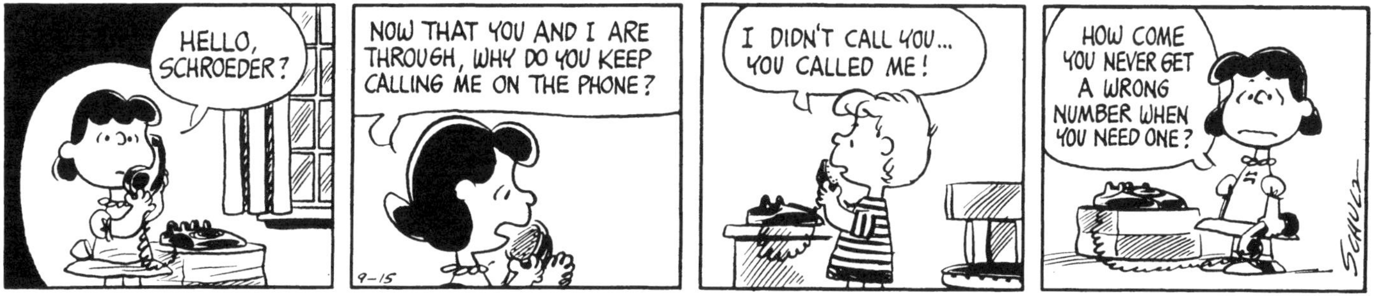
HELLO, SCHROEDER?
NOW THAT YOU AND I ARE THROUGH, WHY DO YOU KEEP CALLING ME ON THE PHONE?
9-15
I DIDN'T CALL YOU... YOU CALLED ME!
HOW COME YOU NEVER GET A WRONG NUMBER WHEN YOU NEED ONE?
SCHULZ

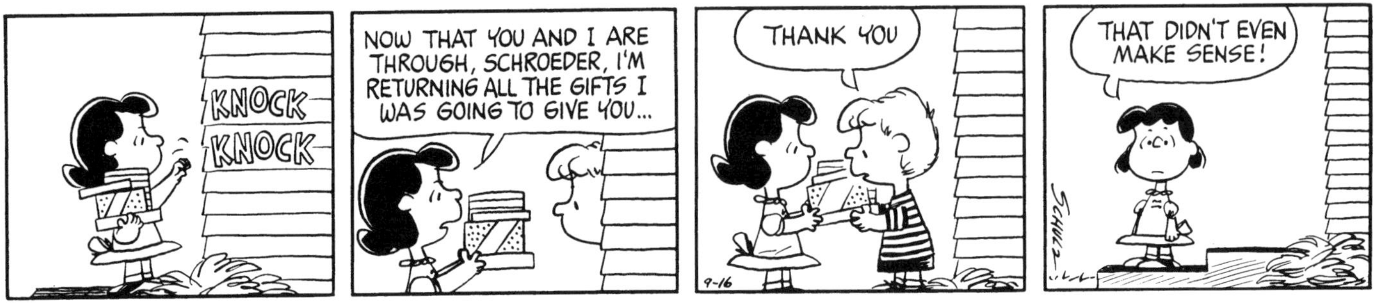
KNOCK
KNOCK
NOW THAT YOU AND I ARE THROUGH, SCHROEDER, I'M RETURNING ALL THE GIFTS I WAS GOING TO GIVE YOU...
THANK YOU
THAT DIDN'T EVEN MAKE SENSE!

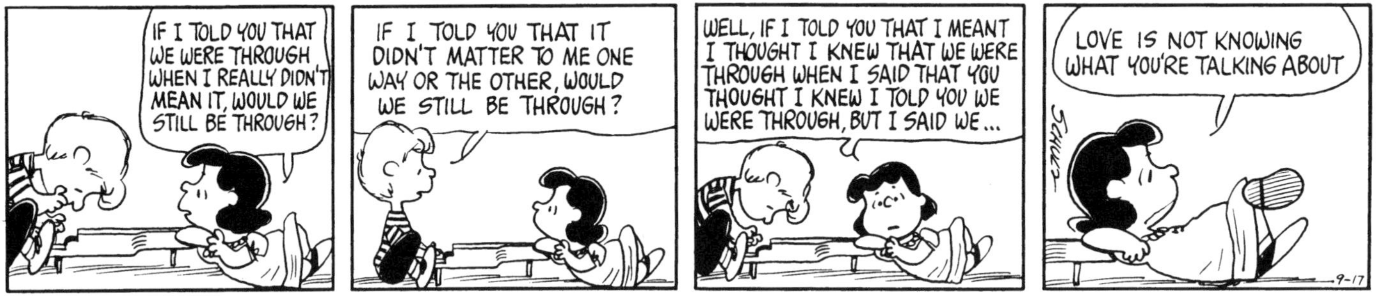
IF I TOLD YOU THAT WE WERE THROUGH WHEN I REALLY DIDN'T MEAN IT, WOULD WE STILL BE THROUGH?
IF I TOLD YOU THAT IT DIDN'T MATTER TO ME ONE WAY OR THE OTHER, WOULD WE STILL BE THROUGH?
WELL, IF I TOLD YOU THAT I MEANT I THOUGHT I KNEW THAT WE WERE THROUGH WHEN I SAID THAT YOU THOUGHT I KNEW I TOLD YOU WE WERE THROUGH, BUT I SAID WE...
LOVE IS NOT KNOWING WHAT YOU'RE TALKING ABOUT

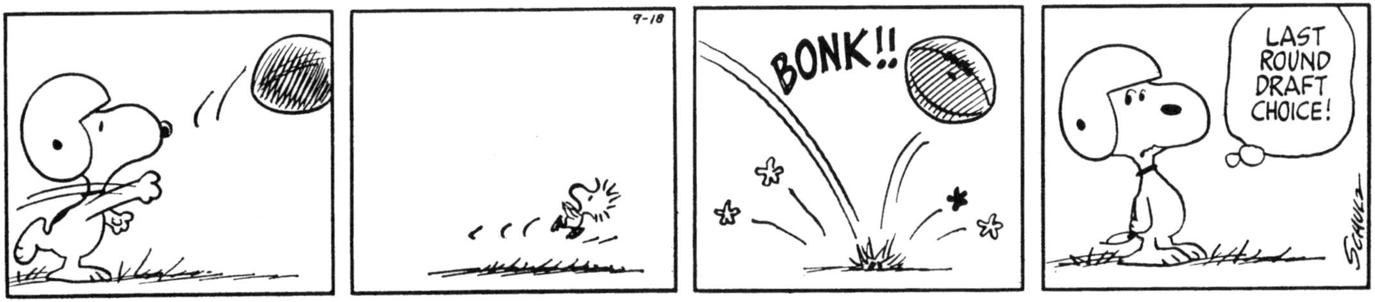
BONK!!
LAST ROUND DRAFT CHOICE!

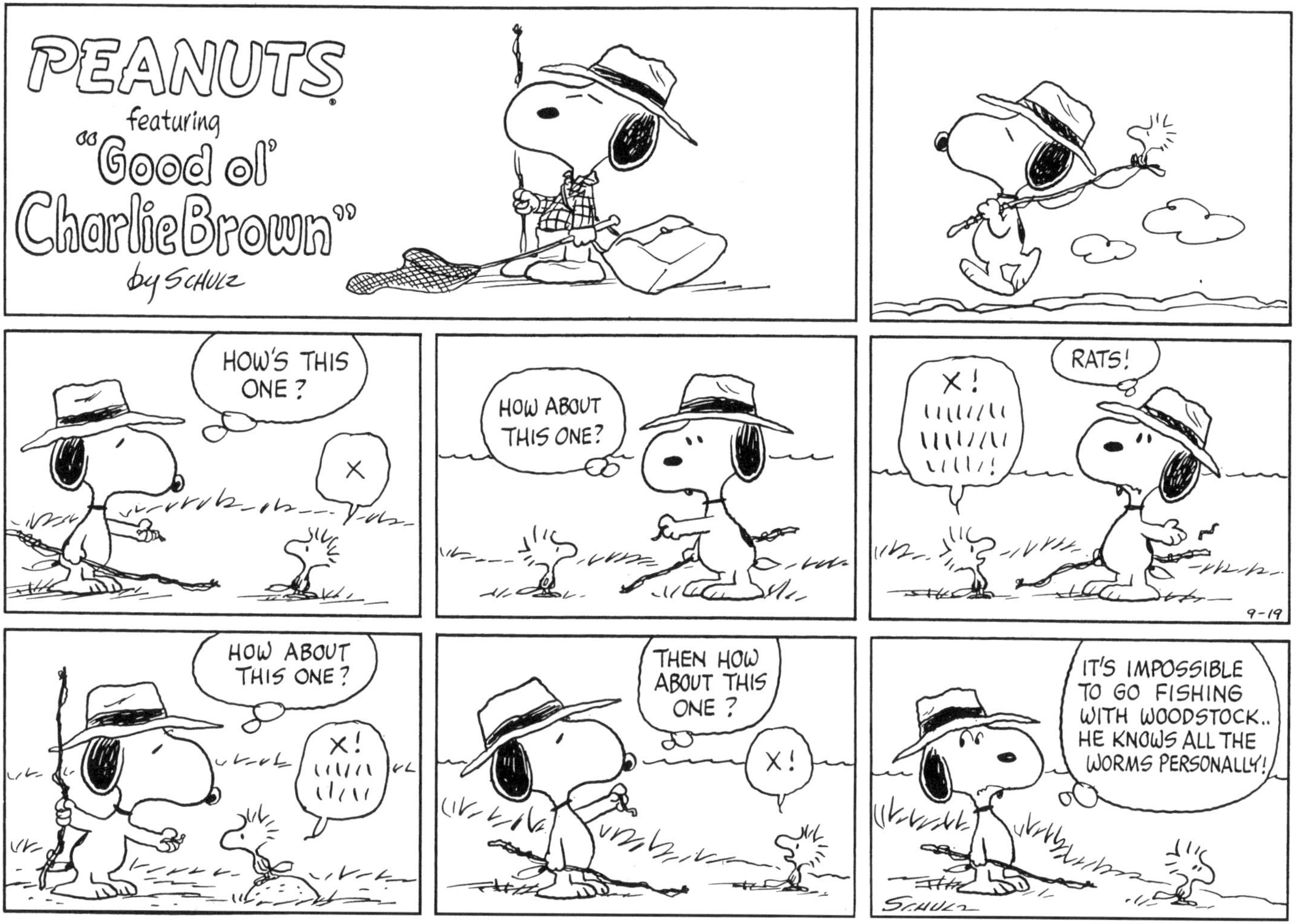
PEANUTS
featuring
"Good ol' Charlie Brown"
by SCHULZ
HOW'S THIS ONE?
X
HOW ABOUT THIS ONE?
X!
RATS!
9-19
HOW ABOUT THIS ONE?
X!
THEN HOW ABOUT THIS ONE?
X!
IT'S IMPOSSIBLE TO GO FISHING WITH WOODSTOCK.. HE KNOWS ALL THE WORMS PERSONALLY!
SCHULZ

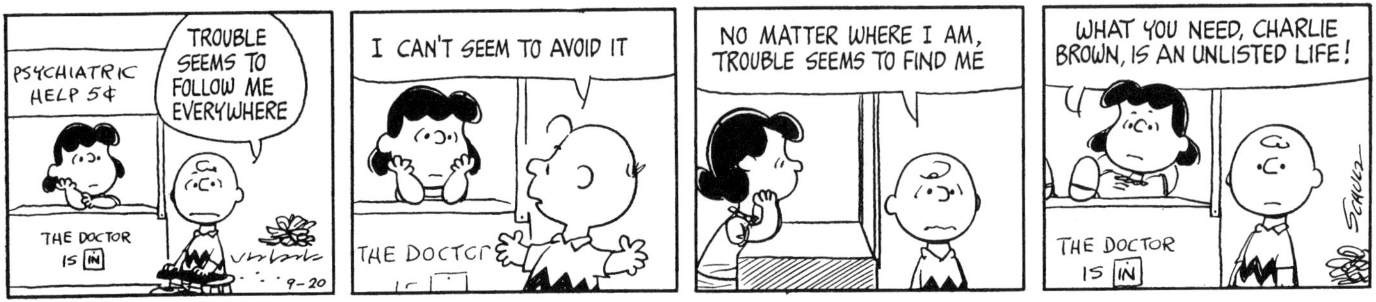
PSYCHIATRIC HELP 5¢
THE DOCTOR IS IN
TROUBLE SEEMS TO FOLLOW ME EVERYWHERE
9-20
I CAN'T SEEM TO AVOID IT
THE DOCTOR
NO MATTER WHERE I AM, TROUBLE SEEMS TO FIND ME
WHAT YOU NEED, CHARLIE BROWN, IS AN UNLISTED LIFE!
THE DOCTOR IS IN
SCHULZ

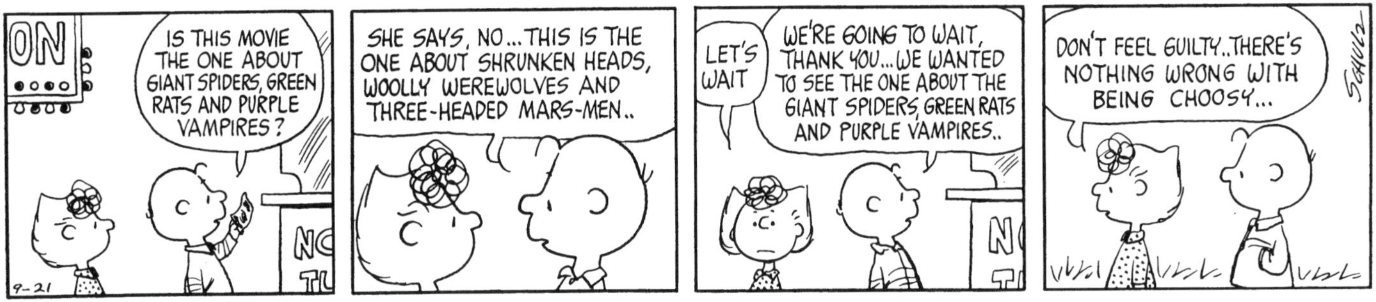
ON
IS THIS MOVIE THE ONE ABOUT GIANT SPIDERS, GREEN RATS AND PURPLE VAMPIRES?
9-21
SHE SAYS, NO... THIS IS THE ONE ABOUT SHRUNKEN HEADS, WOOLLY WEREWOLVES AND THREE-HEADED MARS-MEN..
LET'S WAIT
WE'RE GOING TO WAIT, THANK YOU... WE WANTED TO SEE THE ONE ABOUT THE GIANT SPIDERS, GREEN RATS AND PURPLE VAMPIRES..
DON'T FEEL GUILTY.. THERE'S NOTHING WRONG WITH BEING CHOOSY...
SCHULZ

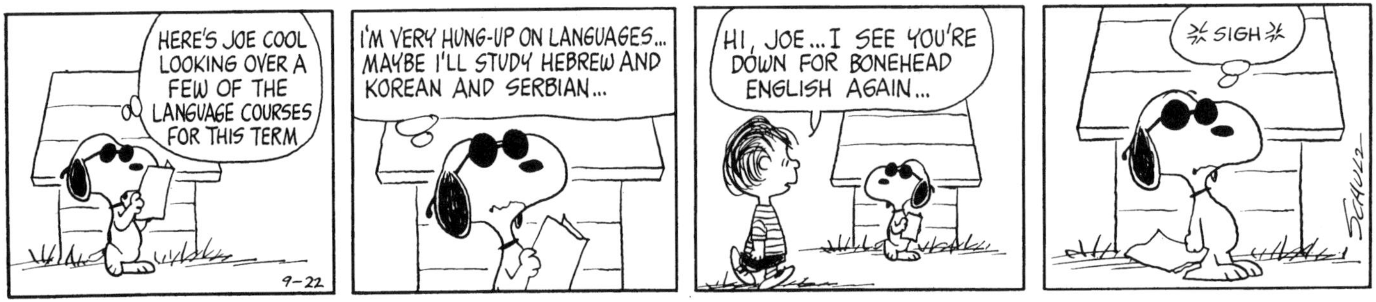
HERE'S JOE COOL LOOKING OVER A FEW OF THE LANGUAGE COURSES FOR THIS TERM
9-22
I'M VERY HUNG-UP ON LANGUAGES... MAYBE I'LL STUDY HEBREW AND KOREAN AND SERBIAN...
HI, JOE... I SEE YOU'RE DOWN FOR BONEHEAD ENGLISH AGAIN...
SIGH
SCHULZ

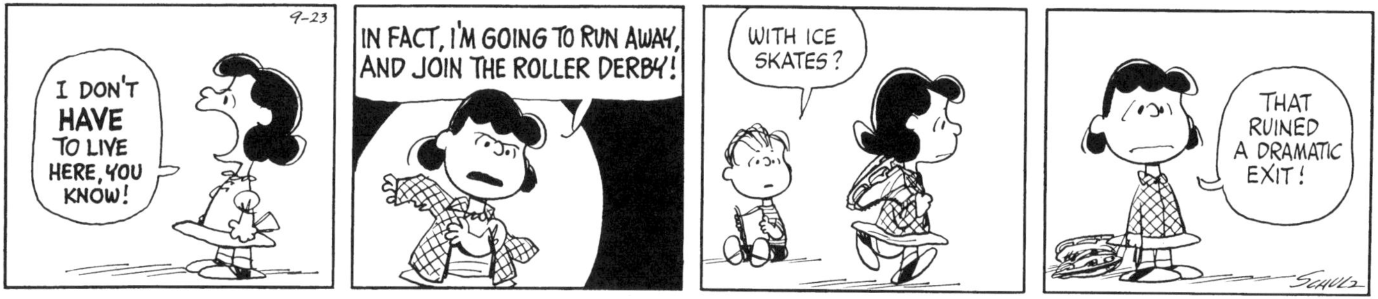
9-23
I DON'T **HAVE** TO LIVE HERE, YOU KNOW!
IN FACT, I'M GOING TO RUN AWAY, AND JOIN THE ROLLER DERBY!
WITH ICE SKATES?
THAT RUINED A DRAMATIC EXIT!

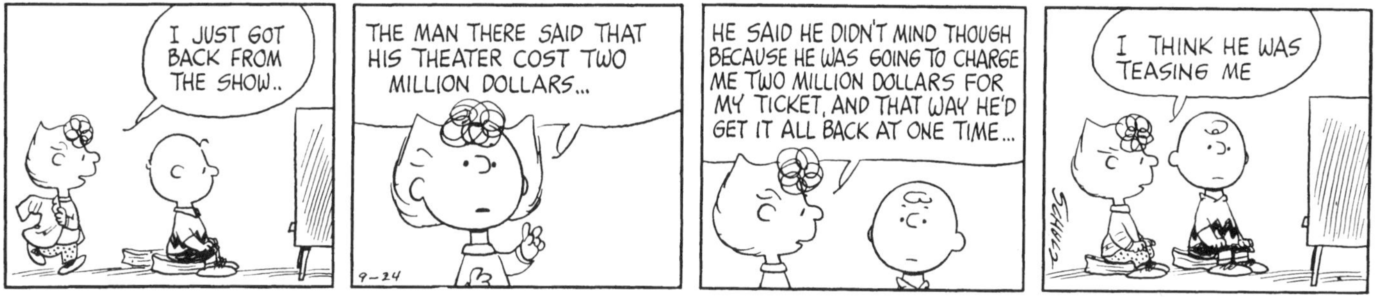
I JUST GOT BACK FROM THE SHOW..
THE MAN THERE SAID THAT HIS THEATER COST TWO MILLION DOLLARS...
9-24
HE SAID HE DIDN'T MIND THOUGH BECAUSE HE WAS GOING TO CHARGE ME TWO MILLION DOLLARS FOR MY TICKET, AND THAT WAY HE'D GET IT ALL BACK AT ONE TIME...
I THINK HE WAS TEASING ME

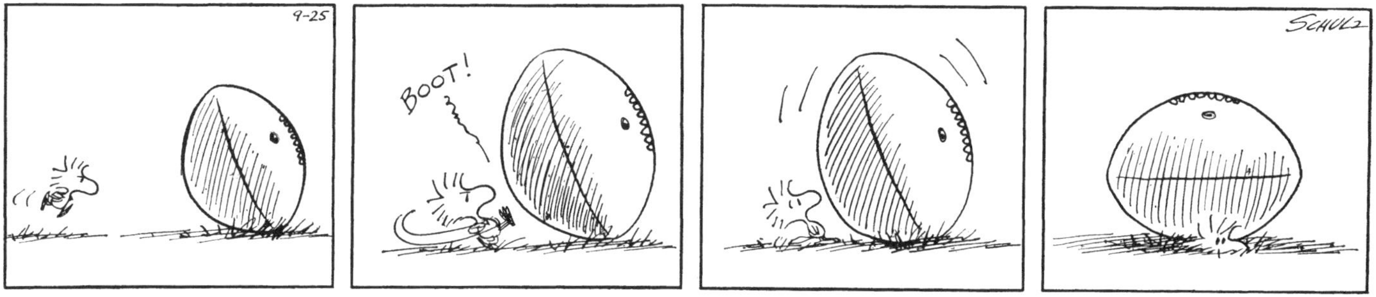
9-25
BOOT!

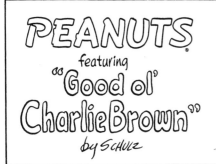

PEANUTS featuring "Good ol' Charlie Brown" by Schulz

CHARLIE BROWNNNNN... ♪♫

I CAN'T BELIEVE IT!

CHARLIE BROWN, I'LL HOLD THE FOOTBALL, AND YOU COME RUNNING UP AND KICK IT...

I CAN'T BELIEVE IT! I CAN'T BELIEVE THAT ANYONE WOULD ACTUALLY THINK I'M THAT STUPID!

BUT YOU DON'T UNDERSTAND, CHARLIE BROWN...I REPRESENT AN ORGANIZATION, AND I'M HOLDING THIS BALL AS A REPRESENTATIVE OF THAT ORGANIZATION

IF SHE REPRESENTS AN ORGANIZATION, THEN I GUESS SHE MUST BE SINCERE...

AAUGH!

WHAK!

THIS YEAR'S FOOTBALL WAS PULLED AWAY FROM YOU THROUGH THE COURTESY OF WOMEN'S LIB!

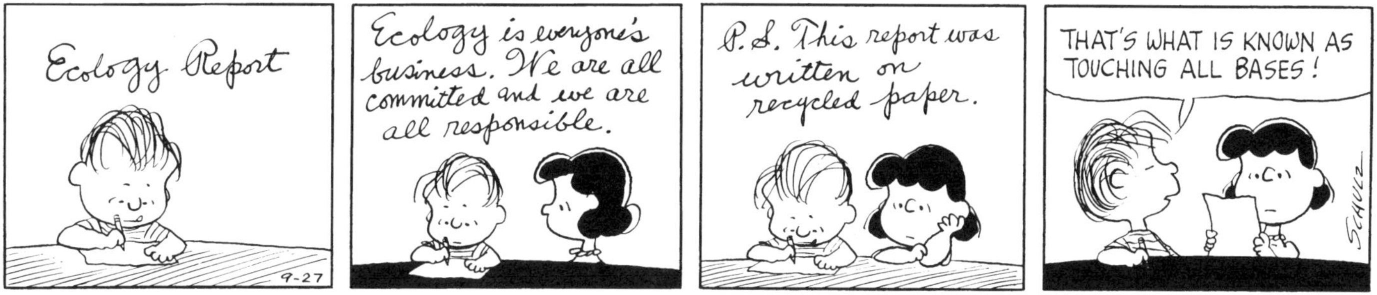
Ecology Report
9-27
Ecology is everyone's business. We are all committed and we are all responsible.
P.S. This report was written on recycled paper.
THAT'S WHAT IS KNOWN AS TOUCHING ALL BASES!
SCHULZ

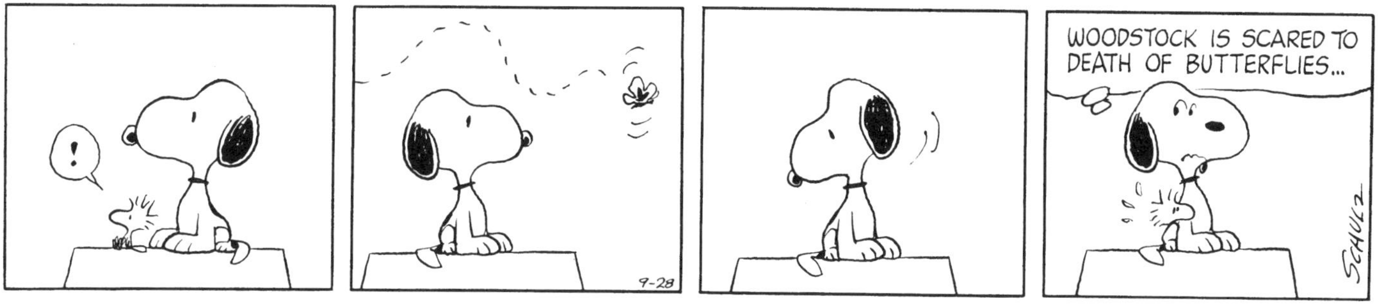
!
9-28
WOODSTOCK IS SCARED TO DEATH OF BUTTERFLIES...
SCHULZ

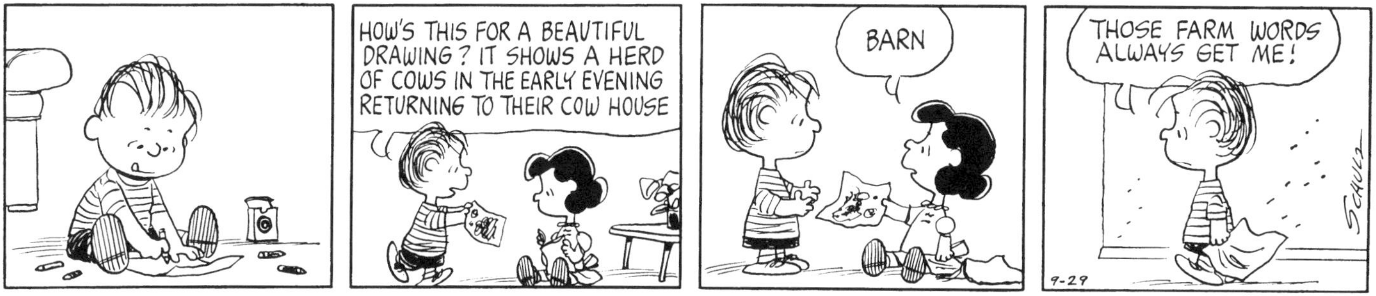
HOW'S THIS FOR A BEAUTIFUL DRAWING? IT SHOWS A HERD OF COWS IN THE EARLY EVENING RETURNING TO THEIR COW HOUSE
BARN
THOSE FARM WORDS ALWAYS GET ME!
9-29
SCHULZ

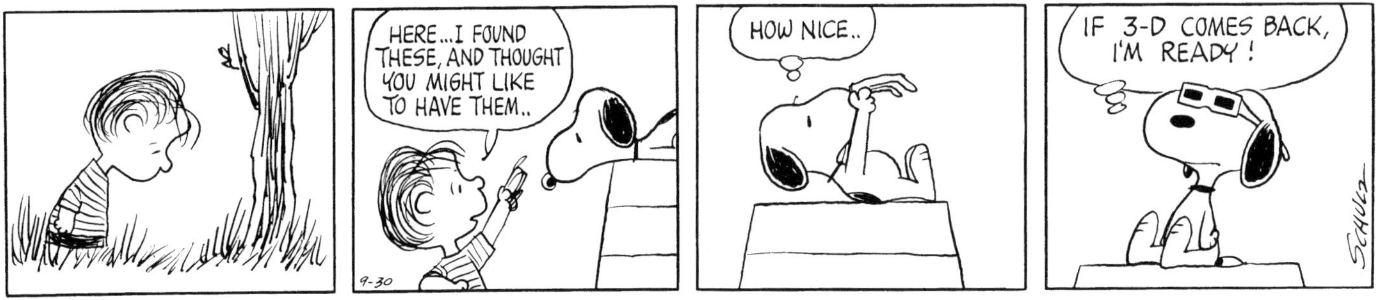
HERE...I FOUND THESE, AND THOUGHT YOU MIGHT LIKE TO HAVE THEM..
9-30
HOW NICE..
IF 3-D COMES BACK, I'M READY!
SCHULZ

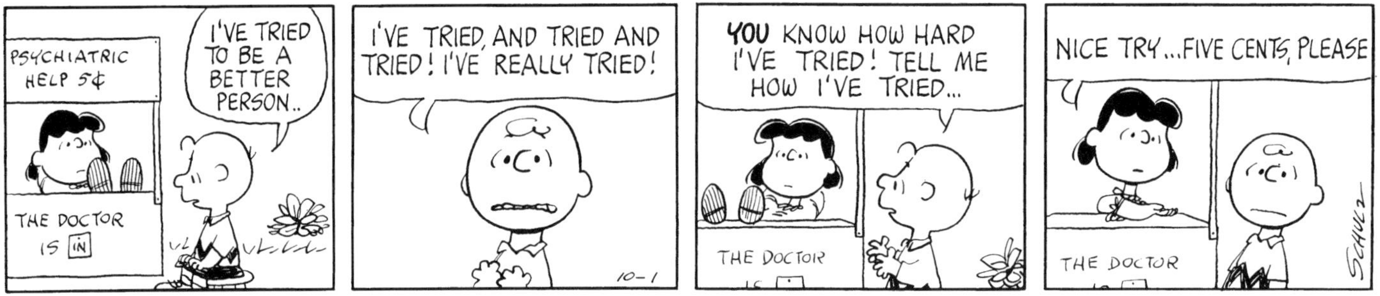
PSYCHIATRIC HELP 5¢
THE DOCTOR IS IN
I'VE TRIED TO BE A BETTER PERSON..
I'VE TRIED, AND TRIED AND TRIED! I'VE REALLY TRIED!
10-1
YOU KNOW HOW HARD I'VE TRIED! TELL ME HOW I'VE TRIED...
THE DOCTOR
NICE TRY...FIVE CENTS, PLEASE
THE DOCTOR
SCHULZ

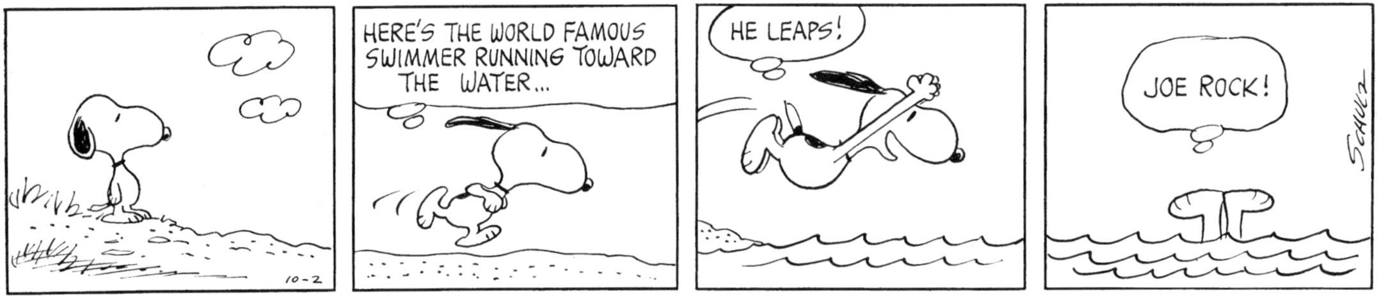
10-2
HERE'S THE WORLD FAMOUS SWIMMER RUNNING TOWARD THE WATER...
HE LEAPS!
JOE ROCK!
SCHULZ

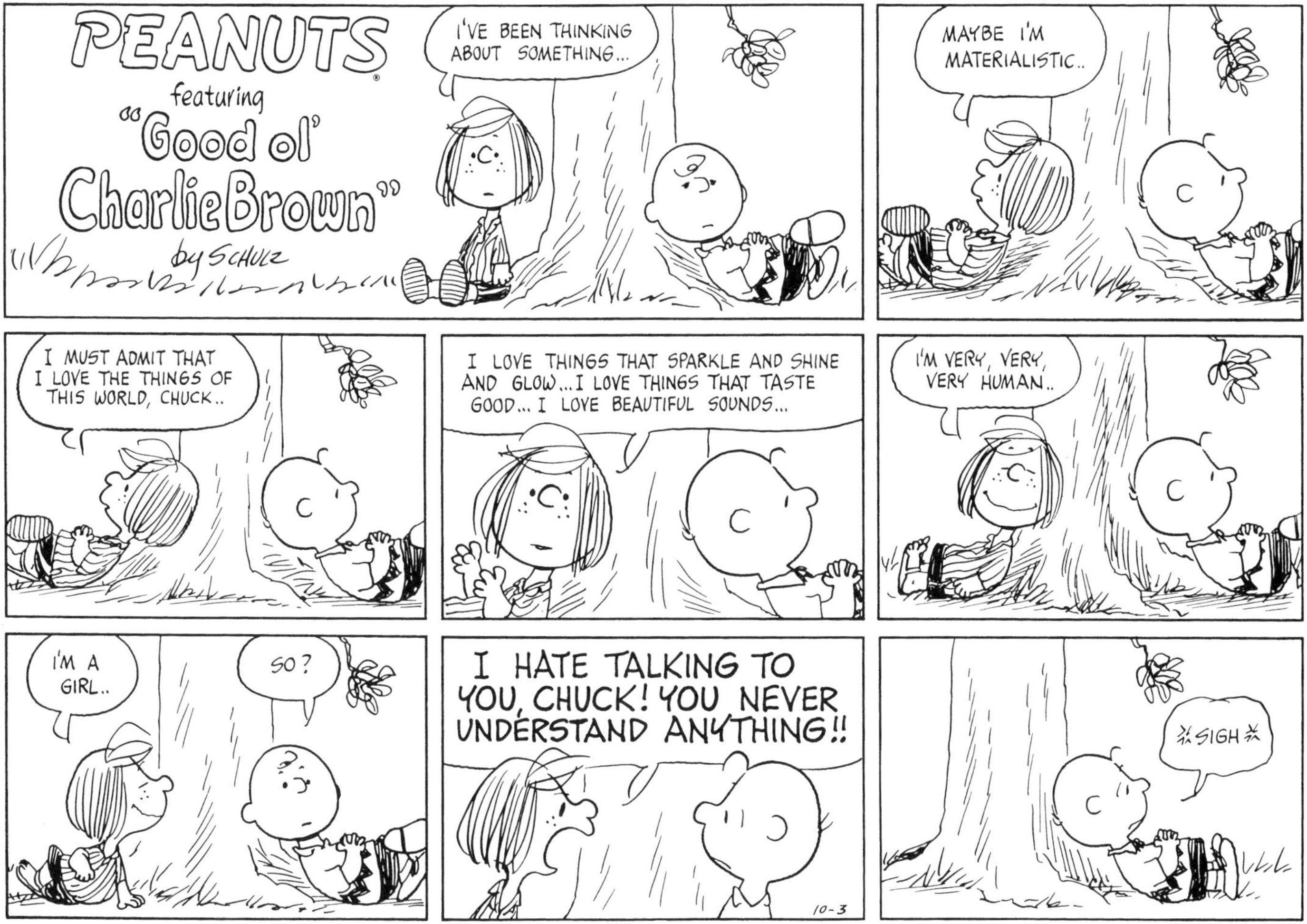
PEANUTS®
featuring "Good ol' Charlie Brown"
by SCHULZ
I'VE BEEN THINKING ABOUT SOMETHING...
MAYBE I'M MATERIALISTIC..
I MUST ADMIT THAT I LOVE THE THINGS OF THIS WORLD, CHUCK..
I LOVE THINGS THAT SPARKLE AND SHINE AND GLOW...I LOVE THINGS THAT TASTE GOOD... I LOVE BEAUTIFUL SOUNDS...
I'M VERY, VERY, VERY HUMAN..
I'M A GIRL..
SO?
I HATE TALKING TO YOU, CHUCK! YOU NEVER UNDERSTAND ANYTHING!!
10-3
SIGH

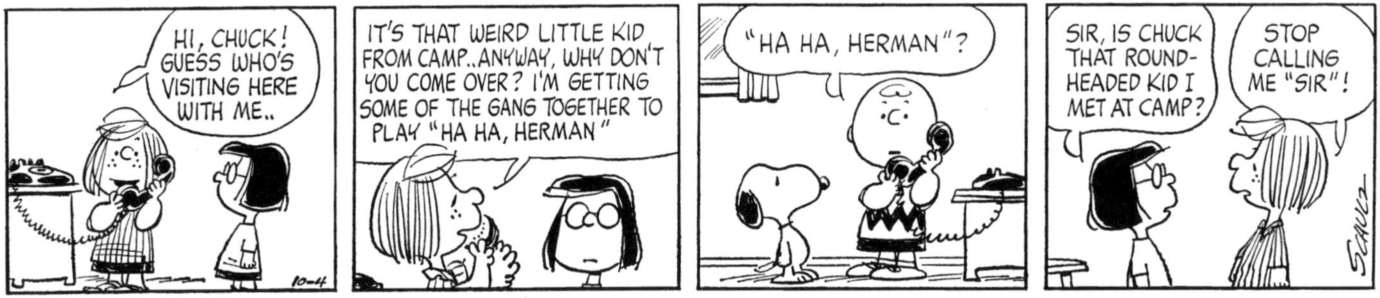
HI, CHUCK! GUESS WHO'S VISITING HERE WITH ME..
IT'S THAT WEIRD LITTLE KID FROM CAMP..ANYWAY, WHY DON'T YOU COME OVER? I'M GETTING SOME OF THE GANG TOGETHER TO PLAY "HA HA, HERMAN"
"HA HA, HERMAN"?
SIR, IS CHUCK THAT ROUND-HEADED KID I MET AT CAMP?
STOP CALLING ME "SIR"!
SCHULZ
10-4

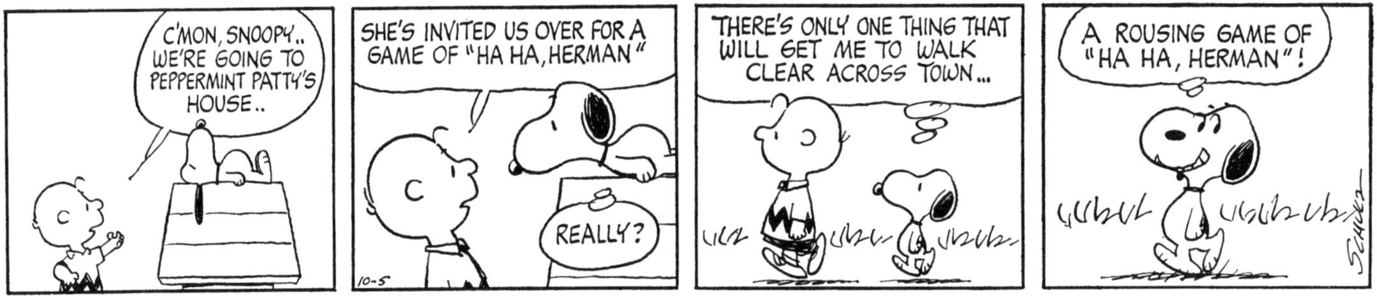
C'MON, SNOOPY.. WE'RE GOING TO PEPPERMINT PATTY'S HOUSE..
SHE'S INVITED US OVER FOR A GAME OF "HA HA, HERMAN"
REALLY?
THERE'S ONLY ONE THING THAT WILL GET ME TO WALK CLEAR ACROSS TOWN...
A ROUSING GAME OF "HA HA, HERMAN"!
SCHULZ
10-5

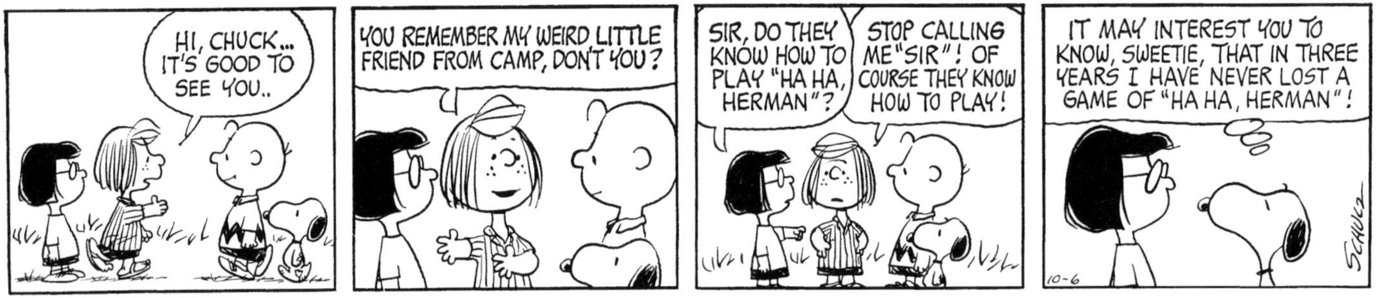
HI, CHUCK... IT'S GOOD TO SEE YOU..
YOU REMEMBER MY WEIRD LITTLE FRIEND FROM CAMP, DON'T YOU?
SIR, DO THEY KNOW HOW TO PLAY "HA HA, HERMAN"?
STOP CALLING ME "SIR"! OF COURSE THEY KNOW HOW TO PLAY!
IT MAY INTEREST YOU TO KNOW, SWEETIE, THAT IN THREE YEARS I HAVE NEVER LOST A GAME OF "HA HA, HERMAN"!
SCHULZ
10-6

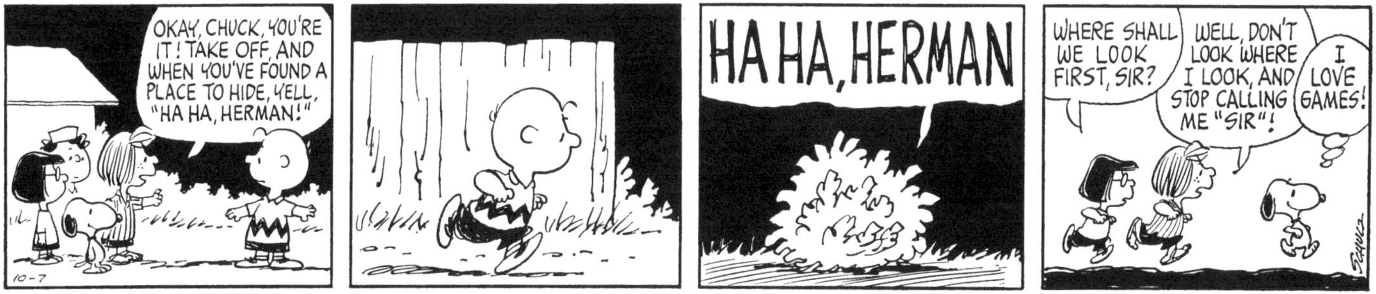
OKAY, CHUCK, YOU'RE IT! TAKE OFF, AND WHEN YOU'VE FOUND A PLACE TO HIDE, YELL, "HA HA, HERMAN!"
10-7
HA HA, HERMAN
WHERE SHALL WE LOOK FIRST, SIR?
WELL, DON'T LOOK WHERE I LOOK, AND STOP CALLING ME "SIR"!
I LOVE GAMES!
SCHULZ

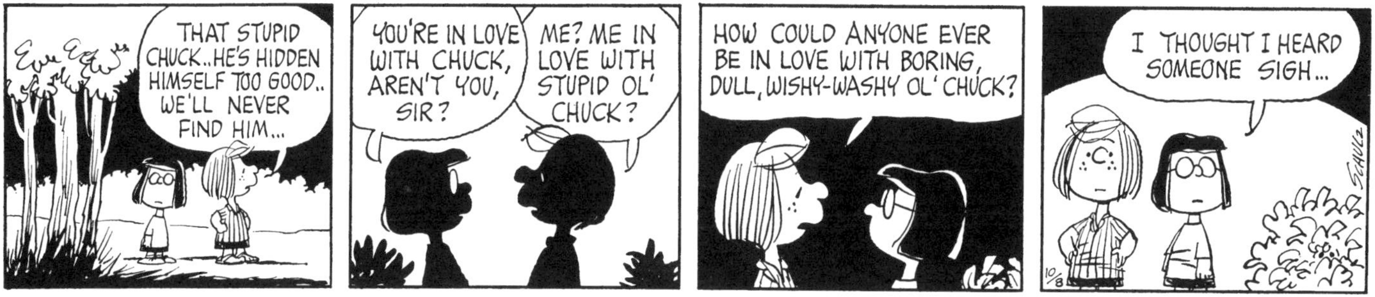
THAT STUPID CHUCK.. HE'S HIDDEN HIMSELF TOO GOOD.. WE'LL NEVER FIND HIM...
YOU'RE IN LOVE WITH CHUCK, AREN'T YOU, SIR?
ME? ME IN LOVE WITH STUPID OL' CHUCK?
HOW COULD ANYONE EVER BE IN LOVE WITH BORING, DULL, WISHY-WASHY OL' CHUCK?
I THOUGHT I HEARD SOMEONE SIGH...
SCHULZ
10/8

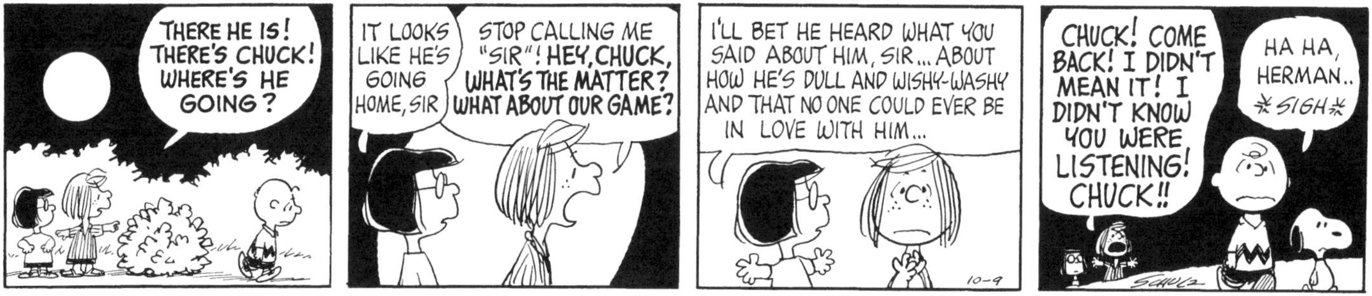
THERE HE IS! THERE'S CHUCK! WHERE'S HE GOING?
IT LOOKS LIKE HE'S GOING HOME, SIR
STOP CALLING ME "SIR"! HEY, CHUCK, WHAT'S THE MATTER? WHAT ABOUT OUR GAME?
I'LL BET HE HEARD WHAT YOU SAID ABOUT HIM, SIR... ABOUT HOW HE'S DULL AND WISHY-WASHY AND THAT NO ONE COULD EVER BE IN LOVE WITH HIM...
10-9
CHUCK! COME BACK! I DIDN'T MEAN IT! I DIDN'T KNOW YOU WERE LISTENING! CHUCK!!
HA HA, HERMAN..
SIGH
SCHULZ

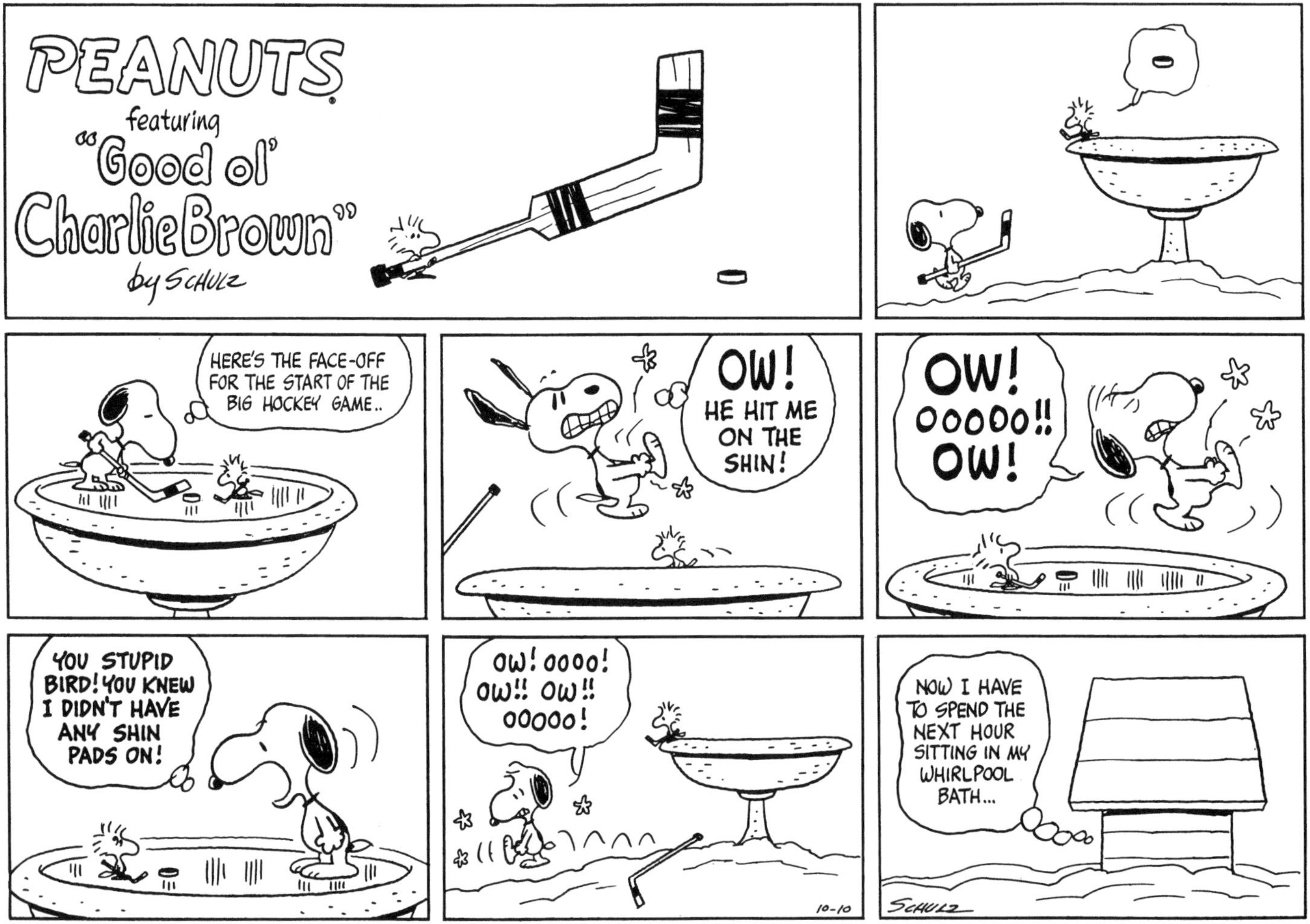
PEANUTS
featuring
"Good ol' Charlie Brown"
by SCHULZ
HERE'S THE FACE-OFF FOR THE START OF THE BIG HOCKEY GAME..
OW! HE HIT ME ON THE SHIN!
OW! OOOOO!! OW!
YOU STUPID BIRD! YOU KNEW I DIDN'T HAVE ANY SHIN PADS ON!
OW! OOOO! OW!! OW!! OOOOO!
10-10
NOW I HAVE TO SPEND THE NEXT HOUR SITTING IN MY WHIRLPOOL BATH...
SCHULZ

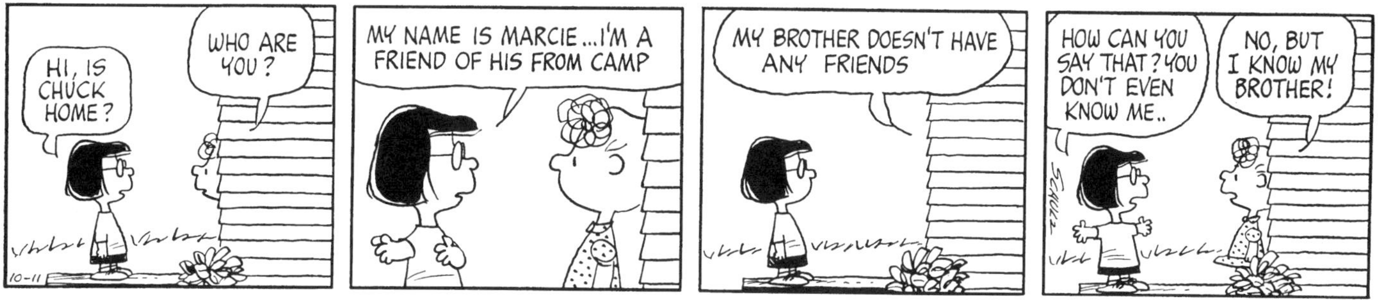
HI, IS CHUCK HOME ?
WHO ARE YOU ?
MY NAME IS MARCIE...I'M A FRIEND OF HIS FROM CAMP
MY BROTHER DOESN'T HAVE ANY FRIENDS
HOW CAN YOU SAY THAT ? YOU DON'T EVEN KNOW ME..
NO, BUT I KNOW MY BROTHER !

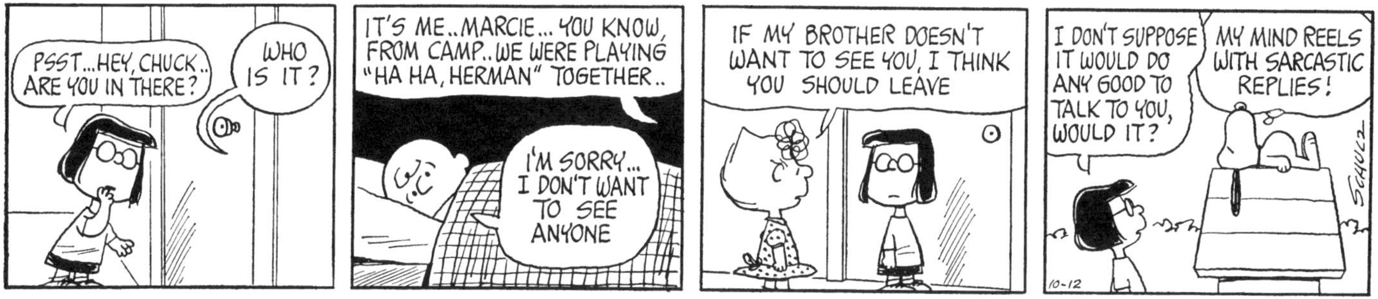
PSST...HEY, CHUCK.. ARE YOU IN THERE ?
WHO IS IT ?
IT'S ME..MARCIE... YOU KNOW, FROM CAMP..WE WERE PLAYING "HA HA, HERMAN" TOGETHER..
I'M SORRY... I DON'T WANT TO SEE ANYONE
IF MY BROTHER DOESN'T WANT TO SEE YOU, I THINK YOU SHOULD LEAVE
I DON'T SUPPOSE IT WOULD DO ANY GOOD TO TALK TO YOU, WOULD IT ?
MY MIND REELS WITH SARCASTIC REPLIES !

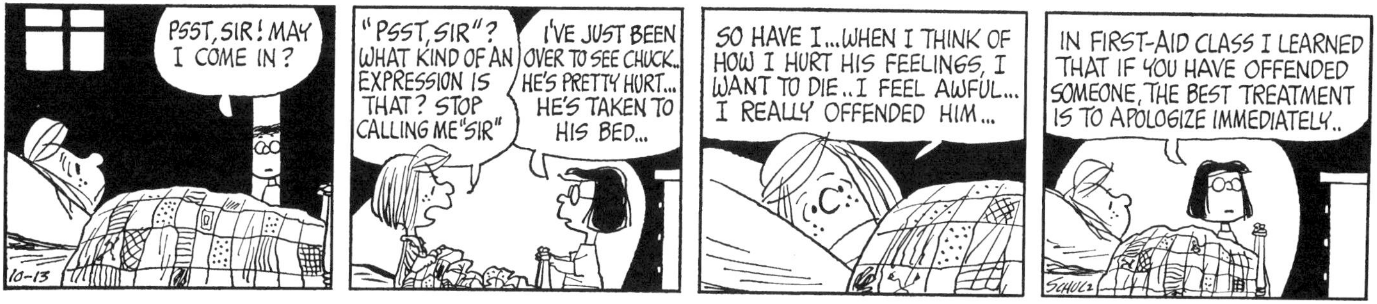
PSST, SIR ! MAY I COME IN ?
"PSST, SIR" ? WHAT KIND OF AN EXPRESSION IS THAT ? STOP CALLING ME "SIR"
I'VE JUST BEEN OVER TO SEE CHUCK.. HE'S PRETTY HURT... HE'S TAKEN TO HIS BED...
SO HAVE I...WHEN I THINK OF HOW I HURT HIS FEELINGS, I WANT TO DIE..I FEEL AWFUL... I REALLY OFFENDED HIM...
IN FIRST-AID CLASS I LEARNED THAT IF YOU HAVE OFFENDED SOMEONE, THE BEST TREATMENT IS TO APOLOGIZE IMMEDIATELY..

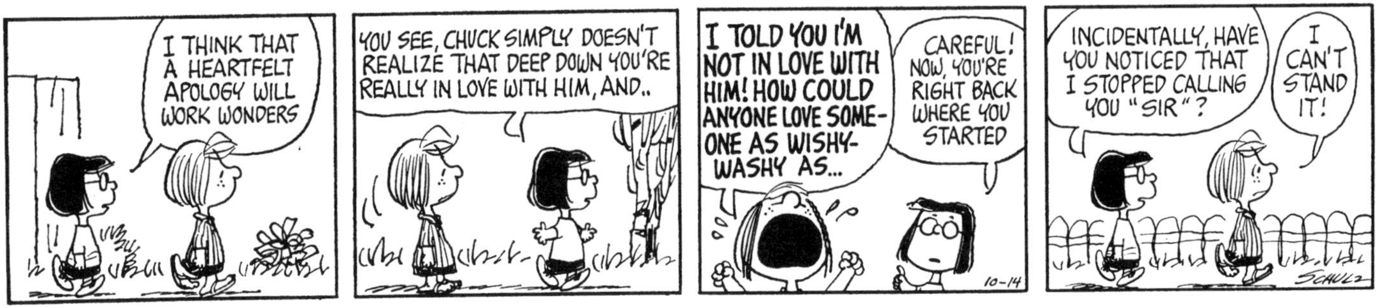
I THINK THAT A HEARTFELT APOLOGY WILL WORK WONDERS
YOU SEE, CHUCK SIMPLY DOESN'T REALIZE THAT DEEP DOWN YOU'RE REALLY IN LOVE WITH HIM, AND..
I TOLD YOU I'M NOT IN LOVE WITH HIM! HOW COULD ANYONE LOVE SOMEONE AS WISHY-WASHY AS...
CAREFUL! NOW, YOU'RE RIGHT BACK WHERE YOU STARTED
10-14
INCIDENTALLY, HAVE YOU NOTICED THAT I STOPPED CALLING YOU "SIR"?
I CAN'T STAND IT!
SCHULZ

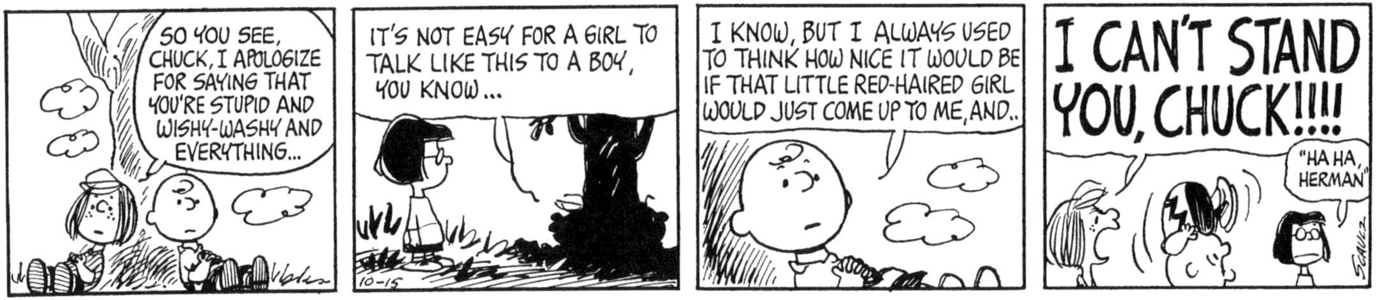
SO YOU SEE, CHUCK, I APOLOGIZE FOR SAYING THAT YOU'RE STUPID AND WISHY-WASHY AND EVERYTHING...
IT'S NOT EASY FOR A GIRL TO TALK LIKE THIS TO A BOY, YOU KNOW...
10-15
I KNOW, BUT I ALWAYS USED TO THINK HOW NICE IT WOULD BE IF THAT LITTLE RED-HAIRED GIRL WOULD JUST COME UP TO ME, AND..
I CAN'T STAND YOU, CHUCK!!!!
"HA HA, HERMAN"
SCHULZ

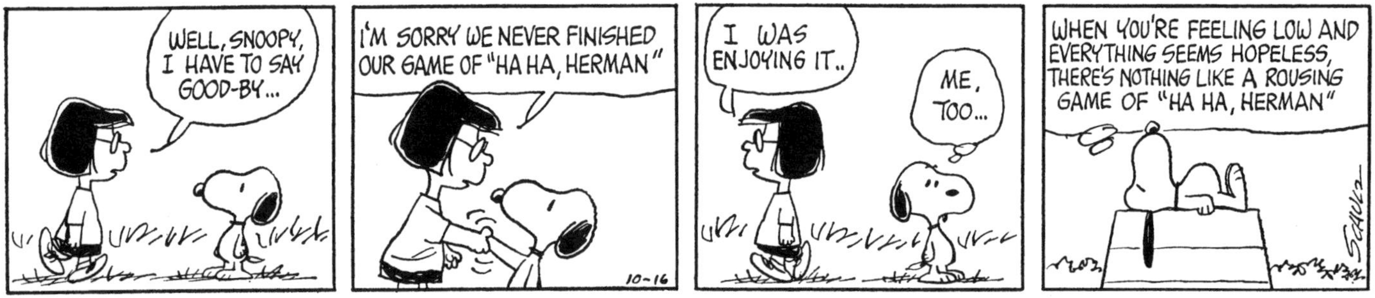
WELL, SNOOPY, I HAVE TO SAY GOOD-BY...
I'M SORRY WE NEVER FINISHED OUR GAME OF "HA HA, HERMAN"
10-16
I WAS ENJOYING IT..
ME, TOO...
WHEN YOU'RE FEELING LOW AND EVERYTHING SEEMS HOPELESS, THERE'S NOTHING LIKE A ROUSING GAME OF "HA HA, HERMAN"
SCHULZ

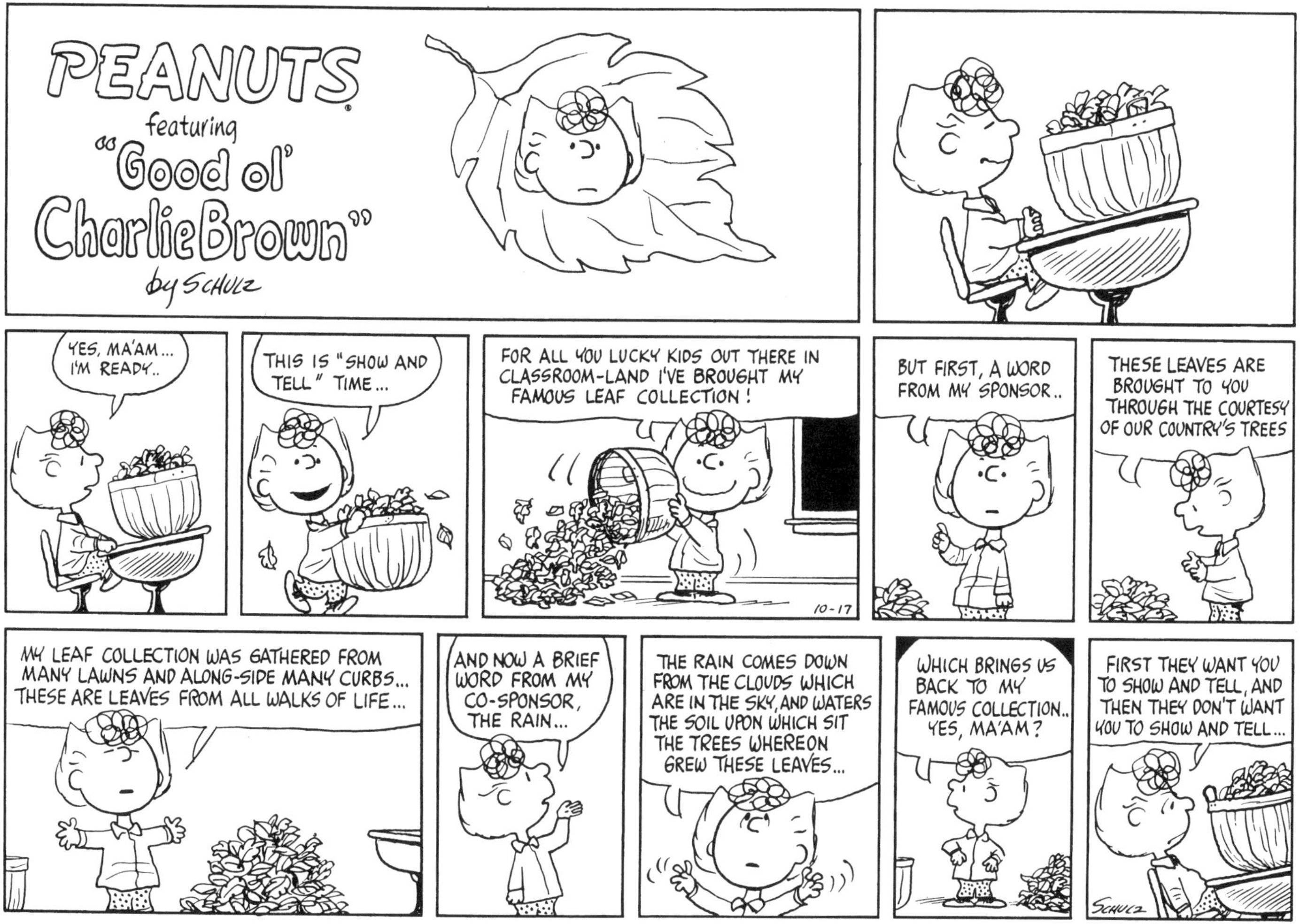
PEANUTS
featuring
"Good ol' Charlie Brown"
by SCHULZ
YES, MA'AM... I'M READY..
THIS IS "SHOW AND TELL" TIME...
FOR ALL YOU LUCKY KIDS OUT THERE IN CLASSROOM-LAND I'VE BROUGHT MY FAMOUS LEAF COLLECTION!
10-17
BUT FIRST, A WORD FROM MY SPONSOR..
THESE LEAVES ARE BROUGHT TO YOU THROUGH THE COURTESY OF OUR COUNTRY'S TREES
MY LEAF COLLECTION WAS GATHERED FROM MANY LAWNS AND ALONG-SIDE MANY CURBS... THESE ARE LEAVES FROM ALL WALKS OF LIFE...
AND NOW A BRIEF WORD FROM MY CO-SPONSOR, THE RAIN...
THE RAIN COMES DOWN FROM THE CLOUDS WHICH ARE IN THE SKY, AND WATERS THE SOIL UPON WHICH SIT THE TREES WHEREON GREW THESE LEAVES...
WHICH BRINGS US BACK TO MY FAMOUS COLLECTION.. YES, MA'AM?
FIRST THEY WANT YOU TO SHOW AND TELL, AND THEN THEY DON'T WANT YOU TO SHOW AND TELL...
SCHULZ

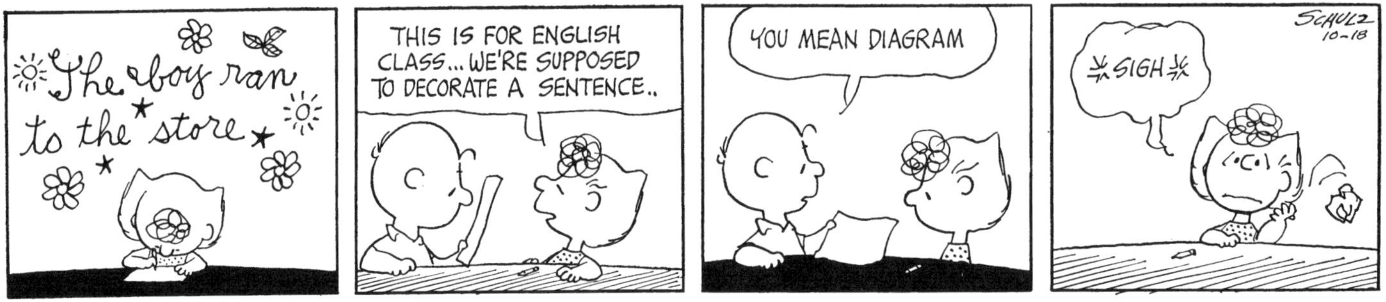
The boy ran to the store
THIS IS FOR ENGLISH CLASS... WE'RE SUPPOSED TO DECORATE A SENTENCE..
YOU MEAN DIAGRAM
SIGH
SCHULZ 10-18

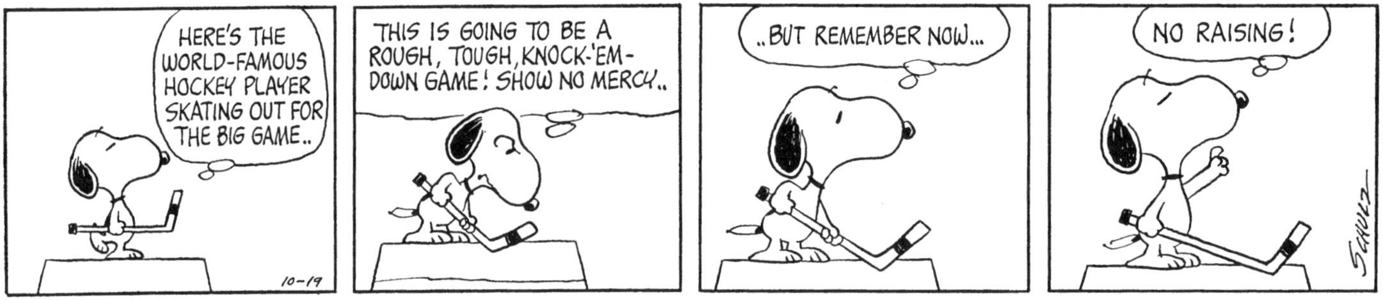
HERE'S THE WORLD-FAMOUS HOCKEY PLAYER SKATING OUT FOR THE BIG GAME..
10-19
THIS IS GOING TO BE A ROUGH, TOUGH, KNOCK-'EM-DOWN GAME! SHOW NO MERCY..
..BUT REMEMBER NOW...
NO RAISING!
SCHULZ

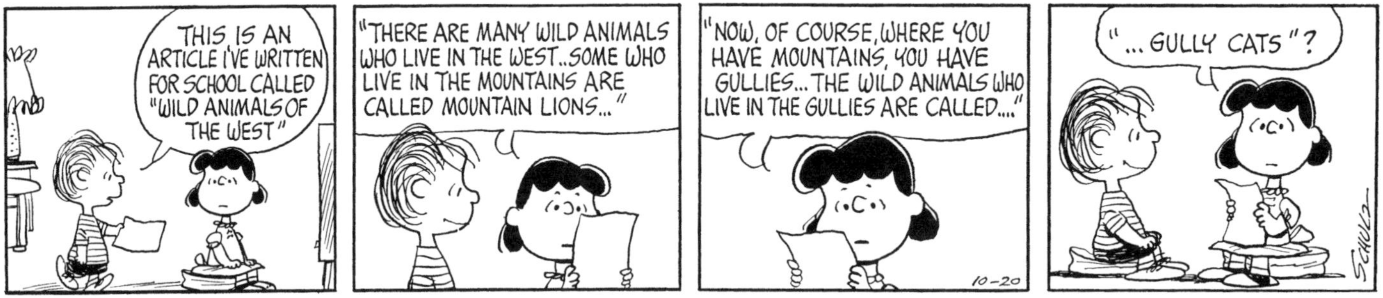
THIS IS AN ARTICLE I'VE WRITTEN FOR SCHOOL CALLED "WILD ANIMALS OF THE WEST"
"THERE ARE MANY WILD ANIMALS WHO LIVE IN THE WEST..SOME WHO LIVE IN THE MOUNTAINS ARE CALLED MOUNTAIN LIONS..."
"NOW, OF COURSE, WHERE YOU HAVE MOUNTAINS, YOU HAVE GULLIES... THE WILD ANIMALS WHO LIVE IN THE GULLIES ARE CALLED...."
10-20
"... GULLY CATS"?
SCHULZ

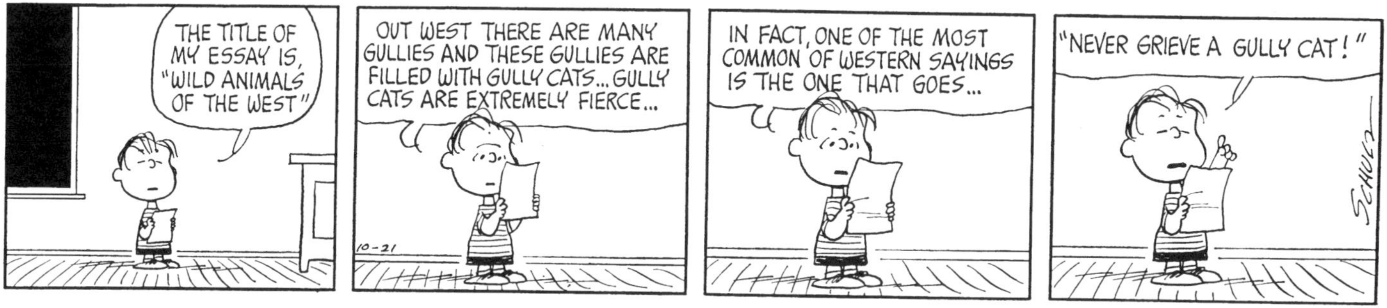
THE TITLE OF MY ESSAY IS, "WILD ANIMALS OF THE WEST"
OUT WEST THERE ARE MANY GULLIES AND THESE GULLIES ARE FILLED WITH GULLY CATS... GULLY CATS ARE EXTREMELY FIERCE...
10-21
IN FACT, ONE OF THE MOST COMMON OF WESTERN SAYINGS IS THE ONE THAT GOES...
"NEVER GRIEVE A GULLY CAT!"
SCHULZ

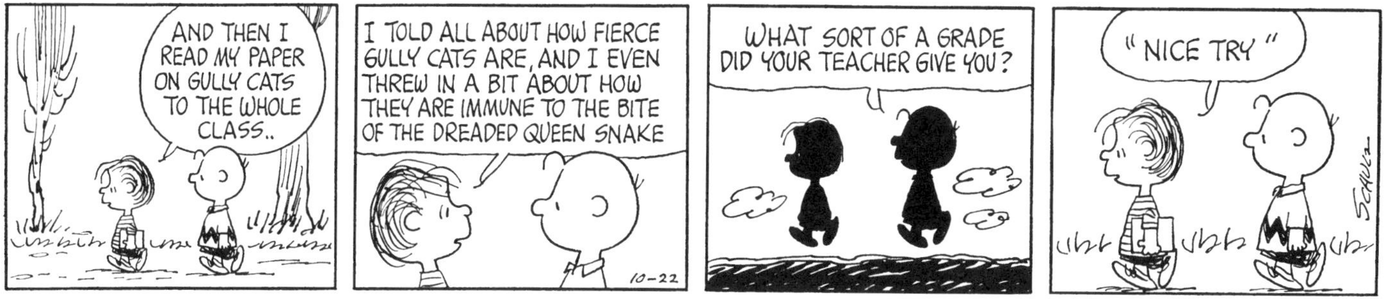
AND THEN I READ MY PAPER ON GULLY CATS TO THE WHOLE CLASS..
I TOLD ALL ABOUT HOW FIERCE GULLY CATS ARE, AND I EVEN THREW IN A BIT ABOUT HOW THEY ARE IMMUNE TO THE BITE OF THE DREADED QUEEN SNAKE
10-22
WHAT SORT OF A GRADE DID YOUR TEACHER GIVE YOU?
"NICE TRY"
SCHULZ

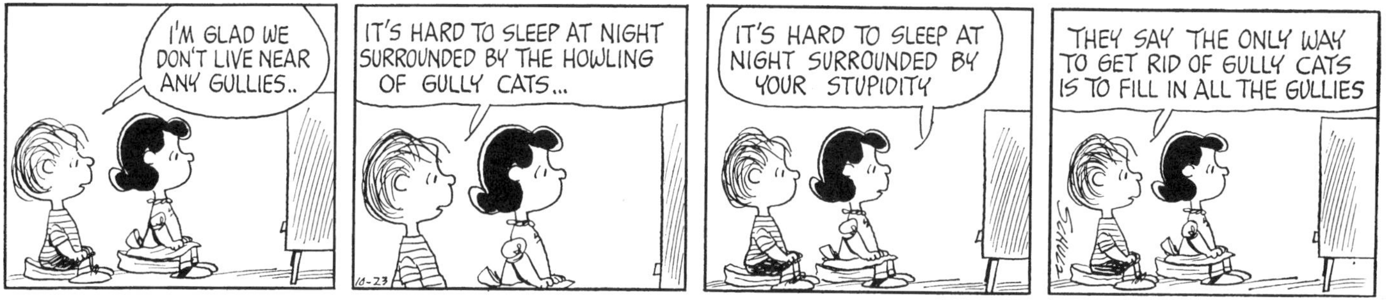
I'M GLAD WE DON'T LIVE NEAR ANY GULLIES..
IT'S HARD TO SLEEP AT NIGHT SURROUNDED BY THE HOWLING OF GULLY CATS...
10-23
IT'S HARD TO SLEEP AT NIGHT SURROUNDED BY YOUR STUPIDITY
THEY SAY THE ONLY WAY TO GET RID OF GULLY CATS IS TO FILL IN ALL THE GULLIES
SCHULZ

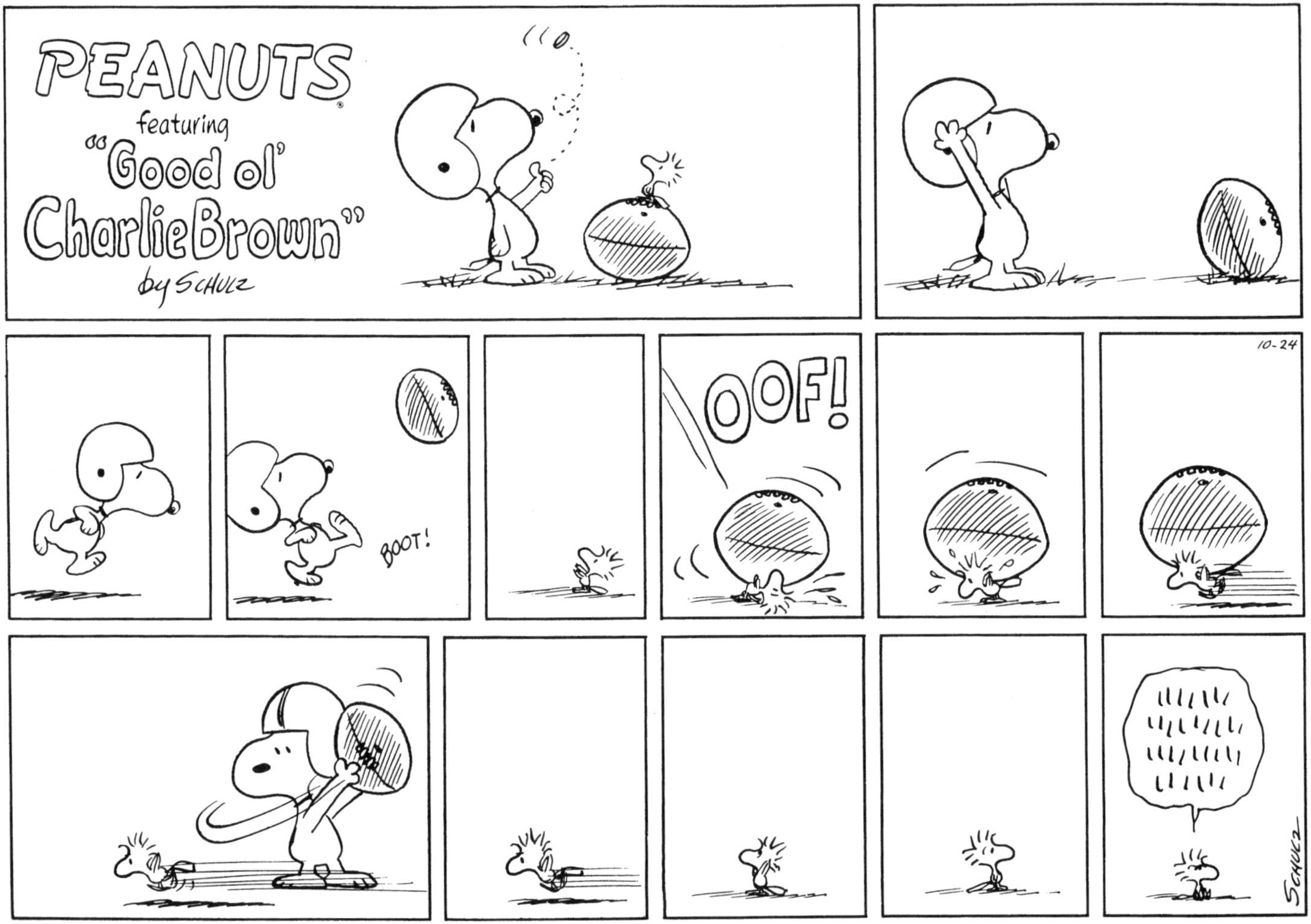
PEANUTS
featuring
"Good ol' Charlie Brown"
by SCHULZ
BOOT!
OOF!
10-24
SCHULZ

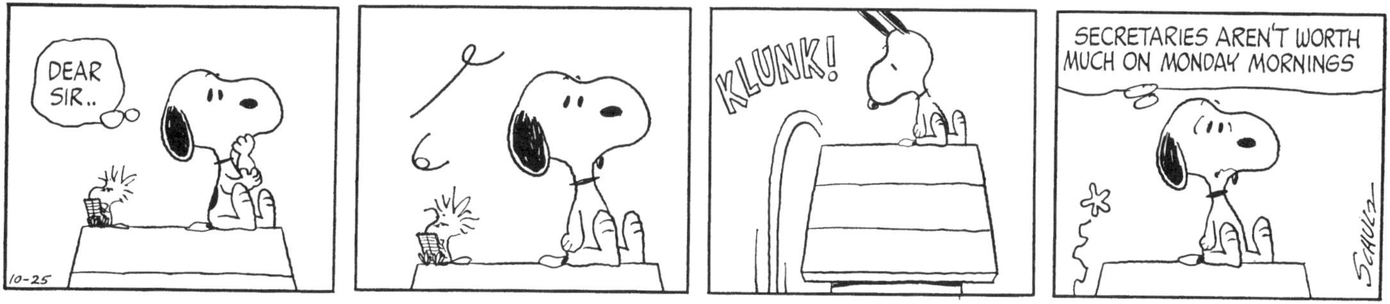
DEAR SIR..
10-25
KLUNK!
SECRETARIES AREN'T WORTH MUCH ON MONDAY MORNINGS
SCHULZ

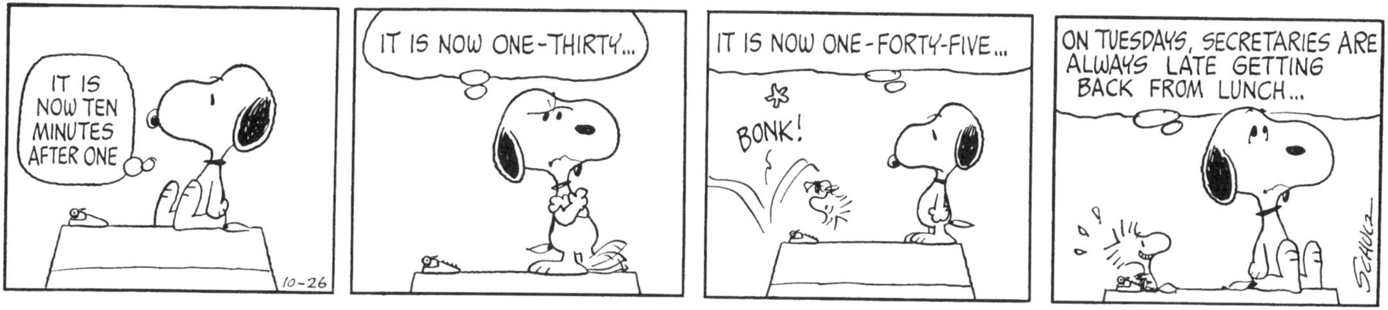
IT IS NOW TEN MINUTES AFTER ONE
10-26
IT IS NOW ONE-THIRTY...
IT IS NOW ONE-FORTY-FIVE...
BONK!
ON TUESDAYS, SECRETARIES ARE ALWAYS LATE GETTING BACK FROM LUNCH...
SCHULZ

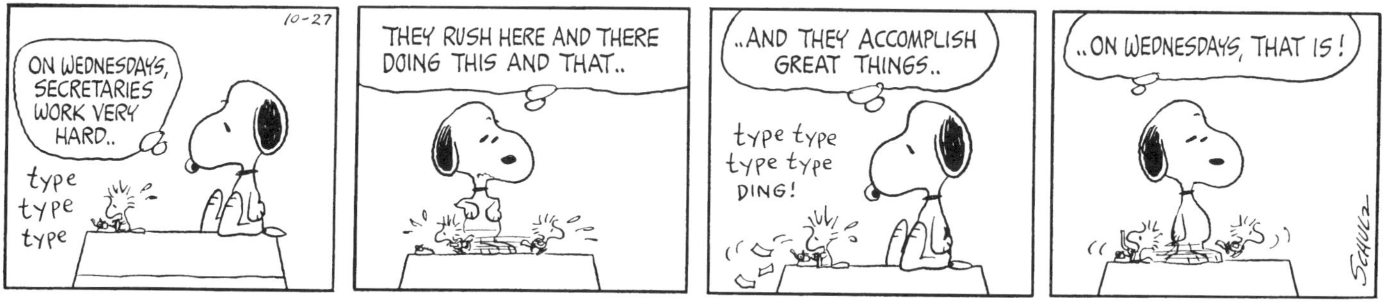
10-27
ON WEDNESDAYS, SECRETARIES WORK VERY HARD..
type type type
THEY RUSH HERE AND THERE DOING THIS AND THAT..
..AND THEY ACCOMPLISH GREAT THINGS..
type type type type DING!
..ON WEDNESDAYS, THAT IS!
SCHULZ

TELEPHONE!

I'LL BET I KNOW WHAT IT IS..

I KNEW IT..

102°

ON THURSDAYS, SECRETARIES ALWAYS CALL IN SICK..

10-28

type type type DING! type type type type DING!

ZIP! BANG! RATTLE RATTLE! type type type type DING!

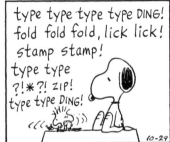

type type type type DING! fold fold fold, lick lick! stamp stamp! type type ?!*?! ZIP! type type DING!

10-29

ON FRIDAY AFTERNOONS AT FOUR O'CLOCK, SECRETARIES MAKE A LOT OF NOISE!

ZOOM!

Z

10-30

Z

AND ON SATURDAYS, SECRETARIES SLEEP 'TIL NOON!

Z

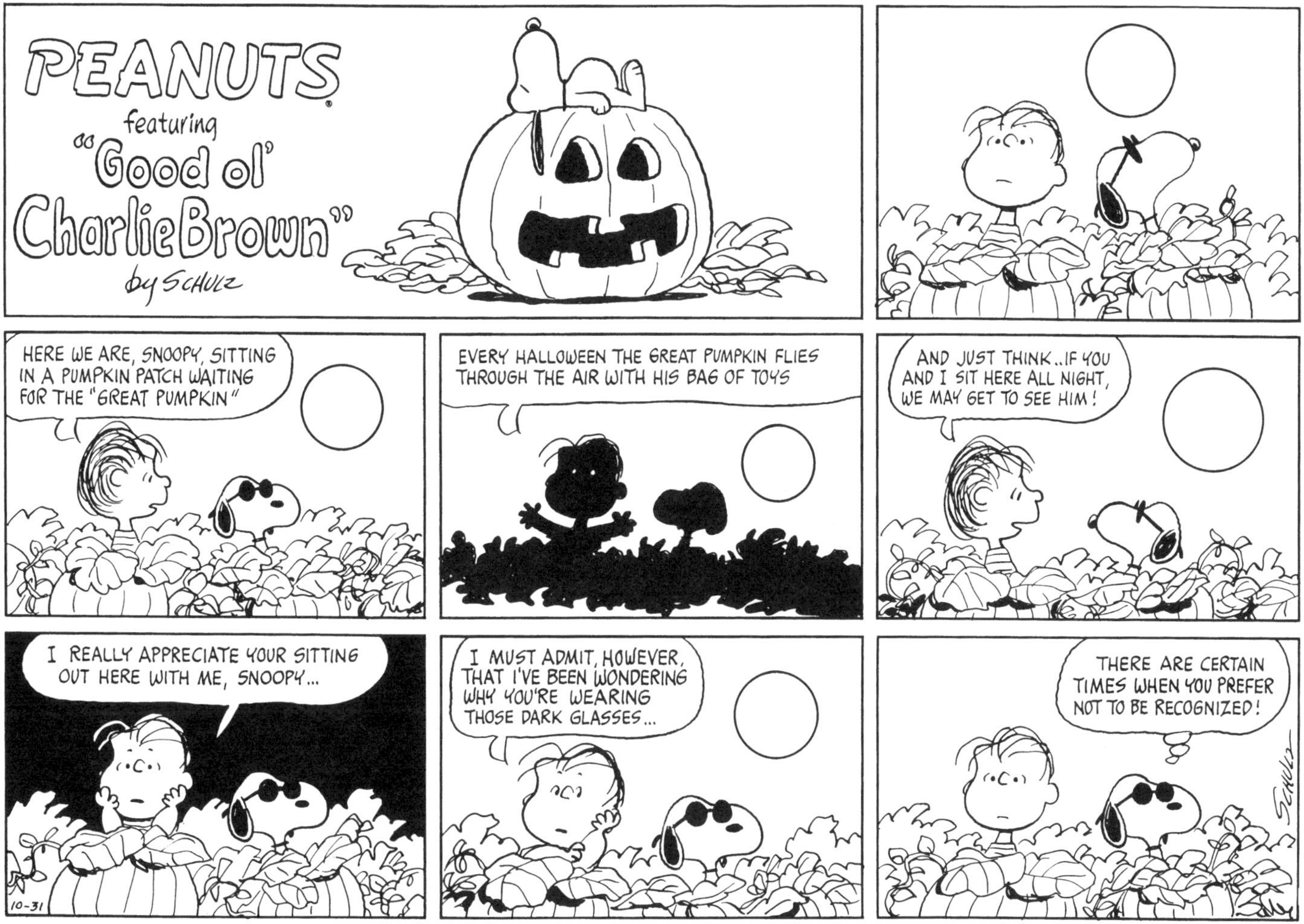
PEANUTS
featuring "Good ol' Charlie Brown"
by SCHULZ
HERE WE ARE, SNOOPY, SITTING IN A PUMPKIN PATCH WAITING FOR THE "GREAT PUMPKIN"
EVERY HALLOWEEN THE GREAT PUMPKIN FLIES THROUGH THE AIR WITH HIS BAG OF TOYS
AND JUST THINK..IF YOU AND I SIT HERE ALL NIGHT, WE MAY GET TO SEE HIM!
I REALLY APPRECIATE YOUR SITTING OUT HERE WITH ME, SNOOPY...
10-31
I MUST ADMIT, HOWEVER, THAT I'VE BEEN WONDERING WHY YOU'RE WEARING THOSE DARK GLASSES...
THERE ARE CERTAIN TIMES WHEN YOU PREFER NOT TO BE RECOGNIZED!
SCHULZ

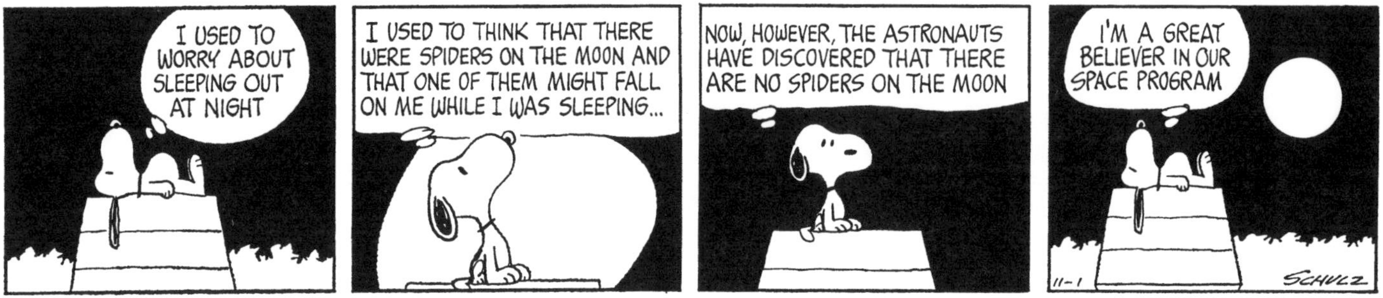
I USED TO WORRY ABOUT SLEEPING OUT AT NIGHT
I USED TO THINK THAT THERE WERE SPIDERS ON THE MOON AND THAT ONE OF THEM MIGHT FALL ON ME WHILE I WAS SLEEPING...
NOW, HOWEVER, THE ASTRONAUTS HAVE DISCOVERED THAT THERE ARE NO SPIDERS ON THE MOON
I'M A GREAT BELIEVER IN OUR SPACE PROGRAM
11-1
SCHULZ

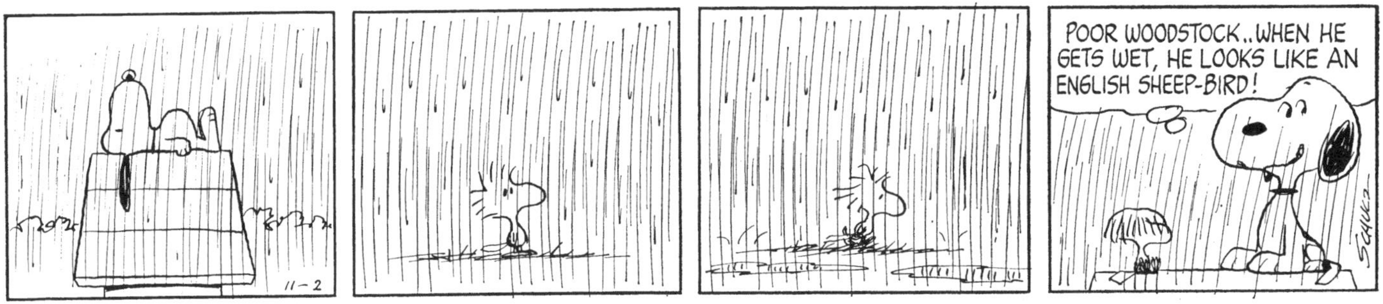
11-2
POOR WOODSTOCK..WHEN HE GETS WET, HE LOOKS LIKE AN ENGLISH SHEEP-BIRD!
SCHULZ

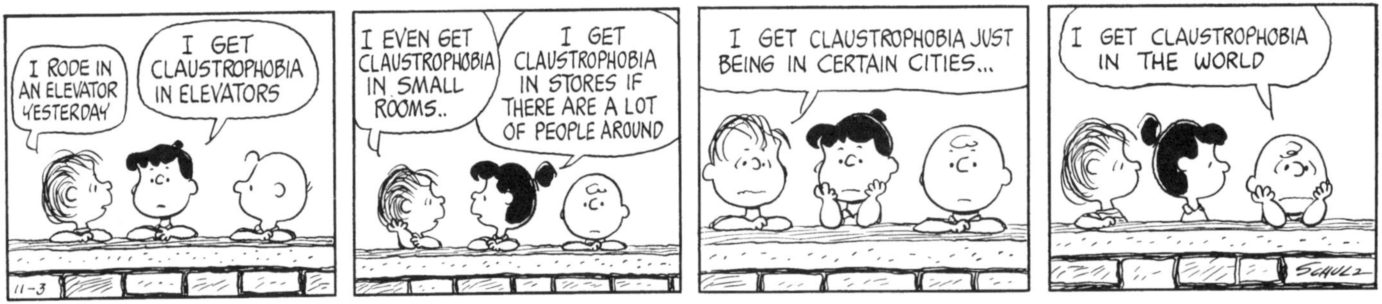
I RODE IN AN ELEVATOR YESTERDAY
I GET CLAUSTROPHOBIA IN ELEVATORS
I EVEN GET CLAUSTROPHOBIA IN SMALL ROOMS..
I GET CLAUSTROPHOBIA IN STORES IF THERE ARE A LOT OF PEOPLE AROUND
I GET CLAUSTROPHOBIA JUST BEING IN CERTAIN CITIES...
I GET CLAUSTROPHOBIA IN THE WORLD
11-3
SCHULZ

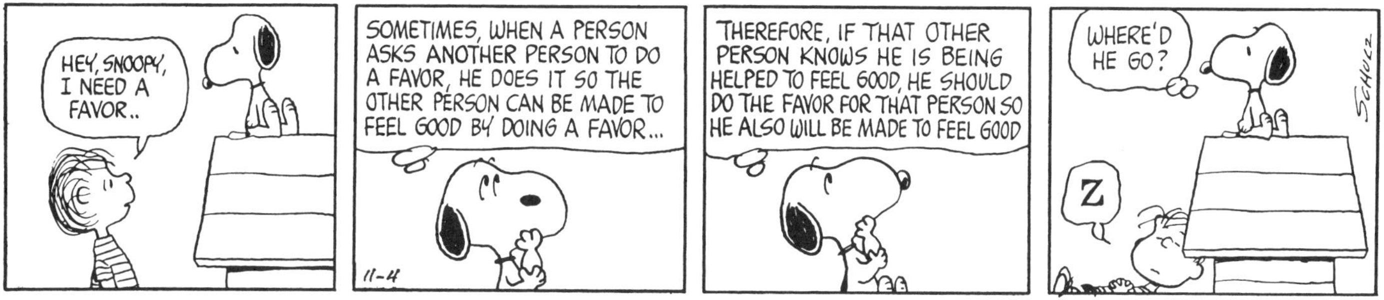
HEY, SNOOPY, I NEED A FAVOR..
SOMETIMES, WHEN A PERSON ASKS ANOTHER PERSON TO DO A FAVOR, HE DOES IT SO THE OTHER PERSON CAN BE MADE TO FEEL GOOD BY DOING A FAVOR...
11-4
THEREFORE, IF THAT OTHER PERSON KNOWS HE IS BEING HELPED TO FEEL GOOD, HE SHOULD DO THE FAVOR FOR THAT PERSON SO HE ALSO WILL BE MADE TO FEEL GOOD
WHERE'D HE GO?
Z

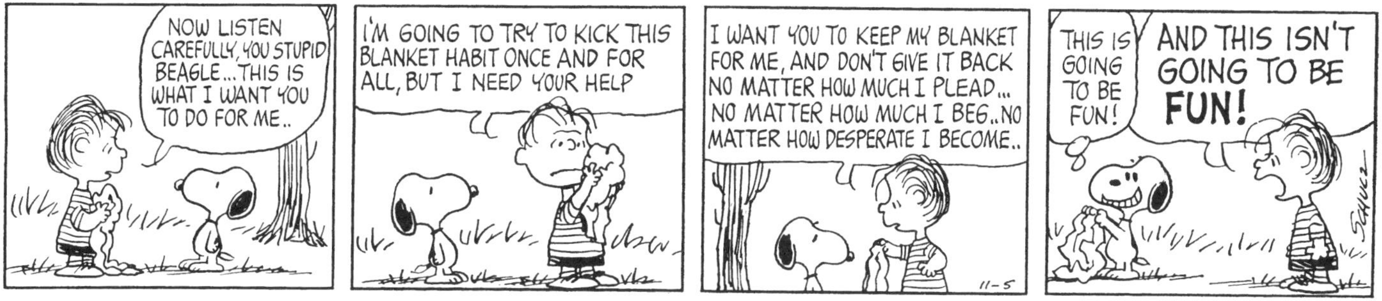
NOW LISTEN CAREFULLY, YOU STUPID BEAGLE...THIS IS WHAT I WANT YOU TO DO FOR ME..
I'M GOING TO TRY TO KICK THIS BLANKET HABIT ONCE AND FOR ALL, BUT I NEED YOUR HELP
I WANT YOU TO KEEP MY BLANKET FOR ME, AND DON'T GIVE IT BACK NO MATTER HOW MUCH I PLEAD... NO MATTER HOW MUCH I BEG..NO MATTER HOW DESPERATE I BECOME..
11-5
THIS IS GOING TO BE FUN!
AND THIS ISN'T GOING TO BE FUN!

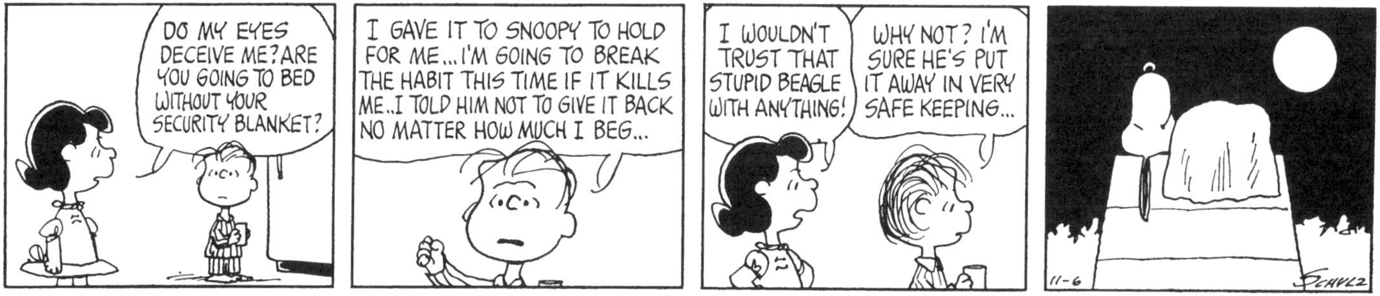
DO MY EYES DECEIVE ME? ARE YOU GOING TO BED WITHOUT YOUR SECURITY BLANKET?
I GAVE IT TO SNOOPY TO HOLD FOR ME... I'M GOING TO BREAK THE HABIT THIS TIME IF IT KILLS ME..I TOLD HIM NOT TO GIVE IT BACK NO MATTER HOW MUCH I BEG...
I WOULDN'T TRUST THAT STUPID BEAGLE WITH ANYTHING!
WHY NOT? I'M SURE HE'S PUT IT AWAY IN VERY SAFE KEEPING...
11-6

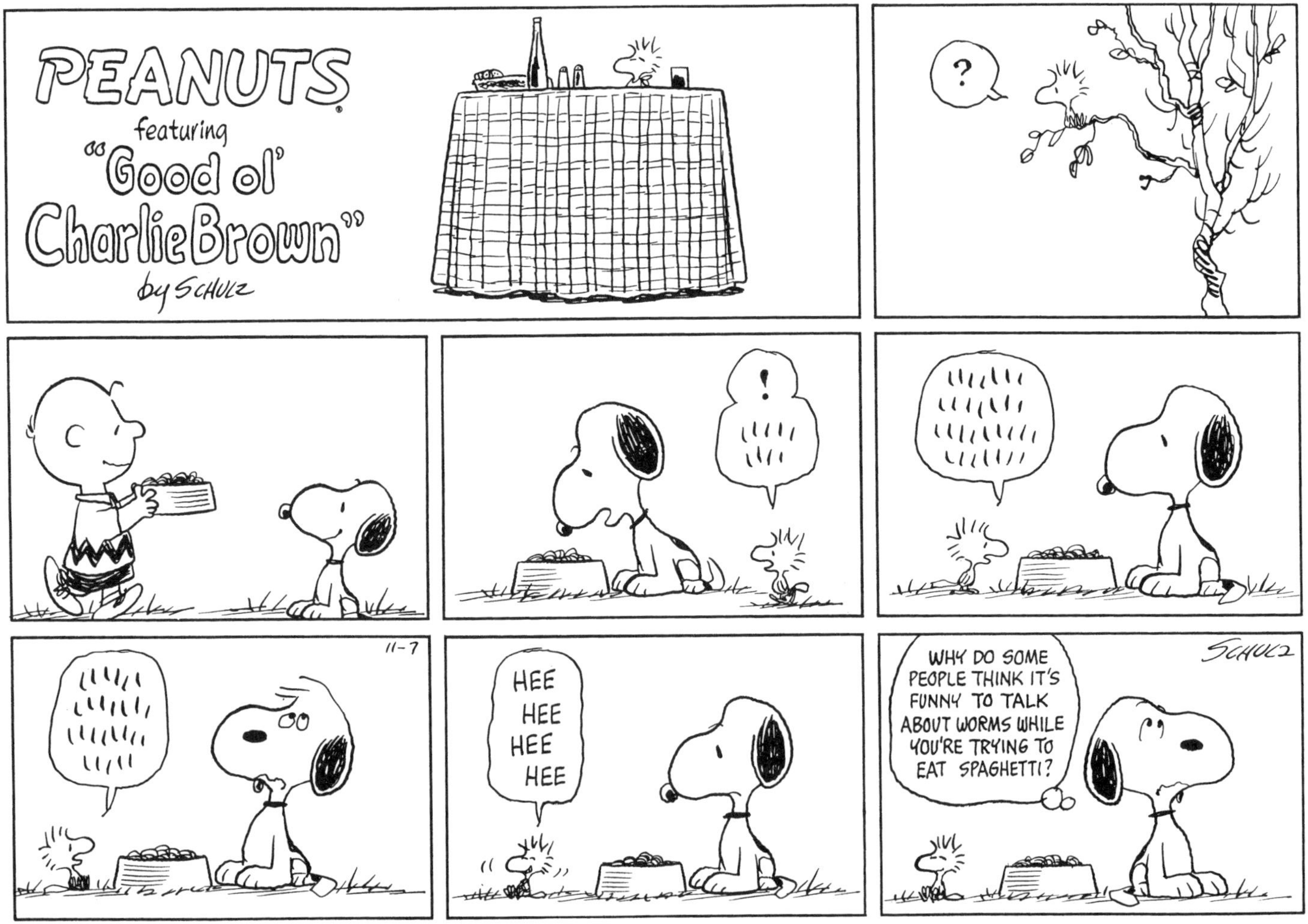
PEANUTS
featuring
"Good ol' Charlie Brown"
by SCHULZ
?
!
11-7
HEE
HEE
HEE
HEE
SCHULZ
WHY DO SOME PEOPLE THINK IT'S FUNNY TO TALK ABOUT WORMS WHILE YOU'RE TRYING TO EAT SPAGHETTI?

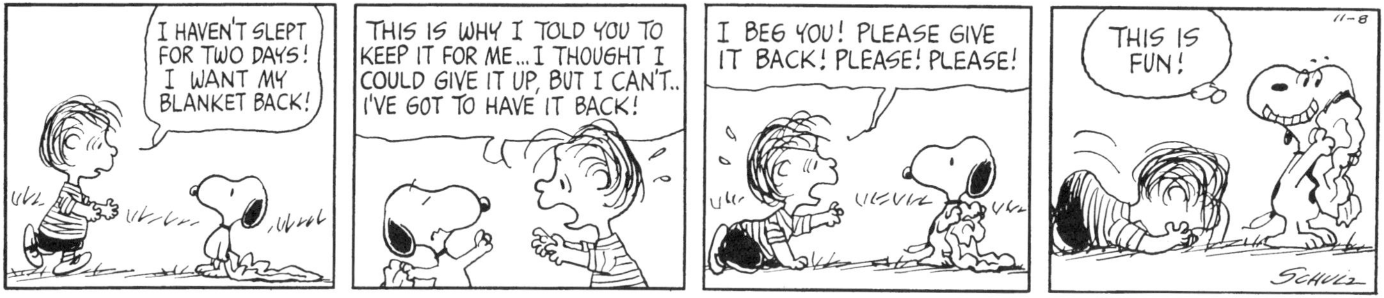
I HAVEN'T SLEPT FOR TWO DAYS! I WANT MY BLANKET BACK!
THIS IS WHY I TOLD YOU TO KEEP IT FOR ME... I THOUGHT I COULD GIVE IT UP, BUT I CAN'T.. I'VE GOT TO HAVE IT BACK!
I BEG YOU! PLEASE GIVE IT BACK! PLEASE! PLEASE!
11-8
THIS IS FUN!
SCHULZ

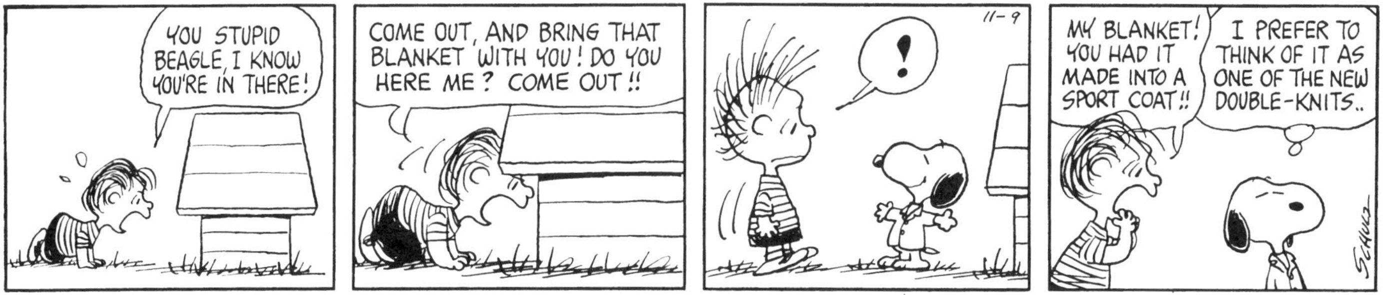
YOU STUPID BEAGLE, I KNOW YOU'RE IN THERE!
COME OUT, AND BRING THAT BLANKET WITH YOU! DO YOU HERE ME? COME OUT!!
11-9
!
MY BLANKET! YOU HAD IT MADE INTO A SPORT COAT!!
I PREFER TO THINK OF IT AS ONE OF THE NEW DOUBLE-KNITS..
SCHULZ

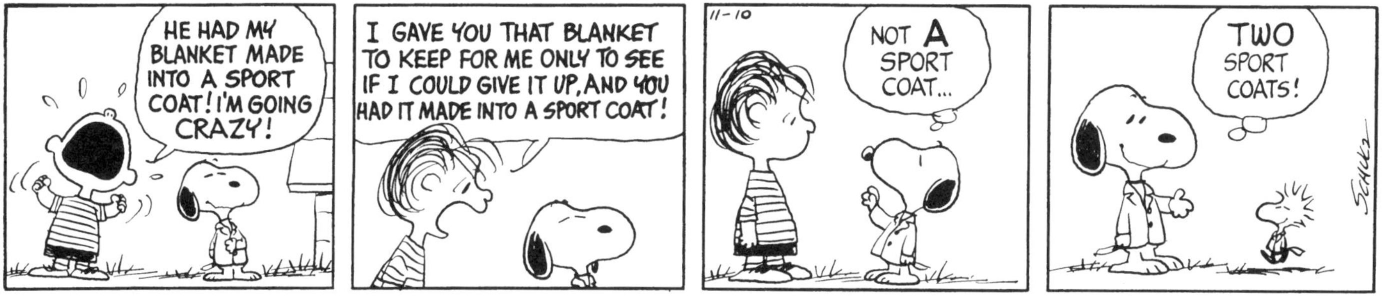
HE HAD MY BLANKET MADE INTO A SPORT COAT! I'M GOING CRAZY!
I GAVE YOU THAT BLANKET TO KEEP FOR ME ONLY TO SEE IF I COULD GIVE IT UP, AND YOU HAD IT MADE INTO A SPORT COAT!
11-10
NOT A SPORT COAT...
TWO SPORT COATS!
SCHULZ

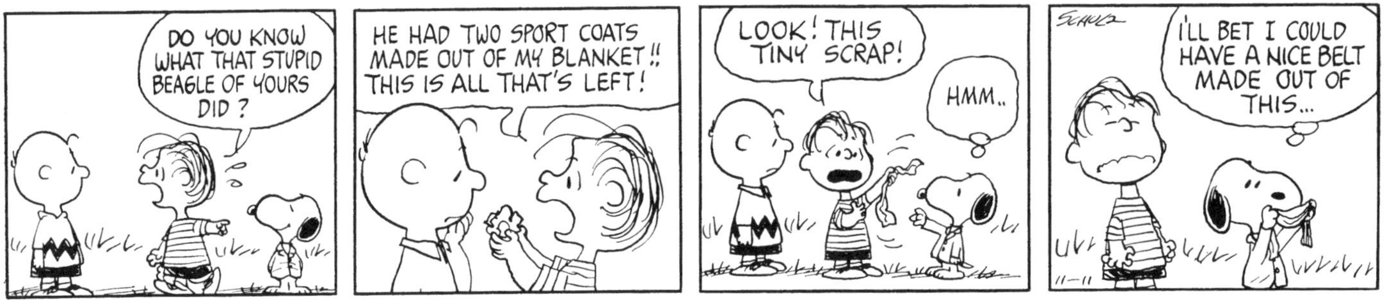
DO YOU KNOW WHAT THAT STUPID BEAGLE OF YOURS DID ?
HE HAD TWO SPORT COATS MADE OUT OF MY BLANKET !! THIS IS ALL THAT'S LEFT !
LOOK ! THIS TINY SCRAP !
HMM..
I'LL BET I COULD HAVE A NICE BELT MADE OUT OF THIS...
11-11

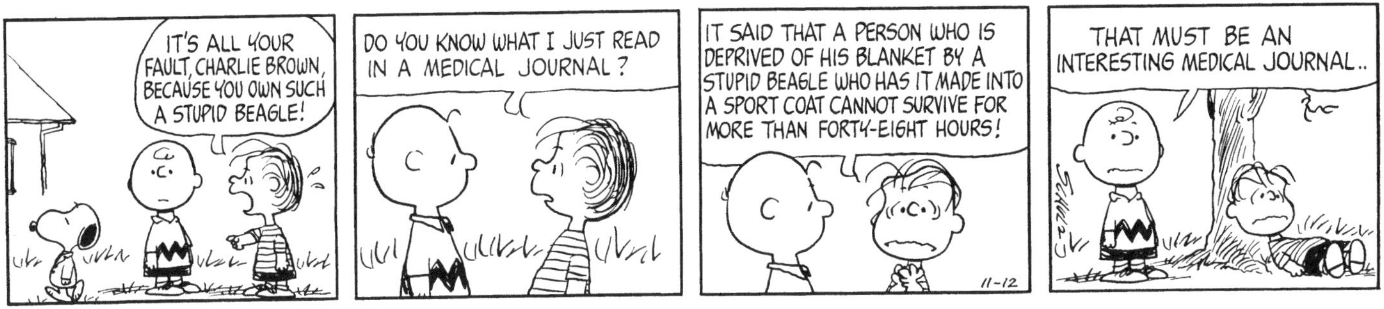
IT'S ALL YOUR FAULT, CHARLIE BROWN, BECAUSE YOU OWN SUCH A STUPID BEAGLE!
DO YOU KNOW WHAT I JUST READ IN A MEDICAL JOURNAL ?
IT SAID THAT A PERSON WHO IS DEPRIVED OF HIS BLANKET BY A STUPID BEAGLE WHO HAS IT MADE INTO A SPORT COAT CANNOT SURVIVE FOR MORE THAN FORTY-EIGHT HOURS !
11-12
THAT MUST BE AN INTERESTING MEDICAL JOURNAL..

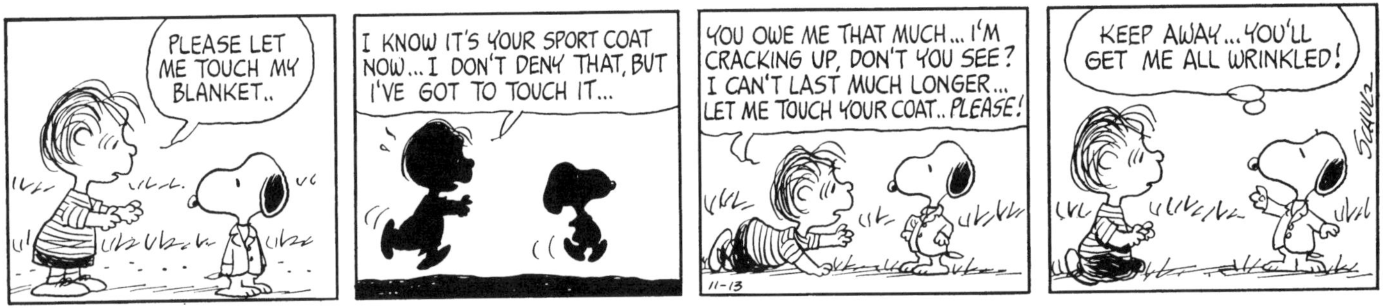
PLEASE LET ME TOUCH MY BLANKET..
I KNOW IT'S YOUR SPORT COAT NOW... I DON'T DENY THAT, BUT I'VE GOT TO TOUCH IT...
YOU OWE ME THAT MUCH... I'M CRACKING UP, DON'T YOU SEE? I CAN'T LAST MUCH LONGER... LET ME TOUCH YOUR COAT.. PLEASE!
11-13
KEEP AWAY... YOU'LL GET ME ALL WRINKLED!

PEANUTS
featuring "Good ol' Charlie Brown"
by Schulz

PSYCHIATRIC HELP 5¢

THE DOCTOR IS IN

I WONDER IF IT'S POSSIBLE REALLY TO MAKE A FRESH START...

PSYCHIATRC HELP 5¢

THE DOCTOR IS IN

SEE THAT PLANE UP THERE?

IT'S FILLED WITH PEOPLE WHO ARE ALL GOING SOMEPLACE..THAT'S WHAT I'D LIKE TO DO.. GO OFF SOMEPLACE, AND START A NEW LIFE...

FORGET IT, CHARLIE BROWN...WHEN YOU GOT OFF THE PLANE, YOU'D STILL BE THE SAME PERSON YOU ARE...

HE DOCTOR

11-14

BUT MAYBE WHEN I GOT TO THIS NEW PLACE, THE NEW PEOPLE WOULD LIKE ME BETTER

ONLY UNTIL THEY GOT TO KNOW YOU, CHARLIE BROWN..THEN YOU'D BE RIGHT BACK WHERE YOU STARTED..

BUT MAYBE THESE NEW PEOPLE WOULD BE MORE UNDERSTANDING

PEOPLE ARE PEOPLE, CHARLIE BROWN...

THE DOCTOR IS IN

WELL, MAYBE I..

FORGET IT, CHARLIE BROWN

BUT..

THE DOCTOR IS IN

NOPE!

UH..

THE DOCTOR IS IN

FIVE CENTS, PLEASE

½ SIGH ½

THE DOCTOR IS IN

ONCE YOU HAVE A PATIENT HOOKED, LAND HIM!

THE DOCTOR IS IN

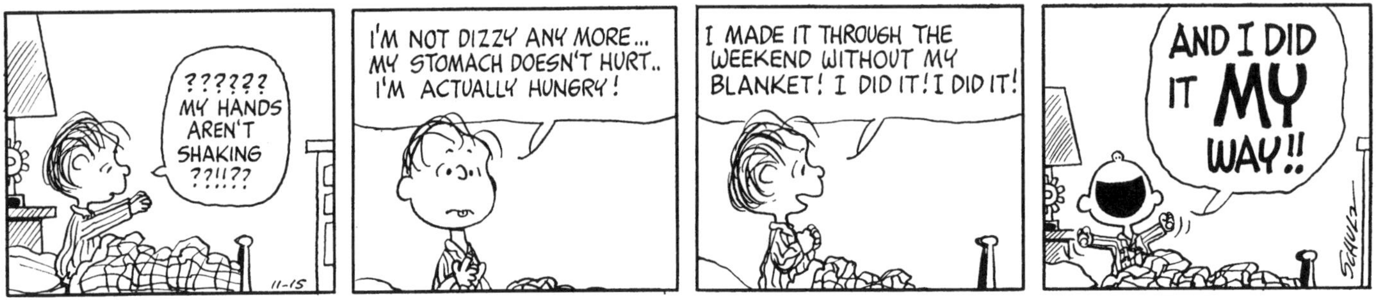
??????
MY HANDS AREN'T SHAKING ??!!??
11-15
I'M NOT DIZZY ANY MORE... MY STOMACH DOESN'T HURT.. I'M ACTUALLY HUNGRY!
I MADE IT THROUGH THE WEEKEND WITHOUT MY BLANKET! I DID IT! I DID IT!
AND I DID IT MY WAY!!
SCHULZ

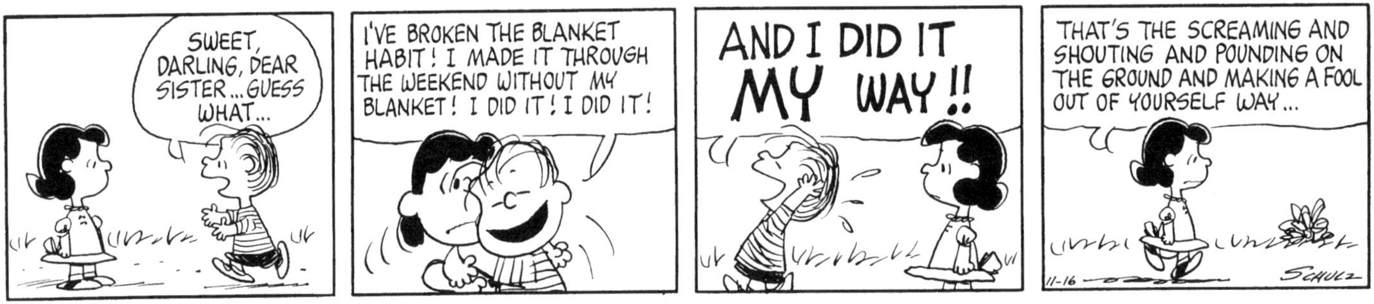
SWEET, DARLING, DEAR SISTER... GUESS WHAT...
I'VE BROKEN THE BLANKET HABIT! I MADE IT THROUGH THE WEEKEND WITHOUT MY BLANKET! I DID IT! I DID IT!
AND I DID IT MY WAY!!
THAT'S THE SCREAMING AND SHOUTING AND POUNDING ON THE GROUND AND MAKING A FOOL OUT OF YOURSELF WAY...
11-16
SCHULZ

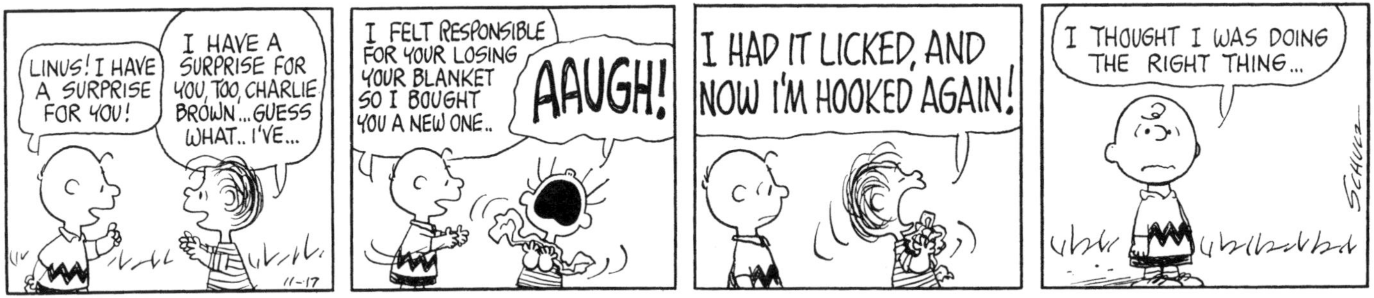
LINUS! I HAVE A SURPRISE FOR YOU!
I HAVE A SURPRISE FOR YOU, TOO, CHARLIE BROWN... GUESS WHAT.. I'VE...
11-17
I FELT RESPONSIBLE FOR YOUR LOSING YOUR BLANKET SO I BOUGHT YOU A NEW ONE..
AAUGH!
I HAD IT LICKED, AND NOW I'M HOOKED AGAIN!
I THOUGHT I WAS DOING THE RIGHT THING...
SCHULZ

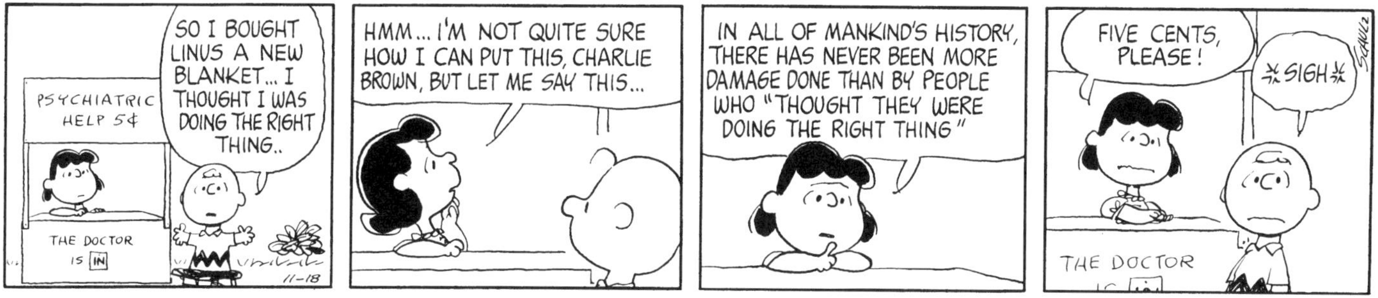
PSYCHIATRIC HELP 5¢
THE DOCTOR IS IN
SO I BOUGHT LINUS A NEW BLANKET... I THOUGHT I WAS DOING THE RIGHT THING..
11-18
HMM... I'M NOT QUITE SURE HOW I CAN PUT THIS, CHARLIE BROWN, BUT LET ME SAY THIS...
IN ALL OF MANKIND'S HISTORY, THERE HAS NEVER BEEN MORE DAMAGE DONE THAN BY PEOPLE WHO "THOUGHT THEY WERE DOING THE RIGHT THING"
FIVE CENTS, PLEASE!
SIGH
SCHULZ
THE DOCTOR

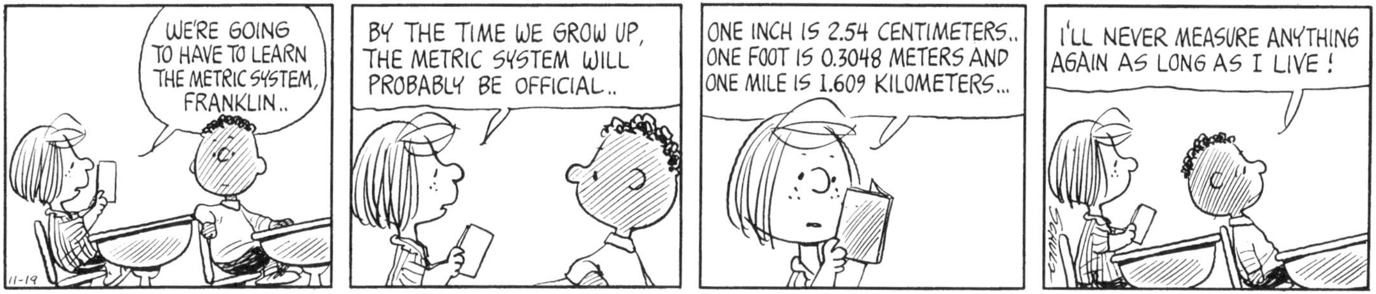
WE'RE GOING TO HAVE TO LEARN THE METRIC SYSTEM, FRANKLIN..
11-19
BY THE TIME WE GROW UP, THE METRIC SYSTEM WILL PROBABLY BE OFFICIAL..
ONE INCH IS 2.54 CENTIMETERS.. ONE FOOT IS 0.3048 METERS AND ONE MILE IS 1.609 KILOMETERS...
I'LL NEVER MEASURE ANYTHING AGAIN AS LONG AS I LIVE!
SCHULZ

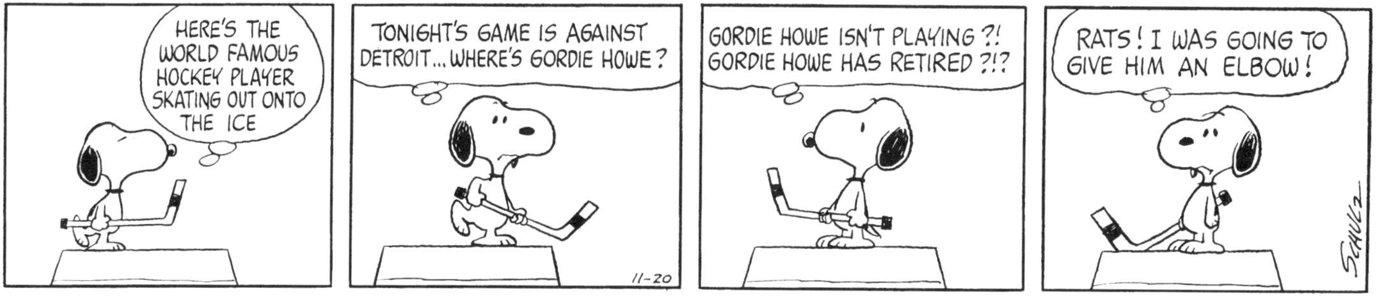
HERE'S THE WORLD FAMOUS HOCKEY PLAYER SKATING OUT ONTO THE ICE
TONIGHT'S GAME IS AGAINST DETROIT... WHERE'S GORDIE HOWE?
11-20
GORDIE HOWE ISN'T PLAYING?! GORDIE HOWE HAS RETIRED?!?
RATS! I WAS GOING TO GIVE HIM AN ELBOW!
SCHULZ

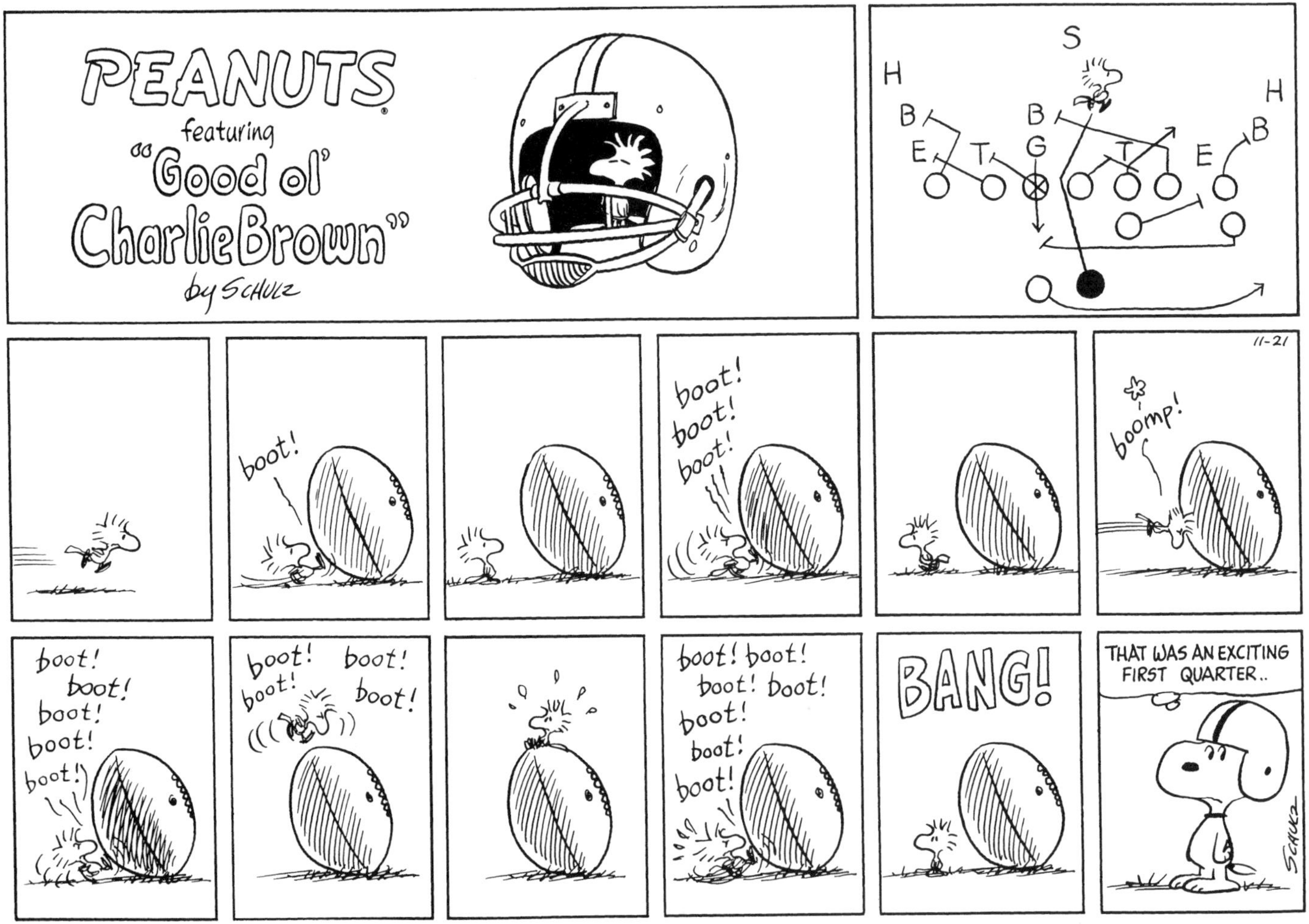
PEANUTS
featuring
"Good ol' CharlieBrown"
by SCHULZ
S
H
H
B
B
B
E
T
G
T
E
11-21
boot!
boot!
boot!
boot!
boomp!
boot!
boot!
boot!
boot!
boot!
boot!
boot!
boot!
boot!
boot! boot!
boot! boot!
boot!
boot!
boot!
BANG!
THAT WAS AN EXCITING FIRST QUARTER..
SCHULZ

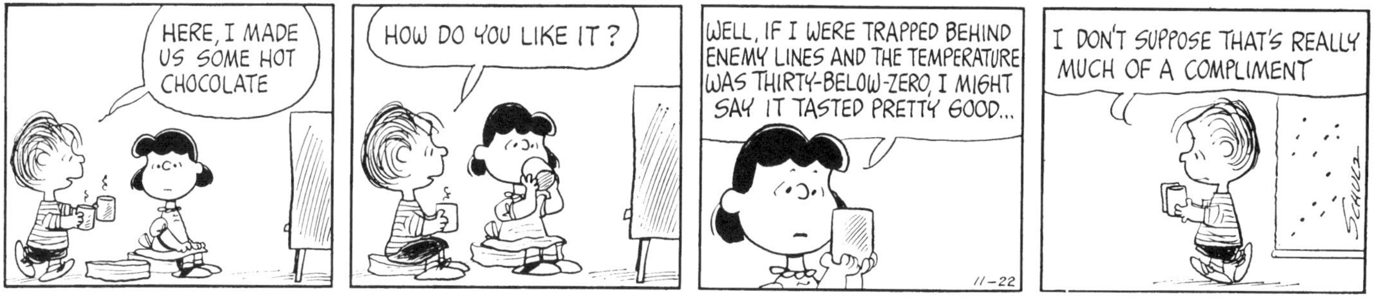
HERE, I MADE US SOME HOT CHOCOLATE
HOW DO YOU LIKE IT ?
WELL, IF I WERE TRAPPED BEHIND ENEMY LINES AND THE TEMPERATURE WAS THIRTY-BELOW-ZERO, I MIGHT SAY IT TASTED PRETTY GOOD...
11-22
I DON'T SUPPOSE THAT'S REALLY MUCH OF A COMPLIMENT
SCHULZ

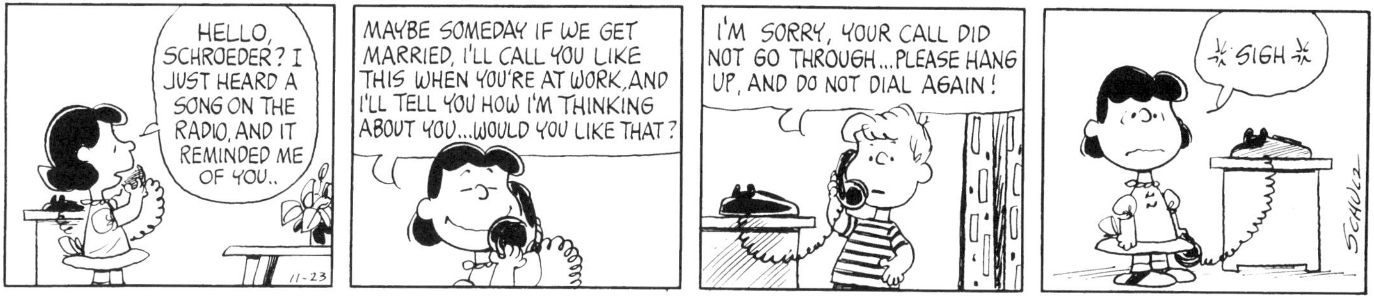
HELLO, SCHROEDER? I JUST HEARD A SONG ON THE RADIO, AND IT REMINDED ME OF YOU..
11-23
MAYBE SOMEDAY IF WE GET MARRIED, I'LL CALL YOU LIKE THIS WHEN YOU'RE AT WORK, AND I'LL TELL YOU HOW I'M THINKING ABOUT YOU...WOULD YOU LIKE THAT?
I'M SORRY, YOUR CALL DID NOT GO THROUGH...PLEASE HANG UP, AND DO NOT DIAL AGAIN!
SIGH
SCHULZ

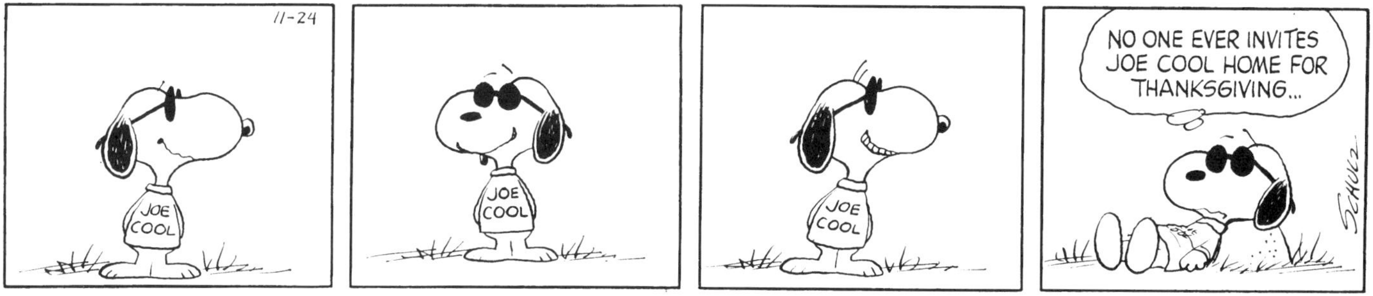
11-24
JOE COOL
JOE COOL
JOE COOL
NO ONE EVER INVITES JOE COOL HOME FOR THANKSGIVING...
SCHULZ

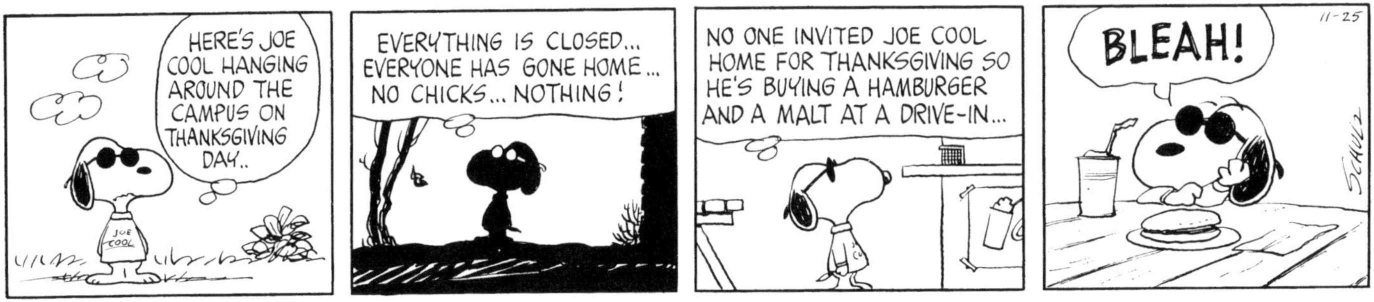
HERE'S JOE COOL HANGING AROUND THE CAMPUS ON THANKSGIVING DAY..
JOE COOL
EVERYTHING IS CLOSED... EVERYONE HAS GONE HOME... NO CHICKS... NOTHING!
NO ONE INVITED JOE COOL HOME FOR THANKSGIVING SO HE'S BUYING A HAMBURGER AND A MALT AT A DRIVE-IN...
11-25
BLEAH!

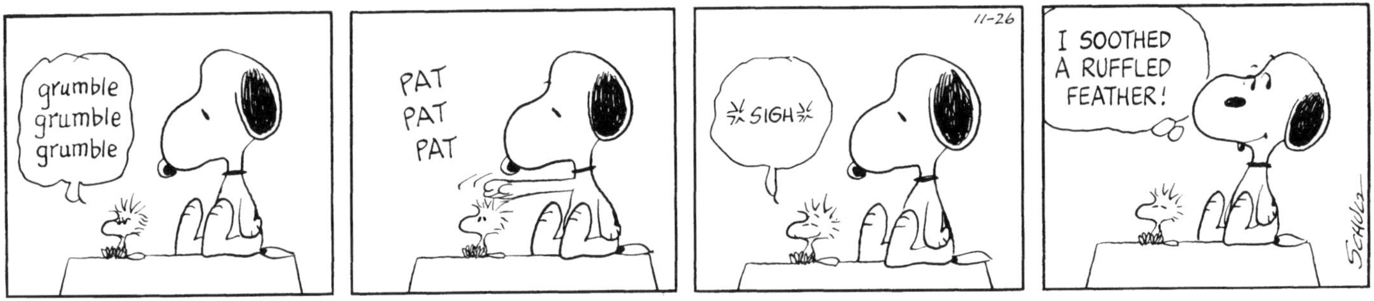
grumble grumble grumble
PAT PAT PAT
11-26
SIGH
I SOOTHED A RUFFLED FEATHER!

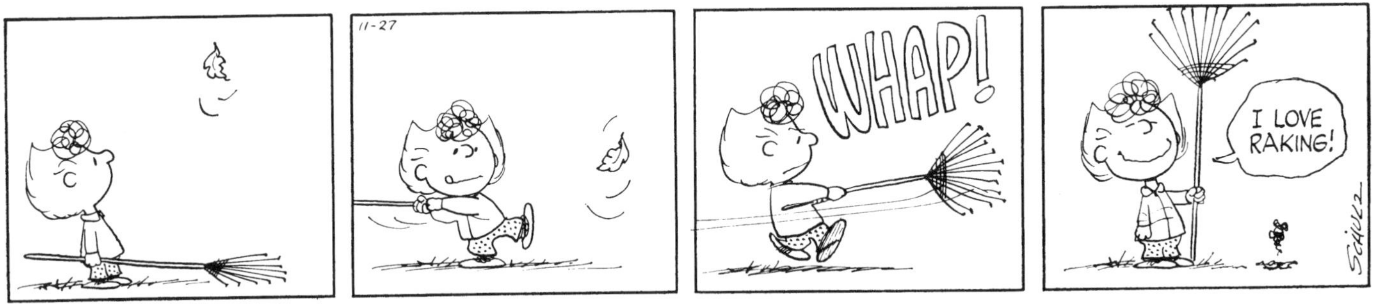
11-27
WHAP!
I LOVE RAKING!

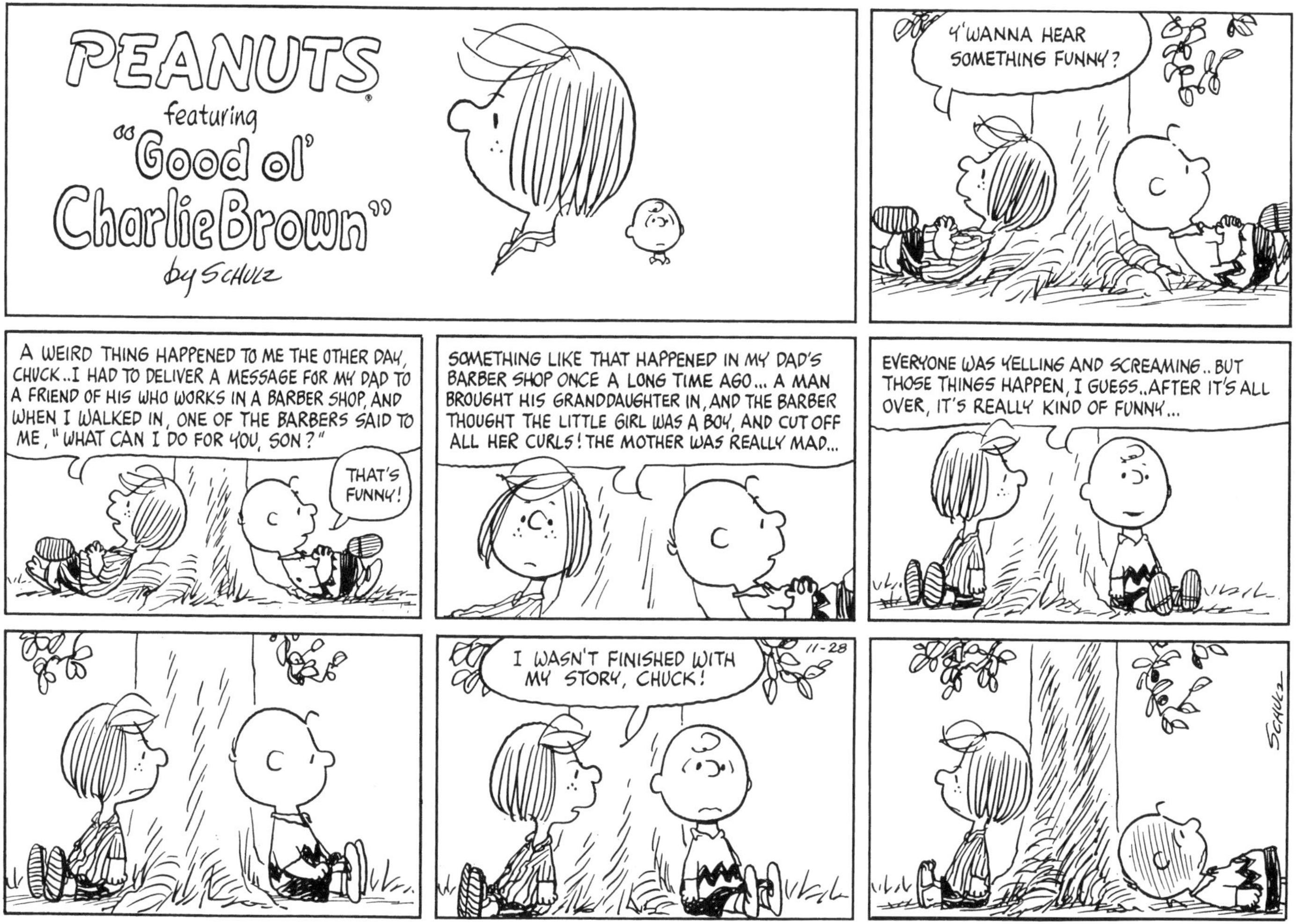
PEANUTS
featuring
"Good ol' Charlie Brown"
by SCHULZ
Y'WANNA HEAR SOMETHING FUNNY?
A WEIRD THING HAPPENED TO ME THE OTHER DAY, CHUCK..I HAD TO DELIVER A MESSAGE FOR MY DAD TO A FRIEND OF HIS WHO WORKS IN A BARBER SHOP, AND WHEN I WALKED IN, ONE OF THE BARBERS SAID TO ME, "WHAT CAN I DO FOR YOU, SON?"
THAT'S FUNNY!
SOMETHING LIKE THAT HAPPENED IN MY DAD'S BARBER SHOP ONCE A LONG TIME AGO... A MAN BROUGHT HIS GRANDDAUGHTER IN, AND THE BARBER THOUGHT THE LITTLE GIRL WAS A BOY, AND CUT OFF ALL HER CURLS! THE MOTHER WAS REALLY MAD...
EVERYONE WAS YELLING AND SCREAMING.. BUT THOSE THINGS HAPPEN, I GUESS..AFTER IT'S ALL OVER, IT'S REALLY KIND OF FUNNY...
I WASN'T FINISHED WITH MY STORY, CHUCK!
11-28
SCHULZ

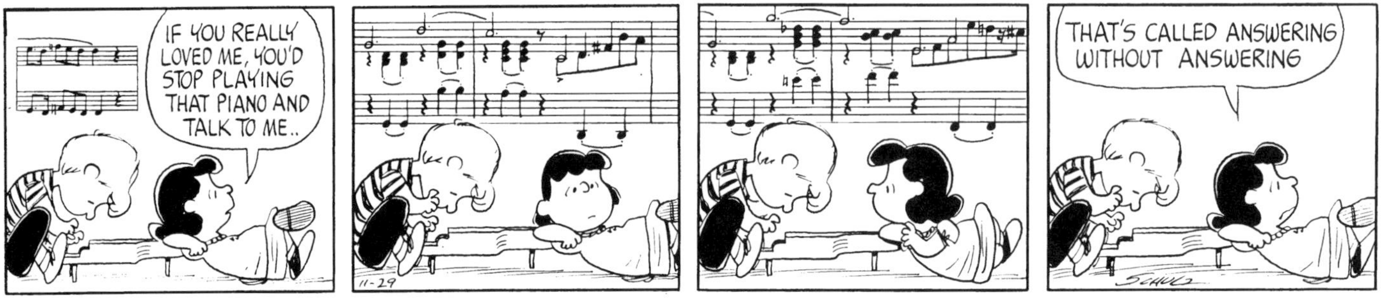
IF YOU REALLY LOVED ME, YOU'D STOP PLAYING THAT PIANO AND TALK TO ME..
11-29
THAT'S CALLED ANSWERING WITHOUT ANSWERING
SCHULZ

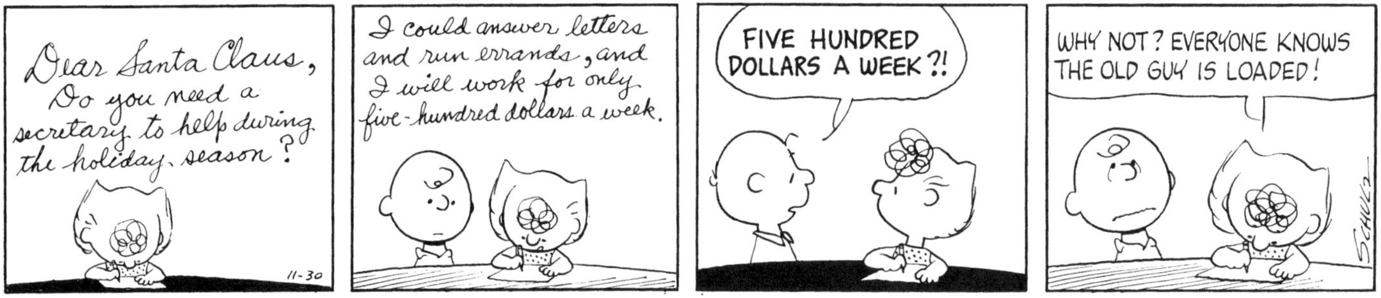
Dear Santa Claus,
Do you need a secretary to help during the holiday season?
11-30
I could answer letters and run errands, and I will work for only five-hundred dollars a week.
FIVE HUNDRED DOLLARS A WEEK?!
WHY NOT? EVERYONE KNOWS THE OLD GUY IS LOADED!
SCHULZ

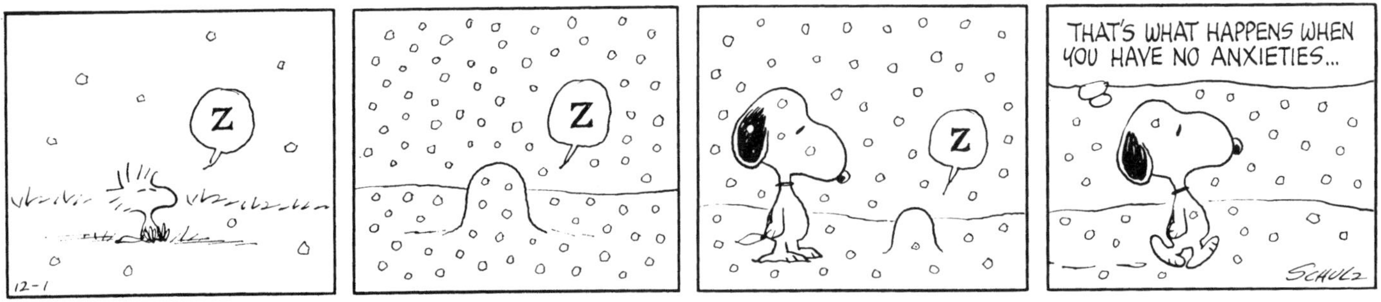
Z
12-1
Z
Z
THAT'S WHAT HAPPENS WHEN YOU HAVE NO ANXIETIES...
SCHULZ

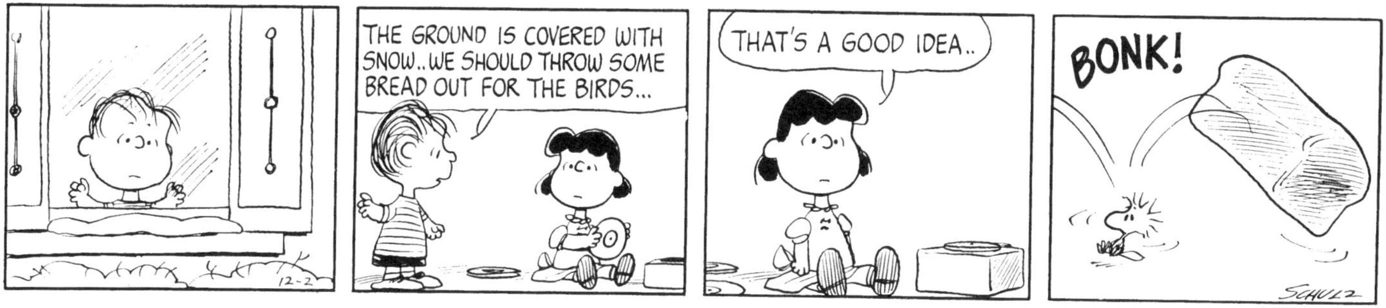
THE GROUND IS COVERED WITH SNOW..WE SHOULD THROW SOME BREAD OUT FOR THE BIRDS...
THAT'S A GOOD IDEA..
BONK!

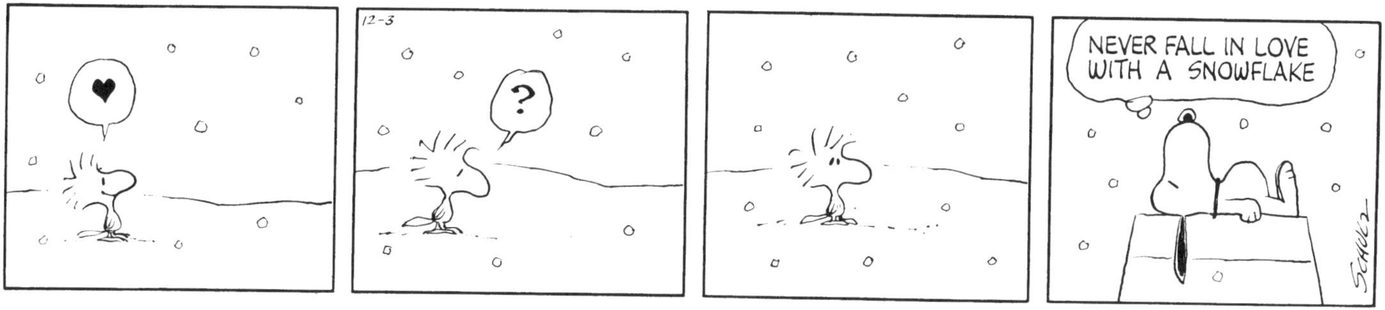
?
NEVER FALL IN LOVE WITH A SNOWFLAKE

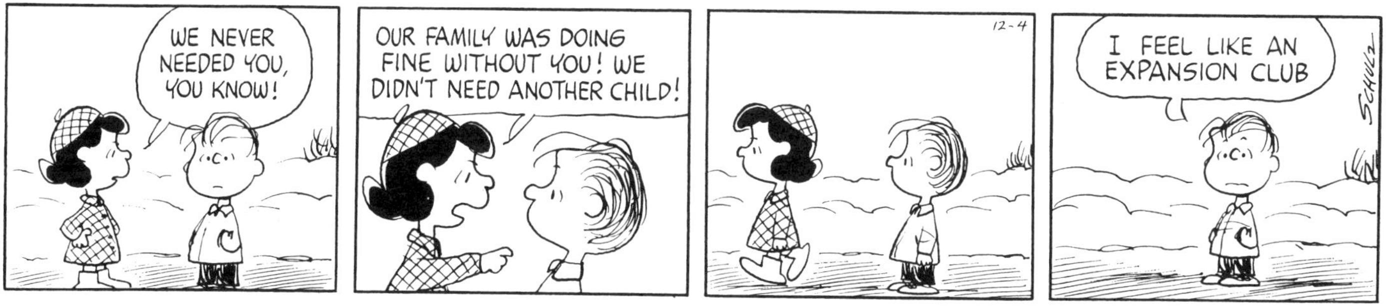
WE NEVER NEEDED YOU, YOU KNOW!
OUR FAMILY WAS DOING FINE WITHOUT YOU! WE DIDN'T NEED ANOTHER CHILD!
I FEEL LIKE AN EXPANSION CLUB

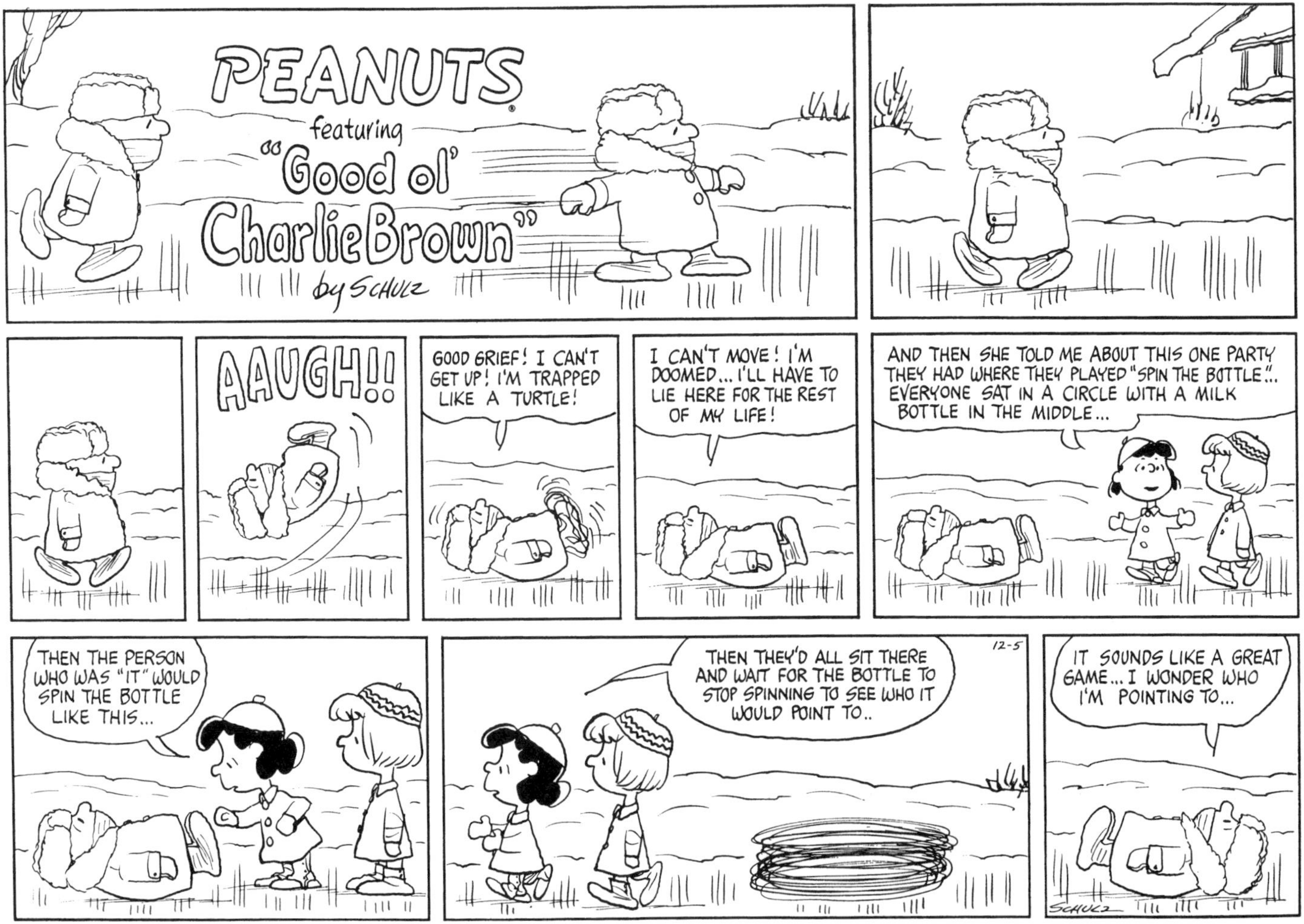
PEANUTS
featuring "Good ol' CharlieBrown"
by SCHULZ
AAUGH!!
GOOD GRIEF! I CAN'T GET UP! I'M TRAPPED LIKE A TURTLE!
I CAN'T MOVE! I'M DOOMED... I'LL HAVE TO LIE HERE FOR THE REST OF MY LIFE!
AND THEN SHE TOLD ME ABOUT THIS ONE PARTY THEY HAD WHERE THEY PLAYED "SPIN THE BOTTLE"... EVERYONE SAT IN A CIRCLE WITH A MILK BOTTLE IN THE MIDDLE...
THEN THE PERSON WHO WAS "IT" WOULD SPIN THE BOTTLE LIKE THIS...
12-5
THEN THEY'D ALL SIT THERE AND WAIT FOR THE BOTTLE TO STOP SPINNING TO SEE WHO IT WOULD POINT TO..
IT SOUNDS LIKE A GREAT GAME... I WONDER WHO I'M POINTING TO...
SCHULZ

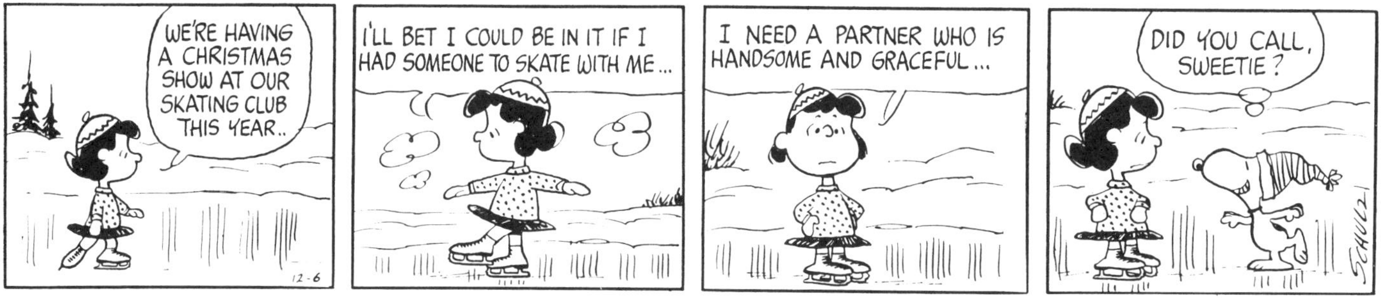
WE'RE HAVING A CHRISTMAS SHOW AT OUR SKATING CLUB THIS YEAR..
12-6
I'LL BET I COULD BE IN IT IF I HAD SOMEONE TO SKATE WITH ME...
I NEED A PARTNER WHO IS HANDSOME AND GRACEFUL...
DID YOU CALL, SWEETIE?
SCHULZ

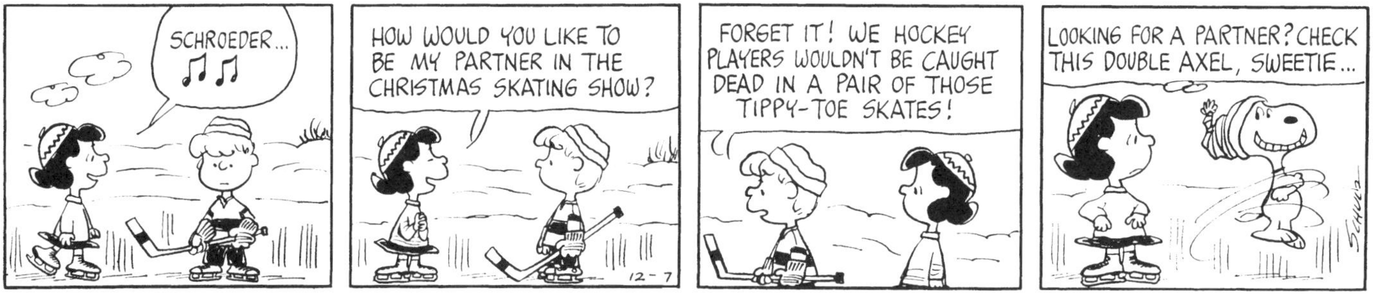
SCHROEDER...
HOW WOULD YOU LIKE TO BE MY PARTNER IN THE CHRISTMAS SKATING SHOW?
12-7
FORGET IT! WE HOCKEY PLAYERS WOULDN'T BE CAUGHT DEAD IN A PAIR OF THOSE TIPPY-TOE SKATES!
LOOKING FOR A PARTNER? CHECK THIS DOUBLE AXEL, SWEETIE...
SCHULZ

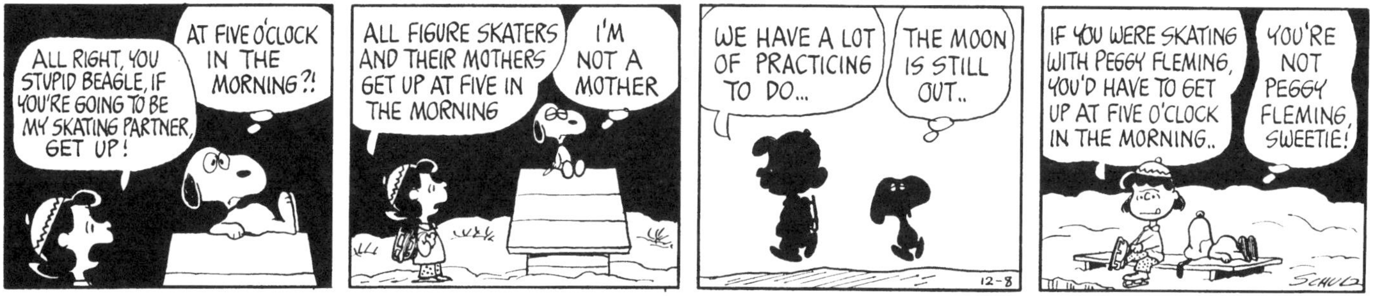
ALL RIGHT, YOU STUPID BEAGLE, IF YOU'RE GOING TO BE MY SKATING PARTNER, GET UP!
AT FIVE O'CLOCK IN THE MORNING?!
ALL FIGURE SKATERS AND THEIR MOTHERS GET UP AT FIVE IN THE MORNING
I'M NOT A MOTHER
WE HAVE A LOT OF PRACTICING TO DO...
THE MOON IS STILL OUT..
12-8
IF YOU WERE SKATING WITH PEGGY FLEMING, YOU'D HAVE TO GET UP AT FIVE O'CLOCK IN THE MORNING..
YOU'RE NOT PEGGY FLEMING, SWEETIE!
SCHULZ

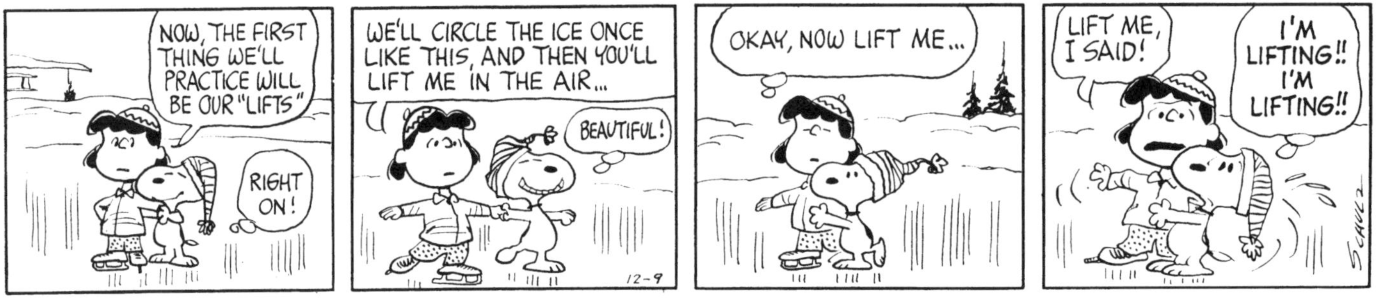
NOW, THE FIRST THING WE'LL PRACTICE WILL BE OUR "LIFTS"
RIGHT ON!
WE'LL CIRCLE THE ICE ONCE LIKE THIS, AND THEN YOU'LL LIFT ME IN THE AIR...
BEAUTIFUL!
12-9
OKAY, NOW LIFT ME...
LIFT ME, I SAID!
I'M LIFTING!! I'M LIFTING!!
SCHULZ

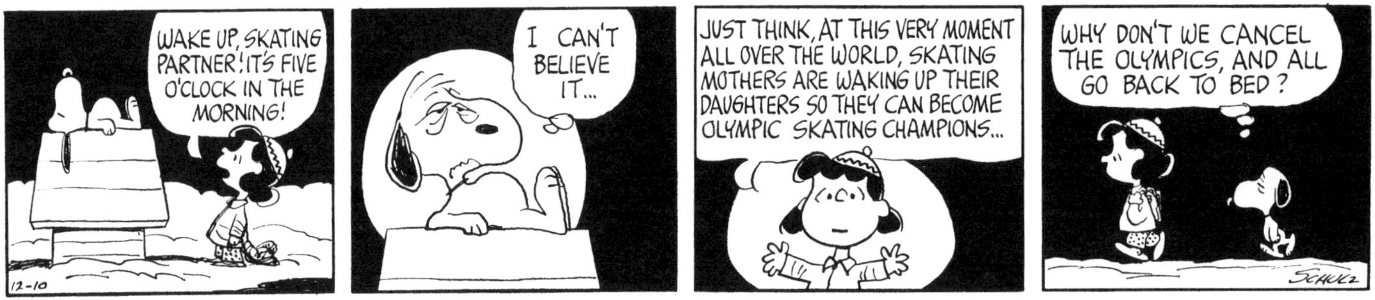
WAKE UP, SKATING PARTNER! IT'S FIVE O'CLOCK IN THE MORNING!
12-10
I CAN'T BELIEVE IT...
JUST THINK, AT THIS VERY MOMENT ALL OVER THE WORLD, SKATING MOTHERS ARE WAKING UP THEIR DAUGHTERS SO THEY CAN BECOME OLYMPIC SKATING CHAMPIONS...
WHY DON'T WE CANCEL THE OLYMPICS, AND ALL GO BACK TO BED?
SCHULZ

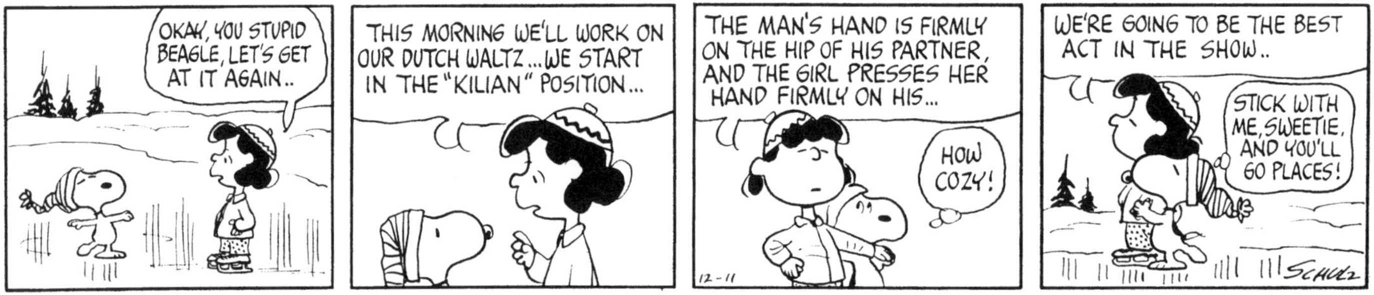
OKAY, YOU STUPID BEAGLE, LET'S GET AT IT AGAIN..
THIS MORNING WE'LL WORK ON OUR DUTCH WALTZ...WE START IN THE "KILIAN" POSITION...
THE MAN'S HAND IS FIRMLY ON THE HIP OF HIS PARTNER, AND THE GIRL PRESSES HER HAND FIRMLY ON HIS...
HOW COZY!
12-11
WE'RE GOING TO BE THE BEST ACT IN THE SHOW..
STICK WITH ME, SWEETIE, AND YOU'LL GO PLACES!
SCHULZ

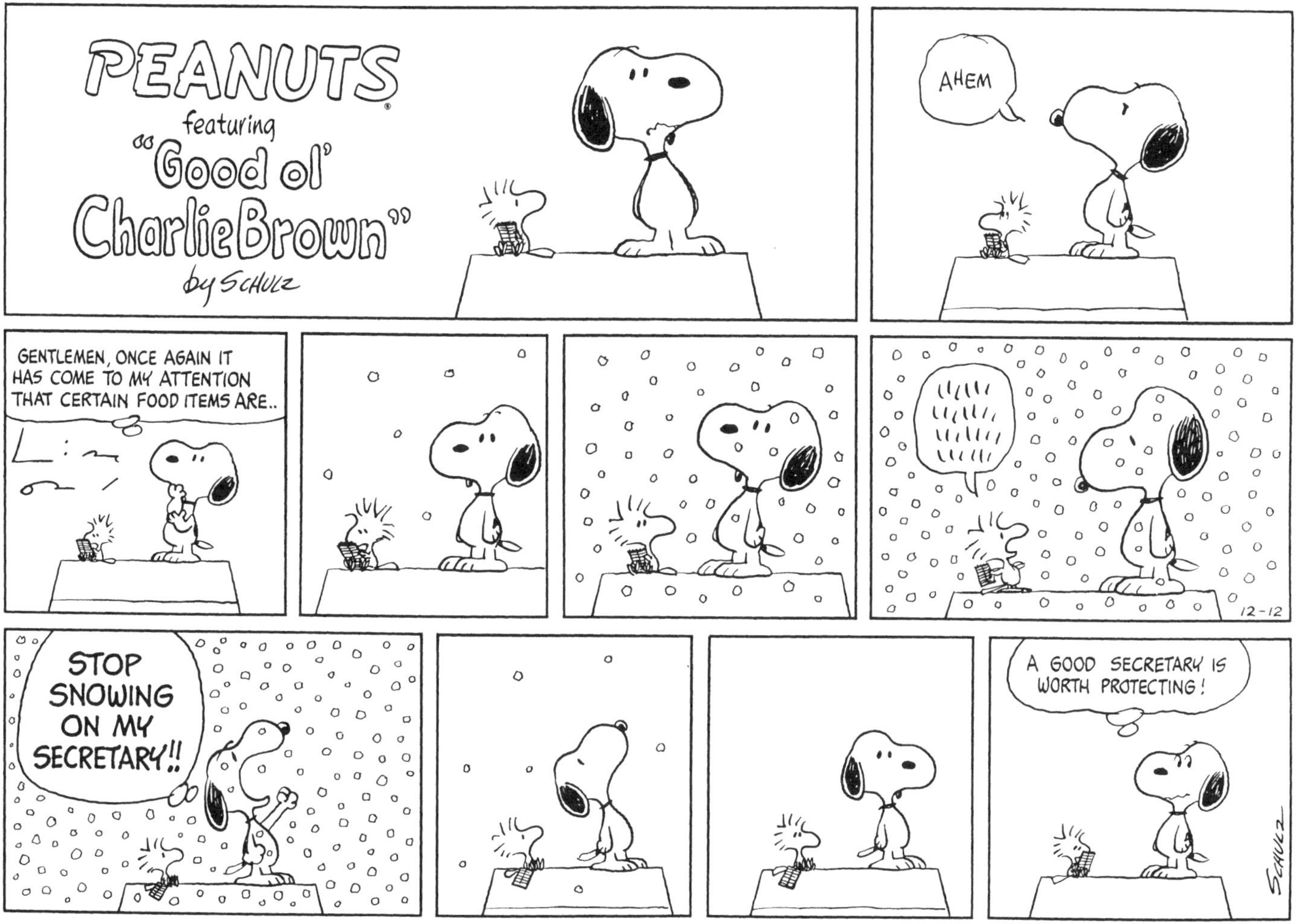
PEANUTS
featuring
"Good ol' Charlie Brown"
by SCHULZ
AHEM
GENTLEMEN, ONCE AGAIN IT HAS COME TO MY ATTENTION THAT CERTAIN FOOD ITEMS ARE..
12-12
STOP SNOWING ON MY SECRETARY!!
A GOOD SECRETARY IS WORTH PROTECTING!
SCHULZ

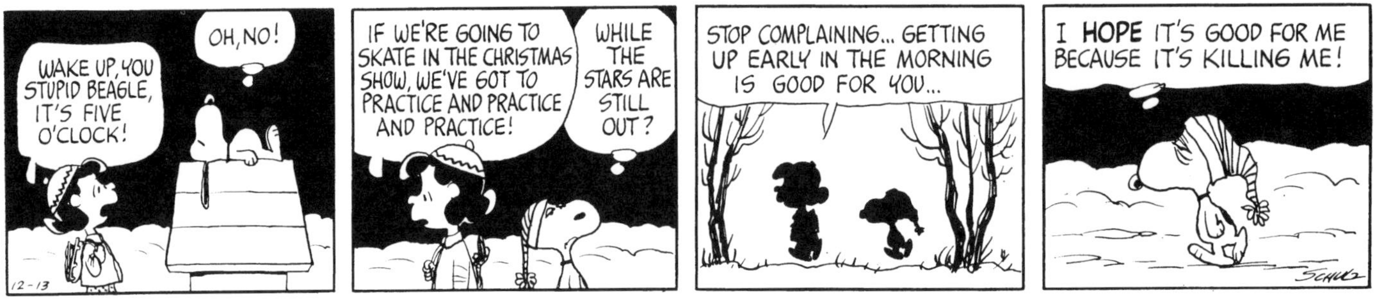

12-13
WAKE UP, YOU STUPID BEAGLE, IT'S FIVE O'CLOCK!
OH, NO!
IF WE'RE GOING TO SKATE IN THE CHRISTMAS SHOW, WE'VE GOT TO PRACTICE AND PRACTICE AND PRACTICE!
WHILE THE STARS ARE STILL OUT?
STOP COMPLAINING... GETTING UP EARLY IN THE MORNING IS GOOD FOR YOU...
I **HOPE** IT'S GOOD FOR ME BECAUSE IT'S KILLING ME!
SCHULZ

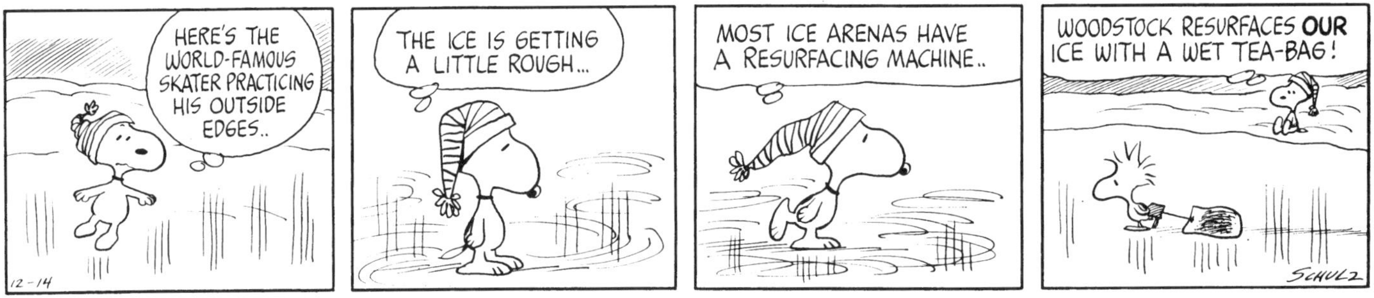

12-14
HERE'S THE WORLD-FAMOUS SKATER PRACTICING HIS OUTSIDE EDGES..
THE ICE IS GETTING A LITTLE ROUGH...
MOST ICE ARENAS HAVE A RESURFACING MACHINE..
WOODSTOCK RESURFACES **OUR** ICE WITH A WET TEA-BAG!
SCHULZ

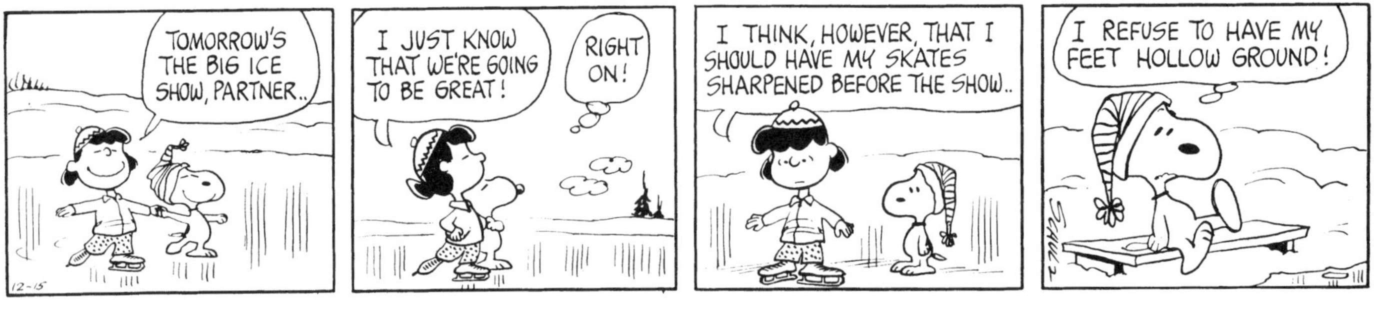

12-15
TOMORROW'S THE BIG ICE SHOW, PARTNER..
I JUST KNOW THAT WE'RE GOING TO BE GREAT!
RIGHT ON!
I THINK, HOWEVER, THAT I SHOULD HAVE MY SKATES SHARPENED BEFORE THE SHOW..
I REFUSE TO HAVE MY FEET HOLLOW GROUND!
SCHULZ

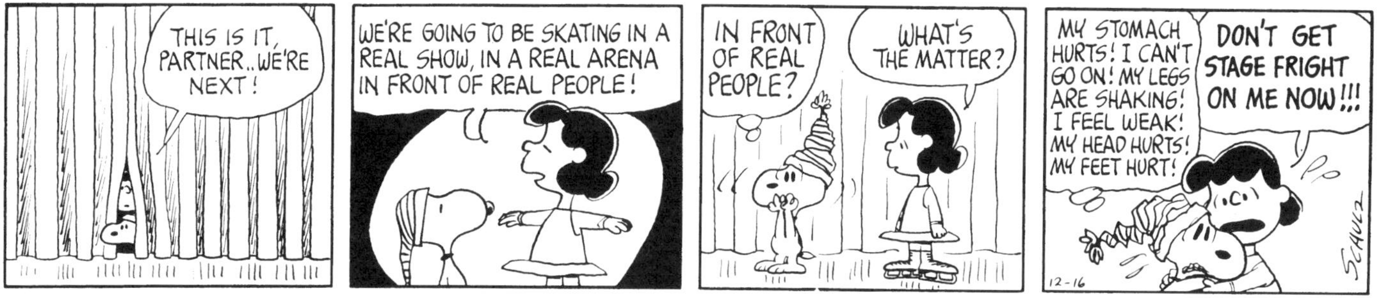
THIS IS IT, PARTNER..WE'RE NEXT!
WE'RE GOING TO BE SKATING IN A REAL SHOW, IN A REAL ARENA IN FRONT OF REAL PEOPLE!
IN FRONT OF REAL PEOPLE?
WHAT'S THE MATTER?
MY STOMACH HURTS! I CAN'T GO ON! MY LEGS ARE SHAKING! I FEEL WEAK! MY HEAD HURTS! MY FEET HURT!
DON'T GET STAGE FRIGHT ON ME NOW!!!
12-16
SCHULZ

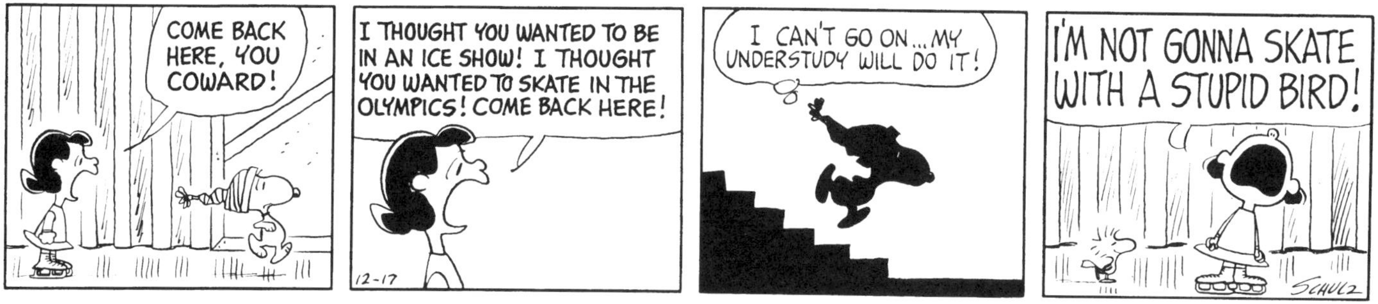
COME BACK HERE, YOU COWARD!
I THOUGHT YOU WANTED TO BE IN AN ICE SHOW! I THOUGHT YOU WANTED TO SKATE IN THE OLYMPICS! COME BACK HERE!
12-17
I CAN'T GO ON... MY UNDERSTUDY WILL DO IT!
I'M NOT GONNA SKATE WITH A STUPID BIRD!
SCHULZ

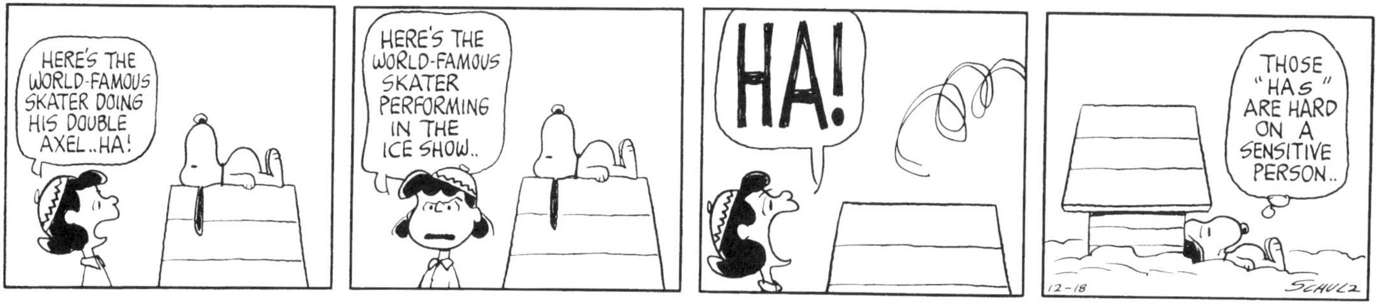
HERE'S THE WORLD-FAMOUS SKATER DOING HIS DOUBLE AXEL..HA!
HERE'S THE WORLD-FAMOUS SKATER PERFORMING IN THE ICE SHOW..
HA!
THOSE "HAs" ARE HARD ON A SENSITIVE PERSON..
12-18
SCHULZ

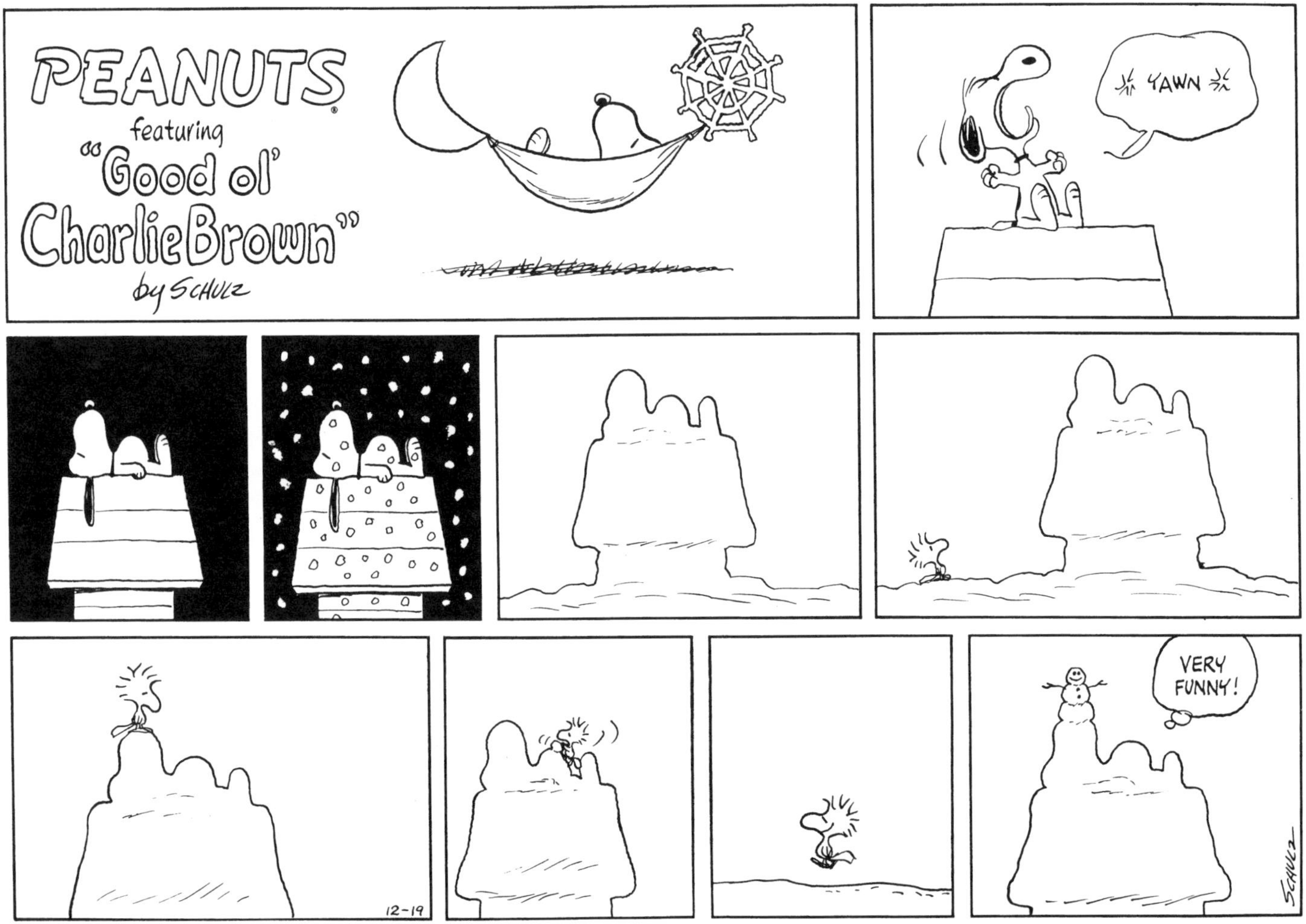
PEANUTS®
featuring
"Good ol' Charlie Brown"
by SCHULZ
☆ YAWN ☆
12-19
VERY FUNNY!
SCHULZ

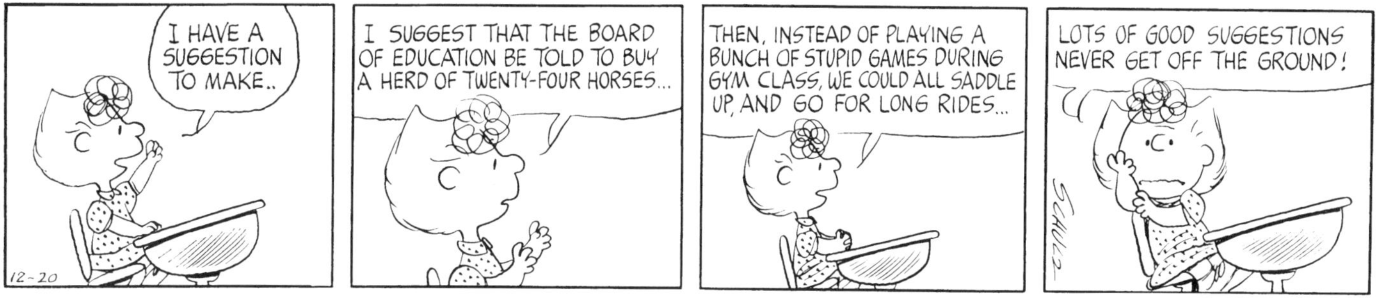
I HAVE A SUGGESTION TO MAKE..
I SUGGEST THAT THE BOARD OF EDUCATION BE TOLD TO BUY A HERD OF TWENTY-FOUR HORSES...
THEN, INSTEAD OF PLAYING A BUNCH OF STUPID GAMES DURING GYM CLASS, WE COULD ALL SADDLE UP, AND GO FOR LONG RIDES...
LOTS OF GOOD SUGGESTIONS NEVER GET OFF THE GROUND!

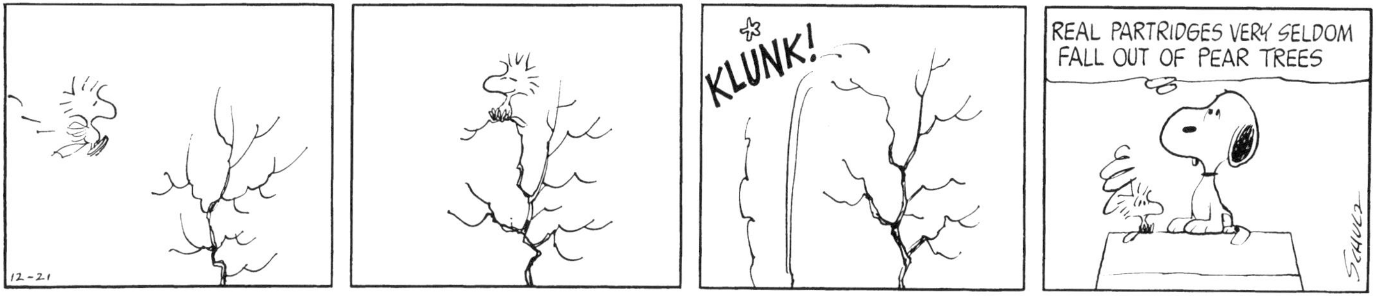
KLUNK!
REAL PARTRIDGES VERY SELDOM FALL OUT OF PEAR TREES

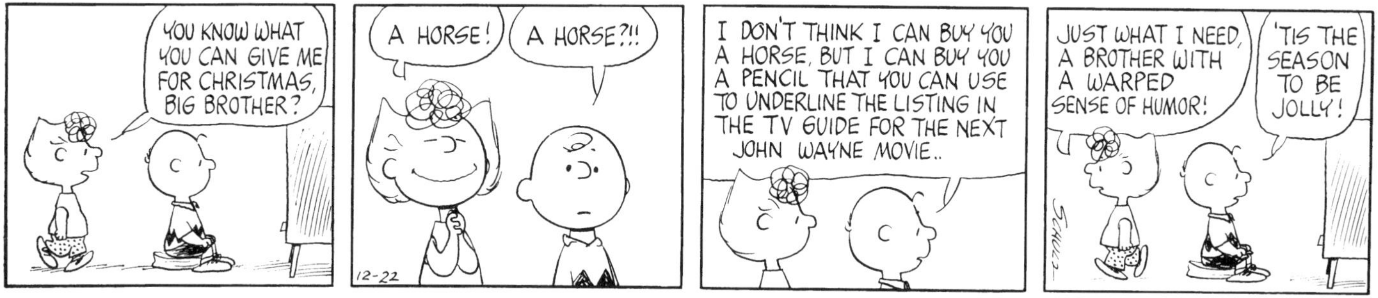
YOU KNOW WHAT YOU CAN GIVE ME FOR CHRISTMAS, BIG BROTHER?
A HORSE!
A HORSE?!!
I DON'T THINK I CAN BUY YOU A HORSE, BUT I CAN BUY YOU A PENCIL THAT YOU CAN USE TO UNDERLINE THE LISTING IN THE TV GUIDE FOR THE NEXT JOHN WAYNE MOVIE..
JUST WHAT I NEED, A BROTHER WITH A WARPED SENSE OF HUMOR!
'TIS THE SEASON TO BE JOLLY!

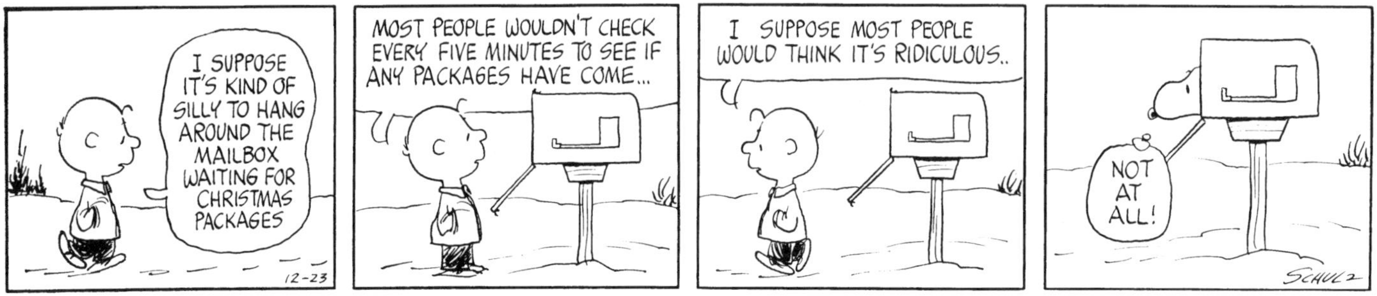
I SUPPOSE IT'S KIND OF SILLY TO HANG AROUND THE MAILBOX WAITING FOR CHRISTMAS PACKAGES
12-23
MOST PEOPLE WOULDN'T CHECK EVERY FIVE MINUTES TO SEE IF ANY PACKAGES HAVE COME...
I SUPPOSE MOST PEOPLE WOULD THINK IT'S RIDICULOUS..
NOT AT ALL!
SCHULZ

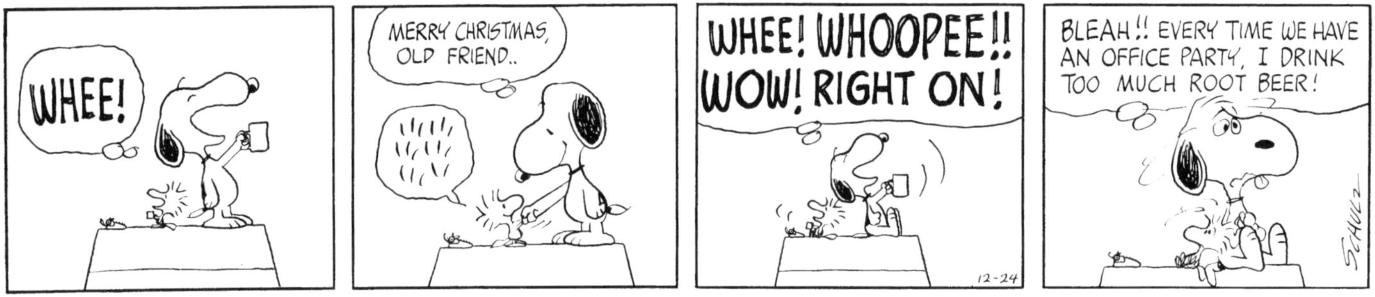
WHEE!
MERRY CHRISTMAS, OLD FRIEND..
WHEE! WHOOPEE!! WOW! RIGHT ON!
12-24
BLEAH!! EVERY TIME WE HAVE AN OFFICE PARTY, I DRINK TOO MUCH ROOT BEER!
SCHULZ

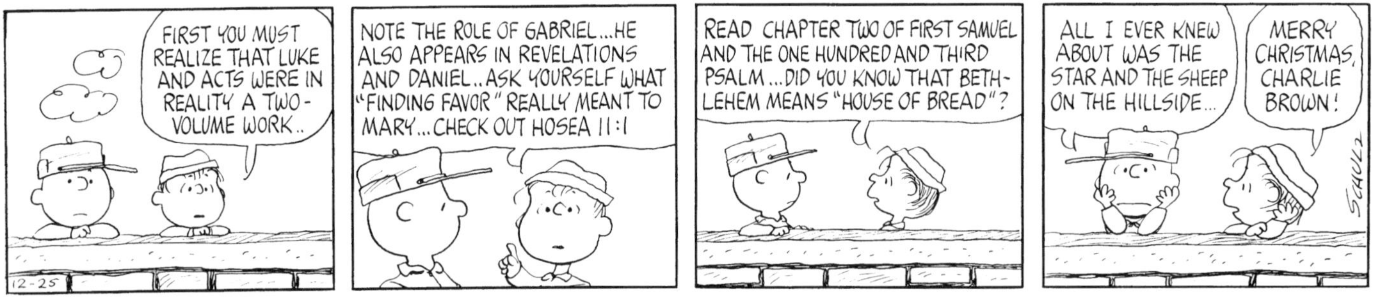
FIRST YOU MUST REALIZE THAT LUKE AND ACTS WERE IN REALITY A TWO-VOLUME WORK..
12-25
NOTE THE ROLE OF GABRIEL...HE ALSO APPEARS IN REVELATIONS AND DANIEL..ASK YOURSELF WHAT "FINDING FAVOR" REALLY MEANT TO MARY...CHECK OUT HOSEA 11:1
READ CHAPTER TWO OF FIRST SAMUEL AND THE ONE HUNDRED AND THIRD PSALM...DID YOU KNOW THAT BETH-LEHEM MEANS "HOUSE OF BREAD"?
ALL I EVER KNEW ABOUT WAS THE STAR AND THE SHEEP ON THE HILLSIDE...
MERRY CHRISTMAS, CHARLIE BROWN!
SCHULZ

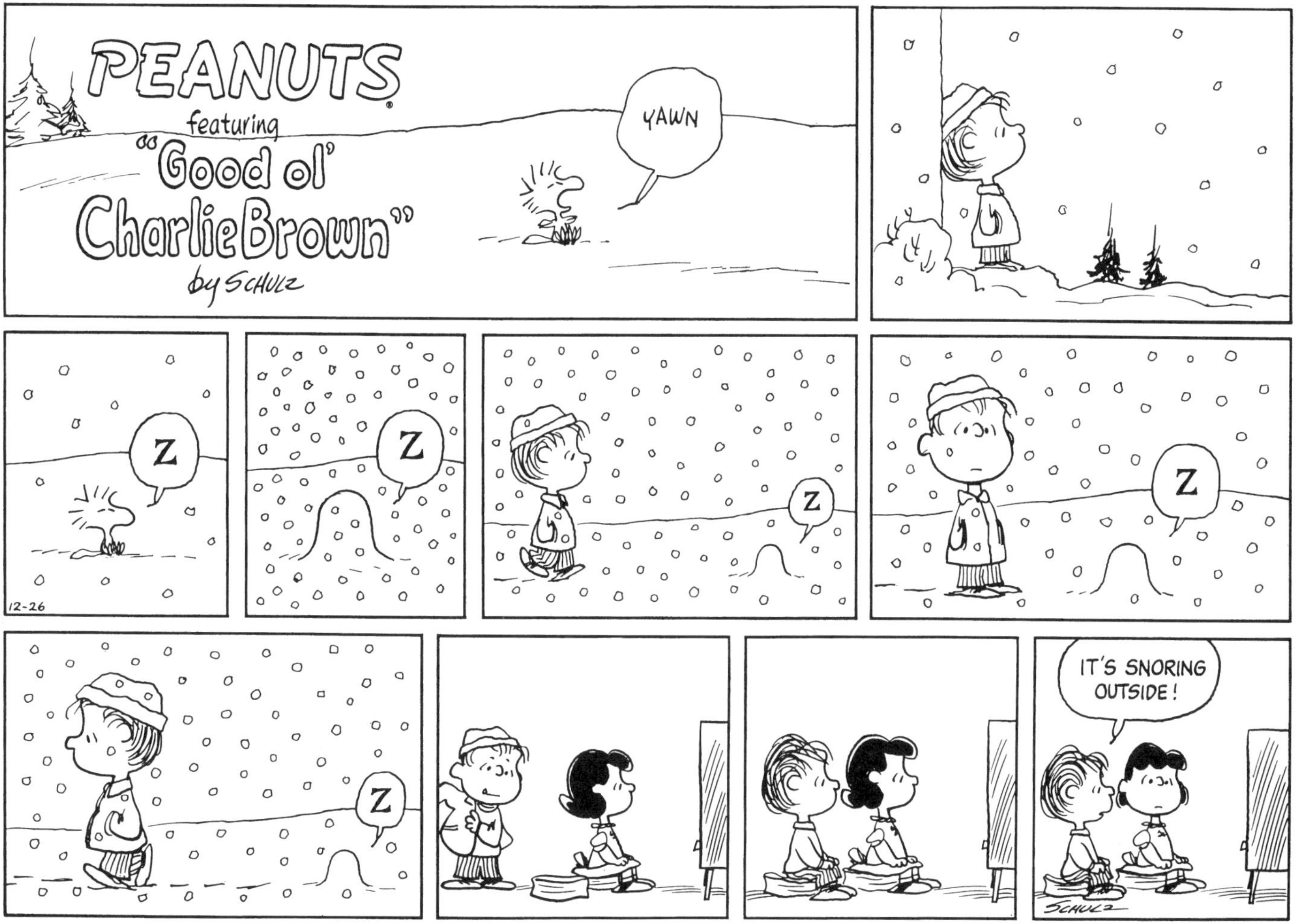
PEANUTS
featuring
"Good ol' CharlieBrown"
by SCHULZ
YAWN
Z
Z
Z
Z
Z
IT'S SNORING OUTSIDE!
SCHULZ

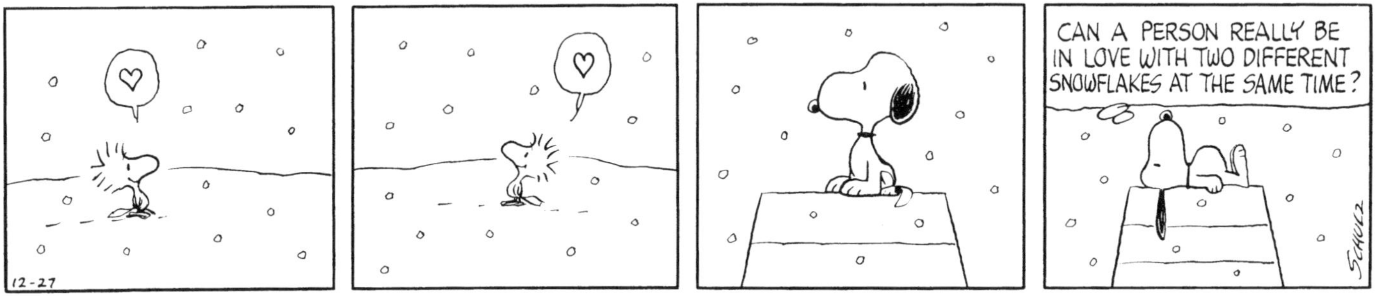
12-27
CAN A PERSON REALLY BE IN LOVE WITH TWO DIFFERENT SNOWFLAKES AT THE SAME TIME?
SCHULZ

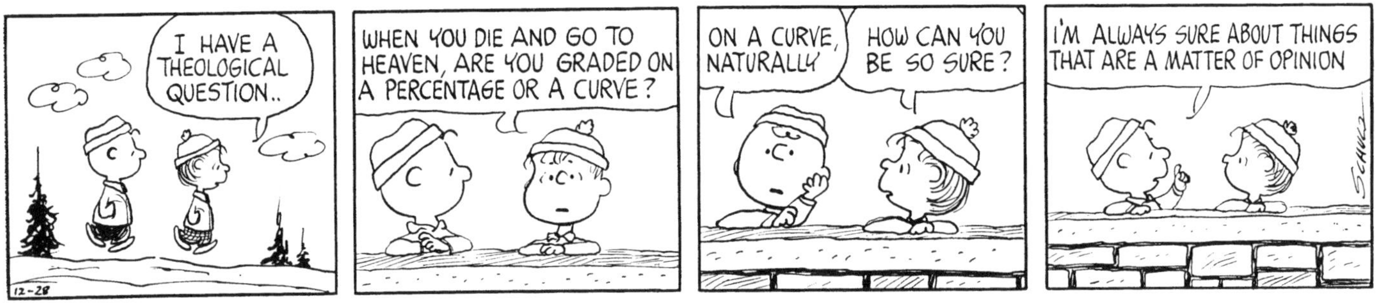
I HAVE A THEOLOGICAL QUESTION..
12-28
WHEN YOU DIE AND GO TO HEAVEN, ARE YOU GRADED ON A PERCENTAGE OR A CURVE?
ON A CURVE, NATURALLY
HOW CAN YOU BE SO SURE?
I'M ALWAYS SURE ABOUT THINGS THAT ARE A MATTER OF OPINION
SCHULZ

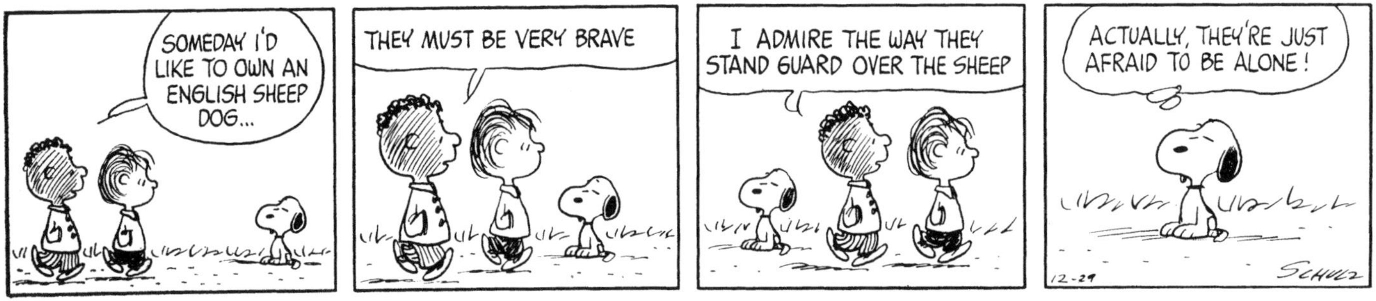
SOMEDAY I'D LIKE TO OWN AN ENGLISH SHEEP DOG...
THEY MUST BE VERY BRAVE
I ADMIRE THE WAY THEY STAND GUARD OVER THE SHEEP
ACTUALLY, THEY'RE JUST AFRAID TO BE ALONE!
12-29
SCHULZ

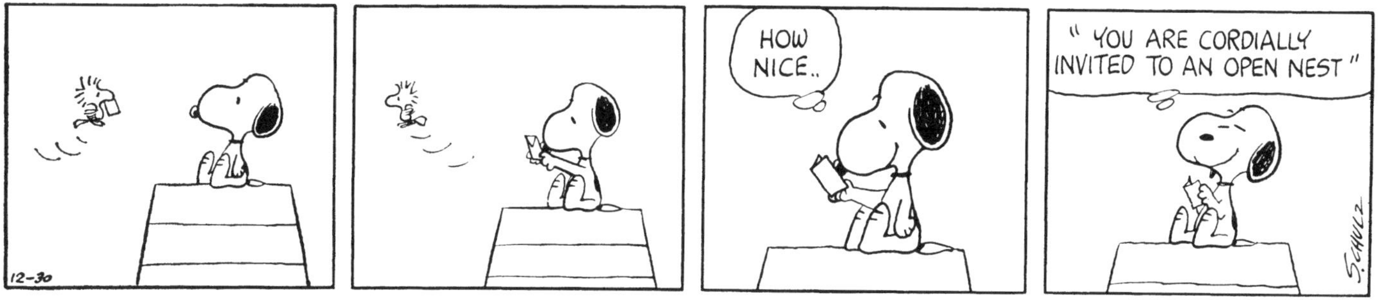
HOW NICE..
" YOU ARE CORDIALLY INVITED TO AN OPEN NEST "

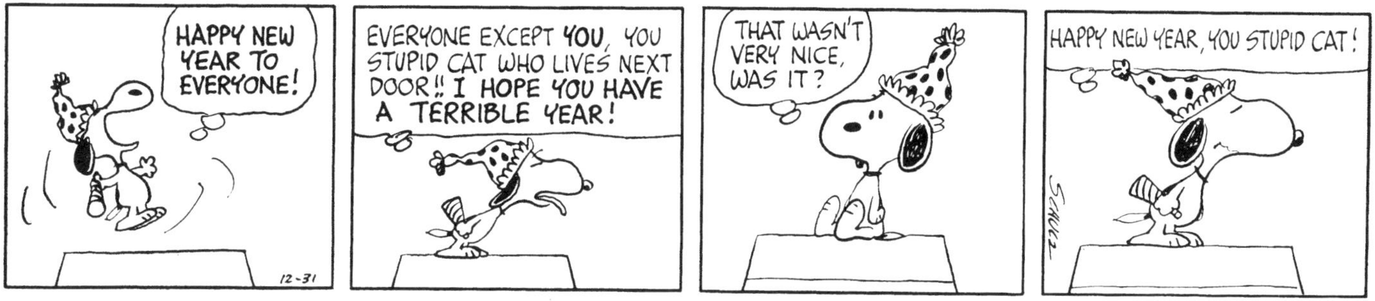
HAPPY NEW YEAR TO EVERYONE!
EVERYONE EXCEPT YOU, YOU STUPID CAT WHO LIVES NEXT DOOR!! I HOPE YOU HAVE A TERRIBLE YEAR!
THAT WASN'T VERY NICE, WAS IT?
HAPPY NEW YEAR, YOU STUPID CAT!

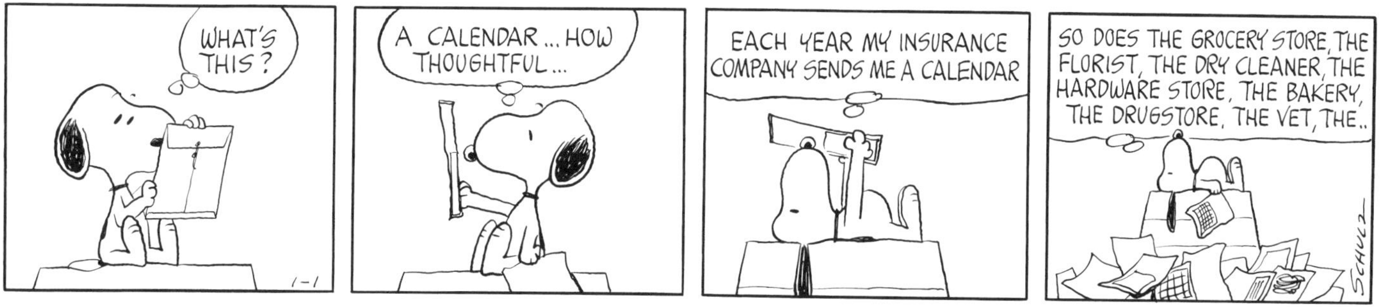
WHAT'S THIS?
A CALENDAR... HOW THOUGHTFUL...
EACH YEAR MY INSURANCE COMPANY SENDS ME A CALENDAR
SO DOES THE GROCERY STORE, THE FLORIST, THE DRY CLEANER, THE HARDWARE STORE, THE BAKERY, THE DRUGSTORE, THE VET, THE..

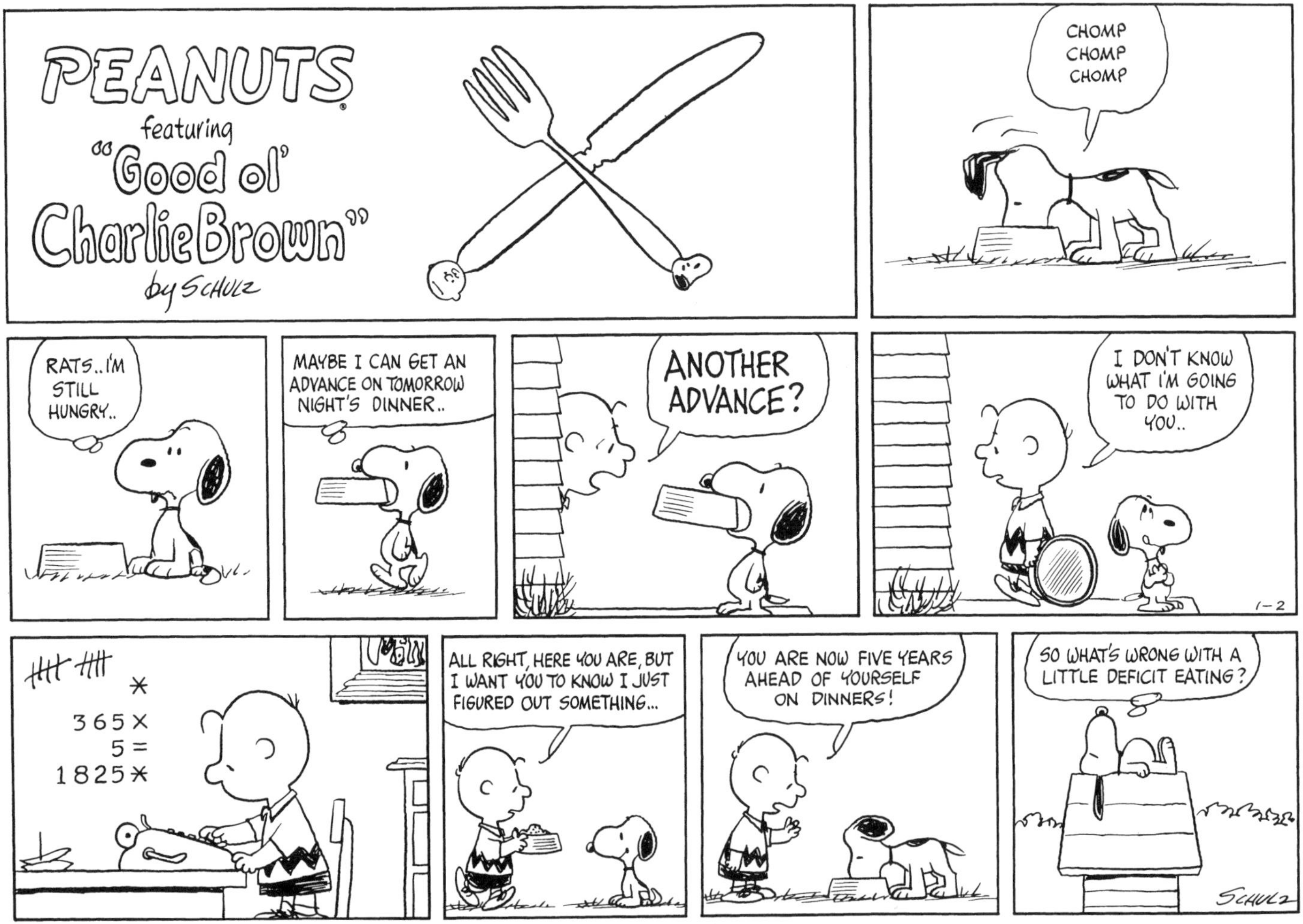
PEANUTS
featuring
"Good ol' CharlieBrown"
by SCHULZ
CHOMP CHOMP CHOMP
RATS..I'M STILL HUNGRY..
MAYBE I CAN GET AN ADVANCE ON TOMORROW NIGHT'S DINNER..
ANOTHER ADVANCE?
I DON'T KNOW WHAT I'M GOING TO DO WITH YOU..
1-2
365 X 5 = 1825
ALL RIGHT, HERE YOU ARE, BUT I WANT YOU TO KNOW I JUST FIGURED OUT SOMETHING...
YOU ARE NOW FIVE YEARS AHEAD OF YOURSELF ON DINNERS!
SO WHAT'S WRONG WITH A LITTLE DEFICIT EATING?
SCHULZ

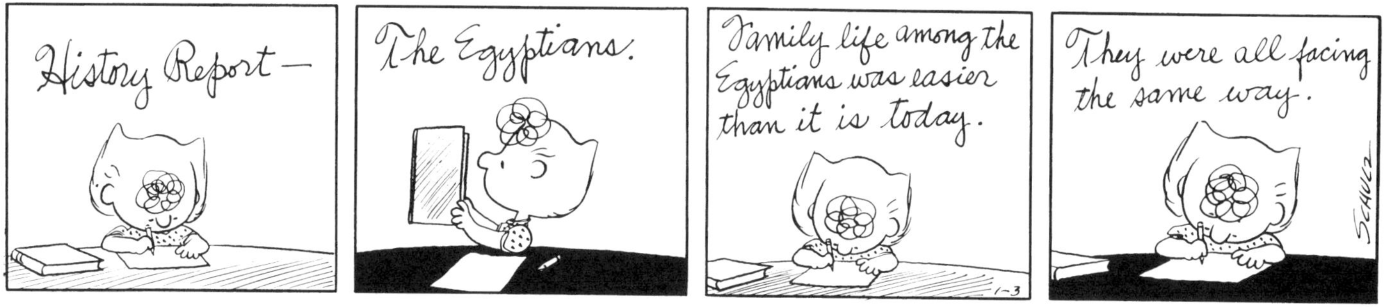
History Report—
The Egyptians.
Family life among the Egyptians was easier than it is today.
They were all facing the same way.

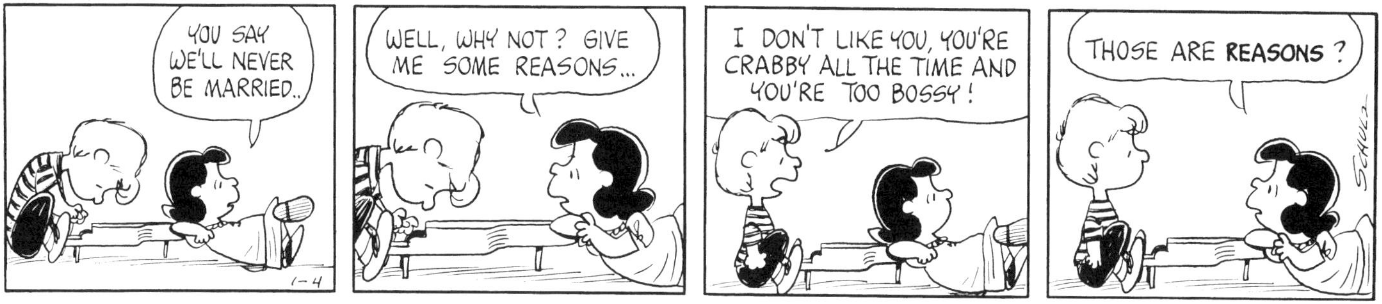
YOU SAY WE'LL NEVER BE MARRIED..
WELL, WHY NOT? GIVE ME SOME REASONS...
I DON'T LIKE YOU, YOU'RE CRABBY ALL THE TIME AND YOU'RE TOO BOSSY!
THOSE ARE **REASONS**?

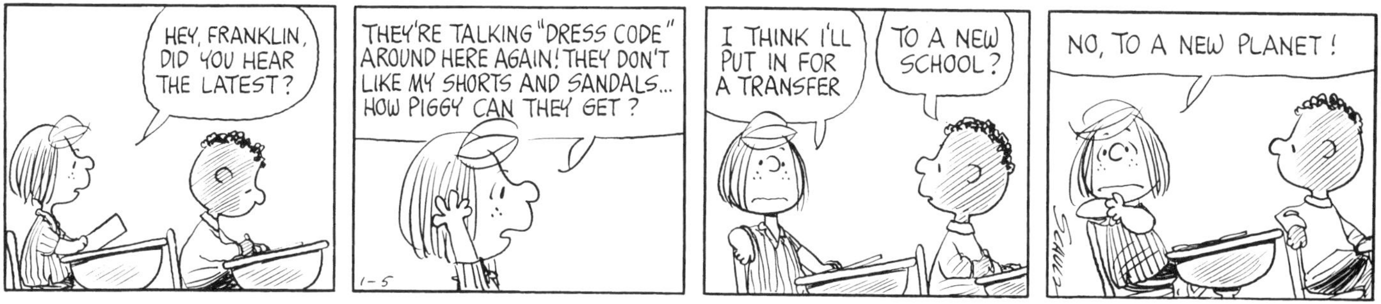
HEY, FRANKLIN, DID YOU HEAR THE LATEST?
THEY'RE TALKING "DRESS CODE" AROUND HERE AGAIN! THEY DON'T LIKE MY SHORTS AND SANDALS... HOW PIGGY CAN THEY GET?
I THINK I'LL PUT IN FOR A TRANSFER
TO A NEW SCHOOL?
NO, TO A NEW PLANET!

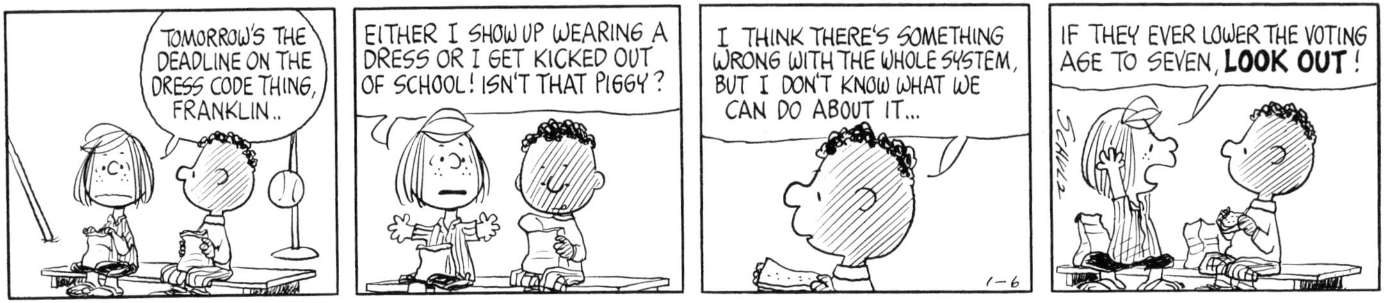
TOMORROW'S THE DEADLINE ON THE DRESS CODE THING, FRANKLIN..
EITHER I SHOW UP WEARING A DRESS OR I GET KICKED OUT OF SCHOOL! ISN'T THAT PIGGY?
I THINK THERE'S SOMETHING WRONG WITH THE WHOLE SYSTEM, BUT I DON'T KNOW WHAT WE CAN DO ABOUT IT...
1-6
IF THEY EVER LOWER THE VOTING AGE TO SEVEN, LOOK OUT!
SCHULZ

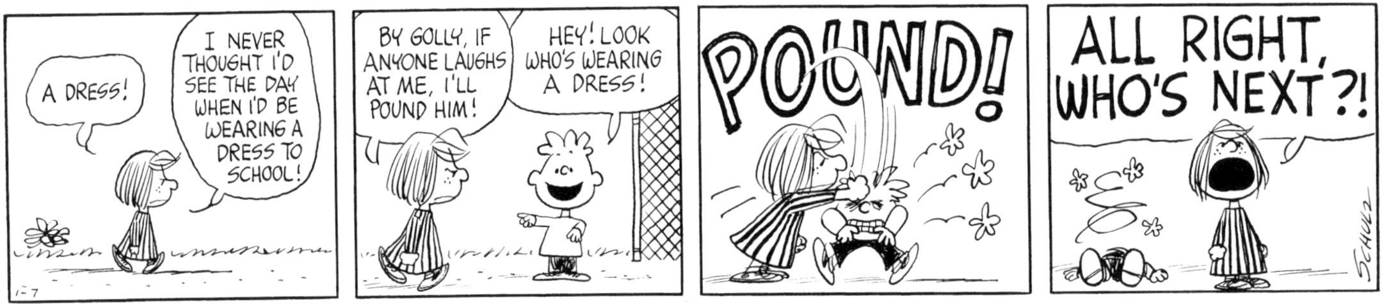
A DRESS!
I NEVER THOUGHT I'D SEE THE DAY WHEN I'D BE WEARING A DRESS TO SCHOOL!
1-7
BY GOLLY, IF ANYONE LAUGHS AT ME, I'LL POUND HIM!
HEY! LOOK WHO'S WEARING A DRESS!
POUND!
ALL RIGHT, WHO'S NEXT?!
SCHULZ

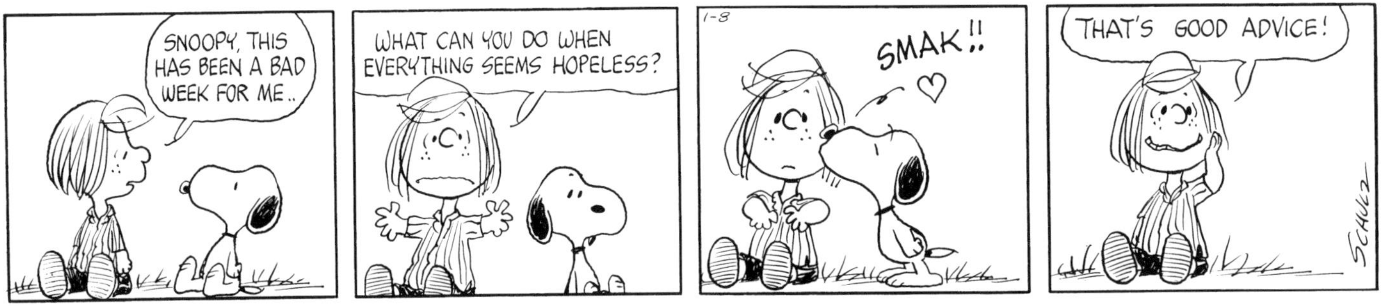
SNOOPY, THIS HAS BEEN A BAD WEEK FOR ME..
WHAT CAN YOU DO WHEN EVERYTHING SEEMS HOPELESS?
1-8
SMAK!!
THAT'S GOOD ADVICE!
SCHULZ

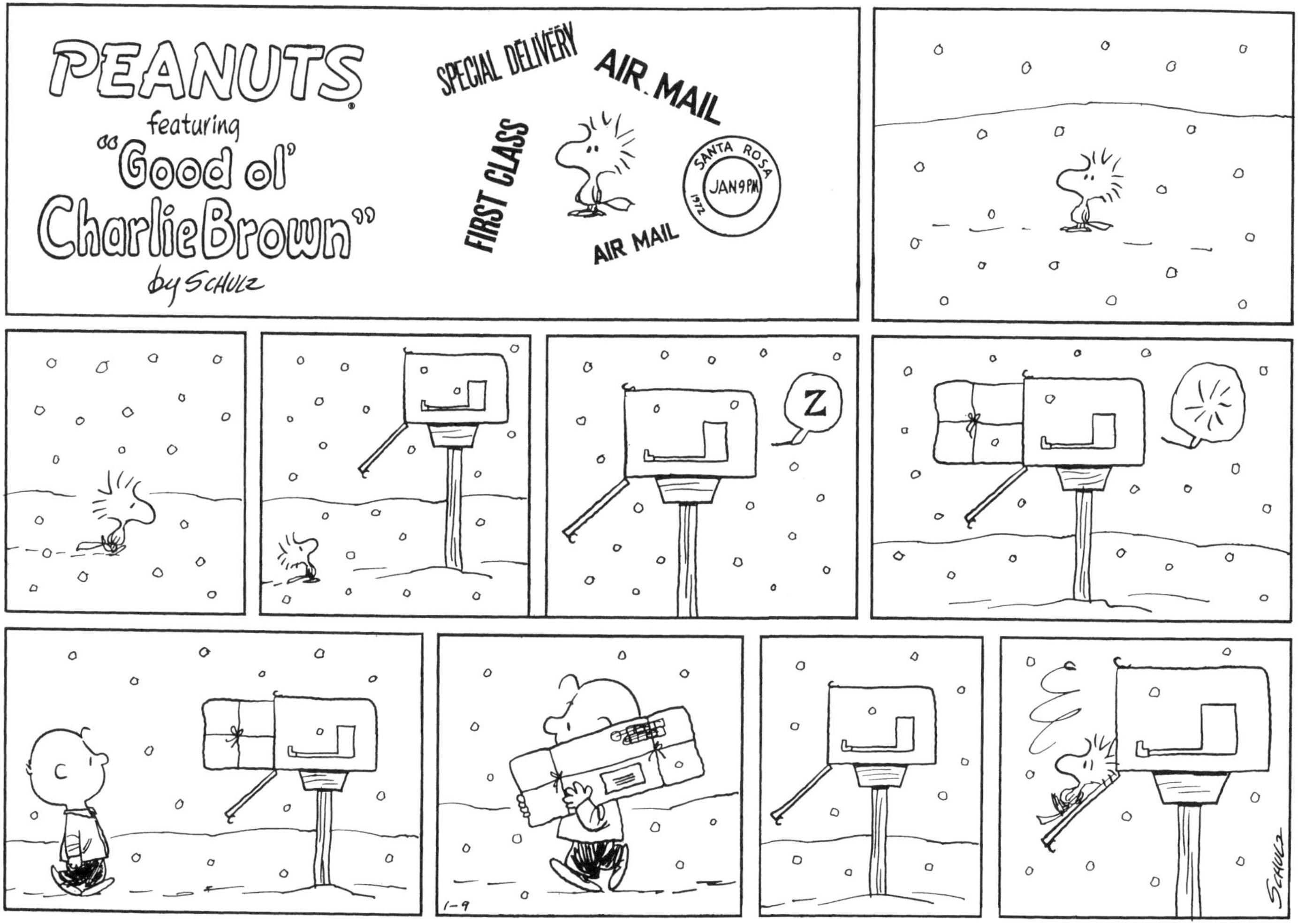

PEANUTS
featuring
"Good ol' Charlie Brown"
by SCHULZ
SPECIAL DELIVERY
AIR MAIL
FIRST CLASS
SANTA ROSA
JAN 9 PM
1972
AIR MAIL
Z
1-9
SCHULZ

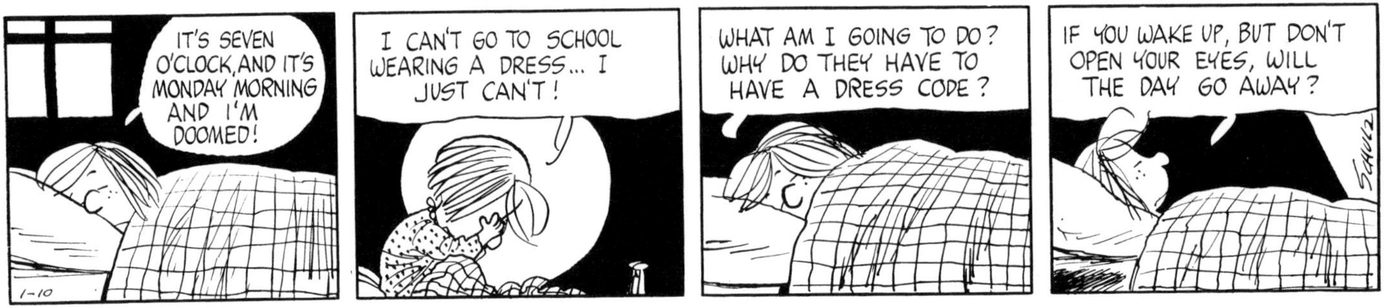
1-10
IT'S SEVEN O'CLOCK, AND IT'S MONDAY MORNING AND I'M DOOMED!
I CAN'T GO TO SCHOOL WEARING A DRESS... I JUST CAN'T!
WHAT AM I GOING TO DO? WHY DO THEY HAVE TO HAVE A DRESS CODE?
IF YOU WAKE UP, BUT DON'T OPEN YOUR EYES, WILL THE DAY GO AWAY?
SCHULZ

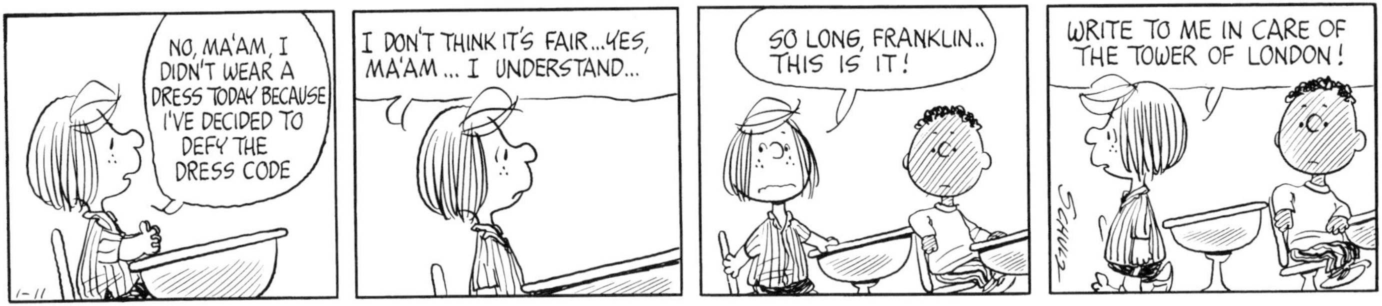
1-11
NO, MA'AM, I DIDN'T WEAR A DRESS TODAY BECAUSE I'VE DECIDED TO DEFY THE DRESS CODE
I DON'T THINK IT'S FAIR...YES, MA'AM ... I UNDERSTAND...
SO LONG, FRANKLIN.. THIS IS IT!
WRITE TO ME IN CARE OF THE TOWER OF LONDON!
SCHULZ

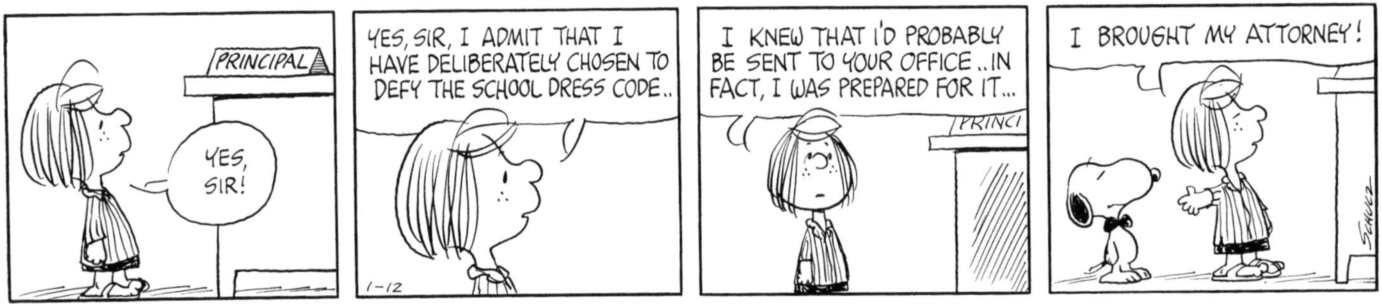
PRINCIPAL
YES, SIR!
1-12
YES, SIR, I ADMIT THAT I HAVE DELIBERATELY CHOSEN TO DEFY THE SCHOOL DRESS CODE..
I KNEW THAT I'D PROBABLY BE SENT TO YOUR OFFICE ..IN FACT, I WAS PREPARED FOR IT...
I BROUGHT MY ATTORNEY!
SCHULZ

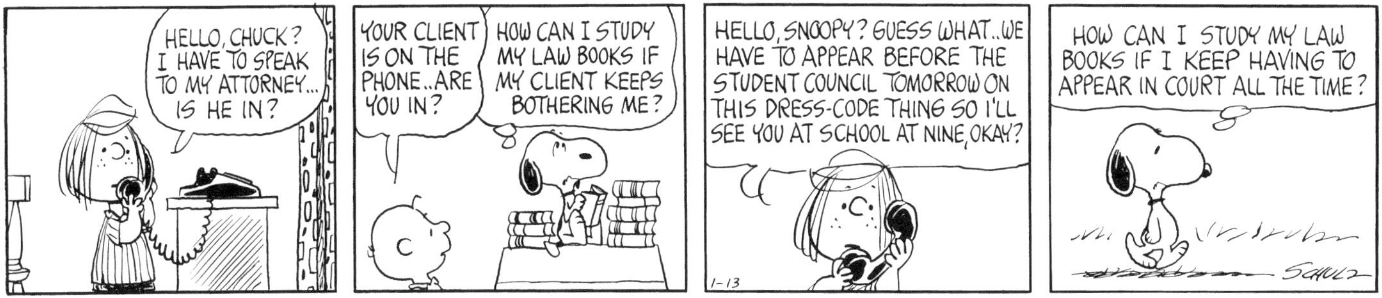
HELLO, CHUCK? I HAVE TO SPEAK TO MY ATTORNEY... IS HE IN?
YOUR CLIENT IS ON THE PHONE..ARE YOU IN?
HOW CAN I STUDY MY LAW BOOKS IF MY CLIENT KEEPS BOTHERING ME?
HELLO, SNOOPY? GUESS WHAT..WE HAVE TO APPEAR BEFORE THE STUDENT COUNCIL TOMORROW ON THIS DRESS-CODE THING SO I'LL SEE YOU AT SCHOOL AT NINE, OKAY?
1-13
HOW CAN I STUDY MY LAW BOOKS IF I KEEP HAVING TO APPEAR IN COURT ALL THE TIME?
SCHULZ

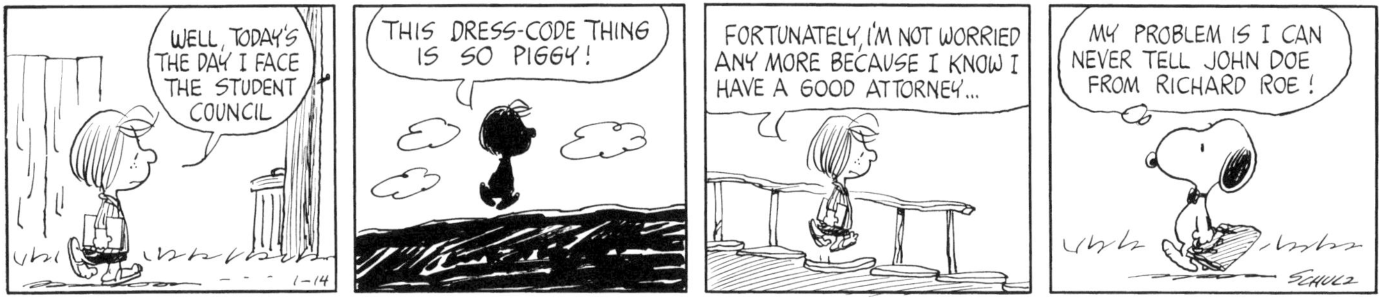
WELL, TODAY'S THE DAY I FACE THE STUDENT COUNCIL
1-14
THIS DRESS-CODE THING IS SO PIGGY!
FORTUNATELY, I'M NOT WORRIED ANY MORE BECAUSE I KNOW I HAVE A GOOD ATTORNEY...
MY PROBLEM IS I CAN NEVER TELL JOHN DOE FROM RICHARD ROE!
SCHULZ

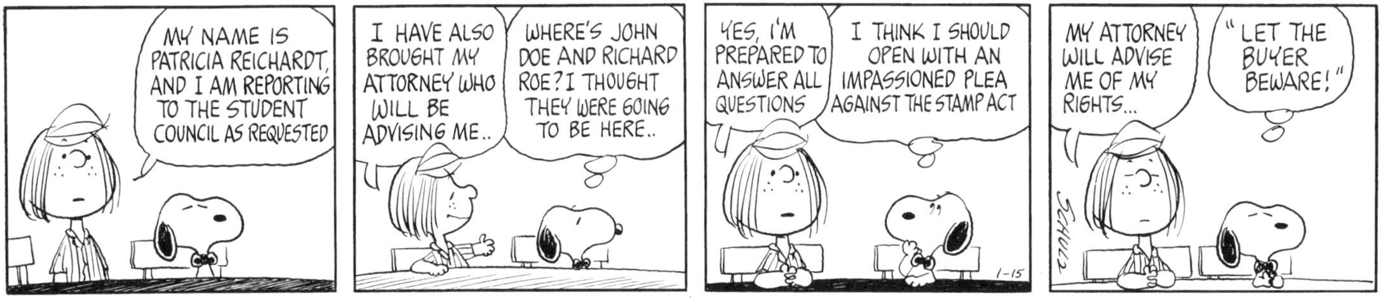
MY NAME IS PATRICIA REICHARDT, AND I AM REPORTING TO THE STUDENT COUNCIL AS REQUESTED
I HAVE ALSO BROUGHT MY ATTORNEY WHO WILL BE ADVISING ME..
WHERE'S JOHN DOE AND RICHARD ROE? I THOUGHT THEY WERE GOING TO BE HERE..
YES, I'M PREPARED TO ANSWER ALL QUESTIONS
I THINK I SHOULD OPEN WITH AN IMPASSIONED PLEA AGAINST THE STAMP ACT
1-15
MY ATTORNEY WILL ADVISE ME OF MY RIGHTS...
"LET THE BUYER BEWARE!"
SCHULZ

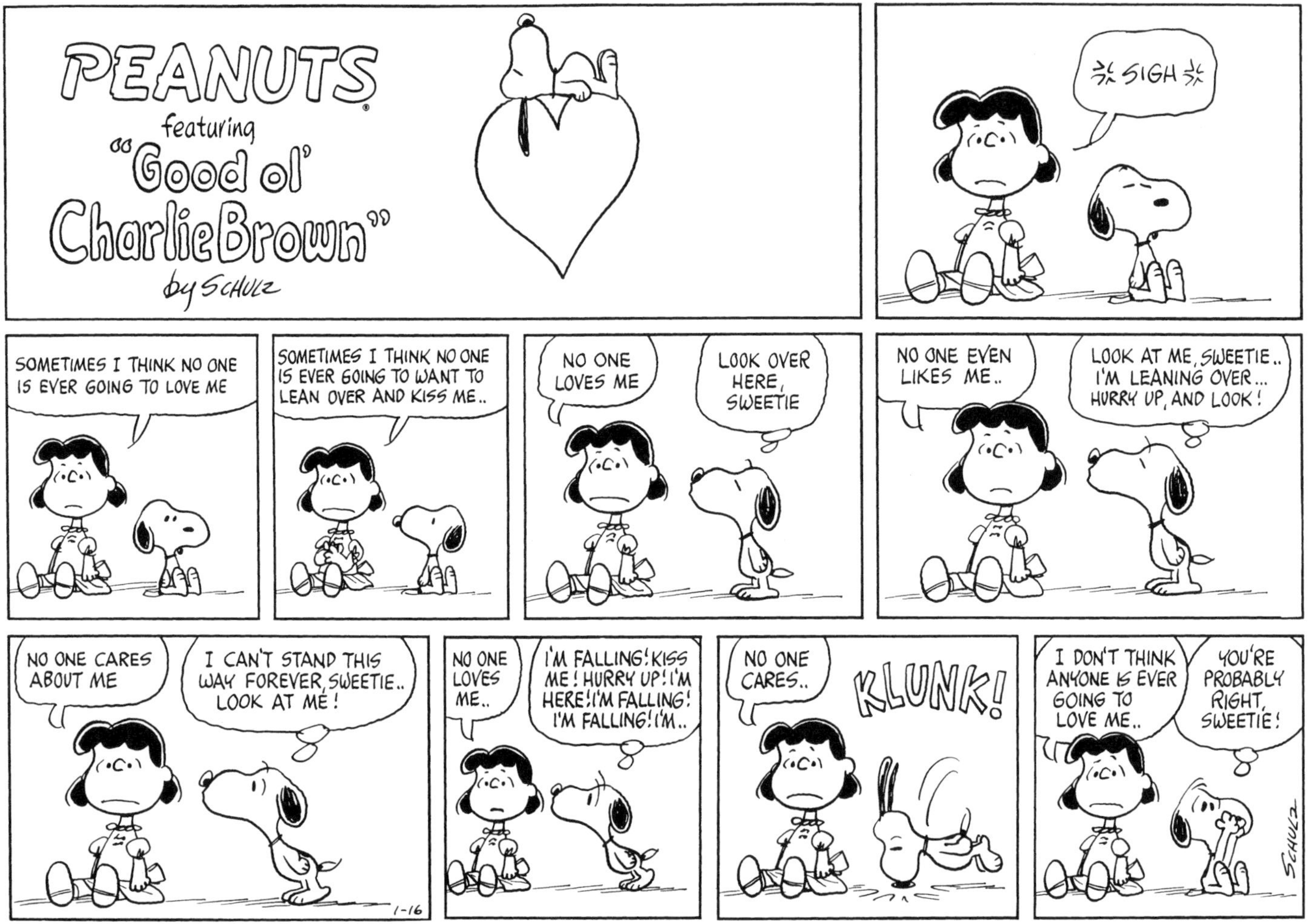
PEANUTS
featuring "Good ol' Charlie Brown"
by SCHULZ
SIGH
SOMETIMES I THINK NO ONE IS EVER GOING TO LOVE ME
SOMETIMES I THINK NO ONE IS EVER GOING TO WANT TO LEAN OVER AND KISS ME..
NO ONE LOVES ME
LOOK OVER HERE, SWEETIE
NO ONE EVEN LIKES ME..
LOOK AT ME, SWEETIE.. I'M LEANING OVER... HURRY UP, AND LOOK!
NO ONE CARES ABOUT ME
I CAN'T STAND THIS WAY FOREVER, SWEETIE.. LOOK AT ME!
1-16
NO ONE LOVES ME..
I'M FALLING! KISS ME! HURRY UP! I'M HERE! I'M FALLING! I'M FALLING! I'M..
NO ONE CARES..
KLUNK!
I DON'T THINK ANYONE IS EVER GOING TO LOVE ME..
YOU'RE PROBABLY RIGHT, SWEETIE!
SCHULZ

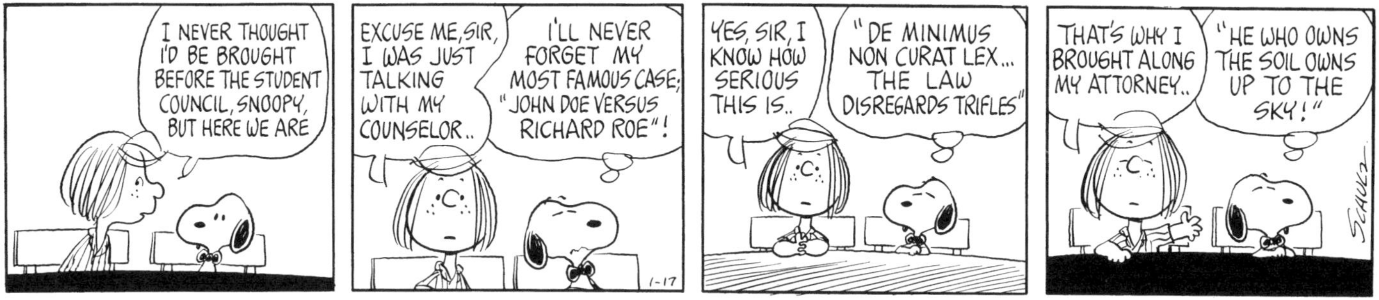
I NEVER THOUGHT I'D BE BROUGHT BEFORE THE STUDENT COUNCIL, SNOOPY, BUT HERE WE ARE
EXCUSE ME, SIR, I WAS JUST TALKING WITH MY COUNSELOR..
I'LL NEVER FORGET MY MOST FAMOUS CASE; "JOHN DOE VERSUS RICHARD ROE"!
1-17
YES, SIR, I KNOW HOW SERIOUS THIS IS..
"DE MINIMUS NON CURAT LEX... THE LAW DISREGARDS TRIFLES"
THAT'S WHY I BROUGHT ALONG MY ATTORNEY..
"HE WHO OWNS THE SOIL OWNS UP TO THE SKY!"
SCHULZ

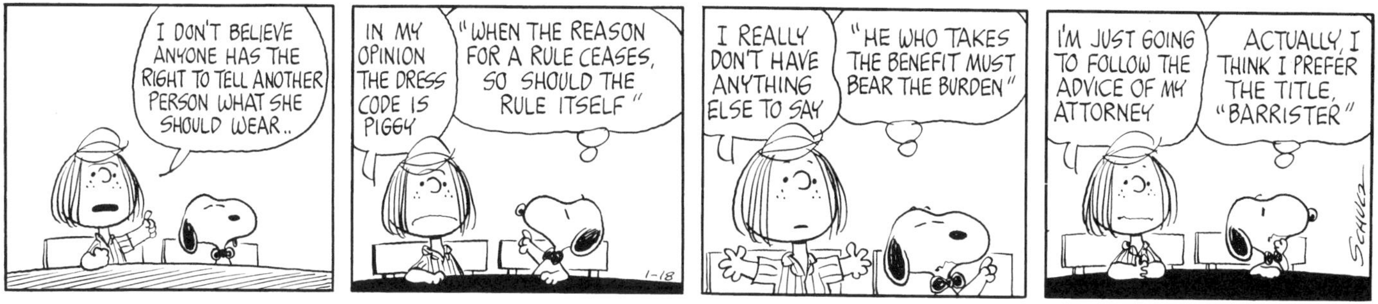
I DON'T BELIEVE ANYONE HAS THE RIGHT TO TELL ANOTHER PERSON WHAT SHE SHOULD WEAR..
IN MY OPINION THE DRESS CODE IS PIGGY
"WHEN THE REASON FOR A RULE CEASES, SO SHOULD THE RULE ITSELF"
1-18
I REALLY DON'T HAVE ANYTHING ELSE TO SAY
"HE WHO TAKES THE BENEFIT MUST BEAR THE BURDEN"
I'M JUST GOING TO FOLLOW THE ADVICE OF MY ATTORNEY
ACTUALLY, I THINK I PREFER THE TITLE, "BARRISTER"
SCHULZ

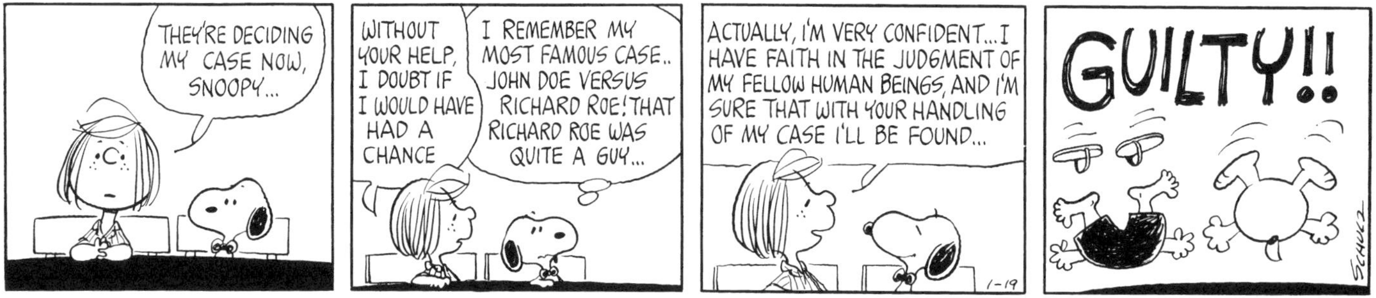
THEY'RE DECIDING MY CASE NOW, SNOOPY...
WITHOUT YOUR HELP, I DOUBT IF I WOULD HAVE HAD A CHANCE
I REMEMBER MY MOST FAMOUS CASE.. JOHN DOE VERSUS RICHARD ROE! THAT RICHARD ROE WAS QUITE A GUY...
ACTUALLY, I'M VERY CONFIDENT...I HAVE FAITH IN THE JUDGMENT OF MY FELLOW HUMAN BEINGS, AND I'M SURE THAT WITH YOUR HANDLING OF MY CASE I'LL BE FOUND...
1-19
GUILTY!!
SCHULZ

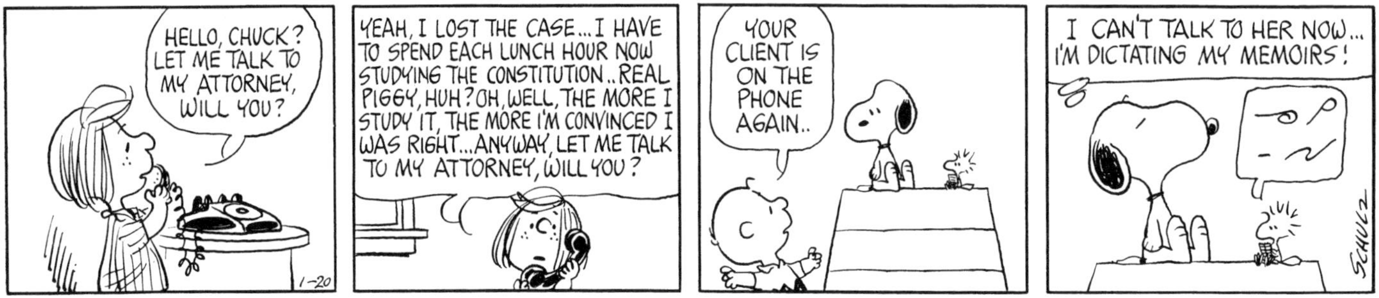
HELLO, CHUCK? LET ME TALK TO MY ATTORNEY, WILL YOU?
1-20
YEAH, I LOST THE CASE...I HAVE TO SPEND EACH LUNCH HOUR NOW STUDYING THE CONSTITUTION..REAL PIGGY, HUH? OH, WELL, THE MORE I STUDY IT, THE MORE I'M CONVINCED I WAS RIGHT...ANYWAY, LET ME TALK TO MY ATTORNEY, WILL YOU?
YOUR CLIENT IS ON THE PHONE AGAIN..
I CAN'T TALK TO HER NOW... I'M DICTATING MY MEMOIRS!
SCHULZ

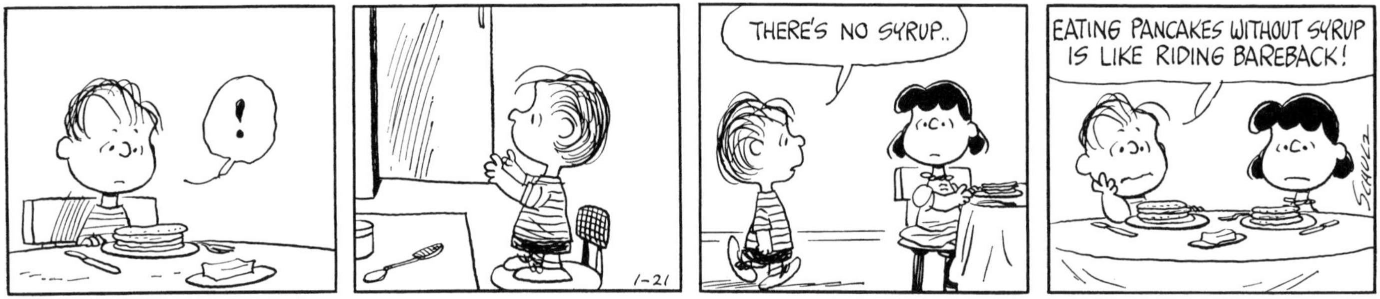
!
1-21
THERE'S NO SYRUP..
EATING PANCAKES WITHOUT SYRUP IS LIKE RIDING BAREBACK!
SCHULZ

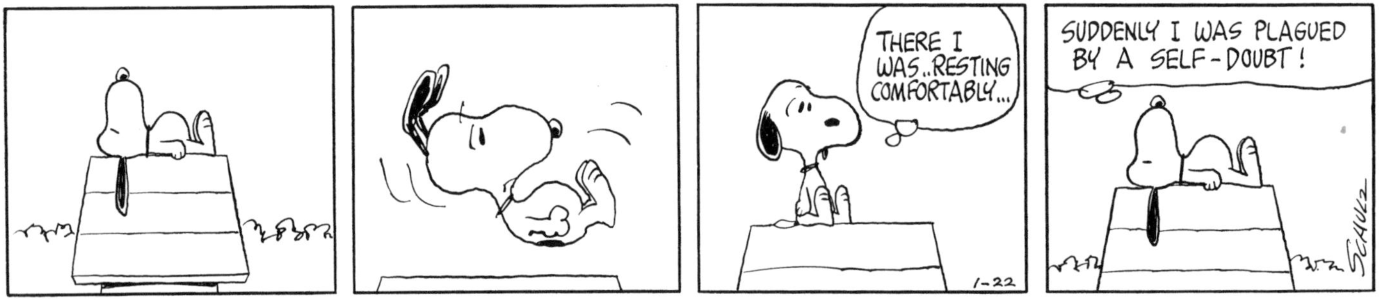
THERE I WAS..RESTING COMFORTABLY...
1-22
SUDDENLY I WAS PLAGUED BY A SELF-DOUBT!
SCHULZ

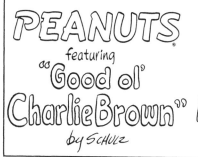

PEANUTS
featuring "Good ol' Charlie Brown"
by Schulz

HERE SHE COMES..

OKAY, CHUCK, I'M ALL SET FOR THE HOCKEY GAME...HOW DO WE PLAY?

WELL, YOU AND I WILL BE CENTERS... WE'LL FACE-OFF HERE IN THE MIDDLE..

LINUS AND SCHROEDER WILL BE WINGS..

THE IDEA IS TO SHOOT THE PUCK BETWEEN THOSE CHUNKS OF SNOW...THE GOALIE, OF COURSE, WILL TRY TO STOP YOU...

WHICH ONE IS THE GOALIE?

THE GOALIE IS THE ONE WEARING THOSE PADS...

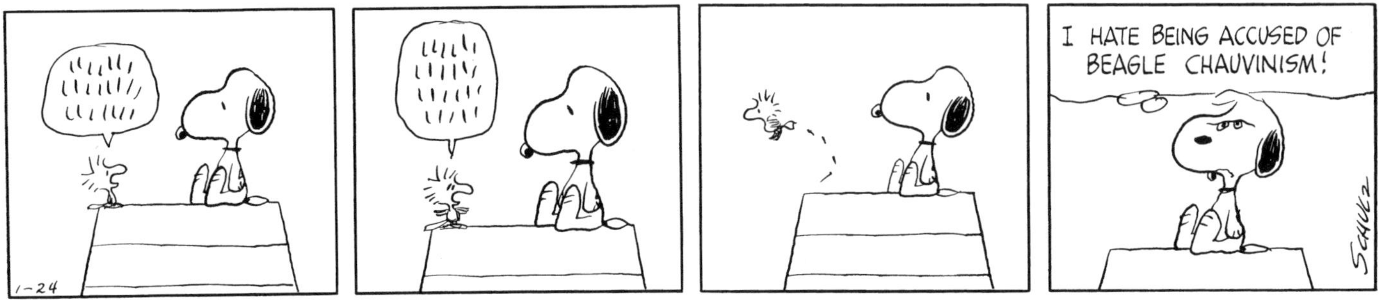
I HATE BEING ACCUSED OF BEAGLE CHAUVINISM!

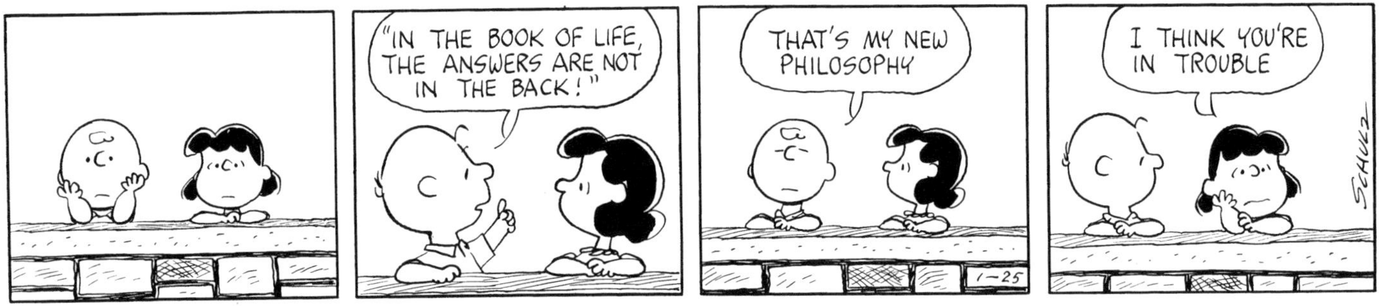
"IN THE BOOK OF LIFE, THE ANSWERS ARE NOT IN THE BACK!"
THAT'S MY NEW PHILOSOPHY
I THINK YOU'RE IN TROUBLE

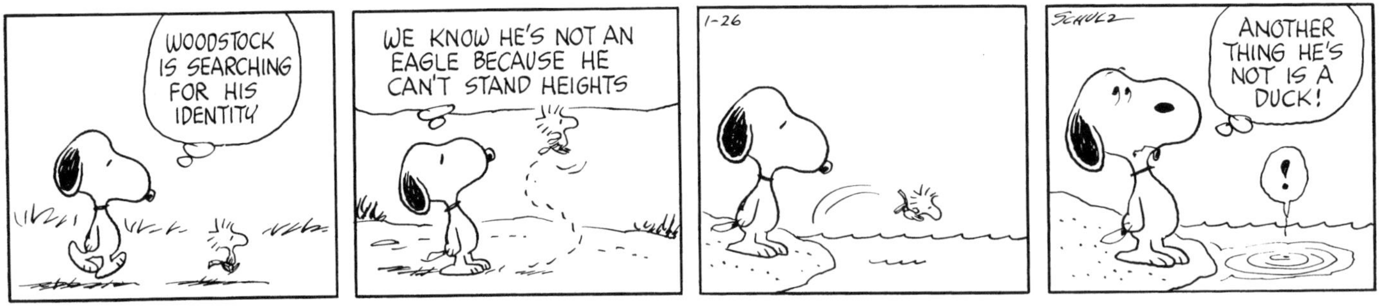
WOODSTOCK IS SEARCHING FOR HIS IDENTITY
WE KNOW HE'S NOT AN EAGLE BECAUSE HE CAN'T STAND HEIGHTS
ANOTHER THING HE'S NOT IS A DUCK!

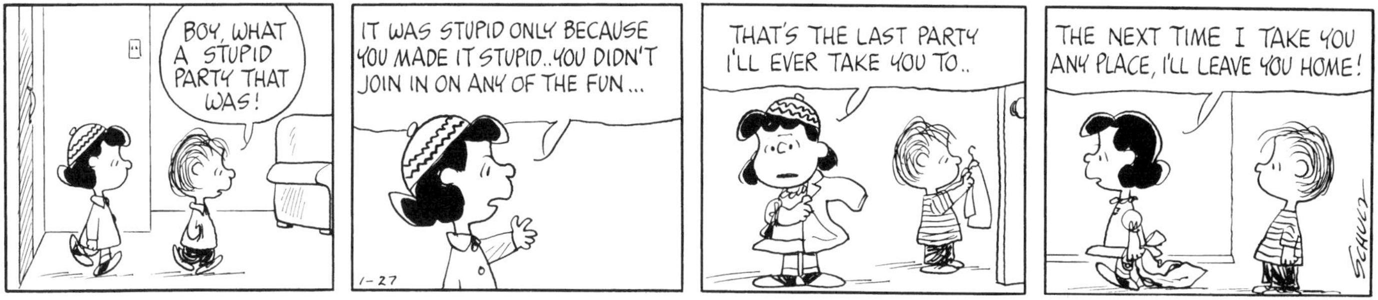
BOY, WHAT A STUPID PARTY THAT WAS!
IT WAS STUPID ONLY BECAUSE YOU MADE IT STUPID..YOU DIDN'T JOIN IN ON ANY OF THE FUN...
1-27
THAT'S THE LAST PARTY I'LL EVER TAKE YOU TO..
THE NEXT TIME I TAKE YOU ANY PLACE, I'LL LEAVE YOU HOME!
SCHULZ

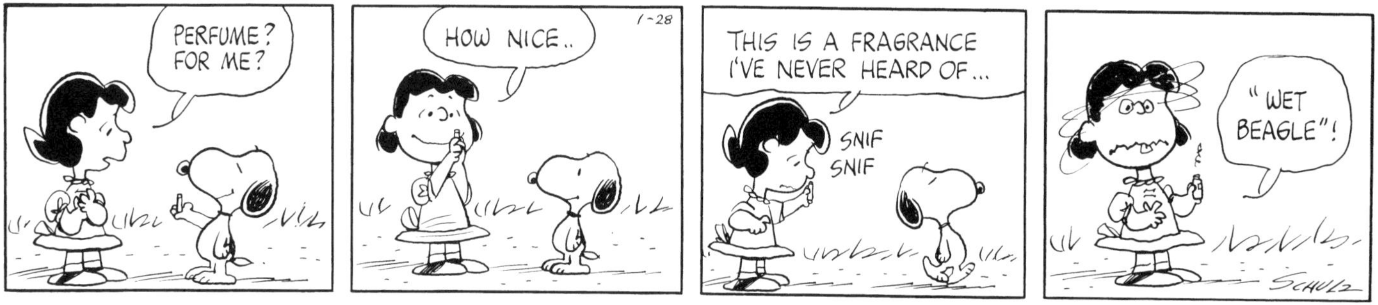
PERFUME? FOR ME?
HOW NICE..
1-28
THIS IS A FRAGRANCE I'VE NEVER HEARD OF...
SNIF SNIF
"WET BEAGLE"!
SCHULZ

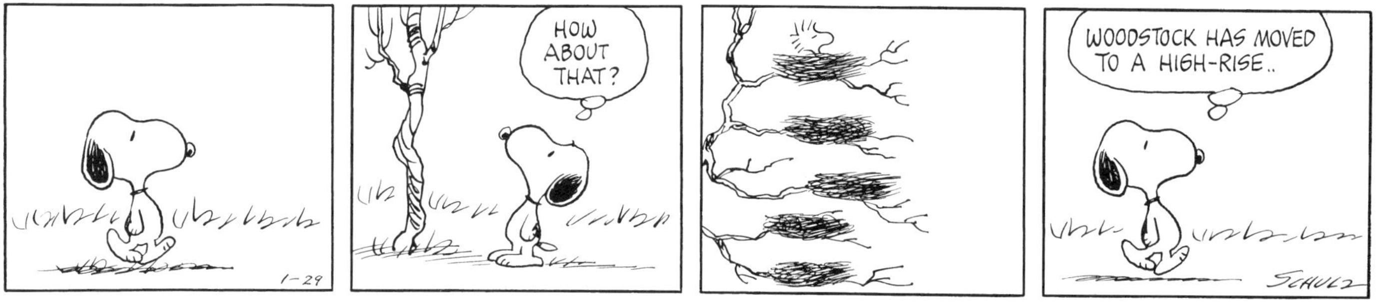
1-29
HOW ABOUT THAT?
WOODSTOCK HAS MOVED TO A HIGH-RISE..
SCHULZ

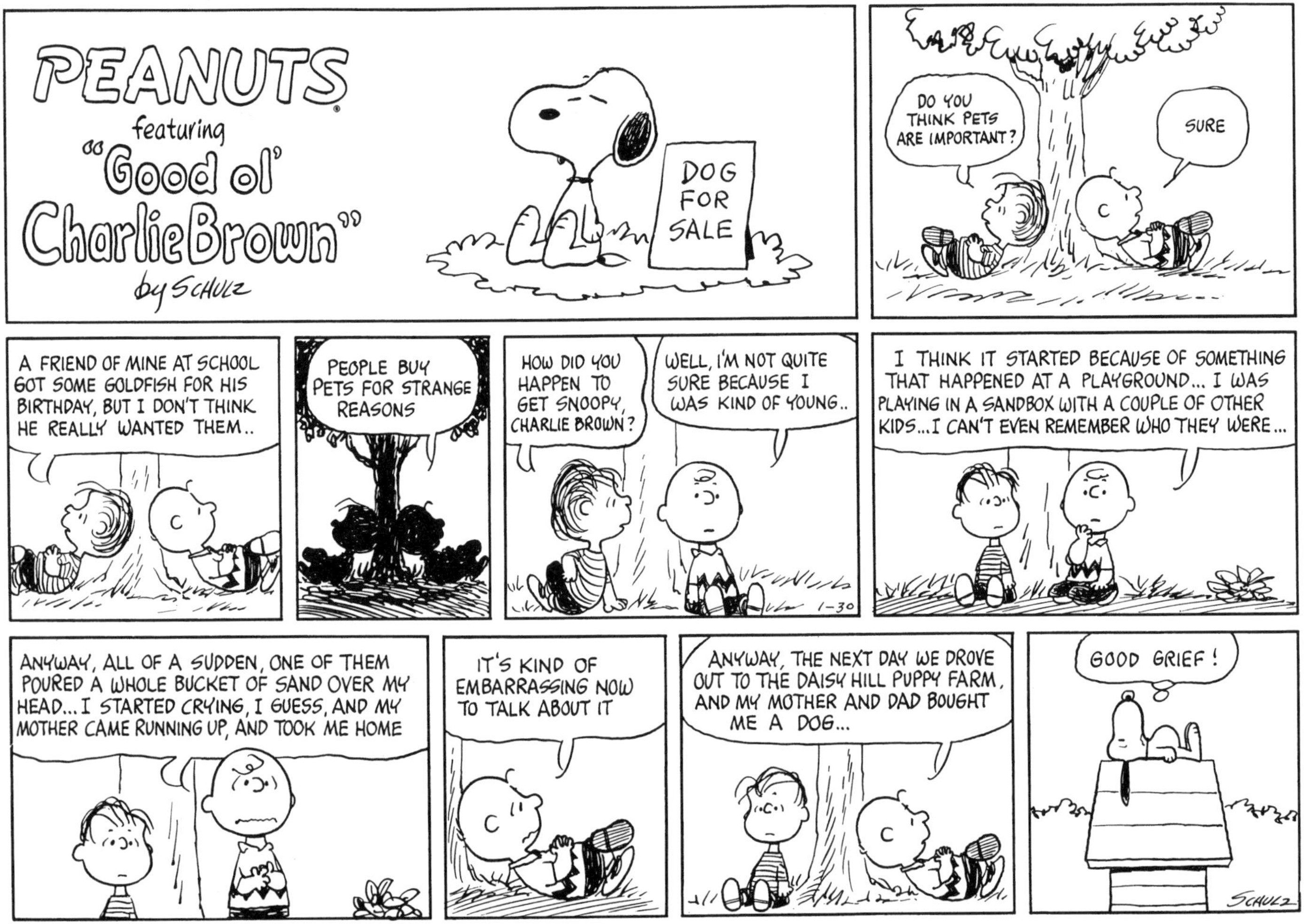
PEANUTS
featuring "Good ol' Charlie Brown"
by SCHULZ
DOG FOR SALE
DO YOU THINK PETS ARE IMPORTANT?
SURE
A FRIEND OF MINE AT SCHOOL GOT SOME GOLDFISH FOR HIS BIRTHDAY, BUT I DON'T THINK HE REALLY WANTED THEM..
PEOPLE BUY PETS FOR STRANGE REASONS
HOW DID YOU HAPPEN TO GET SNOOPY, CHARLIE BROWN?
WELL, I'M NOT QUITE SURE BECAUSE I WAS KIND OF YOUNG..
1-30
I THINK IT STARTED BECAUSE OF SOMETHING THAT HAPPENED AT A PLAYGROUND... I WAS PLAYING IN A SANDBOX WITH A COUPLE OF OTHER KIDS...I CAN'T EVEN REMEMBER WHO THEY WERE...
ANYWAY, ALL OF A SUDDEN, ONE OF THEM POURED A WHOLE BUCKET OF SAND OVER MY HEAD...I STARTED CRYING, I GUESS, AND MY MOTHER CAME RUNNING UP, AND TOOK ME HOME
IT'S KIND OF EMBARRASSING NOW TO TALK ABOUT IT
ANYWAY, THE NEXT DAY WE DROVE OUT TO THE DAISY HILL PUPPY FARM, AND MY MOTHER AND DAD BOUGHT ME A DOG...
GOOD GRIEF!
SCHULZ

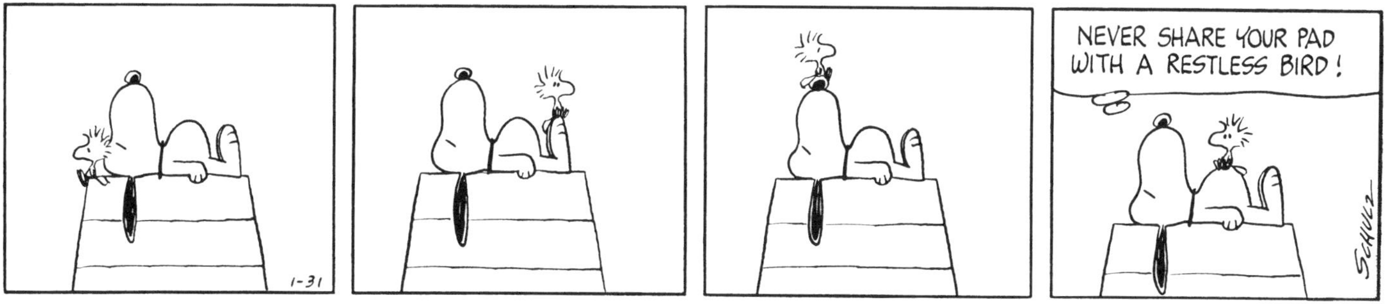
1-31
NEVER SHARE YOUR PAD WITH A RESTLESS BIRD!
SCHULZ

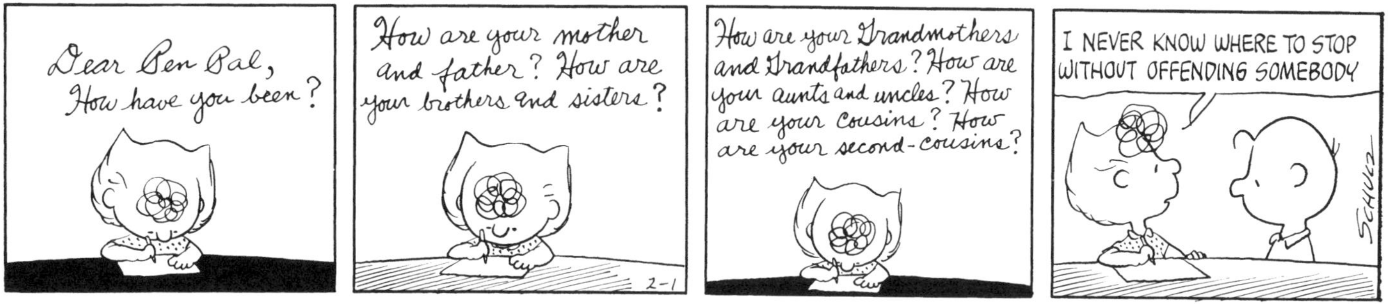
Dear Pen Pal, How have you been?
How are your mother and father? How are your brothers and sisters?
2-1
How are your Grandmothers and Grandfathers? How are your aunts and uncles? How are your cousins? How are your second-cousins?
I NEVER KNOW WHERE TO STOP WITHOUT OFFENDING SOMEBODY
SCHULZ

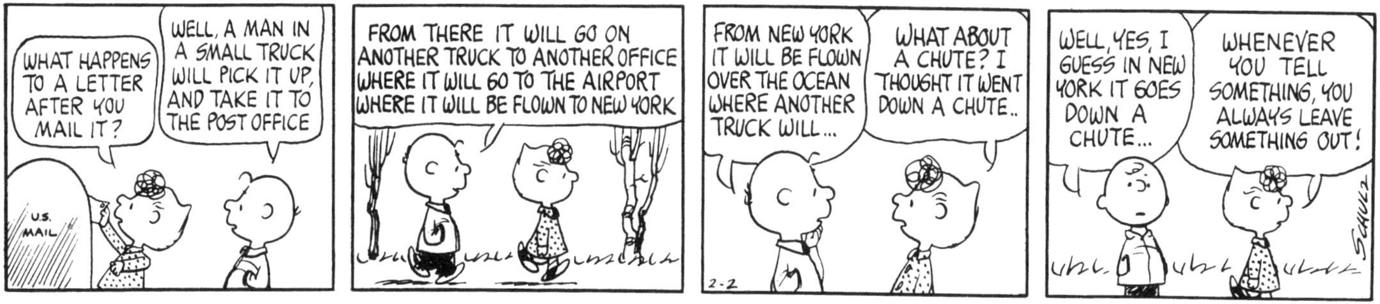
WHAT HAPPENS TO A LETTER AFTER YOU MAIL IT?
WELL, A MAN IN A SMALL TRUCK WILL PICK IT UP, AND TAKE IT TO THE POST OFFICE
U.S. MAIL
FROM THERE IT WILL GO ON ANOTHER TRUCK TO ANOTHER OFFICE WHERE IT WILL GO TO THE AIRPORT WHERE IT WILL BE FLOWN TO NEW YORK
FROM NEW YORK IT WILL BE FLOWN OVER THE OCEAN WHERE ANOTHER TRUCK WILL...
WHAT ABOUT A CHUTE? I THOUGHT IT WENT DOWN A CHUTE..
2-2
WELL, YES, I GUESS IN NEW YORK IT GOES DOWN A CHUTE...
WHENEVER YOU TELL SOMETHING, YOU ALWAYS LEAVE SOMETHING OUT!
SCHULZ

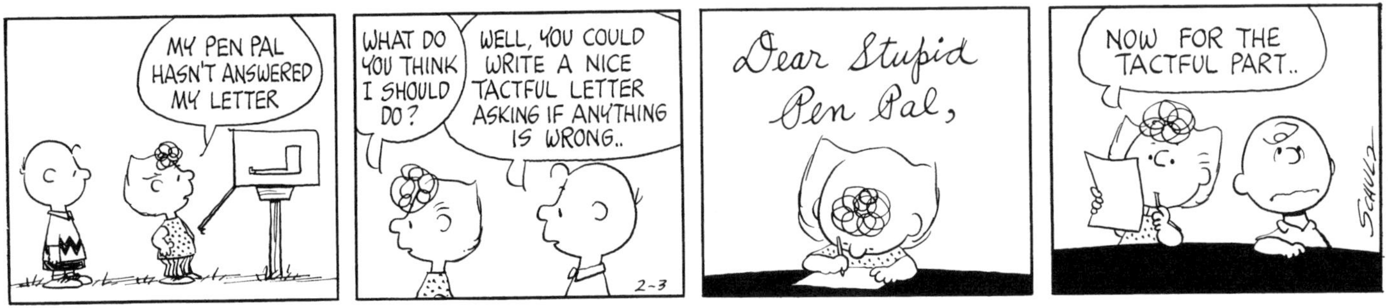
MY PEN PAL HASN'T ANSWERED MY LETTER
WHAT DO YOU THINK I SHOULD DO?
WELL, YOU COULD WRITE A NICE TACTFUL LETTER ASKING IF ANYTHING IS WRONG..
Dear Stupid Pen Pal,
NOW FOR THE TACTFUL PART..

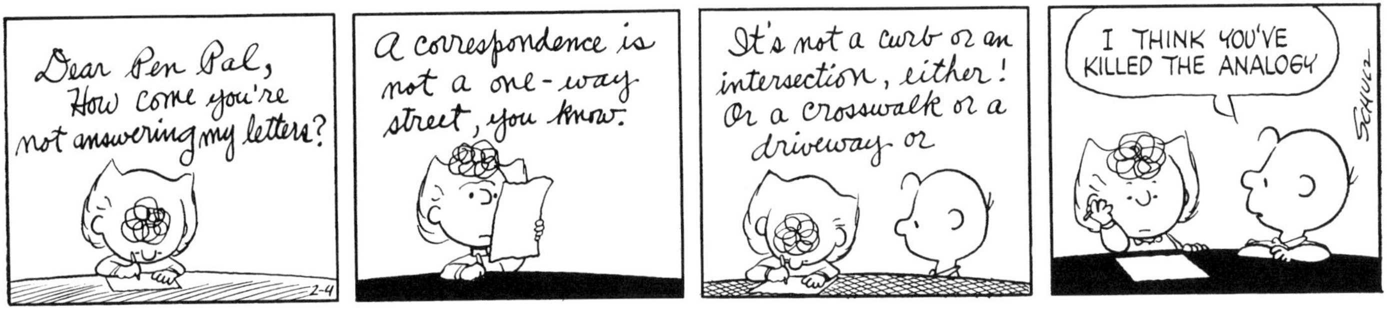
Dear Pen Pal,
How come you're not answering my letters?
A correspondence is not a one-way street, you know.
It's not a curb or an intersection, either! Or a crosswalk or a driveway or
I THINK YOU'VE KILLED THE ANALOGY

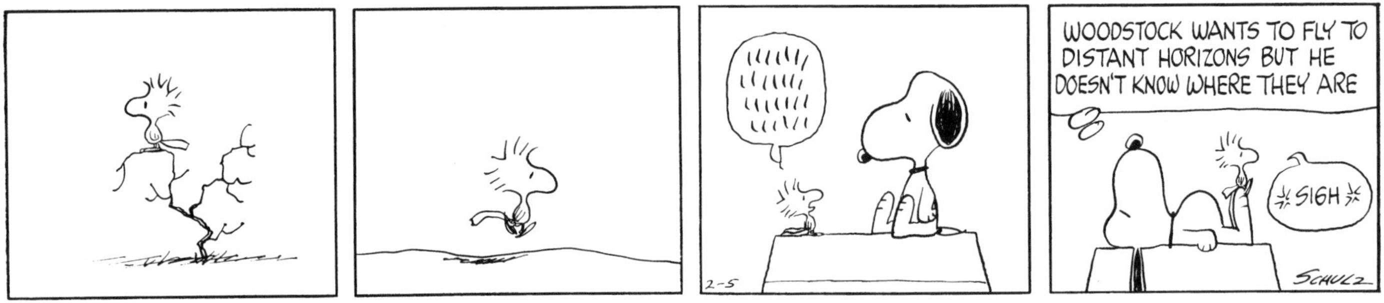
WOODSTOCK WANTS TO FLY TO DISTANT HORIZONS BUT HE DOESN'T KNOW WHERE THEY ARE
SIGH

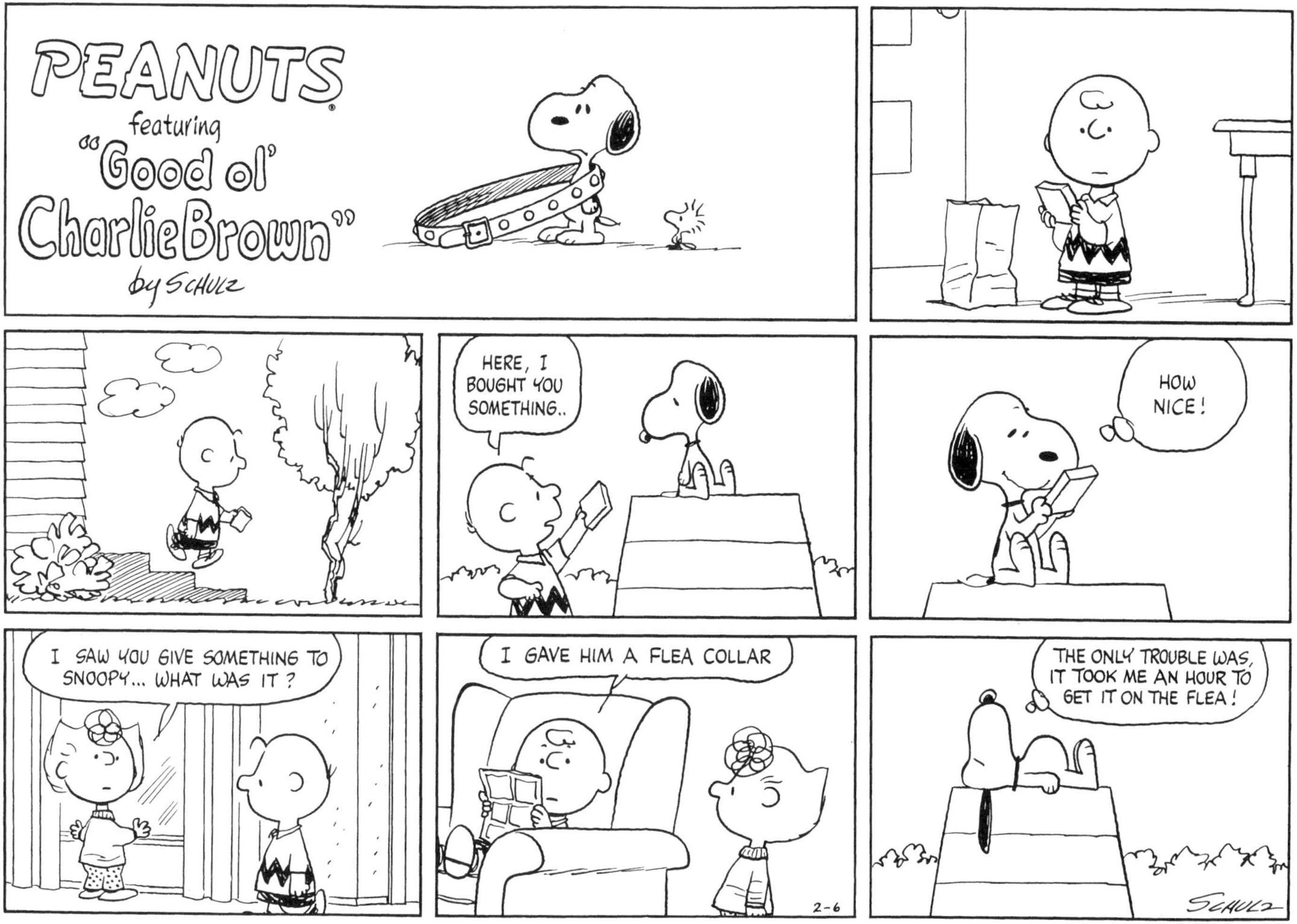
PEANUTS
featuring
"Good ol' CharlieBrown"
by SCHULZ
HERE, I BOUGHT YOU SOMETHING..
HOW NICE!
I SAW YOU GIVE SOMETHING TO SNOOPY... WHAT WAS IT?
I GAVE HIM A FLEA COLLAR
2-6
THE ONLY TROUBLE WAS, IT TOOK ME AN HOUR TO GET IT ON THE FLEA!
SCHULZ

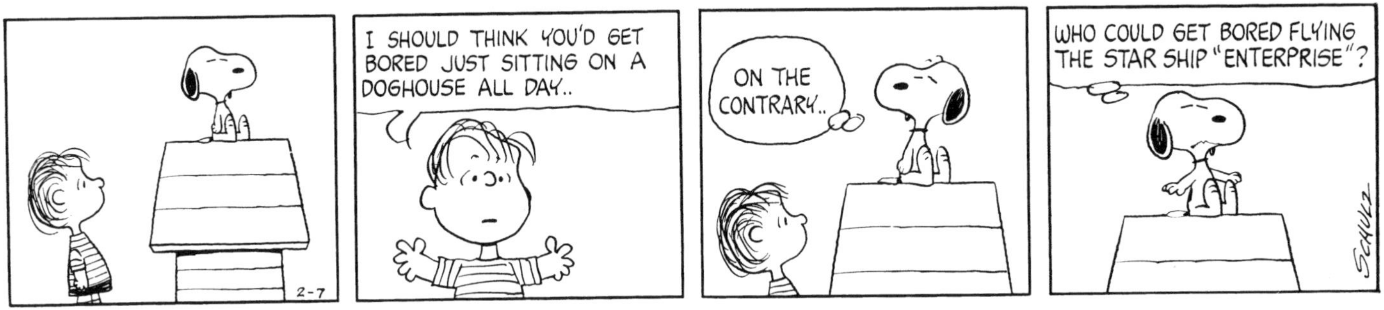
2-7
I SHOULD THINK YOU'D GET BORED JUST SITTING ON A DOGHOUSE ALL DAY..
ON THE CONTRARY..
WHO COULD GET BORED FLYING THE STAR SHIP "ENTERPRISE"?
SCHULZ

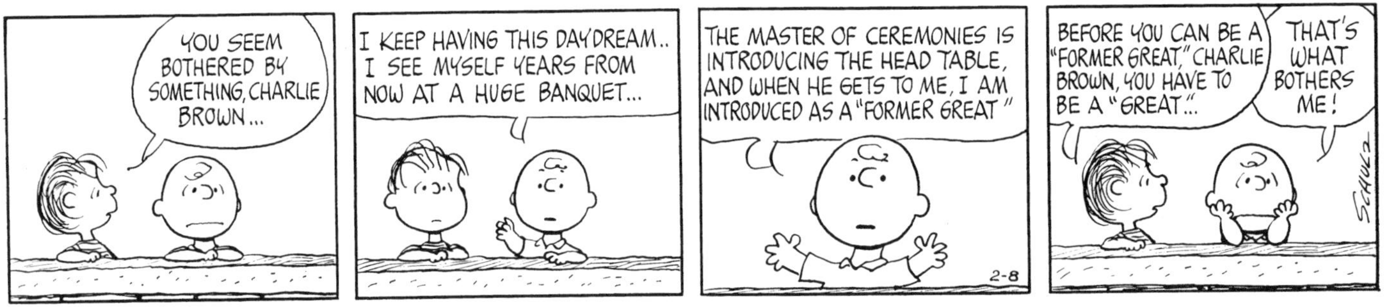
YOU SEEM BOTHERED BY SOMETHING, CHARLIE BROWN...
I KEEP HAVING THIS DAYDREAM.. I SEE MYSELF YEARS FROM NOW AT A HUGE BANQUET...
THE MASTER OF CEREMONIES IS INTRODUCING THE HEAD TABLE, AND WHEN HE GETS TO ME, I AM INTRODUCED AS A "FORMER GREAT"
2-8
BEFORE YOU CAN BE A "FORMER GREAT," CHARLIE BROWN, YOU HAVE TO BE A "GREAT."..
THAT'S WHAT BOTHERS ME!
SCHULZ

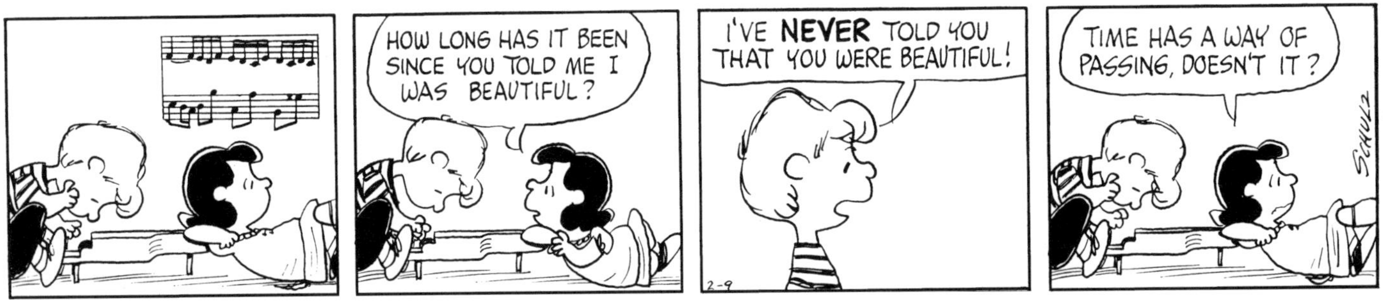
HOW LONG HAS IT BEEN SINCE YOU TOLD ME I WAS BEAUTIFUL?
I'VE **NEVER** TOLD YOU THAT YOU WERE BEAUTIFUL!
2-9
TIME HAS A WAY OF PASSING, DOESN'T IT?
SCHULZ

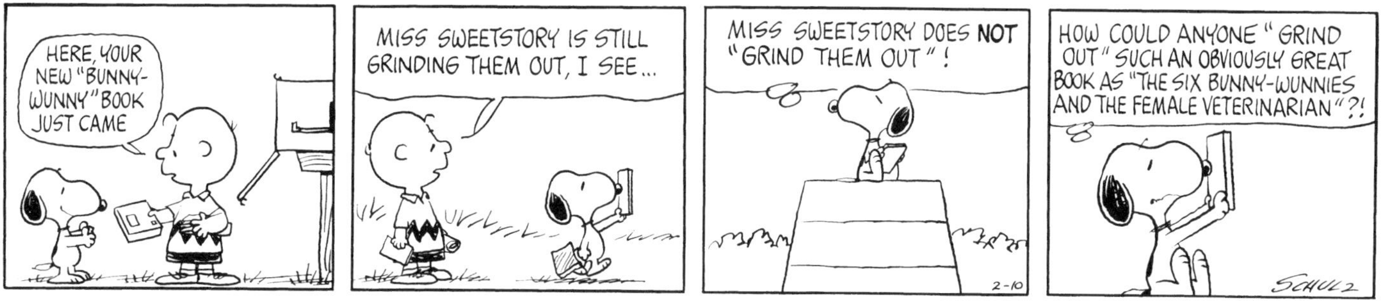
HERE, YOUR NEW "BUNNY-WUNNY" BOOK JUST CAME
MISS SWEETSTORY IS STILL GRINDING THEM OUT, I SEE...
MISS SWEETSTORY DOES **NOT** "GRIND THEM OUT"!
2-10
HOW COULD ANYONE "GRIND OUT" SUCH AN OBVIOUSLY GREAT BOOK AS "THE SIX BUNNY-WUNNIES AND THE FEMALE VETERINARIAN"?!
SCHULZ

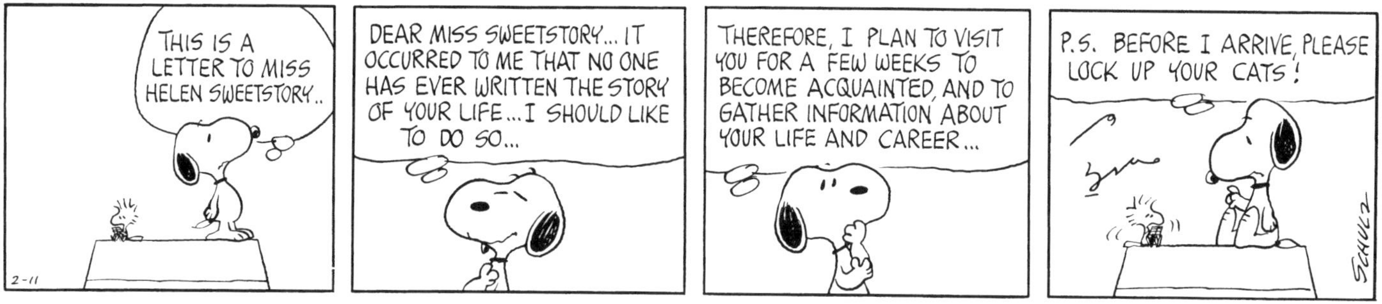
THIS IS A LETTER TO MISS HELEN SWEETSTORY..
2-11
DEAR MISS SWEETSTORY... IT OCCURRED TO ME THAT NO ONE HAS EVER WRITTEN THE STORY OF YOUR LIFE...I SHOULD LIKE TO DO SO...
THEREFORE, I PLAN TO VISIT YOU FOR A FEW WEEKS TO BECOME ACQUAINTED, AND TO GATHER INFORMATION ABOUT YOUR LIFE AND CAREER...
P.S. BEFORE I ARRIVE, PLEASE LOCK UP YOUR CATS!
SCHULZ

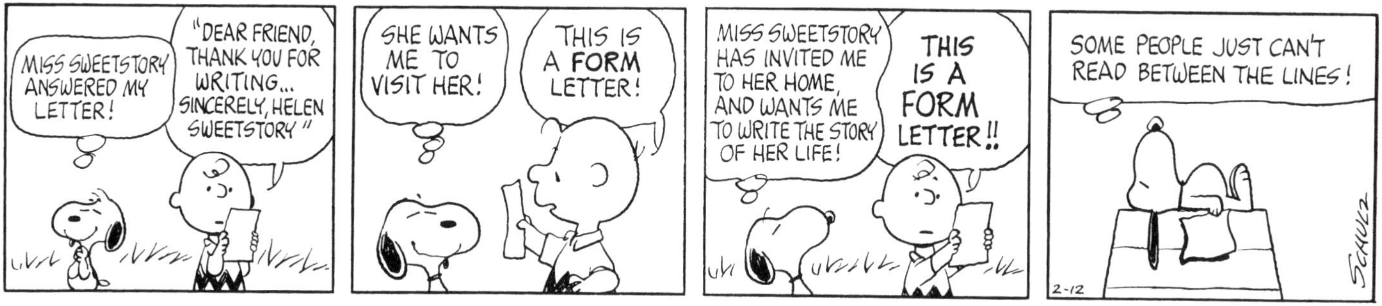
MISS SWEETSTORY ANSWERED MY LETTER!
"DEAR FRIEND, THANK YOU FOR WRITING... SINCERELY, HELEN SWEETSTORY"
SHE WANTS ME TO VISIT HER!
THIS IS A **FORM** LETTER!
MISS SWEETSTORY HAS INVITED ME TO HER HOME, AND WANTS ME TO WRITE THE STORY OF HER LIFE!
THIS IS A FORM LETTER!!
SOME PEOPLE JUST CAN'T READ BETWEEN THE LINES!
2-12
SCHULZ

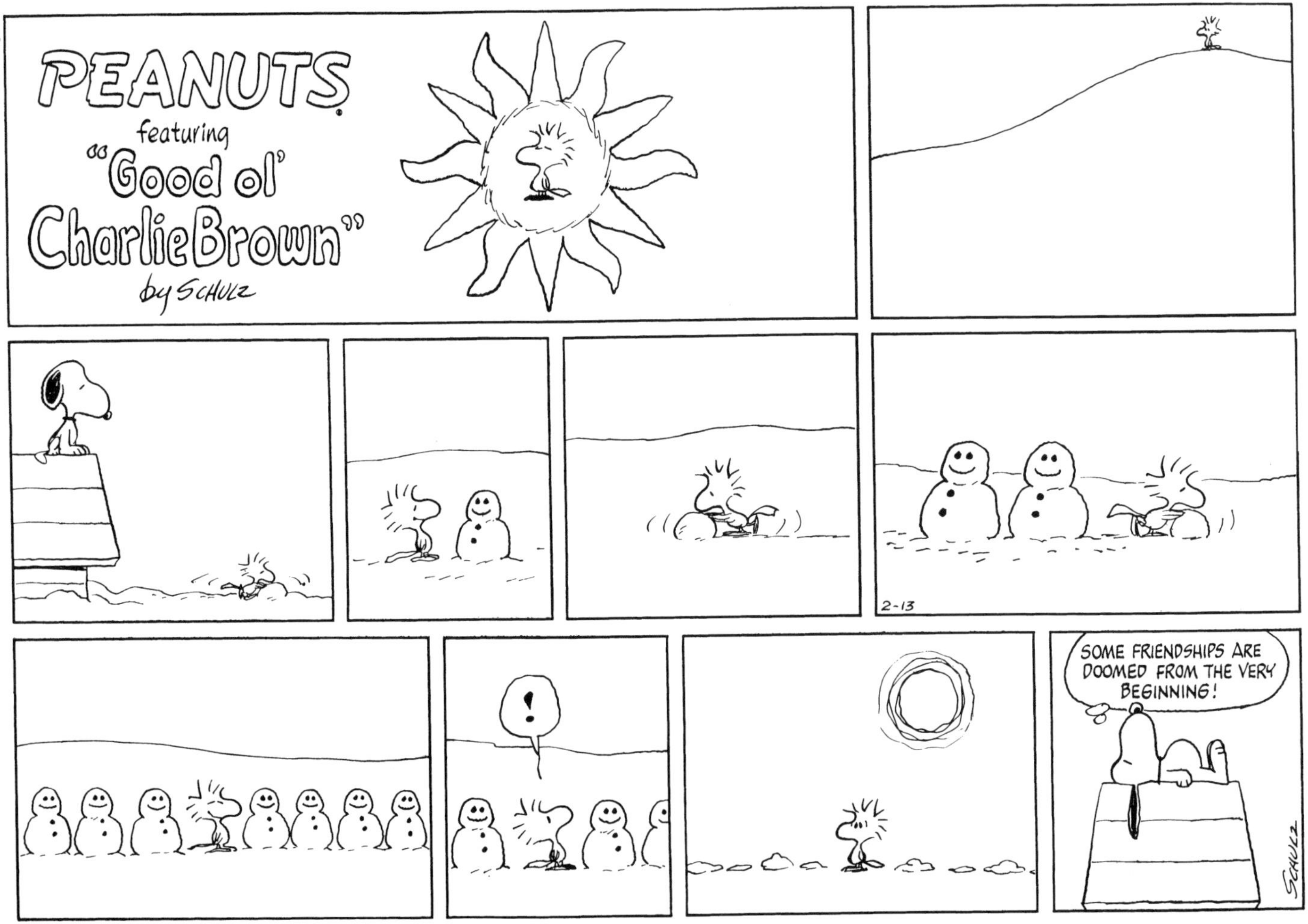
PEANUTS
featuring
"Good ol' CharlieBrown"
by SCHULZ
2-13
!
SOME FRIENDSHIPS ARE DOOMED FROM THE VERY BEGINNING!
SCHULZ

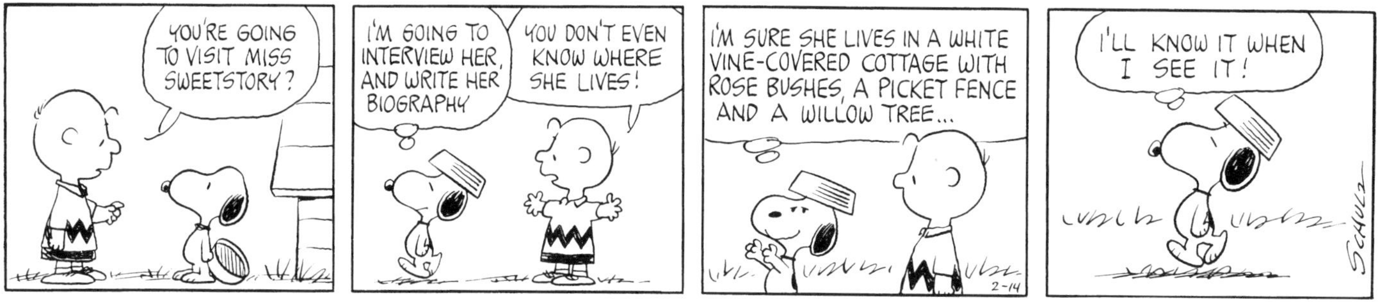
YOU'RE GOING TO VISIT MISS SWEETSTORY?
I'M GOING TO INTERVIEW HER, AND WRITE HER BIOGRAPHY
YOU DON'T EVEN KNOW WHERE SHE LIVES!
I'M SURE SHE LIVES IN A WHITE VINE-COVERED COTTAGE WITH ROSE BUSHES, A PICKET FENCE AND A WILLOW TREE...
2-14
I'LL KNOW IT WHEN I SEE IT!
SCHULZ

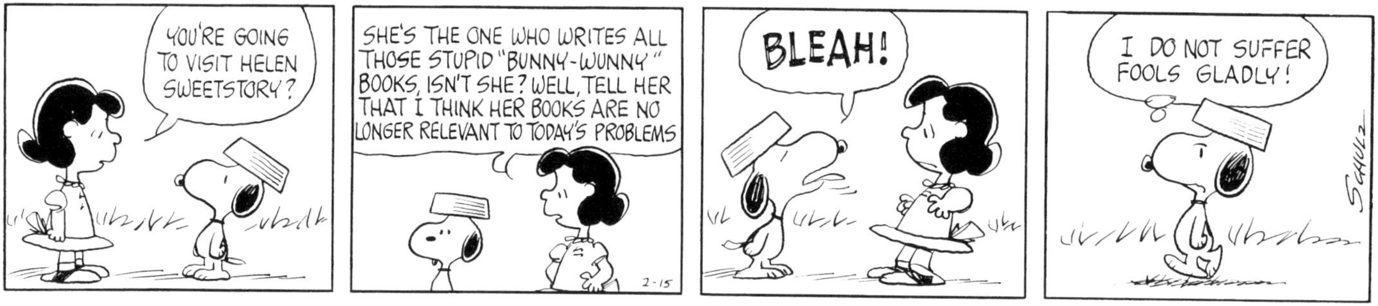
YOU'RE GOING TO VISIT HELEN SWEETSTORY?
SHE'S THE ONE WHO WRITES ALL THOSE STUPID "BUNNY-WUNNY" BOOKS, ISN'T SHE? WELL, TELL HER THAT I THINK HER BOOKS ARE NO LONGER RELEVANT TO TODAY'S PROBLEMS
2-15
BLEAH!
I DO NOT SUFFER FOOLS GLADLY!
SCHULZ

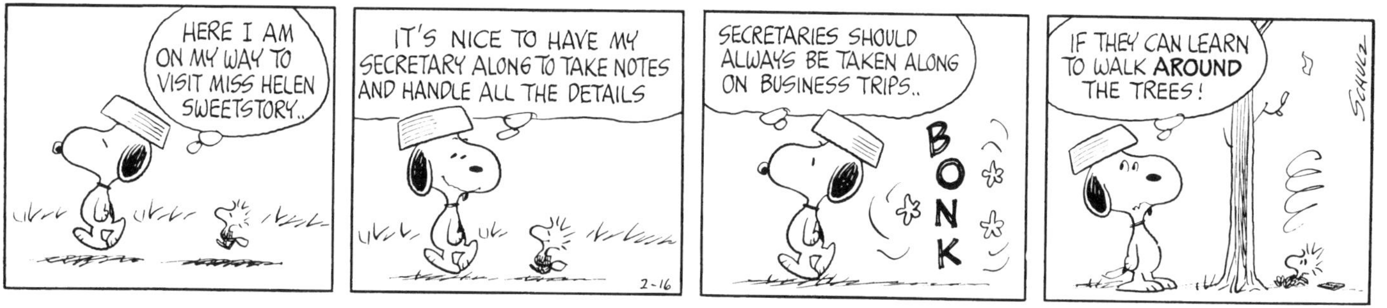
HERE I AM ON MY WAY TO VISIT MISS HELEN SWEETSTORY..
IT'S NICE TO HAVE MY SECRETARY ALONG TO TAKE NOTES AND HANDLE ALL THE DETAILS
2-16
SECRETARIES SHOULD ALWAYS BE TAKEN ALONG ON BUSINESS TRIPS..
BONK
IF THEY CAN LEARN TO WALK **AROUND** THE TREES!
SCHULZ

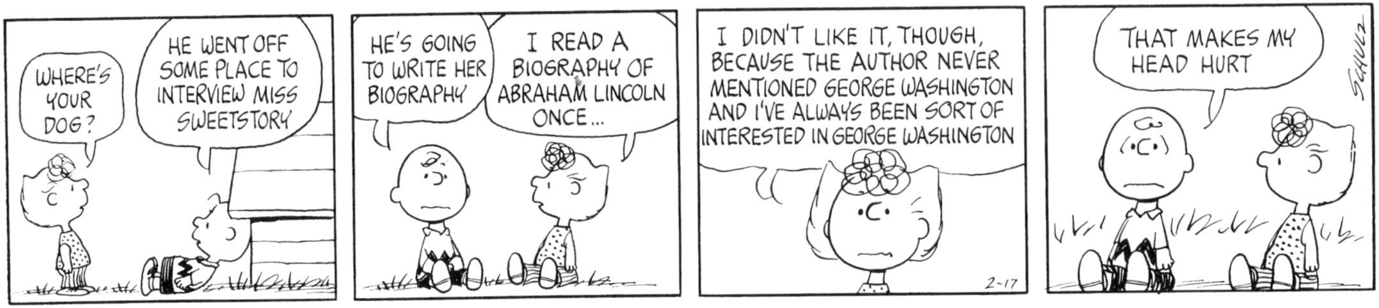
WHERE'S YOUR DOG?
HE WENT OFF SOME PLACE TO INTERVIEW MISS SWEETSTORY
HE'S GOING TO WRITE HER BIOGRAPHY
I READ A BIOGRAPHY OF ABRAHAM LINCOLN ONCE...
I DIDN'T LIKE IT, THOUGH, BECAUSE THE AUTHOR NEVER MENTIONED GEORGE WASHINGTON AND I'VE ALWAYS BEEN SORT OF INTERESTED IN GEORGE WASHINGTON
2-17
THAT MAKES MY HEAD HURT
SCHULZ

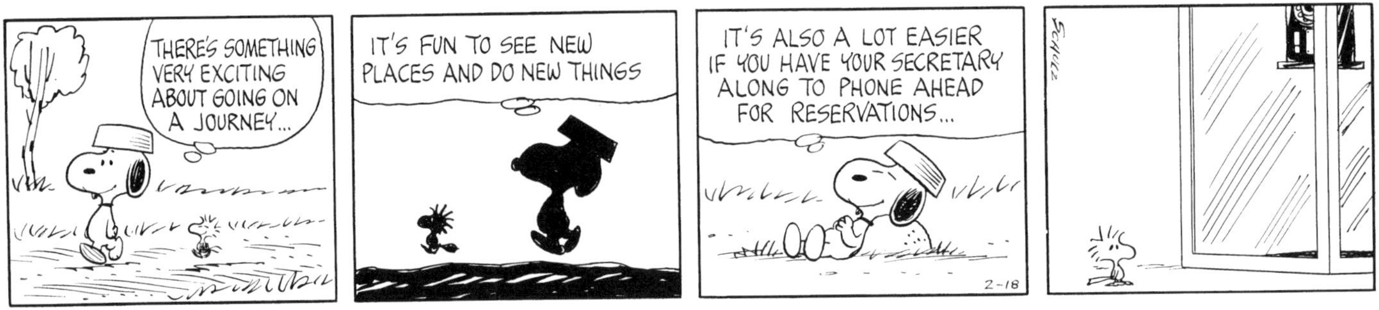
THERE'S SOMETHING VERY EXCITING ABOUT GOING ON A JOURNEY...
IT'S FUN TO SEE NEW PLACES AND DO NEW THINGS
IT'S ALSO A LOT EASIER IF YOU HAVE YOUR SECRETARY ALONG TO PHONE AHEAD FOR RESERVATIONS...
2-18
SCHULZ

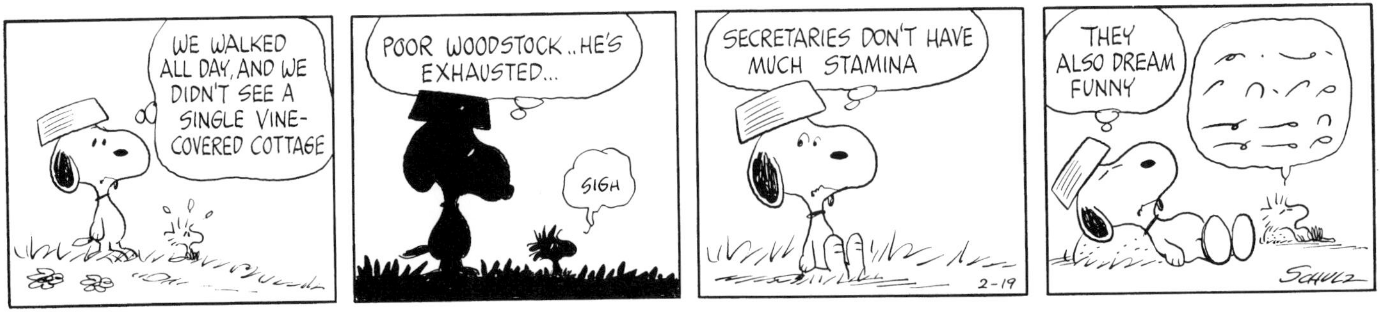
WE WALKED ALL DAY, AND WE DIDN'T SEE A SINGLE VINE-COVERED COTTAGE
POOR WOODSTOCK..HE'S EXHAUSTED...
SIGH
SECRETARIES DON'T HAVE MUCH STAMINA
2-19
THEY ALSO DREAM FUNNY
SCHULZ

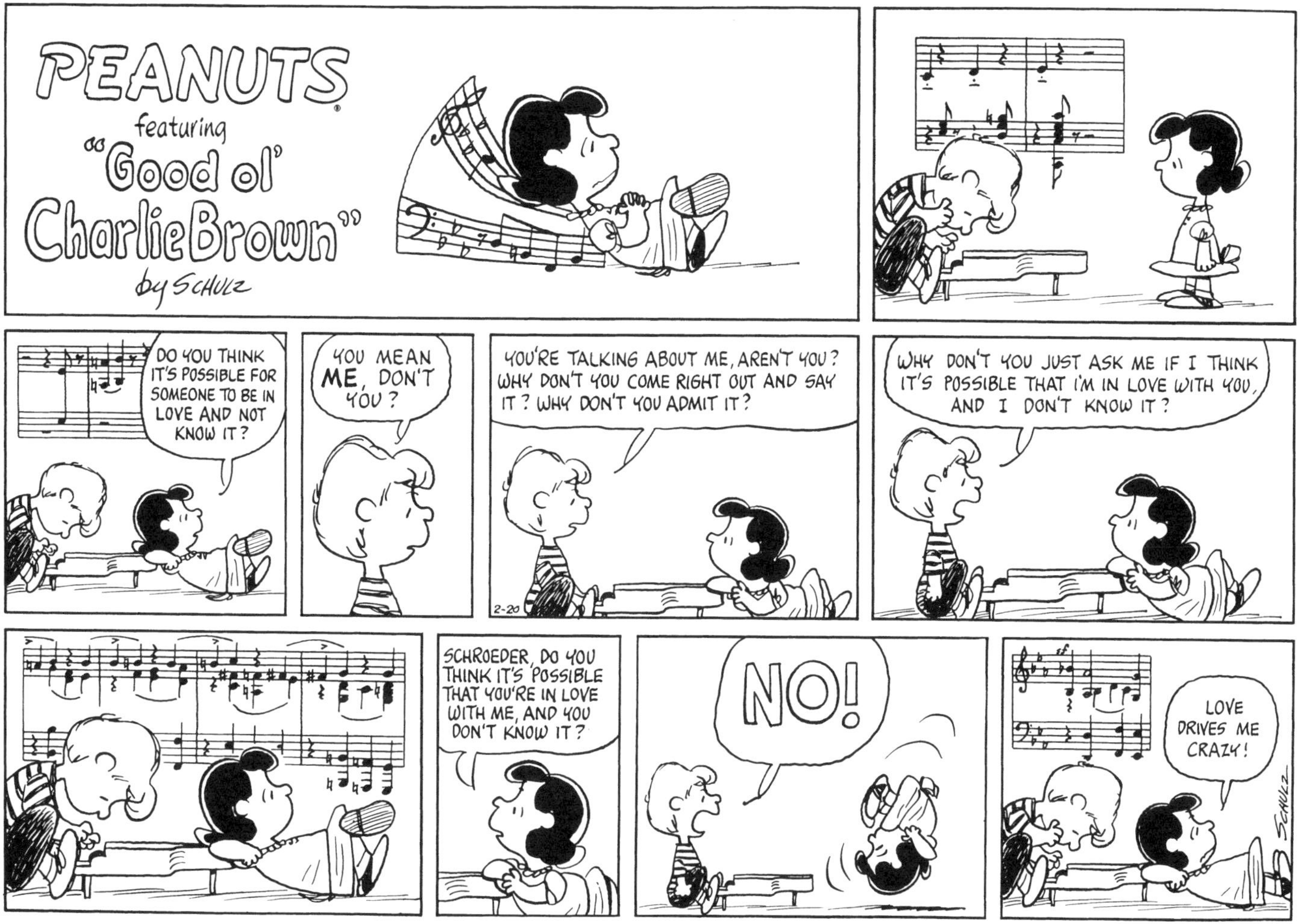
PEANUTS
featuring
"Good ol' CharlieBrown"
by SCHULZ
DO YOU THINK IT'S POSSIBLE FOR SOMEONE TO BE IN LOVE AND NOT KNOW IT?
YOU MEAN ME, DON'T YOU?
YOU'RE TALKING ABOUT ME, AREN'T YOU? WHY DON'T YOU COME RIGHT OUT AND SAY IT? WHY DON'T YOU ADMIT IT?
2-20
WHY DON'T YOU JUST ASK ME IF I THINK IT'S POSSIBLE THAT I'M IN LOVE WITH YOU, AND I DON'T KNOW IT?
SCHROEDER, DO YOU THINK IT'S POSSIBLE THAT YOU'RE IN LOVE WITH ME, AND YOU DON'T KNOW IT?
NO!
LOVE DRIVES ME CRAZY!
SCHULZ

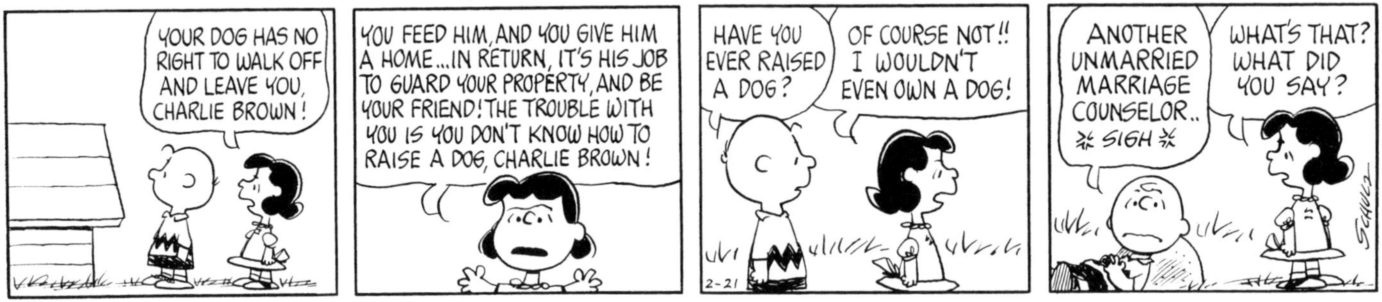
YOUR DOG HAS NO RIGHT TO WALK OFF AND LEAVE YOU, CHARLIE BROWN!
YOU FEED HIM, AND YOU GIVE HIM A HOME...IN RETURN, IT'S HIS JOB TO GUARD YOUR PROPERTY, AND BE YOUR FRIEND! THE TROUBLE WITH YOU IS YOU DON'T KNOW HOW TO RAISE A DOG, CHARLIE BROWN!
HAVE YOU EVER RAISED A DOG?
OF COURSE NOT!! I WOULDN'T EVEN OWN A DOG!
2-21
ANOTHER UNMARRIED MARRIAGE COUNSELOR..
SIGH
WHAT'S THAT? WHAT DID YOU SAY?
SCHULZ

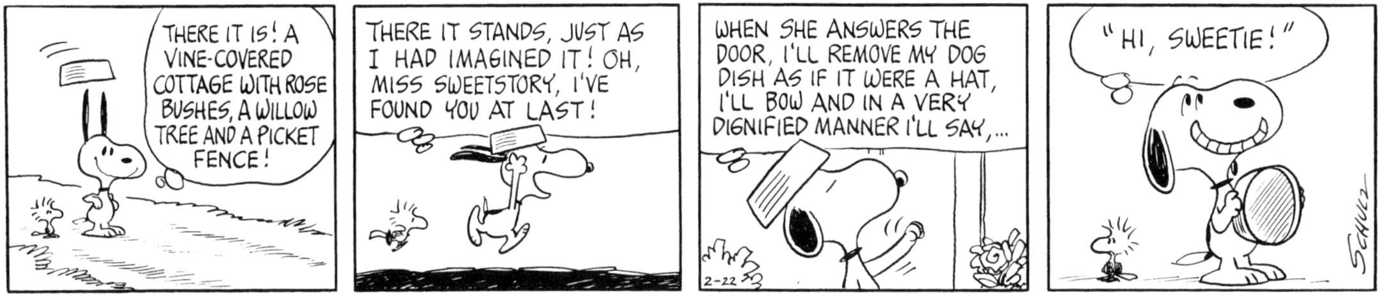
THERE IT IS! A VINE-COVERED COTTAGE WITH ROSE BUSHES, A WILLOW TREE AND A PICKET FENCE!
THERE IT STANDS, JUST AS I HAD IMAGINED IT! OH, MISS SWEETSTORY, I'VE FOUND YOU AT LAST!
WHEN SHE ANSWERS THE DOOR, I'LL REMOVE MY DOG DISH AS IF IT WERE A HAT, I'LL BOW AND IN A VERY DIGNIFIED MANNER I'LL SAY,...
2-22
"HI, SWEETIE!"
SCHULZ

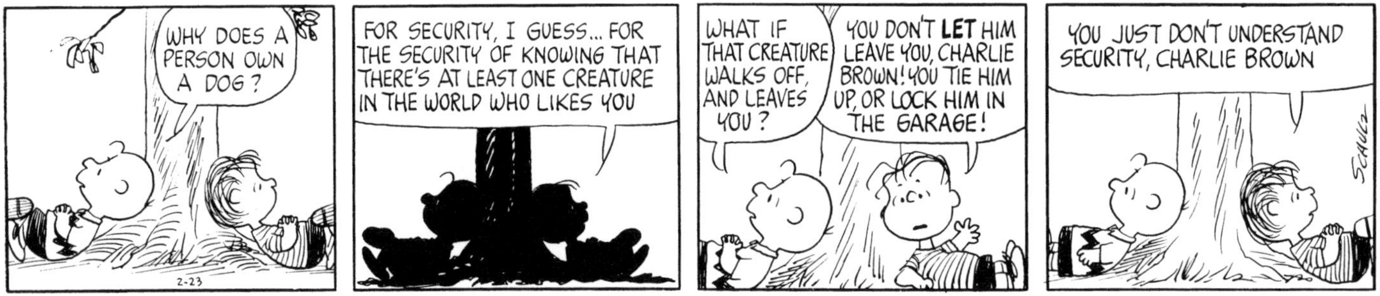
WHY DOES A PERSON OWN A DOG?
2-23
FOR SECURITY, I GUESS... FOR THE SECURITY OF KNOWING THAT THERE'S AT LEAST ONE CREATURE IN THE WORLD WHO LIKES YOU
WHAT IF THAT CREATURE WALKS OFF, AND LEAVES YOU?
YOU DON'T LET HIM LEAVE YOU, CHARLIE BROWN! YOU TIE HIM UP, OR LOCK HIM IN THE GARAGE!
YOU JUST DON'T UNDERSTAND SECURITY, CHARLIE BROWN
SCHULZ

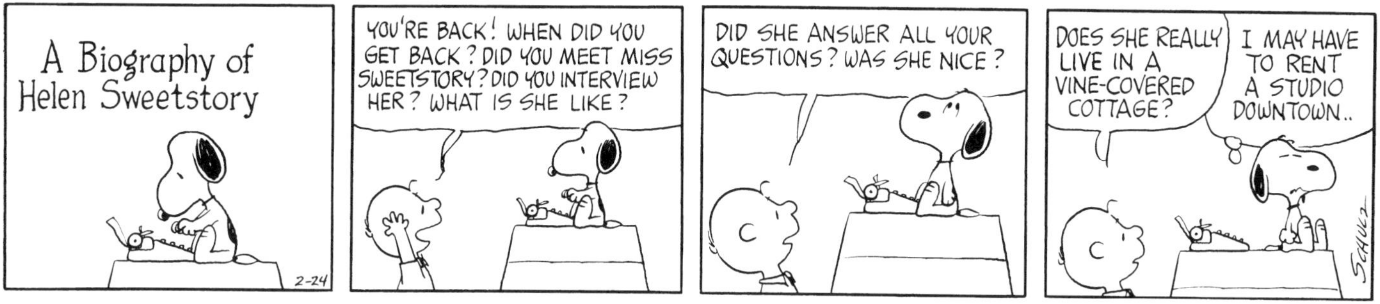
A Biography of Helen Sweetstory
2-24
YOU'RE BACK! WHEN DID YOU GET BACK? DID YOU MEET MISS SWEETSTORY? DID YOU INTERVIEW HER? WHAT IS SHE LIKE?
DID SHE ANSWER ALL YOUR QUESTIONS? WAS SHE NICE?
DOES SHE REALLY LIVE IN A VINE-COVERED COTTAGE?
I MAY HAVE TO RENT A STUDIO DOWNTOWN..
SCHULZ

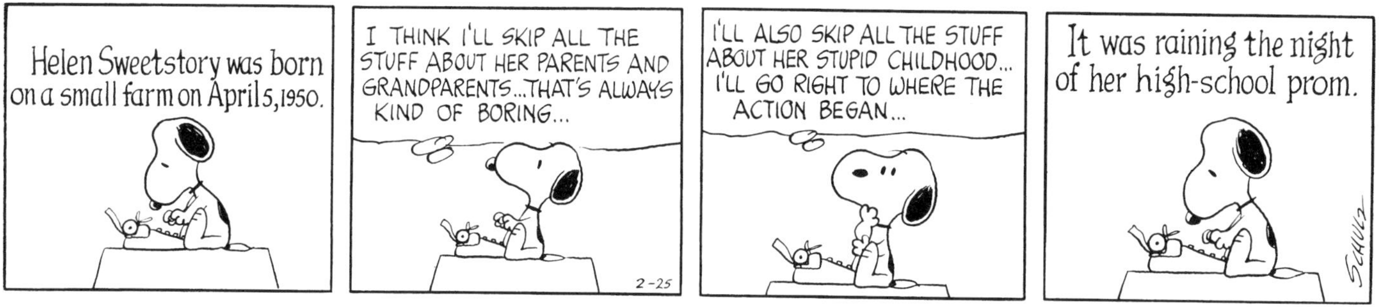
Helen Sweetstory was born on a small farm on April 5, 1950.
I THINK I'LL SKIP ALL THE STUFF ABOUT HER PARENTS AND GRANDPARENTS...THAT'S ALWAYS KIND OF BORING...
2-25
I'LL ALSO SKIP ALL THE STUFF ABOUT HER STUPID CHILDHOOD... I'LL GO RIGHT TO WHERE THE ACTION BEGAN...
It was raining the night of her high-school prom.
SCHULZ

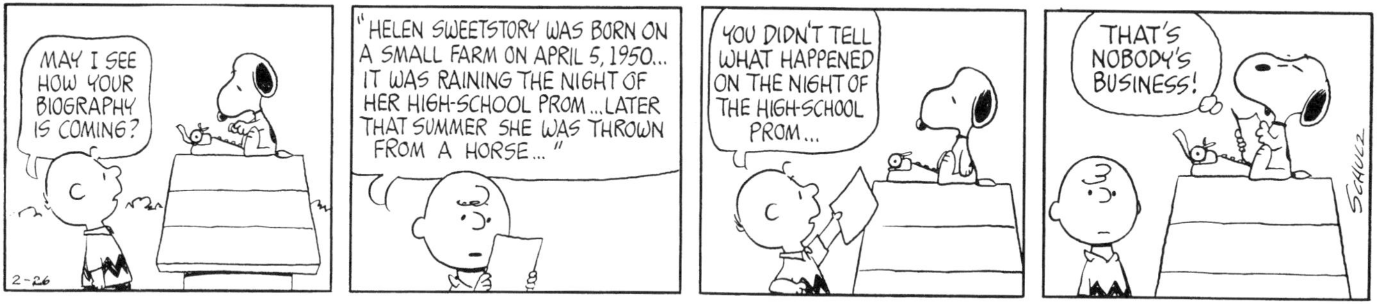
MAY I SEE HOW YOUR BIOGRAPHY IS COMING?
2-26
"HELEN SWEETSTORY WAS BORN ON A SMALL FARM ON APRIL 5, 1950... IT WAS RAINING THE NIGHT OF HER HIGH-SCHOOL PROM...LATER THAT SUMMER SHE WAS THROWN FROM A HORSE..."
YOU DIDN'T TELL WHAT HAPPENED ON THE NIGHT OF THE HIGH-SCHOOL PROM...
THAT'S NOBODY'S BUSINESS!
SCHULZ

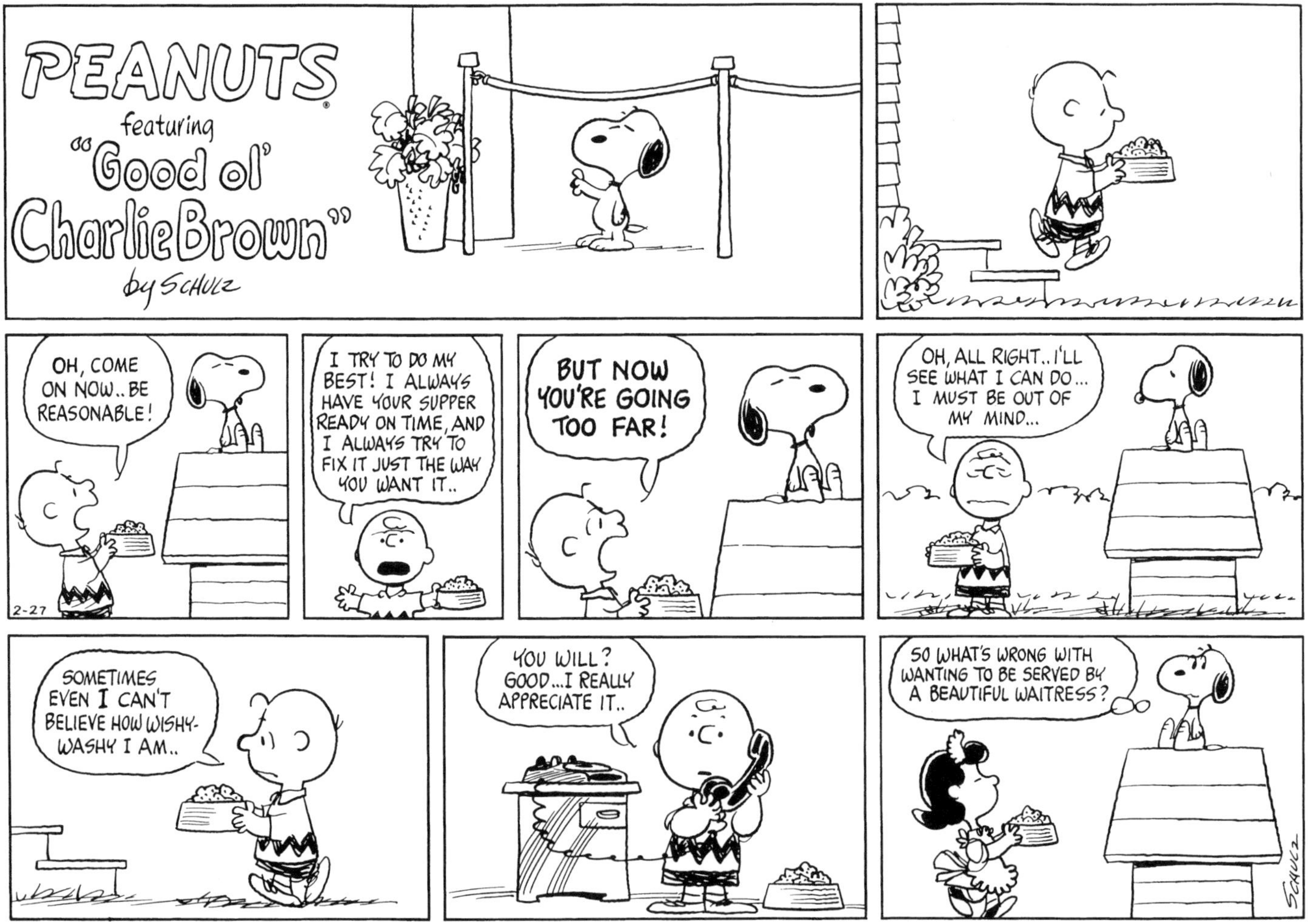
PEANUTS
featuring
"Good ol' CharlieBrown"
by SCHULZ
OH, COME ON NOW.. BE REASONABLE!
2-27
I TRY TO DO MY BEST! I ALWAYS HAVE YOUR SUPPER READY ON TIME, AND I ALWAYS TRY TO FIX IT JUST THE WAY YOU WANT IT..
BUT NOW YOU'RE GOING TOO FAR!
OH, ALL RIGHT.. I'LL SEE WHAT I CAN DO... I MUST BE OUT OF MY MIND...
SOMETIMES EVEN I CAN'T BELIEVE HOW WISHY-WASHY I AM..
YOU WILL? GOOD...I REALLY APPRECIATE IT..
SO WHAT'S WRONG WITH WANTING TO BE SERVED BY A BEAUTIFUL WAITRESS?
SCHULZ

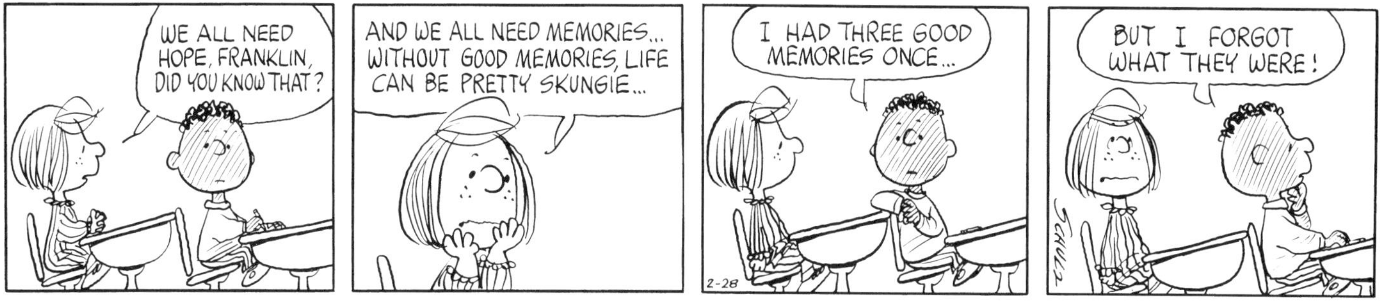
WE ALL NEED HOPE, FRANKLIN, DID YOU KNOW THAT?
AND WE ALL NEED MEMORIES... WITHOUT GOOD MEMORIES, LIFE CAN BE PRETTY SKUNGIE...
I HAD THREE GOOD MEMORIES ONCE...
BUT I FORGOT WHAT THEY WERE!

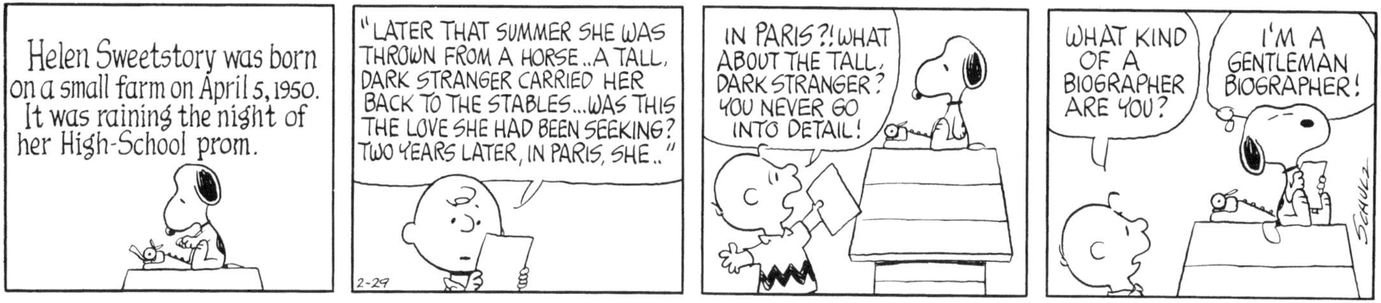
Helen Sweetstory was born on a small farm on April 5, 1950. It was raining the night of her High-School prom.
"LATER THAT SUMMER SHE WAS THROWN FROM A HORSE.. A TALL, DARK STRANGER CARRIED HER BACK TO THE STABLES... WAS THIS THE LOVE SHE HAD BEEN SEEKING? TWO YEARS LATER, IN PARIS, SHE.."
IN PARIS?! WHAT ABOUT THE TALL, DARK STRANGER? YOU NEVER GO INTO DETAIL!
WHAT KIND OF A BIOGRAPHER ARE YOU?
I'M A GENTLEMAN BIOGRAPHER!

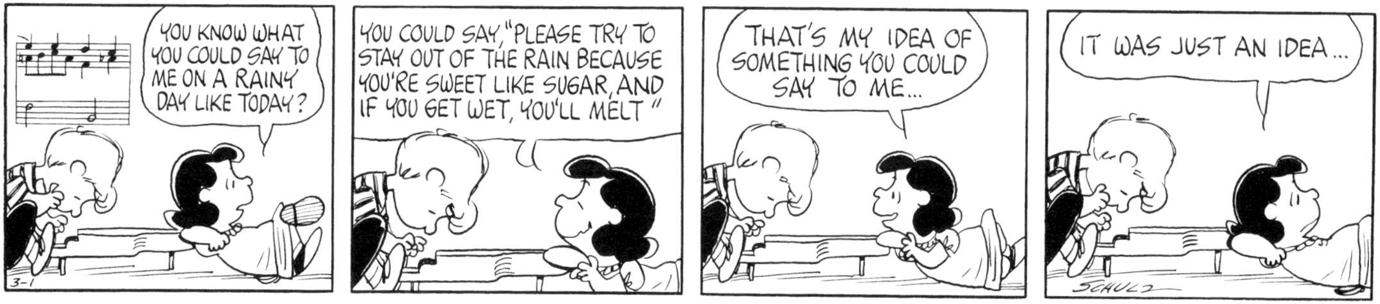
YOU KNOW WHAT YOU COULD SAY TO ME ON A RAINY DAY LIKE TODAY?
YOU COULD SAY, "PLEASE TRY TO STAY OUT OF THE RAIN BECAUSE YOU'RE SWEET LIKE SUGAR, AND IF YOU GET WET, YOU'LL MELT"
THAT'S MY IDEA OF SOMETHING YOU COULD SAY TO ME...
IT WAS JUST AN IDEA...

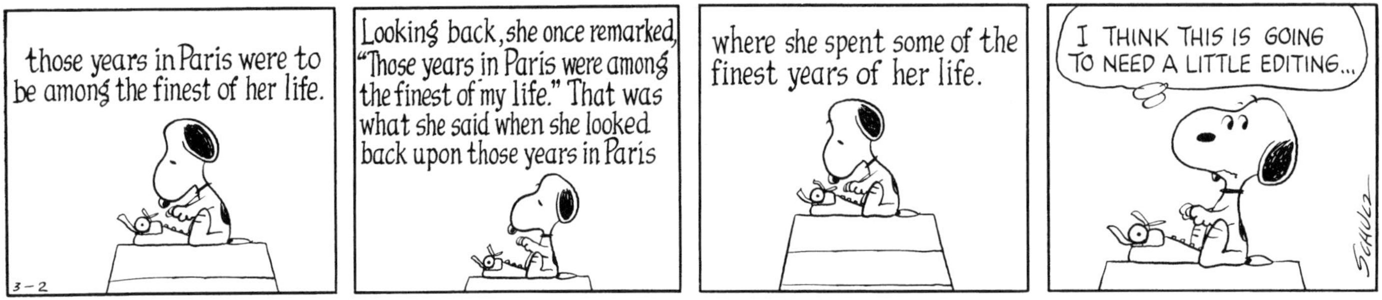
those years in Paris were to be among the finest of her life.
3-2
Looking back, she once remarked, "Those years in Paris were among the finest of my life." That was what she said when she looked back upon those years in Paris
where she spent some of the finest years of her life.
I THINK THIS IS GOING TO NEED A LITTLE EDITING...
SCHULZ

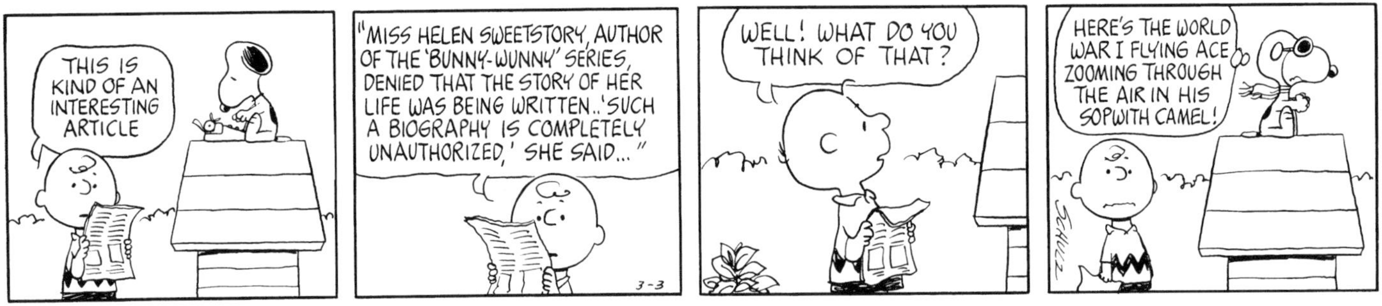
THIS IS KIND OF AN INTERESTING ARTICLE
"MISS HELEN SWEETSTORY, AUTHOR OF THE 'BUNNY-WUNNY' SERIES, DENIED THAT THE STORY OF HER LIFE WAS BEING WRITTEN..'SUCH A BIOGRAPHY IS COMPLETELY UNAUTHORIZED,' SHE SAID..."
3-3
WELL! WHAT DO YOU THINK OF THAT?
HERE'S THE WORLD WAR I FLYING ACE ZOOMING THROUGH THE AIR IN HIS SOPWITH CAMEL!
SCHULZ

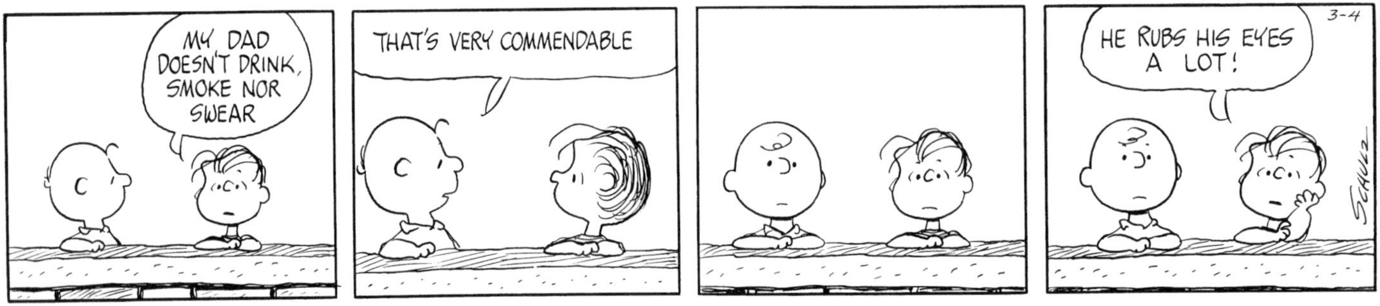
MY DAD DOESN'T DRINK, SMOKE NOR SWEAR
THAT'S VERY COMMENDABLE
3-4
HE RUBS HIS EYES A LOT!
SCHULZ

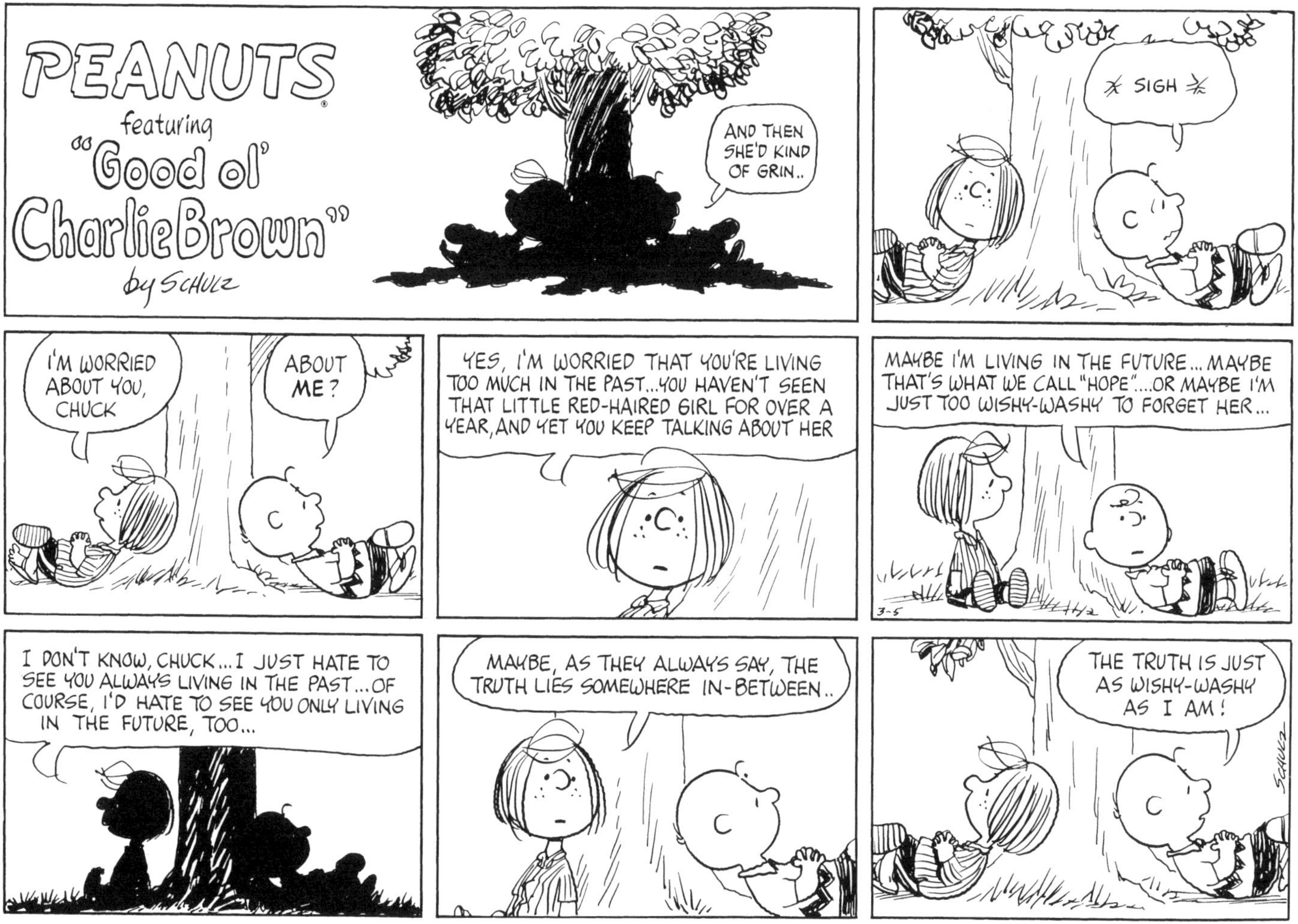
PEANUTS
featuring "Good ol' CharlieBrown"
by SCHULZ
AND THEN SHE'D KIND OF GRIN..
SIGH
I'M WORRIED ABOUT YOU, CHUCK
ABOUT ME?
YES, I'M WORRIED THAT YOU'RE LIVING TOO MUCH IN THE PAST...YOU HAVEN'T SEEN THAT LITTLE RED-HAIRED GIRL FOR OVER A YEAR, AND YET YOU KEEP TALKING ABOUT HER
MAYBE I'M LIVING IN THE FUTURE... MAYBE THAT'S WHAT WE CALL "HOPE"....OR MAYBE I'M JUST TOO WISHY-WASHY TO FORGET HER...
3-5
I DON'T KNOW, CHUCK...I JUST HATE TO SEE YOU ALWAYS LIVING IN THE PAST...OF COURSE, I'D HATE TO SEE YOU ONLY LIVING IN THE FUTURE, TOO...
MAYBE, AS THEY ALWAYS SAY, THE TRUTH LIES SOMEWHERE IN-BETWEEN..
THE TRUTH IS JUST AS WISHY-WASHY AS I AM!
SCHULZ

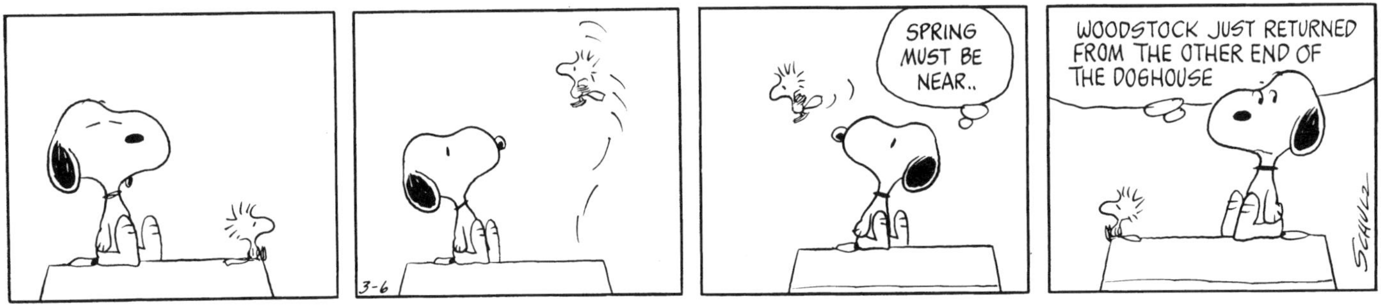
3-6
SPRING MUST BE NEAR..
WOODSTOCK JUST RETURNED FROM THE OTHER END OF THE DOGHOUSE
SCHULZ

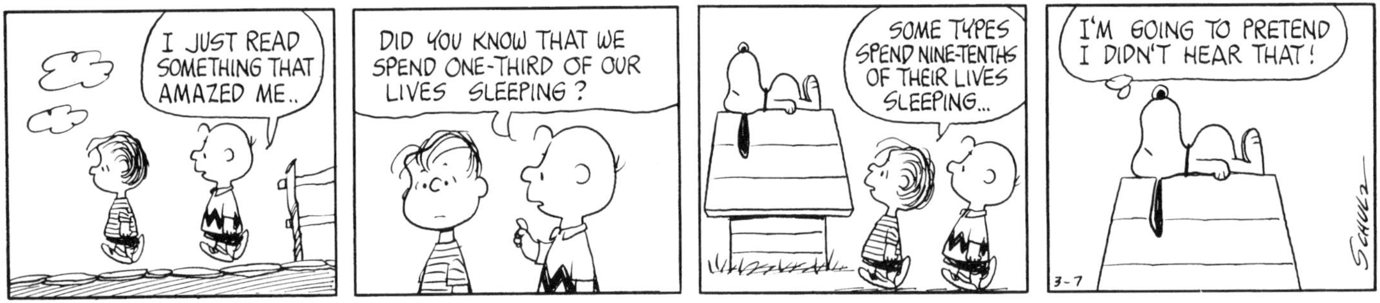
I JUST READ SOMETHING THAT AMAZED ME..
DID YOU KNOW THAT WE SPEND ONE-THIRD OF OUR LIVES SLEEPING?
SOME TYPES SPEND NINE-TENTHS OF THEIR LIVES SLEEPING...
I'M GOING TO PRETEND I DIDN'T HEAR THAT!
3-7
SCHULZ

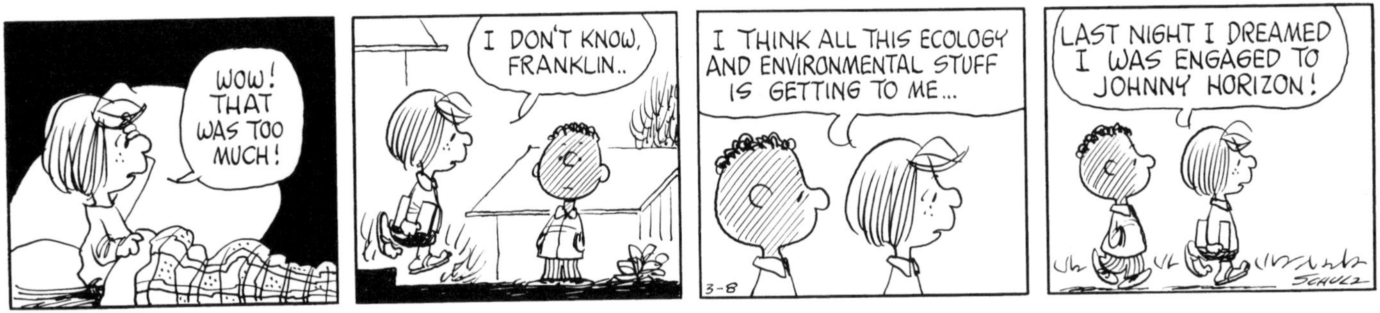
WOW! THAT WAS TOO MUCH!
I DON'T KNOW, FRANKLIN..
I THINK ALL THIS ECOLOGY AND ENVIRONMENTAL STUFF IS GETTING TO ME...
3-8
LAST NIGHT I DREAMED I WAS ENGAGED TO JOHNNY HORIZON!
SCHULZ

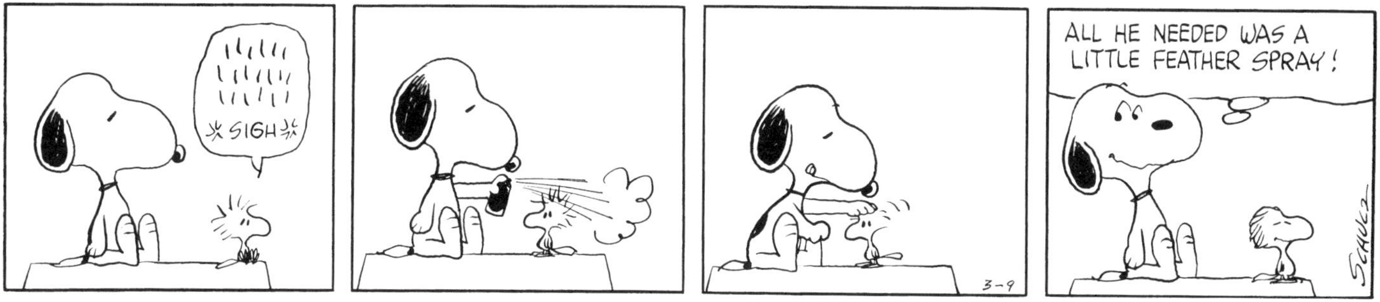
SIGH
3-9
ALL HE NEEDED WAS A LITTLE FEATHER SPRAY!
SCHULZ

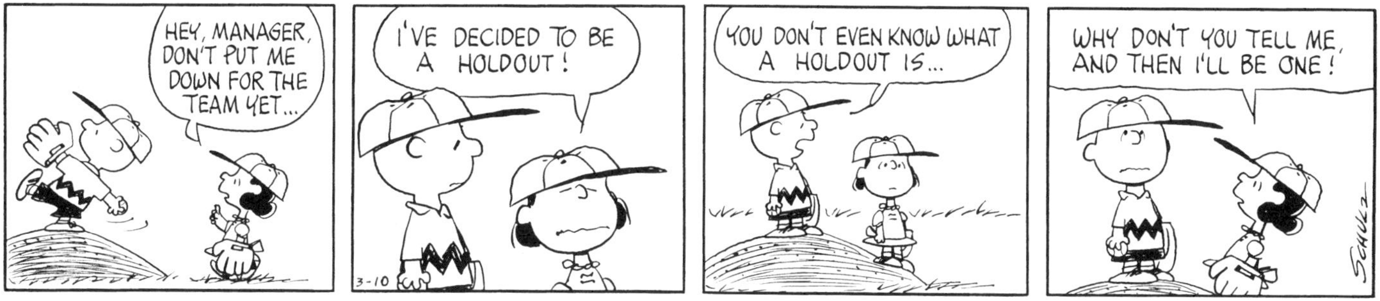
HEY, MANAGER, DON'T PUT ME DOWN FOR THE TEAM YET...
I'VE DECIDED TO BE A HOLDOUT!
3-10
YOU DON'T EVEN KNOW WHAT A HOLDOUT IS...
WHY DON'T YOU TELL ME, AND THEN I'LL BE ONE!
SCHULZ

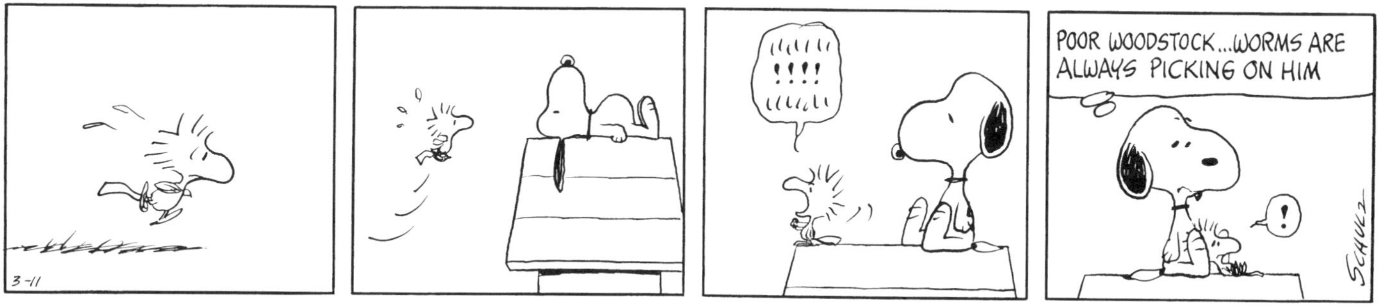
3-11
!!!!
POOR WOODSTOCK...WORMS ARE ALWAYS PICKING ON HIM
!
SCHULZ

PEANUTS
featuring
"Good ol' Charlie Brown"
by SCHULZ

SEVEN O'CLOCK, SALLY... TIME TO GET UP!

GOOD GRIEF... I'VE GOT TO HURRY...

The Incas

3-12

The Incas were people who lived a long time ago in Incaland.

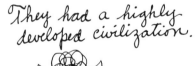

They had a highly developed civilization.

They would still be here today, but they lacked motel facilities.

SOME OF MY BEST TERM PAPERS HAVE BEEN WRITTEN BEFORE BREAKFAST!

March

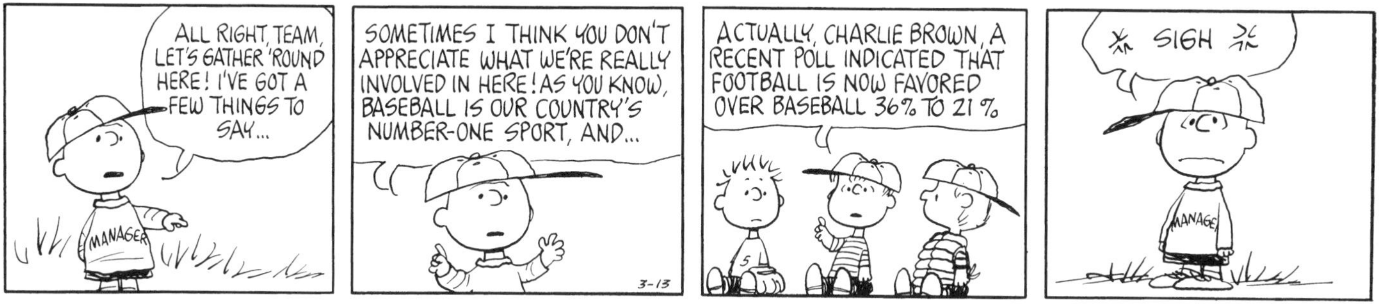
ALL RIGHT, TEAM, LET'S GATHER 'ROUND HERE! I'VE GOT A FEW THINGS TO SAY...
MANAGER
SOMETIMES I THINK YOU DON'T APPRECIATE WHAT WE'RE REALLY INVOLVED IN HERE! AS YOU KNOW, BASEBALL IS OUR COUNTRY'S NUMBER-ONE SPORT, AND...
3-13
ACTUALLY, CHARLIE BROWN, A RECENT POLL INDICATED THAT FOOTBALL IS NOW FAVORED OVER BASEBALL 36% TO 21%
SIGH
MANAGER

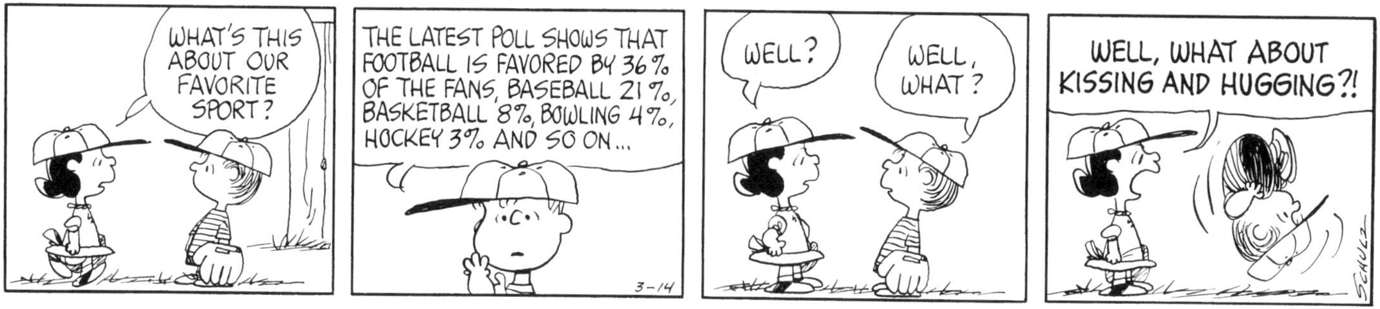
WHAT'S THIS ABOUT OUR FAVORITE SPORT?
THE LATEST POLL SHOWS THAT FOOTBALL IS FAVORED BY 36% OF THE FANS, BASEBALL 21%, BASKETBALL 8%, BOWLING 4%, HOCKEY 3% AND SO ON...
3-14
WELL?
WELL, WHAT?
WELL, WHAT ABOUT KISSING AND HUGGING?!
SCHULZ

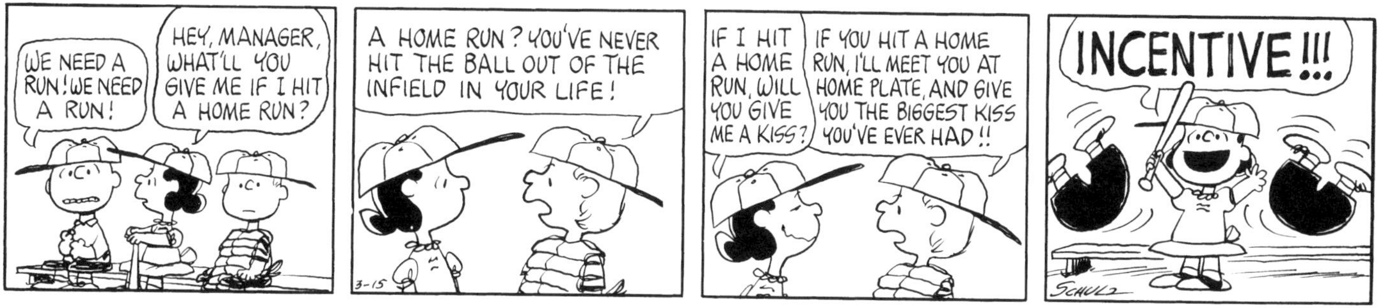
WE NEED A RUN! WE NEED A RUN!
HEY, MANAGER, WHAT'LL YOU GIVE ME IF I HIT A HOME RUN?
A HOME RUN? YOU'VE NEVER HIT THE BALL OUT OF THE INFIELD IN YOUR LIFE!
3-15
IF I HIT A HOME RUN, WILL YOU GIVE ME A KISS?
IF YOU HIT A HOME RUN, I'LL MEET YOU AT HOME PLATE, AND GIVE YOU THE BIGGEST KISS YOU'VE EVER HAD!!
INCENTIVE!!!
SCHULZ

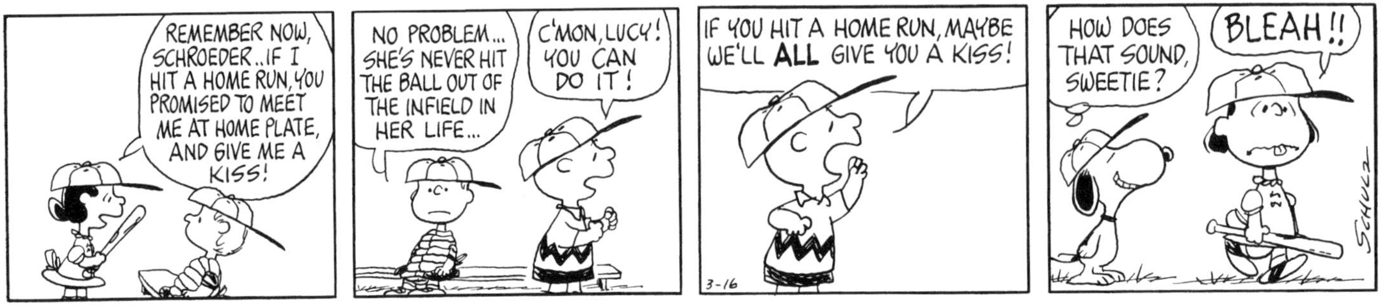
REMEMBER NOW, SCHROEDER..IF I HIT A HOME RUN, YOU PROMISED TO MEET ME AT HOME PLATE, AND GIVE ME A KISS!
NO PROBLEM... SHE'S NEVER HIT THE BALL OUT OF THE INFIELD IN HER LIFE...
C'MON, LUCY! YOU CAN DO IT!
IF YOU HIT A HOME RUN, MAYBE WE'LL **ALL** GIVE YOU A KISS!
3-16
HOW DOES THAT SOUND, SWEETIE?
BLEAH!!
SCHULZ

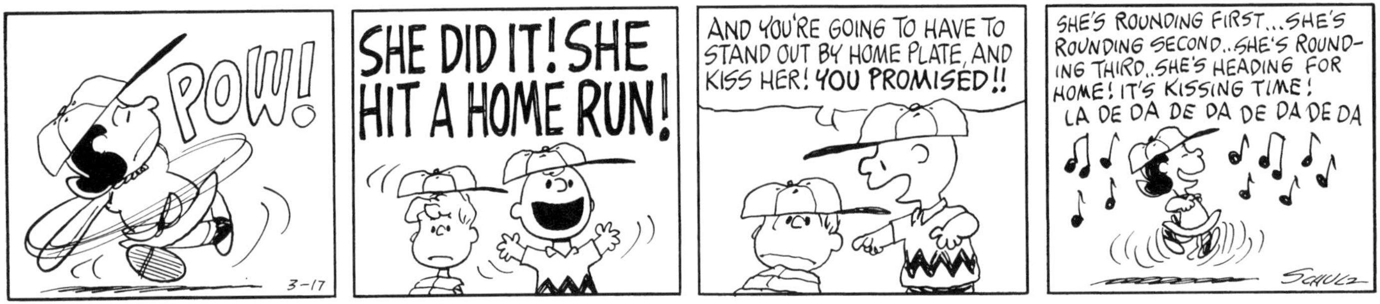
POW!
3-17
SHE DID IT! SHE HIT A HOME RUN!
AND YOU'RE GOING TO HAVE TO STAND OUT BY HOME PLATE, AND KISS HER! **YOU PROMISED!!**
SHE'S ROUNDING FIRST...SHE'S ROUNDING SECOND..SHE'S ROUNDING THIRD..SHE'S HEADING FOR HOME! IT'S KISSING TIME!
LA DE DA DE DA DE DA DE DA
SCHULZ

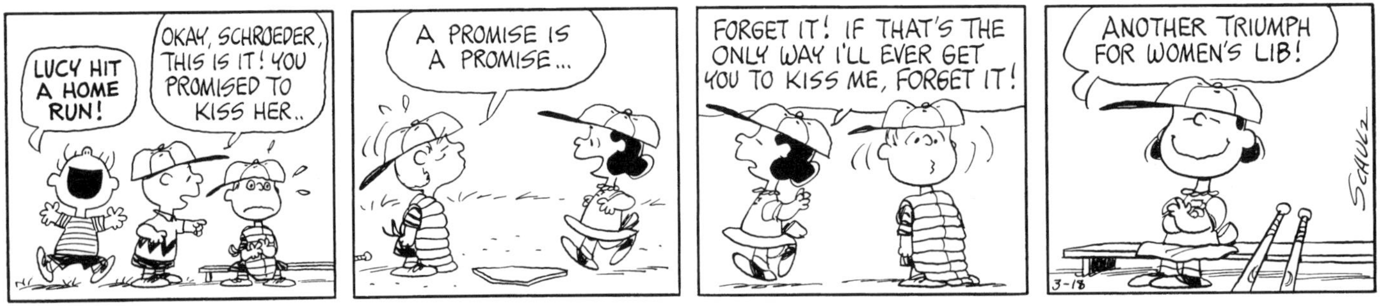
LUCY HIT A HOME RUN!
OKAY, SCHROEDER, THIS IS IT! YOU PROMISED TO KISS HER..
A PROMISE IS A PROMISE...
FORGET IT! IF THAT'S THE ONLY WAY I'LL EVER GET YOU TO KISS ME, FORGET IT!
ANOTHER TRIUMPH FOR WOMEN'S LIB!
SCHULZ
3-18

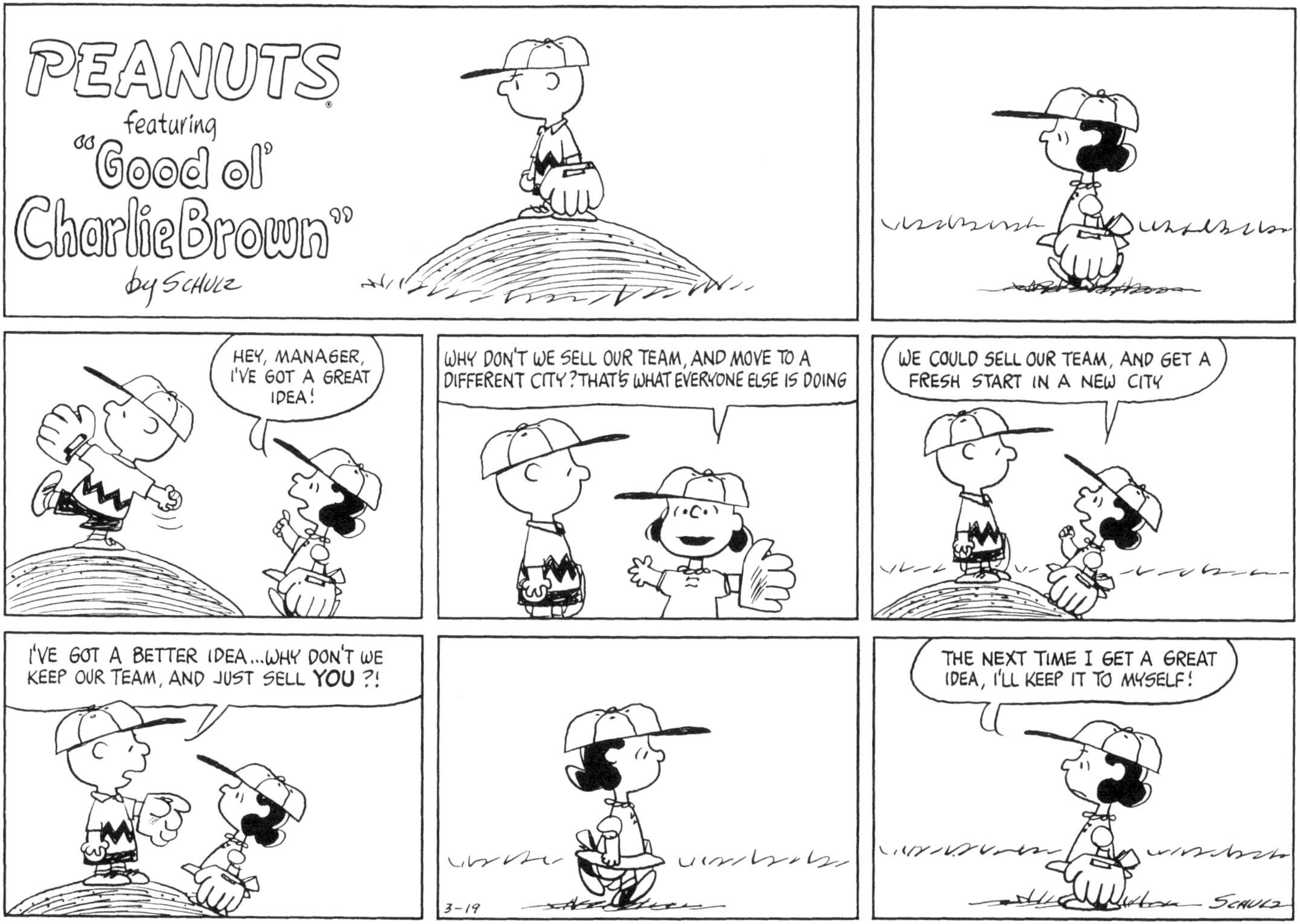
PEANUTS
featuring
"Good ol' Charlie Brown"
by SCHULZ
HEY, MANAGER, I'VE GOT A GREAT IDEA!
WHY DON'T WE SELL OUR TEAM, AND MOVE TO A DIFFERENT CITY? THAT'S WHAT EVERYONE ELSE IS DOING
WE COULD SELL OUR TEAM, AND GET A FRESH START IN A NEW CITY
I'VE GOT A BETTER IDEA...WHY DON'T WE KEEP OUR TEAM, AND JUST SELL YOU ?!
3-19
THE NEXT TIME I GET A GREAT IDEA, I'LL KEEP IT TO MYSELF!
SCHULZ

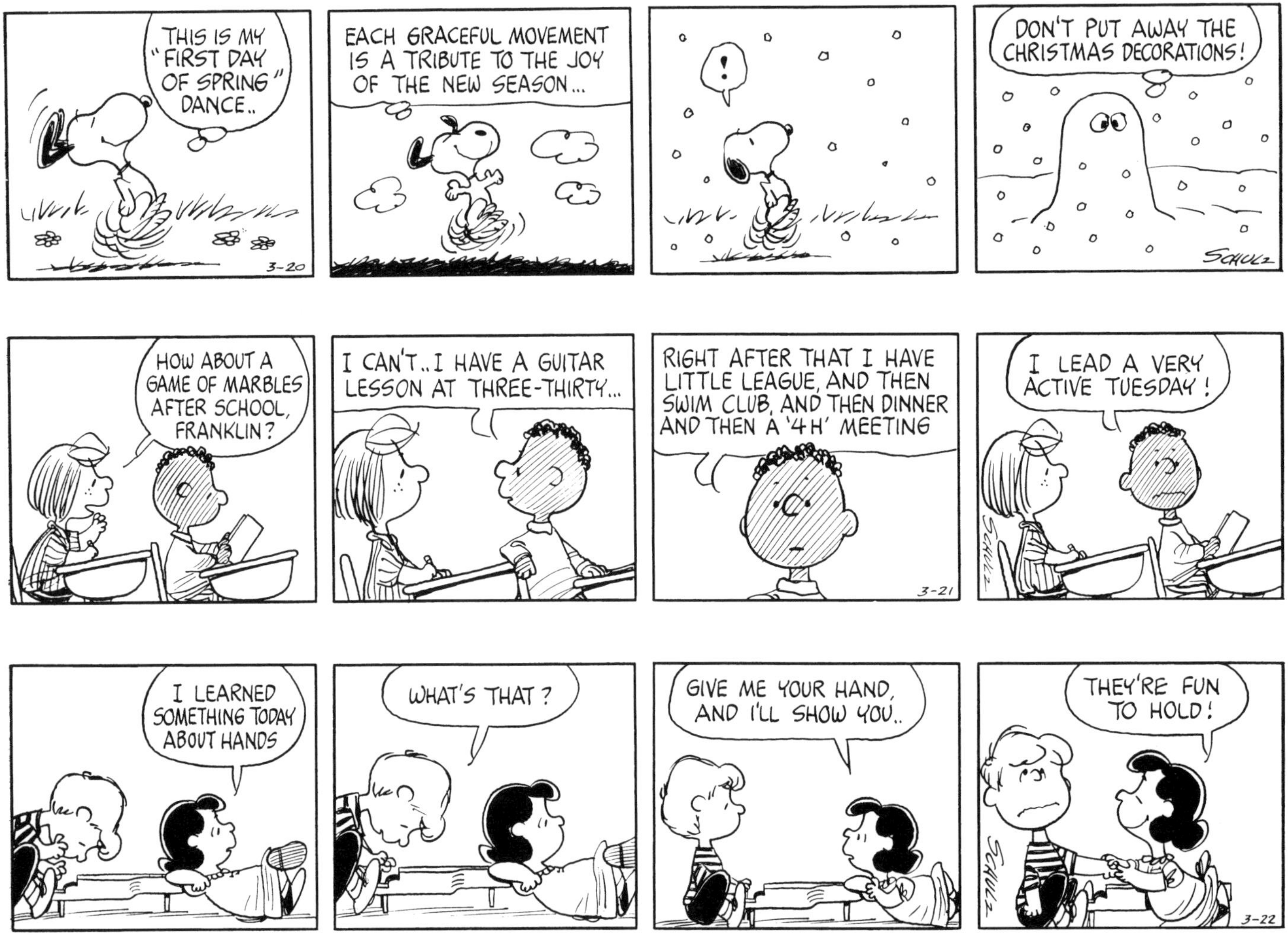

THIS IS MY "FIRST DAY OF SPRING" DANCE..
EACH GRACEFUL MOVEMENT IS A TRIBUTE TO THE JOY OF THE NEW SEASON...
!
DON'T PUT AWAY THE CHRISTMAS DECORATIONS!
SCHULZ
3-20
HOW ABOUT A GAME OF MARBLES AFTER SCHOOL, FRANKLIN?
I CAN'T.. I HAVE A GUITAR LESSON AT THREE-THIRTY...
RIGHT AFTER THAT I HAVE LITTLE LEAGUE, AND THEN SWIM CLUB, AND THEN DINNER AND THEN A '4 H' MEETING
I LEAD A VERY ACTIVE TUESDAY!
SCHULZ
3-21
I LEARNED SOMETHING TODAY ABOUT HANDS
WHAT'S THAT?
GIVE ME YOUR HAND, AND I'LL SHOW YOU..
THEY'RE FUN TO HOLD!
SCHULZ
3-22

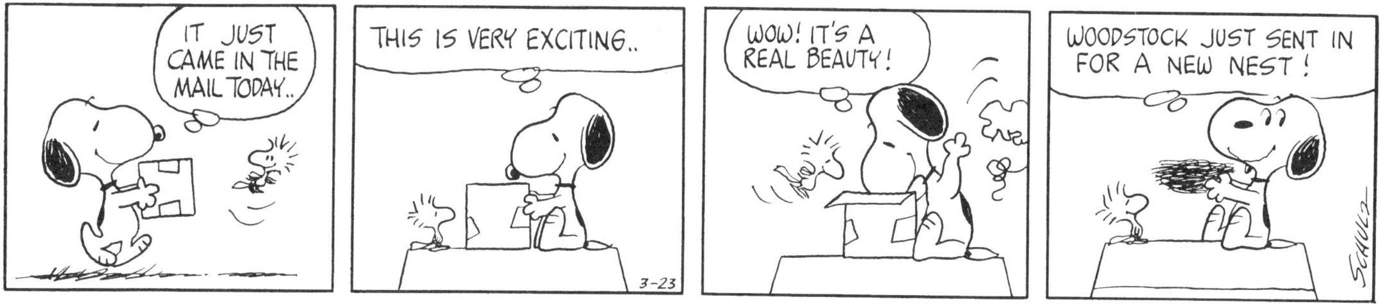
IT JUST CAME IN THE MAIL TODAY..
THIS IS VERY EXCITING..
3-23
WOW! IT'S A REAL BEAUTY!
WOODSTOCK JUST SENT IN FOR A NEW NEST!
SCHULZ

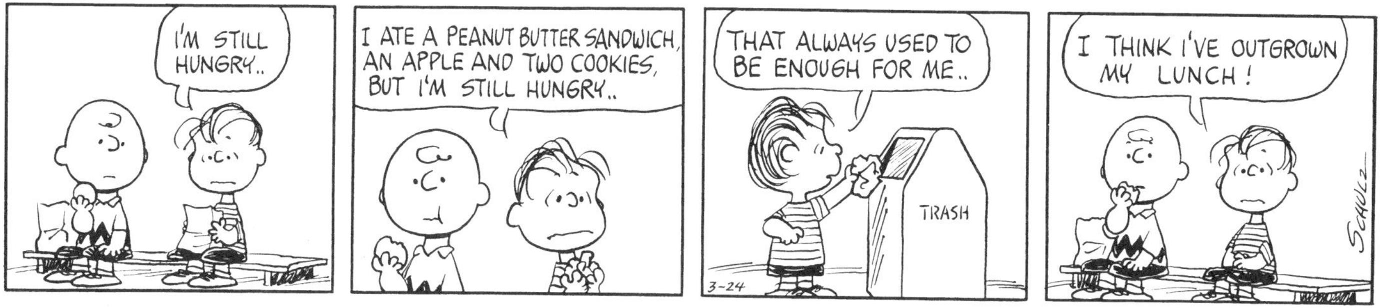
I'M STILL HUNGRY..
I ATE A PEANUT BUTTER SANDWICH, AN APPLE AND TWO COOKIES, BUT I'M STILL HUNGRY..
THAT ALWAYS USED TO BE ENOUGH FOR ME..
TRASH
3-24
I THINK I'VE OUTGROWN MY LUNCH!
SCHULZ

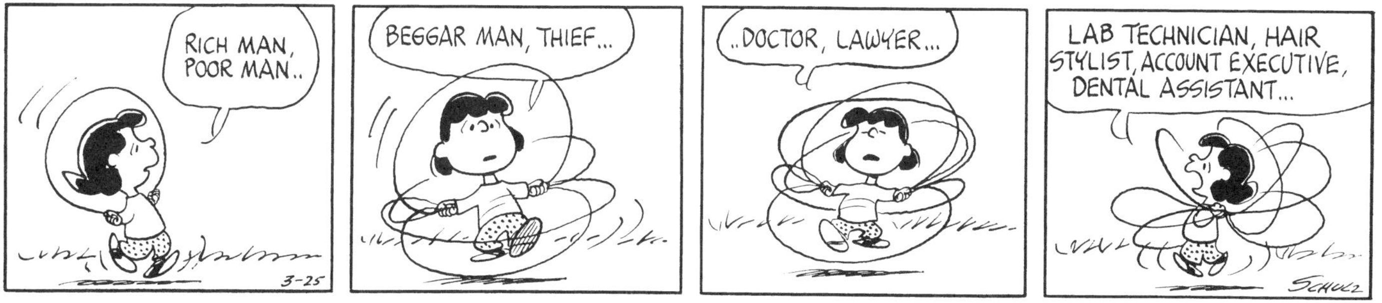
RICH MAN, POOR MAN..
3-25
BEGGAR MAN, THIEF...
..DOCTOR, LAWYER...
LAB TECHNICIAN, HAIR STYLIST, ACCOUNT EXECUTIVE, DENTAL ASSISTANT...
SCHULZ

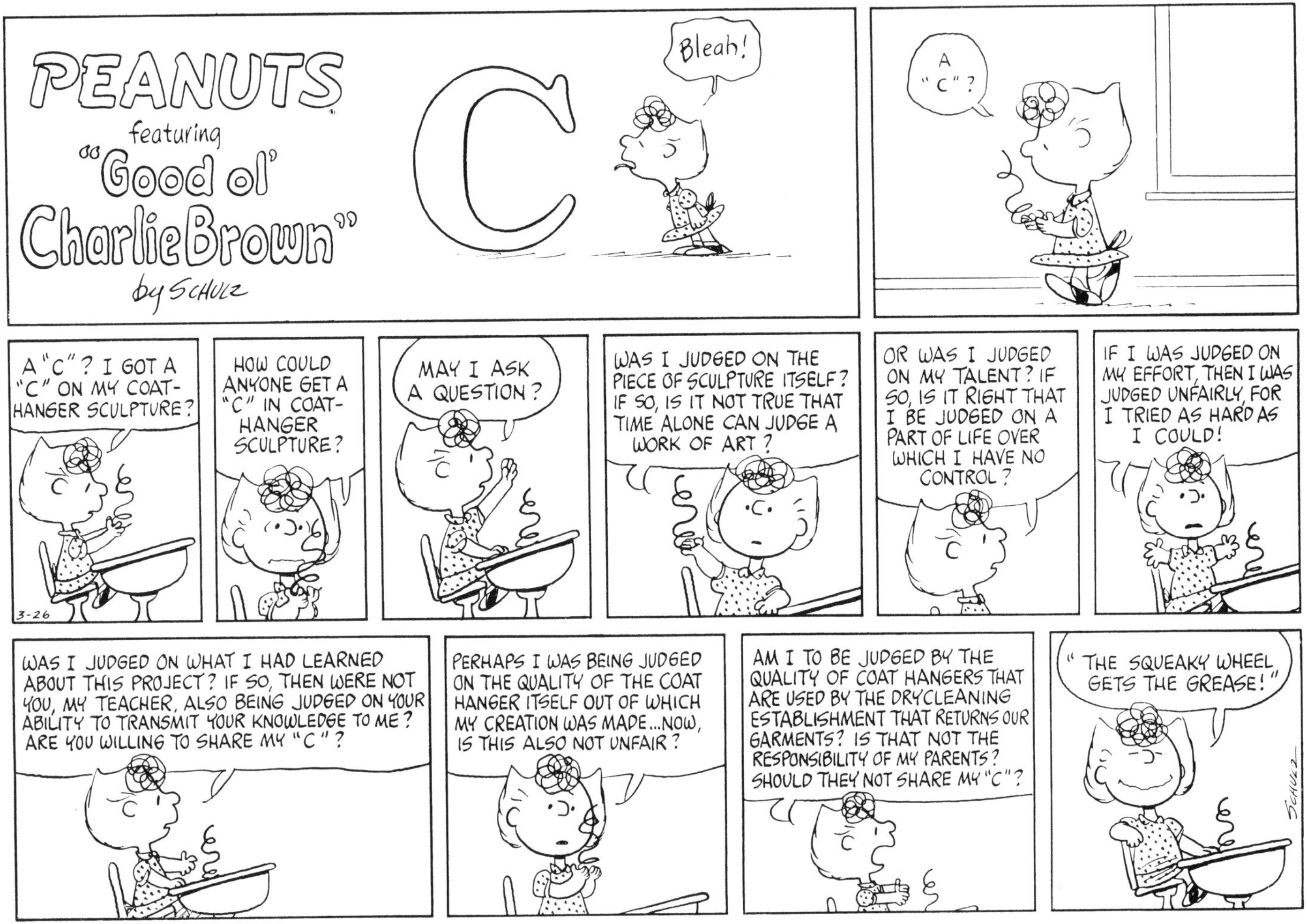
PEANUTS
featuring "Good ol' Charlie Brown"
by SCHULZ
C
Bleah!
A "C"?
A "C"? I GOT A "C" ON MY COAT-HANGER SCULPTURE?
3-26
HOW COULD ANYONE GET A "C" IN COAT-HANGER SCULPTURE?
MAY I ASK A QUESTION?
WAS I JUDGED ON THE PIECE OF SCULPTURE ITSELF? IF SO, IS IT NOT TRUE THAT TIME ALONE CAN JUDGE A WORK OF ART?
OR WAS I JUDGED ON MY TALENT? IF SO, IS IT RIGHT THAT I BE JUDGED ON A PART OF LIFE OVER WHICH I HAVE NO CONTROL?
IF I WAS JUDGED ON MY EFFORT, THEN I WAS JUDGED UNFAIRLY, FOR I TRIED AS HARD AS I COULD!
WAS I JUDGED ON WHAT I HAD LEARNED ABOUT THIS PROJECT? IF SO, THEN WERE NOT YOU, MY TEACHER, ALSO BEING JUDGED ON YOUR ABILITY TO TRANSMIT YOUR KNOWLEDGE TO ME? ARE YOU WILLING TO SHARE MY "C"?
PERHAPS I WAS BEING JUDGED ON THE QUALITY OF THE COAT HANGER ITSELF OUT OF WHICH MY CREATION WAS MADE...NOW, IS THIS ALSO NOT UNFAIR?
AM I TO BE JUDGED BY THE QUALITY OF COAT HANGERS THAT ARE USED BY THE DRYCLEANING ESTABLISHMENT THAT RETURNS OUR GARMENTS? IS THAT NOT THE RESPONSIBILITY OF MY PARENTS? SHOULD THEY NOT SHARE MY "C"?
"THE SQUEAKY WHEEL GETS THE GREASE!"
SCHULZ

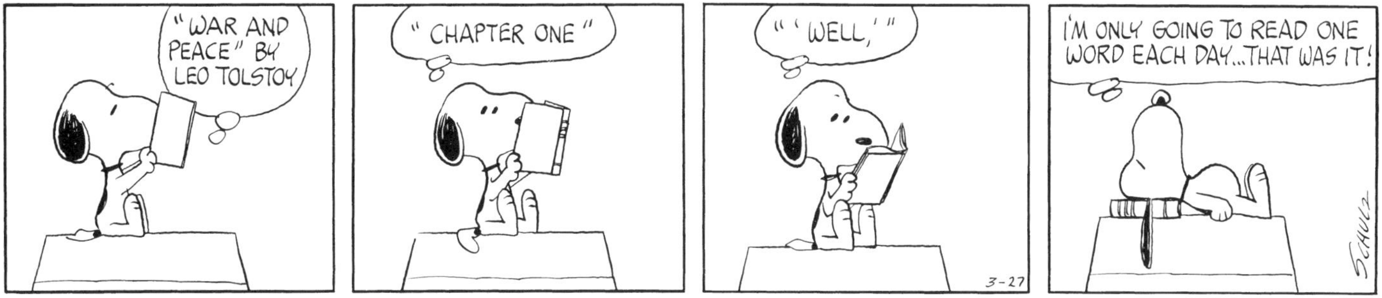
"WAR AND PEACE" BY LEO TOLSTOY
" CHAPTER ONE "
" 'WELL,' "
3-27
I'M ONLY GOING TO READ ONE WORD EACH DAY...THAT WAS IT!
SCHULZ

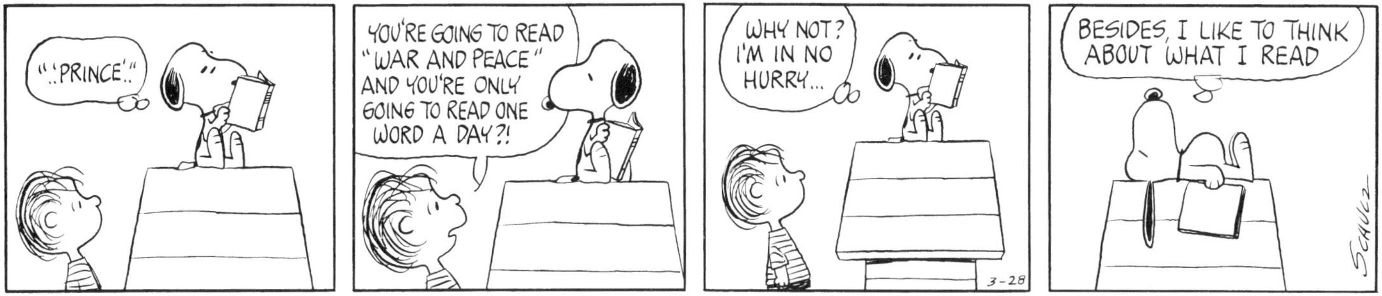
"..'PRINCE'.."
YOU'RE GOING TO READ "WAR AND PEACE" AND YOU'RE ONLY GOING TO READ ONE WORD A DAY?!
WHY NOT? I'M IN NO HURRY...
3-28
BESIDES, I LIKE TO THINK ABOUT WHAT I READ
SCHULZ

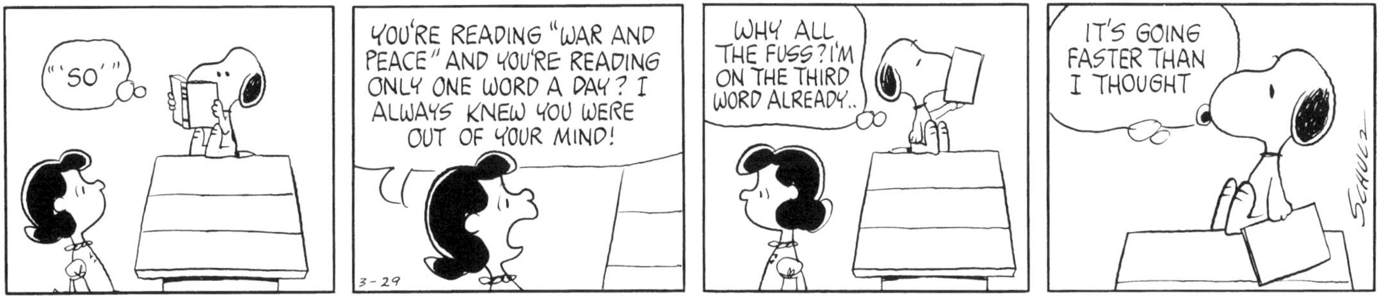
" 'SO' "
YOU'RE READING "WAR AND PEACE" AND YOU'RE READING ONLY ONE WORD A DAY? I ALWAYS KNEW YOU WERE OUT OF YOUR MIND!
3-29
WHY ALL THE FUSS? I'M ON THE THIRD WORD ALREADY..
IT'S GOING FASTER THAN I THOUGHT
SCHULZ

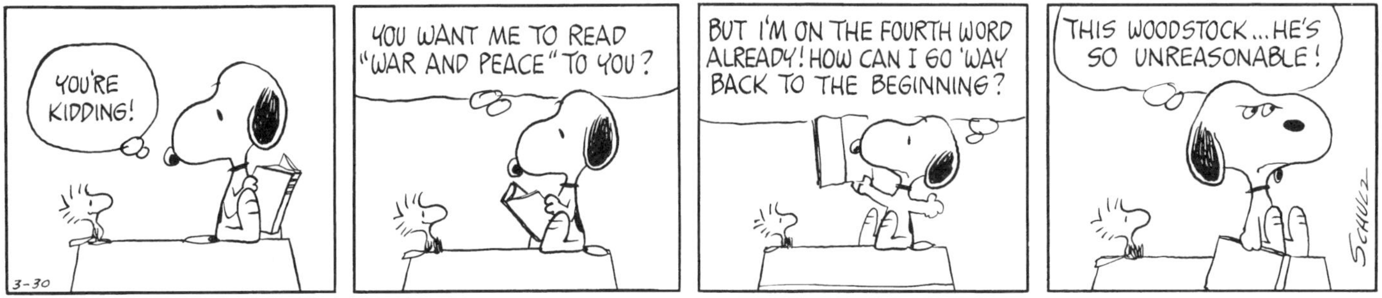
YOU'RE KIDDING!
YOU WANT ME TO READ "WAR AND PEACE" TO YOU?
BUT I'M ON THE FOURTH WORD ALREADY! HOW CAN I GO 'WAY BACK TO THE BEGINNING?
THIS WOODSTOCK... HE'S SO UNREASONABLE!
3-30
SCHULZ

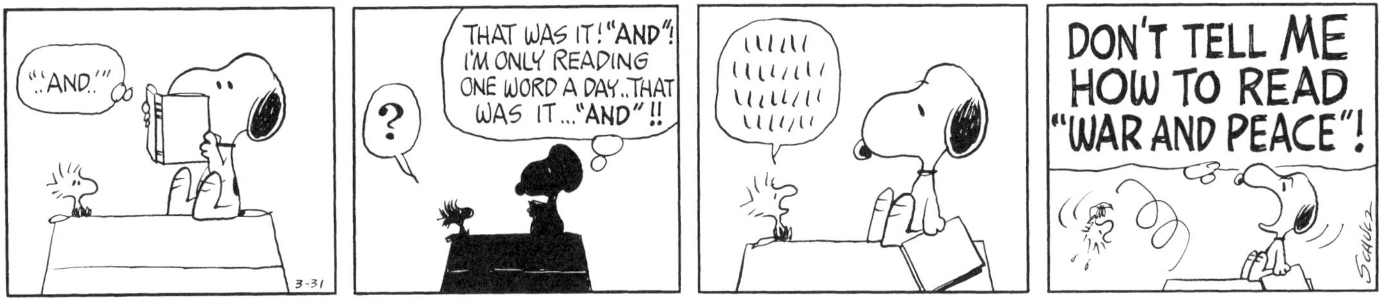
"..AND.."
?
THAT WAS IT! "AND"! I'M ONLY READING ONE WORD A DAY.. THAT WAS IT... "AND"!!
DON'T TELL ME HOW TO READ "WAR AND PEACE"!
3-31
SCHULZ

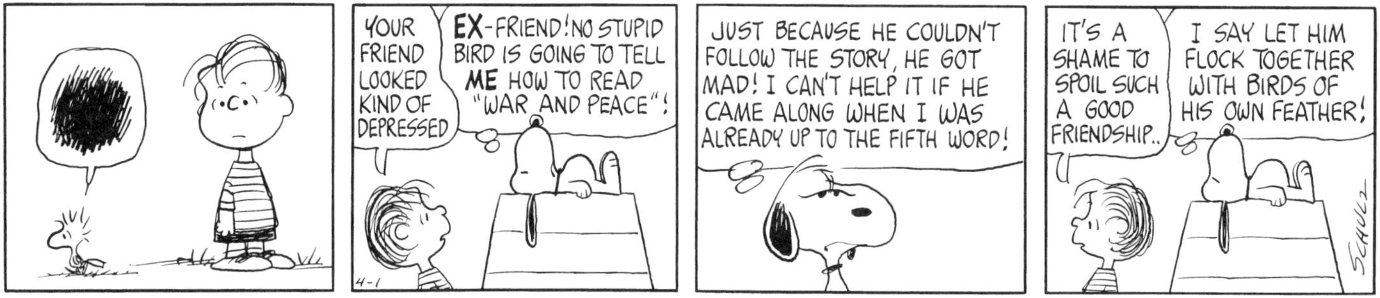
YOUR FRIEND LOOKED KIND OF DEPRESSED
EX-FRIEND! NO STUPID BIRD IS GOING TO TELL ME HOW TO READ "WAR AND PEACE"!
JUST BECAUSE HE COULDN'T FOLLOW THE STORY, HE GOT MAD! I CAN'T HELP IT IF HE CAME ALONG WHEN I WAS ALREADY UP TO THE FIFTH WORD!
IT'S A SHAME TO SPOIL SUCH A GOOD FRIENDSHIP..
I SAY LET HIM FLOCK TOGETHER WITH BIRDS OF HIS OWN FEATHER!
4-1
SCHULZ

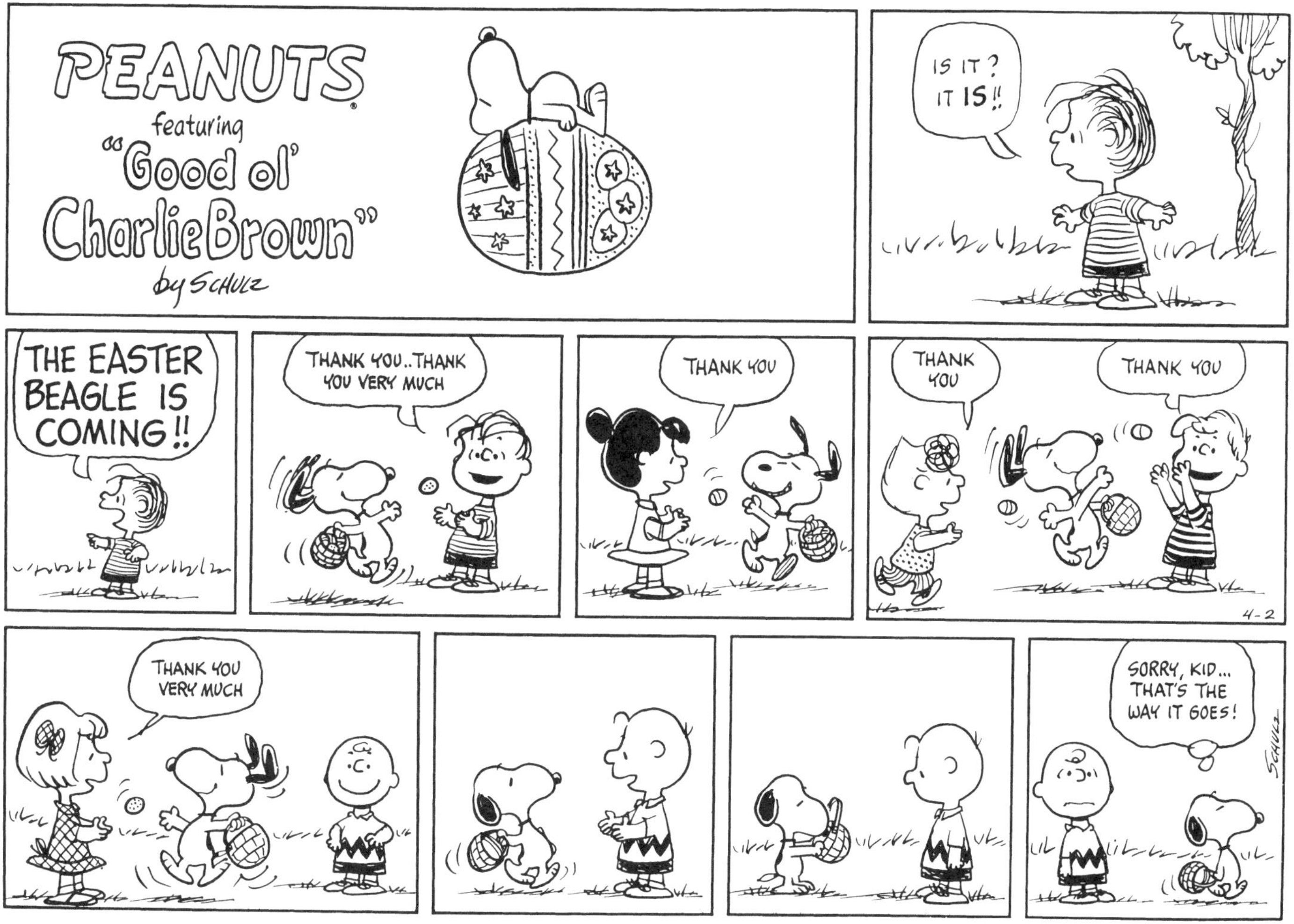
PEANUTS
featuring
"Good ol' Charlie Brown"
by SCHULZ
IS IT? IT IS!!
THE EASTER BEAGLE IS COMING!!
THANK YOU..THANK YOU VERY MUCH
THANK YOU
THANK YOU
THANK YOU
4-2
THANK YOU VERY MUCH
SORRY, KID... THAT'S THE WAY IT GOES!
SCHULZ

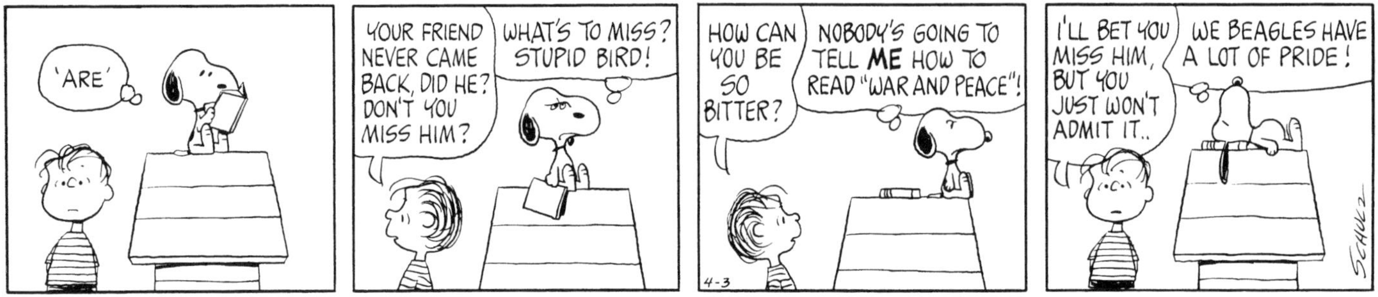
'ARE'
YOUR FRIEND NEVER CAME BACK, DID HE? DON'T YOU MISS HIM?
WHAT'S TO MISS? STUPID BIRD!
HOW CAN YOU BE SO BITTER?
NOBODY'S GOING TO TELL **ME** HOW TO READ "WAR AND PEACE"!
4-3
I'LL BET YOU MISS HIM, BUT YOU JUST WON'T ADMIT IT..
WE BEAGLES HAVE A LOT OF PRIDE!
SCHULZ

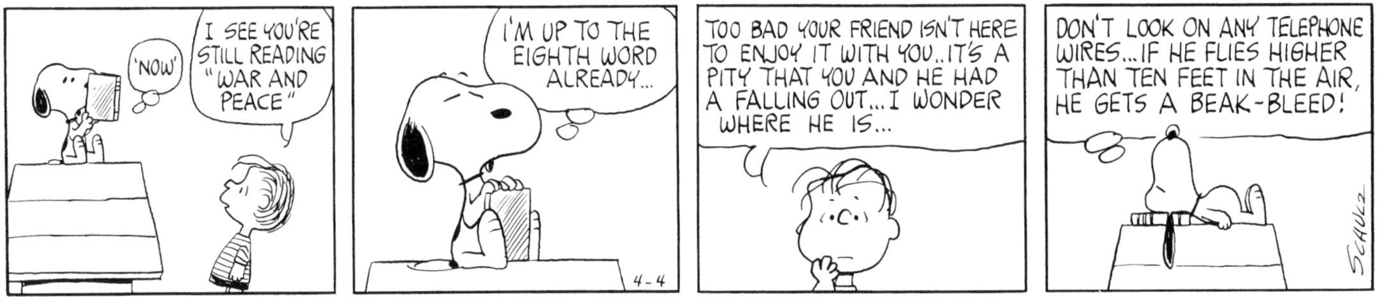
'NOW'
I SEE YOU'RE STILL READING "WAR AND PEACE"
I'M UP TO THE EIGHTH WORD ALREADY...
4-4
TOO BAD YOUR FRIEND ISN'T HERE TO ENJOY IT WITH YOU..IT'S A PITY THAT YOU AND HE HAD A FALLING OUT...I WONDER WHERE HE IS...
DON'T LOOK ON ANY TELEPHONE WIRES...IF HE FLIES HIGHER THAN TEN FEET IN THE AIR, HE GETS A BEAK-BLEED!
SCHULZ

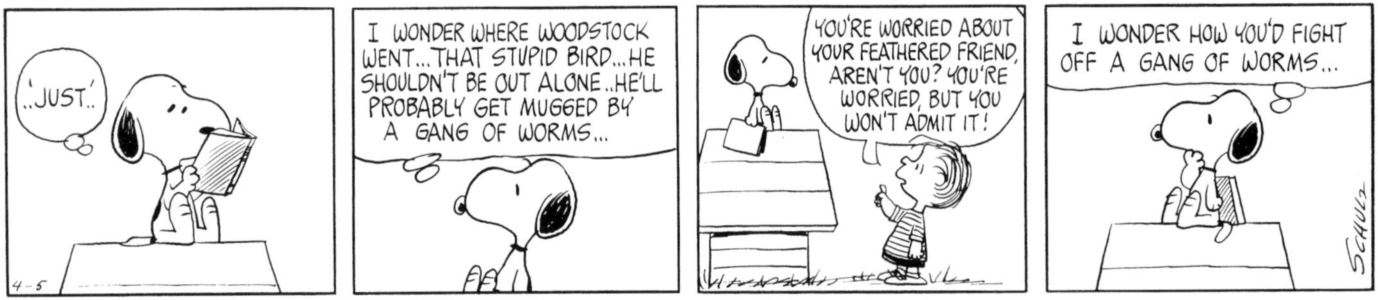
'..JUST'..
4-5
I WONDER WHERE WOODSTOCK WENT...THAT STUPID BIRD...HE SHOULDN'T BE OUT ALONE..HE'LL PROBABLY GET MUGGED BY A GANG OF WORMS...
YOU'RE WORRIED ABOUT YOUR FEATHERED FRIEND, AREN'T YOU? YOU'RE WORRIED, BUT YOU WON'T ADMIT IT!
I WONDER HOW YOU'D FIGHT OFF A GANG OF WORMS...
SCHULZ

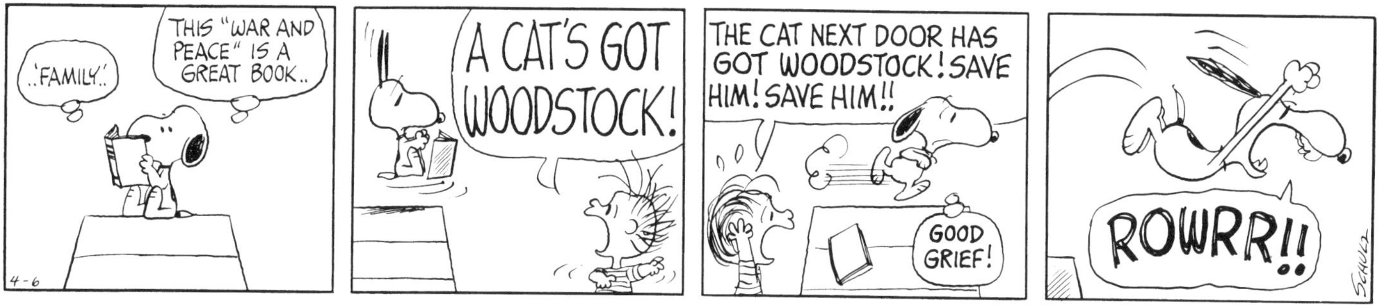
..'FAMILY'..
THIS "WAR AND PEACE" IS A GREAT BOOK..
4-6
A CAT'S GOT WOODSTOCK!
THE CAT NEXT DOOR HAS GOT WOODSTOCK! SAVE HIM! SAVE HIM!!
GOOD GRIEF!
ROWRR!!
SCHULZ

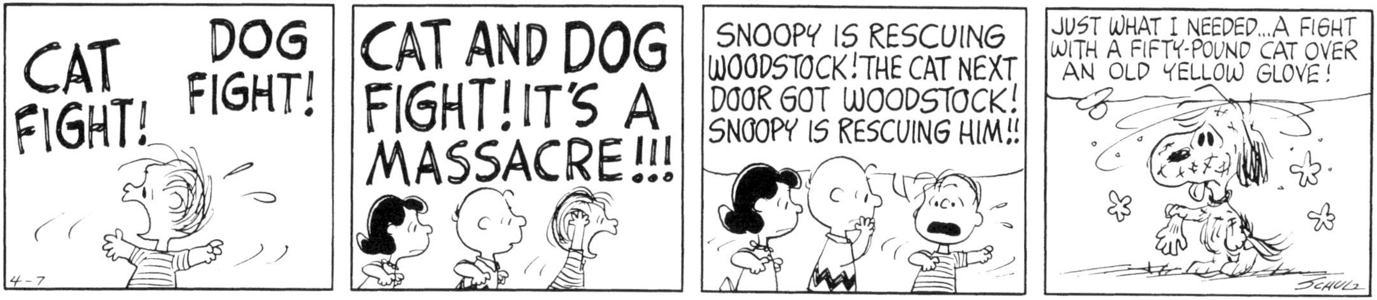
CAT FIGHT!
DOG FIGHT!
4-7
CAT AND DOG FIGHT! IT'S A MASSACRE!!!
SNOOPY IS RESCUING WOODSTOCK! THE CAT NEXT DOOR GOT WOODSTOCK! SNOOPY IS RESCUING HIM!!
JUST WHAT I NEEDED...A FIGHT WITH A FIFTY-POUND CAT OVER AN OLD YELLOW GLOVE!
SCHULZ

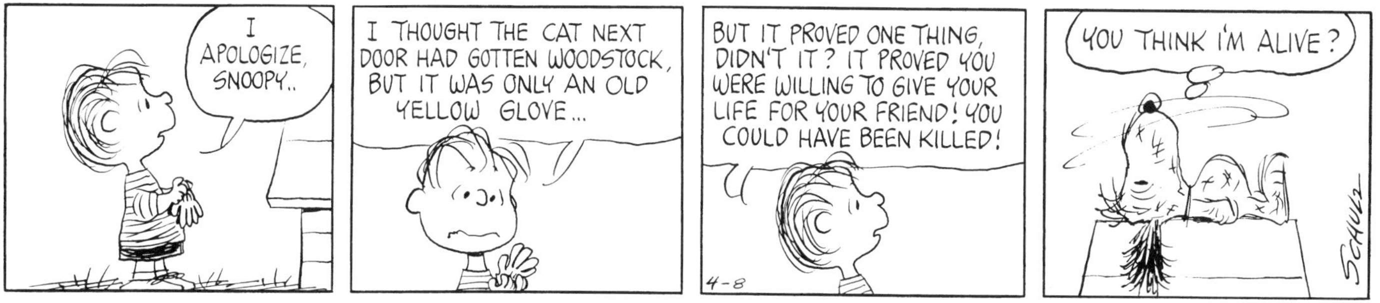
I APOLOGIZE, SNOOPY..
I THOUGHT THE CAT NEXT DOOR HAD GOTTEN WOODSTOCK, BUT IT WAS ONLY AN OLD YELLOW GLOVE...
BUT IT PROVED ONE THING, DIDN'T IT? IT PROVED YOU WERE WILLING TO GIVE YOUR LIFE FOR YOUR FRIEND! YOU COULD HAVE BEEN KILLED!
4-8
YOU THINK I'M ALIVE?
SCHULZ

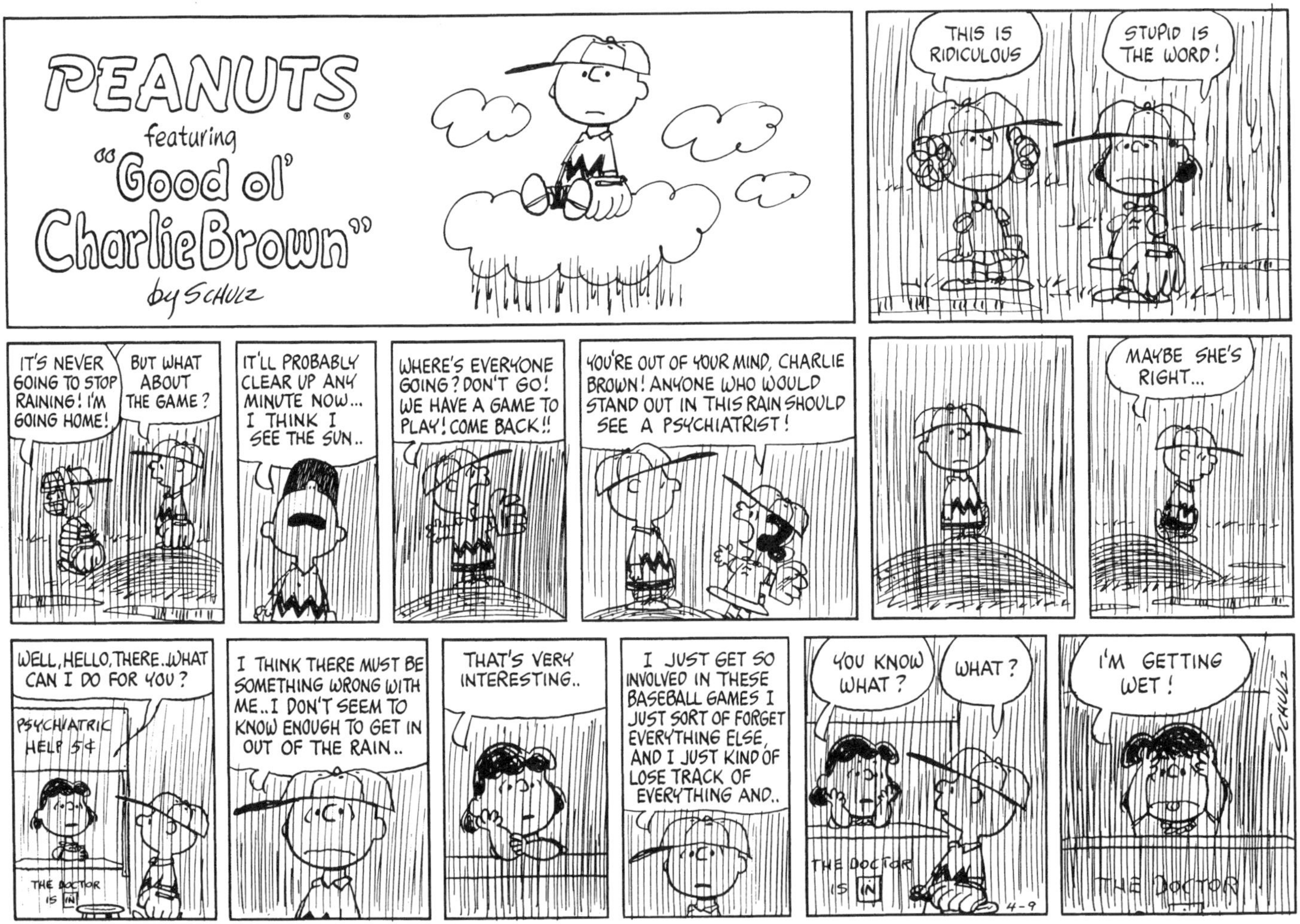
PEANUTS
featuring "Good ol' Charlie Brown"
by SCHULZ
THIS IS RIDICULOUS
STUPID IS THE WORD!
IT'S NEVER GOING TO STOP RAINING! I'M GOING HOME!
BUT WHAT ABOUT THE GAME?
IT'LL PROBABLY CLEAR UP ANY MINUTE NOW... I THINK I SEE THE SUN..
WHERE'S EVERYONE GOING? DON'T GO! WE HAVE A GAME TO PLAY! COME BACK!!
YOU'RE OUT OF YOUR MIND, CHARLIE BROWN! ANYONE WHO WOULD STAND OUT IN THIS RAIN SHOULD SEE A PSYCHIATRIST!
MAYBE SHE'S RIGHT...
WELL, HELLO, THERE..WHAT CAN I DO FOR YOU?
PSYCHIATRIC HELP 5¢
THE DOCTOR IS IN
I THINK THERE MUST BE SOMETHING WRONG WITH ME..I DON'T SEEM TO KNOW ENOUGH TO GET IN OUT OF THE RAIN..
THAT'S VERY INTERESTING..
I JUST GET SO INVOLVED IN THESE BASEBALL GAMES I JUST SORT OF FORGET EVERYTHING ELSE, AND I JUST KIND OF LOSE TRACK OF EVERYTHING AND..
YOU KNOW WHAT?
WHAT?
THE DOCTOR IS IN
4-9
I'M GETTING WET!
SCHULZ
THE DOCTOR

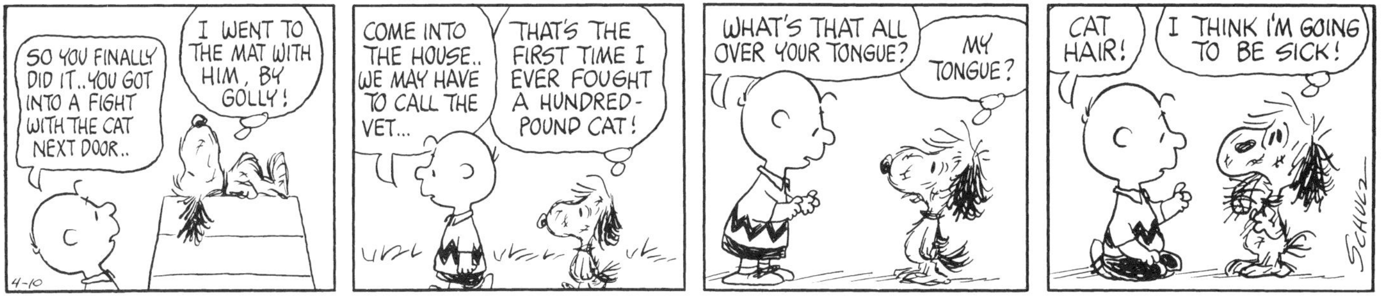
SO YOU FINALLY DID IT..YOU GOT INTO A FIGHT WITH THE CAT NEXT DOOR..
I WENT TO THE MAT WITH HIM, BY GOLLY!
COME INTO THE HOUSE.. WE MAY HAVE TO CALL THE VET...
THAT'S THE FIRST TIME I EVER FOUGHT A HUNDRED-POUND CAT!
WHAT'S THAT ALL OVER YOUR TONGUE?
MY TONGUE?
CAT HAIR!
I THINK I'M GOING TO BE SICK!
4-10
SCHULZ

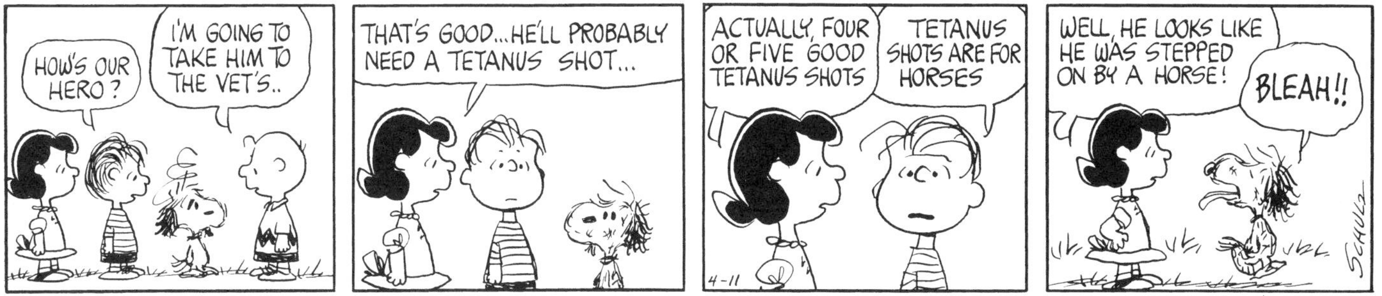
HOW'S OUR HERO?
I'M GOING TO TAKE HIM TO THE VET'S..
THAT'S GOOD...HE'LL PROBABLY NEED A TETANUS SHOT...
ACTUALLY, FOUR OR FIVE GOOD TETANUS SHOTS
TETANUS SHOTS ARE FOR HORSES
WELL, HE LOOKS LIKE HE WAS STEPPED ON BY A HORSE!
BLEAH!!
4-11
SCHULZ

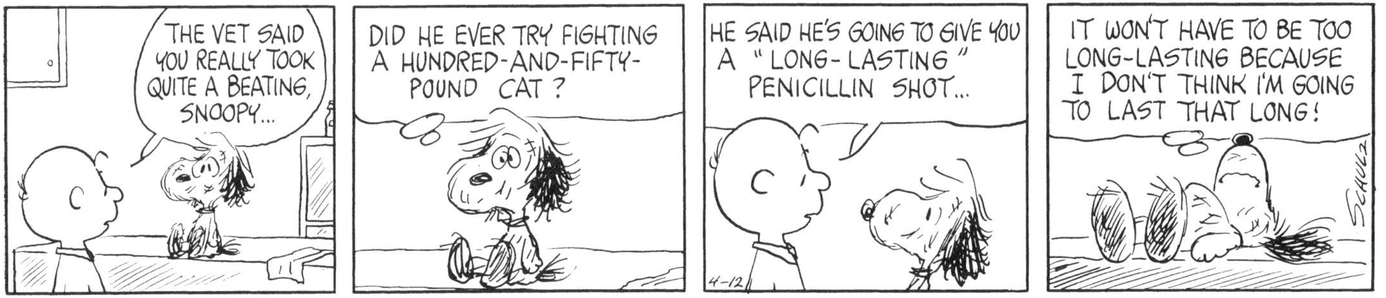
THE VET SAID YOU REALLY TOOK QUITE A BEATING, SNOOPY...
DID HE EVER TRY FIGHTING A HUNDRED-AND-FIFTY-POUND CAT?
HE SAID HE'S GOING TO GIVE YOU A "LONG-LASTING" PENICILLIN SHOT...
IT WON'T HAVE TO BE TOO LONG-LASTING BECAUSE I DON'T THINK I'M GOING TO LAST THAT LONG!
4-12
SCHULZ

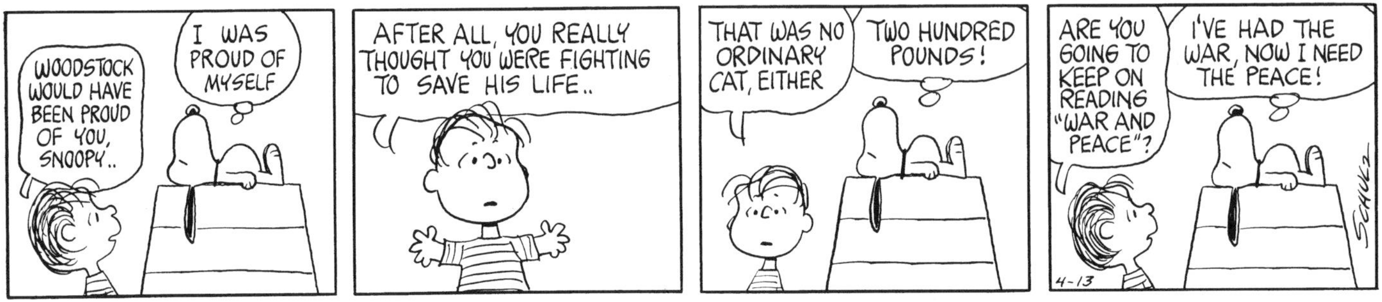
WOODSTOCK WOULD HAVE BEEN PROUD OF YOU, SNOOPY..
I WAS PROUD OF MYSELF
AFTER ALL, YOU REALLY THOUGHT YOU WERE FIGHTING TO SAVE HIS LIFE..
THAT WAS NO ORDINARY CAT, EITHER
TWO HUNDRED POUNDS!
ARE YOU GOING TO KEEP ON READING "WAR AND PEACE"?
I'VE HAD THE WAR, NOW I NEED THE PEACE!
SCHULZ
4-13

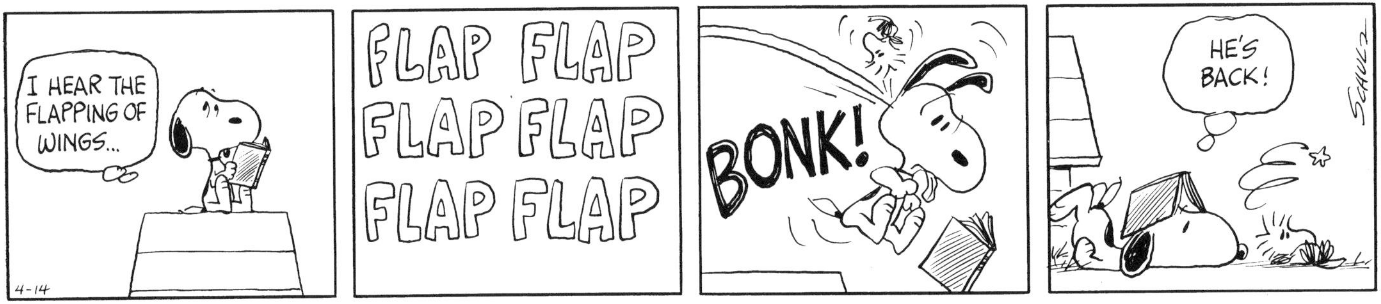
I HEAR THE FLAPPING OF WINGS...
4-14
FLAP FLAP FLAP FLAP FLAP FLAP
BONK!
HE'S BACK!
SCHULZ

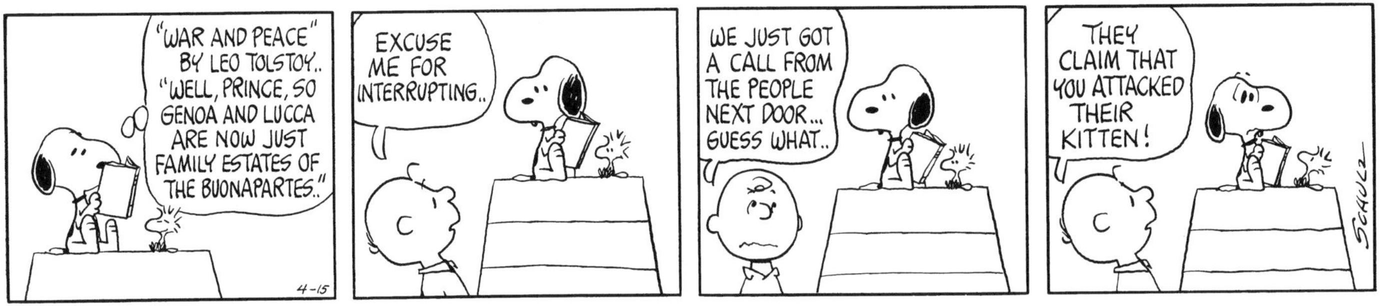
"WAR AND PEACE" BY LEO TOLSTOY.. "WELL, PRINCE, SO GENOA AND LUCCA ARE NOW JUST FAMILY ESTATES OF THE BUONAPARTES.."
4-15
EXCUSE ME FOR INTERRUPTING..
WE JUST GOT A CALL FROM THE PEOPLE NEXT DOOR... GUESS WHAT..
THEY CLAIM THAT YOU ATTACKED THEIR KITTEN!
SCHULZ

PEANUTS®
featuring
"Good ol' CharlieBrown"
by Schulz

I HAVE A QUESTION..

WHAT DO YOU THINK THE SECRET OF LIVING IS, CHUCK?

THE SECRET OF LIVING IS TO OWN A CONVERTIBLE AND A LAKE..

A CONVERTIBLE AND A LAKE?

IF THE SUN IS SHINING, YOU CAN RIDE AROUND IN YOUR CONVERTIBLE AND BE HAPPY... IF IT STARTS TO RAIN, IT WON'T SPOIL YOUR DAY BECAUSE YOU CAN JUST SAY, "OH, WELL, THE RAIN WILL FILL UP MY LAKE!"

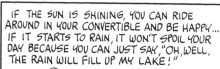

WHAT DO YOU THINK THE SECRET OF LIVING IS, SNOOPY?

SMAK!

A CONVERTIBLE AND A LAKE..I DON'T KNOW ABOUT YOU, CHUCK...

IF YOUR LAKE IS DRYING UP, YOU CAN SAY, "OH, WELL, THIS IS NICE WEATHER FOR RIDING IN A CONVERTIBLE.."

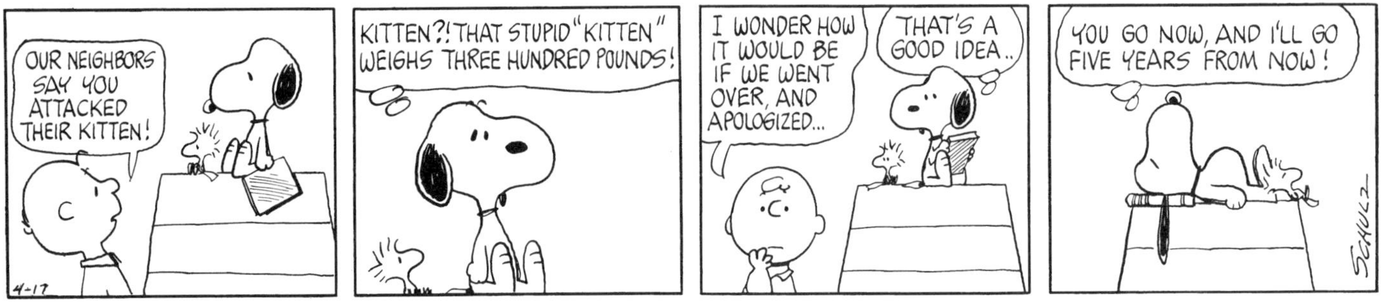
OUR NEIGHBORS SAY YOU ATTACKED THEIR KITTEN!
KITTEN?! THAT STUPID "KITTEN" WEIGHS THREE HUNDRED POUNDS!
I WONDER HOW IT WOULD BE IF WE WENT OVER, AND APOLOGIZED...
THAT'S A GOOD IDEA..
YOU GO NOW, AND I'LL GO FIVE YEARS FROM NOW!
SCHULZ

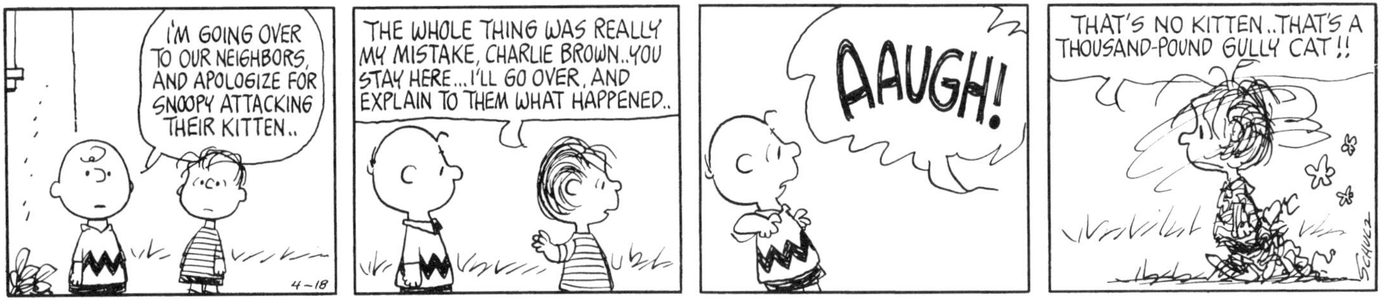
I'M GOING OVER TO OUR NEIGHBORS, AND APOLOGIZE FOR SNOOPY ATTACKING THEIR KITTEN..
THE WHOLE THING WAS REALLY MY MISTAKE, CHARLIE BROWN..YOU STAY HERE...I'LL GO OVER, AND EXPLAIN TO THEM WHAT HAPPENED..
AAUGH!
THAT'S NO KITTEN..THAT'S A THOUSAND-POUND GULLY CAT!!
SCHULZ

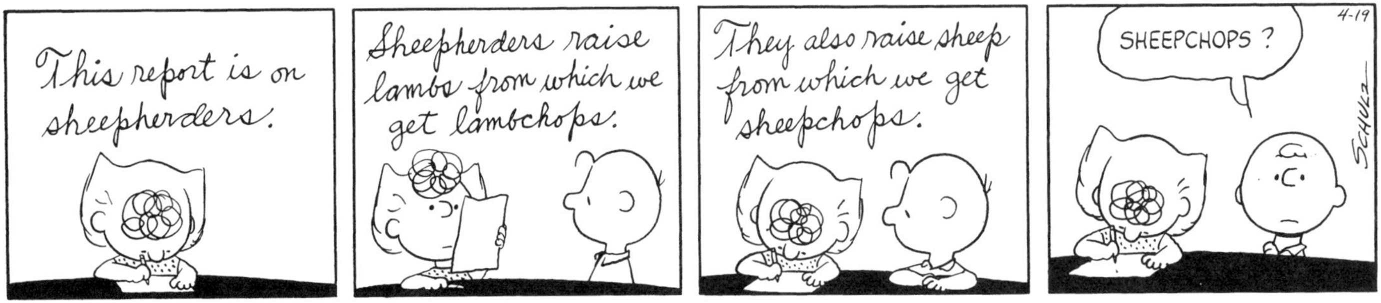
This report is on sheepherders.
Sheepherders raise lambs from which we get lambchops.
They also raise sheep from which we get sheepchops.
SHEEPCHOPS ?
SCHULZ

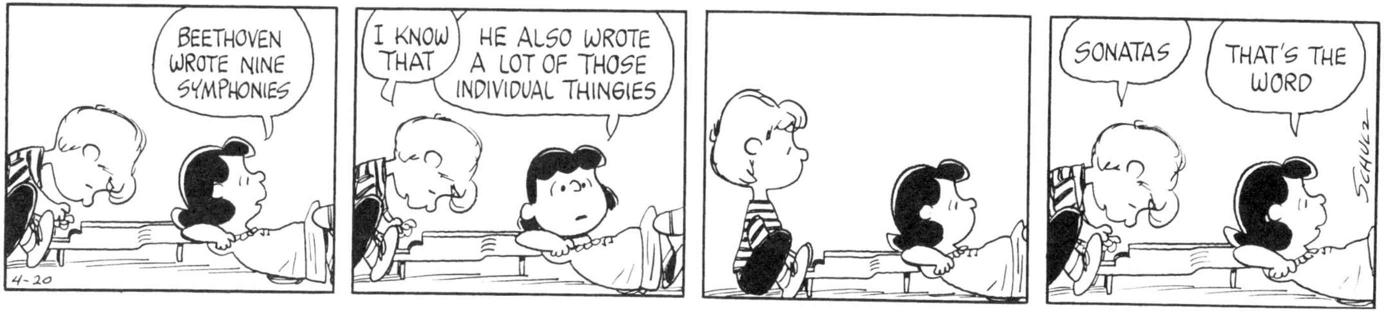
BEETHOVEN WROTE NINE SYMPHONIES
I KNOW THAT
HE ALSO WROTE A LOT OF THOSE INDIVIDUAL THINGIES
SONATAS
THAT'S THE WORD

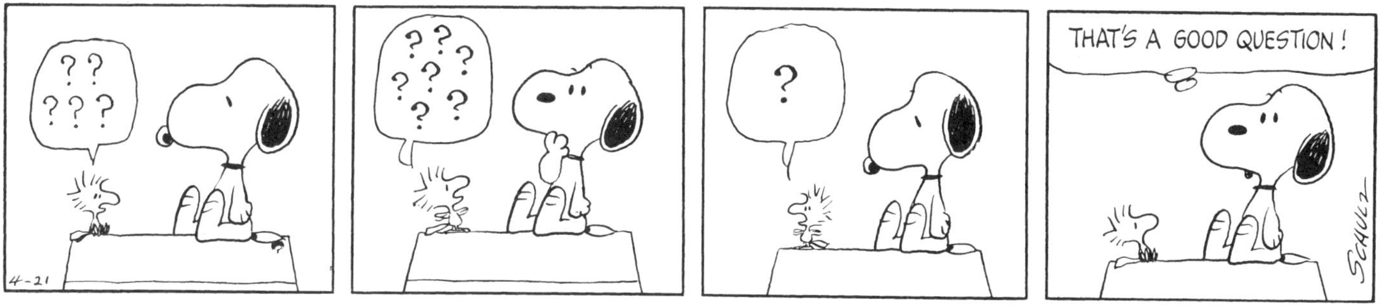
? ? ? ? ?
? ? ? ? ? ? ?
?
THAT'S A GOOD QUESTION !

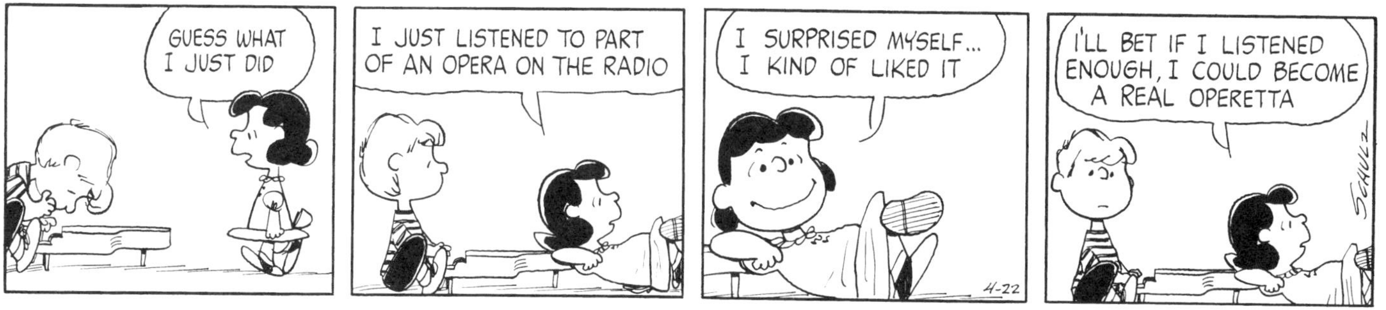
GUESS WHAT I JUST DID
I JUST LISTENED TO PART OF AN OPERA ON THE RADIO
I SURPRISED MYSELF... I KIND OF LIKED IT
I'LL BET IF I LISTENED ENOUGH, I COULD BECOME A REAL OPERETTA

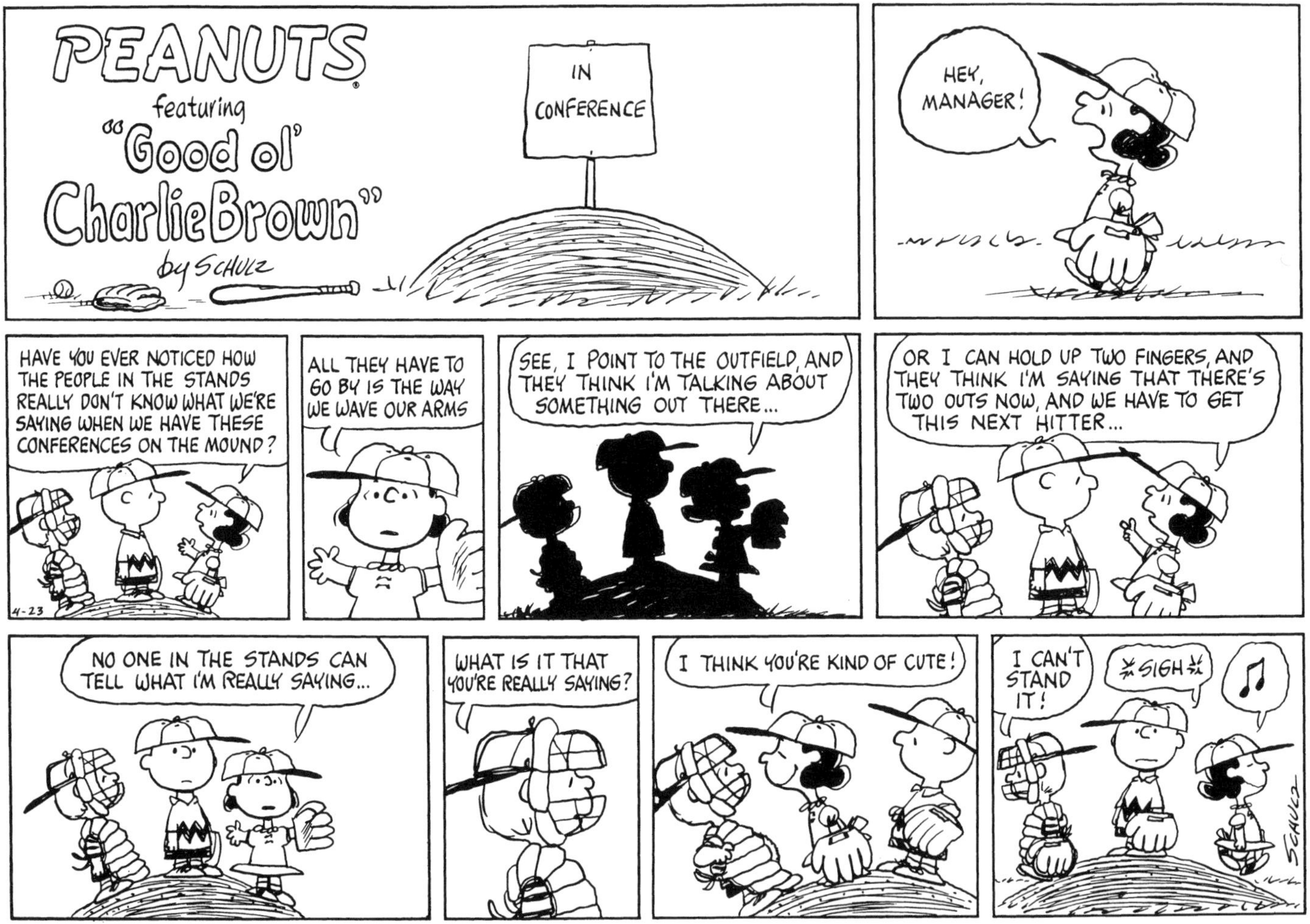
PEANUTS
featuring
"Good ol' CharlieBrown"
by SCHULZ
IN CONFERENCE
HEY, MANAGER!
HAVE YOU EVER NOTICED HOW THE PEOPLE IN THE STANDS REALLY DON'T KNOW WHAT WE'RE SAYING WHEN WE HAVE THESE CONFERENCES ON THE MOUND?
4-23
ALL THEY HAVE TO GO BY IS THE WAY WE WAVE OUR ARMS
SEE, I POINT TO THE OUTFIELD, AND THEY THINK I'M TALKING ABOUT SOMETHING OUT THERE...
OR I CAN HOLD UP TWO FINGERS, AND THEY THINK I'M SAYING THAT THERE'S TWO OUTS NOW, AND WE HAVE TO GET THIS NEXT HITTER...
NO ONE IN THE STANDS CAN TELL WHAT I'M REALLY SAYING...
WHAT IS IT THAT YOU'RE REALLY SAYING?
I THINK YOU'RE KIND OF CUTE!
I CAN'T STAND IT!
SIGH
♪
SCHULZ

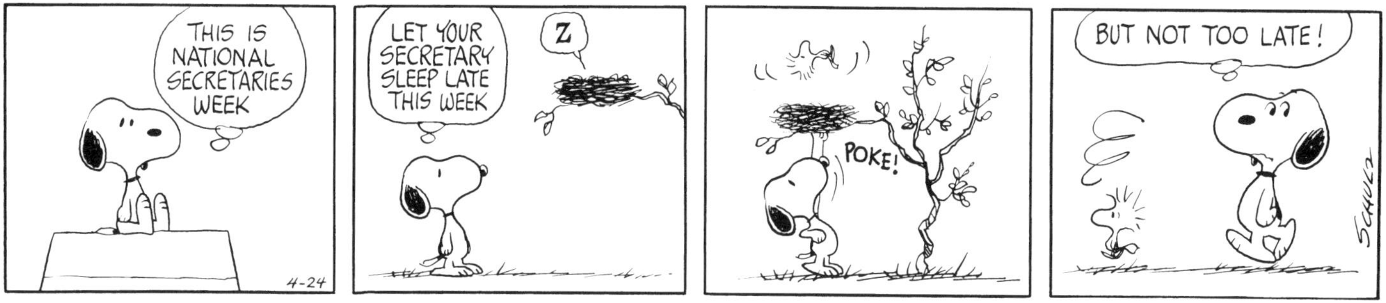
THIS IS NATIONAL SECRETARIES WEEK
LET YOUR SECRETARY SLEEP LATE THIS WEEK
Z
POKE!
BUT NOT TOO LATE!

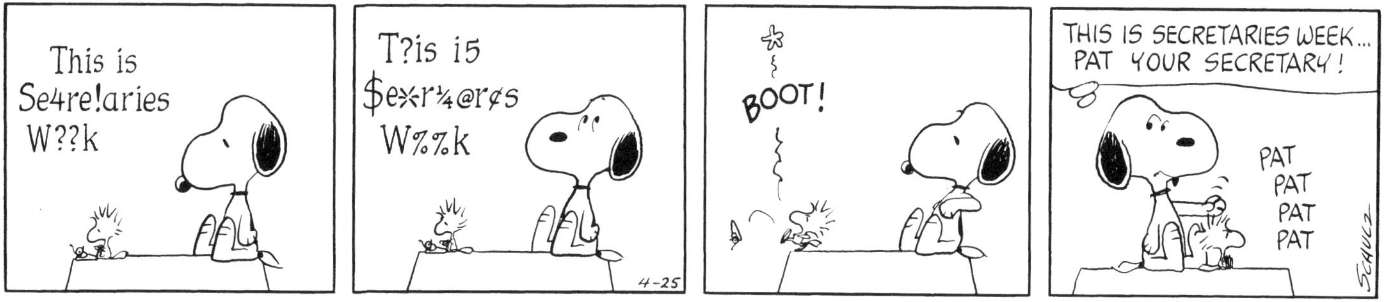
This is Se4re!aries W??k
T?is i5 $e✻r¼@r¢s W%%k
BOOT!
THIS IS SECRETARIES WEEK... PAT YOUR SECRETARY!
PAT PAT PAT PAT

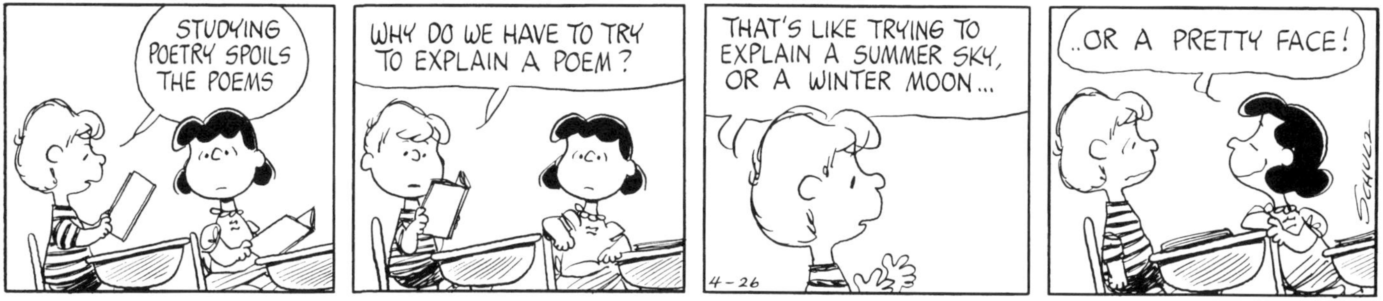
STUDYING POETRY SPOILS THE POEMS
WHY DO WE HAVE TO TRY TO EXPLAIN A POEM?
THAT'S LIKE TRYING TO EXPLAIN A SUMMER SKY, OR A WINTER MOON...
..OR A PRETTY FACE!

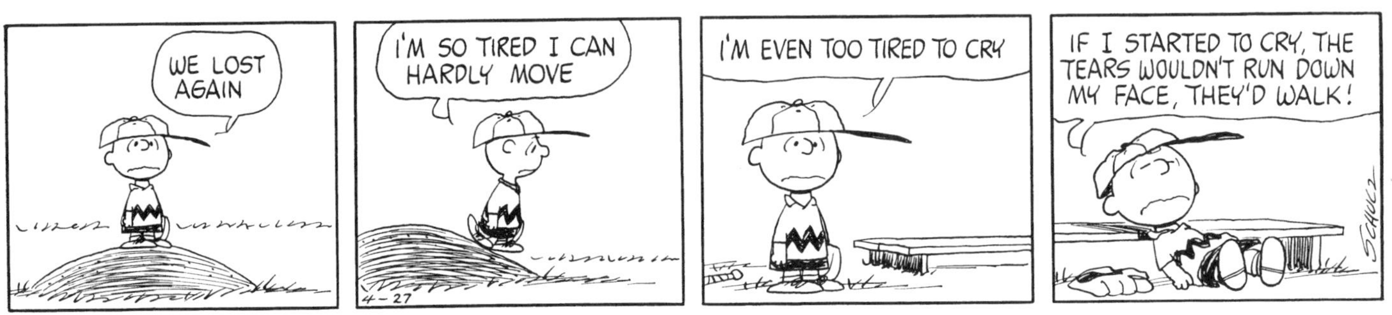
WE LOST AGAIN
I'M SO TIRED I CAN HARDLY MOVE
4-27
I'M EVEN TOO TIRED TO CRY
IF I STARTED TO CRY, THE TEARS WOULDN'T RUN DOWN MY FACE, THEY'D WALK!
SCHULZ

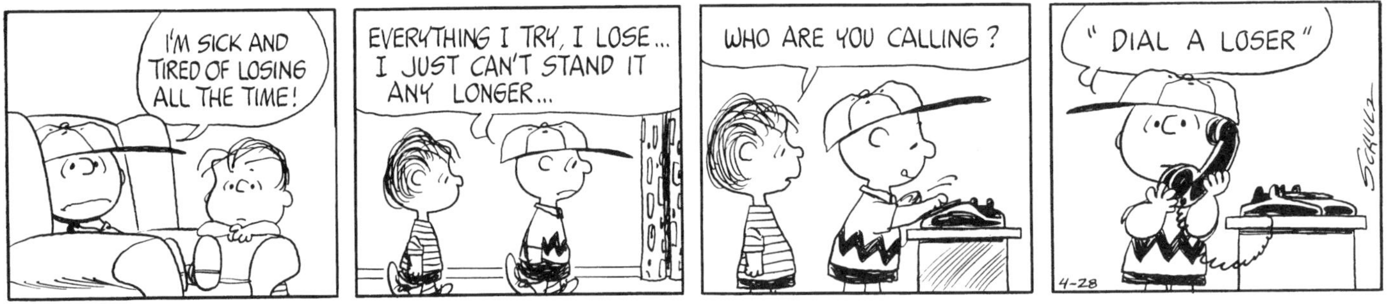
I'M SICK AND TIRED OF LOSING ALL THE TIME!
EVERYTHING I TRY, I LOSE... I JUST CAN'T STAND IT ANY LONGER...
WHO ARE YOU CALLING?
" DIAL A LOSER "
SCHULZ
4-28

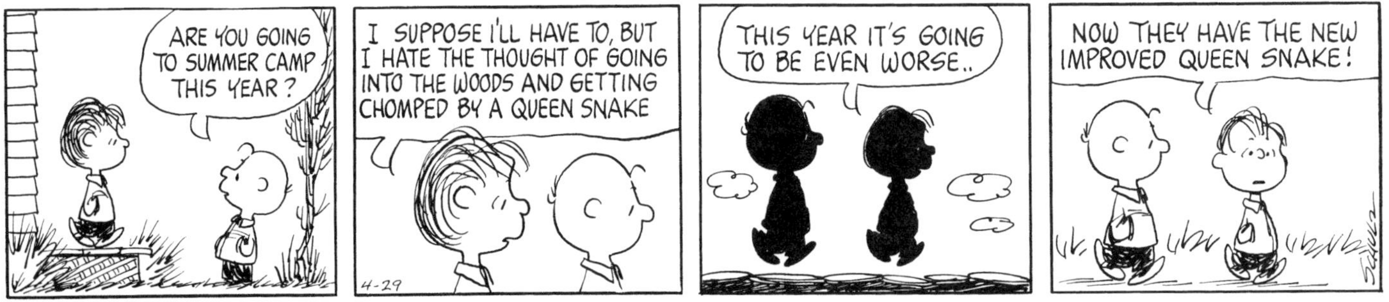
ARE YOU GOING TO SUMMER CAMP THIS YEAR?
I SUPPOSE I'LL HAVE TO, BUT I HATE THE THOUGHT OF GOING INTO THE WOODS AND GETTING CHOMPED BY A QUEEN SNAKE
4-29
THIS YEAR IT'S GOING TO BE EVEN WORSE..
NOW THEY HAVE THE NEW IMPROVED QUEEN SNAKE!
SCHULZ

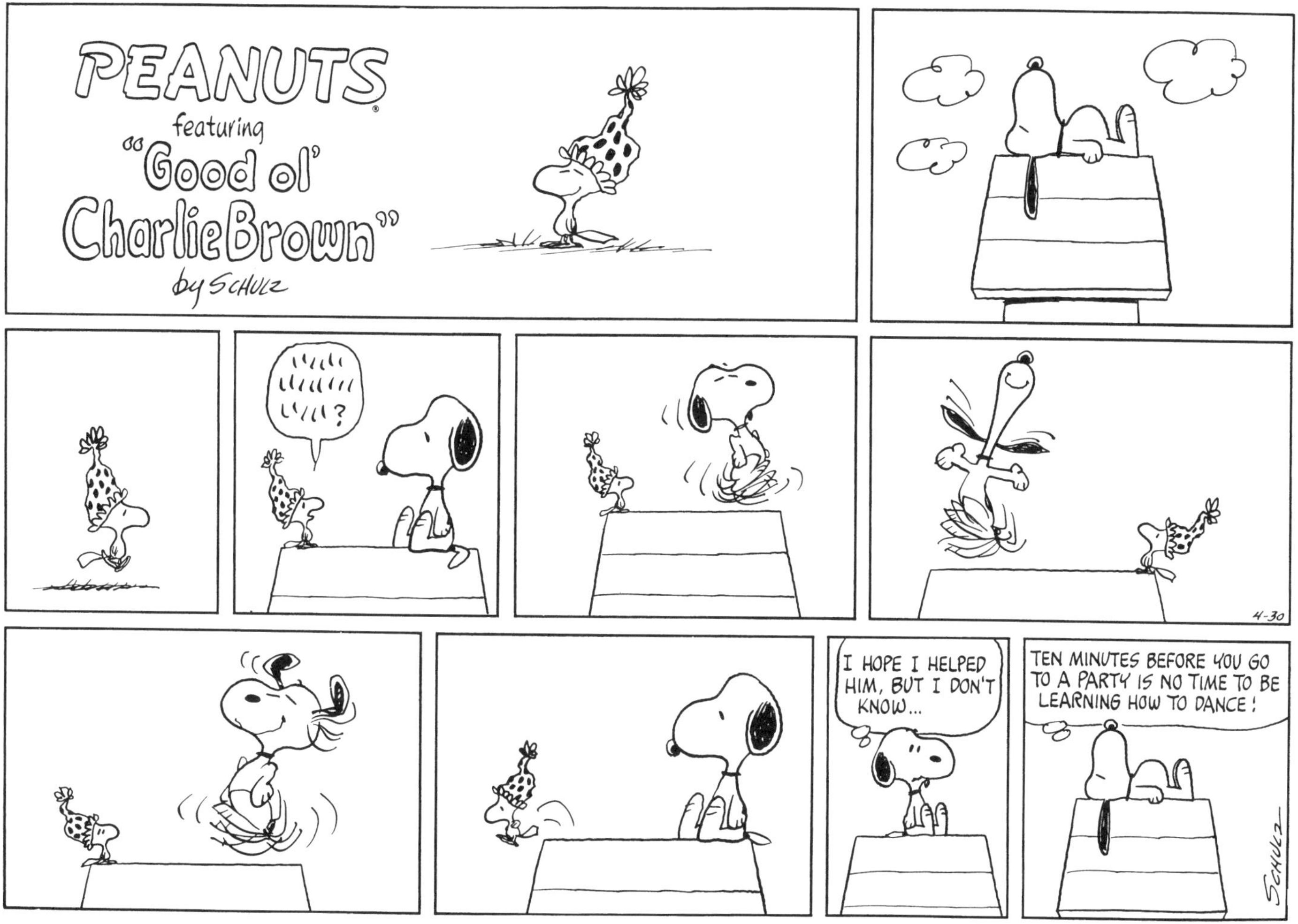
PEANUTS
featuring "Good ol' Charlie Brown"
by SCHULZ
I HOPE I HELPED HIM, BUT I DON'T KNOW...
TEN MINUTES BEFORE YOU GO TO A PARTY IS NO TIME TO BE LEARNING HOW TO DANCE!
4-30
SCHULZ

THE SOFT RAINS OF APRIL ARE OVER..

THE WARM SUN OF MAY FAVORS THE EARTH..

EVERYTHING IS GROWING!

ALL RIGHT, WHO PLANTED THE FLOWER?!

I LEARNED TWO THINGS IN SCHOOL TODAY

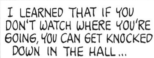

I LEARNED THAT IF YOU DON'T WATCH WHERE YOU'RE GOING, YOU CAN GET KNOCKED DOWN IN THE HALL...

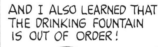

AND I ALSO LEARNED THAT THE DRINKING FOUNTAIN IS OUT OF ORDER!

IT'S NOT OFTEN THAT YOU CAN LEARN TWO NEW THINGS IN ONE DAY!

Report; Agriculture

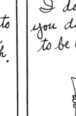
This report is on melons. Melons have to be planted between May 15th and June 5th.

I don't know what you do if you happen to be out of town.

I'm glad I'm not a melon farmer.

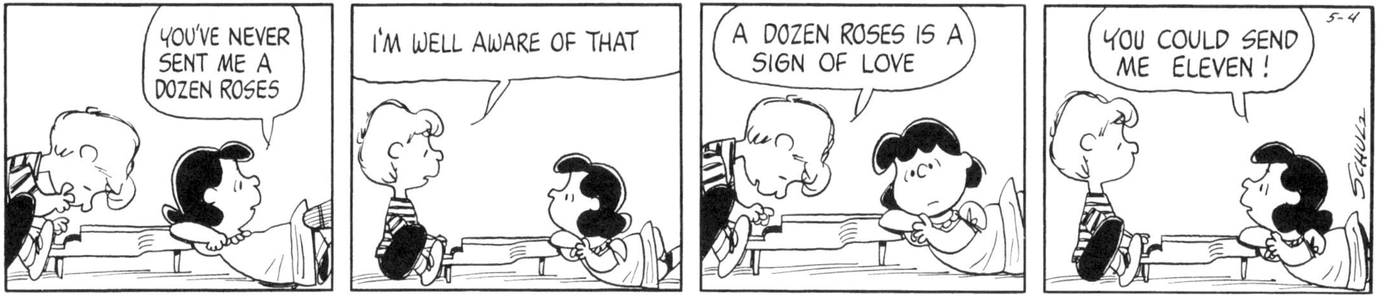
YOU'VE NEVER SENT ME A DOZEN ROSES
I'M WELL AWARE OF THAT
A DOZEN ROSES IS A SIGN OF LOVE
YOU COULD SEND ME ELEVEN!
5-4
SCHULZ

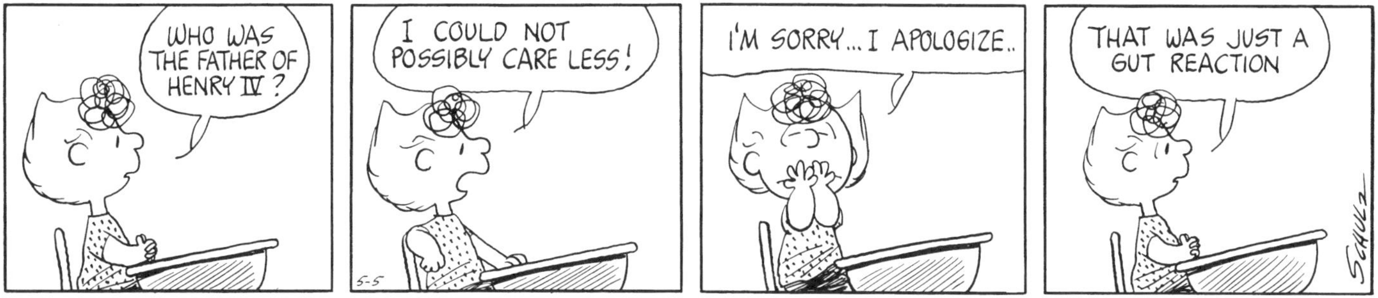
WHO WAS THE FATHER OF HENRY IV?
I COULD NOT POSSIBLY CARE LESS!
5-5
I'M SORRY... I APOLOGIZE..
THAT WAS JUST A GUT REACTION
SCHULZ

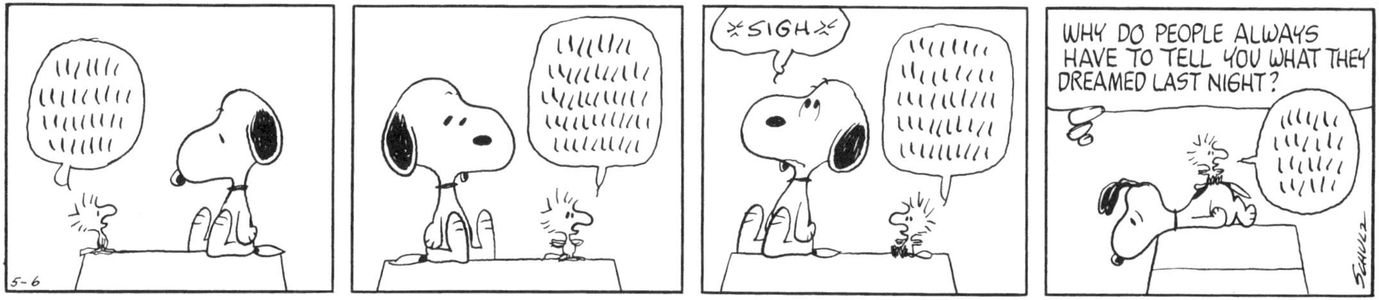
5-6
SIGH
WHY DO PEOPLE ALWAYS HAVE TO TELL YOU WHAT THEY DREAMED LAST NIGHT?
SCHULZ

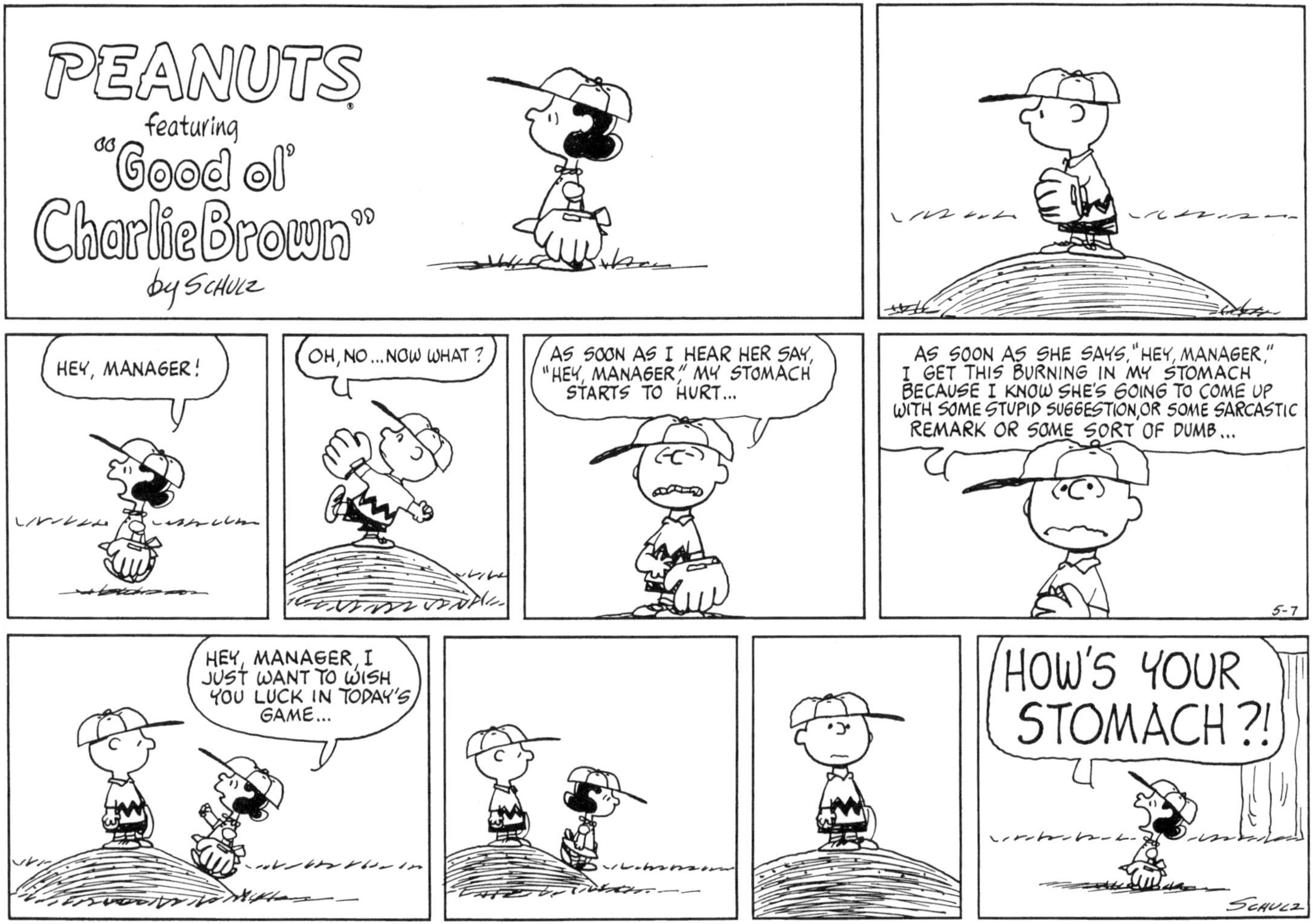
PEANUTS
featuring "Good ol' CharlieBrown"
by SCHULZ
HEY, MANAGER!
OH, NO...NOW WHAT?
AS SOON AS I HEAR HER SAY, "HEY, MANAGER," MY STOMACH STARTS TO HURT...
AS SOON AS SHE SAYS, "HEY, MANAGER," I GET THIS BURNING IN MY STOMACH BECAUSE I KNOW SHE'S GOING TO COME UP WITH SOME STUPID SUGGESTION, OR SOME SARCASTIC REMARK OR SOME SORT OF DUMB...
5-7
HEY, MANAGER, I JUST WANT TO WISH YOU LUCK IN TODAY'S GAME...
HOW'S YOUR STOMACH?!
SCHULZ

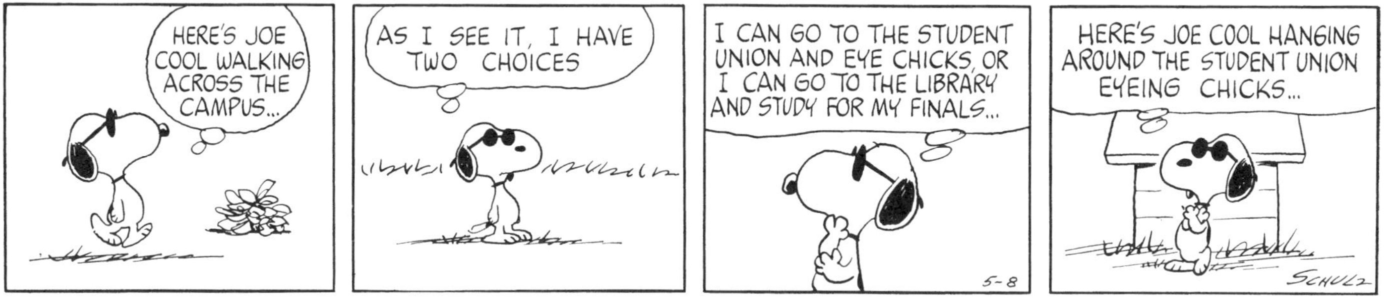
HERE'S JOE COOL WALKING ACROSS THE CAMPUS...
AS I SEE IT, I HAVE TWO CHOICES
I CAN GO TO THE STUDENT UNION AND EYE CHICKS, OR I CAN GO TO THE LIBRARY AND STUDY FOR MY FINALS...
HERE'S JOE COOL HANGING AROUND THE STUDENT UNION EYEING CHICKS...

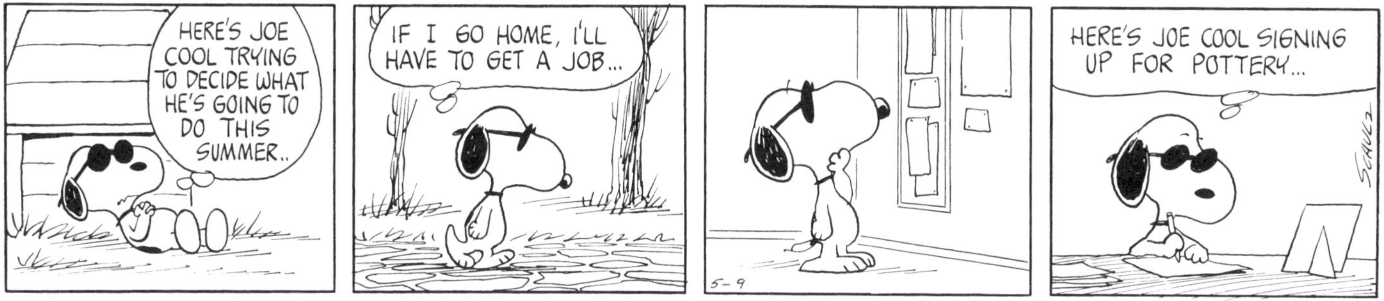
HERE'S JOE COOL TRYING TO DECIDE WHAT HE'S GOING TO DO THIS SUMMER..
IF I GO HOME, I'LL HAVE TO GET A JOB...
HERE'S JOE COOL SIGNING UP FOR POTTERY...

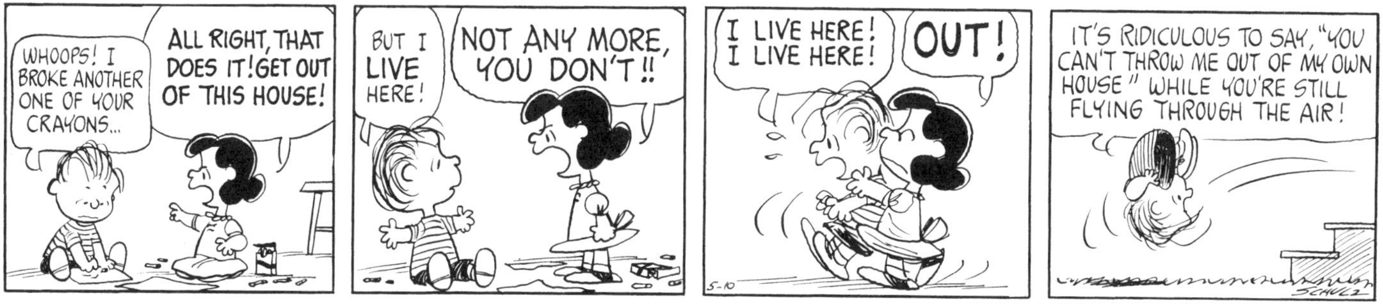
WHOOPS! I BROKE ANOTHER ONE OF YOUR CRAYONS...
ALL RIGHT, THAT DOES IT! GET OUT OF THIS HOUSE!
BUT I LIVE HERE!
NOT ANY MORE, YOU DON'T!!
I LIVE HERE! I LIVE HERE!
OUT!
IT'S RIDICULOUS TO SAY, "YOU CAN'T THROW ME OUT OF MY OWN HOUSE" WHILE YOU'RE STILL FLYING THROUGH THE AIR!

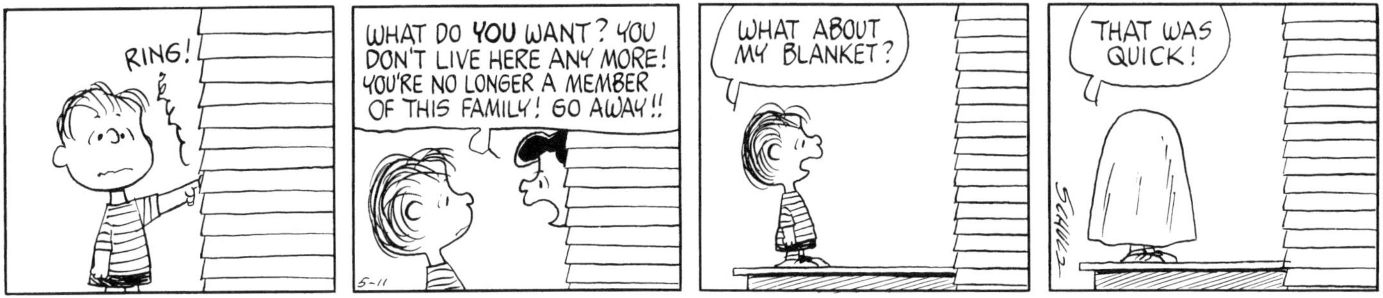
RING!
WHAT DO YOU WANT? YOU DON'T LIVE HERE ANY MORE! YOU'RE NO LONGER A MEMBER OF THIS FAMILY! GO AWAY!!
5-11
WHAT ABOUT MY BLANKET?
THAT WAS QUICK!
SCHULZ

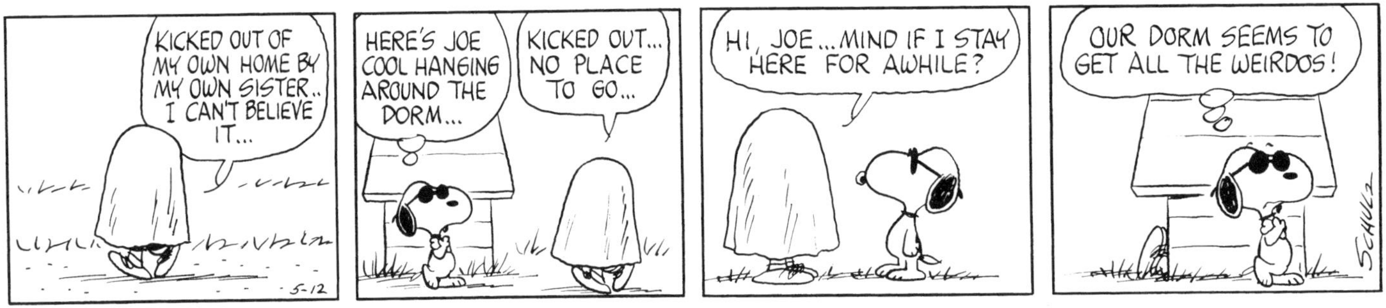
KICKED OUT OF MY OWN HOME BY MY OWN SISTER.. I CAN'T BELIEVE IT...
5-12
HERE'S JOE COOL HANGING AROUND THE DORM...
KICKED OUT... NO PLACE TO GO...
HI, JOE...MIND IF I STAY HERE FOR AWHILE?
OUR DORM SEEMS TO GET ALL THE WEIRDOS!
SCHULZ

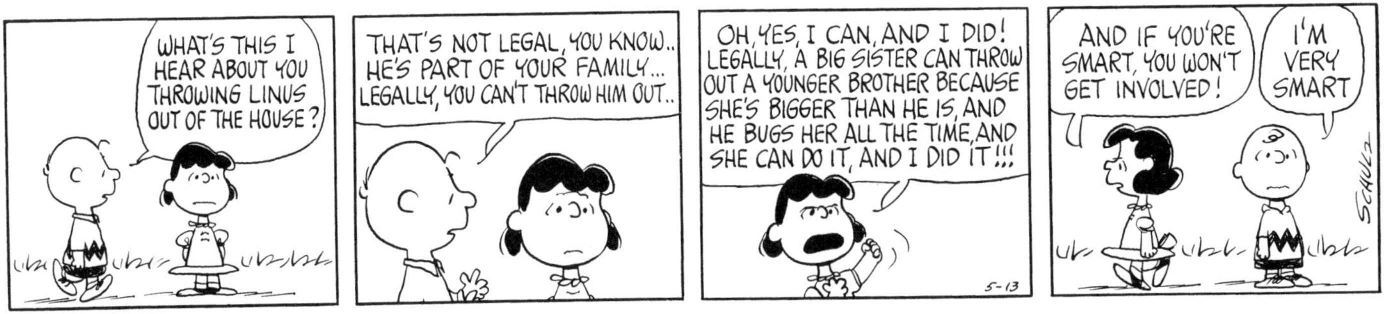
WHAT'S THIS I HEAR ABOUT YOU THROWING LINUS OUT OF THE HOUSE?
THAT'S NOT LEGAL, YOU KNOW.. HE'S PART OF YOUR FAMILY... LEGALLY, YOU CAN'T THROW HIM OUT..
OH, YES, I CAN, AND I DID! LEGALLY, A BIG SISTER CAN THROW OUT A YOUNGER BROTHER BECAUSE SHE'S BIGGER THAN HE IS, AND HE BUGS HER ALL THE TIME, AND SHE CAN DO IT, AND I DID IT!!!
5-13
AND IF YOU'RE SMART, YOU WON'T GET INVOLVED!
I'M VERY SMART
SCHULZ

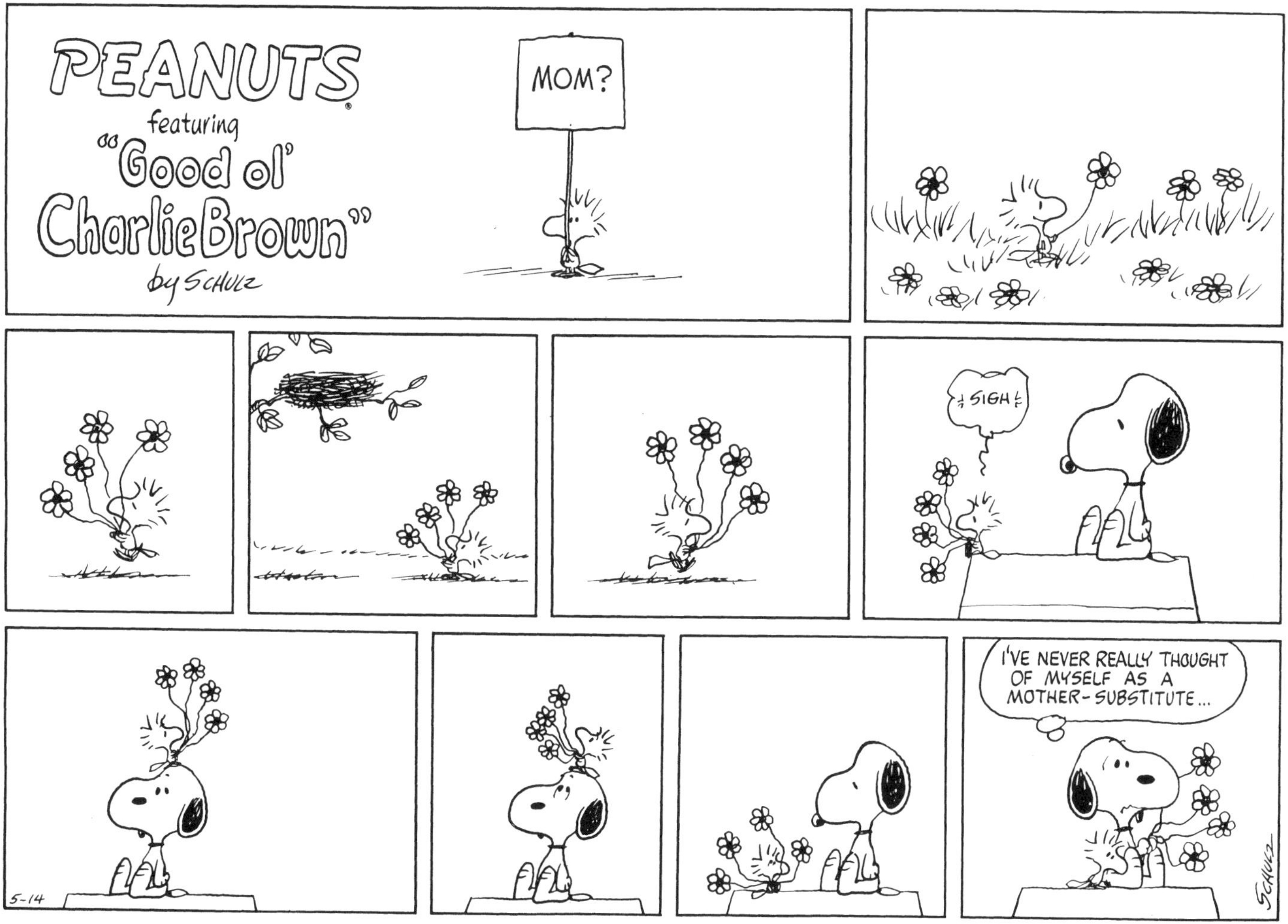
PEANUTS
featuring
"Good ol' Charlie Brown"
by SCHULZ
MOM?
SIGH
I'VE NEVER REALLY THOUGHT OF MYSELF AS A MOTHER-SUBSTITUTE...
5-14
SCHULZ

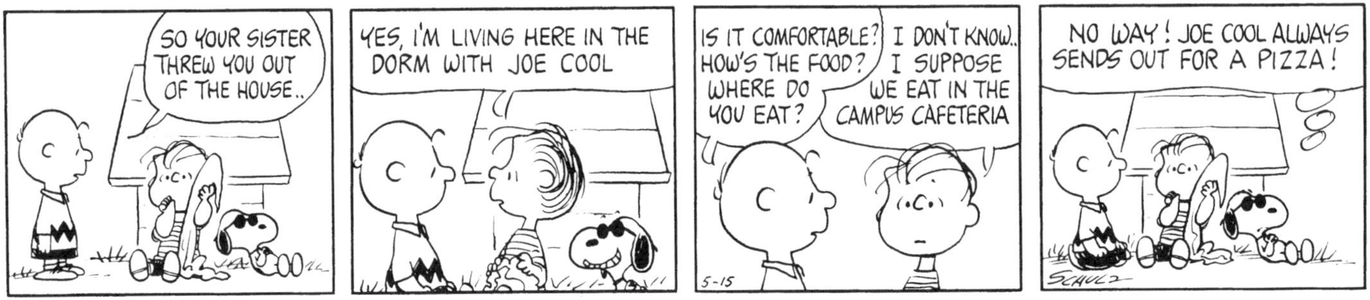

SO YOUR SISTER THREW YOU OUT OF THE HOUSE..
YES, I'M LIVING HERE IN THE DORM WITH JOE COOL
IS IT COMFORTABLE? HOW'S THE FOOD? WHERE DO YOU EAT?
I DON'T KNOW.. I SUPPOSE WE EAT IN THE CAMPUS CAFETERIA
5-15
NO WAY! JOE COOL ALWAYS SENDS OUT FOR A PIZZA!
SCHULZ

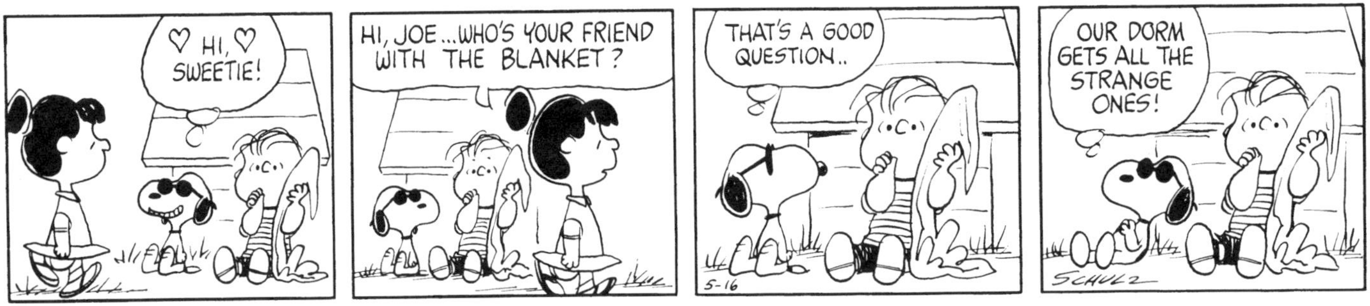

♡ HI, ♡ SWEETIE!
HI, JOE...WHO'S YOUR FRIEND WITH THE BLANKET?
THAT'S A GOOD QUESTION..
5-16
OUR DORM GETS ALL THE STRANGE ONES!
SCHULZ

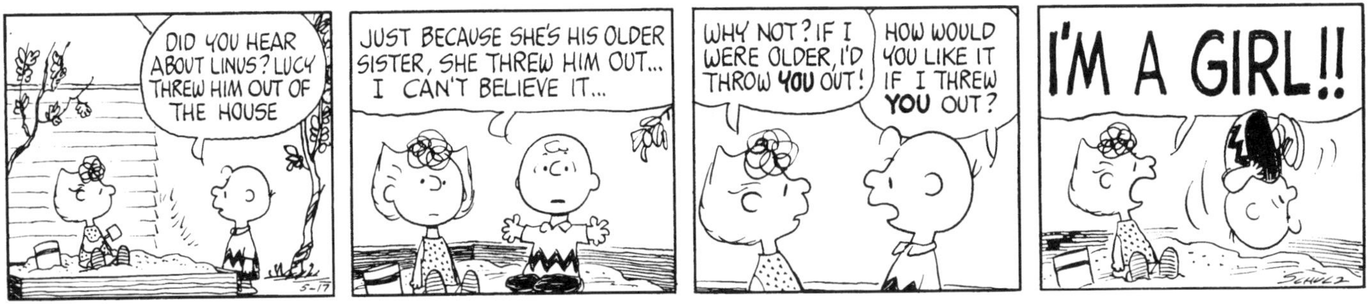

DID YOU HEAR ABOUT LINUS? LUCY THREW HIM OUT OF THE HOUSE
5-17
JUST BECAUSE SHE'S HIS OLDER SISTER, SHE THREW HIM OUT... I CAN'T BELIEVE IT...
WHY NOT? IF I WERE OLDER, I'D THROW YOU OUT!
HOW WOULD YOU LIKE IT IF I THREW YOU OUT?
I'M A GIRL!!
SCHULZ

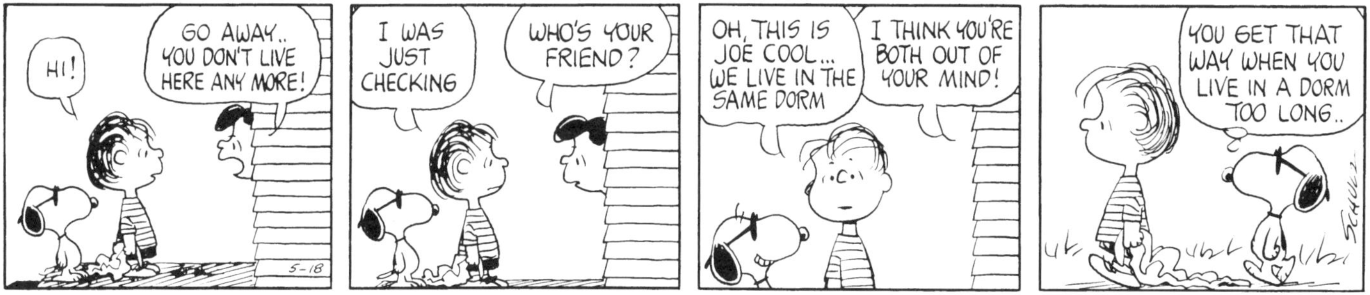
HI!
GO AWAY.. YOU DON'T LIVE HERE ANY MORE!
5-18
I WAS JUST CHECKING
WHO'S YOUR FRIEND?
OH, THIS IS JOE COOL... WE LIVE IN THE SAME DORM
I THINK YOU'RE BOTH OUT OF YOUR MIND!
YOU GET THAT WAY WHEN YOU LIVE IN A DORM TOO LONG..
SCHULZ

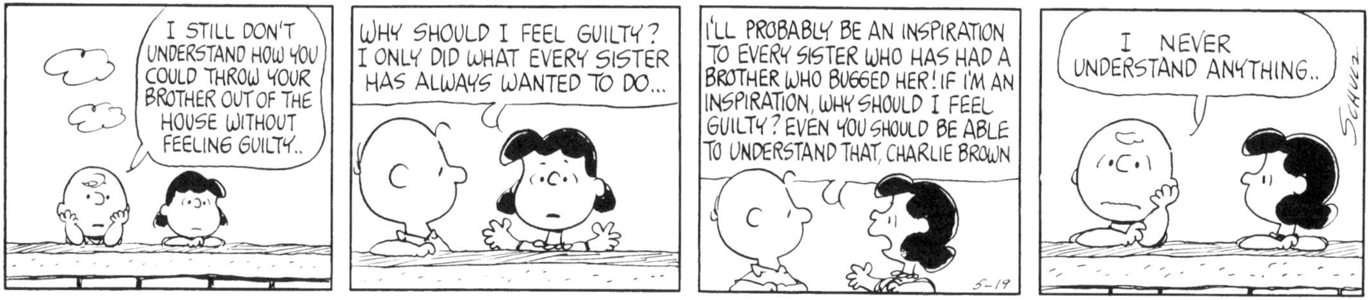
I STILL DON'T UNDERSTAND HOW YOU COULD THROW YOUR BROTHER OUT OF THE HOUSE WITHOUT FEELING GUILTY..
WHY SHOULD I FEEL GUILTY? I ONLY DID WHAT EVERY SISTER HAS ALWAYS WANTED TO DO...
I'LL PROBABLY BE AN INSPIRATION TO EVERY SISTER WHO HAS HAD A BROTHER WHO BUGGED HER! IF I'M AN INSPIRATION, WHY SHOULD I FEEL GUILTY? EVEN YOU SHOULD BE ABLE TO UNDERSTAND THAT, CHARLIE BROWN
5-19
I NEVER UNDERSTAND ANYTHING..
SCHULZ

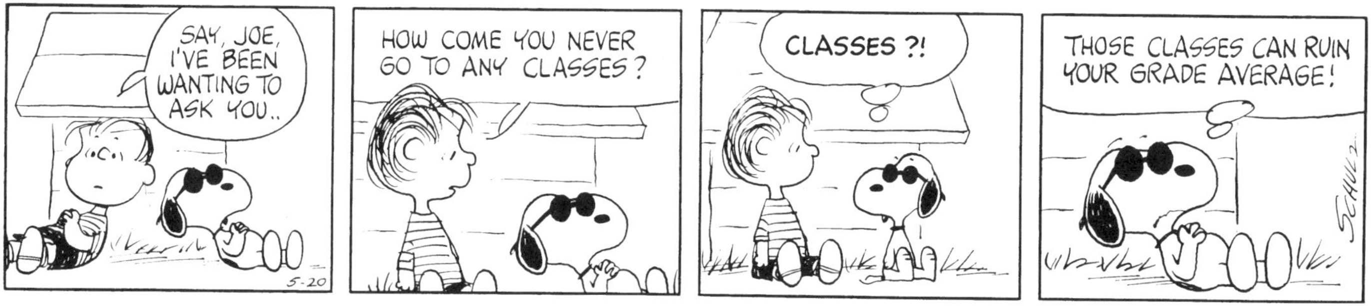
SAY, JOE, I'VE BEEN WANTING TO ASK YOU..
5-20
HOW COME YOU NEVER GO TO ANY CLASSES?
CLASSES?!
THOSE CLASSES CAN RUIN YOUR GRADE AVERAGE!
SCHULZ

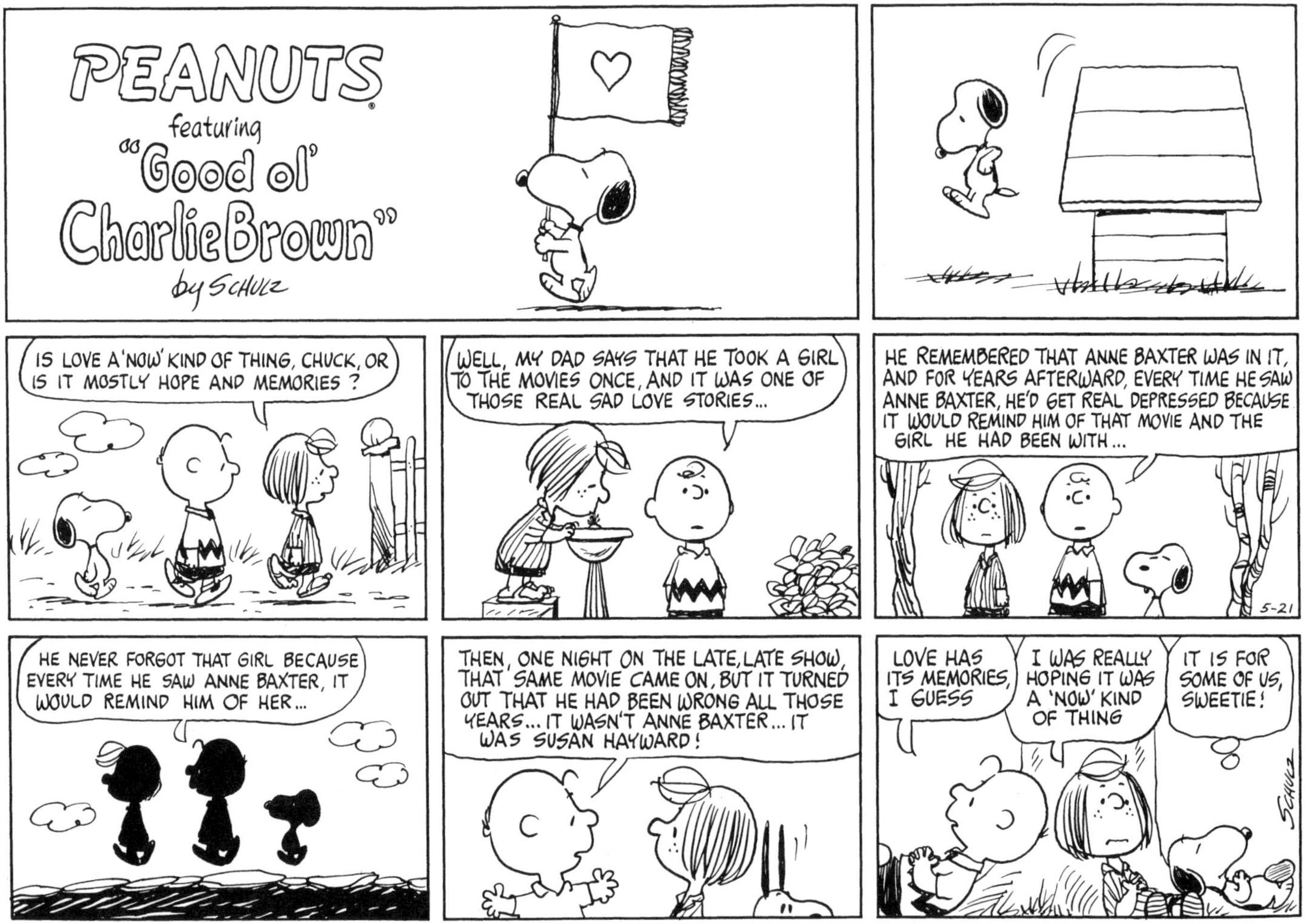
PEANUTS
featuring
"Good ol' Charlie Brown"
by SCHULZ
IS LOVE A 'NOW' KIND OF THING, CHUCK, OR IS IT MOSTLY HOPE AND MEMORIES ?
WELL, MY DAD SAYS THAT HE TOOK A GIRL TO THE MOVIES ONCE, AND IT WAS ONE OF THOSE REAL SAD LOVE STORIES...
HE REMEMBERED THAT ANNE BAXTER WAS IN IT, AND FOR YEARS AFTERWARD, EVERY TIME HE SAW ANNE BAXTER, HE'D GET REAL DEPRESSED BECAUSE IT WOULD REMIND HIM OF THAT MOVIE AND THE GIRL HE HAD BEEN WITH...
5-21
HE NEVER FORGOT THAT GIRL BECAUSE EVERY TIME HE SAW ANNE BAXTER, IT WOULD REMIND HIM OF HER...
THEN, ONE NIGHT ON THE LATE, LATE SHOW, THAT SAME MOVIE CAME ON, BUT IT TURNED OUT THAT HE HAD BEEN WRONG ALL THOSE YEARS... IT WASN'T ANNE BAXTER... IT WAS SUSAN HAYWARD!
LOVE HAS ITS MEMORIES, I GUESS
I WAS REALLY HOPING IT WAS A 'NOW' KIND OF THING
IT IS FOR SOME OF US, SWEETIE!
SCHULZ

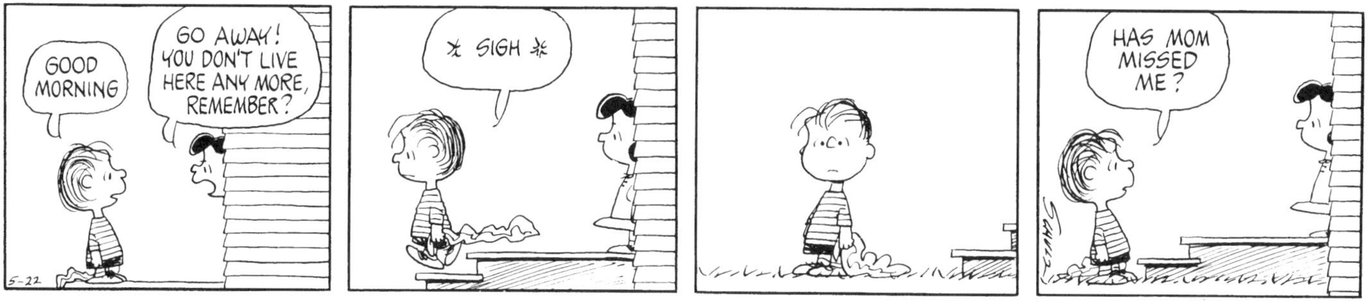
GOOD MORNING
GO AWAY! YOU DON'T LIVE HERE ANY MORE, REMEMBER?
* SIGH *
HAS MOM MISSED ME?
5-22
SCHULZ

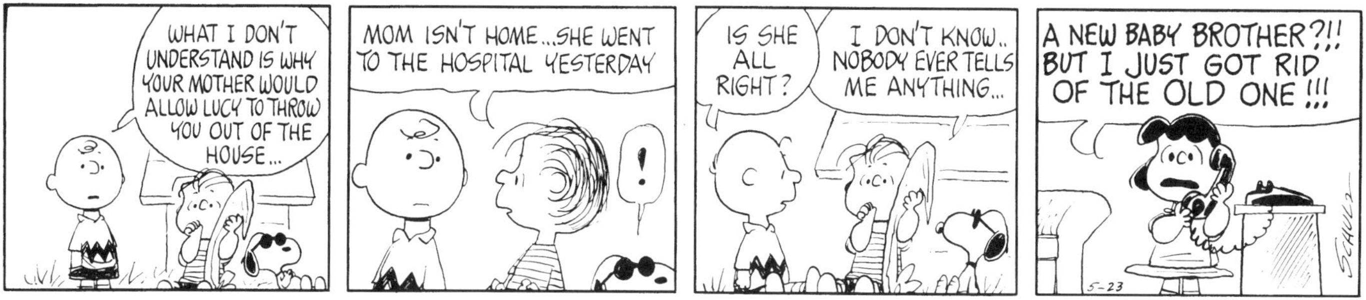
WHAT I DON'T UNDERSTAND IS WHY YOUR MOTHER WOULD ALLOW LUCY TO THROW YOU OUT OF THE HOUSE...
MOM ISN'T HOME...SHE WENT TO THE HOSPITAL YESTERDAY
!
IS SHE ALL RIGHT?
I DON'T KNOW.. NOBODY EVER TELLS ME ANYTHING...
A NEW BABY BROTHER?!! BUT I JUST GOT RID OF THE OLD ONE!!!
5-23
SCHULZ

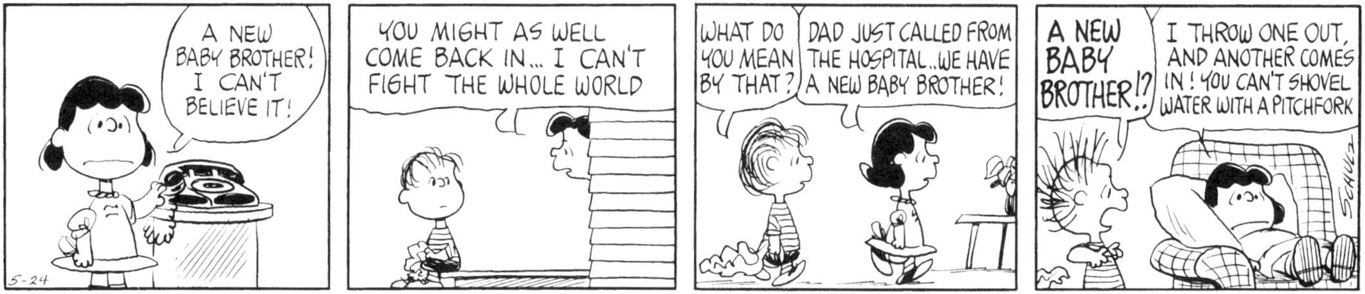
A NEW BABY BROTHER! I CAN'T BELIEVE IT!
YOU MIGHT AS WELL COME BACK IN... I CAN'T FIGHT THE WHOLE WORLD
WHAT DO YOU MEAN BY THAT?
DAD JUST CALLED FROM THE HOSPITAL..WE HAVE A NEW BABY BROTHER!
A NEW BABY BROTHER!?
I THROW ONE OUT, AND ANOTHER COMES IN! YOU CAN'T SHOVEL WATER WITH A PITCHFORK
5-24
SCHULZ

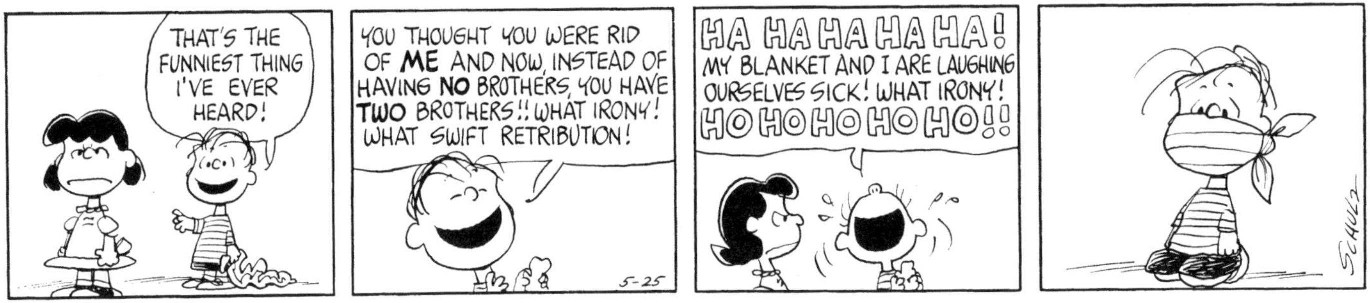
THAT'S THE FUNNIEST THING I'VE EVER HEARD!
YOU THOUGHT YOU WERE RID OF ME AND NOW, INSTEAD OF HAVING NO BROTHERS, YOU HAVE TWO BROTHERS!! WHAT IRONY! WHAT SWIFT RETRIBUTION!
5-25
HA HA HA HA HA! MY BLANKET AND I ARE LAUGHING OURSELVES SICK! WHAT IRONY! HO HO HO HO HO HO!!
SCHULZ

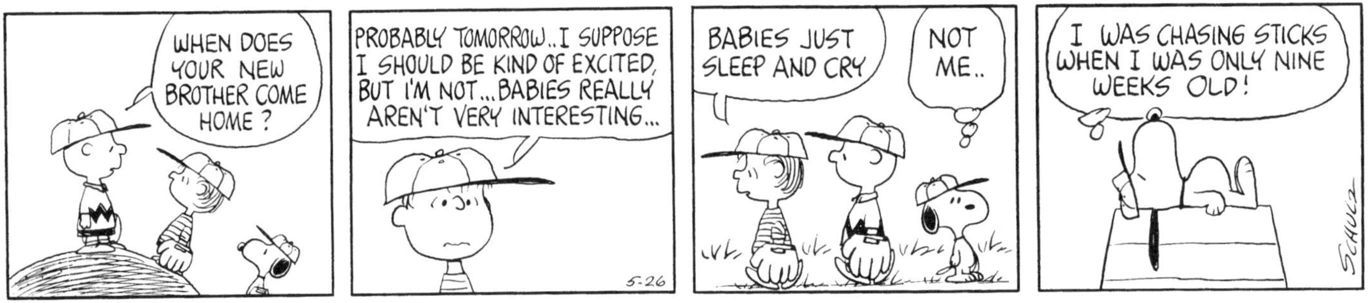
WHEN DOES YOUR NEW BROTHER COME HOME?
PROBABLY TOMORROW..I SUPPOSE I SHOULD BE KIND OF EXCITED, BUT I'M NOT...BABIES REALLY AREN'T VERY INTERESTING...
5-26
BABIES JUST SLEEP AND CRY
NOT ME..
I WAS CHASING STICKS WHEN I WAS ONLY NINE WEEKS OLD!
SCHULZ

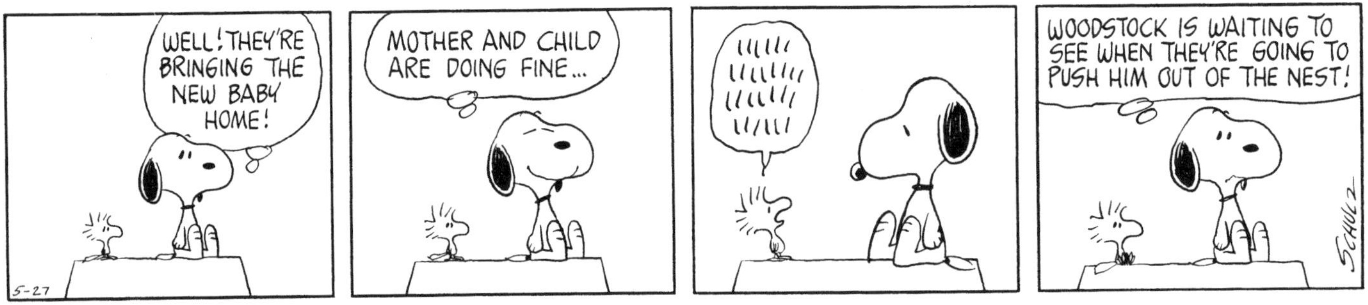
WELL! THEY'RE BRINGING THE NEW BABY HOME!
5-27
MOTHER AND CHILD ARE DOING FINE...
WOODSTOCK IS WAITING TO SEE WHEN THEY'RE GOING TO PUSH HIM OUT OF THE NEST!
SCHULZ

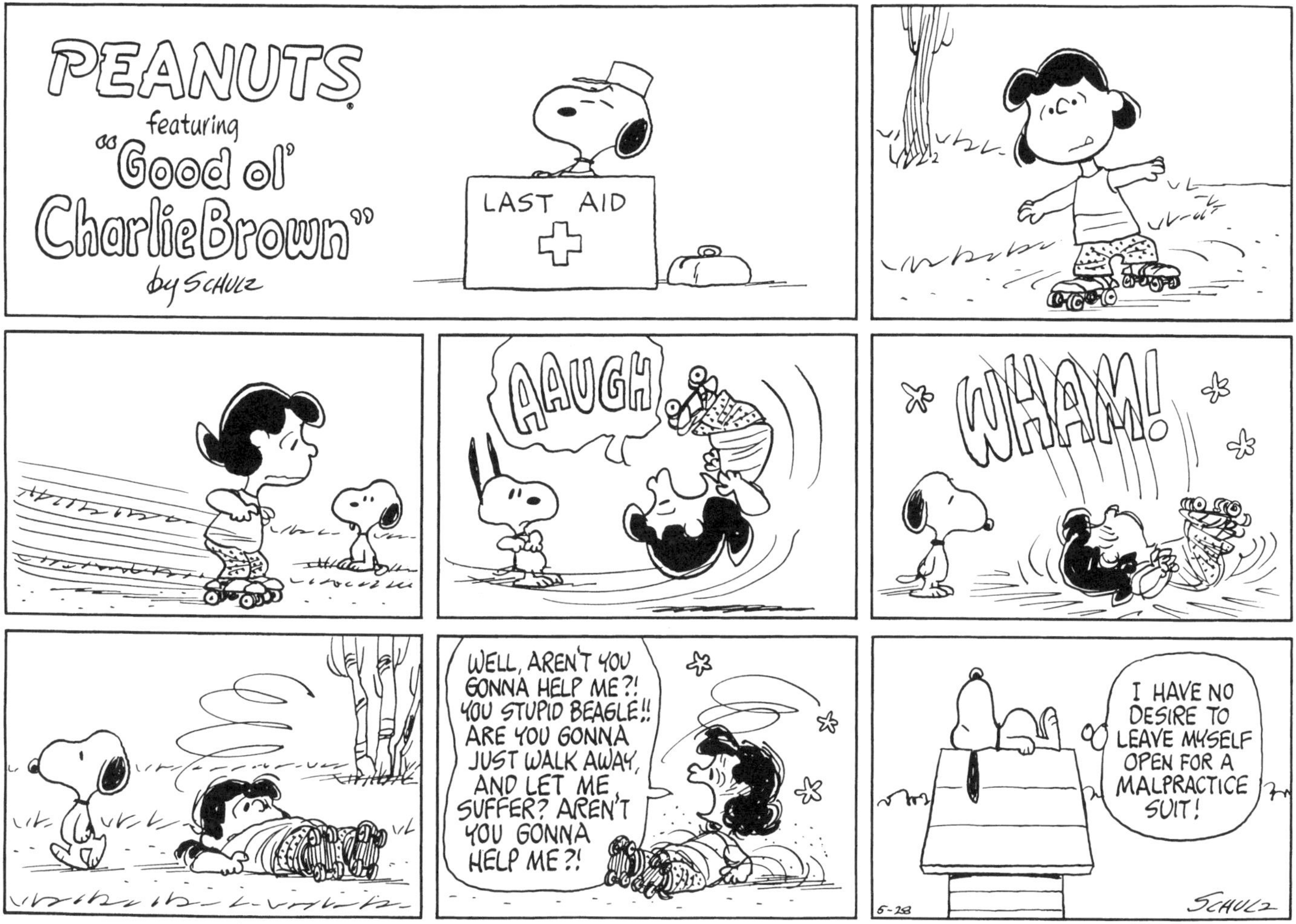
PEANUTS
featuring
"Good ol' Charlie Brown"
by SCHULZ
LAST AID
AAUGH
WHAM!
WELL, AREN'T YOU GONNA HELP ME?! YOU STUPID BEAGLE!! ARE YOU GONNA JUST WALK AWAY, AND LET ME SUFFER? AREN'T YOU GONNA HELP ME?!
I HAVE NO DESIRE TO LEAVE MYSELF OPEN FOR A MALPRACTICE SUIT!
5-28
SCHULZ

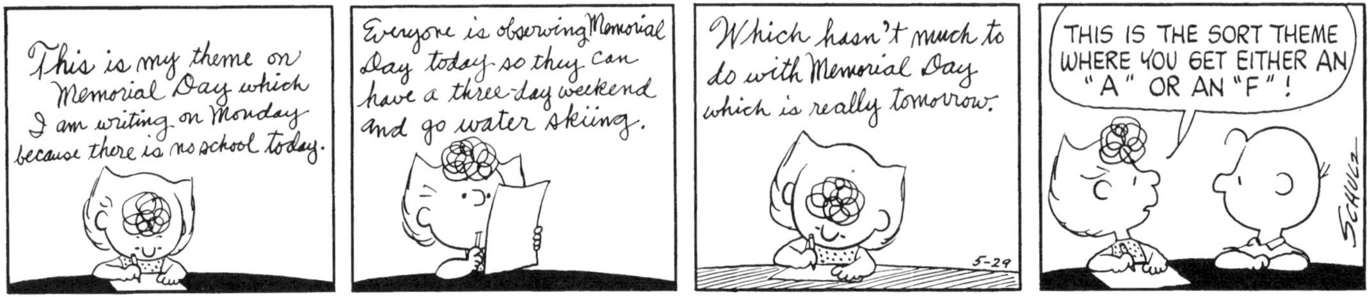
This is my theme on Memorial Day which I am writing on Monday because there is no school today.
Everyone is observing Memorial Day today so they can have a three-day weekend and go water skiing.
Which hasn't much to do with Memorial Day which is really tomorrow.
THIS IS THE SORT THEME WHERE YOU GET EITHER AN "A" OR AN "F"!

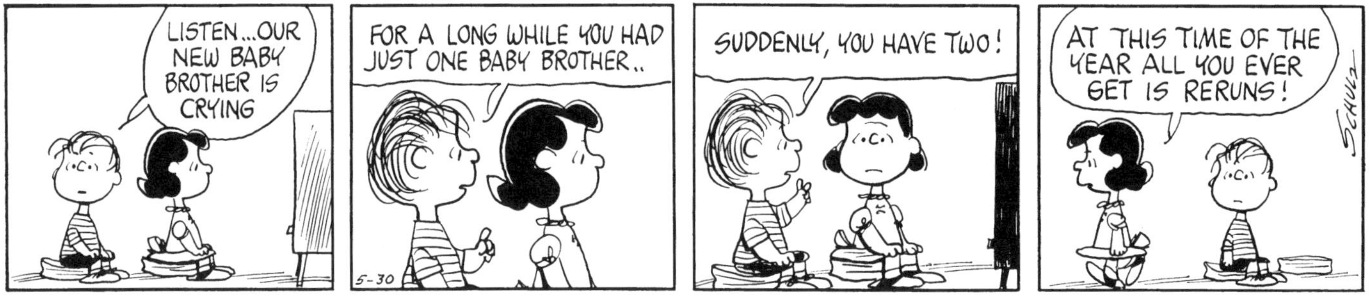
LISTEN...OUR NEW BABY BROTHER IS CRYING
FOR A LONG WHILE YOU HAD JUST ONE BABY BROTHER..
SUDDENLY, YOU HAVE TWO!
AT THIS TIME OF THE YEAR ALL YOU EVER GET IS RERUNS!

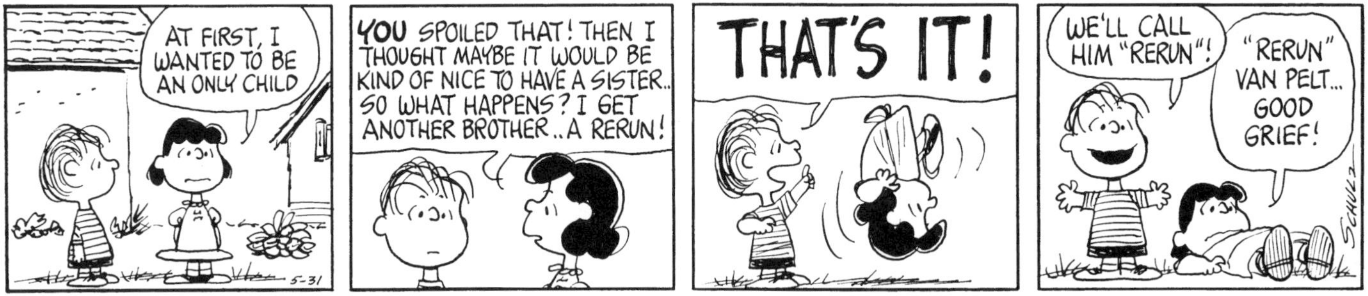
AT FIRST, I WANTED TO BE AN ONLY CHILD
YOU SPOILED THAT! THEN I THOUGHT MAYBE IT WOULD BE KIND OF NICE TO HAVE A SISTER.. SO WHAT HAPPENS? I GET ANOTHER BROTHER..A RERUN!
THAT'S IT!
WE'LL CALL HIM "RERUN"!
"RERUN" VAN PELT... GOOD GRIEF!

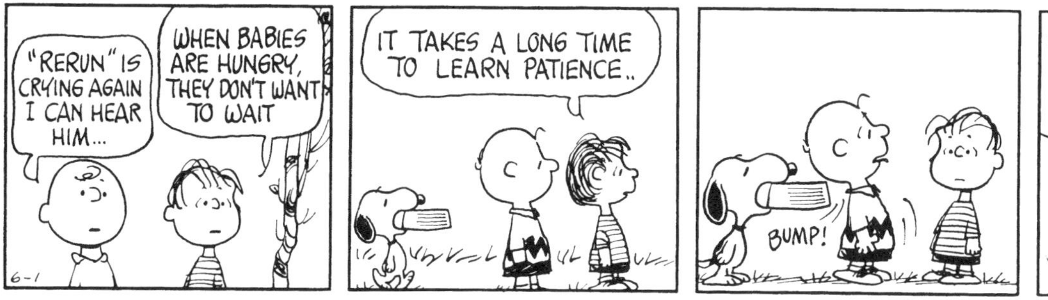

"RERUN" IS CRYING AGAIN I CAN HEAR HIM...
WHEN BABIES ARE HUNGRY, THEY DON'T WANT TO WAIT
IT TAKES A LONG TIME TO LEARN PATIENCE..
BUMP!
SOME PEOPLE I KNOW NEVER LEARN ANY PATIENCE!
I'M VERY PATIENT...IT'S MY STOMACH THAT'S CRABBY!

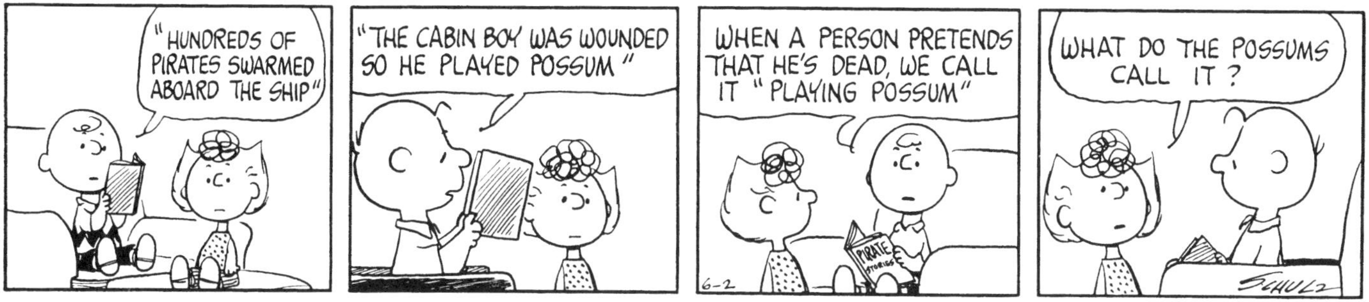

"HUNDREDS OF PIRATES SWARMED ABOARD THE SHIP"
"THE CABIN BOY WAS WOUNDED SO HE PLAYED POSSUM"
WHEN A PERSON PRETENDS THAT HE'S DEAD, WE CALL IT "PLAYING POSSUM"
PIRATE STORIES
WHAT DO THE POSSUMS CALL IT ?

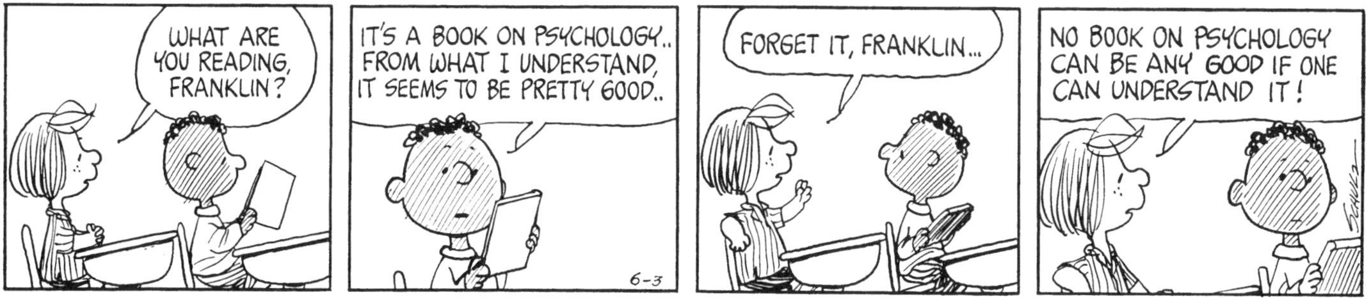

WHAT ARE YOU READING, FRANKLIN?
IT'S A BOOK ON PSYCHOLOGY.. FROM WHAT I UNDERSTAND, IT SEEMS TO BE PRETTY GOOD..
FORGET IT, FRANKLIN...
NO BOOK ON PSYCHOLOGY CAN BE ANY GOOD IF ONE CAN UNDERSTAND IT!

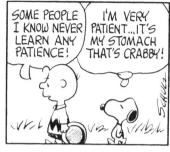

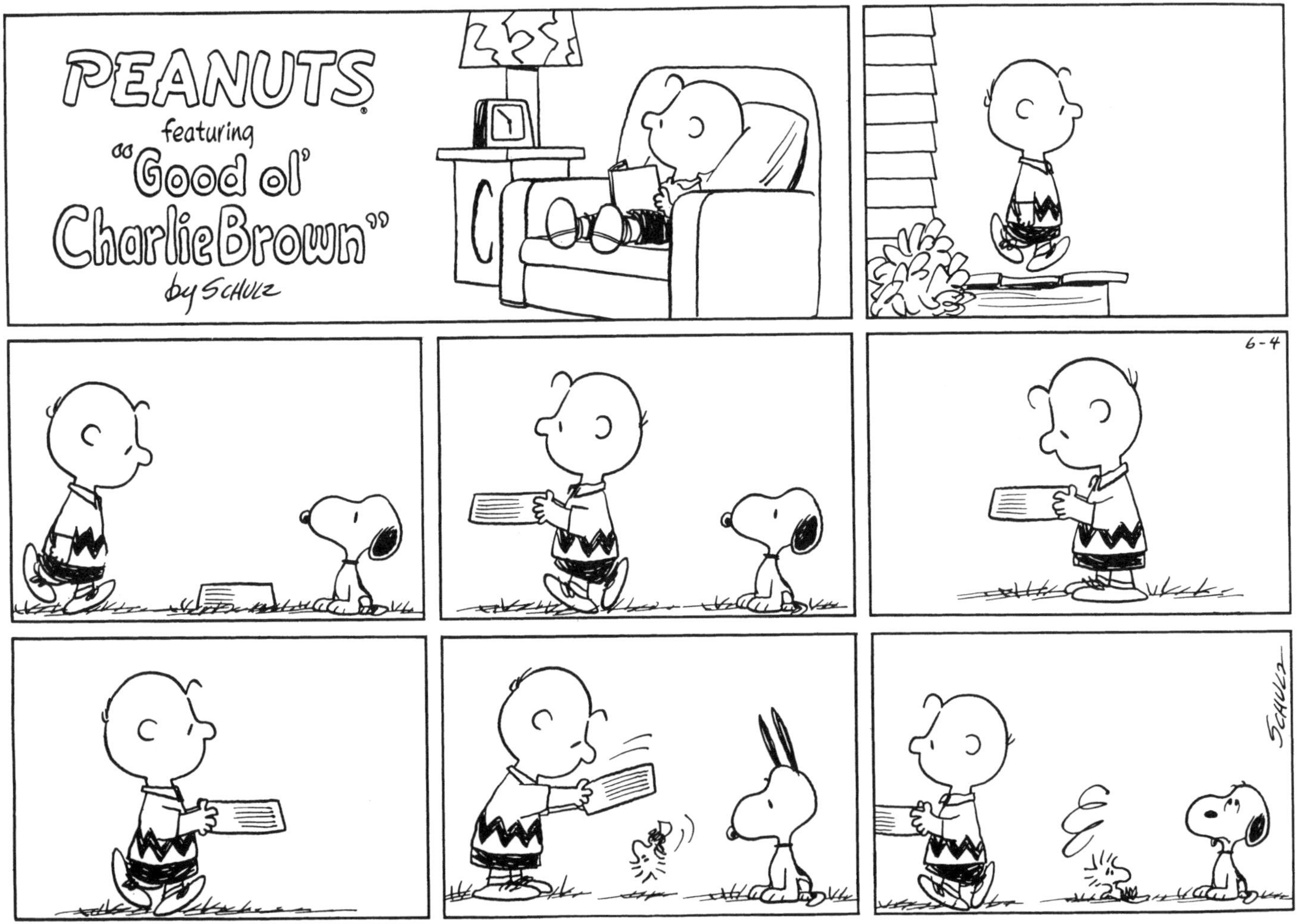
PEANUTS
featuring
"Good ol' CharlieBrown"
by SCHULZ
6-4
SCHULZ

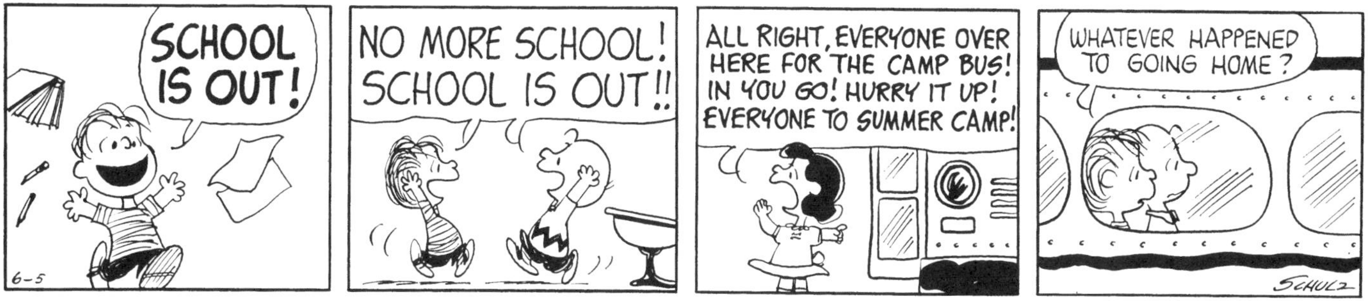
SCHOOL IS OUT!
NO MORE SCHOOL! SCHOOL IS OUT!!
ALL RIGHT, EVERYONE OVER HERE FOR THE CAMP BUS! IN YOU GO! HURRY IT UP! EVERYONE TO SUMMER CAMP!
WHATEVER HAPPENED TO GOING HOME?
6-5
SCHULZ

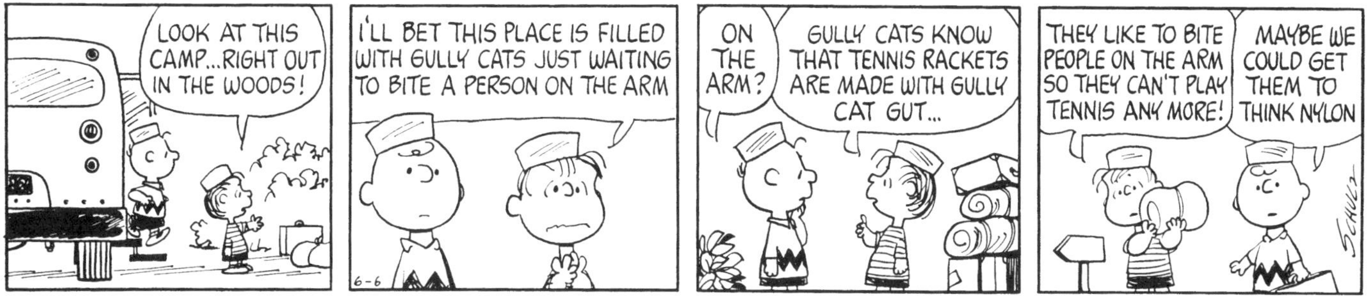
LOOK AT THIS CAMP...RIGHT OUT IN THE WOODS!
I'LL BET THIS PLACE IS FILLED WITH GULLY CATS JUST WAITING TO BITE A PERSON ON THE ARM
6-6
ON THE ARM?
GULLY CATS KNOW THAT TENNIS RACKETS ARE MADE WITH GULLY CAT GUT...
THEY LIKE TO BITE PEOPLE ON THE ARM SO THEY CAN'T PLAY TENNIS ANY MORE!
MAYBE WE COULD GET THEM TO THINK NYLON
SCHULZ

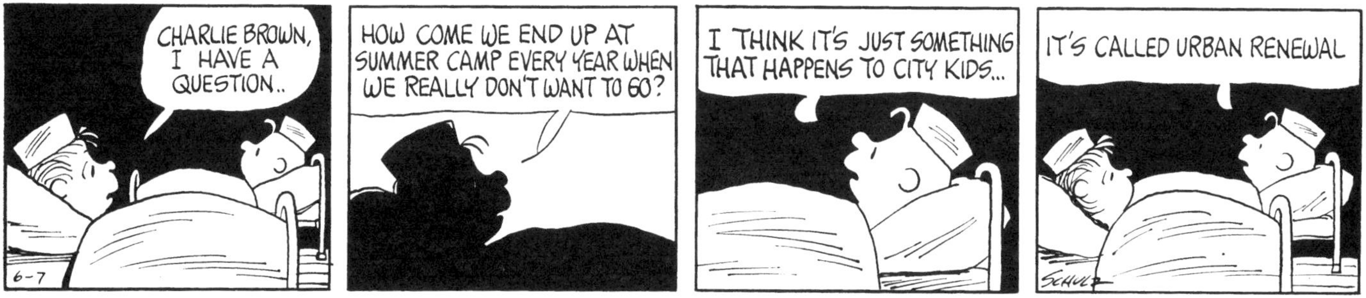
CHARLIE BROWN, I HAVE A QUESTION..
6-7
HOW COME WE END UP AT SUMMER CAMP EVERY YEAR WHEN WE REALLY DON'T WANT TO GO?
I THINK IT'S JUST SOMETHING THAT HAPPENS TO CITY KIDS...
IT'S CALLED URBAN RENEWAL
SCHULZ

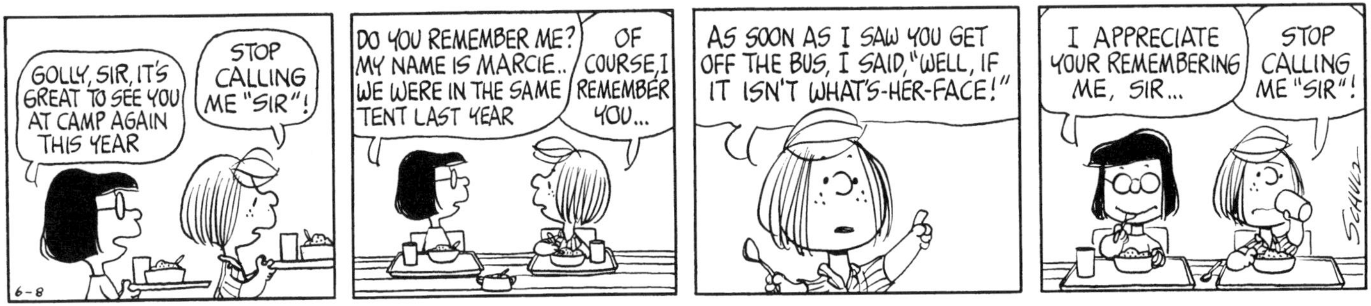
GOLLY, SIR, IT'S GREAT TO SEE YOU AT CAMP AGAIN THIS YEAR
STOP CALLING ME "SIR"!
6-8
DO YOU REMEMBER ME? MY NAME IS MARCIE.. WE WERE IN THE SAME TENT LAST YEAR
OF COURSE, I REMEMBER YOU...
AS SOON AS I SAW YOU GET OFF THE BUS, I SAID, "WELL, IF IT ISN'T WHAT'S-HER-FACE!"
I APPRECIATE YOUR REMEMBERING ME, SIR...
STOP CALLING ME "SIR"!
SCHULZ

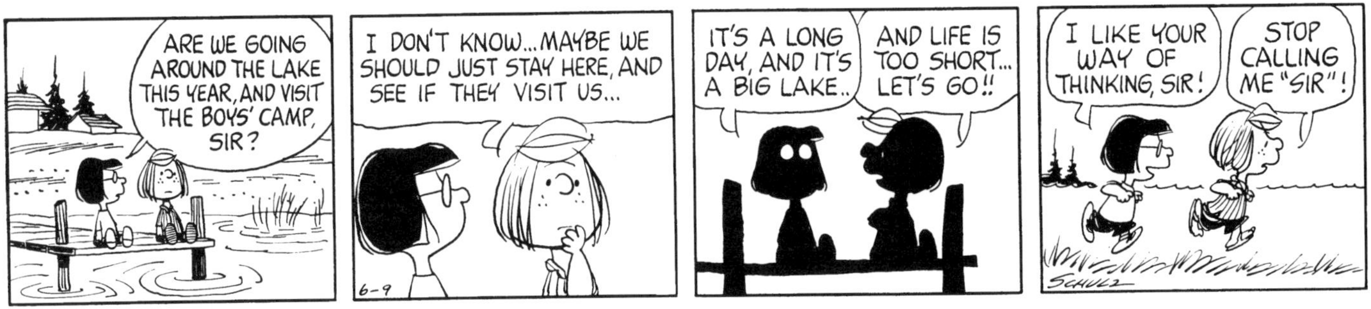
ARE WE GOING AROUND THE LAKE THIS YEAR, AND VISIT THE BOYS' CAMP, SIR?
I DON'T KNOW... MAYBE WE SHOULD JUST STAY HERE, AND SEE IF THEY VISIT US...
6-9
IT'S A LONG DAY, AND IT'S A BIG LAKE..
AND LIFE IS TOO SHORT... LET'S GO!!
I LIKE YOUR WAY OF THINKING, SIR!
STOP CALLING ME "SIR"!
SCHULZ

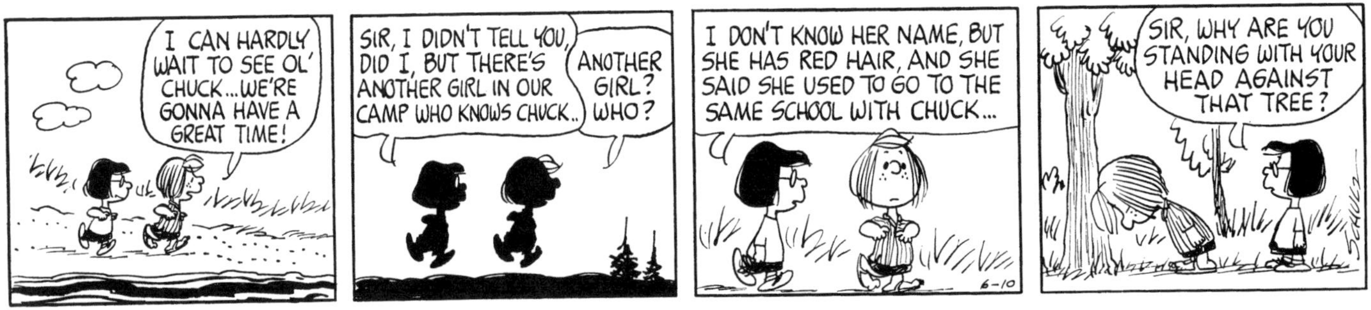
I CAN HARDLY WAIT TO SEE OL' CHUCK... WE'RE GONNA HAVE A GREAT TIME!
SIR, I DIDN'T TELL YOU, DID I, BUT THERE'S ANOTHER GIRL IN OUR CAMP WHO KNOWS CHUCK..
ANOTHER GIRL? WHO?
I DON'T KNOW HER NAME, BUT SHE HAS RED HAIR, AND SHE SAID SHE USED TO GO TO THE SAME SCHOOL WITH CHUCK...
6-10
SIR, WHY ARE YOU STANDING WITH YOUR HEAD AGAINST THAT TREE?
SCHULZ

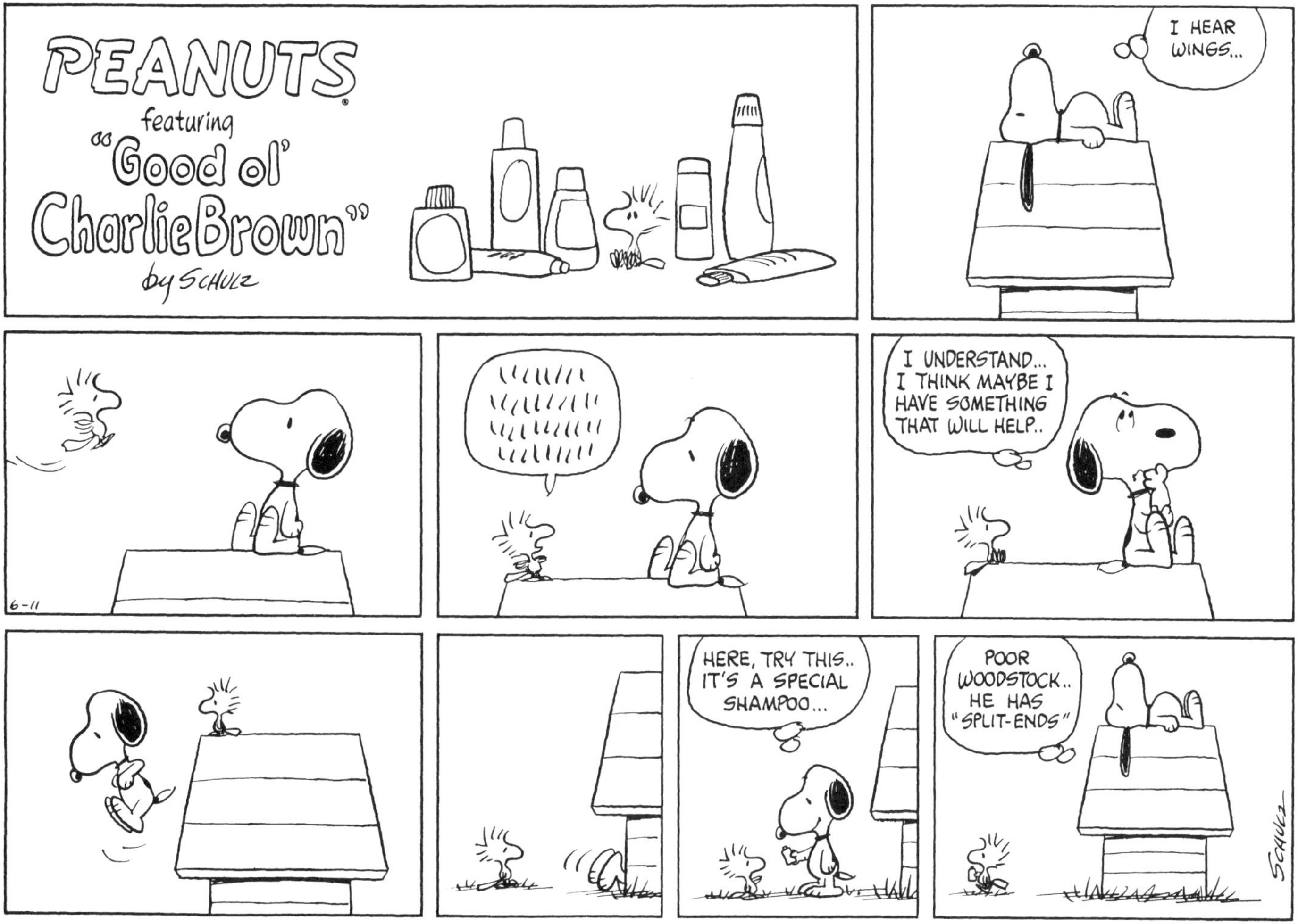
PEANUTS
featuring
"Good ol' CharlieBrown"
by SCHULZ
I HEAR WINGS...
6-11
I UNDERSTAND... I THINK MAYBE I HAVE SOMETHING THAT WILL HELP..
HERE, TRY THIS.. IT'S A SPECIAL SHAMPOO...
POOR WOODSTOCK.. HE HAS "SPLIT-ENDS"
SCHULZ

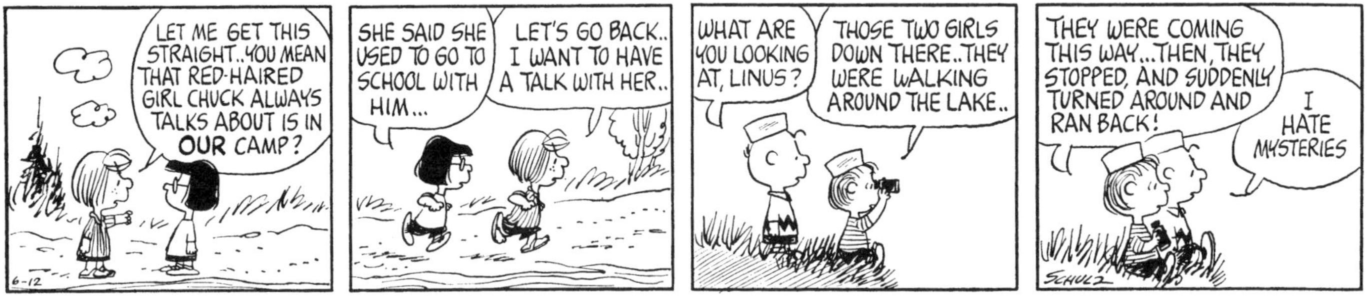
LET ME GET THIS STRAIGHT..YOU MEAN THAT RED-HAIRED GIRL CHUCK ALWAYS TALKS ABOUT IS IN **OUR** CAMP?
SHE SAID SHE USED TO GO TO SCHOOL WITH HIM...
LET'S GO BACK.. I WANT TO HAVE A TALK WITH HER..
WHAT ARE YOU LOOKING AT, LINUS?
THOSE TWO GIRLS DOWN THERE..THEY WERE WALKING AROUND THE LAKE..
THEY WERE COMING THIS WAY...THEN, THEY STOPPED, AND SUDDENLY TURNED AROUND AND RAN BACK!
I HATE MYSTERIES

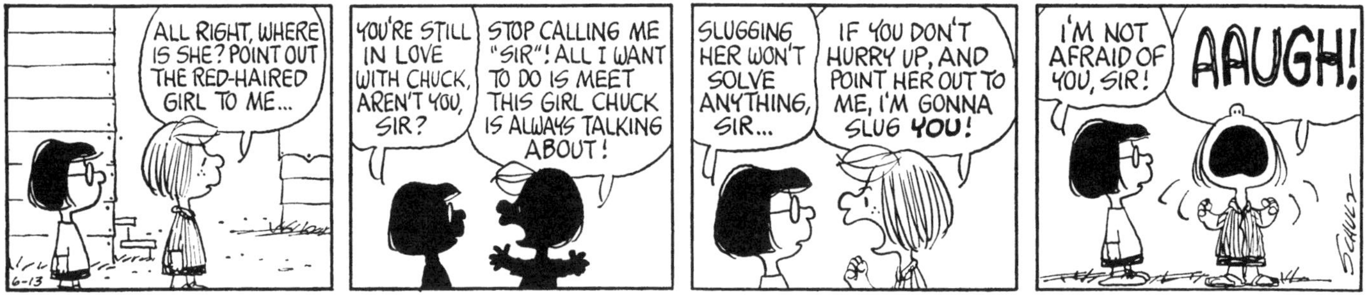
ALL RIGHT, WHERE IS SHE? POINT OUT THE RED-HAIRED GIRL TO ME...
YOU'RE STILL IN LOVE WITH CHUCK, AREN'T YOU, SIR?
STOP CALLING ME "SIR"! ALL I WANT TO DO IS MEET THIS GIRL CHUCK IS ALWAYS TALKING ABOUT!
SLUGGING HER WON'T SOLVE ANYTHING, SIR...
IF YOU DON'T HURRY UP, AND POINT HER OUT TO ME, I'M GONNA SLUG **YOU**!
I'M NOT AFRAID OF YOU, SIR!
AAUGH!

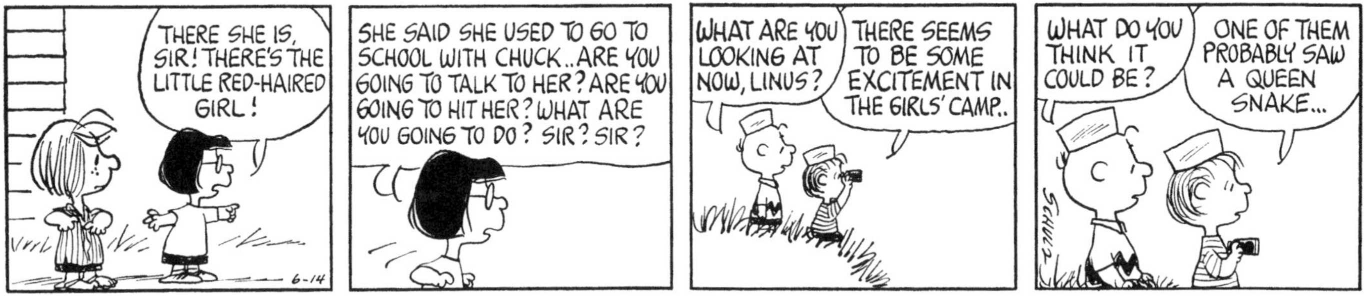
THERE SHE IS, SIR! THERE'S THE LITTLE RED-HAIRED GIRL!
SHE SAID SHE USED TO GO TO SCHOOL WITH CHUCK..ARE YOU GOING TO TALK TO HER? ARE YOU GOING TO HIT HER? WHAT ARE YOU GOING TO DO? SIR? SIR?
WHAT ARE YOU LOOKING AT NOW, LINUS?
THERE SEEMS TO BE SOME EXCITEMENT IN THE GIRLS' CAMP..
WHAT DO YOU THINK IT COULD BE?
ONE OF THEM PROBABLY SAW A QUEEN SNAKE...

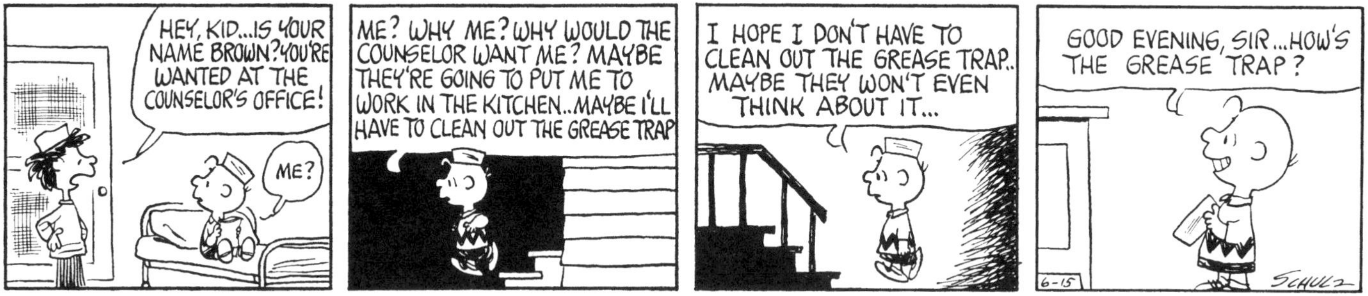
HEY, KID...IS YOUR NAME BROWN? YOU'RE WANTED AT THE COUNSELOR'S OFFICE!
ME?
ME? WHY ME? WHY WOULD THE COUNSELOR WANT ME? MAYBE THEY'RE GOING TO PUT ME TO WORK IN THE KITCHEN..MAYBE I'LL HAVE TO CLEAN OUT THE GREASE TRAP
I HOPE I DON'T HAVE TO CLEAN OUT THE GREASE TRAP.. MAYBE THEY WON'T EVEN THINK ABOUT IT...
GOOD EVENING, SIR...HOW'S THE GREASE TRAP?
6-15
SCHULZ

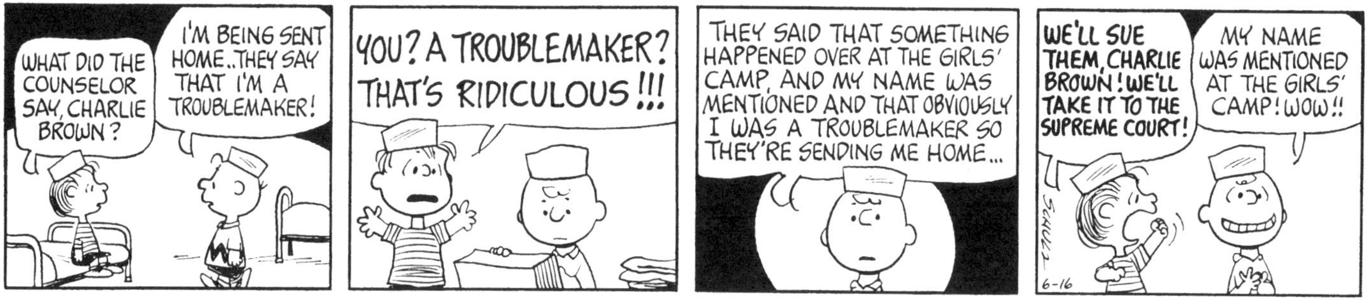
WHAT DID THE COUNSELOR SAY, CHARLIE BROWN?
I'M BEING SENT HOME..THEY SAY THAT I'M A TROUBLEMAKER!
YOU? A TROUBLEMAKER? THAT'S RIDICULOUS!!!
THEY SAID THAT SOMETHING HAPPENED OVER AT THE GIRLS' CAMP, AND MY NAME WAS MENTIONED AND THAT OBVIOUSLY I WAS A TROUBLEMAKER SO THEY'RE SENDING ME HOME...
WE'LL SUE THEM, CHARLIE BROWN! WE'LL TAKE IT TO THE SUPREME COURT!
MY NAME WAS MENTIONED AT THE GIRLS' CAMP! WOW!!
SCHULZ
6-16

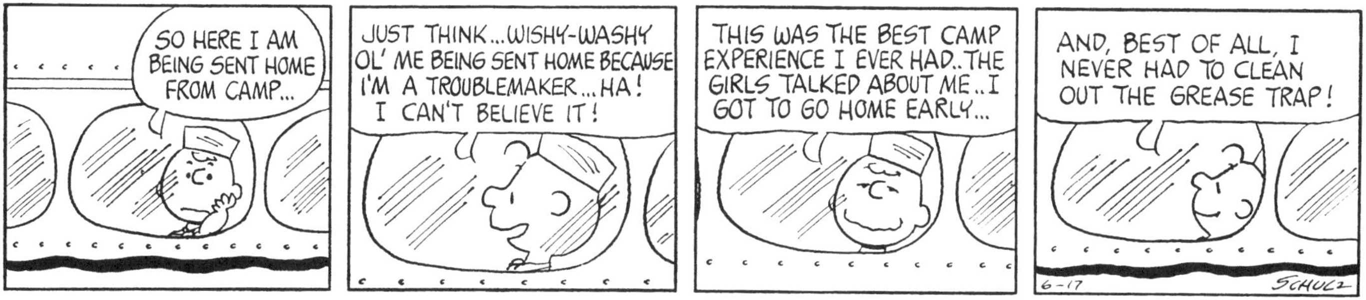
SO HERE I AM BEING SENT HOME FROM CAMP...
JUST THINK...WISHY-WASHY OL' ME BEING SENT HOME BECAUSE I'M A TROUBLEMAKER...HA! I CAN'T BELIEVE IT!
THIS WAS THE BEST CAMP EXPERIENCE I EVER HAD..THE GIRLS TALKED ABOUT ME..I GOT TO GO HOME EARLY...
AND, BEST OF ALL, I NEVER HAD TO CLEAN OUT THE GREASE TRAP!
6-17
SCHULZ

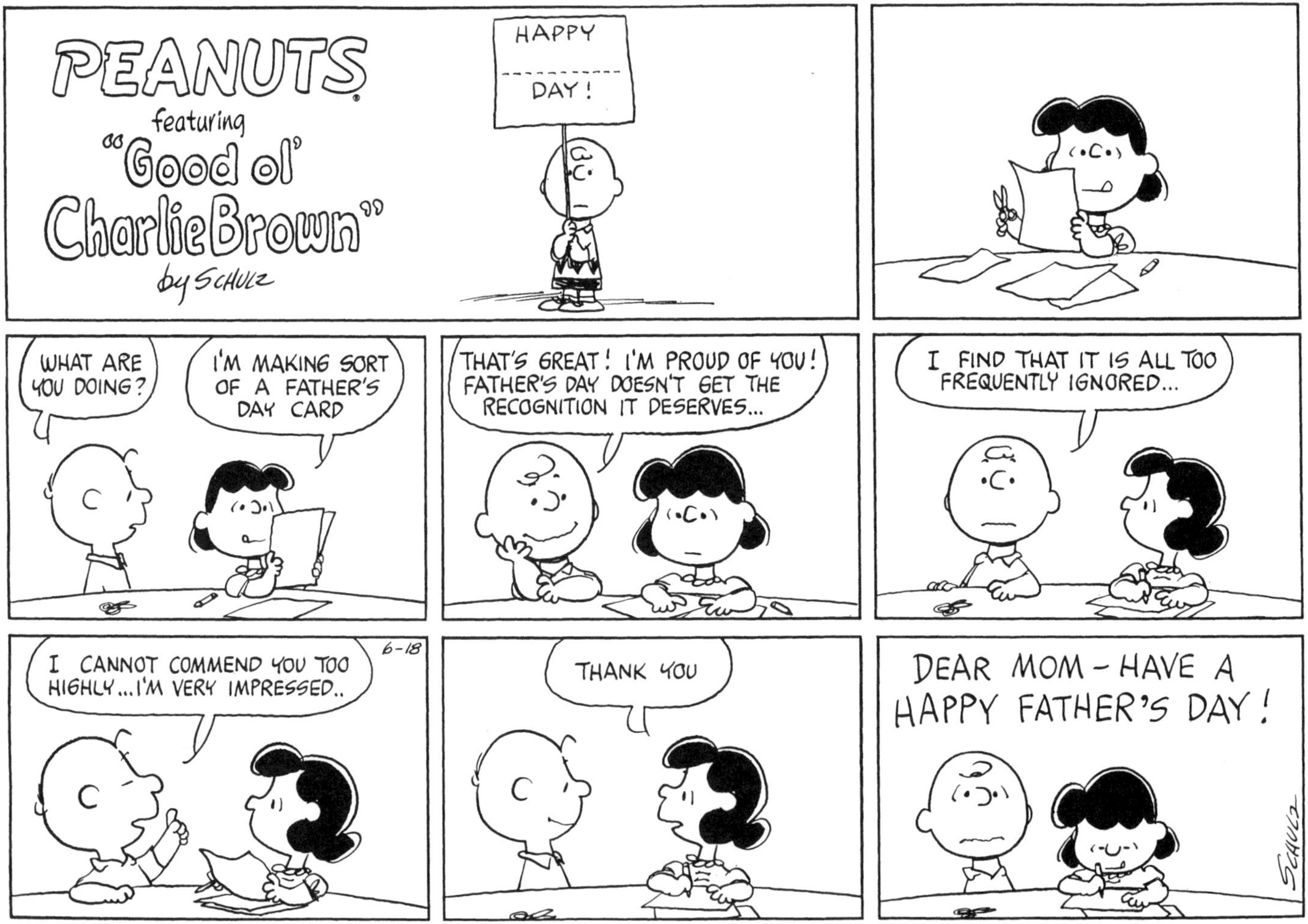
PEANUTS
featuring
"Good ol' Charlie Brown"
by SCHULZ
HAPPY
DAY!
WHAT ARE YOU DOING?
I'M MAKING SORT OF A FATHER'S DAY CARD
THAT'S GREAT! I'M PROUD OF YOU! FATHER'S DAY DOESN'T GET THE RECOGNITION IT DESERVES...
I FIND THAT IT IS ALL TOO FREQUENTLY IGNORED...
6-18
I CANNOT COMMEND YOU TOO HIGHLY...I'M VERY IMPRESSED..
THANK YOU
DEAR MOM - HAVE A HAPPY FATHER'S DAY!
SCHULZ

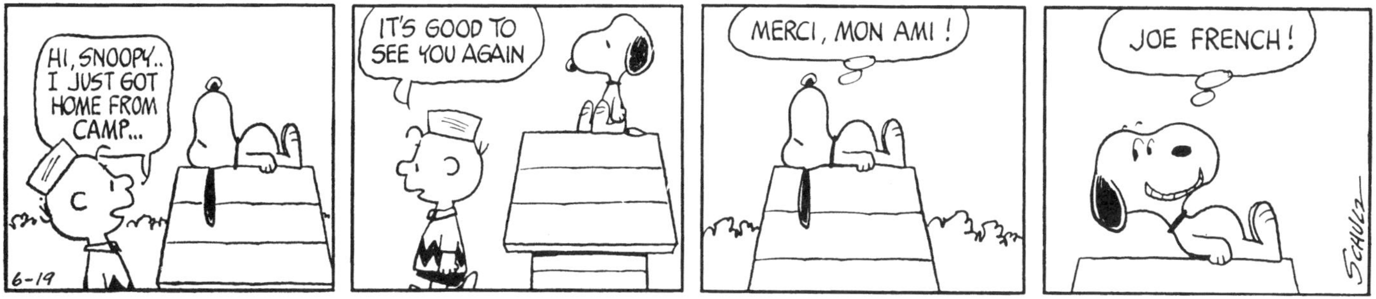
HI, SNOOPY.. I JUST GOT HOME FROM CAMP...
6-19
IT'S GOOD TO SEE YOU AGAIN
MERCI, MON AMI !
JOE FRENCH !
SCHULZ

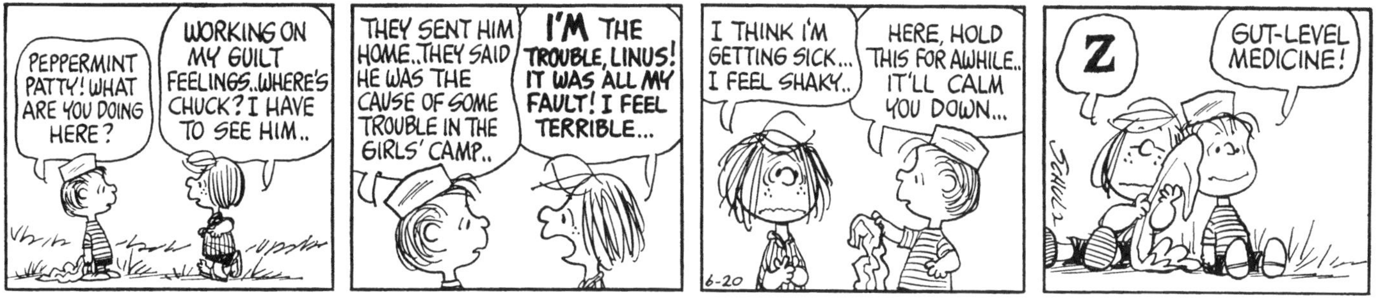
PEPPERMINT PATTY! WHAT ARE YOU DOING HERE ?
WORKING ON MY GUILT FEELINGS..WHERE'S CHUCK? I HAVE TO SEE HIM..
THEY SENT HIM HOME..THEY SAID HE WAS THE CAUSE OF SOME TROUBLE IN THE GIRLS' CAMP..
I'M THE TROUBLE, LINUS! IT WAS ALL MY FAULT! I FEEL TERRIBLE...
I THINK I'M GETTING SICK... I FEEL SHAKY..
HERE, HOLD THIS FOR AWHILE.. IT'LL CALM YOU DOWN...
6-20
Z
GUT-LEVEL MEDICINE!
SCHULZ

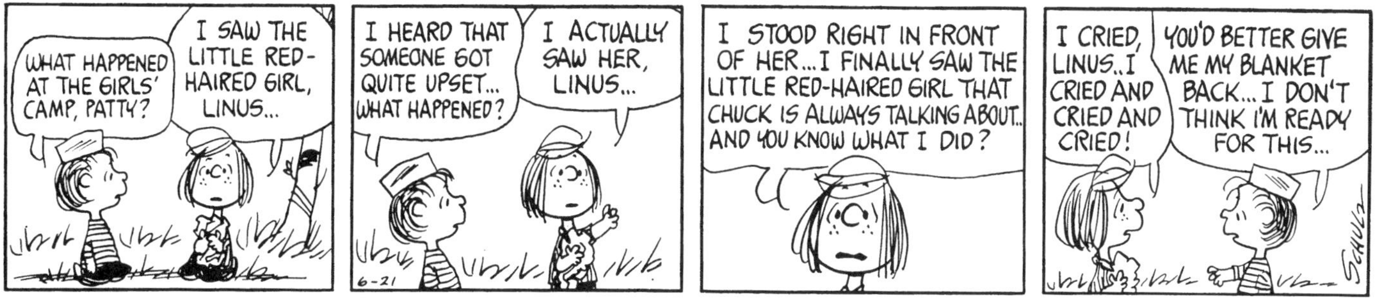
WHAT HAPPENED AT THE GIRLS' CAMP, PATTY?
I SAW THE LITTLE RED-HAIRED GIRL, LINUS...
I HEARD THAT SOMEONE GOT QUITE UPSET... WHAT HAPPENED?
I ACTUALLY SAW HER, LINUS...
6-21
I STOOD RIGHT IN FRONT OF HER...I FINALLY SAW THE LITTLE RED-HAIRED GIRL THAT CHUCK IS ALWAYS TALKING ABOUT.. AND YOU KNOW WHAT I DID?
I CRIED, LINUS..I CRIED AND CRIED AND CRIED!
YOU'D BETTER GIVE ME MY BLANKET BACK...I DON'T THINK I'M READY FOR THIS...
SCHULZ

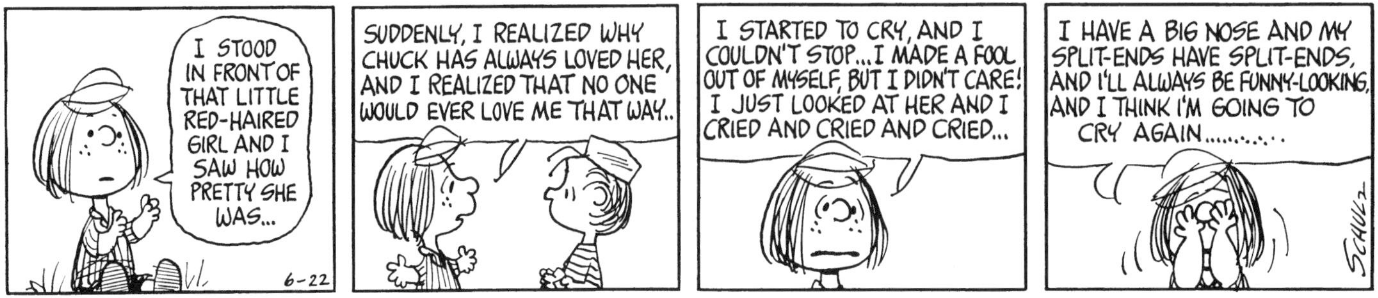
I STOOD IN FRONT OF THAT LITTLE RED-HAIRED GIRL AND I SAW HOW PRETTY SHE WAS...
6-22
SUDDENLY, I REALIZED WHY CHUCK HAS ALWAYS LOVED HER, AND I REALIZED THAT NO ONE WOULD EVER LOVE ME THAT WAY..
I STARTED TO CRY, AND I COULDN'T STOP...I MADE A FOOL OUT OF MYSELF, BUT I DIDN'T CARE! I JUST LOOKED AT HER AND I CRIED AND CRIED AND CRIED...
I HAVE A BIG NOSE AND MY SPLIT-ENDS HAVE SPLIT-ENDS, AND I'LL ALWAYS BE FUNNY-LOOKING, AND I THINK I'M GOING TO CRY AGAIN..........

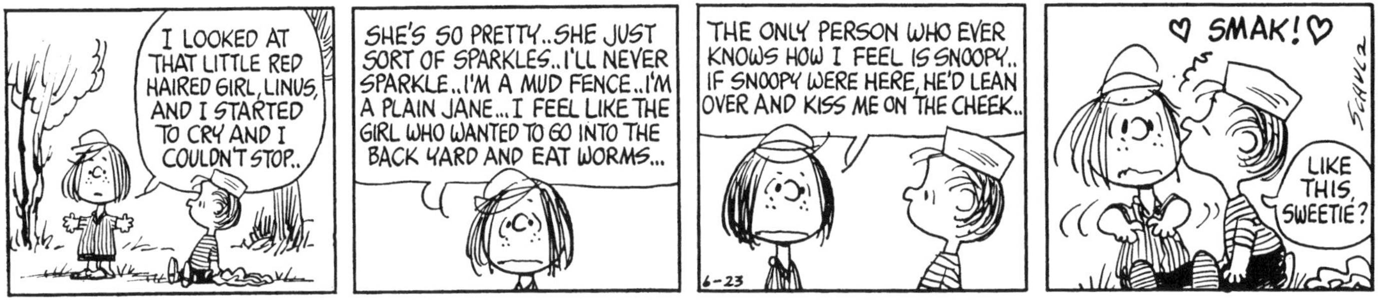
I LOOKED AT THAT LITTLE RED HAIRED GIRL, LINUS, AND I STARTED TO CRY AND I COULDN'T STOP..
SHE'S SO PRETTY..SHE JUST SORT OF SPARKLES..I'LL NEVER SPARKLE..I'M A MUD FENCE..I'M A PLAIN JANE...I FEEL LIKE THE GIRL WHO WANTED TO GO INTO THE BACK YARD AND EAT WORMS...
THE ONLY PERSON WHO EVER KNOWS HOW I FEEL IS SNOOPY.. IF SNOOPY WERE HERE, HE'D LEAN OVER AND KISS ME ON THE CHEEK..
6-23
SMAK!
LIKE THIS, SWEETIE?

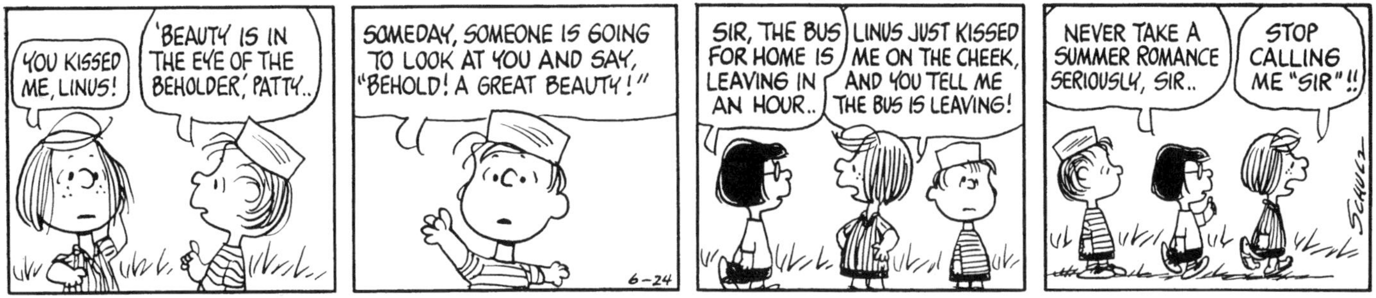
YOU KISSED ME, LINUS!
'BEAUTY IS IN THE EYE OF THE BEHOLDER,' PATTY..
SOMEDAY, SOMEONE IS GOING TO LOOK AT YOU AND SAY, "BEHOLD! A GREAT BEAUTY!"
6-24
SIR, THE BUS FOR HOME IS LEAVING IN AN HOUR..
LINUS JUST KISSED ME ON THE CHEEK, AND YOU TELL ME THE BUS IS LEAVING!
NEVER TAKE A SUMMER ROMANCE SERIOUSLY, SIR..
STOP CALLING ME "SIR"!!

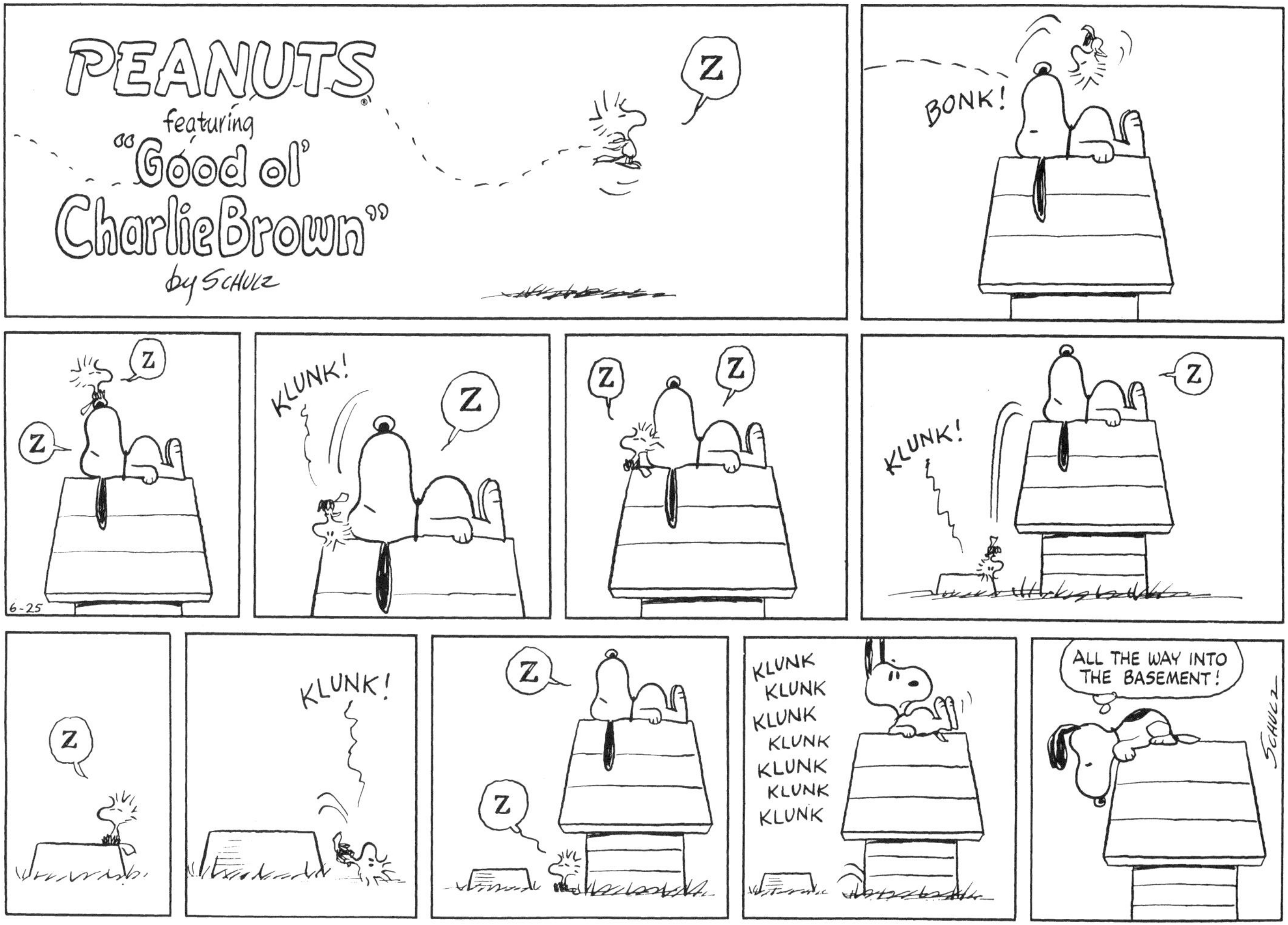
PEANUTS
featuring
"Good ol' Charlie Brown"
by SCHULZ
Z
BONK!
6-25
Z
Z
KLUNK!
Z
Z
Z
KLUNK!
Z
Z
KLUNK!
Z
Z
KLUNK
KLUNK
KLUNK
KLUNK
KLUNK
KLUNK
KLUNK
ALL THE WAY INTO THE BASEMENT!
SCHULZ

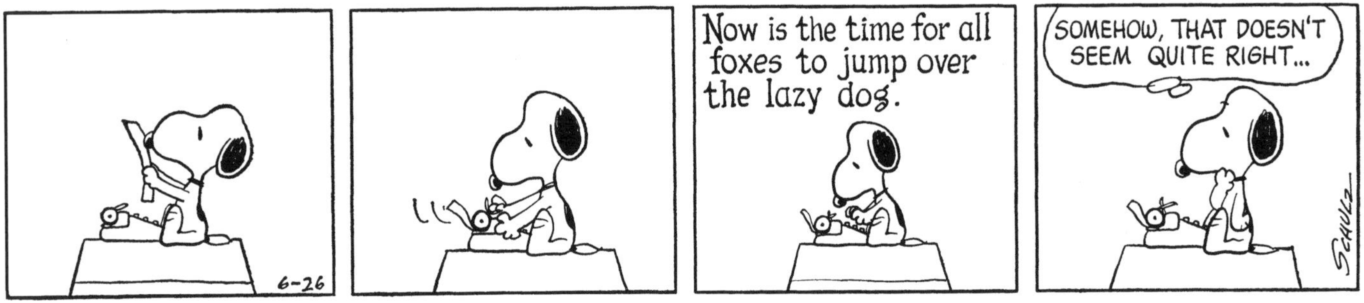
6-26
Now is the time for all foxes to jump over the lazy dog.
SOMEHOW, THAT DOESN'T SEEM QUITE RIGHT...
SCHULZ

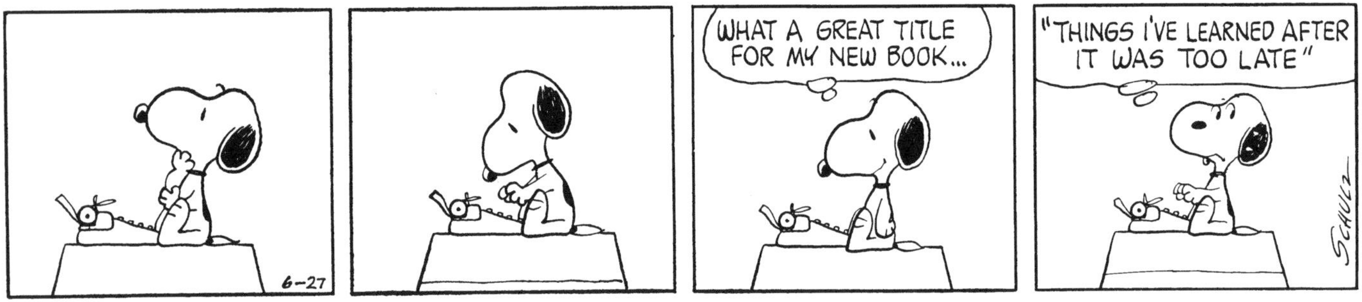
6-27
WHAT A GREAT TITLE FOR MY NEW BOOK...
"THINGS I'VE LEARNED AFTER IT WAS TOO LATE"
SCHULZ

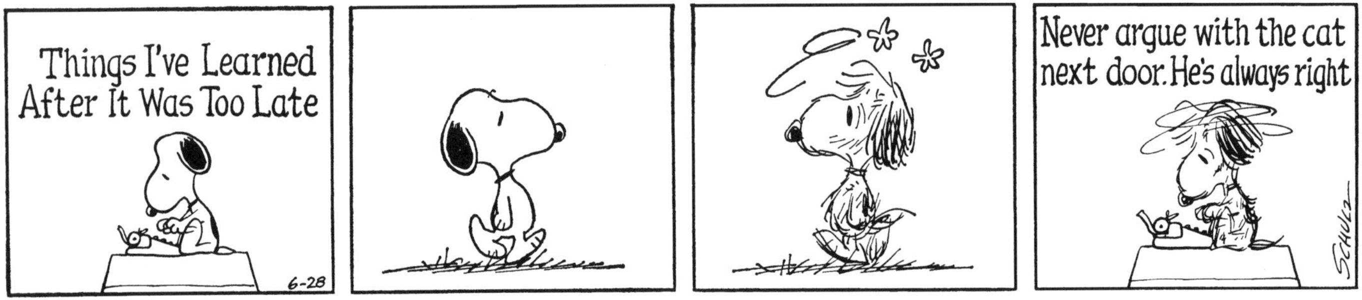
Things I've Learned After It Was Too Late
6-28
Never argue with the cat next door. He's always right
SCHULZ

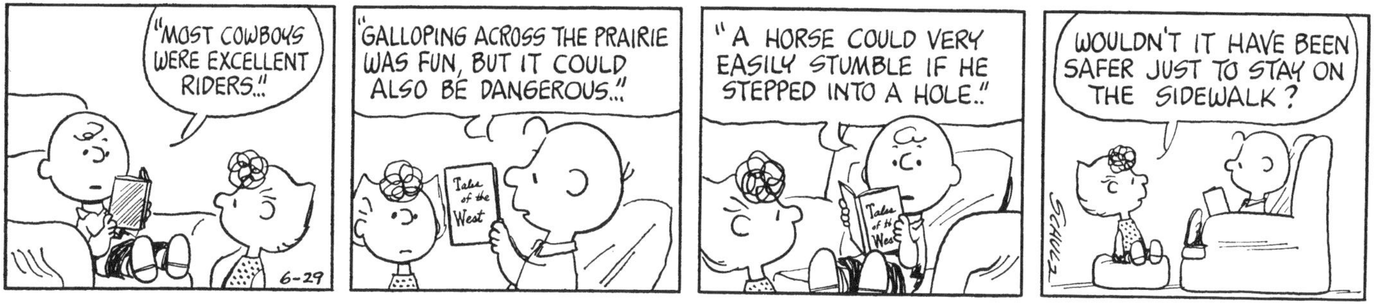
"MOST COWBOYS WERE EXCELLENT RIDERS.."
6-29
"GALLOPING ACROSS THE PRAIRIE WAS FUN, BUT IT COULD ALSO BE DANGEROUS.."
Tales of the West
"A HORSE COULD VERY EASILY STUMBLE IF HE STEPPED INTO A HOLE.."
WOULDN'T IT HAVE BEEN SAFER JUST TO STAY ON THE SIDEWALK?
SCHULZ

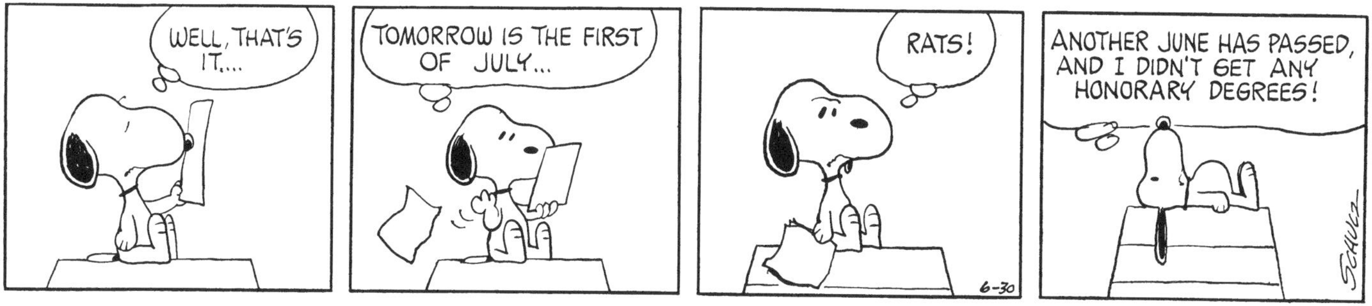
WELL, THAT'S IT....
TOMORROW IS THE FIRST OF JULY...
RATS!
6-30
ANOTHER JUNE HAS PASSED, AND I DIDN'T GET ANY HONORARY DEGREES!
SCHULZ

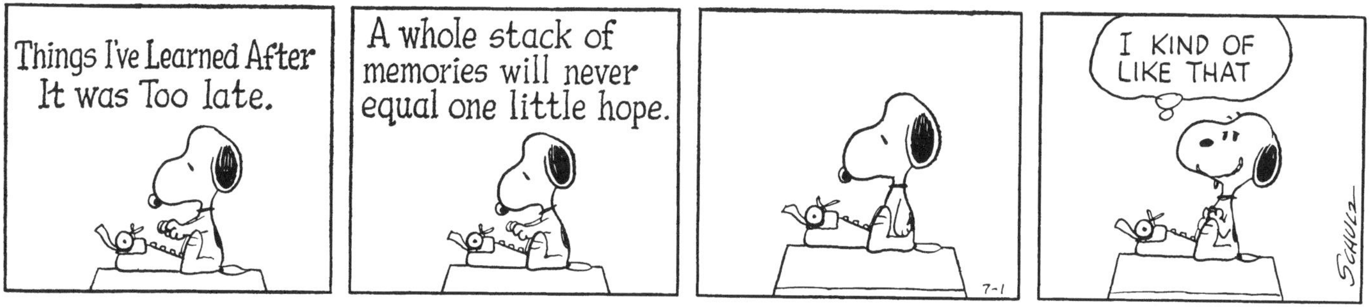
Things I've Learned After It was Too late.
A whole stack of memories will never equal one little hope.
7-1
I KIND OF LIKE THAT
SCHULZ

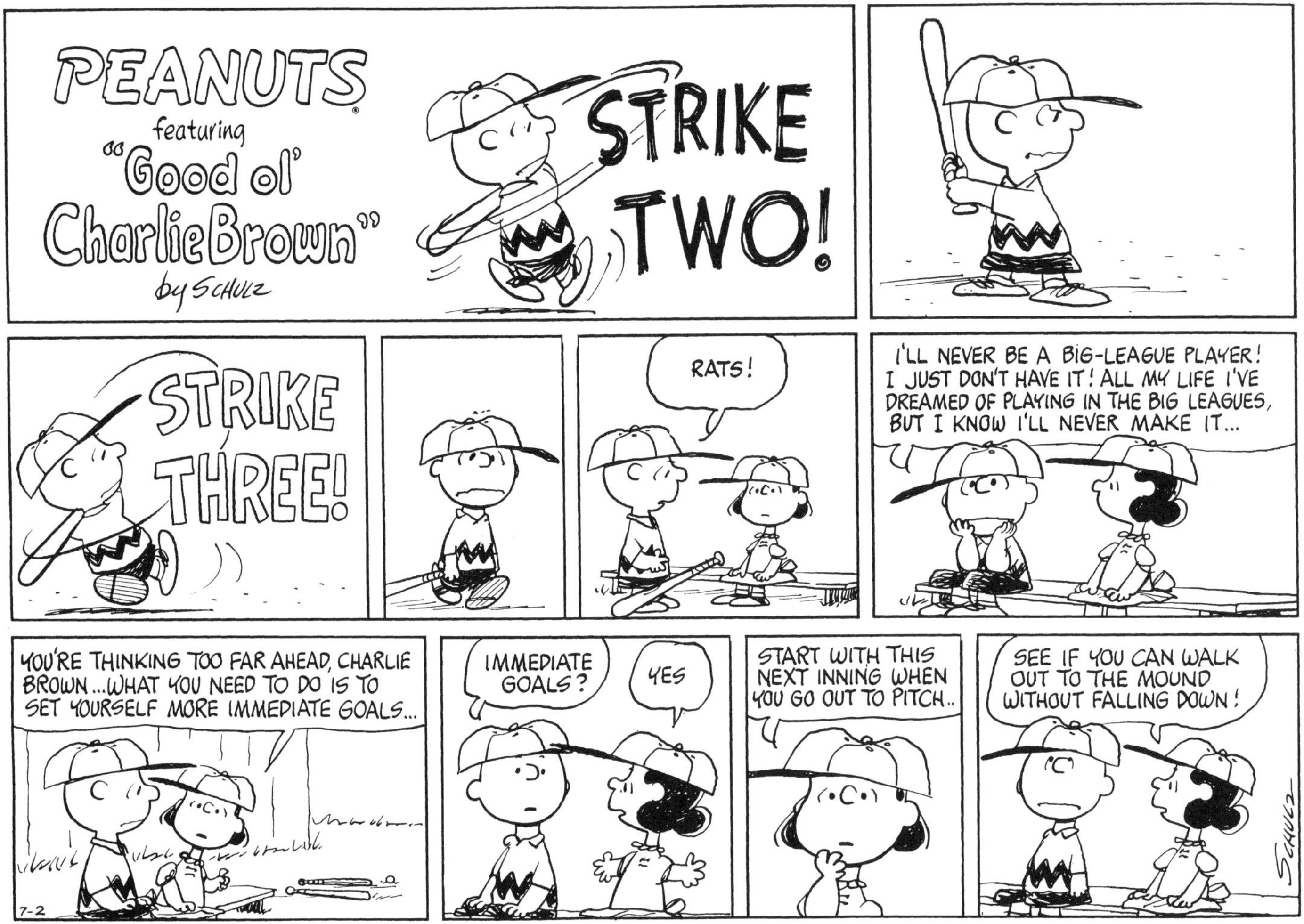
PEANUTS
featuring
"Good ol' Charlie Brown"
by SCHULZ
STRIKE TWO!
STRIKE THREE!
RATS!
I'LL NEVER BE A BIG-LEAGUE PLAYER! I JUST DON'T HAVE IT! ALL MY LIFE I'VE DREAMED OF PLAYING IN THE BIG LEAGUES, BUT I KNOW I'LL NEVER MAKE IT...
YOU'RE THINKING TOO FAR AHEAD, CHARLIE BROWN...WHAT YOU NEED TO DO IS TO SET YOURSELF MORE IMMEDIATE GOALS...
7-2
IMMEDIATE GOALS?
YES
START WITH THIS NEXT INNING WHEN YOU GO OUT TO PITCH..
SEE IF YOU CAN WALK OUT TO THE MOUND WITHOUT FALLING DOWN!
SCHULZ

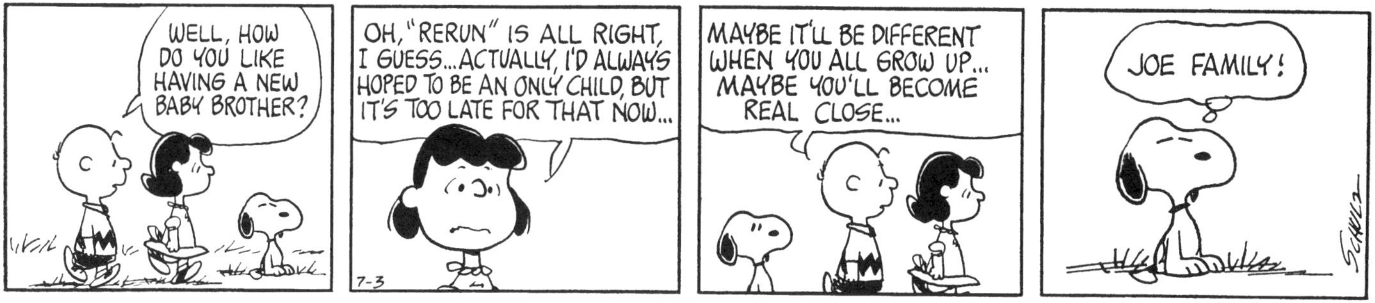
WELL, HOW DO YOU LIKE HAVING A NEW BABY BROTHER?
OH, "RERUN" IS ALL RIGHT, I GUESS...ACTUALLY, I'D ALWAYS HOPED TO BE AN ONLY CHILD, BUT IT'S TOO LATE FOR THAT NOW...
7-3
MAYBE IT'LL BE DIFFERENT WHEN YOU ALL GROW UP... MAYBE YOU'LL BECOME REAL CLOSE...
JOE FAMILY!
SCHULZ

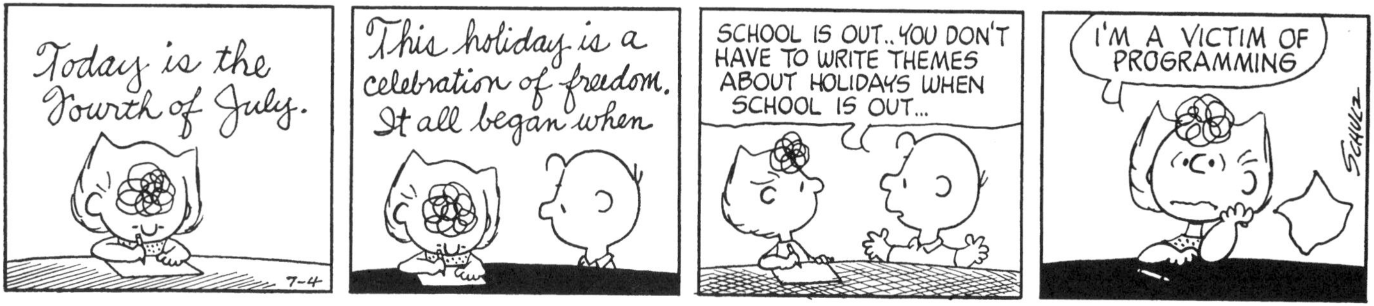
Today is the Fourth of July.
7-4
This holiday is a celebration of freedom. It all began when
SCHOOL IS OUT..YOU DON'T HAVE TO WRITE THEMES ABOUT HOLIDAYS WHEN SCHOOL IS OUT...
I'M A VICTIM OF PROGRAMMING
SCHULZ

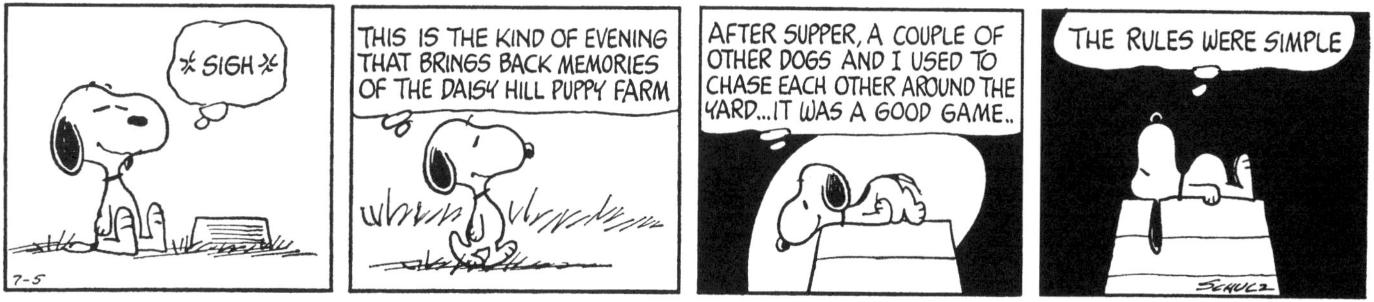
SIGH
7-5
THIS IS THE KIND OF EVENING THAT BRINGS BACK MEMORIES OF THE DAISY HILL PUPPY FARM
AFTER SUPPER, A COUPLE OF OTHER DOGS AND I USED TO CHASE EACH OTHER AROUND THE YARD...IT WAS A GOOD GAME..
THE RULES WERE SIMPLE
SCHULZ

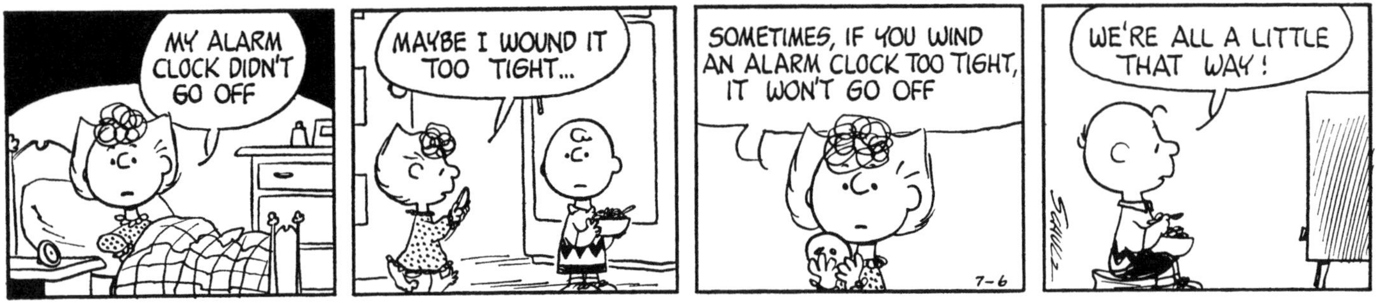
MY ALARM CLOCK DIDN'T GO OFF
MAYBE I WOUND IT TOO TIGHT...
SOMETIMES, IF YOU WIND AN ALARM CLOCK TOO TIGHT, IT WON'T GO OFF
WE'RE ALL A LITTLE THAT WAY!
7-6
SCHULZ

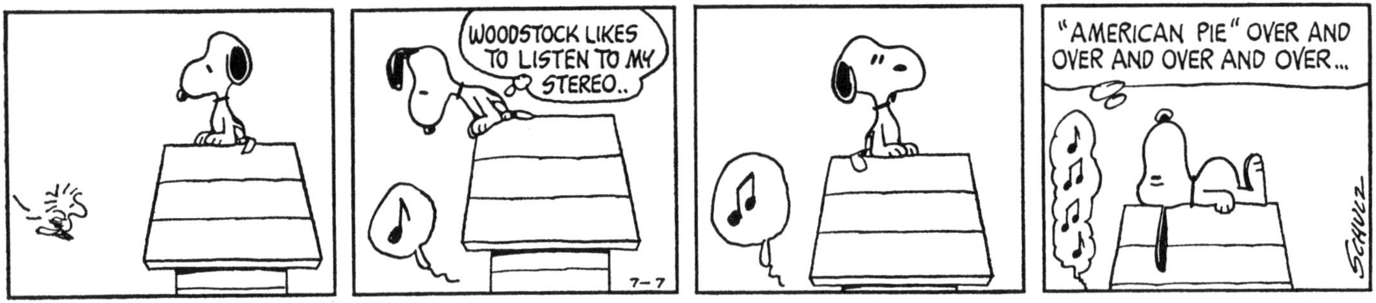
WOODSTOCK LIKES TO LISTEN TO MY STEREO..
7-7
"AMERICAN PIE" OVER AND OVER AND OVER AND OVER...
SCHULZ

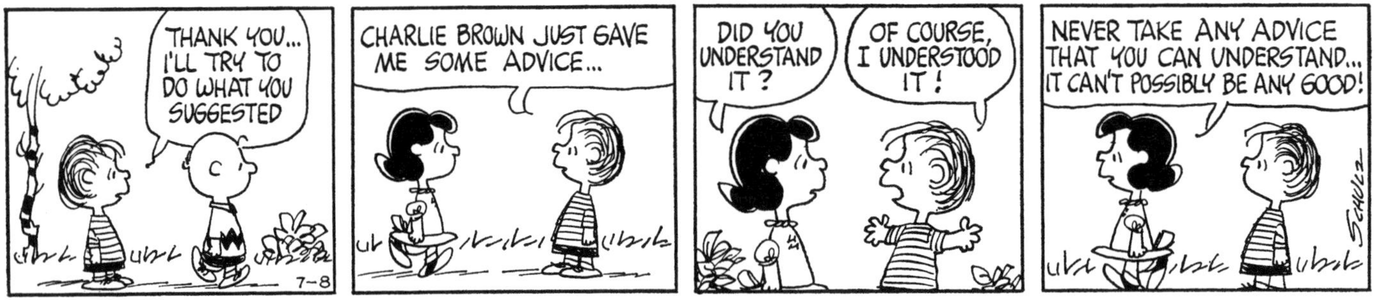
THANK YOU... I'LL TRY TO DO WHAT YOU SUGGESTED
7-8
CHARLIE BROWN JUST GAVE ME SOME ADVICE...
DID YOU UNDERSTAND IT?
OF COURSE, I UNDERSTOOD IT!
NEVER TAKE ANY ADVICE THAT YOU CAN UNDERSTAND... IT CAN'T POSSIBLY BE ANY GOOD!
SCHULZ

PEANUTS
featuring
"Good ol' CharlieBrown"
by SCHULZ

I SAW A MOVIE RECENTLY ABOUT A BOY AND HIS DOG

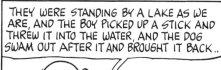

THEY WERE STANDING BY A LAKE AS WE ARE, AND THE BOY PICKED UP A STICK AND THREW IT INTO THE WATER, AND THE DOG SWAM OUT AFTER IT AND BROUGHT IT BACK..

I'M GOING TO HAVE TO STOP WATCHING THOSE MOVIES

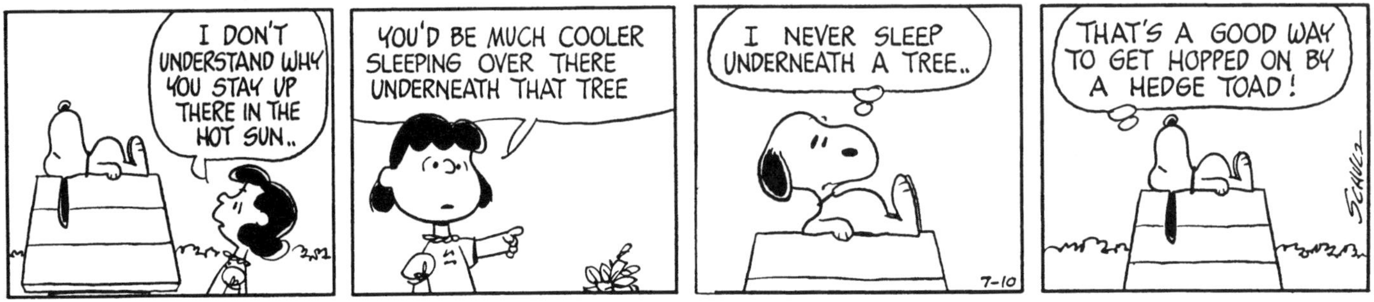

I DON'T UNDERSTAND WHY YOU STAY UP THERE IN THE HOT SUN..
YOU'D BE MUCH COOLER SLEEPING OVER THERE UNDERNEATH THAT TREE
I NEVER SLEEP UNDERNEATH A TREE..
THAT'S A GOOD WAY TO GET HOPPED ON BY A HEDGE TOAD!

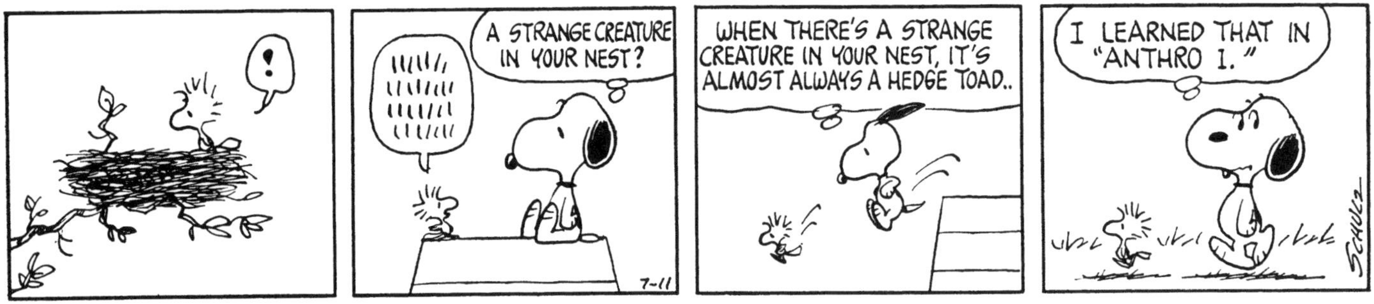

!
A STRANGE CREATURE IN YOUR NEST?
WHEN THERE'S A STRANGE CREATURE IN YOUR NEST, IT'S ALMOST ALWAYS A HEDGE TOAD..
I LEARNED THAT IN "ANTHRO I."

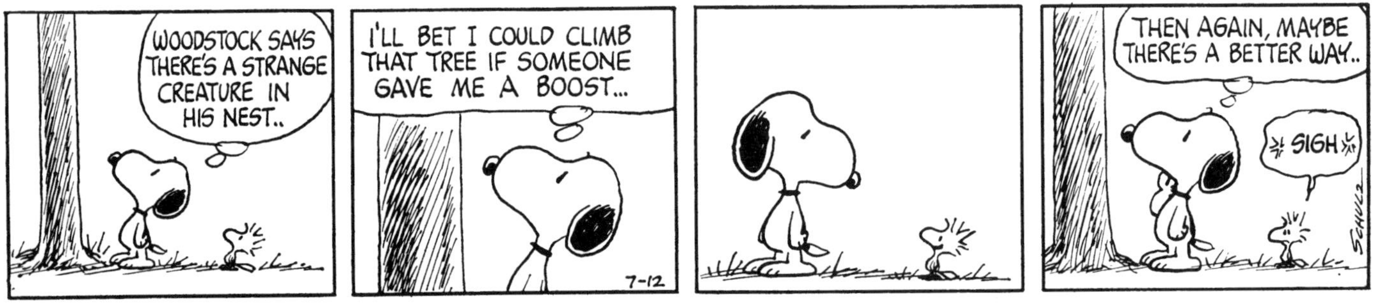

WOODSTOCK SAYS THERE'S A STRANGE CREATURE IN HIS NEST..
I'LL BET I COULD CLIMB THAT TREE IF SOMEONE GAVE ME A BOOST...
THEN AGAIN, MAYBE THERE'S A BETTER WAY..
SIGH

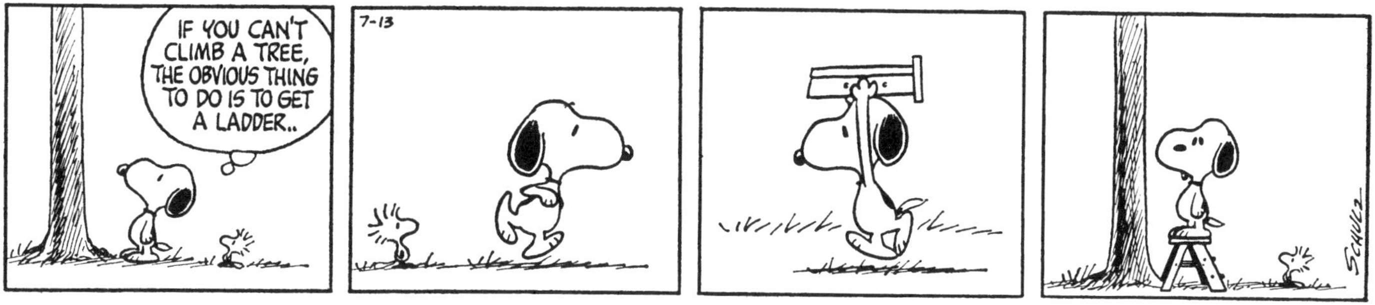
IF YOU CAN'T CLIMB A TREE, THE OBVIOUS THING TO DO IS TO GET A LADDER..
7-13
SCHULZ

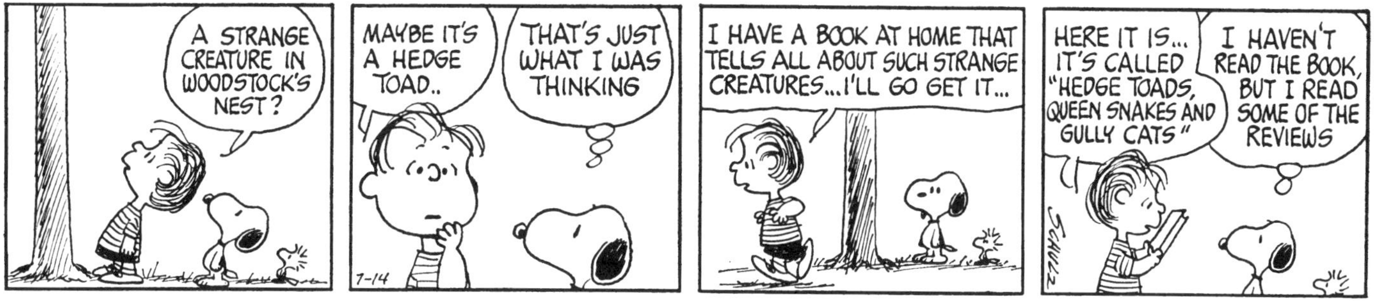
A STRANGE CREATURE IN WOODSTOCK'S NEST?
MAYBE IT'S A HEDGE TOAD..
THAT'S JUST WHAT I WAS THINKING
7-14
I HAVE A BOOK AT HOME THAT TELLS ALL ABOUT SUCH STRANGE CREATURES...I'LL GO GET IT...
HERE IT IS... IT'S CALLED "HEDGE TOADS, QUEEN SNAKES AND GULLY CATS"
I HAVEN'T READ THE BOOK, BUT I READ SOME OF THE REVIEWS
SCHULZ

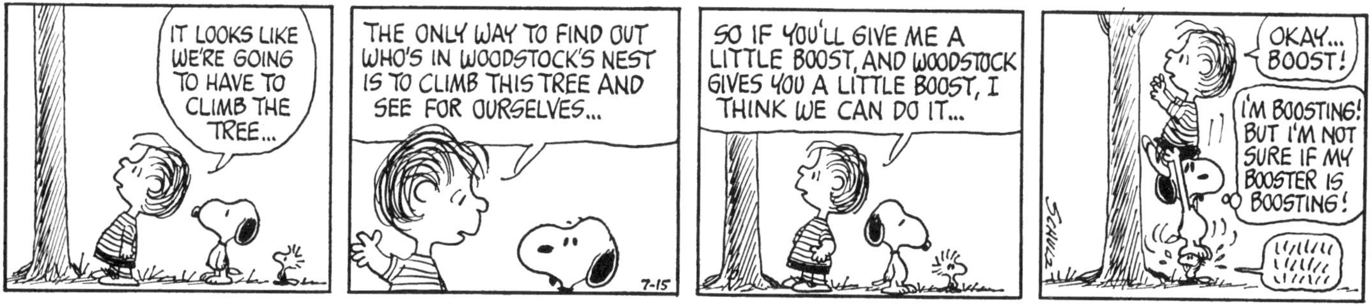
IT LOOKS LIKE WE'RE GOING TO HAVE TO CLIMB THE TREE...
THE ONLY WAY TO FIND OUT WHO'S IN WOODSTOCK'S NEST IS TO CLIMB THIS TREE AND SEE FOR OURSELVES...
7-15
SO IF YOU'LL GIVE ME A LITTLE BOOST, AND WOODSTOCK GIVES YOU A LITTLE BOOST, I THINK WE CAN DO IT...
OKAY... BOOST!
I'M BOOSTING! BUT I'M NOT SURE IF MY BOOSTER IS BOOSTING!
SCHULZ

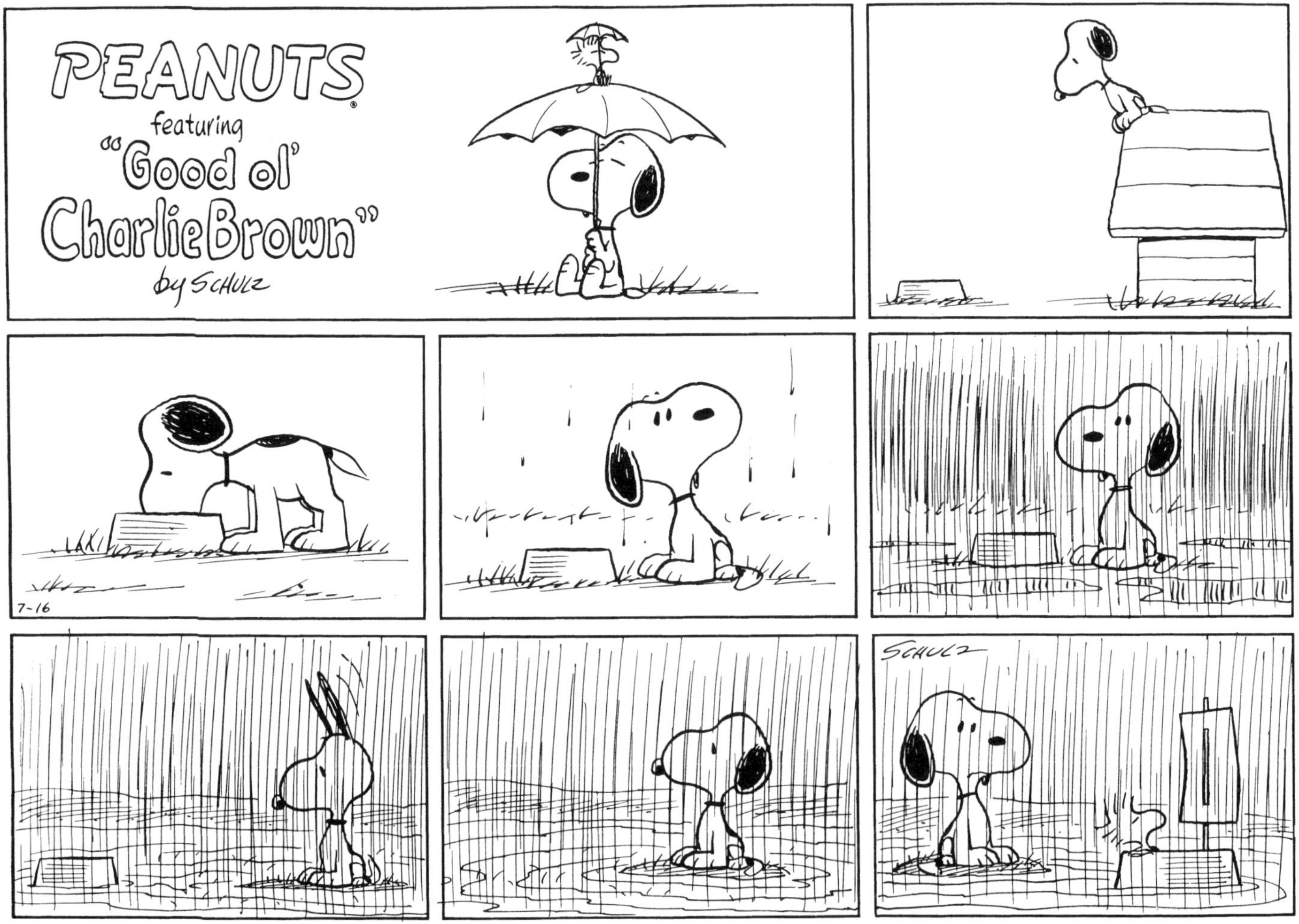
PEANUTS
featuring
"Good ol' Charlie Brown"
by SCHULZ
7-16
SCHULZ

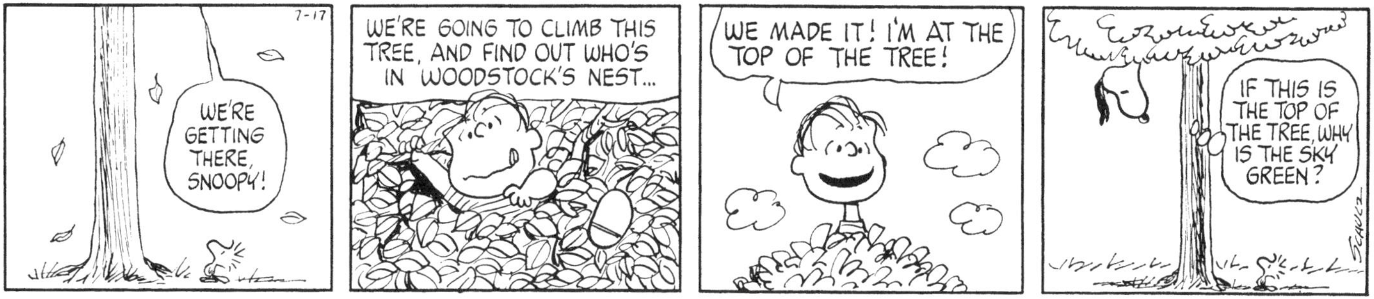
7-17
WE'RE GETTING THERE, SNOOPY!
WE'RE GOING TO CLIMB THIS TREE, AND FIND OUT WHO'S IN WOODSTOCK'S NEST...
WE MADE IT! I'M AT THE TOP OF THE TREE!
IF THIS IS THE TOP OF THE TREE, WHY IS THE SKY GREEN?
SCHULZ

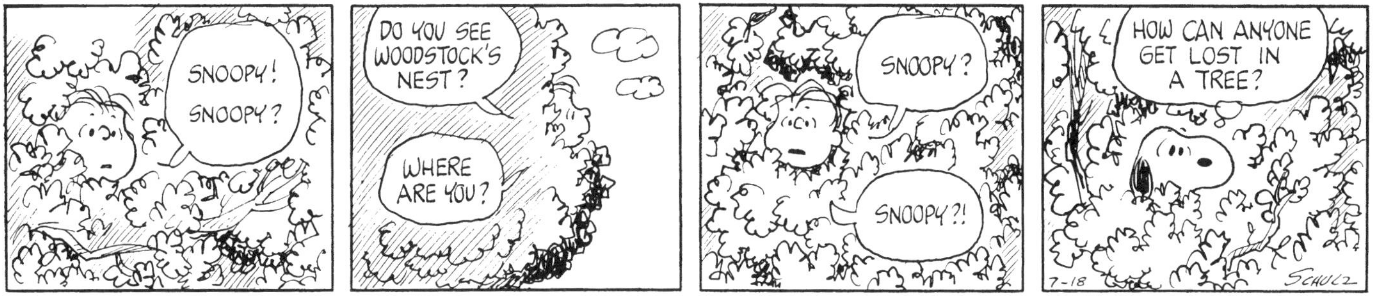
SNOOPY!
SNOOPY?
DO YOU SEE WOODSTOCK'S NEST?
WHERE ARE YOU?
SNOOPY?
SNOOPY?!
HOW CAN ANYONE GET LOST IN A TREE?
7-18
SCHULZ

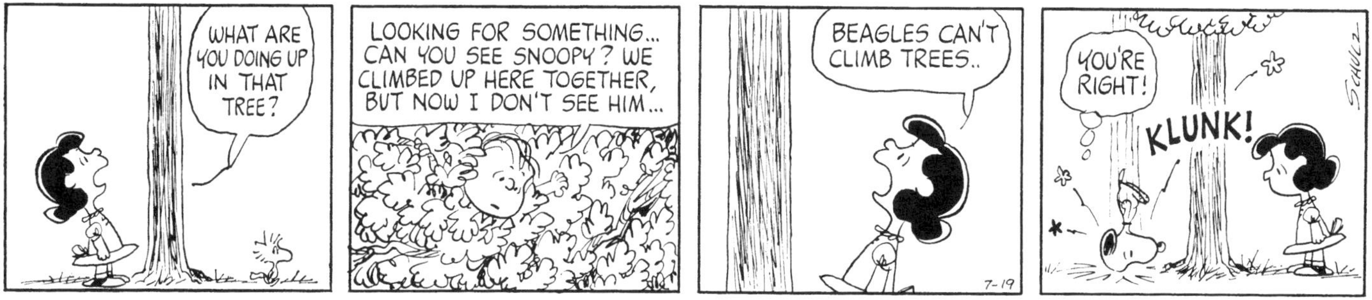
WHAT ARE YOU DOING UP IN THAT TREE?
LOOKING FOR SOMETHING... CAN YOU SEE SNOOPY? WE CLIMBED UP HERE TOGETHER, BUT NOW I DON'T SEE HIM...
BEAGLES CAN'T CLIMB TREES..
7-19
YOU'RE RIGHT!
KLUNK!
SCHULZ

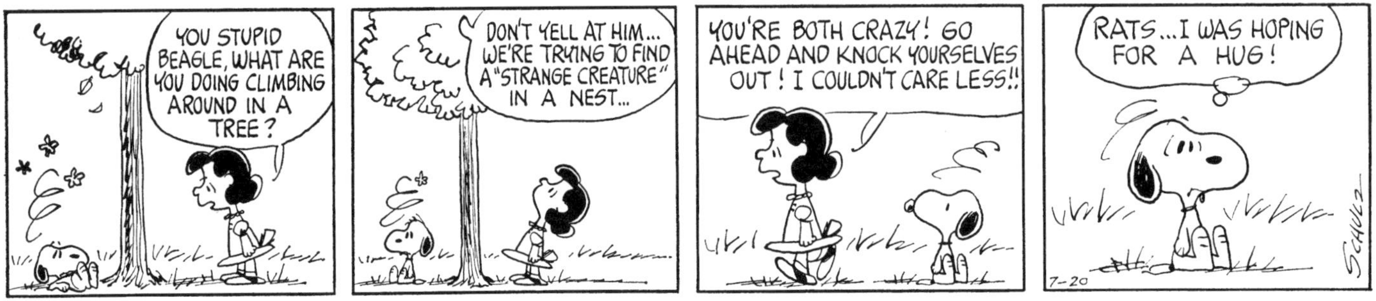
YOU STUPID BEAGLE, WHAT ARE YOU DOING CLIMBING AROUND IN A TREE?
DON'T YELL AT HIM... WE'RE TRYING TO FIND A "STRANGE CREATURE" IN A NEST...
YOU'RE BOTH CRAZY! GO AHEAD AND KNOCK YOURSELVES OUT! I COULDN'T CARE LESS!!
RATS...I WAS HOPING FOR A HUG!
7-20
SCHULZ

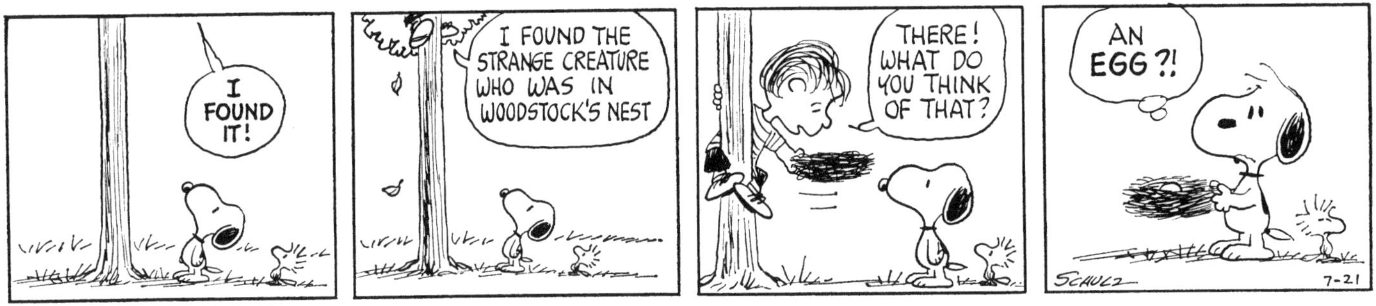
I FOUND IT!
I FOUND THE STRANGE CREATURE WHO WAS IN WOODSTOCK'S NEST
THERE! WHAT DO YOU THINK OF THAT?
AN EGG?!
SCHULZ
7-21

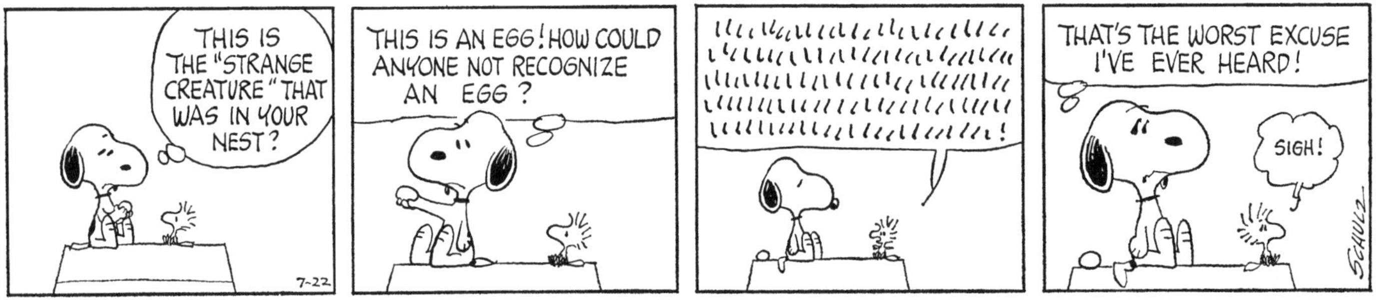
THIS IS THE "STRANGE CREATURE" THAT WAS IN YOUR NEST?
7-22
THIS IS AN EGG! HOW COULD ANYONE NOT RECOGNIZE AN EGG?
THAT'S THE WORST EXCUSE I'VE EVER HEARD!
SIGH!
SCHULZ

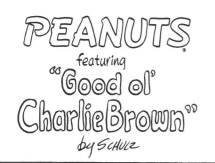

PEANUTS featuring "Good ol' CharlieBrown" by SCHULZ

PSYCHIATRIC HELP 5¢

THE DOCTOR IS [WAY OUT]

PSYCHIATRIC HELP 5¢

I NEED SOME ADVICE

THE DOCTOR IS [IN]

GOOD.. THAT'S WHAT I'M HERE FOR..

THE DOCTOR IS [IN]

THERE'S THIS BOY I KIND OF LIKE, SEE, BUT HE NEVER PAYS ANY ATTENTION TO ME.. IS IT BECAUSE I'M UNATTRACTIVE?

THE DOCTOR IS [IN]

7-23

HELP 5¢

NONSENSE! YOU'RE A VERY BEAUTIFUL YOUNG GIRL, AND YOU SHOULDN'T HAVE TO CHASE AFTER ANYONE!

THE DOCTOR

DO YOU REALLY THINK SO?

HE DOCTOR IS [IN]

OF COURSE! WOULD I LIE TO YOU?

THE DOCTOR IS [IN]

MY PSYCHIATRIST SAYS, "BLEAH!!"

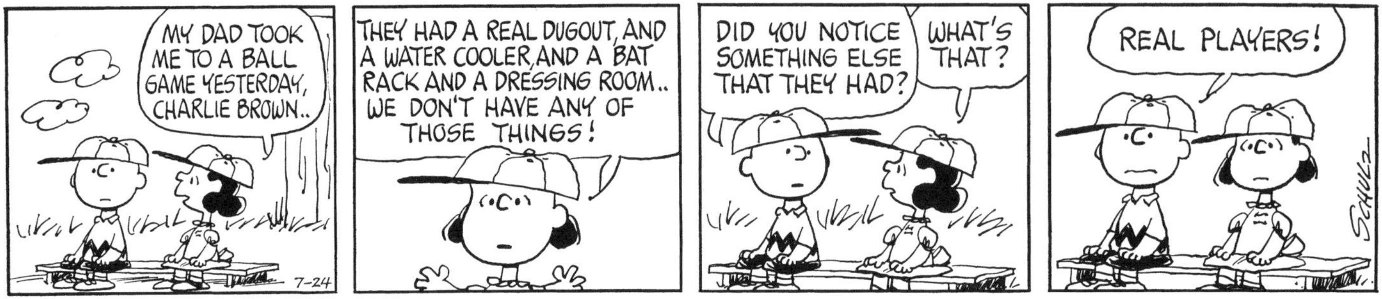
MY DAD TOOK ME TO A BALL GAME YESTERDAY, CHARLIE BROWN..
THEY HAD A REAL DUGOUT, AND A WATER COOLER, AND A BAT RACK AND A DRESSING ROOM.. WE DON'T HAVE ANY OF THOSE THINGS!
DID YOU NOTICE SOMETHING ELSE THAT THEY HAD?
WHAT'S THAT?
REAL PLAYERS!
7-24
SCHULZ

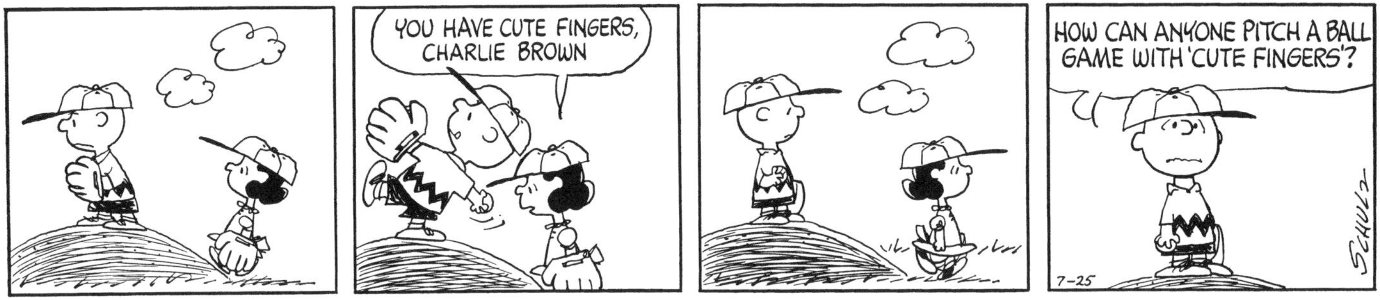
YOU HAVE CUTE FINGERS, CHARLIE BROWN
HOW CAN ANYONE PITCH A BALL GAME WITH 'CUTE FINGERS'?
7-25
SCHULZ

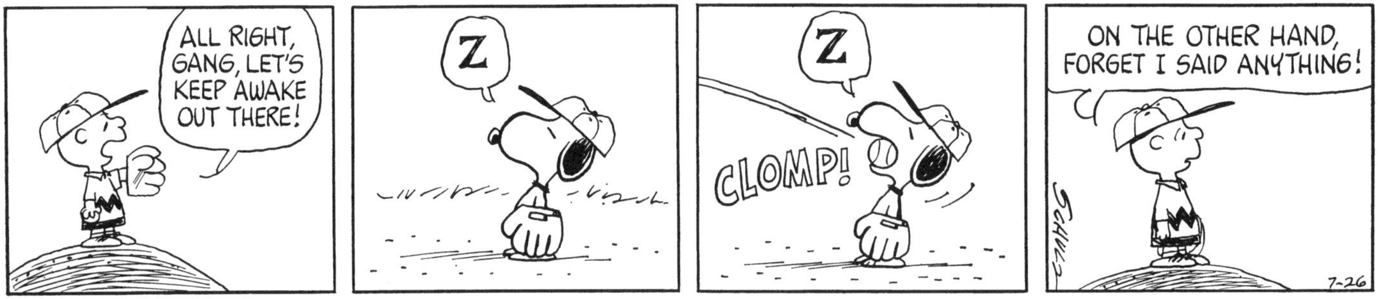
ALL RIGHT, GANG, LET'S KEEP AWAKE OUT THERE!
Z
Z
CLOMP!
SCHULZ
ON THE OTHER HAND, FORGET I SAID ANYTHING!
7-26

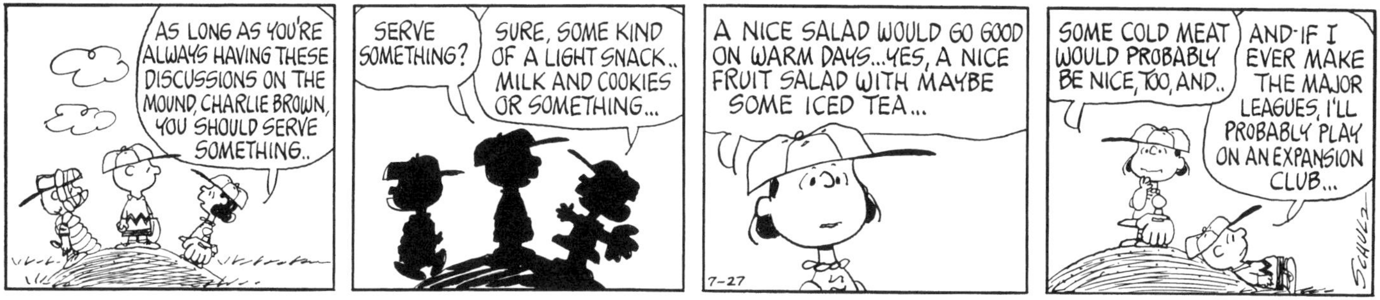
AS LONG AS YOU'RE ALWAYS HAVING THESE DISCUSSIONS ON THE MOUND, CHARLIE BROWN, YOU SHOULD SERVE SOMETHING..
SERVE SOMETHING?
SURE, SOME KIND OF A LIGHT SNACK.. MILK AND COOKIES OR SOMETHING...
A NICE SALAD WOULD GO GOOD ON WARM DAYS...YES, A NICE FRUIT SALAD WITH MAYBE SOME ICED TEA...
7-27
SOME COLD MEAT WOULD PROBABLY BE NICE, TOO, AND..
AND IF I EVER MAKE THE MAJOR LEAGUES, I'LL PROBABLY PLAY ON AN EXPANSION CLUB...
SCHULZ

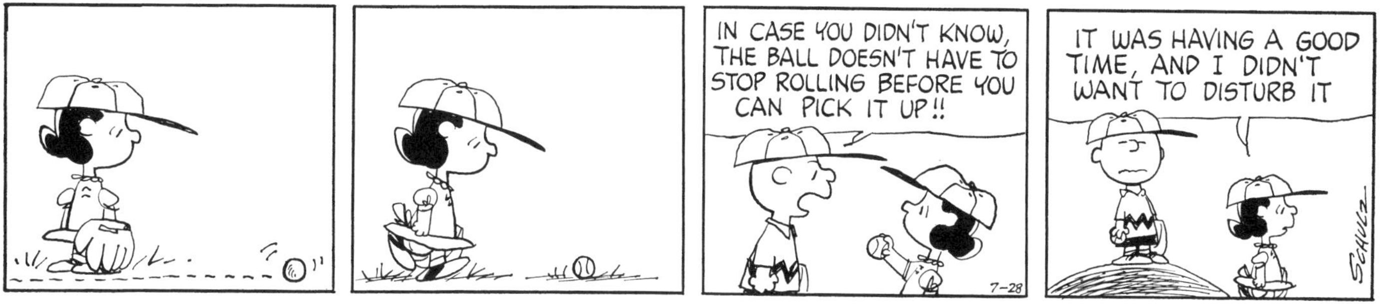
IN CASE YOU DIDN'T KNOW, THE BALL DOESN'T HAVE TO STOP ROLLING BEFORE YOU CAN PICK IT UP!!
7-28
IT WAS HAVING A GOOD TIME, AND I DIDN'T WANT TO DISTURB IT
SCHULZ

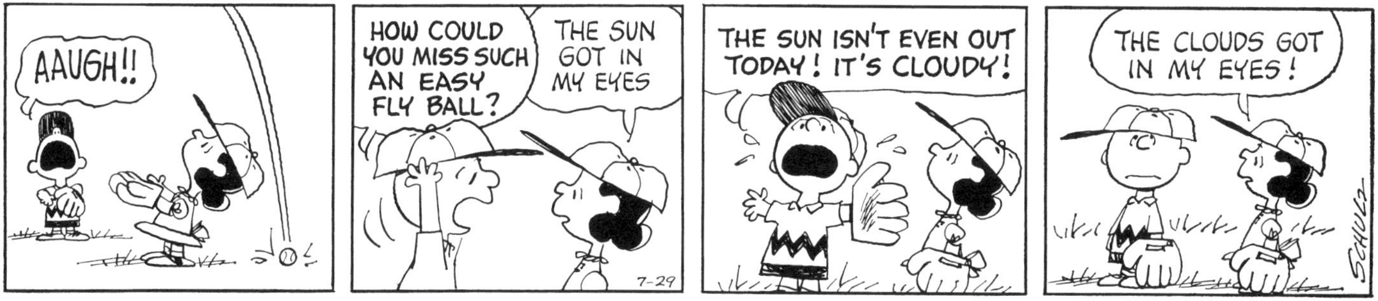
AAUGH!!
HOW COULD YOU MISS SUCH AN EASY FLY BALL?
THE SUN GOT IN MY EYES
7-29
THE SUN ISN'T EVEN OUT TODAY! IT'S CLOUDY!
THE CLOUDS GOT IN MY EYES!
SCHULZ

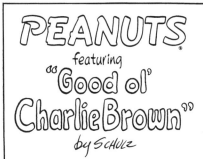

PEANUTS featuring "Good ol' CharlieBrown" by SCHULZ

Z, z (zeta)

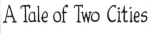

A Tale of Two Cities

REALLY?

Of Human Bondage

7-30

YOU'RE KIDDING!

Heart of Darkness

I CAN'T BELIEVE IT!!

I HAVE A GREAT IDEA FOR A NOVEL, BUT ALL THE GOOD TITLES ARE TAKEN!

July/August

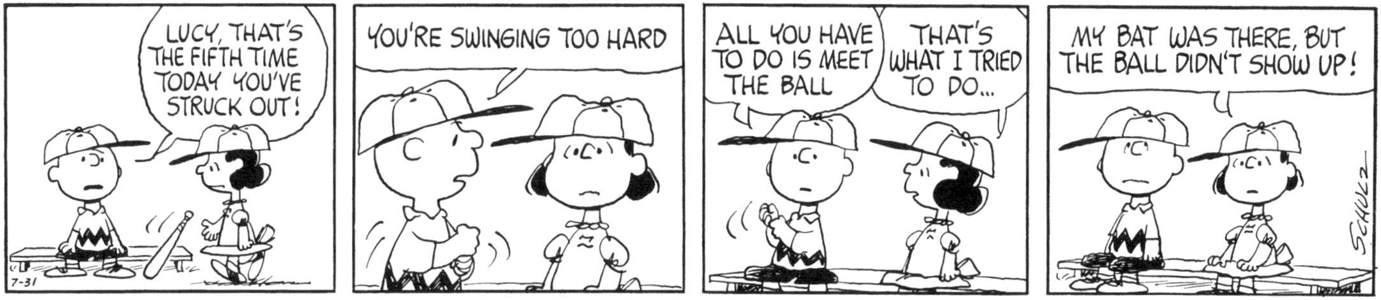
LUCY, THAT'S THE FIFTH TIME TODAY YOU'VE STRUCK OUT!
7-31
YOU'RE SWINGING TOO HARD
ALL YOU HAVE TO DO IS MEET THE BALL
THAT'S WHAT I TRIED TO DO...
MY BAT WAS THERE, BUT THE BALL DIDN'T SHOW UP!
SCHULZ

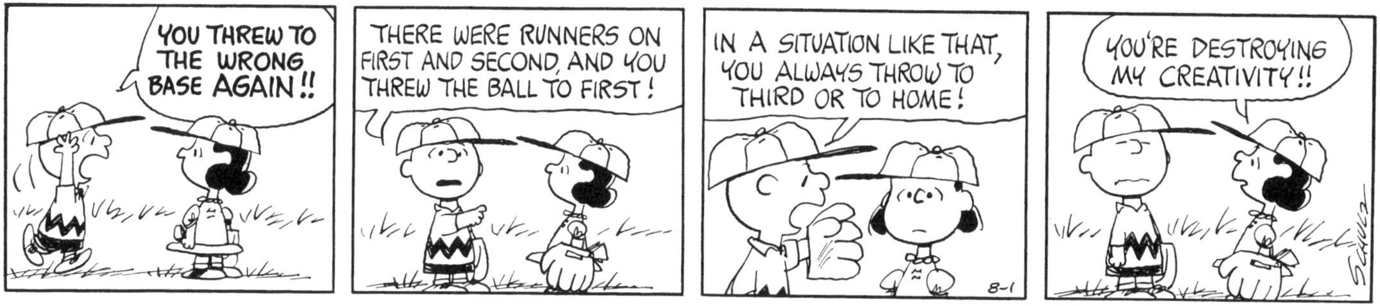
YOU THREW TO THE WRONG BASE AGAIN!!
THERE WERE RUNNERS ON FIRST AND SECOND, AND YOU THREW THE BALL TO FIRST!
IN A SITUATION LIKE THAT, YOU ALWAYS THROW TO THIRD OR TO HOME!
8-1
YOU'RE DESTROYING MY CREATIVITY!!
SCHULZ

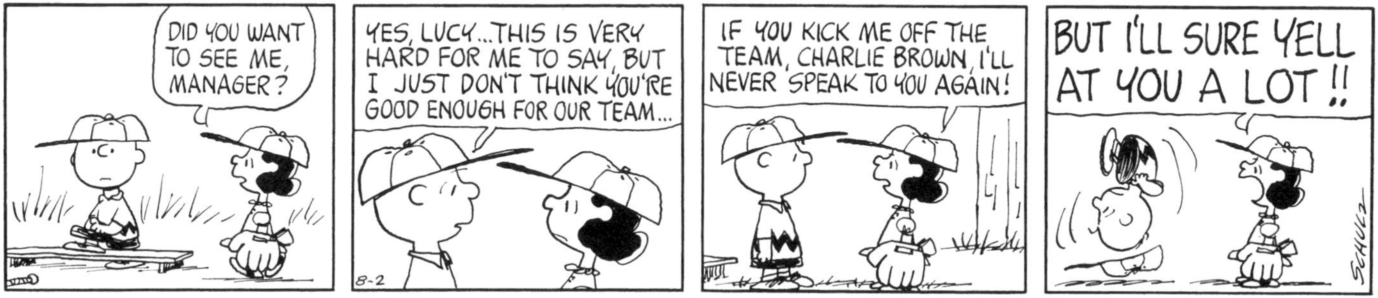
DID YOU WANT TO SEE ME, MANAGER?
YES, LUCY...THIS IS VERY HARD FOR ME TO SAY, BUT I JUST DON'T THINK YOU'RE GOOD ENOUGH FOR OUR TEAM...
8-2
IF YOU KICK ME OFF THE TEAM, CHARLIE BROWN, I'LL NEVER SPEAK TO YOU AGAIN!
BUT I'LL SURE YELL AT YOU A LOT!!
SCHULZ

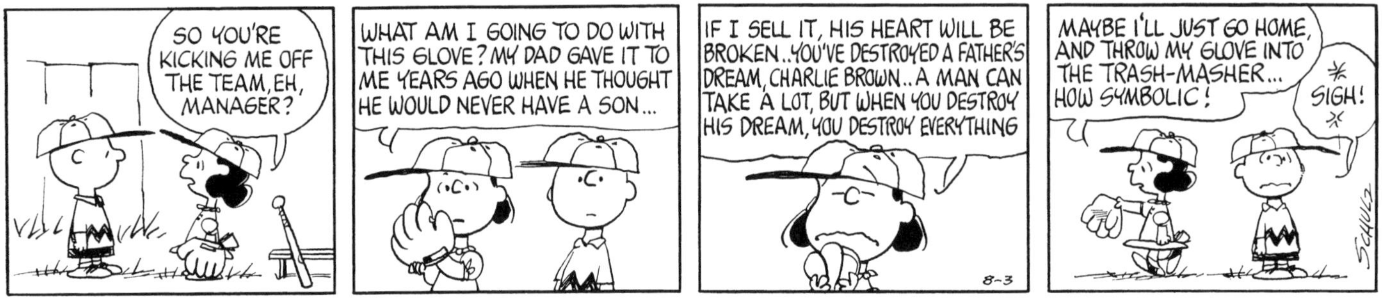
SO YOU'RE KICKING ME OFF THE TEAM, EH, MANAGER?
WHAT AM I GOING TO DO WITH THIS GLOVE? MY DAD GAVE IT TO ME YEARS AGO WHEN HE THOUGHT HE WOULD NEVER HAVE A SON...
IF I SELL IT, HIS HEART WILL BE BROKEN..YOU'VE DESTROYED A FATHER'S DREAM, CHARLIE BROWN.. A MAN CAN TAKE A LOT, BUT WHEN YOU DESTROY HIS DREAM, YOU DESTROY EVERYTHING
8-3
MAYBE I'LL JUST GO HOME, AND THROW MY GLOVE INTO THE TRASH-MASHER... HOW SYMBOLIC!
SIGH!
SCHULZ

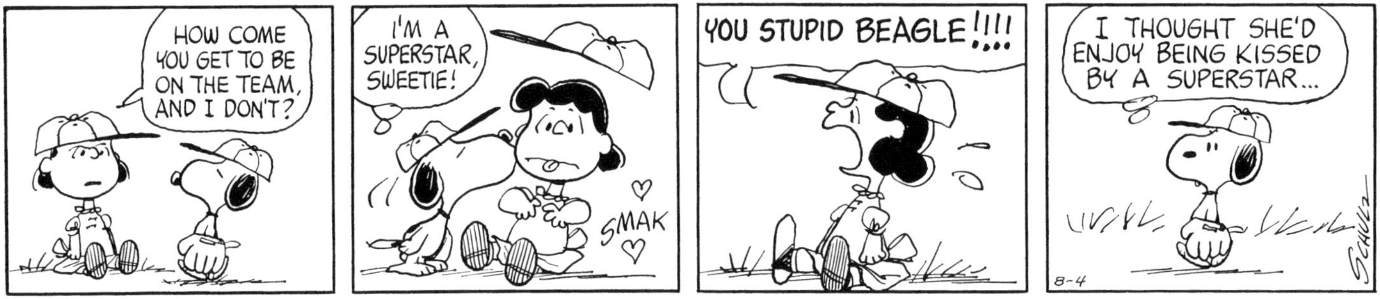
HOW COME YOU GET TO BE ON THE TEAM, AND I DON'T?
I'M A SUPERSTAR, SWEETIE!
SMAK
YOU STUPID BEAGLE!!!!
I THOUGHT SHE'D ENJOY BEING KISSED BY A SUPERSTAR...
8-4
SCHULZ

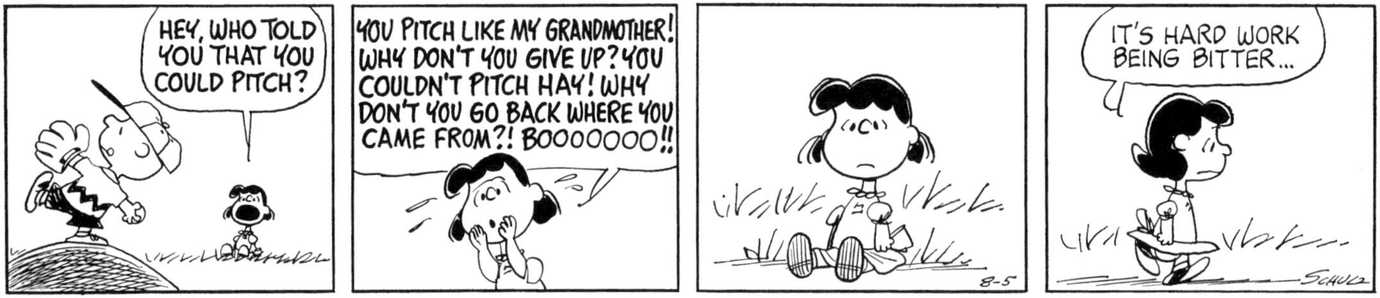
HEY, WHO TOLD YOU THAT YOU COULD PITCH?
YOU PITCH LIKE MY GRANDMOTHER! WHY DON'T YOU GIVE UP? YOU COULDN'T PITCH HAY! WHY DON'T YOU GO BACK WHERE YOU CAME FROM?! BOOOOOOO!!
8-5
IT'S HARD WORK BEING BITTER...
SCHULZ

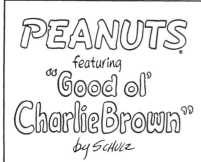

PEANUTS featuring "Good ol' CharlieBrown" by Schulz

LATELY EVERYTHING SEEMS TO BOTHER ME...

HOW DO YOU MEAN?

WHAT DO YOU THINK SECURITY IS, CHUCK?

SECURITY?

SECURITY IS SLEEPING IN THE BACK SEAT OF THE CAR...

WHEN YOU'RE A LITTLE KID, AND YOU'VE BEEN SOMEWHERE WITH YOUR MOM AND DAD, AND IT'S NIGHT, AND YOU'RE RIDING HOME IN THE CAR, YOU CAN SLEEP IN THE BACK SEAT..

YOU DON'T HAVE TO WORRY ABOUT ANYTHING... YOUR MOM AND DAD ARE IN THE FRONT SEAT, AND THEY DO ALL THE WORRYING...THEY TAKE CARE OF EVERYTHING...

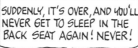

THAT'S REAL NEAT!

BUT IT DOESN'T LAST! SUDDENLY, YOU'RE GROWN UP, AND IT CAN NEVER BE THAT WAY AGAIN!

SUDDENLY, IT'S OVER, AND YOU'LL NEVER GET TO SLEEP IN THE BACK SEAT AGAIN! NEVER!

NEVER?

ABSOLUTELY NEVER!

HOLD MY HAND, CHUCK!!

1972

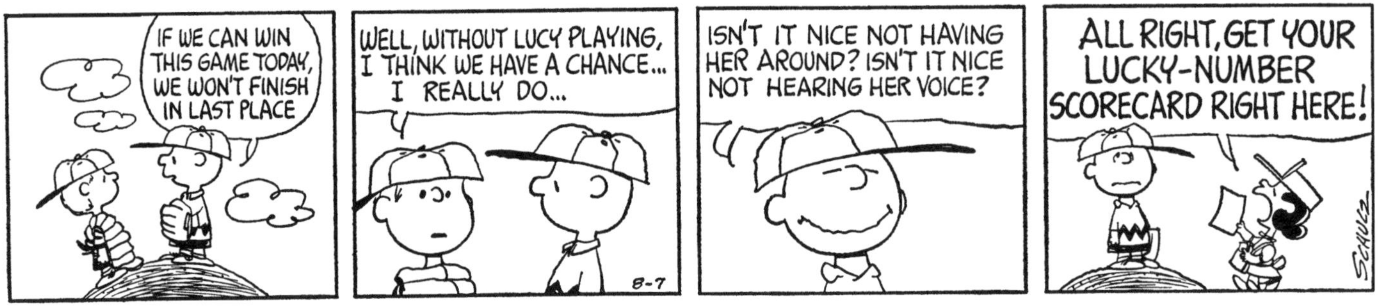
IF WE CAN WIN THIS GAME TODAY, WE WON'T FINISH IN LAST PLACE
WELL, WITHOUT LUCY PLAYING, I THINK WE HAVE A CHANCE... I REALLY DO...
8-7
ISN'T IT NICE NOT HAVING HER AROUND? ISN'T IT NICE NOT HEARING HER VOICE?
ALL RIGHT, GET YOUR LUCKY-NUMBER SCORECARD RIGHT HERE!
SCHULZ

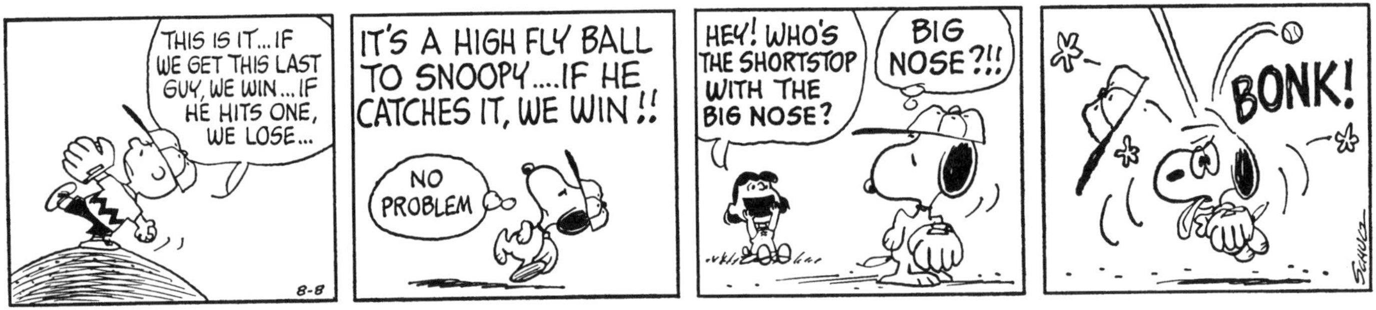
THIS IS IT...IF WE GET THIS LAST GUY, WE WIN...IF HE HITS ONE, WE LOSE...
8-8
IT'S A HIGH FLY BALL TO SNOOPY....IF HE CATCHES IT, WE WIN!!
NO PROBLEM
HEY! WHO'S THE SHORTSTOP WITH THE BIG NOSE?
BIG NOSE?!!
BONK!
SCHULZ

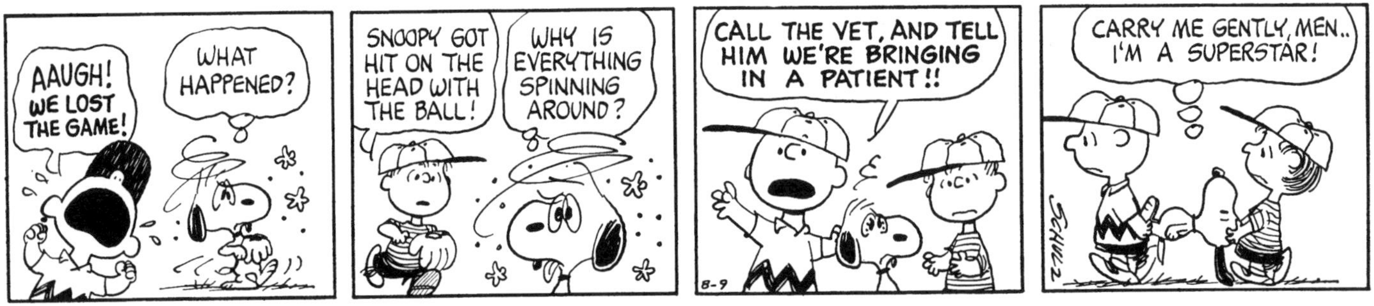
AAUGH! WE LOST THE GAME!
WHAT HAPPENED?
SNOOPY GOT HIT ON THE HEAD WITH THE BALL!
WHY IS EVERYTHING SPINNING AROUND?
CALL THE VET, AND TELL HIM WE'RE BRINGING IN A PATIENT!!
8-9
CARRY ME GENTLY, MEN.. I'M A SUPERSTAR!
SCHULZ

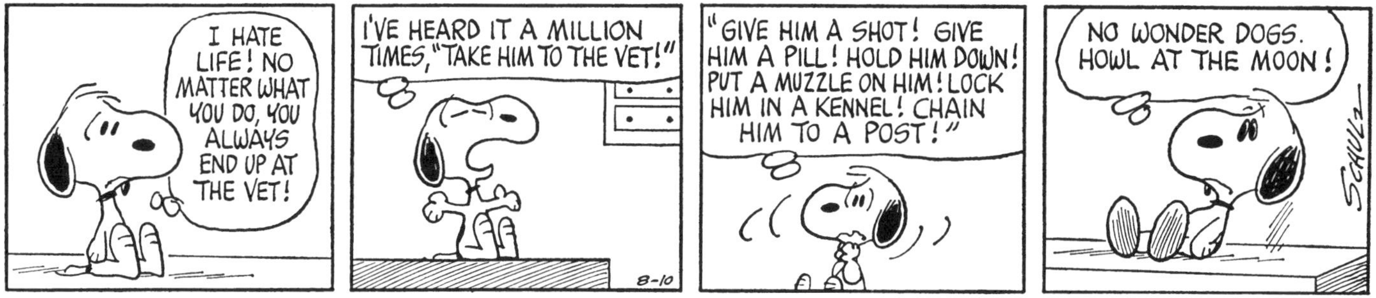
I HATE LIFE! NO MATTER WHAT YOU DO, YOU ALWAYS END UP AT THE VET!
I'VE HEARD IT A MILLION TIMES, "TAKE HIM TO THE VET!"
8-10
"GIVE HIM A SHOT! GIVE HIM A PILL! HOLD HIM DOWN! PUT A MUZZLE ON HIM! LOCK HIM IN A KENNEL! CHAIN HIM TO A POST!"
NO WONDER DOGS. HOWL AT THE MOON!
SCHULZ

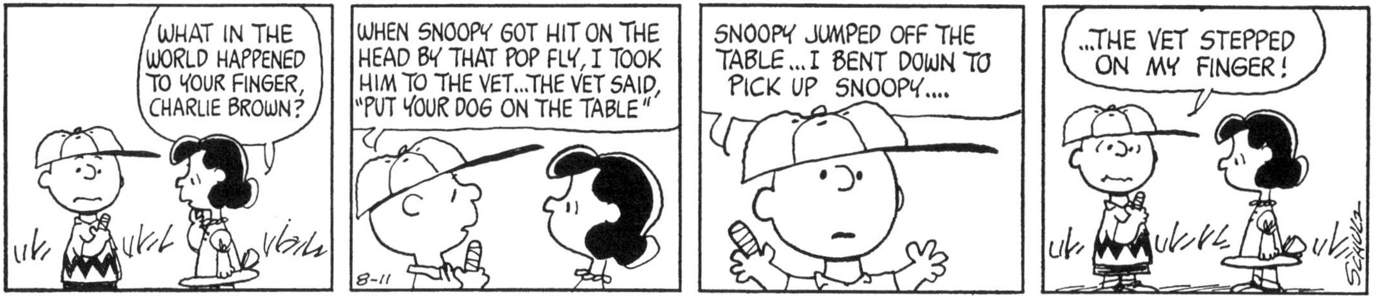
WHAT IN THE WORLD HAPPENED TO YOUR FINGER, CHARLIE BROWN?
WHEN SNOOPY GOT HIT ON THE HEAD BY THAT POP FLY, I TOOK HIM TO THE VET...THE VET SAID, "PUT YOUR DOG ON THE TABLE"
8-11
SNOOPY JUMPED OFF THE TABLE...I BENT DOWN TO PICK UP SNOOPY....
...THE VET STEPPED ON MY FINGER!
SCHULZ

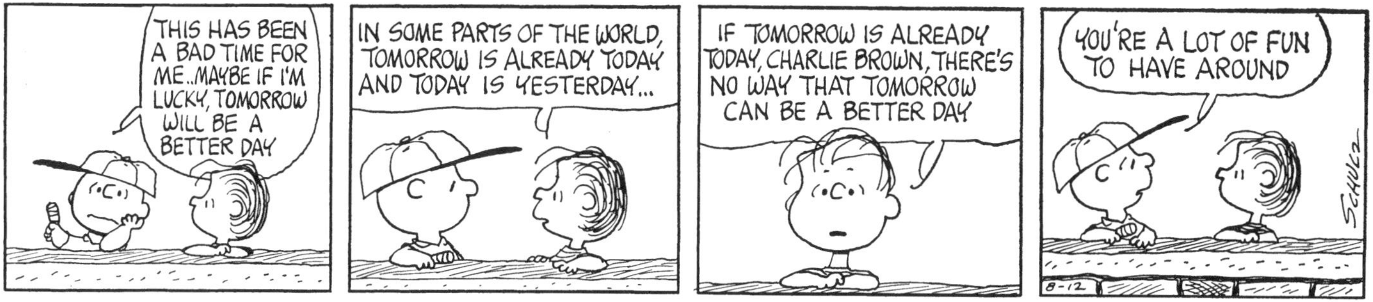
THIS HAS BEEN A BAD TIME FOR ME..MAYBE IF I'M LUCKY, TOMORROW WILL BE A BETTER DAY
IN SOME PARTS OF THE WORLD, TOMORROW IS ALREADY TODAY AND TODAY IS YESTERDAY...
IF TOMORROW IS ALREADY TODAY, CHARLIE BROWN, THERE'S NO WAY THAT TOMORROW CAN BE A BETTER DAY
YOU'RE A LOT OF FUN TO HAVE AROUND
SCHULZ
8-12

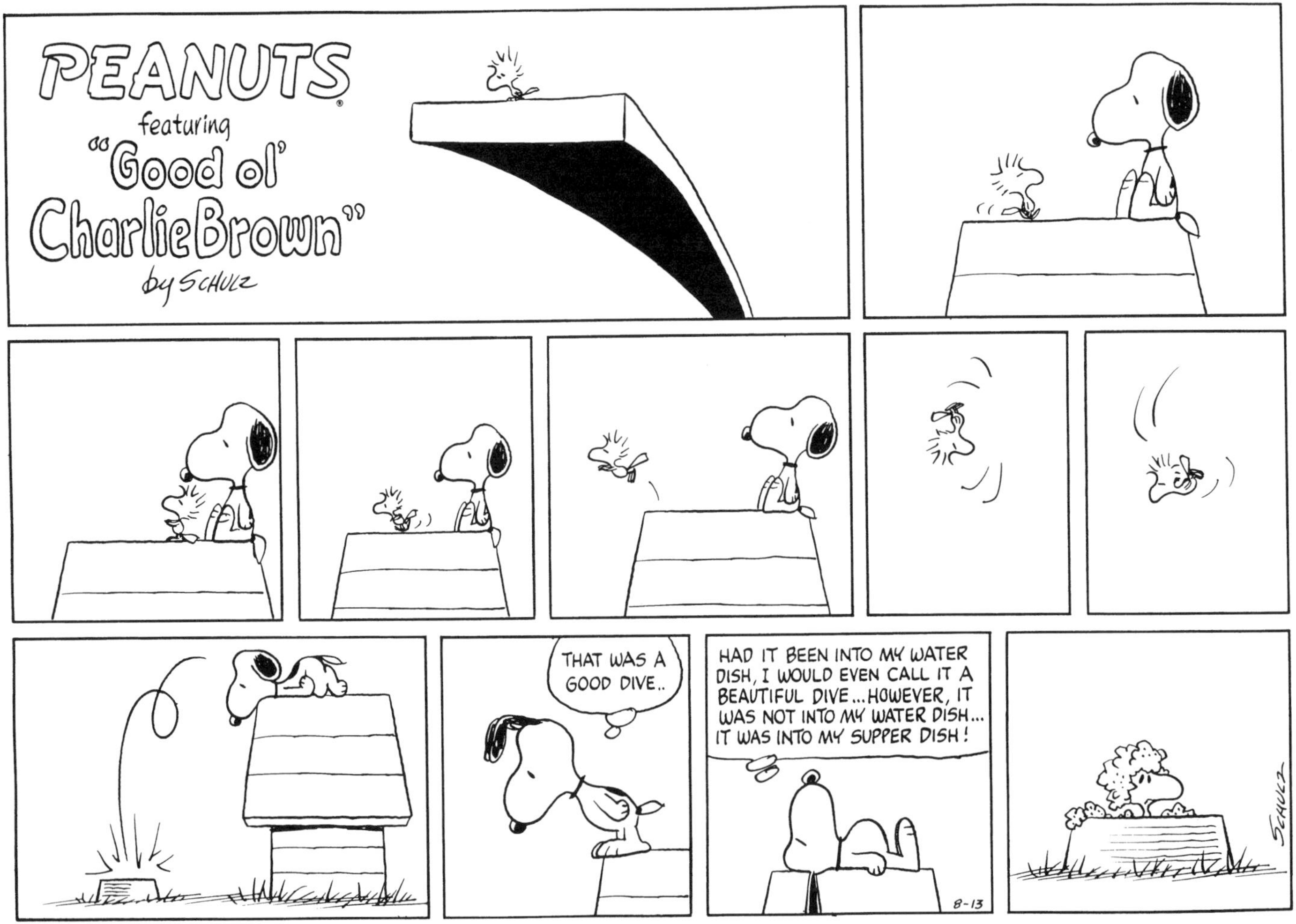
PEANUTS
featuring
"Good ol' Charlie Brown"
by SCHULZ
THAT WAS A GOOD DIVE..
HAD IT BEEN INTO MY WATER DISH, I WOULD EVEN CALL IT A BEAUTIFUL DIVE...HOWEVER, IT WAS NOT INTO MY WATER DISH... IT WAS INTO MY SUPPER DISH!
8-13
SCHULZ

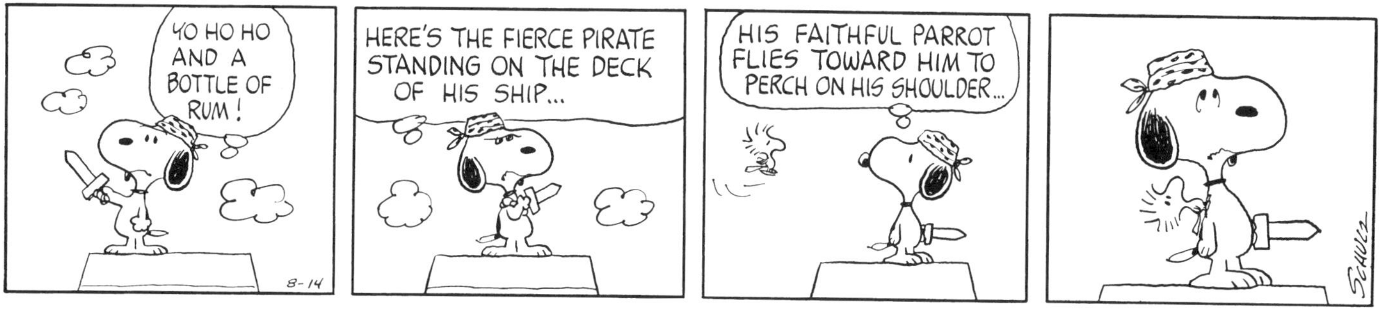
YO HO HO AND A BOTTLE OF RUM!
8-14
HERE'S THE FIERCE PIRATE STANDING ON THE DECK OF HIS SHIP...
HIS FAITHFUL PARROT FLIES TOWARD HIM TO PERCH ON HIS SHOULDER...
SCHULZ

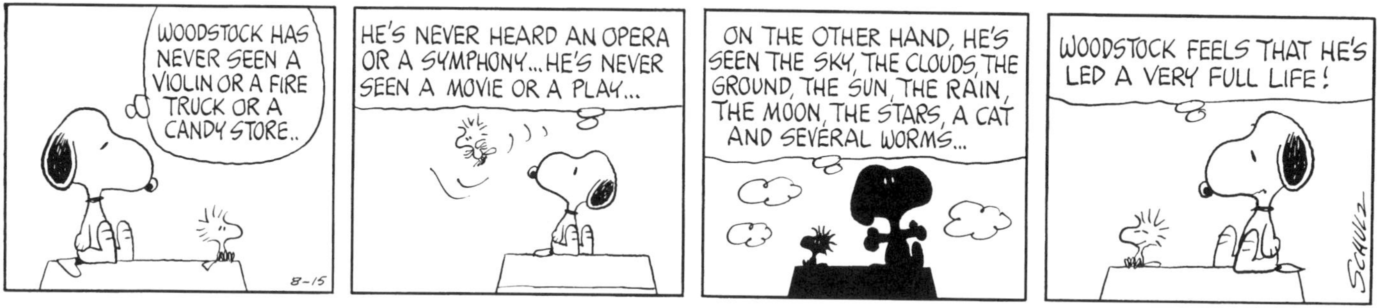
WOODSTOCK HAS NEVER SEEN A VIOLIN OR A FIRE TRUCK OR A CANDY STORE..
8-15
HE'S NEVER HEARD AN OPERA OR A SYMPHONY... HE'S NEVER SEEN A MOVIE OR A PLAY...
ON THE OTHER HAND, HE'S SEEN THE SKY, THE CLOUDS, THE GROUND, THE SUN, THE RAIN, THE MOON, THE STARS, A CAT AND SEVERAL WORMS...
WOODSTOCK FEELS THAT HE'S LED A VERY FULL LIFE!
SCHULZ

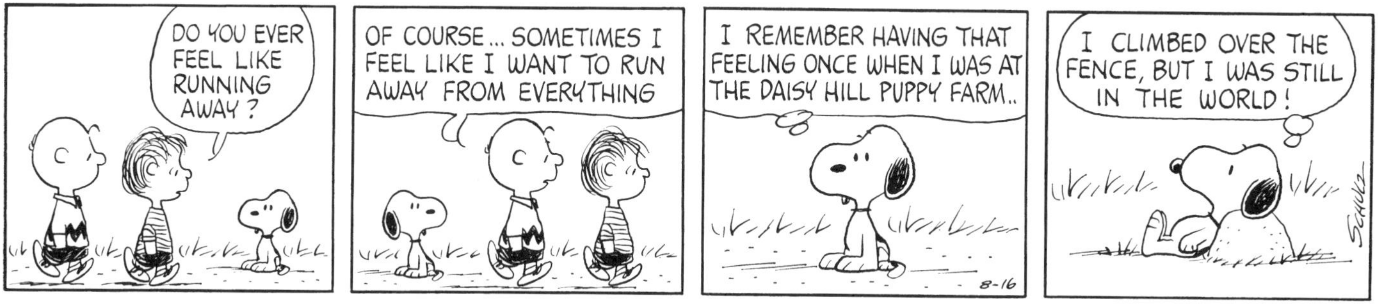
DO YOU EVER FEEL LIKE RUNNING AWAY?
OF COURSE... SOMETIMES I FEEL LIKE I WANT TO RUN AWAY FROM EVERYTHING
I REMEMBER HAVING THAT FEELING ONCE WHEN I WAS AT THE DAISY HILL PUPPY FARM..
8-16
I CLIMBED OVER THE FENCE, BUT I WAS STILL IN THE WORLD!
SCHULZ

I'M TIRED... I ONLY HAD TEN HOURS SLEEP LAST NIGHT

TEN HOURS SHOULD BE PLENTY

NOT FOR ME... I HAVE BIG EYES..

IT'S A MEDICAL FACT THAT PEOPLE WITH BIG EYES NEED MORE SLEEP THAN PEOPLE WITH SMALL EYES...

PEOPLE WITH BIG STOMACHS NEED MORE FOOD, DON'T THEY?

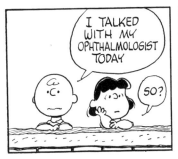

I TALKED WITH MY OPHTHALMOLOGIST TODAY

SO?

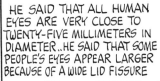

HE SAID THAT ALL HUMAN EYES ARE VERY CLOSE TO TWENTY-FIVE MILLIMETERS IN DIAMETER..HE SAID THAT SOME PEOPLE'S EYES APPEAR LARGER BECAUSE OF A WIDE LID FISSURE

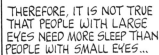

THEREFORE, IT IS NOT TRUE THAT PEOPLE WITH LARGE EYES NEED MORE SLEEP THAN PEOPLE WITH SMALL EYES...

I KNOW A KID IN SCHOOL WHO BELONGS TO FOUR BOOK CLUBS!

RATS! I NEVER FIND ANY ARROWHEADS!

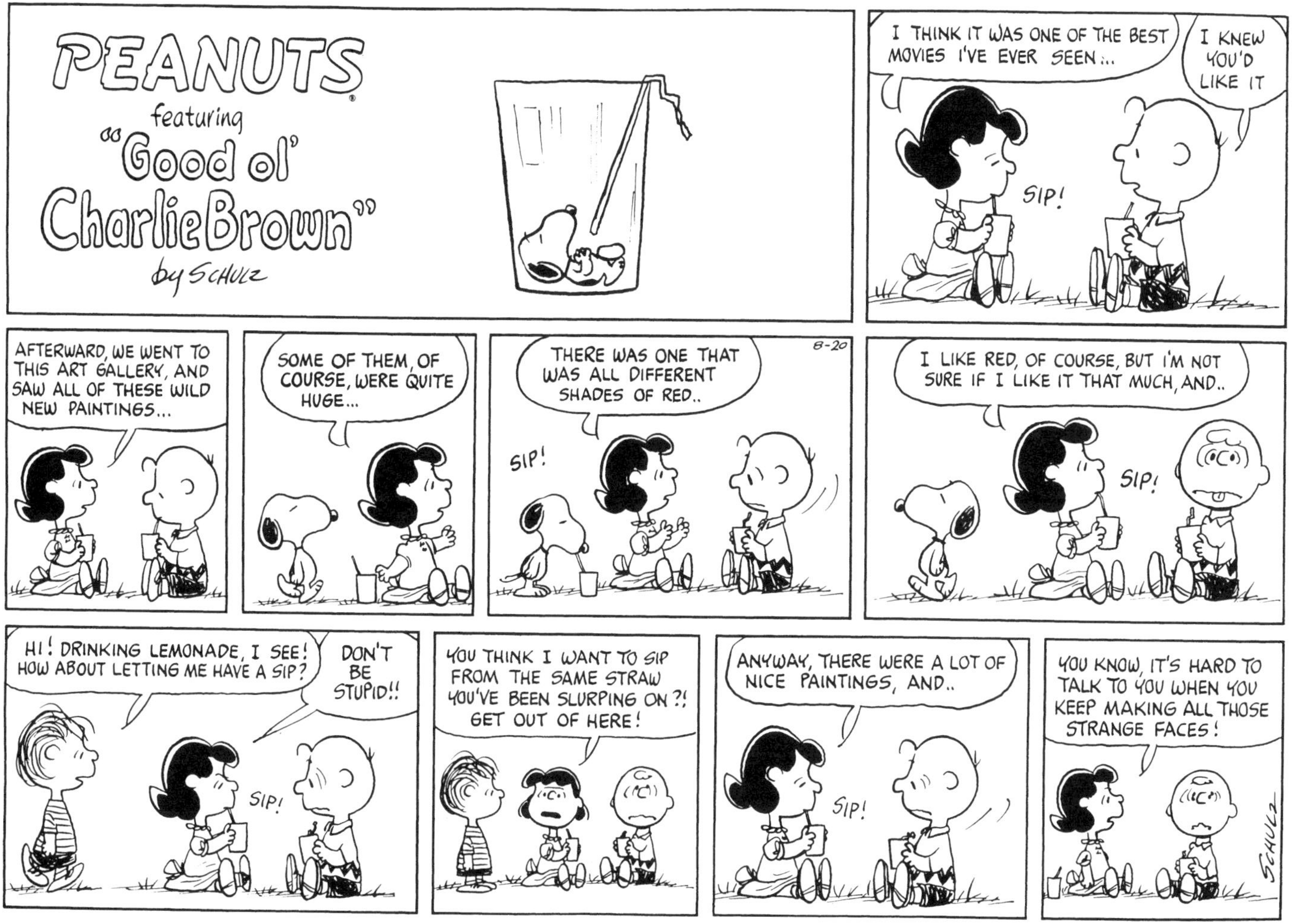
PEANUTS
featuring "Good ol' CharlieBrown"
by SCHULZ
I THINK IT WAS ONE OF THE BEST MOVIES I'VE EVER SEEN...
I KNEW YOU'D LIKE IT
SIP!
AFTERWARD, WE WENT TO THIS ART GALLERY, AND SAW ALL OF THESE WILD NEW PAINTINGS...
SOME OF THEM, OF COURSE, WERE QUITE HUGE...
8-20
THERE WAS ONE THAT WAS ALL DIFFERENT SHADES OF RED..
SIP!
I LIKE RED, OF COURSE, BUT I'M NOT SURE IF I LIKE IT THAT MUCH, AND..
SIP!
HI! DRINKING LEMONADE, I SEE! HOW ABOUT LETTING ME HAVE A SIP?
DON'T BE STUPID!!
SIP!
YOU THINK I WANT TO SIP FROM THE SAME STRAW YOU'VE BEEN SLURPING ON?! GET OUT OF HERE!
ANYWAY, THERE WERE A LOT OF NICE PAINTINGS, AND..
SIP!
SCHULZ
YOU KNOW, IT'S HARD TO TALK TO YOU WHEN YOU KEEP MAKING ALL THOSE STRANGE FACES!

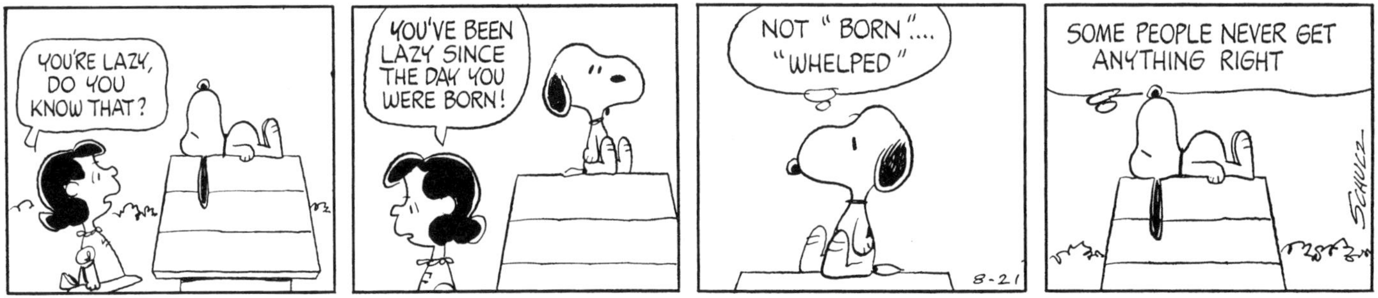
YOU'RE LAZY, DO YOU KNOW THAT?
YOU'VE BEEN LAZY SINCE THE DAY YOU WERE BORN!
NOT "BORN"... "WHELPED"
8-21
SOME PEOPLE NEVER GET ANYTHING RIGHT
SCHULZ

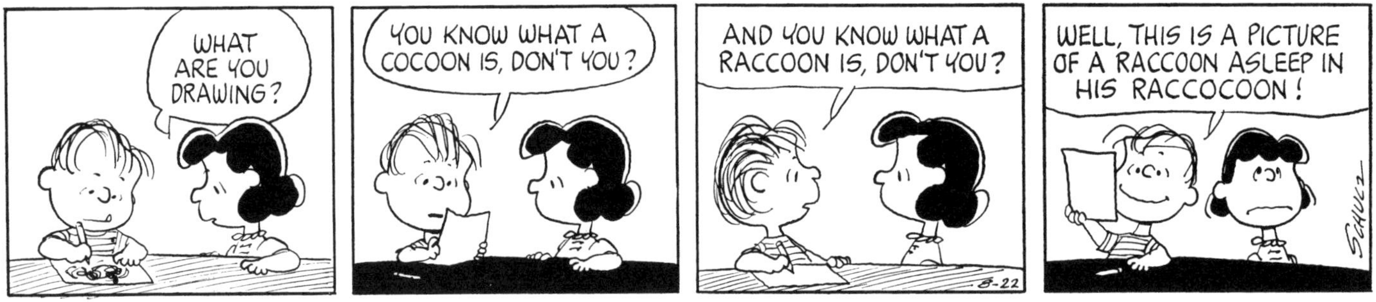
WHAT ARE YOU DRAWING?
YOU KNOW WHAT A COCOON IS, DON'T YOU?
AND YOU KNOW WHAT A RACCOON IS, DON'T YOU?
8-22
WELL, THIS IS A PICTURE OF A RACCOON ASLEEP IN HIS RACCOCOON!
SCHULZ

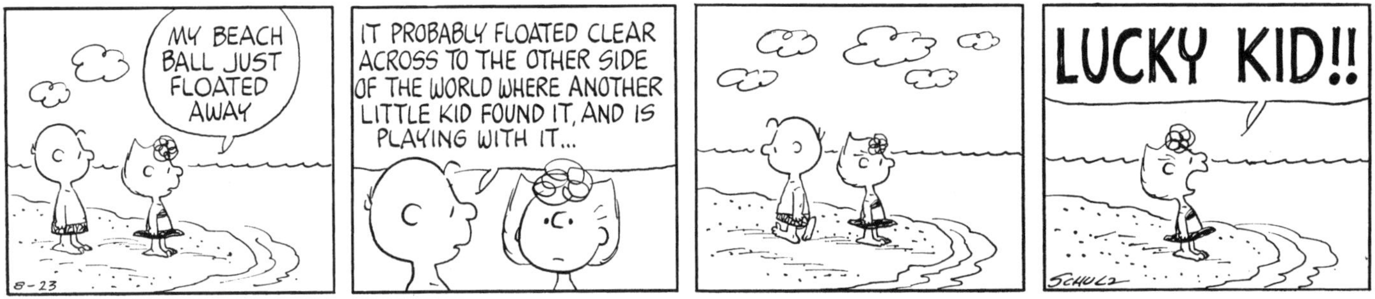
MY BEACH BALL JUST FLOATED AWAY
8-23
IT PROBABLY FLOATED CLEAR ACROSS TO THE OTHER SIDE OF THE WORLD WHERE ANOTHER LITTLE KID FOUND IT, AND IS PLAYING WITH IT...
LUCKY KID!!
SCHULZ

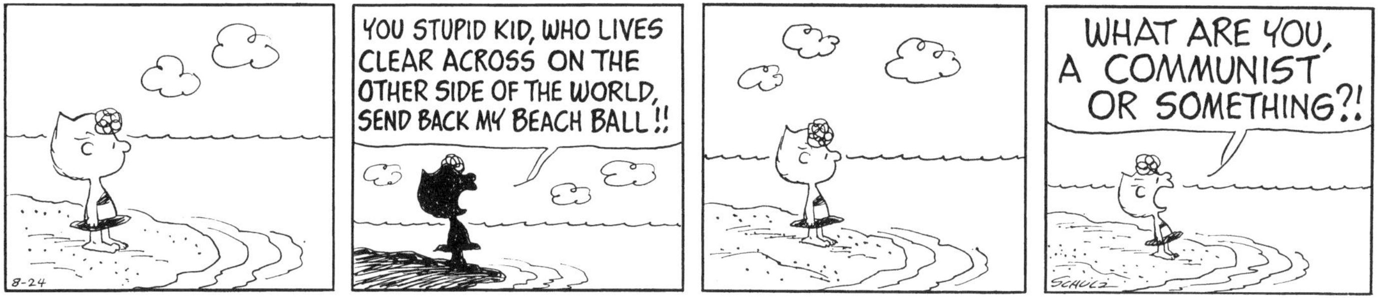
8-24
YOU STUPID KID, WHO LIVES CLEAR ACROSS ON THE OTHER SIDE OF THE WORLD, SEND BACK MY BEACH BALL!!
WHAT ARE YOU, A COMMUNIST OR SOMETHING?!
SCHULZ

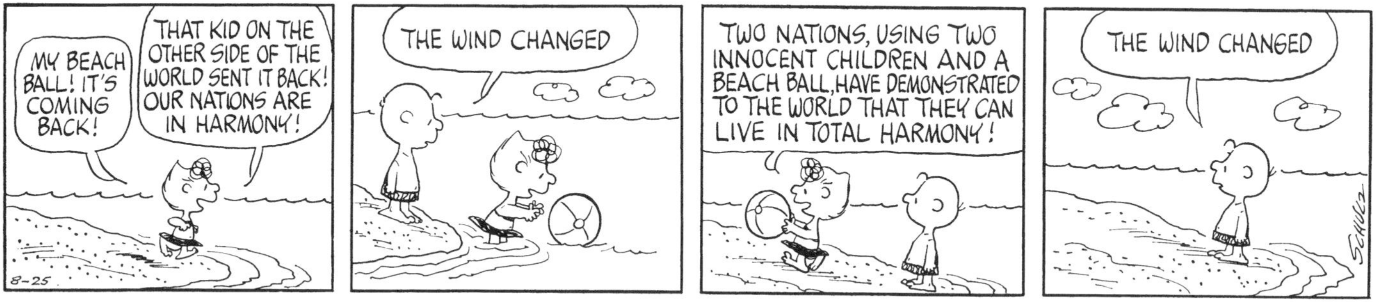
MY BEACH BALL! IT'S COMING BACK!
THAT KID ON THE OTHER SIDE OF THE WORLD SENT IT BACK! OUR NATIONS ARE IN HARMONY!
8-25
THE WIND CHANGED
TWO NATIONS, USING TWO INNOCENT CHILDREN AND A BEACH BALL, HAVE DEMONSTRATED TO THE WORLD THAT THEY CAN LIVE IN TOTAL HARMONY!
THE WIND CHANGED
SCHULZ

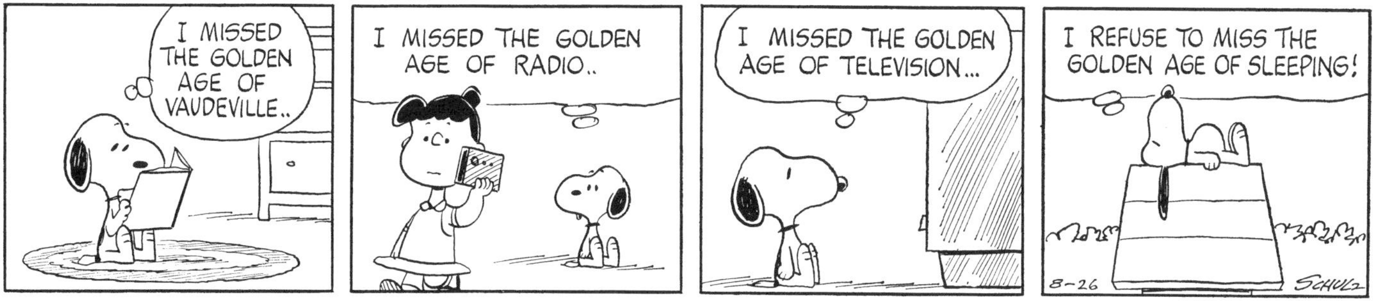
I MISSED THE GOLDEN AGE OF VAUDEVILLE..
I MISSED THE GOLDEN AGE OF RADIO..
I MISSED THE GOLDEN AGE OF TELEVISION...
I REFUSE TO MISS THE GOLDEN AGE OF SLEEPING!
8-26
SCHULZ

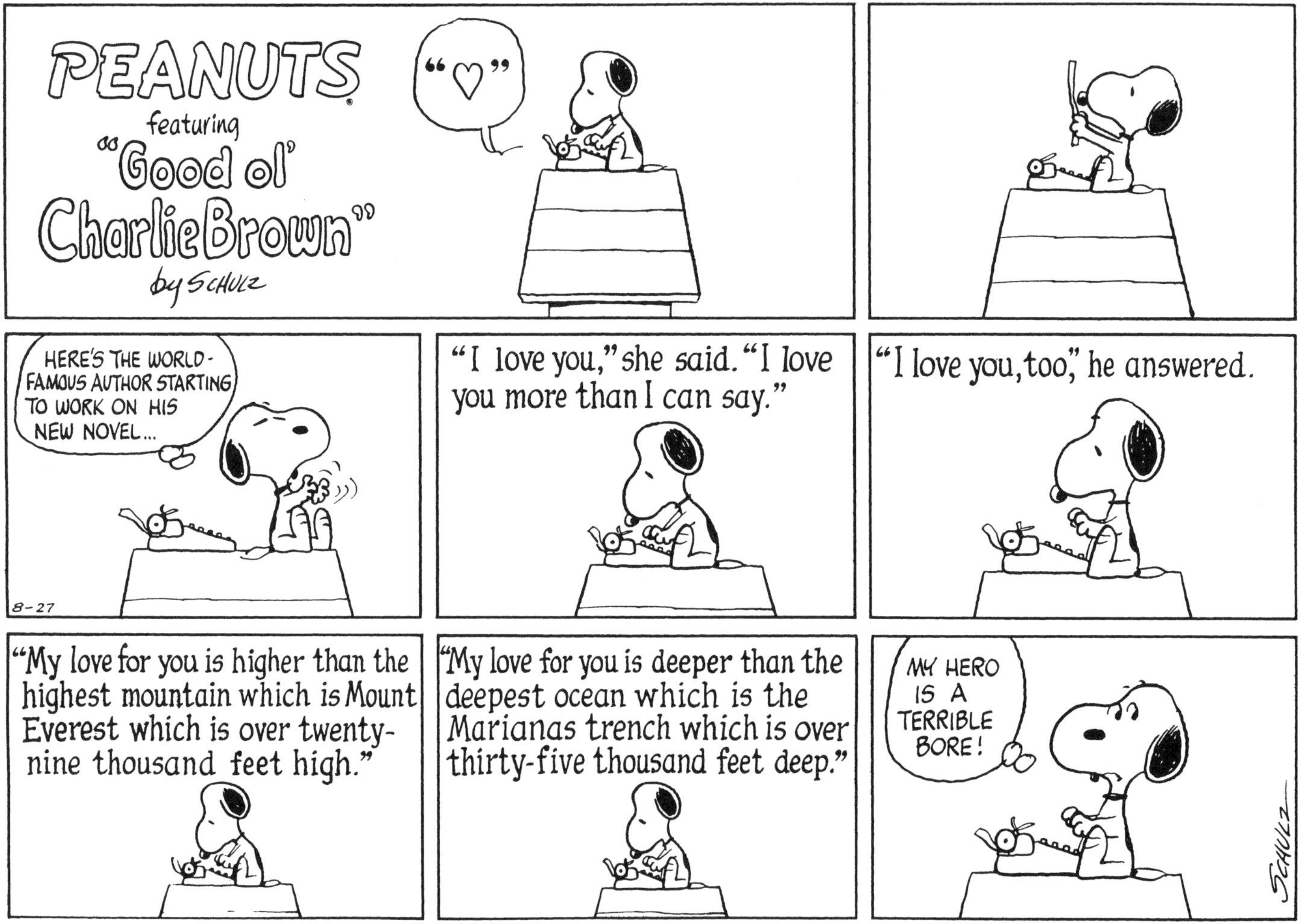
PEANUTS
featuring
"Good ol' CharlieBrown"
by SCHULZ
"♡"
HERE'S THE WORLD-FAMOUS AUTHOR STARTING TO WORK ON HIS NEW NOVEL...
8-27
"I love you," she said. "I love you more than I can say."
"I love you, too," he answered.
"My love for you is higher than the highest mountain which is Mount Everest which is over twenty-nine thousand feet high."
"My love for you is deeper than the deepest ocean which is the Marianas trench which is over thirty-five thousand feet deep."
MY HERO IS A TERRIBLE BORE!
SCHULZ

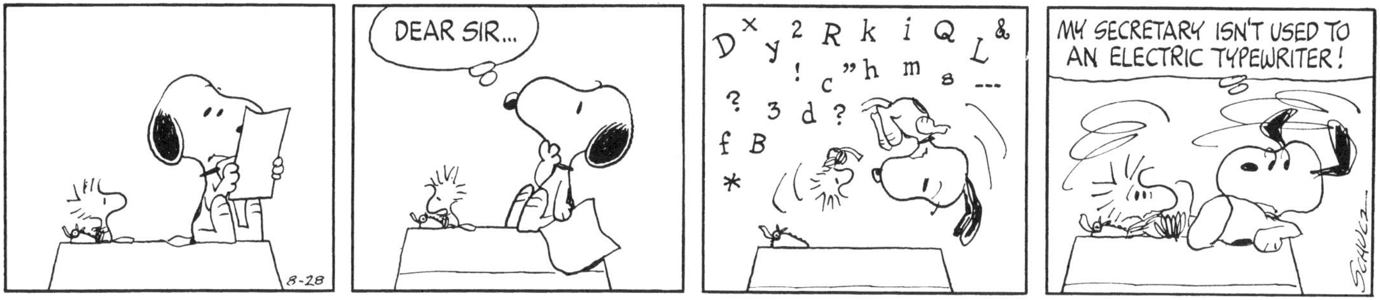
8-28
DEAR SIR...
D x y 2 R k i Q & L
! c " h m s ---
? 3 d ?
f B
*
MY SECRETARY ISN'T USED TO AN ELECTRIC TYPEWRITER!
SCHULZ

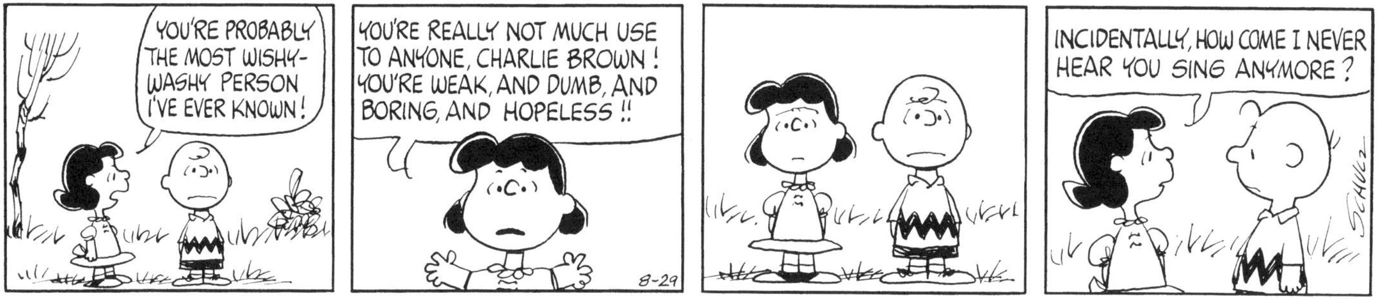
YOU'RE PROBABLY THE MOST WISHY-WASHY PERSON I'VE EVER KNOWN!
YOU'RE REALLY NOT MUCH USE TO ANYONE, CHARLIE BROWN! YOU'RE WEAK, AND DUMB, AND BORING, AND HOPELESS!!
8-29
INCIDENTALLY, HOW COME I NEVER HEAR YOU SING ANYMORE?
SCHULZ

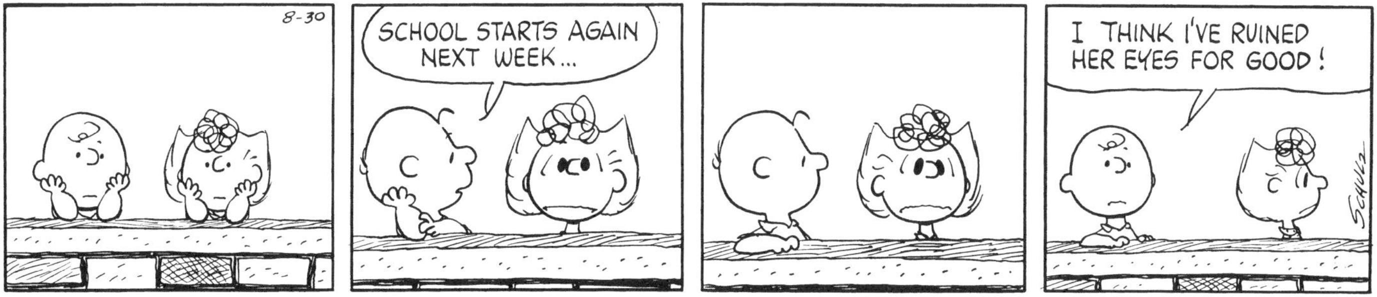
8-30
SCHOOL STARTS AGAIN NEXT WEEK...
I THINK I'VE RUINED HER EYES FOR GOOD!
SCHULZ

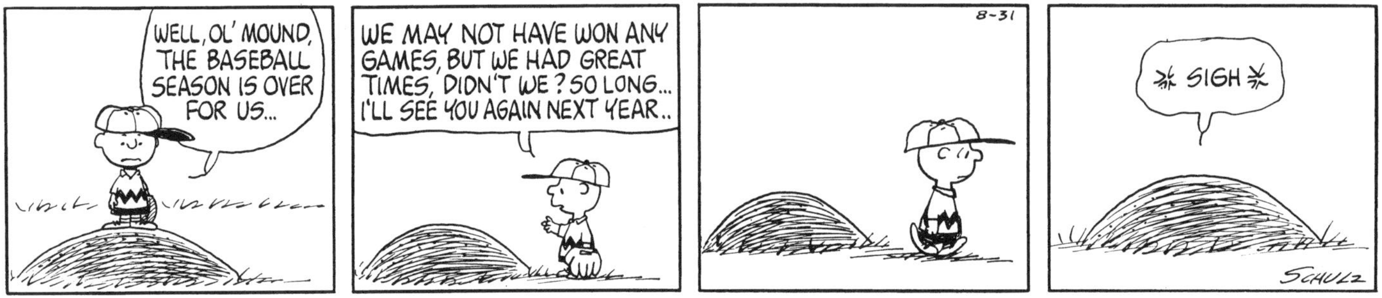
WELL, OL' MOUND, THE BASEBALL SEASON IS OVER FOR US...
WE MAY NOT HAVE WON ANY GAMES, BUT WE HAD GREAT TIMES, DIDN'T WE? SO LONG... I'LL SEE YOU AGAIN NEXT YEAR..
8-31
SIGH
SCHULZ

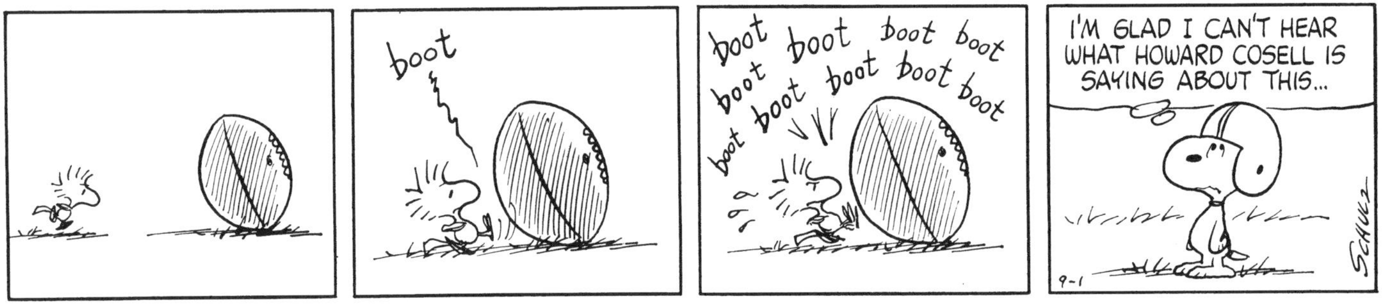
boot
boot boot boot boot boot boot boot boot boot boot
I'M GLAD I CAN'T HEAR WHAT HOWARD COSELL IS SAYING ABOUT THIS...
9-1
SCHULZ

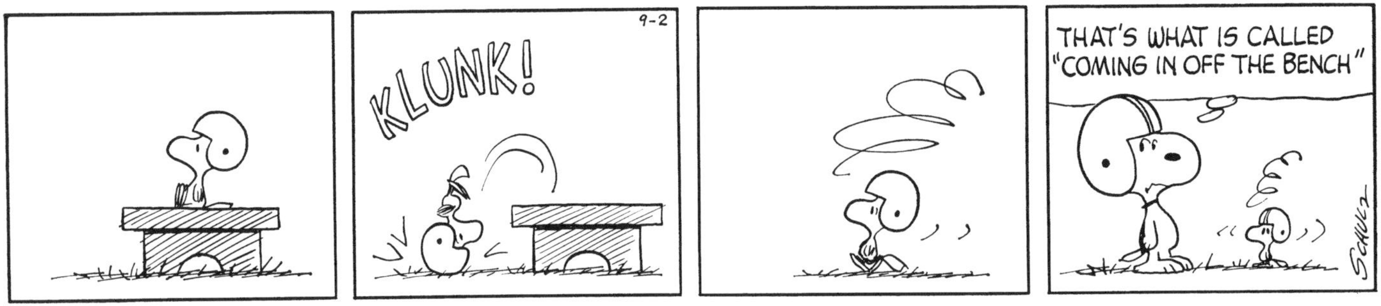
9-2
KLUNK!
THAT'S WHAT IS CALLED "COMING IN OFF THE BENCH"
SCHULZ

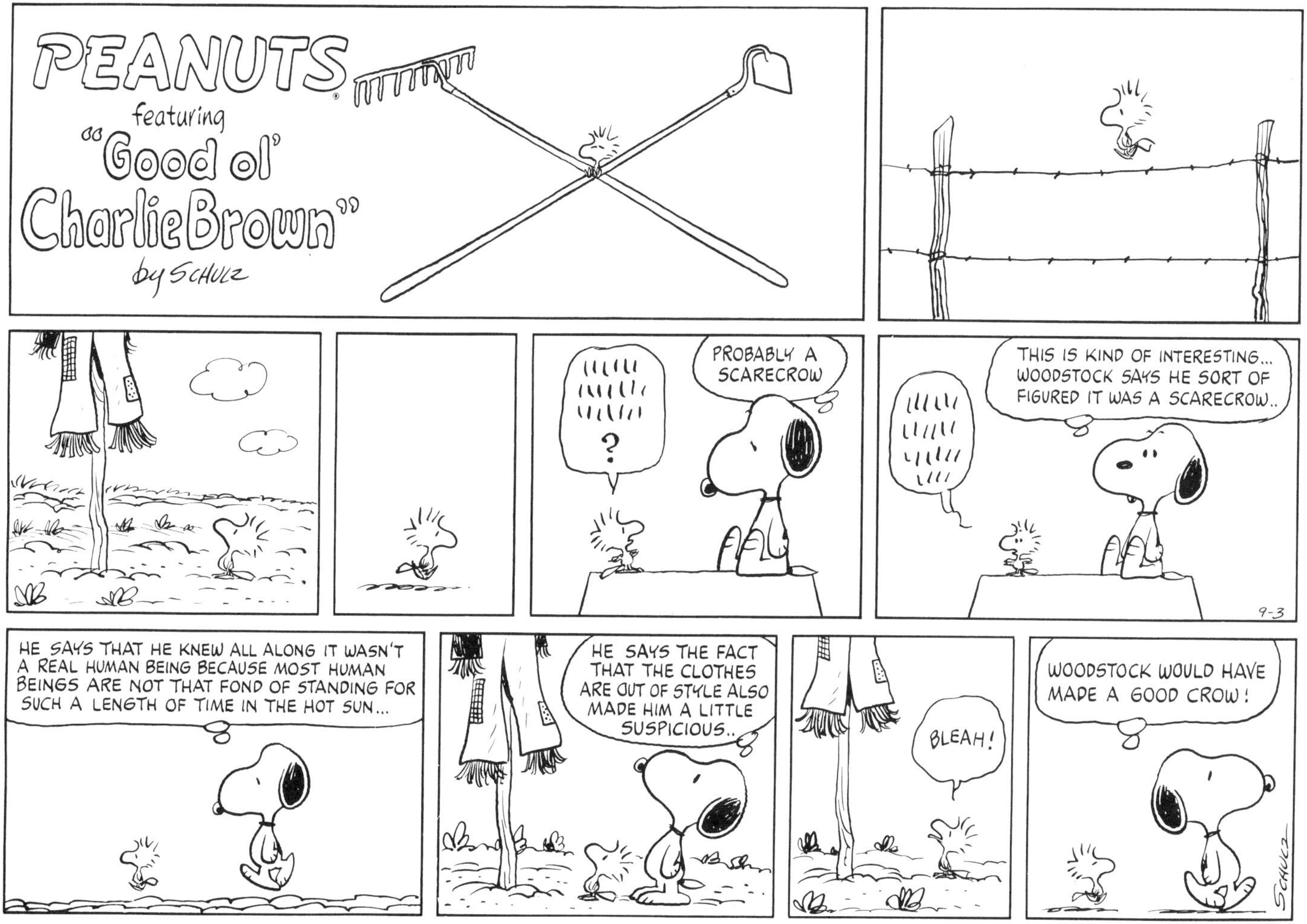
PEANUTS
featuring
"Good ol' Charlie Brown"
by SCHULZ
?
PROBABLY A SCARECROW
THIS IS KIND OF INTERESTING... WOODSTOCK SAYS HE SORT OF FIGURED IT WAS A SCARECROW..
9-3
HE SAYS THAT HE KNEW ALL ALONG IT WASN'T A REAL HUMAN BEING BECAUSE MOST HUMAN BEINGS ARE NOT THAT FOND OF STANDING FOR SUCH A LENGTH OF TIME IN THE HOT SUN...
HE SAYS THE FACT THAT THE CLOTHES ARE OUT OF STYLE ALSO MADE HIM A LITTLE SUSPICIOUS..
BLEAH!
WOODSTOCK WOULD HAVE MADE A GOOD CROW!
SCHULZ

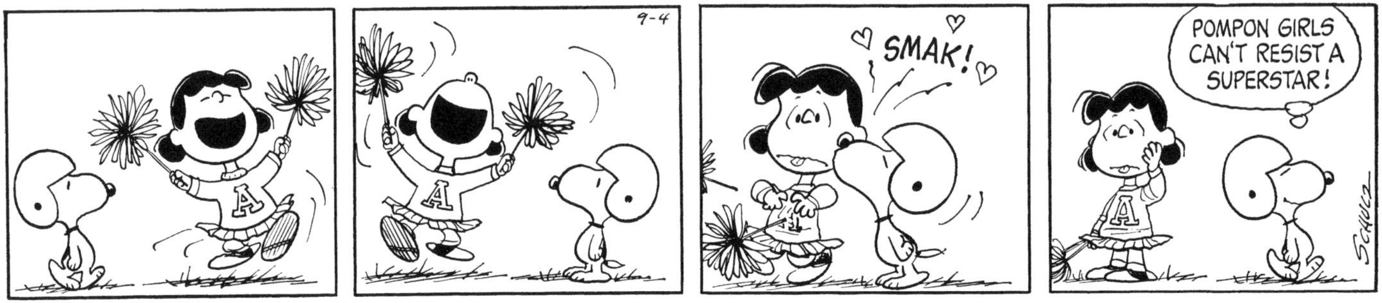
9-4
SMAK!
POMPON GIRLS CAN'T RESIST A SUPERSTAR!

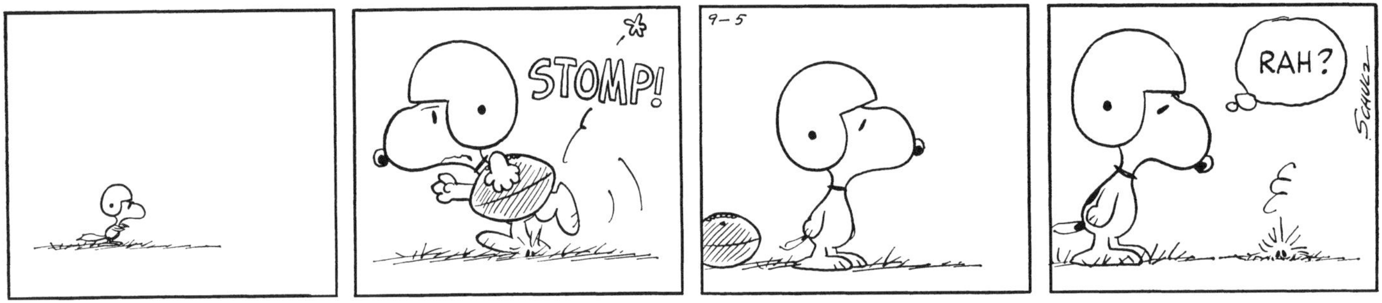
STOMP!
9-5
RAH?

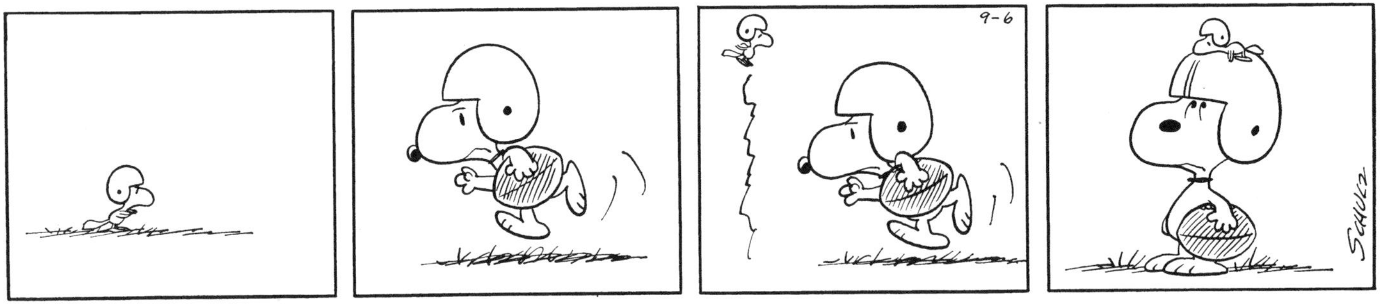
9-6

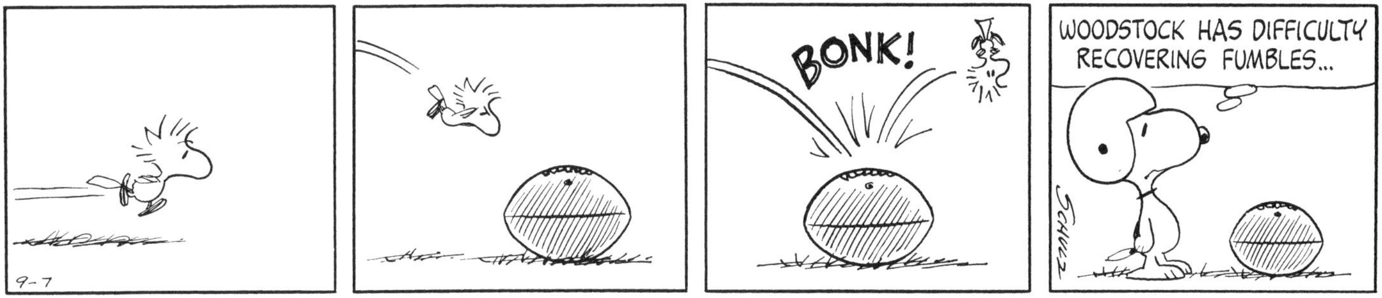
9-7
BONK!
WOODSTOCK HAS DIFFICULTY RECOVERING FUMBLES...
SCHULZ

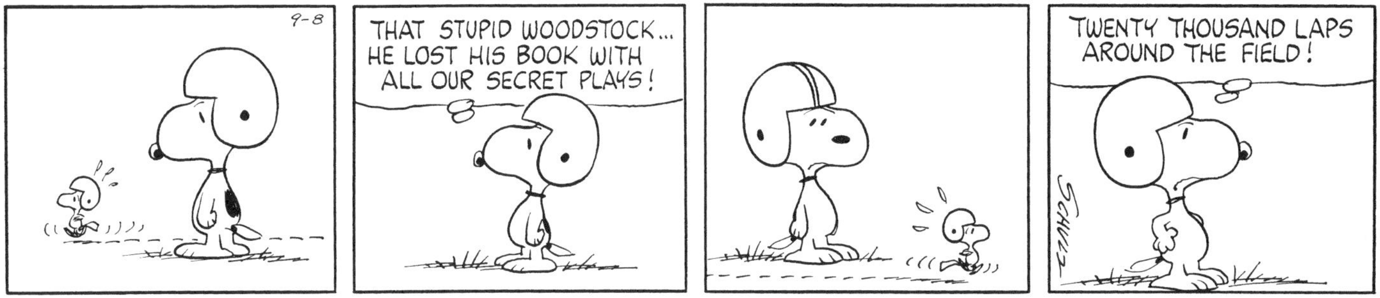
9-8
THAT STUPID WOODSTOCK... HE LOST HIS BOOK WITH ALL OUR SECRET PLAYS!
TWENTY THOUSAND LAPS AROUND THE FIELD!
SCHULZ

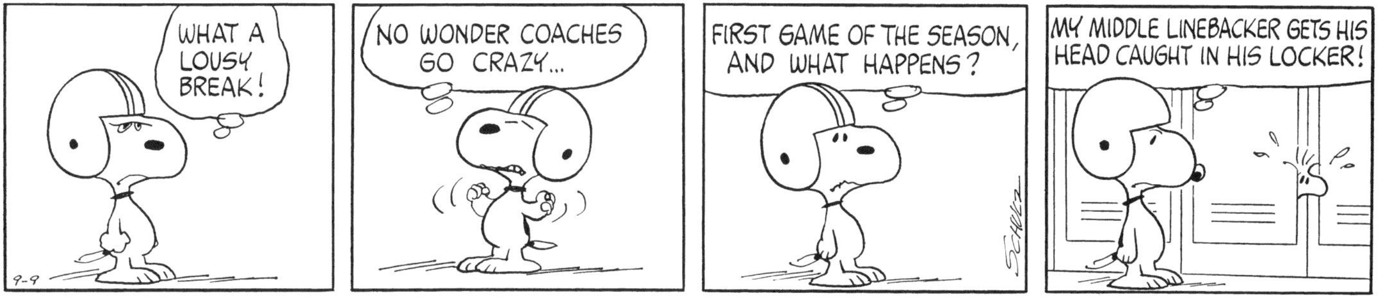
WHAT A LOUSY BREAK!
9-9
NO WONDER COACHES GO CRAZY...
FIRST GAME OF THE SEASON, AND WHAT HAPPENS?
SCHULZ
MY MIDDLE LINEBACKER GETS HIS HEAD CAUGHT IN HIS LOCKER!

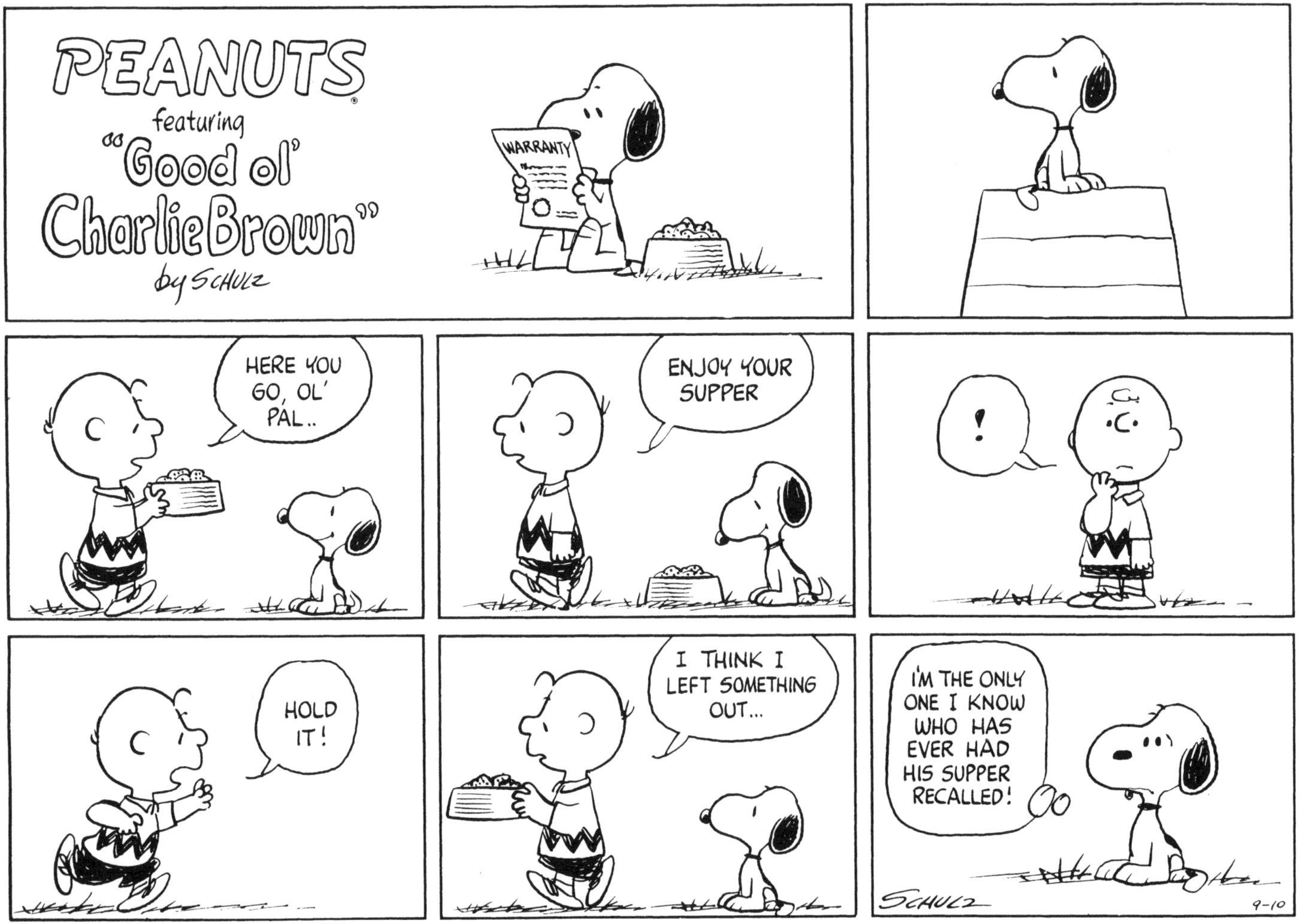
PEANUTS
featuring
"Good ol' Charlie Brown"
by SCHULZ
WARRANTY
HERE YOU GO, OL' PAL..
ENJOY YOUR SUPPER
!
HOLD IT!
I THINK I LEFT SOMETHING OUT...
I'M THE ONLY ONE I KNOW WHO HAS EVER HAD HIS SUPPER RECALLED!
SCHULZ
9-10

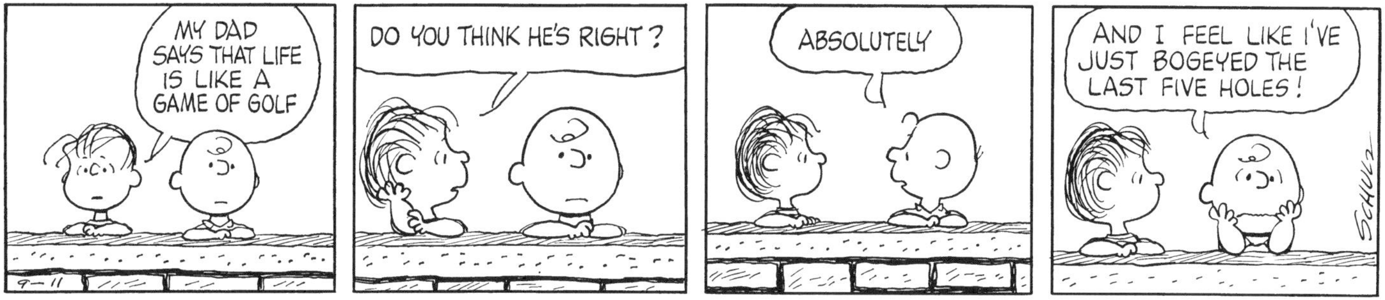
MY DAD SAYS THAT LIFE IS LIKE A GAME OF GOLF
9-11
DO YOU THINK HE'S RIGHT?
ABSOLUTELY
AND I FEEL LIKE I'VE JUST BOGEYED THE LAST FIVE HOLES!
SCHULZ

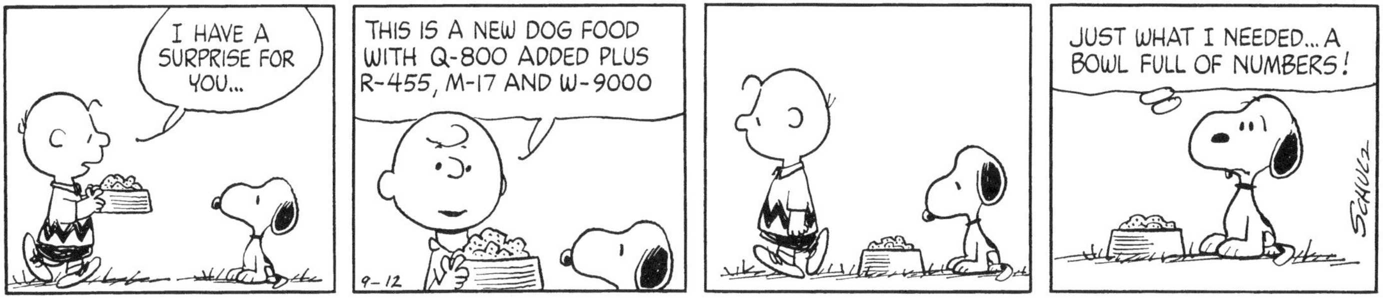
I HAVE A SURPRISE FOR YOU...
THIS IS A NEW DOG FOOD WITH Q-800 ADDED PLUS R-455, M-17 AND W-9000
9-12
JUST WHAT I NEEDED... A BOWL FULL OF NUMBERS!
SCHULZ

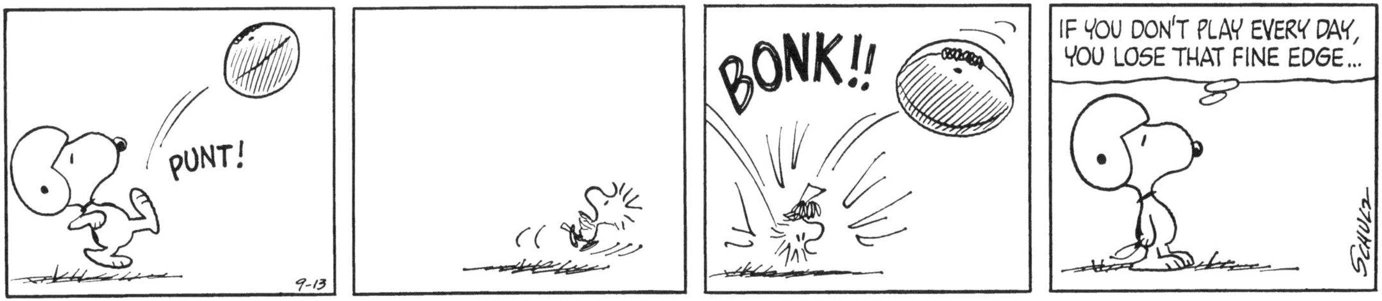
PUNT!
9-13
BONK!!
IF YOU DON'T PLAY EVERY DAY, YOU LOSE THAT FINE EDGE...
SCHULZ

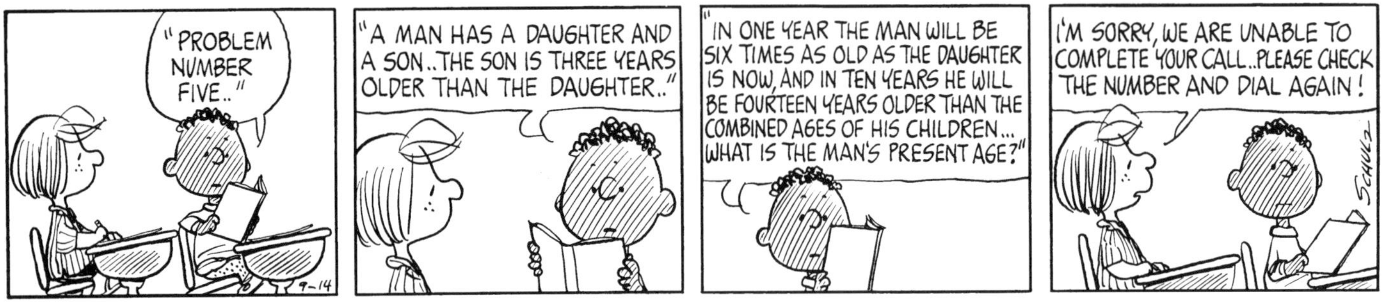
"PROBLEM NUMBER FIVE.."
"A MAN HAS A DAUGHTER AND A SON..THE SON IS THREE YEARS OLDER THAN THE DAUGHTER.."
"IN ONE YEAR THE MAN WILL BE SIX TIMES AS OLD AS THE DAUGHTER IS NOW, AND IN TEN YEARS HE WILL BE FOURTEEN YEARS OLDER THAN THE COMBINED AGES OF HIS CHILDREN... WHAT IS THE MAN'S PRESENT AGE?"
I'M SORRY, WE ARE UNABLE TO COMPLETE YOUR CALL..PLEASE CHECK THE NUMBER AND DIAL AGAIN!
9-14
SCHULZ

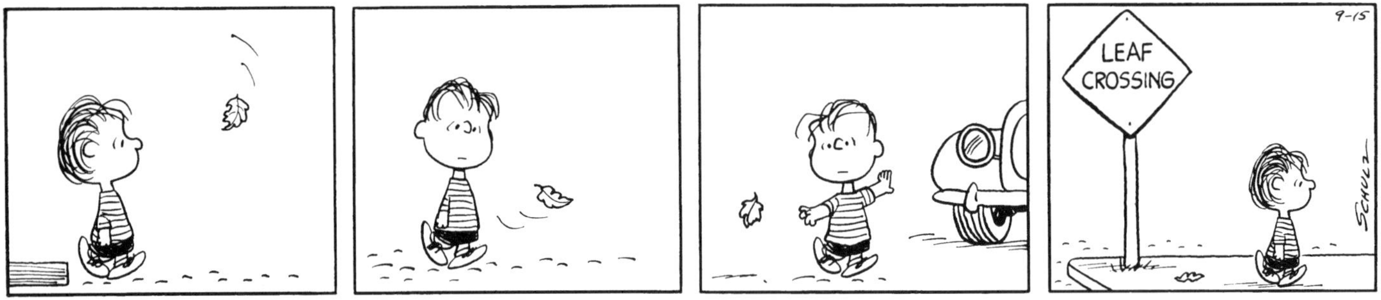
9-15
LEAF CROSSING
SCHULZ

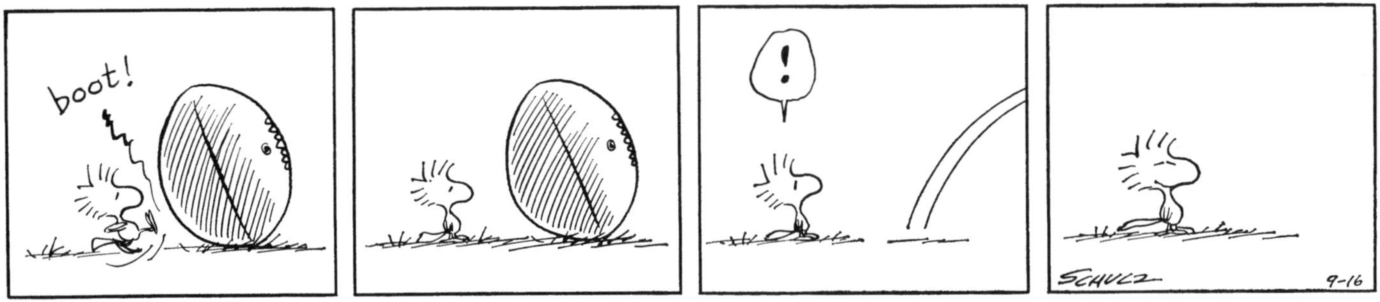
boot!
!
SCHULZ
9-16

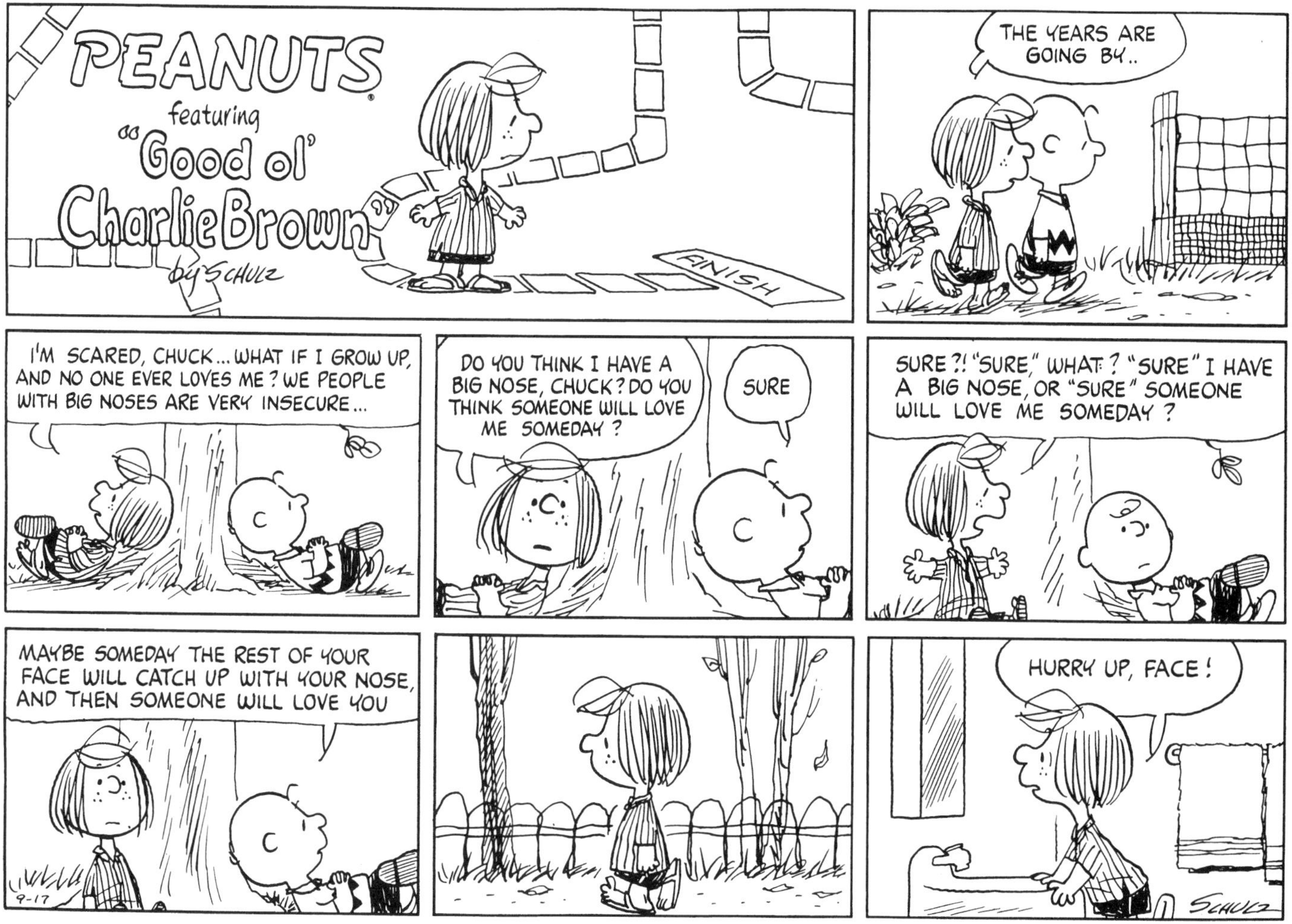
PEANUTS
featuring
"Good ol' CharlieBrown"
by SCHULZ
FINISH
THE YEARS ARE GOING BY..
I'M SCARED, CHUCK... WHAT IF I GROW UP, AND NO ONE EVER LOVES ME? WE PEOPLE WITH BIG NOSES ARE VERY INSECURE...
DO YOU THINK I HAVE A BIG NOSE, CHUCK? DO YOU THINK SOMEONE WILL LOVE ME SOMEDAY?
SURE
SURE?! "SURE," WHAT? "SURE" I HAVE A BIG NOSE, OR "SURE" SOMEONE WILL LOVE ME SOMEDAY?
MAYBE SOMEDAY THE REST OF YOUR FACE WILL CATCH UP WITH YOUR NOSE, AND THEN SOMEONE WILL LOVE YOU
9-17
HURRY UP, FACE!
SCHULZ

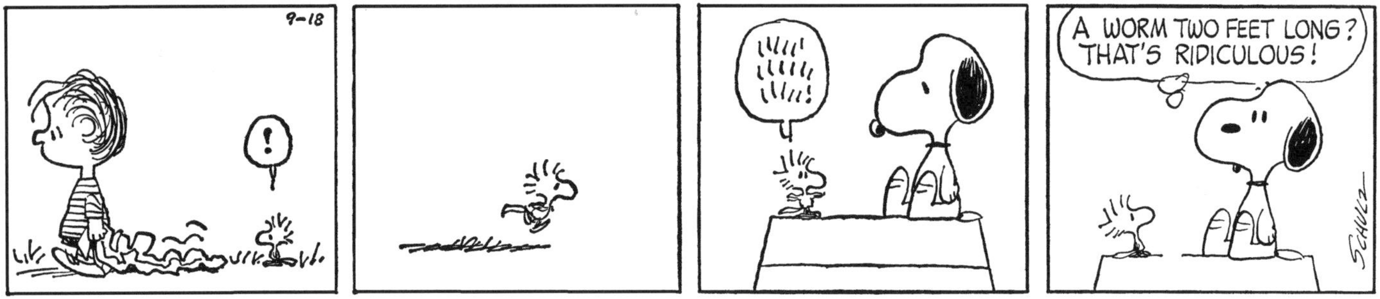
9-18
!
A WORM TWO FEET LONG? THAT'S RIDICULOUS!
SCHULZ

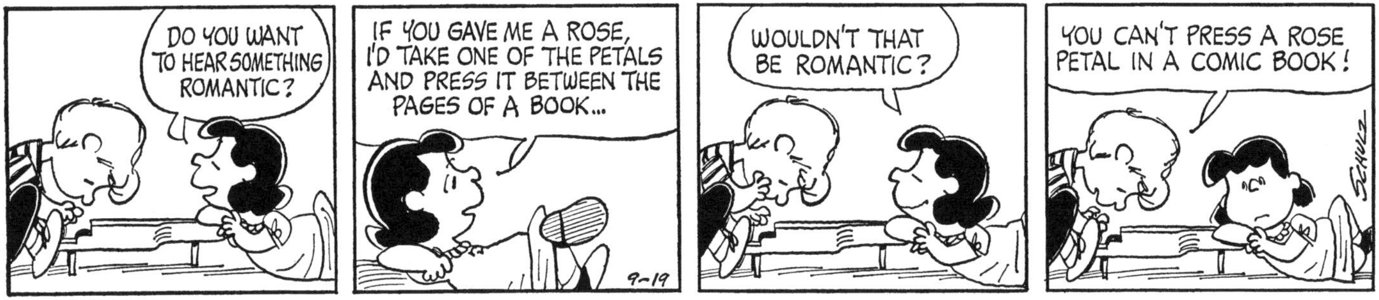
DO YOU WANT TO HEAR SOMETHING ROMANTIC?
IF YOU GAVE ME A ROSE, I'D TAKE ONE OF THE PETALS AND PRESS IT BETWEEN THE PAGES OF A BOOK...
9-19
WOULDN'T THAT BE ROMANTIC?
YOU CAN'T PRESS A ROSE PETAL IN A COMIC BOOK!
SCHULZ

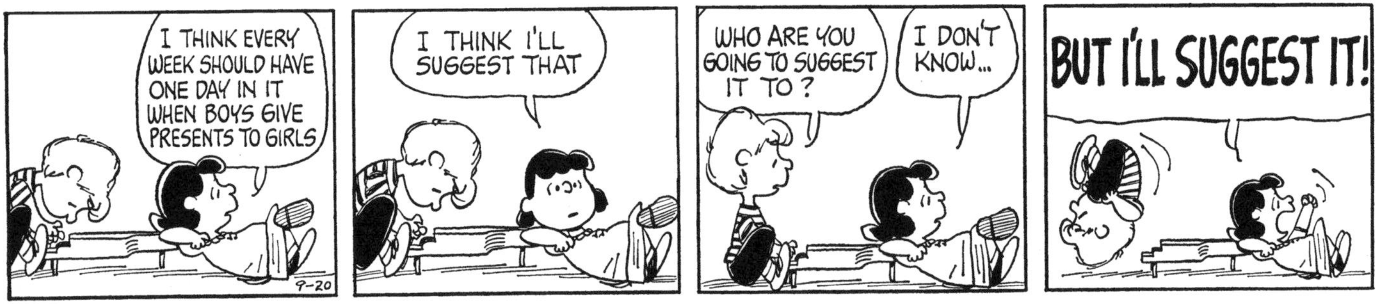
I THINK EVERY WEEK SHOULD HAVE ONE DAY IN IT WHEN BOYS GIVE PRESENTS TO GIRLS
9-20
I THINK I'LL SUGGEST THAT
WHO ARE YOU GOING TO SUGGEST IT TO?
I DON'T KNOW...
BUT I'LL SUGGEST IT!

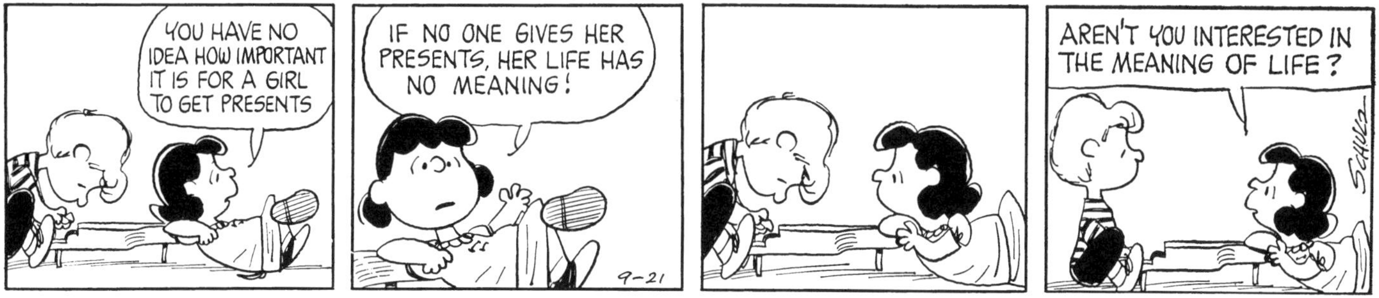
YOU HAVE NO IDEA HOW IMPORTANT IT IS FOR A GIRL TO GET PRESENTS
IF NO ONE GIVES HER PRESENTS, HER LIFE HAS NO MEANING!
9-21
AREN'T YOU INTERESTED IN THE MEANING OF LIFE?
SCHULZ

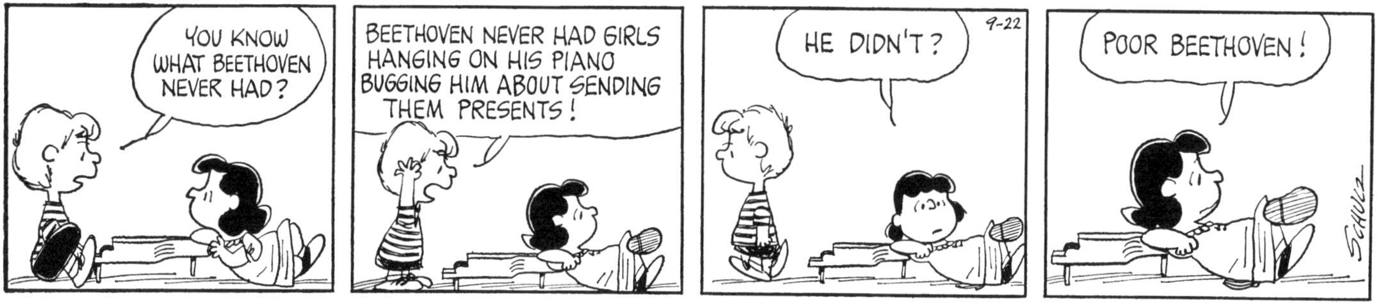
YOU KNOW WHAT BEETHOVEN NEVER HAD?
BEETHOVEN NEVER HAD GIRLS HANGING ON HIS PIANO BUGGING HIM ABOUT SENDING THEM PRESENTS!
9-22
HE DIDN'T?
POOR BEETHOVEN!
SCHULZ

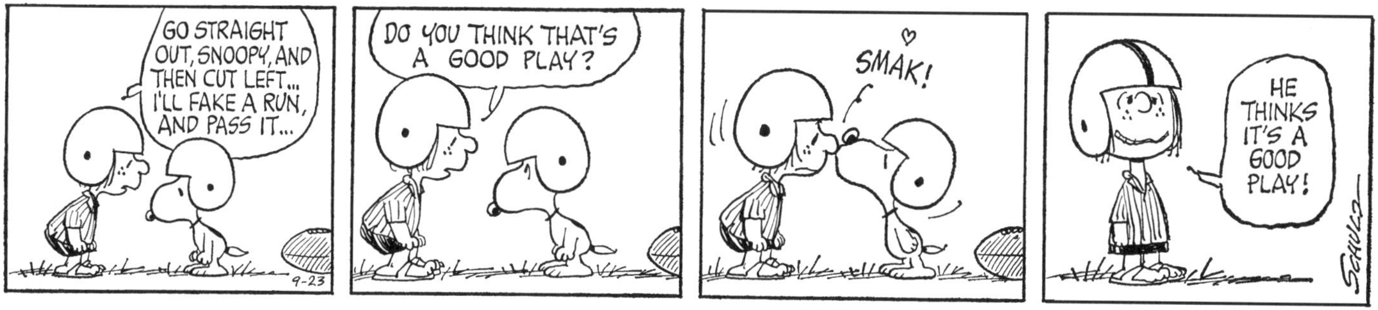
GO STRAIGHT OUT, SNOOPY, AND THEN CUT LEFT... I'LL FAKE A RUN, AND PASS IT...
9-23
DO YOU THINK THAT'S A GOOD PLAY?
SMAK!
HE THINKS IT'S A GOOD PLAY!
SCHULZ

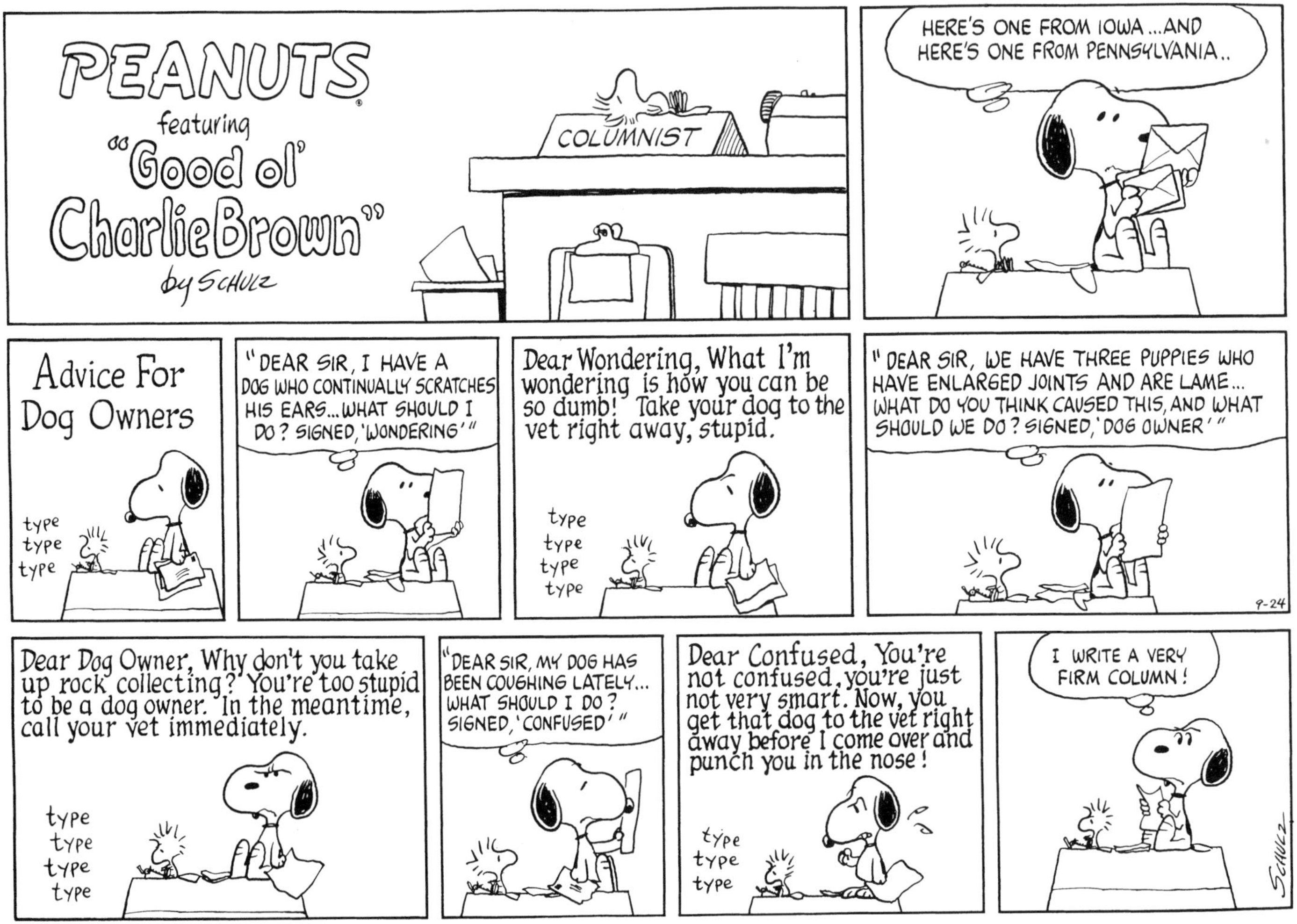
PEANUTS
featuring
"Good ol' Charlie Brown"
by SCHULZ
COLUMNIST
HERE'S ONE FROM IOWA...AND HERE'S ONE FROM PENNSYLVANIA..
Advice For Dog Owners
type
type
type
"DEAR SIR, I HAVE A DOG WHO CONTINUALLY SCRATCHES HIS EARS...WHAT SHOULD I DO? SIGNED, 'WONDERING'"
Dear Wondering, What I'm wondering is how you can be so dumb! Take your dog to the vet right away, stupid.
type
type
type
type
"DEAR SIR, WE HAVE THREE PUPPIES WHO HAVE ENLARGED JOINTS AND ARE LAME... WHAT DO YOU THINK CAUSED THIS, AND WHAT SHOULD WE DO? SIGNED, 'DOG OWNER'"
9-24
Dear Dog Owner, Why don't you take up rock collecting? You're too stupid to be a dog owner. In the meantime, call your vet immediately.
type
type
type
type
"DEAR SIR, MY DOG HAS BEEN COUGHING LATELY... WHAT SHOULD I DO? SIGNED, 'CONFUSED'"
Dear Confused, You're not confused, you're just not very smart. Now, you get that dog to the vet right away before I come over and punch you in the nose!
type
type
type
I WRITE A VERY FIRM COLUMN!
SCHULZ

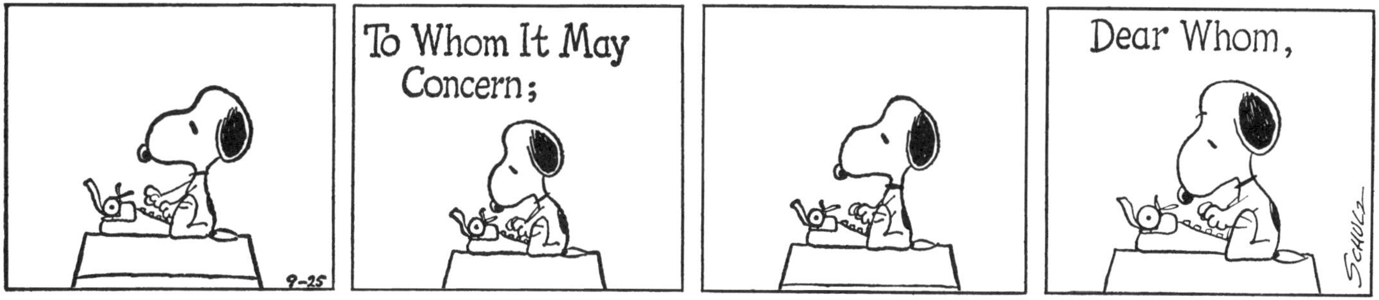

To Whom It May Concern;
Dear Whom,

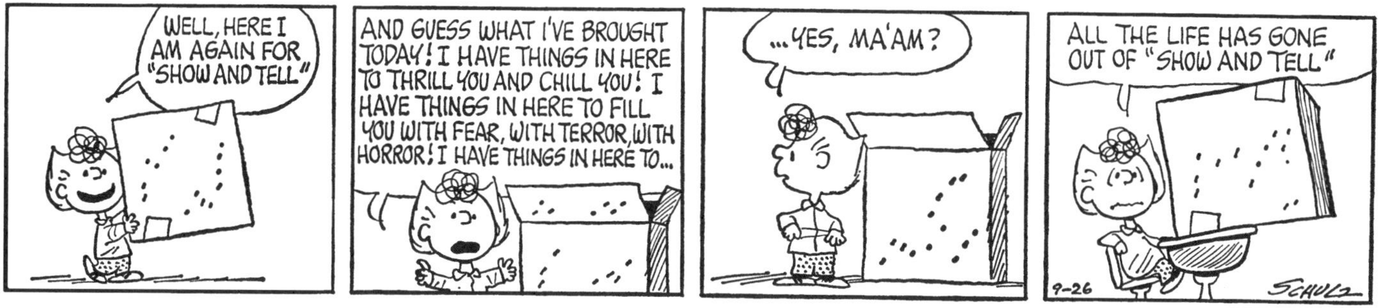

WELL, HERE I AM AGAIN FOR "SHOW AND TELL"
AND GUESS WHAT I'VE BROUGHT TODAY! I HAVE THINGS IN HERE TO THRILL YOU AND CHILL YOU! I HAVE THINGS IN HERE TO FILL YOU WITH FEAR, WITH TERROR, WITH HORROR! I HAVE THINGS IN HERE TO...
...YES, MA'AM?
ALL THE LIFE HAS GONE OUT OF "SHOW AND TELL"

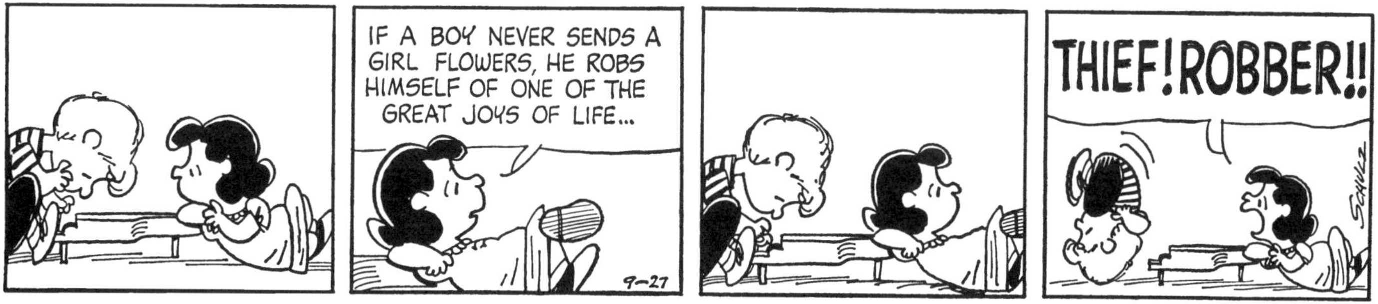

IF A BOY NEVER SENDS A GIRL FLOWERS, HE ROBS HIMSELF OF ONE OF THE GREAT JOYS OF LIFE...
THIEF! ROBBER!!

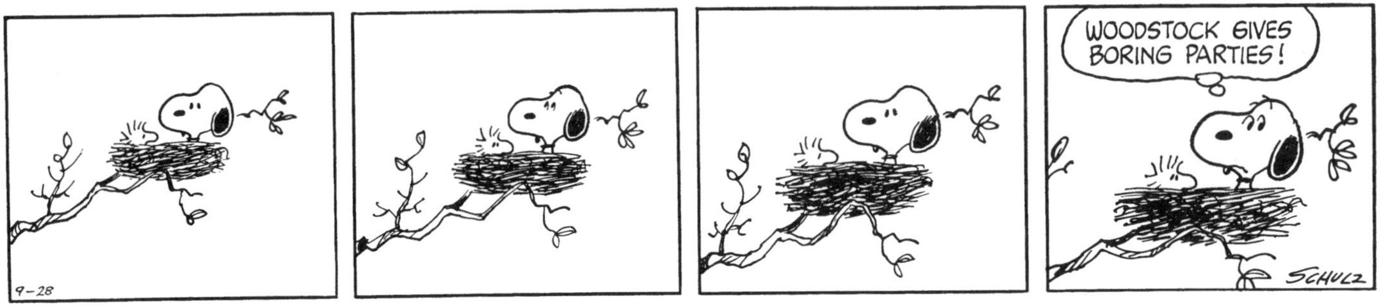
WOODSTOCK GIVES BORING PARTIES!

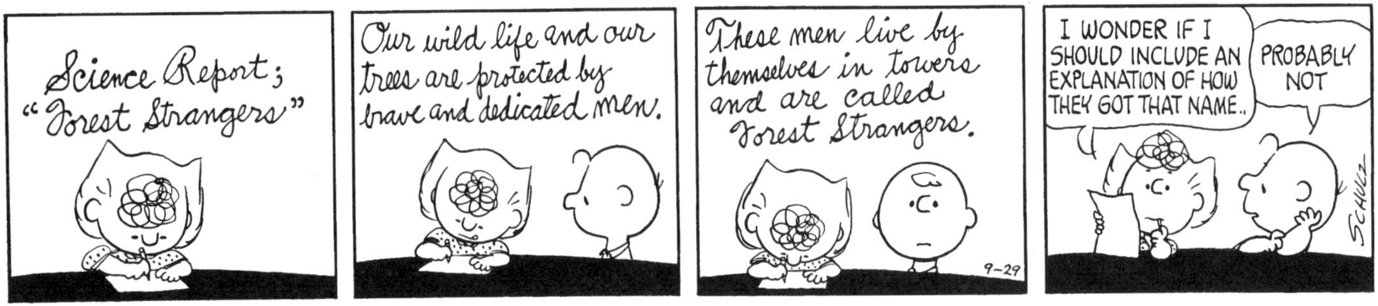
Science Report; "Forest Strangers"
Our wild life and our trees are protected by brave and dedicated men.
These men live by themselves in towers and are called Forest Strangers.
I WONDER IF I SHOULD INCLUDE AN EXPLANATION OF HOW THEY GOT THAT NAME..
PROBABLY NOT

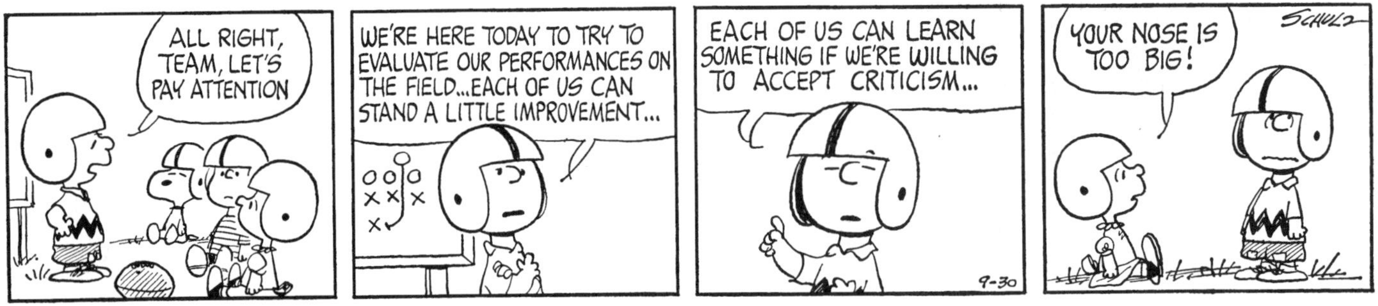
ALL RIGHT, TEAM, LET'S PAY ATTENTION
WE'RE HERE TODAY TO TRY TO EVALUATE OUR PERFORMANCES ON THE FIELD...EACH OF US CAN STAND A LITTLE IMPROVEMENT...
EACH OF US CAN LEARN SOMETHING IF WE'RE WILLING TO ACCEPT CRITICISM...
YOUR NOSE IS TOO BIG!

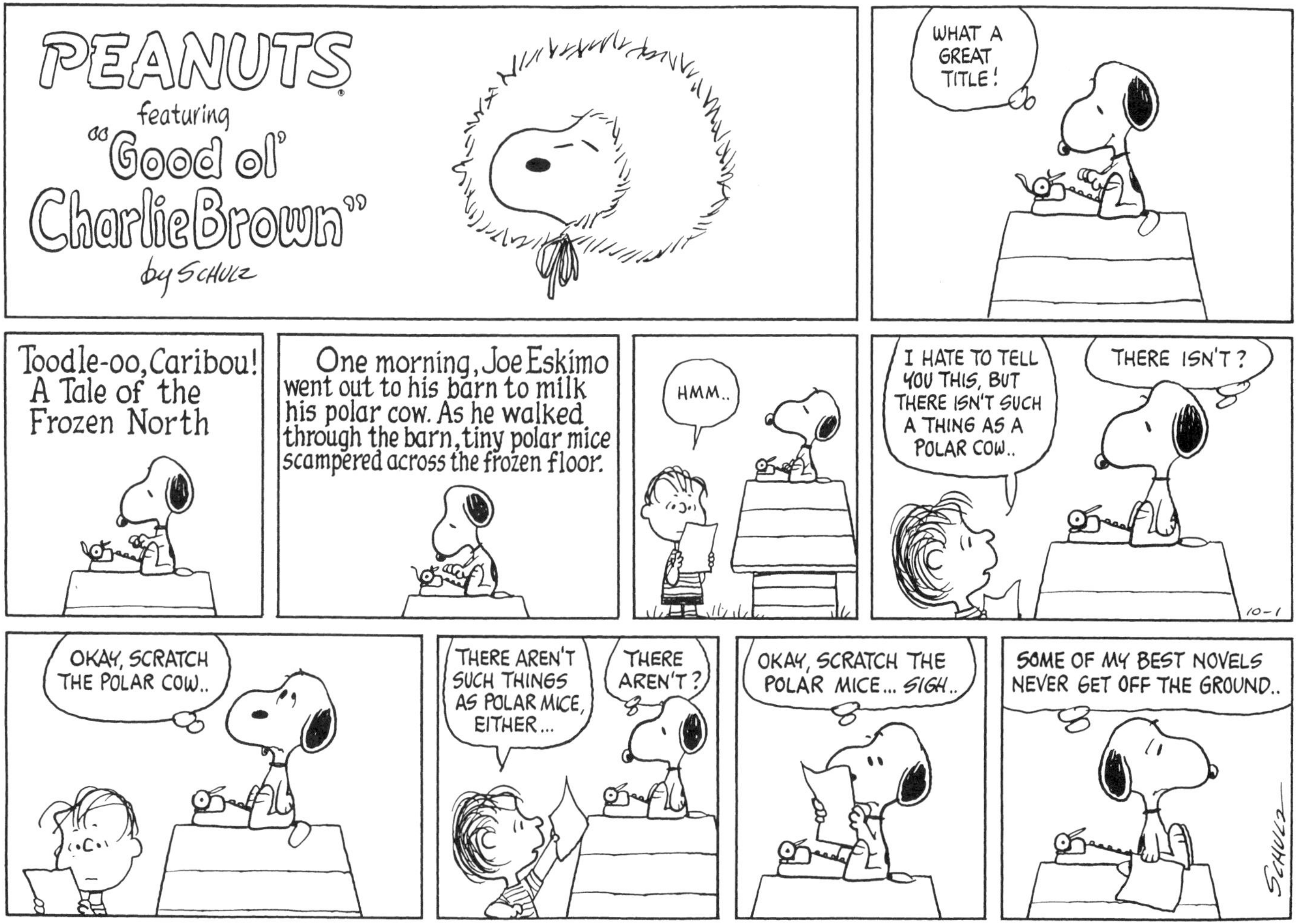
PEANUTS
featuring "Good ol' Charlie Brown"
by SCHULZ
WHAT A GREAT TITLE!
Toodle-oo, Caribou! A Tale of the Frozen North
One morning, Joe Eskimo went out to his barn to milk his polar cow. As he walked through the barn, tiny polar mice scampered across the frozen floor.
HMM..
I HATE TO TELL YOU THIS, BUT THERE ISN'T SUCH A THING AS A POLAR COW..
THERE ISN'T?
10-1
OKAY, SCRATCH THE POLAR COW..
THERE AREN'T SUCH THINGS AS POLAR MICE, EITHER...
THERE AREN'T?
OKAY, SCRATCH THE POLAR MICE... SIGH..
SOME OF MY BEST NOVELS NEVER GET OFF THE GROUND..
SCHULZ

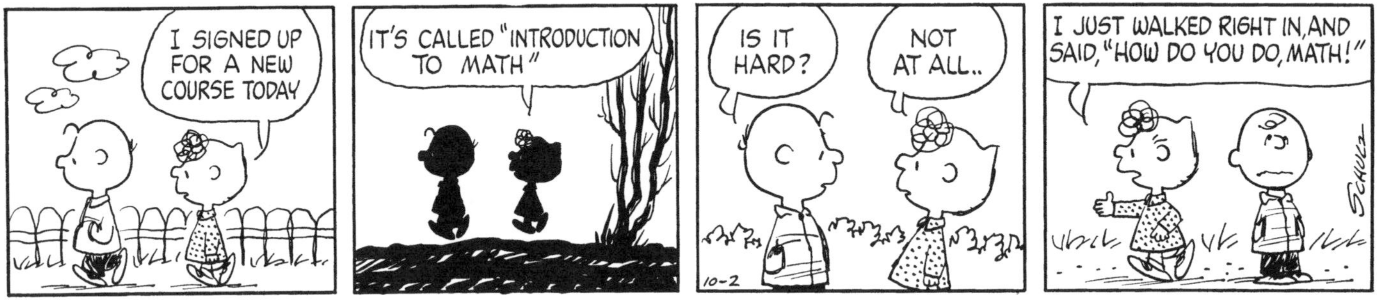
I SIGNED UP FOR A NEW COURSE TODAY
IT'S CALLED "INTRODUCTION TO MATH"
IS IT HARD?
NOT AT ALL..
I JUST WALKED RIGHT IN, AND SAID, "HOW DO YOU DO, MATH!"
SCHULZ

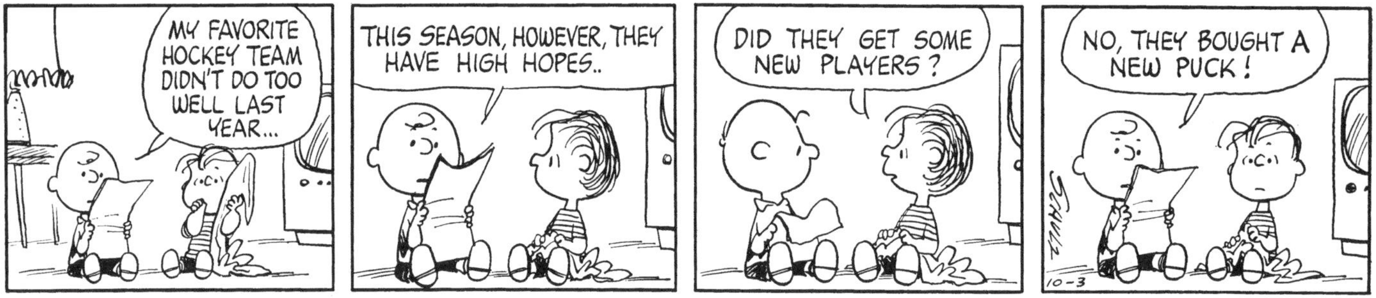
MY FAVORITE HOCKEY TEAM DIDN'T DO TOO WELL LAST YEAR...
THIS SEASON, HOWEVER, THEY HAVE HIGH HOPES..
DID THEY GET SOME NEW PLAYERS?
NO, THEY BOUGHT A NEW PUCK!
SCHULZ

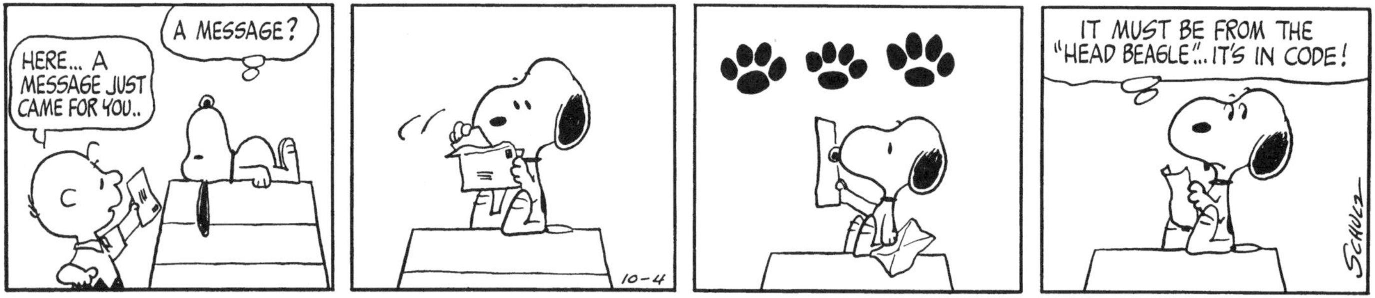
HERE... A MESSAGE JUST CAME FOR YOU..
A MESSAGE?
IT MUST BE FROM THE "HEAD BEAGLE"... IT'S IN CODE!
SCHULZ

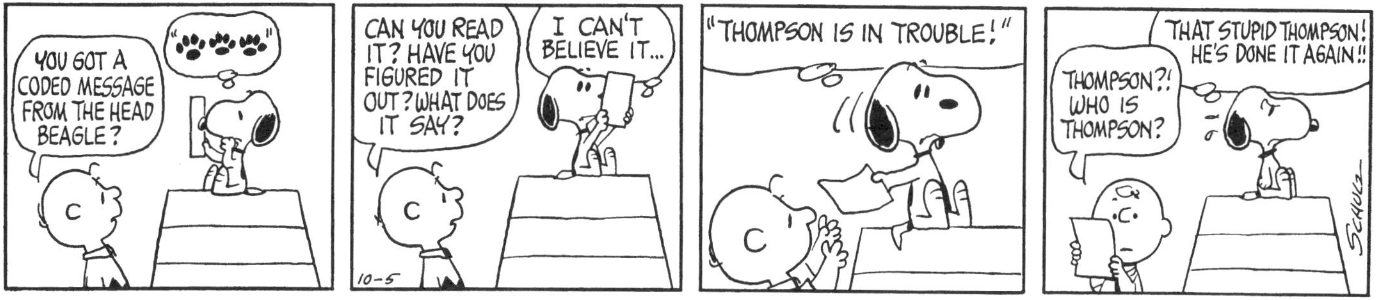
YOU GOT A CODED MESSAGE FROM THE HEAD BEAGLE?
"🐾🐾🐾"
CAN YOU READ IT? HAVE YOU FIGURED IT OUT? WHAT DOES IT SAY?
I CAN'T BELIEVE IT...
10-5
"THOMPSON IS IN TROUBLE!"
THAT STUPID THOMPSON! HE'S DONE IT AGAIN!!
THOMPSON?! WHO IS THOMPSON?
SCHULZ

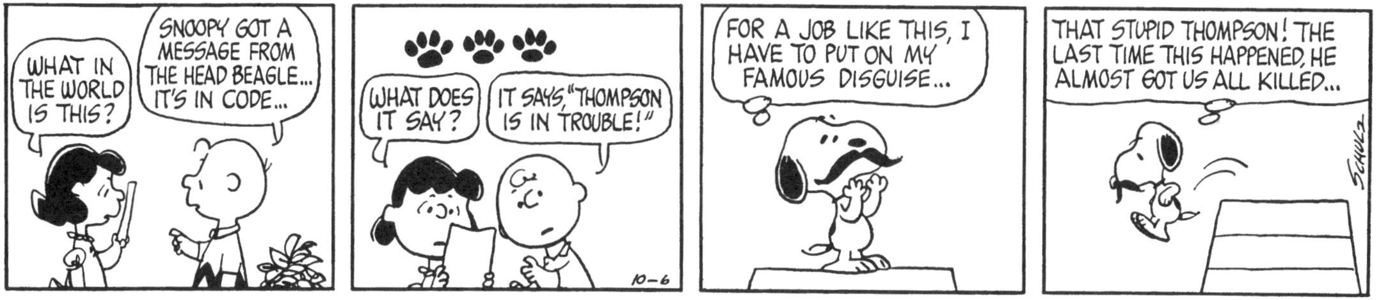
WHAT IN THE WORLD IS THIS?
SNOOPY GOT A MESSAGE FROM THE HEAD BEAGLE... IT'S IN CODE...
WHAT DOES IT SAY?
IT SAYS, "THOMPSON IS IN TROUBLE!"
10-6
FOR A JOB LIKE THIS, I HAVE TO PUT ON MY FAMOUS DISGUISE...
THAT STUPID THOMPSON! THE LAST TIME THIS HAPPENED, HE ALMOST GOT US ALL KILLED...
SCHULZ

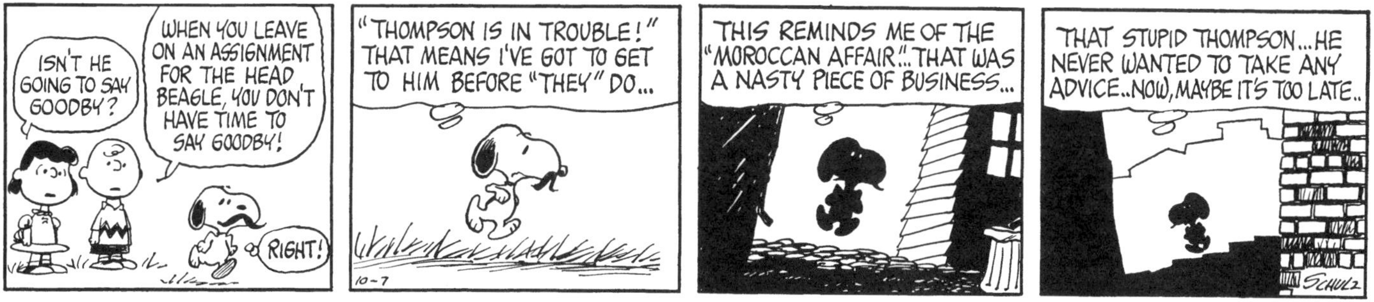
ISN'T HE GOING TO SAY GOODBY?
WHEN YOU LEAVE ON AN ASSIGNMENT FOR THE HEAD BEAGLE, YOU DON'T HAVE TIME TO SAY GOODBY!
RIGHT!
"THOMPSON IS IN TROUBLE!" THAT MEANS I'VE GOT TO GET TO HIM BEFORE "THEY" DO...
10-7
THIS REMINDS ME OF THE "MOROCCAN AFFAIR"... THAT WAS A NASTY PIECE OF BUSINESS...
THAT STUPID THOMPSON... HE NEVER WANTED TO TAKE ANY ADVICE.. NOW, MAYBE IT'S TOO LATE..
SCHULZ

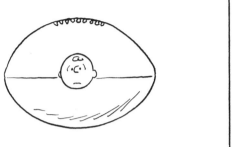

PEANUTS
featuring
"Good ol' Charlie Brown"
by Schulz

♫ CHARLIE BROWNNNNN ♫

I'LL HOLD THE FOOTBALL, CHARLIE BROWN, AND YOU COME RUNNING UP, AND KICK IT..

I CAN'T

I NEVER DO ANYTHING WITHOUT CONSULTING MY PSYCHIATRIST...

WELL, YOU GO TALK WITH YOUR PSYCHIATRIST, AND SEE WHAT YOU WANT TO DO...OKAY?

PSYCHIATRIC HELP 5¢

THE DOCTOR IS IN

I HAVE A STRANGE PROBLEM

THERE'S THIS GIRL, SEE, AND SHE'S ALWAYS TRYING TO GET ME TO KICK THIS FOOTBALL, BUT SHE ALSO ALWAYS PULLS IT AWAY AND I LAND ON MY BACK AND KILL MYSELF...

SHE SOUNDS LIKE AN INTERESTING GIRL...SORT OF A FUN TYPE...

I GET THE IMPRESSION THAT YOU HAVE A REAL NEED TO KICK THIS FOOTBALL...I THINK YOU SHOULD TRY IT!

I THINK YOU SHOULD TRY IT BECAUSE IN MEDICAL TERMS, YOU HAVE WHAT WE CALL THE "NEED TO NEED TO TRY IT"

10-8

I'M GLAD I TALKED WITH MY PSYCHIATRIST BECAUSE THIS YEAR I'M GONNA KICK THAT BALL CLEAR TO THE MOON!

AUGH!

WHAM

UNFORTUNATELY, CHARLIE BROWN, YOUR AVERAGE PSYCHIATRIST KNOWS VERY LITTLE ABOUT KICKING FOOTBALLS

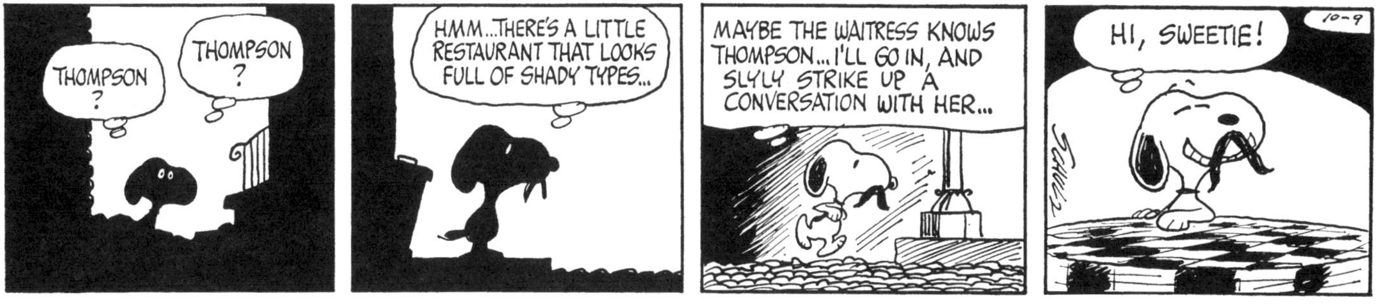
THOMPSON ?
THOMPSON ?
HMM...THERE'S A LITTLE RESTAURANT THAT LOOKS FULL OF SHADY TYPES...
MAYBE THE WAITRESS KNOWS THOMPSON... I'LL GO IN, AND SLYLY STRIKE UP A CONVERSATION WITH HER...
10-9
HI, SWEETIE!

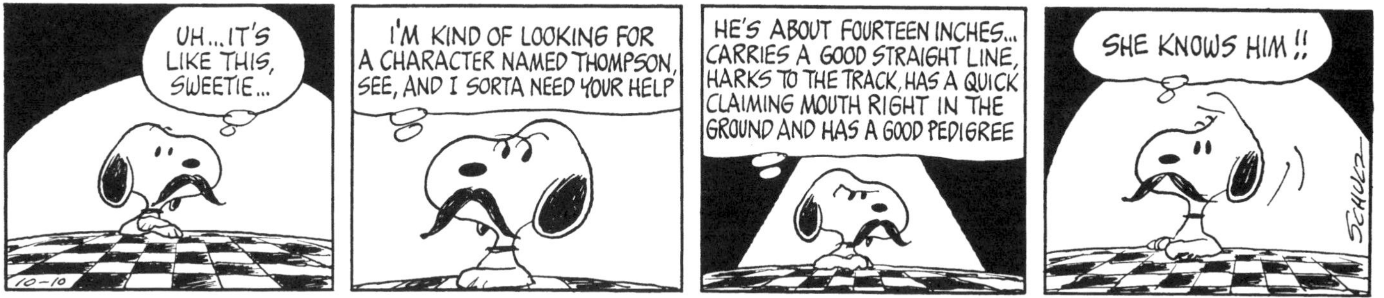
UH...IT'S LIKE THIS, SWEETIE...
10-10
I'M KIND OF LOOKING FOR A CHARACTER NAMED THOMPSON, SEE, AND I SORTA NEED YOUR HELP
HE'S ABOUT FOURTEEN INCHES... CARRIES A GOOD STRAIGHT LINE, HARKS TO THE TRACK, HAS A QUICK CLAIMING MOUTH RIGHT IN THE GROUND AND HAS A GOOD PEDIGREE
SHE KNOWS HIM !!

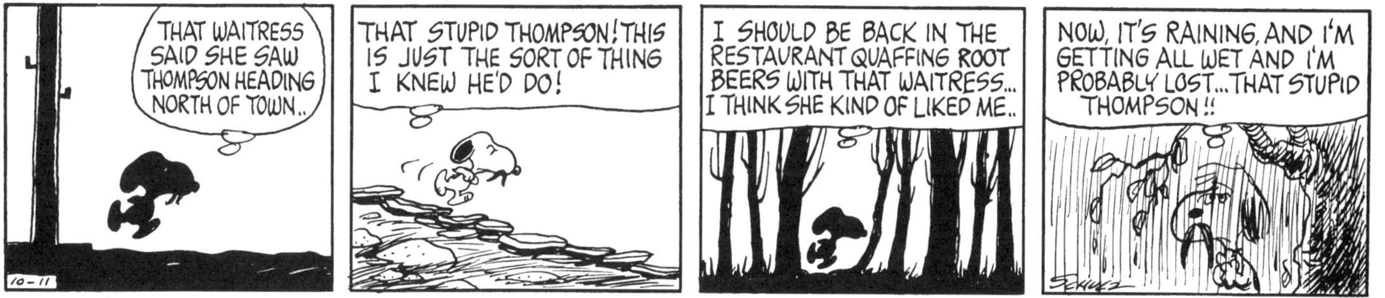
THAT WAITRESS SAID SHE SAW THOMPSON HEADING NORTH OF TOWN..
10-11
THAT STUPID THOMPSON! THIS IS JUST THE SORT OF THING I KNEW HE'D DO!
I SHOULD BE BACK IN THE RESTAURANT QUAFFING ROOT BEERS WITH THAT WAITRESS... I THINK SHE KIND OF LIKED ME..
NOW, IT'S RAINING, AND I'M GETTING ALL WET AND I'M PROBABLY LOST...THAT STUPID THOMPSON !!

THOMPSON?
THOMPSON, WHERE ARE YOU?
THOMPSON?
10-12
!
TOO LATE!
POOR THOMPSON!

Report to the Head Beagle
10-13
Subject: Our Beagle in the field, Thompson.
Subject attempted to subdue ten-thousand rabbits by himself. End came quickly.
Rabbit-tat-tat, and it was all over!

I WAS SORRY TO HEAR ABOUT THOMPSON..
POOR THOMPSON
10-14
I SUPPOSE YOU'LL NEVER KNOW WHAT REALLY HAPPENED, WILL YOU?
ON THE CONTRARY
I KNOW EXACTLY WHAT HAPPENED...
THOSE RABBITS MADE HIM AN OFFER HE COULDN'T REFUSE!

PEANUTS featuring "Good ol' CharlieBrown" by Schulz

type
type
type
type

Toodle-oo, Caribou! A Tale of the Frozen North

The stall was empty! "Someone has stolen my polar cow!" shouted Joe Eskimo.

"This is the work of Joe Jacket, who hates me!"

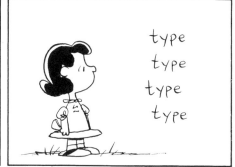

MAY I SEE HOW YOUR NEW NOVEL IS COMING ALONG?

BE MY GUEST..

10-15

"JOE ESKIMO AND JOE JACKET WERE RIVALS FOR THE HEART OF SALLY SNOW WHO LIVED SOUTH OF THE ICEBERG....JOE ESKIMO THOUGHT BACK TO THE NIGHT HE FIRST SHOOK HER HAND"

"'I THINK YOU ARE VERY NICE,' HE HAD TOLD HER, AND THEY SHOOK HANDS."

THEY SHOOK HANDS?

I THINK YOUR LOVE SCENE NEEDS A LITTLE SOMETHING..

I ALWAYS GET SO EMBARRASSED..

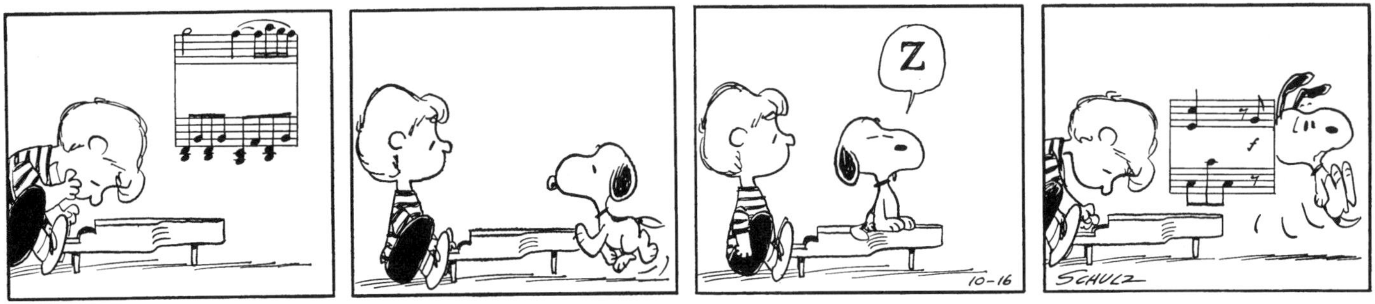
Z
10-16
SCHULZ

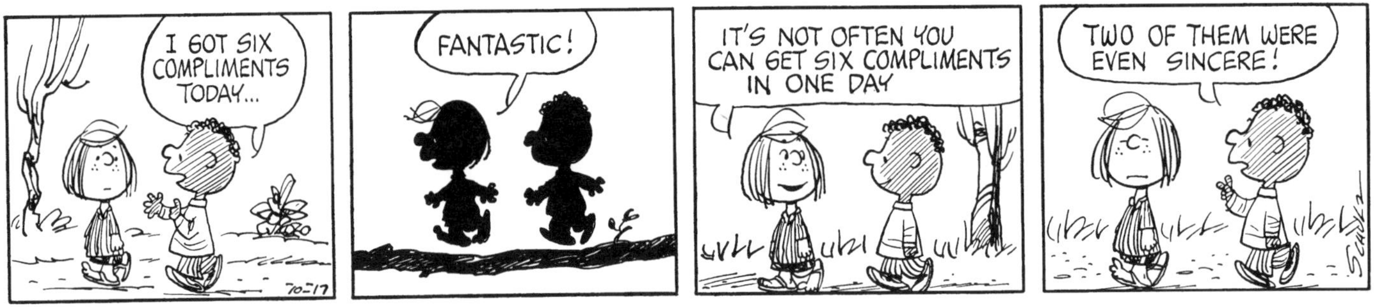
I GOT SIX COMPLIMENTS TODAY...
FANTASTIC!
IT'S NOT OFTEN YOU CAN GET SIX COMPLIMENTS IN ONE DAY
TWO OF THEM WERE EVEN SINCERE!
SCHULZ

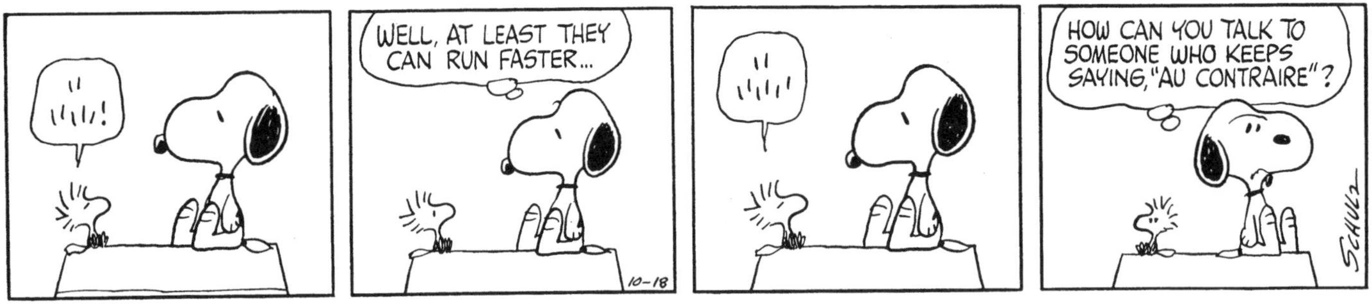
WELL, AT LEAST THEY CAN RUN FASTER...
10-18
HOW CAN YOU TALK TO SOMEONE WHO KEEPS SAYING, "AU CONTRAIRE"?
SCHULZ

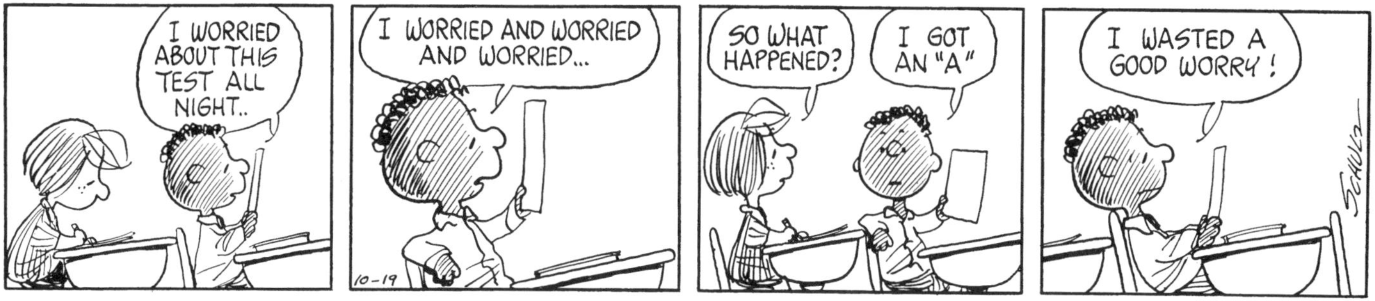

I WORRIED ABOUT THIS TEST ALL NIGHT..
I WORRIED AND WORRIED AND WORRIED...
10-19
SO WHAT HAPPENED?
I GOT AN "A"
I WASTED A GOOD WORRY!
SCHULZ

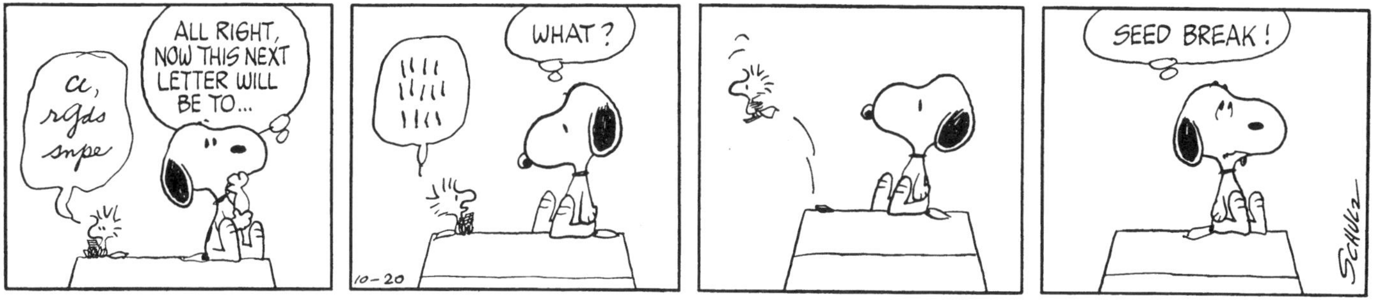

ALL RIGHT, NOW THIS NEXT LETTER WILL BE TO...
WHAT?
10-20
SEED BREAK!
SCHULZ

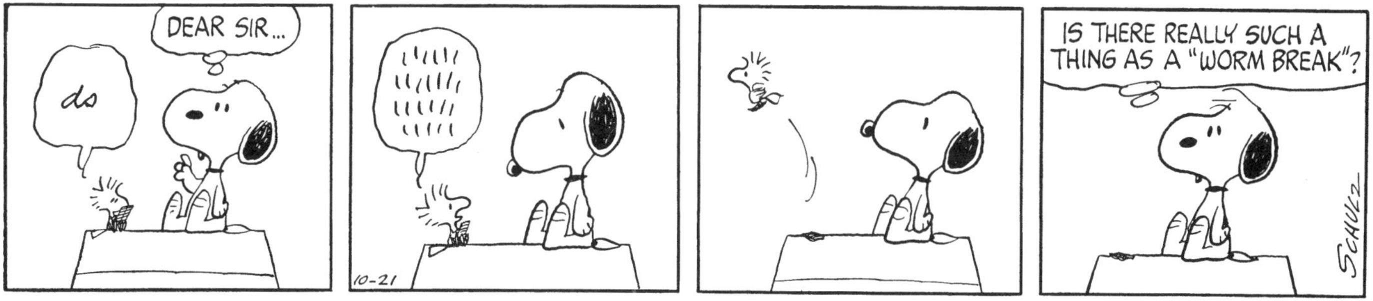

DEAR SIR...
ds
10-21
IS THERE REALLY SUCH A THING AS A "WORM BREAK"?
SCHULZ

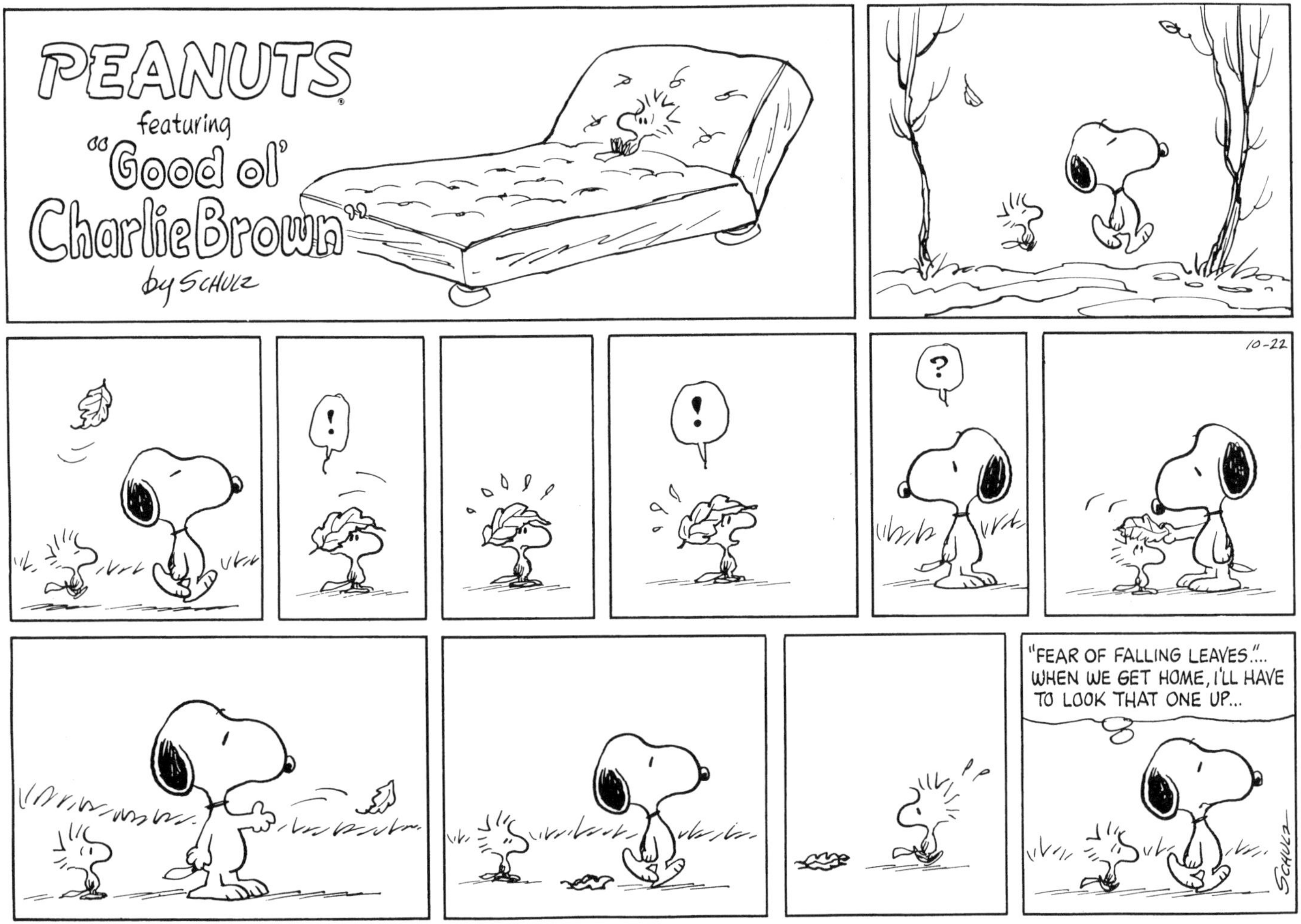
PEANUTS
featuring
"Good ol' Charlie Brown"
by SCHULZ
10-22
?
"FEAR OF FALLING LEAVES."...
WHEN WE GET HOME, I'LL HAVE
TO LOOK THAT ONE UP...
SCHULZ

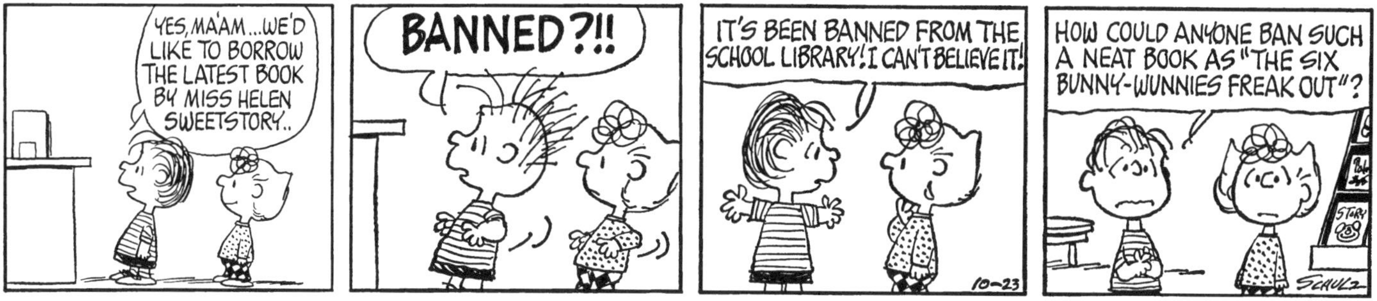
YES, MA'AM...WE'D LIKE TO BORROW THE LATEST BOOK BY MISS HELEN SWEETSTORY..
BANNED?!!
IT'S BEEN BANNED FROM THE SCHOOL LIBRARY! I CAN'T BELIEVE IT!
10-23
HOW COULD ANYONE BAN SUCH A NEAT BOOK AS "THE SIX BUNNY-WUNNIES FREAK OUT"?

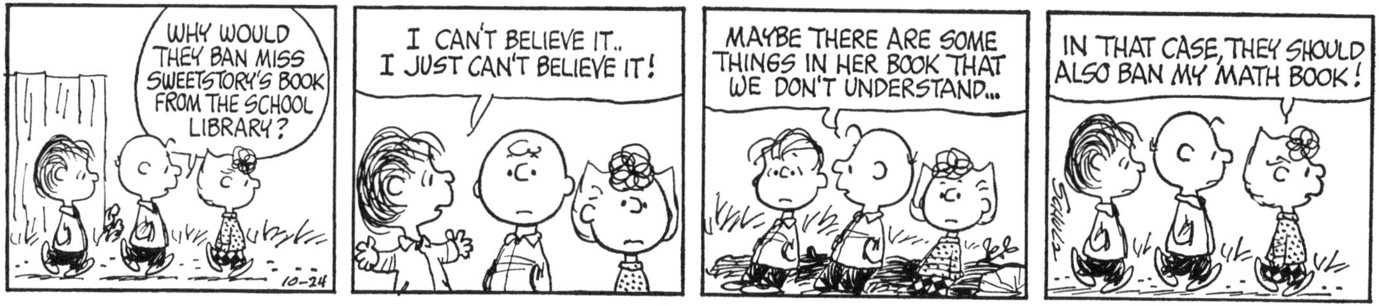
WHY WOULD THEY BAN MISS SWEETSTORY'S BOOK FROM THE SCHOOL LIBRARY?
10-24
I CAN'T BELIEVE IT.. I JUST CAN'T BELIEVE IT!
MAYBE THERE ARE SOME THINGS IN HER BOOK THAT WE DON'T UNDERSTAND...
IN THAT CASE, THEY SHOULD ALSO BAN MY MATH BOOK!

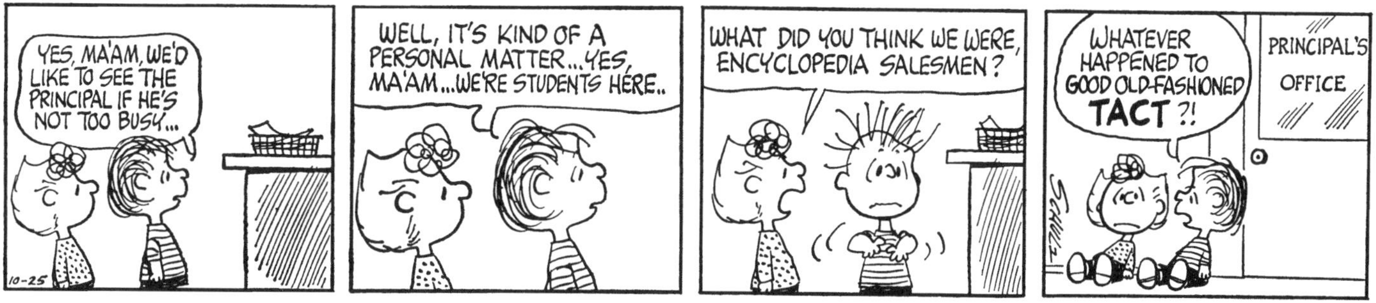
YES, MA'AM, WE'D LIKE TO SEE THE PRINCIPAL IF HE'S NOT TOO BUSY...
10-25
WELL, IT'S KIND OF A PERSONAL MATTER...YES, MA'AM...WE'RE STUDENTS HERE..
WHAT DID YOU THINK WE WERE, ENCYCLOPEDIA SALESMEN?
WHATEVER HAPPENED TO GOOD OLD-FASHIONED TACT?!
PRINCIPAL'S OFFICE

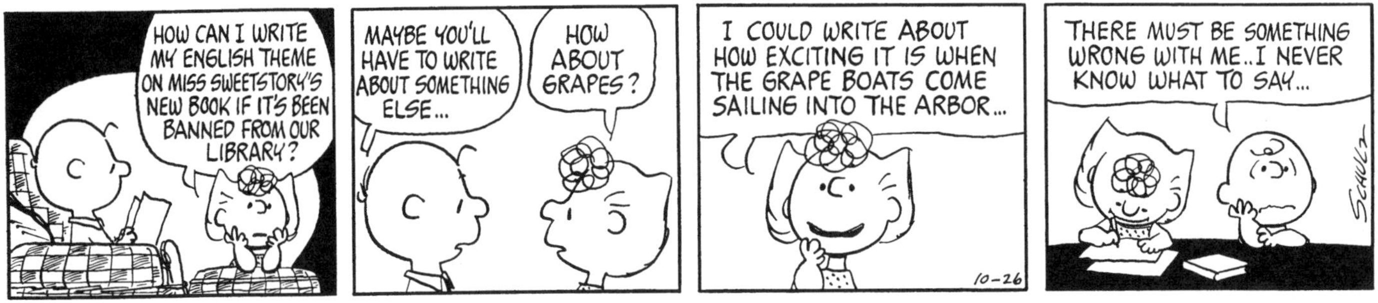
HOW CAN I WRITE MY ENGLISH THEME ON MISS SWEETSTORY'S NEW BOOK IF IT'S BEEN BANNED FROM OUR LIBRARY?
MAYBE YOU'LL HAVE TO WRITE ABOUT SOMETHING ELSE...
HOW ABOUT GRAPES?
I COULD WRITE ABOUT HOW EXCITING IT IS WHEN THE GRAPE BOATS COME SAILING INTO THE ARBOR...
10-26
THERE MUST BE SOMETHING WRONG WITH ME..I NEVER KNOW WHAT TO SAY...
SCHULZ

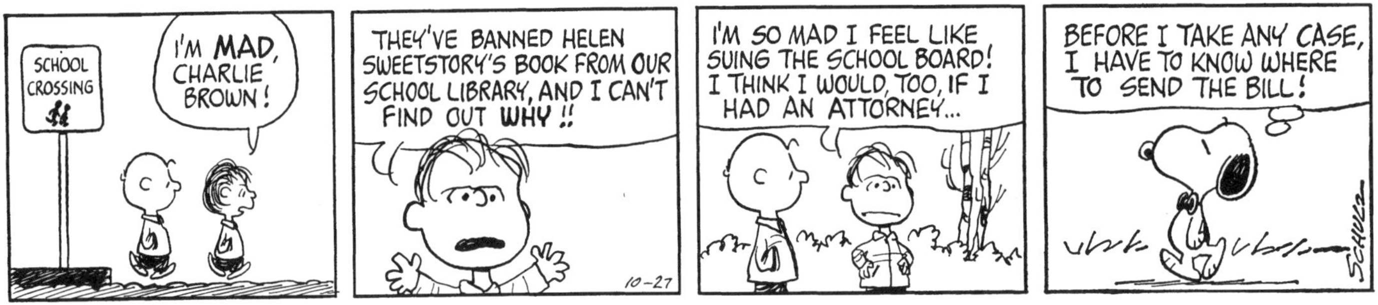
SCHOOL CROSSING
I'M MAD, CHARLIE BROWN!
THEY'VE BANNED HELEN SWEETSTORY'S BOOK FROM OUR SCHOOL LIBRARY, AND I CAN'T FIND OUT WHY!!
10-27
I'M SO MAD I FEEL LIKE SUING THE SCHOOL BOARD! I THINK I WOULD, TOO, IF I HAD AN ATTORNEY...
BEFORE I TAKE ANY CASE, I HAVE TO KNOW WHERE TO SEND THE BILL!
SCHULZ

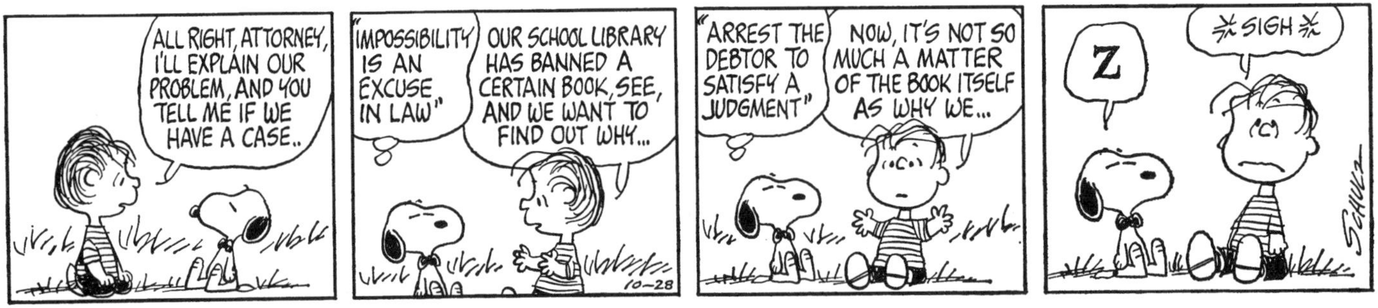
ALL RIGHT, ATTORNEY, I'LL EXPLAIN OUR PROBLEM, AND YOU TELL ME IF WE HAVE A CASE..
"IMPOSSIBILITY IS AN EXCUSE IN LAW"
OUR SCHOOL LIBRARY HAS BANNED A CERTAIN BOOK, SEE, AND WE WANT TO FIND OUT WHY...
10-28
"ARREST THE DEBTOR TO SATISFY A JUDGMENT"
NOW, IT'S NOT SO MUCH A MATTER OF THE BOOK ITSELF AS WHY WE...
Z
SIGH
SCHULZ

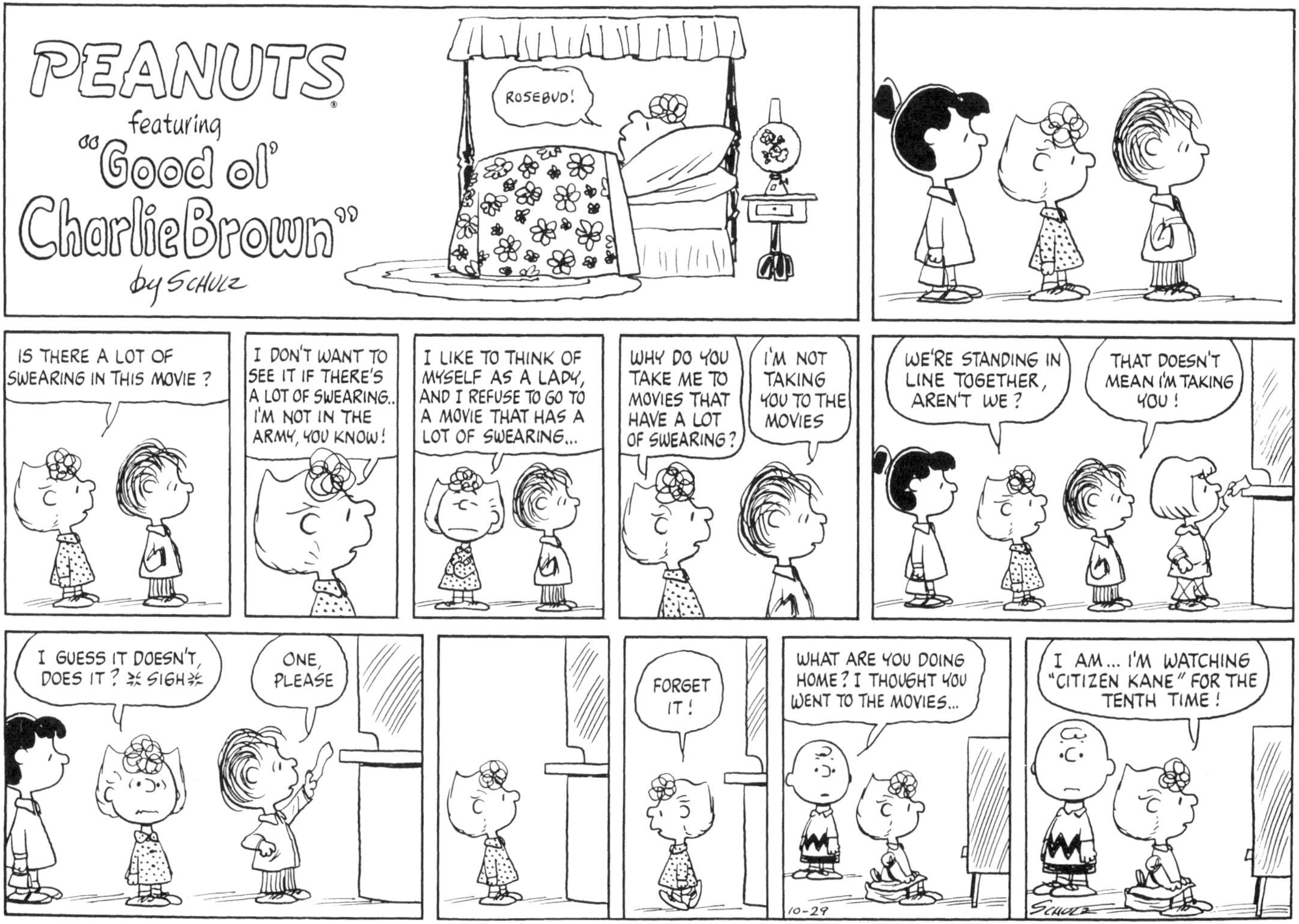
PEANUTS
featuring
"Good ol' Charlie Brown"
by SCHULZ
ROSEBUD!
IS THERE A LOT OF SWEARING IN THIS MOVIE ?
I DON'T WANT TO SEE IT IF THERE'S A LOT OF SWEARING.. I'M NOT IN THE ARMY, YOU KNOW!
I LIKE TO THINK OF MYSELF AS A LADY, AND I REFUSE TO GO TO A MOVIE THAT HAS A LOT OF SWEARING...
WHY DO YOU TAKE ME TO MOVIES THAT HAVE A LOT OF SWEARING?
I'M NOT TAKING YOU TO THE MOVIES
WE'RE STANDING IN LINE TOGETHER, AREN'T WE ?
THAT DOESN'T MEAN I'M TAKING YOU !
I GUESS IT DOESN'T, DOES IT ? SIGH
ONE, PLEASE
FORGET IT !
WHAT ARE YOU DOING HOME? I THOUGHT YOU WENT TO THE MOVIES...
10-29
I AM... I'M WATCHING "CITIZEN KANE" FOR THE TENTH TIME !
SCHULZ

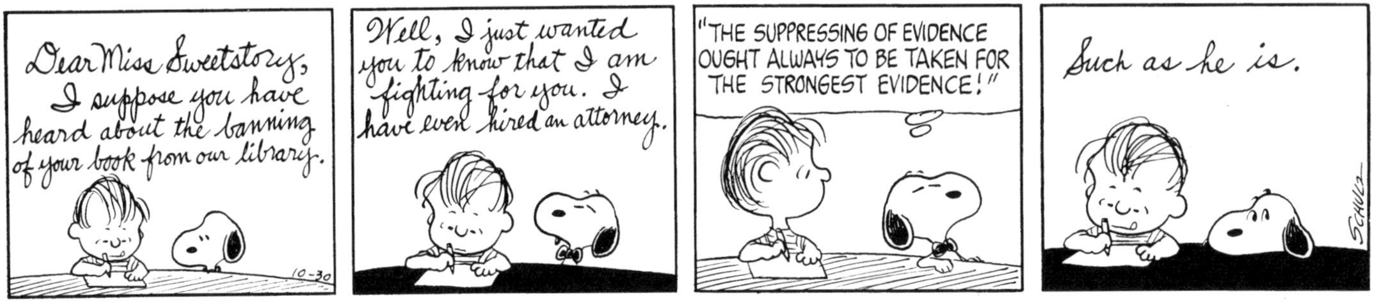
Dear Miss Sweetstory,
I suppose you have heard about the banning of your book from our library.
10-30
Well, I just wanted you to know that I am fighting for you. I have even hired an attorney.
"THE SUPPRESSING OF EVIDENCE OUGHT ALWAYS TO BE TAKEN FOR THE STRONGEST EVIDENCE!"
Such as he is.
SCHULZ

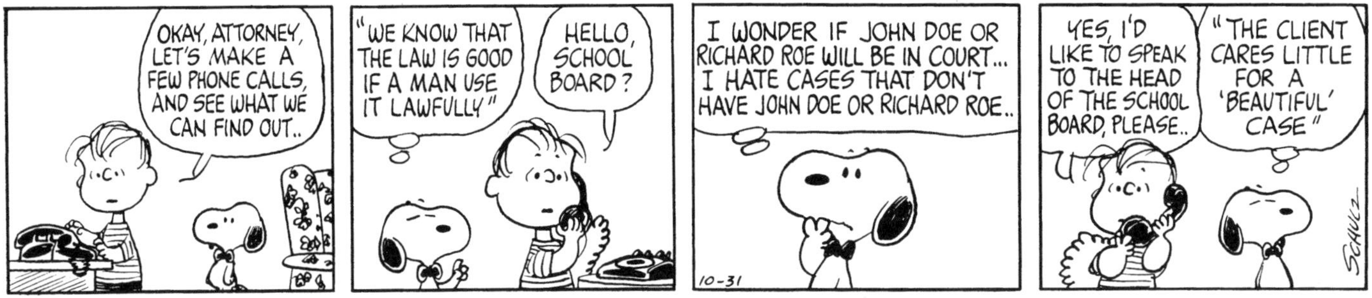
OKAY, ATTORNEY, LET'S MAKE A FEW PHONE CALLS, AND SEE WHAT WE CAN FIND OUT..
"WE KNOW THAT THE LAW IS GOOD IF A MAN USE IT LAWFULLY"
HELLO, SCHOOL BOARD?
I WONDER IF JOHN DOE OR RICHARD ROE WILL BE IN COURT... I HATE CASES THAT DON'T HAVE JOHN DOE OR RICHARD ROE..
10-31
YES, I'D LIKE TO SPEAK TO THE HEAD OF THE SCHOOL BOARD, PLEASE..
"THE CLIENT CARES LITTLE FOR A 'BEAUTIFUL' CASE"
SCHULZ

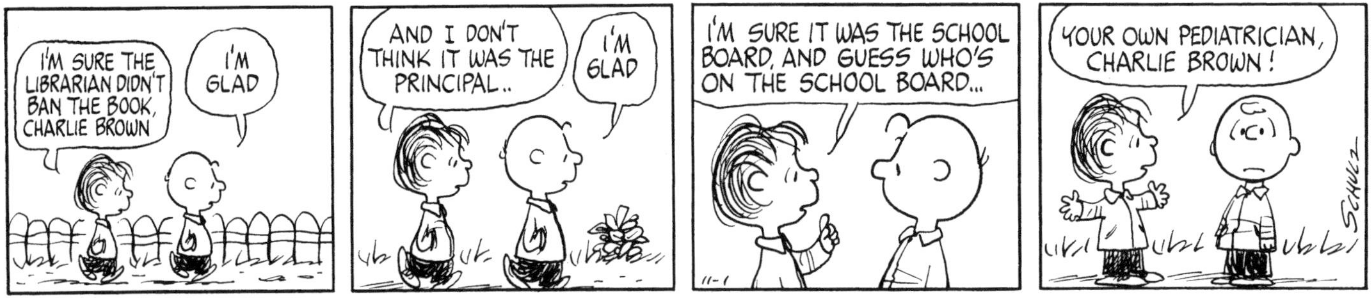
I'M SURE THE LIBRARIAN DIDN'T BAN THE BOOK, CHARLIE BROWN
I'M GLAD
AND I DON'T THINK IT WAS THE PRINCIPAL..
I'M GLAD
I'M SURE IT WAS THE SCHOOL BOARD, AND GUESS WHO'S ON THE SCHOOL BOARD...
11-1
YOUR OWN PEDIATRICIAN, CHARLIE BROWN!
SCHULZ

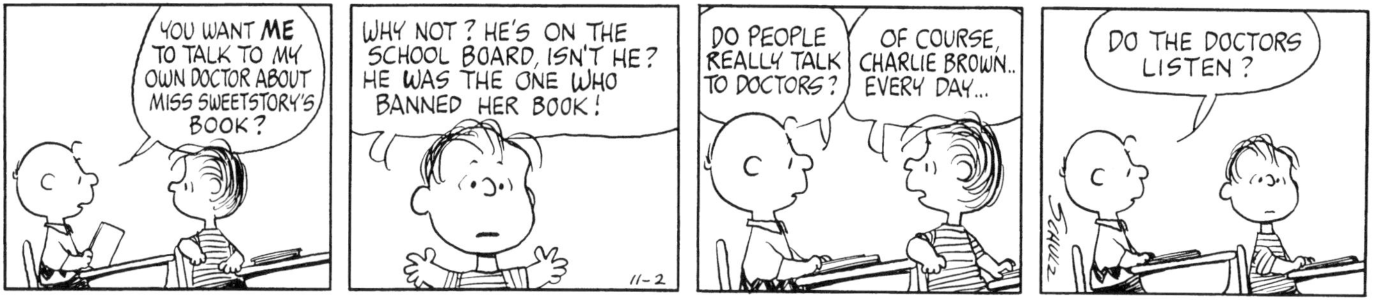
YOU WANT ME TO TALK TO MY OWN DOCTOR ABOUT MISS SWEETSTORY'S BOOK?
WHY NOT? HE'S ON THE SCHOOL BOARD, ISN'T HE? HE WAS THE ONE WHO BANNED HER BOOK!
11-2
DO PEOPLE REALLY TALK TO DOCTORS?
OF COURSE, CHARLIE BROWN.. EVERY DAY...
DO THE DOCTORS LISTEN?
SCHULZ

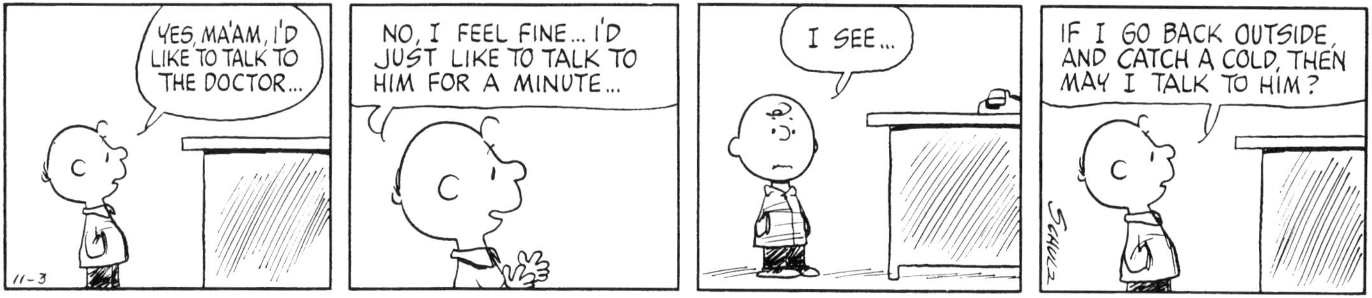
YES, MA'AM, I'D LIKE TO TALK TO THE DOCTOR...
11-3
NO, I FEEL FINE... I'D JUST LIKE TO TALK TO HIM FOR A MINUTE...
I SEE...
IF I GO BACK OUTSIDE AND CATCH A COLD, THEN MAY I TALK TO HIM?
SCHULZ

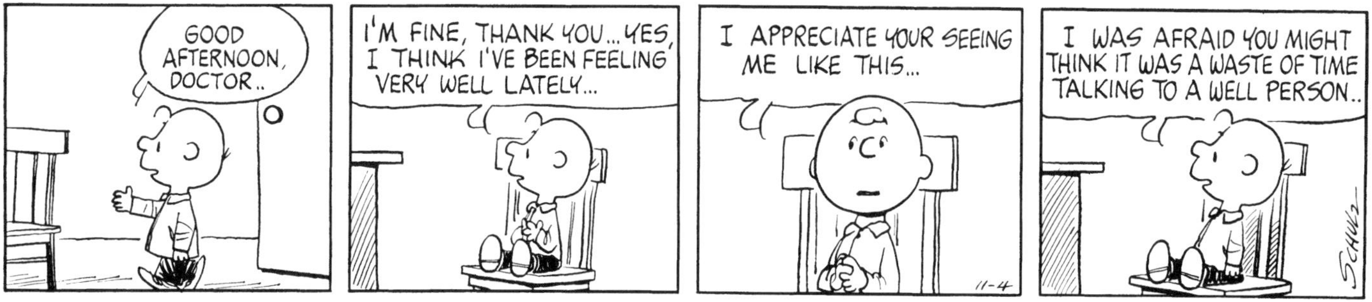
GOOD AFTERNOON, DOCTOR..
I'M FINE, THANK YOU... YES, I THINK I'VE BEEN FEELING VERY WELL LATELY...
I APPRECIATE YOUR SEEING ME LIKE THIS...
11-4
I WAS AFRAID YOU MIGHT THINK IT WAS A WASTE OF TIME TALKING TO A WELL PERSON..
SCHULZ

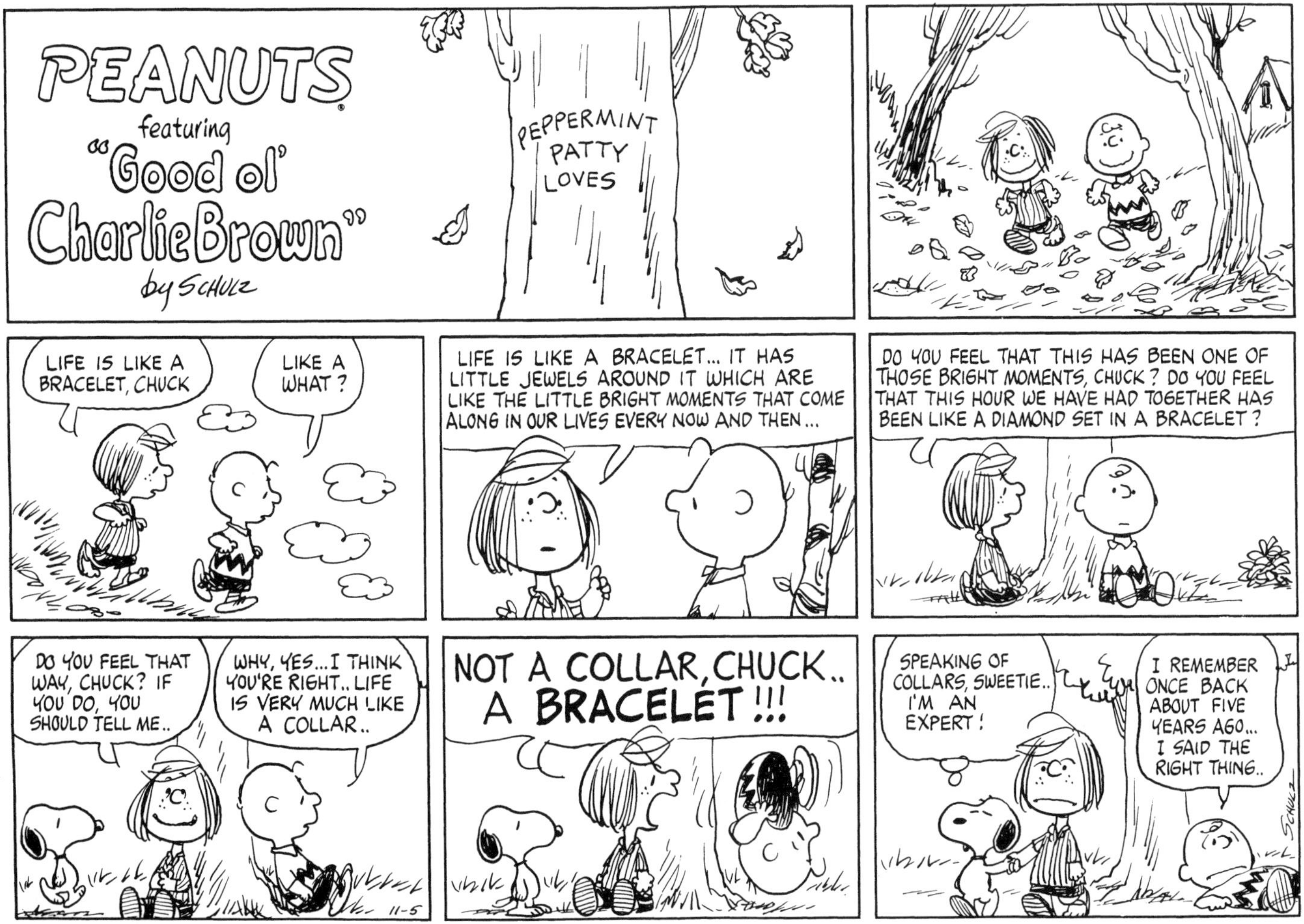
PEANUTS
featuring "Good ol' Charlie Brown"
by SCHULZ
PEPPERMINT PATTY LOVES
LIFE IS LIKE A BRACELET, CHUCK
LIKE A WHAT ?
LIFE IS LIKE A BRACELET... IT HAS LITTLE JEWELS AROUND IT WHICH ARE LIKE THE LITTLE BRIGHT MOMENTS THAT COME ALONG IN OUR LIVES EVERY NOW AND THEN...
DO YOU FEEL THAT THIS HAS BEEN ONE OF THOSE BRIGHT MOMENTS, CHUCK ? DO YOU FEEL THAT THIS HOUR WE HAVE HAD TOGETHER HAS BEEN LIKE A DIAMOND SET IN A BRACELET ?
DO YOU FEEL THAT WAY, CHUCK? IF YOU DO, YOU SHOULD TELL ME..
WHY, YES... I THINK YOU'RE RIGHT.. LIFE IS VERY MUCH LIKE A COLLAR..
11-5
NOT A COLLAR, CHUCK.. A BRACELET !!!
SPEAKING OF COLLARS, SWEETIE.. I'M AN EXPERT !
I REMEMBER ONCE BACK ABOUT FIVE YEARS AGO... I SAID THE RIGHT THING..
SCHULZ

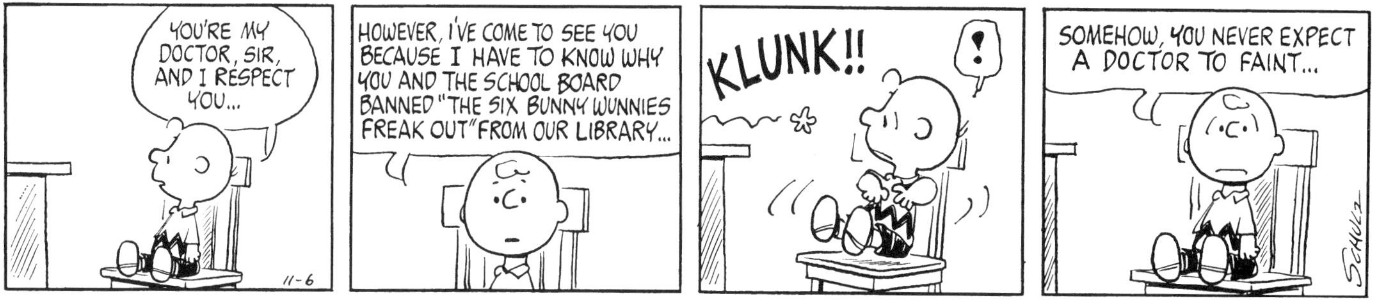
YOU'RE MY DOCTOR, SIR, AND I RESPECT YOU...
HOWEVER, I'VE COME TO SEE YOU BECAUSE I HAVE TO KNOW WHY YOU AND THE SCHOOL BOARD BANNED "THE SIX BUNNY WUNNIES FREAK OUT" FROM OUR LIBRARY...
KLUNK!!
!
SOMEHOW, YOU NEVER EXPECT A DOCTOR TO FAINT...

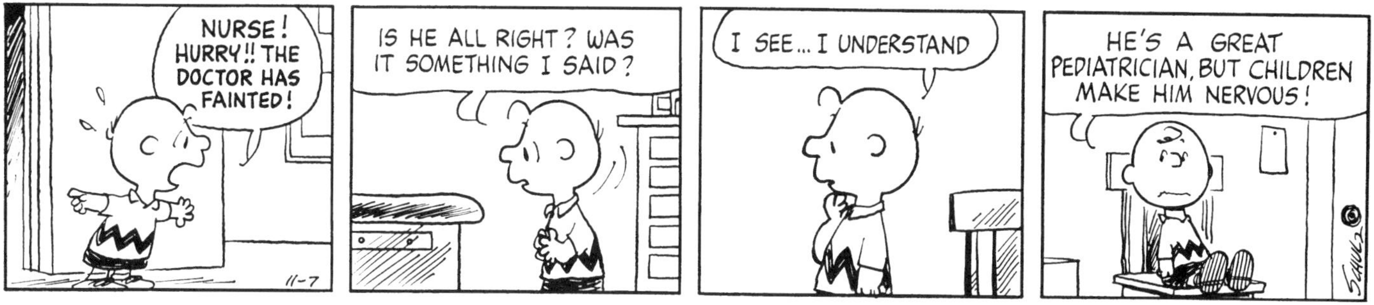
NURSE! HURRY!! THE DOCTOR HAS FAINTED!
IS HE ALL RIGHT? WAS IT SOMETHING I SAID?
I SEE... I UNDERSTAND
HE'S A GREAT PEDIATRICIAN, BUT CHILDREN MAKE HIM NERVOUS!

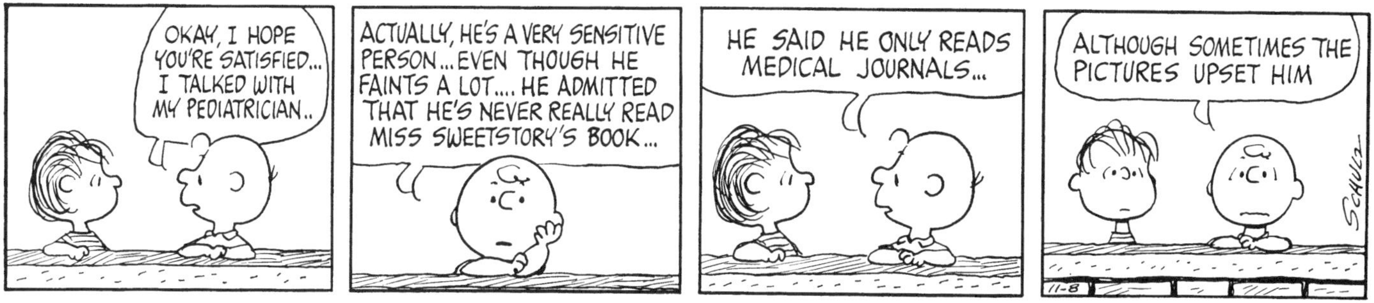
OKAY, I HOPE YOU'RE SATISFIED... I TALKED WITH MY PEDIATRICIAN..
ACTUALLY, HE'S A VERY SENSITIVE PERSON... EVEN THOUGH HE FAINTS A LOT.... HE ADMITTED THAT HE'S NEVER REALLY READ MISS SWEETSTORY'S BOOK...
HE SAID HE ONLY READS MEDICAL JOURNALS...
ALTHOUGH SOMETIMES THE PICTURES UPSET HIM

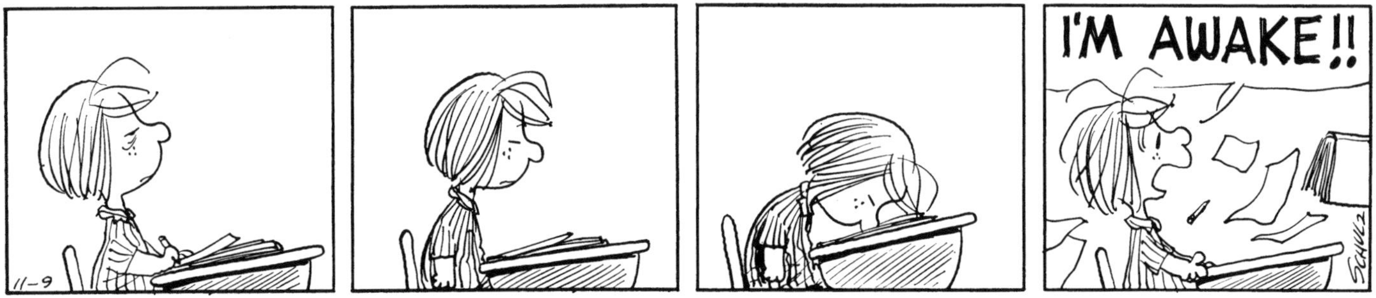
11-9
I'M AWAKE!!
SCHULZ

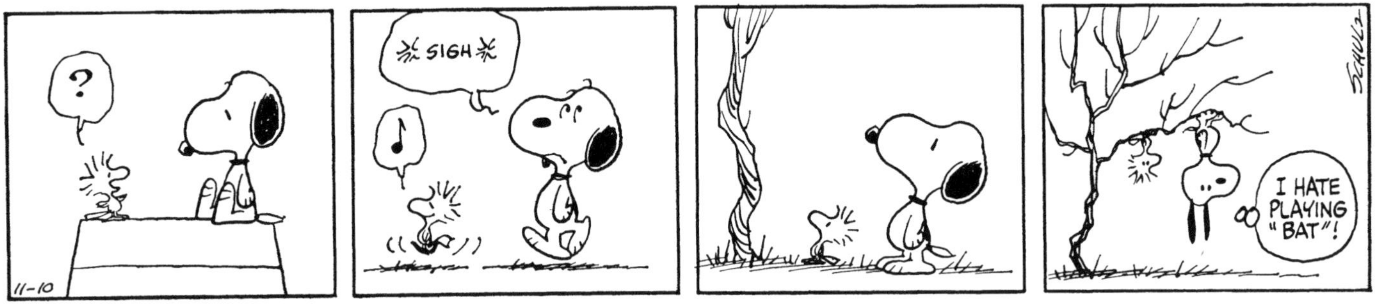
11-10
?
SIGH
♪
I HATE PLAYING "BAT"!
SCHULZ

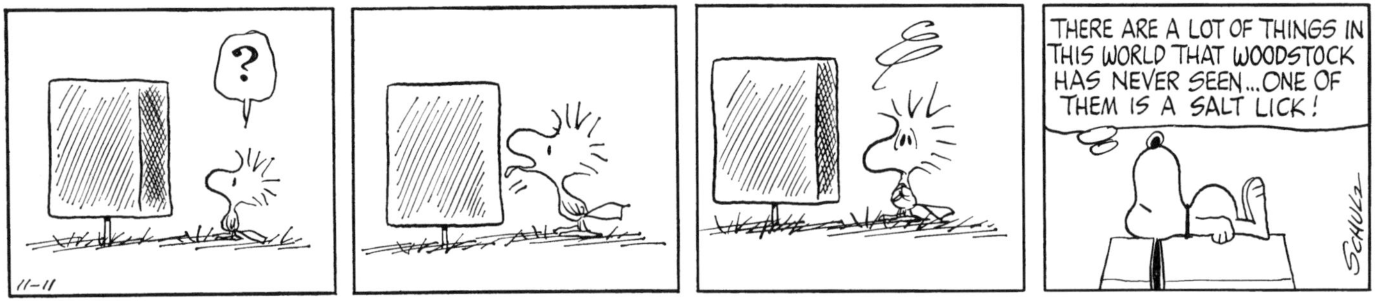
11-11
?
THERE ARE A LOT OF THINGS IN THIS WORLD THAT WOODSTOCK HAS NEVER SEEN...ONE OF THEM IS A SALT LICK!
SCHULZ

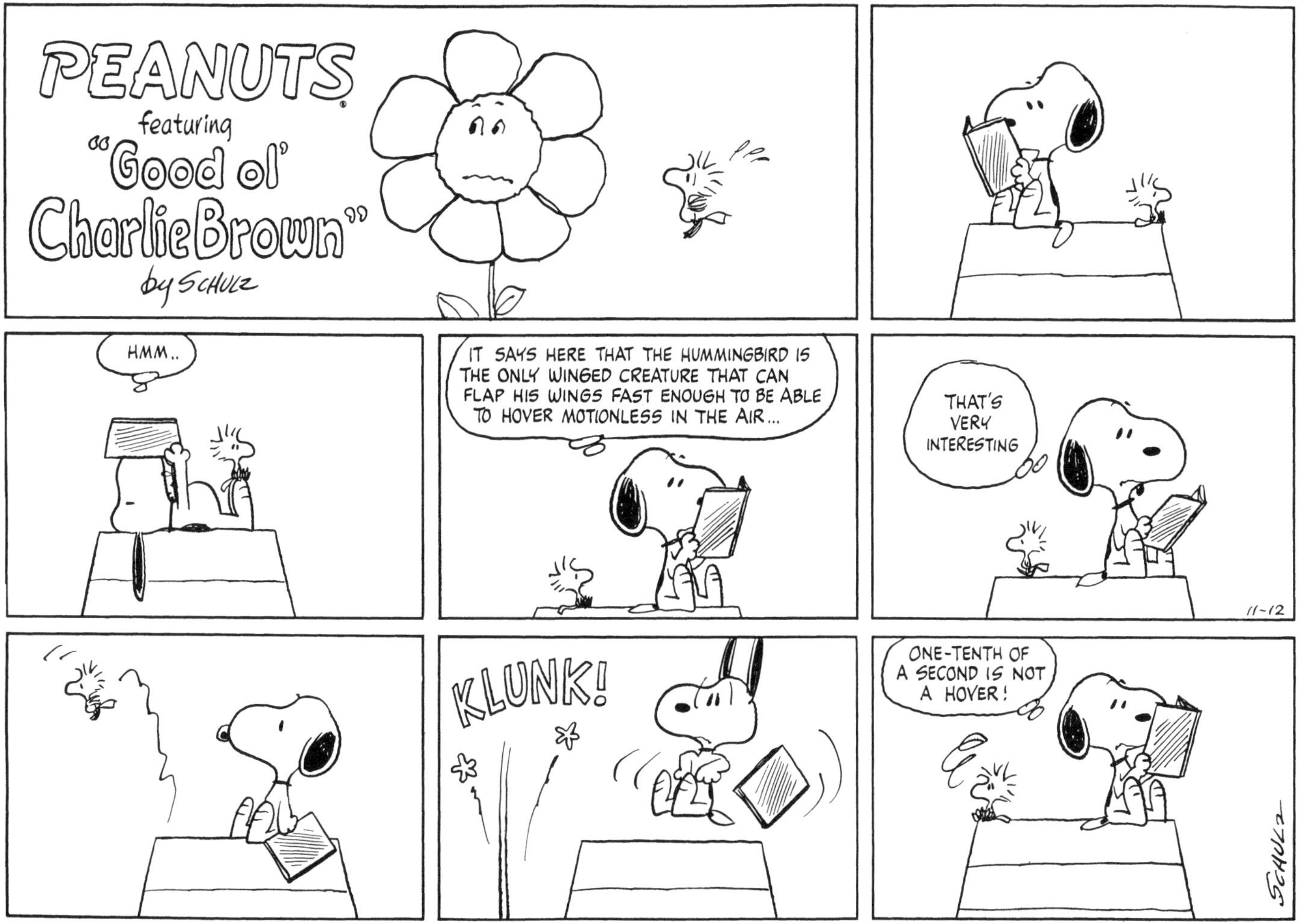
PEANUTS
featuring "Good ol' Charlie Brown"
by SCHULZ
HMM..
IT SAYS HERE THAT THE HUMMINGBIRD IS THE ONLY WINGED CREATURE THAT CAN FLAP HIS WINGS FAST ENOUGH TO BE ABLE TO HOVER MOTIONLESS IN THE AIR...
THAT'S VERY INTERESTING
11-12
KLUNK!
ONE-TENTH OF A SECOND IS NOT A HOVER!
SCHULZ

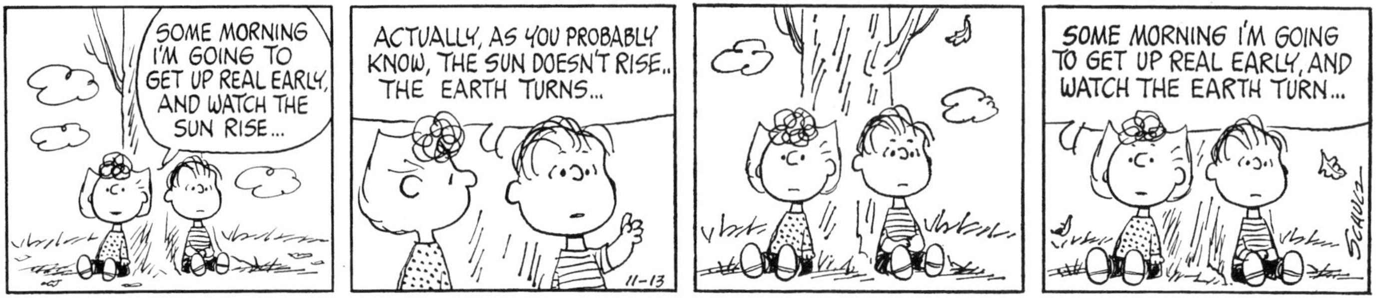
SOME MORNING I'M GOING TO GET UP REAL EARLY, AND WATCH THE SUN RISE...
ACTUALLY, AS YOU PROBABLY KNOW, THE SUN DOESN'T RISE.. THE EARTH TURNS...
SOME MORNING I'M GOING TO GET UP REAL EARLY, AND WATCH THE EARTH TURN...

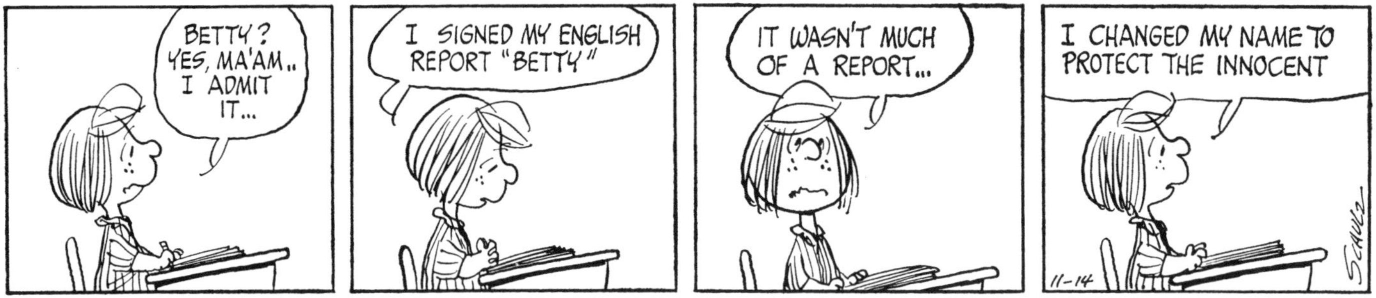
BETTY? YES, MA'AM.. I ADMIT IT...
I SIGNED MY ENGLISH REPORT "BETTY"
IT WASN'T MUCH OF A REPORT...
I CHANGED MY NAME TO PROTECT THE INNOCENT

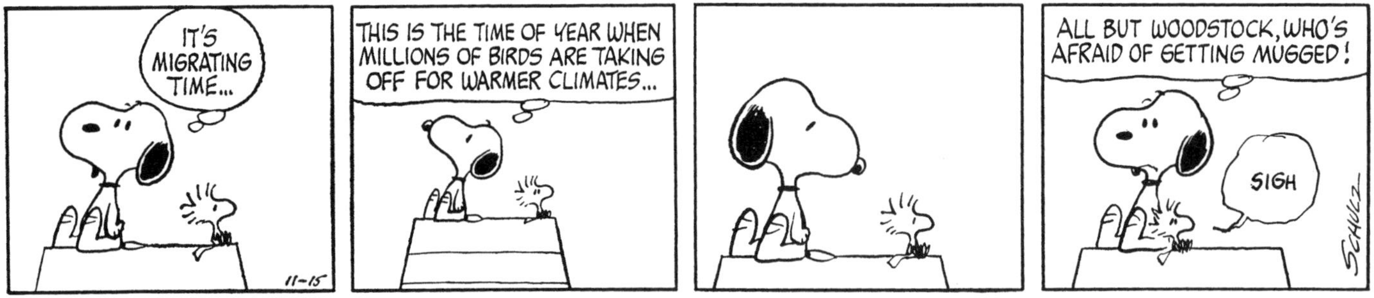
IT'S MIGRATING TIME...
THIS IS THE TIME OF YEAR WHEN MILLIONS OF BIRDS ARE TAKING OFF FOR WARMER CLIMATES...
ALL BUT WOODSTOCK, WHO'S AFRAID OF GETTING MUGGED!
SIGH

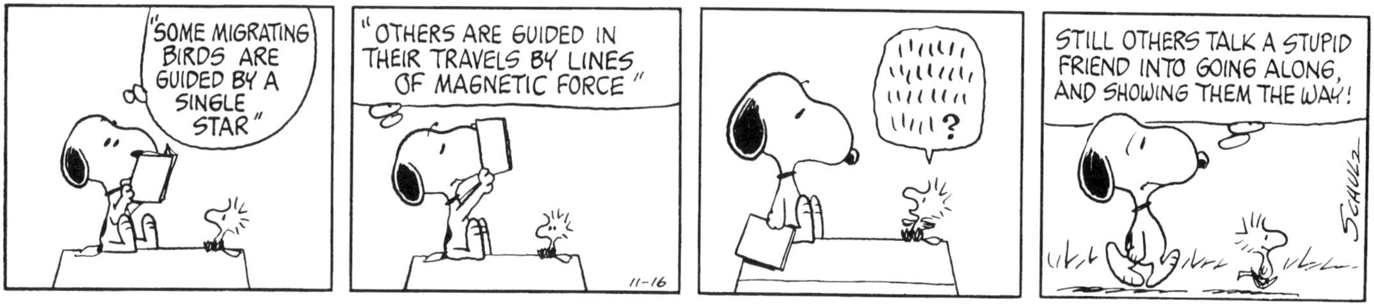
"SOME MIGRATING BIRDS ARE GUIDED BY A SINGLE STAR"
"OTHERS ARE GUIDED IN THEIR TRAVELS BY LINES OF MAGNETIC FORCE"
11-16
?
STILL OTHERS TALK A STUPID FRIEND INTO GOING ALONG, AND SHOWING THEM THE WAY!
SCHULZ

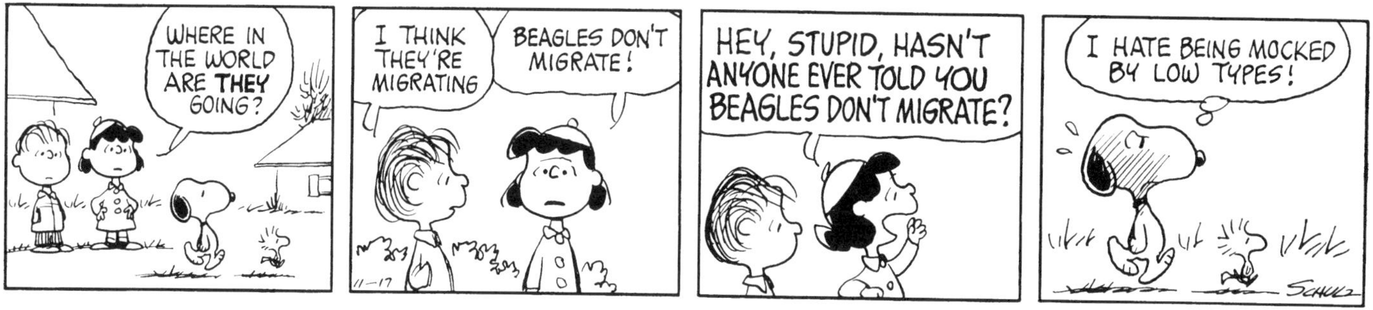
WHERE IN THE WORLD ARE **THEY** GOING?
I THINK THEY'RE MIGRATING
BEAGLES DON'T MIGRATE!
11-17
HEY, STUPID, HASN'T ANYONE EVER TOLD YOU BEAGLES DON'T MIGRATE?
I HATE BEING MOCKED BY LOW TYPES!
SCHULZ

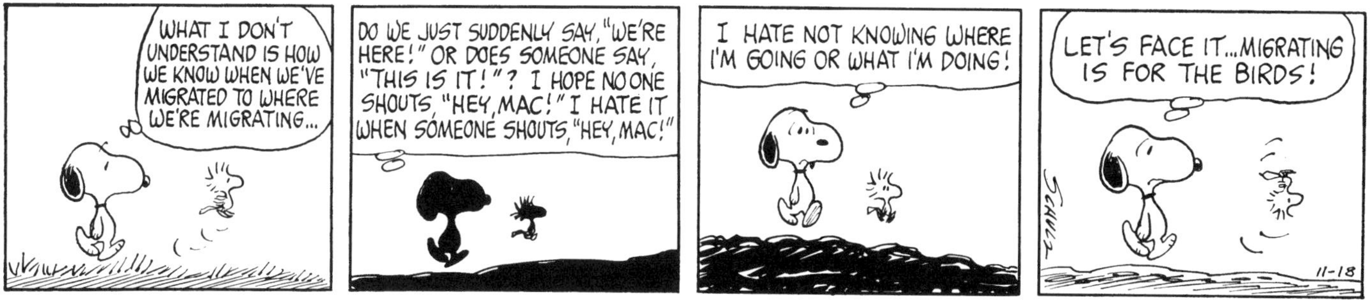
WHAT I DON'T UNDERSTAND IS HOW WE KNOW WHEN WE'VE MIGRATED TO WHERE WE'RE MIGRATING...
DO WE JUST SUDDENLY SAY, "WE'RE HERE!" OR DOES SOMEONE SAY, "THIS IS IT!"? I HOPE NO ONE SHOUTS, "HEY, MAC!" I HATE IT WHEN SOMEONE SHOUTS, "HEY, MAC!"
I HATE NOT KNOWING WHERE I'M GOING OR WHAT I'M DOING!
LET'S FACE IT...MIGRATING IS FOR THE BIRDS!
SCHULZ
11-18

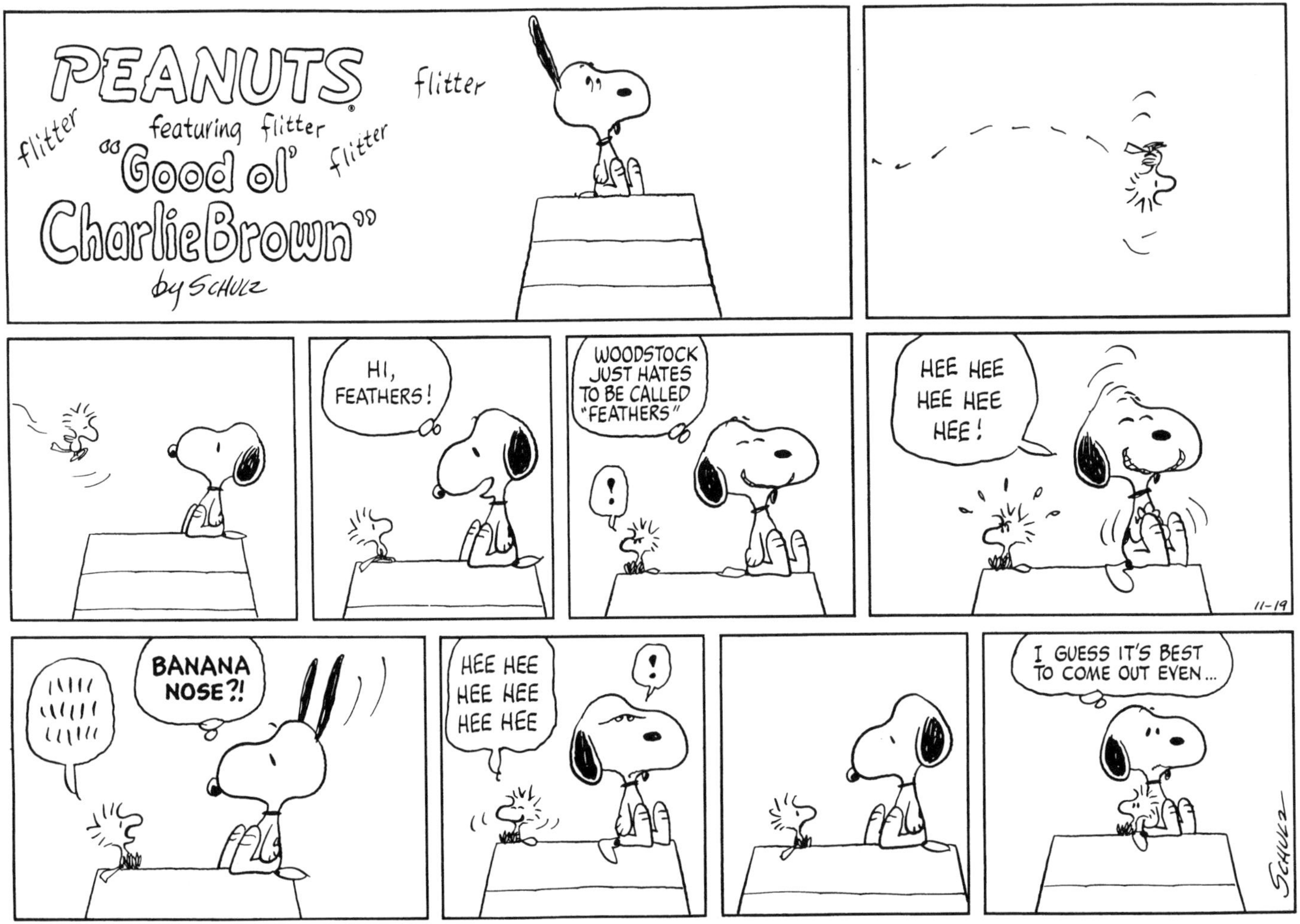
PEANUTS
featuring
"Good ol' Charlie Brown"
by SCHULZ
flitter
flitter
flitter
flitter
HI, FEATHERS!
WOODSTOCK JUST HATES TO BE CALLED "FEATHERS"
!
HEE HEE HEE HEE HEE!
11-19
BANANA NOSE?!
HEE HEE HEE HEE HEE HEE
!
I GUESS IT'S BEST TO COME OUT EVEN...
SCHULZ

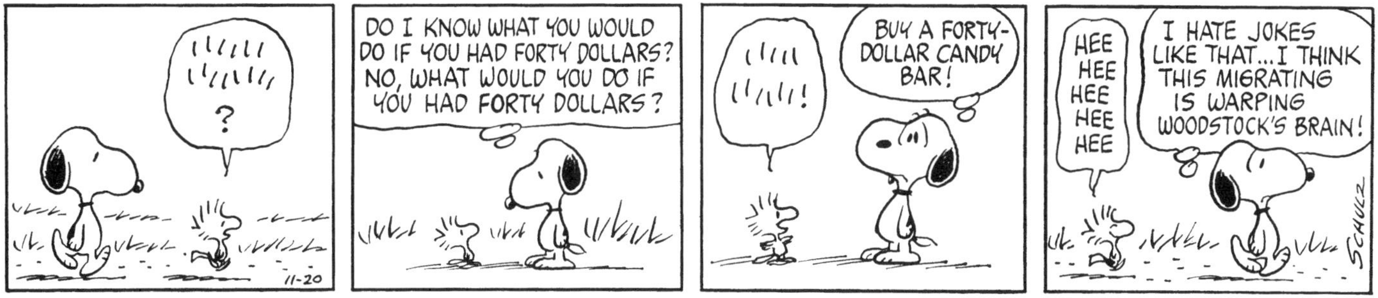

?
11-20
DO I KNOW WHAT YOU WOULD DO IF YOU HAD FORTY DOLLARS? NO, WHAT WOULD YOU DO IF YOU HAD FORTY DOLLARS?
BUY A FORTY-DOLLAR CANDY BAR!
HEE HEE HEE HEE HEE
I HATE JOKES LIKE THAT... I THINK THIS MIGRATING IS WARPING WOODSTOCK'S BRAIN!
SCHULZ

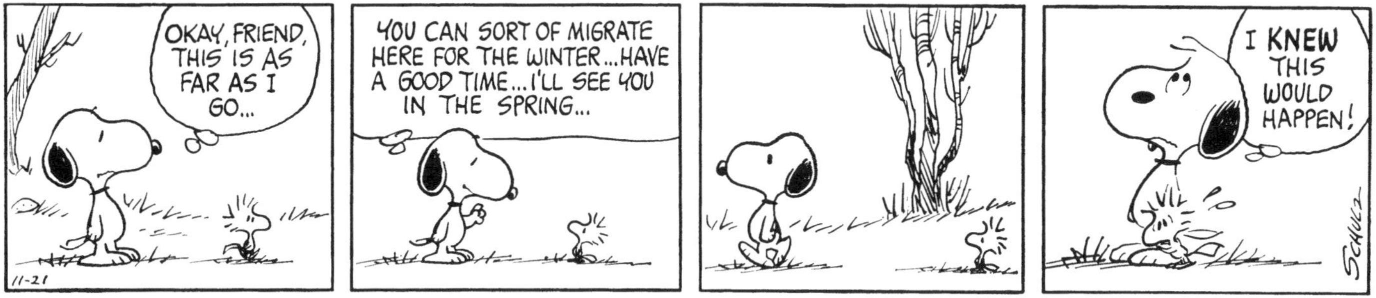

OKAY, FRIEND, THIS IS AS FAR AS I GO...
11-21
YOU CAN SORT OF MIGRATE HERE FOR THE WINTER... HAVE A GOOD TIME... I'LL SEE YOU IN THE SPRING...
I KNEW THIS WOULD HAPPEN!
SCHULZ

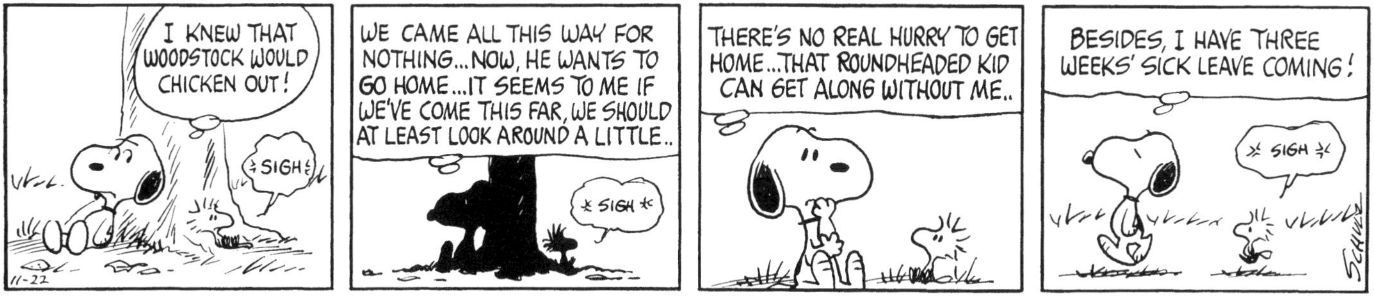

I KNEW THAT WOODSTOCK WOULD CHICKEN OUT!
SIGH
11-22
WE CAME ALL THIS WAY FOR NOTHING... NOW, HE WANTS TO GO HOME... IT SEEMS TO ME IF WE'VE COME THIS FAR, WE SHOULD AT LEAST LOOK AROUND A LITTLE..
SIGH
THERE'S NO REAL HURRY TO GET HOME... THAT ROUNDHEADED KID CAN GET ALONG WITHOUT ME..
BESIDES, I HAVE THREE WEEKS' SICK LEAVE COMING!
SIGH
SCHULZ

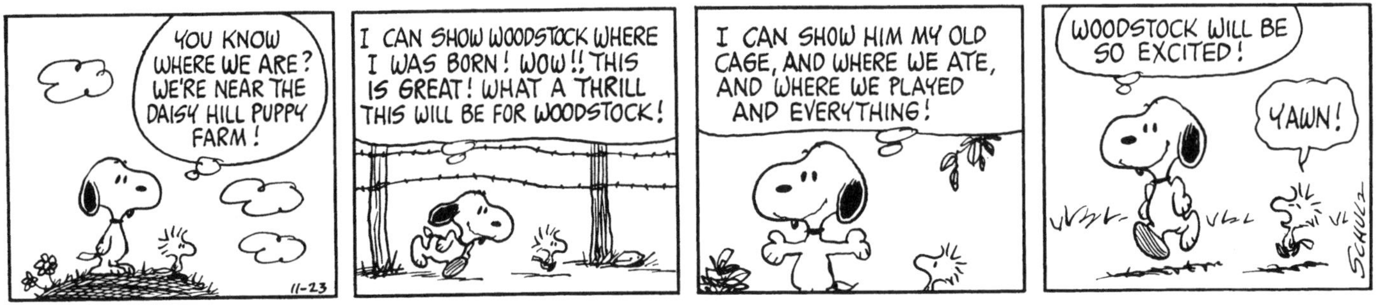
YOU KNOW WHERE WE ARE? WE'RE NEAR THE DAISY HILL PUPPY FARM!
11-23
I CAN SHOW WOODSTOCK WHERE I WAS BORN! WOW!! THIS IS GREAT! WHAT A THRILL THIS WILL BE FOR WOODSTOCK!
I CAN SHOW HIM MY OLD CAGE, AND WHERE WE ATE, AND WHERE WE PLAYED AND EVERYTHING!
WOODSTOCK WILL BE SO EXCITED!
YAWN!

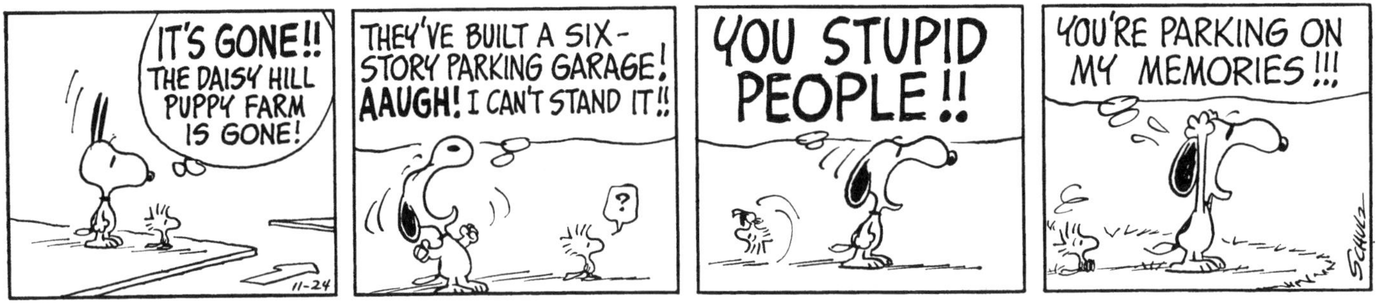
IT'S GONE!! THE DAISY HILL PUPPY FARM IS GONE!
11-24
THEY'VE BUILT A SIX-STORY PARKING GARAGE! AAUGH! I CAN'T STAND IT!!
?
YOU STUPID PEOPLE!!
YOU'RE PARKING ON MY MEMORIES!!!

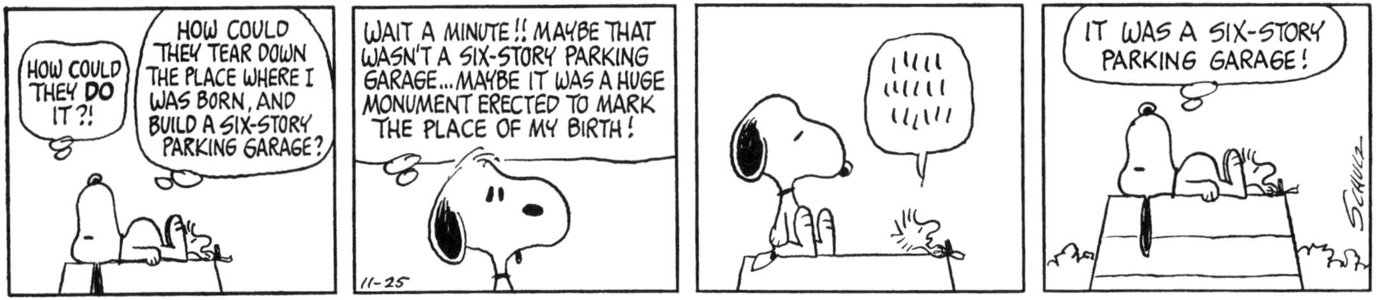
HOW COULD THEY DO IT?!
HOW COULD THEY TEAR DOWN THE PLACE WHERE I WAS BORN, AND BUILD A SIX-STORY PARKING GARAGE?
WAIT A MINUTE!! MAYBE THAT WASN'T A SIX-STORY PARKING GARAGE... MAYBE IT WAS A HUGE MONUMENT ERECTED TO MARK THE PLACE OF MY BIRTH!
11-25
IT WAS A SIX-STORY PARKING GARAGE!

PEANUTS
featuring
"Good ol' CharlieBrown"
by SCHULZ

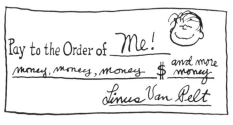

Pay to the Order of __Me!__

money, money, money $ _and more money_

Linus Van Pelt

HA!! LOOK AT THAT!

IT'S STARTING TO SNOW, AND I'M **READY**!

I'M GOING TO BE THE FIRST KID IN THE NEIGHBORHOOD TO SHOVEL WALKS..

I'M GOING FROM HOUSE TO HOUSE, AND I'M GOING TO SHOVEL EVERY SIDEWALK AND DRIVEWAY THAT I CAN FIND!

WILL YOU MAKE A LOT OF MONEY?

YOU BET I'LL MAKE A LOT OF MONEY! AND YOU THINK I'LL SPEND IT RIGHT AWAY, DON'T YOU? WELL, I WON'T!

I'LL PROBABLY PUT IT ALL IN A SAVINGS ACCOUNT, AND JUST LIVE OFF THE INTEREST, OR MAYBE I'LL BUY AN ANNUITY PAYABLE AT AGE TWELVE, OR MAYBE I'LL INVEST IT ALL IN SOME MUTUAL FUNDS, OR EVEN BUY SOME STOCK IN ONE OF OUR LOCAL COMPANIES THAT SEEMS TO BE GETTING BIGGER, OR...

11-26

..OR MAYBE I'LL... I'LL...

I REMEMBER READING ABOUT ABRAHAM LINCOLN, AND HOW HE USED TO DO HIS HOMEWORK WITH A PIECE OF COAL ON THE BACK OF A SHOVEL...

FORGET IT!

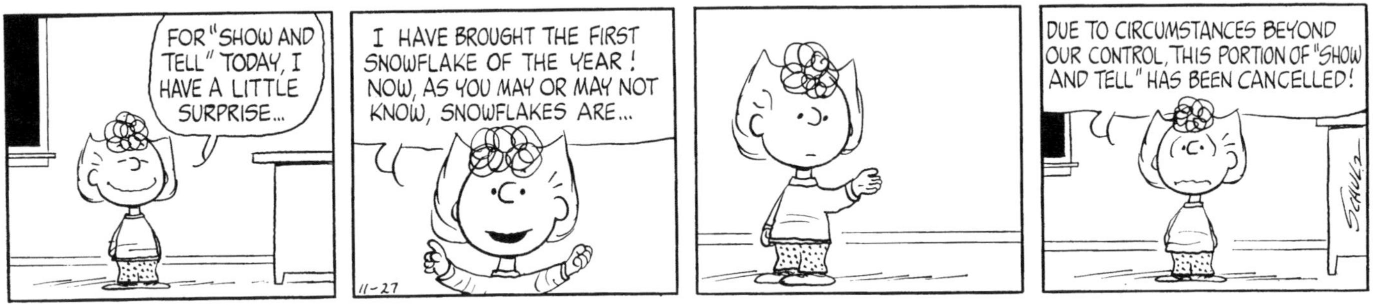
FOR "SHOW AND TELL" TODAY, I HAVE A LITTLE SURPRISE...
I HAVE BROUGHT THE FIRST SNOWFLAKE OF THE YEAR! NOW, AS YOU MAY OR MAY NOT KNOW, SNOWFLAKES ARE...
DUE TO CIRCUMSTANCES BEYOND OUR CONTROL, THIS PORTION OF "SHOW AND TELL" HAS BEEN CANCELLED!
11-27
SCHULZ

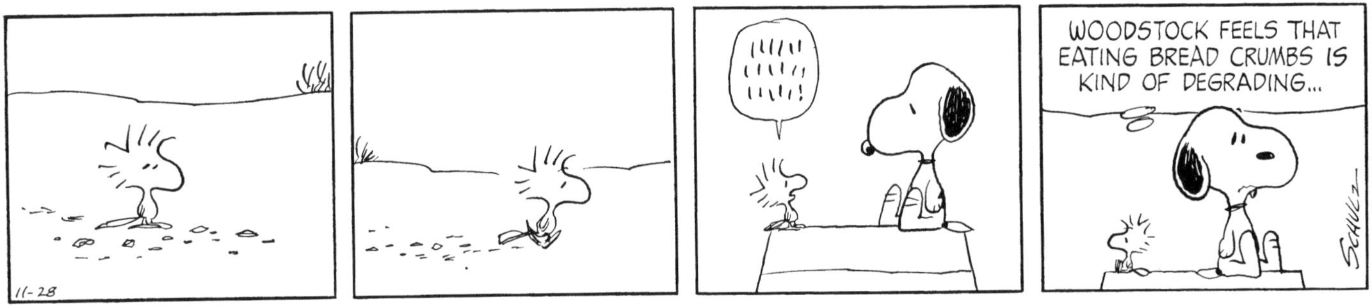
11-28
WOODSTOCK FEELS THAT EATING BREAD CRUMBS IS KIND OF DEGRADING...
SCHULZ

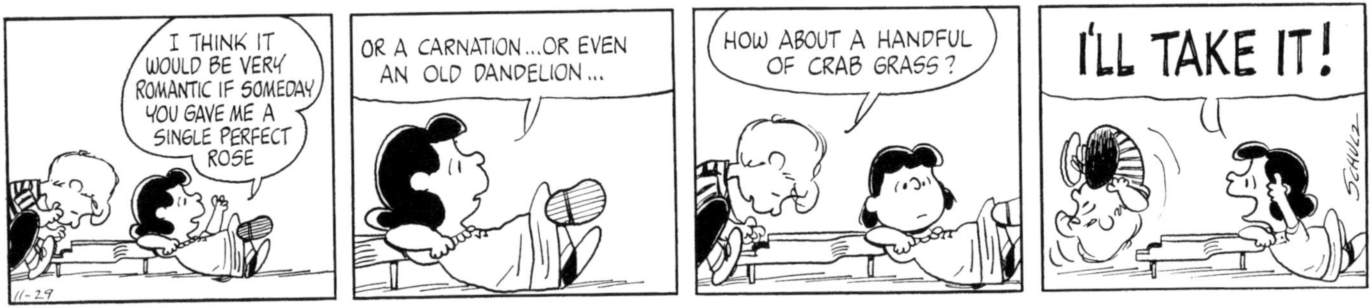
I THINK IT WOULD BE VERY ROMANTIC IF SOMEDAY YOU GAVE ME A SINGLE PERFECT ROSE
11-29
OR A CARNATION...OR EVEN AN OLD DANDELION...
HOW ABOUT A HANDFUL OF CRAB GRASS?
I'LL TAKE IT!
SCHULZ

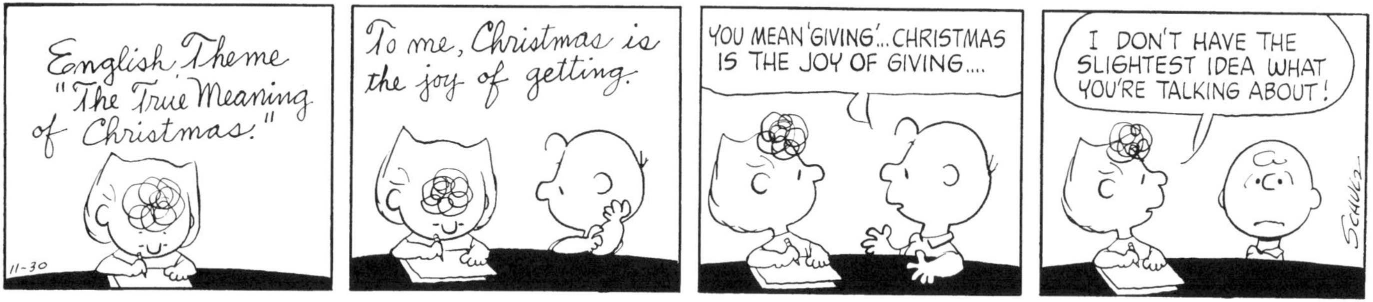
English Theme "The True Meaning of Christmas."
11-30
To me, Christmas is the joy of getting.
YOU MEAN 'GIVING'... CHRISTMAS IS THE JOY OF GIVING....
I DON'T HAVE THE SLIGHTEST IDEA WHAT YOU'RE TALKING ABOUT!
SCHULZ

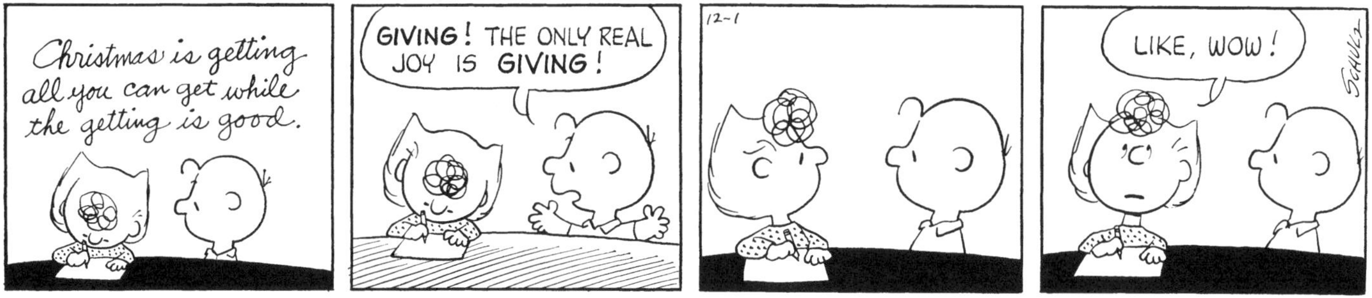
Christmas is getting all you can get while the getting is good.
GIVING! THE ONLY REAL JOY IS GIVING!
12-1
LIKE, WOW!
SCHULZ

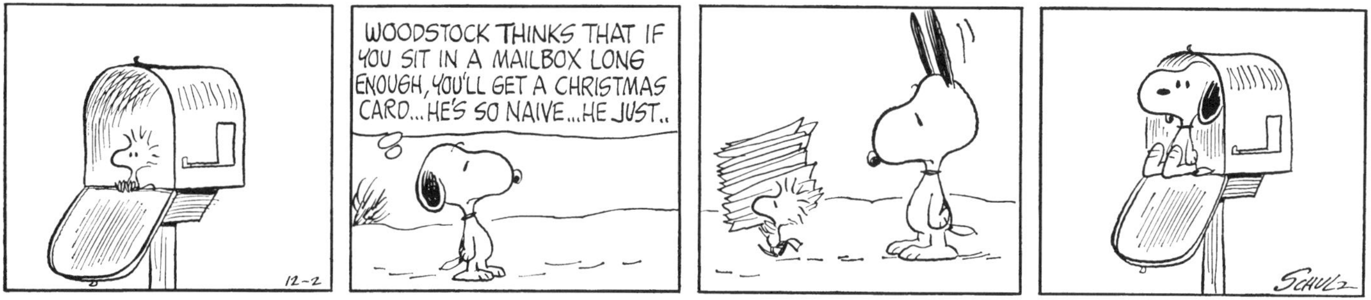
12-2
WOODSTOCK THINKS THAT IF YOU SIT IN A MAILBOX LONG ENOUGH, YOU'LL GET A CHRISTMAS CARD... HE'S SO NAIVE... HE JUST..
SCHULZ

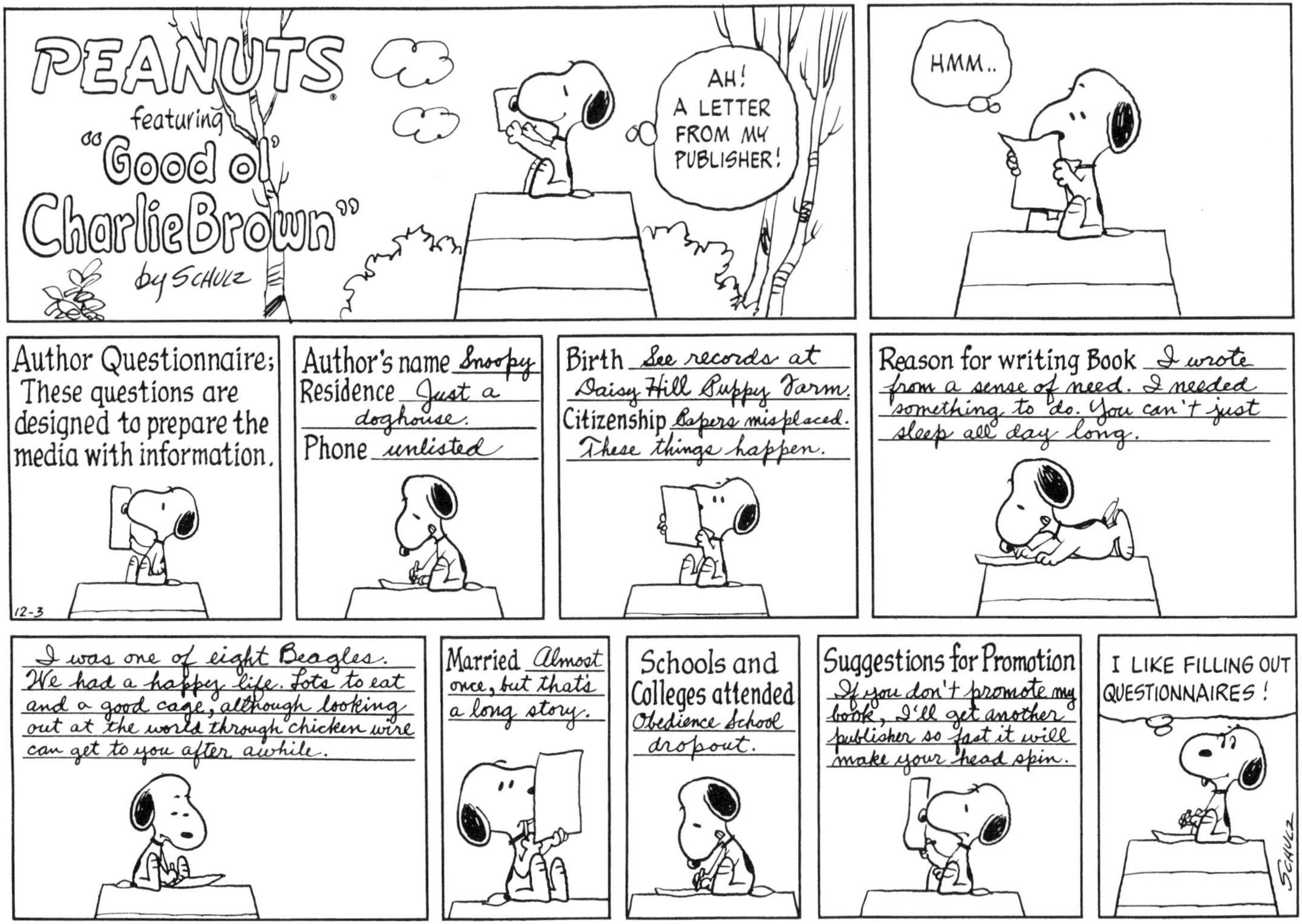
PEANUTS
featuring "Good ol' Charlie Brown"
by SCHULZ
AH! A LETTER FROM MY PUBLISHER!
HMM..
Author Questionnaire; These questions are designed to prepare the media with information.
12-3
Author's name Snoopy
Residence Just a doghouse.
Phone unlisted
Birth See records at Daisy Hill Puppy Farm.
Citizenship Papers misplaced. These things happen.
Reason for writing Book I wrote from a sense of need. I needed something to do. You can't just sleep all day long.
I was one of eight Beagles. We had a happy life. Lots to eat and a good cage, although looking out at the world through chicken wire can get to you after awhile.
Married Almost once, but that's a long story.
Schools and Colleges attended Obedience School dropout.
Suggestions for Promotion If you don't promote my book, I'll get another publisher so fast it will make your head spin.
I LIKE FILLING OUT QUESTIONNAIRES!
SCHULZ

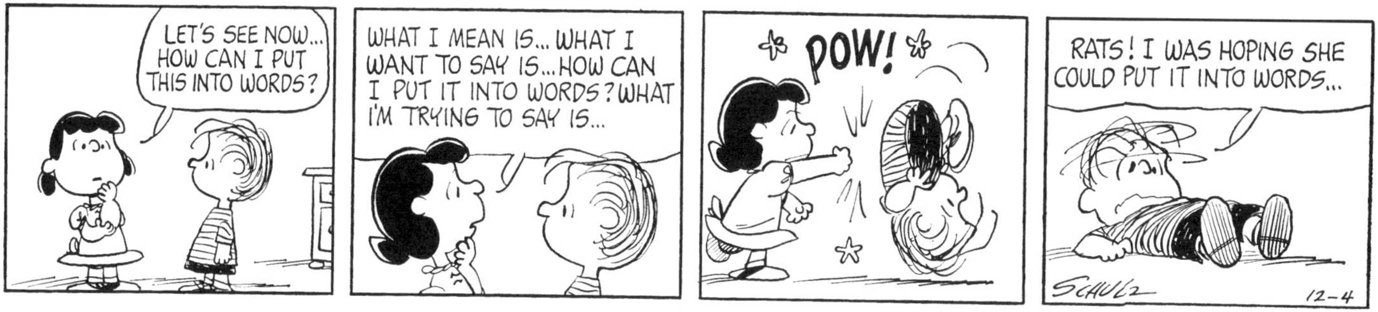
LET'S SEE NOW... HOW CAN I PUT THIS INTO WORDS?
WHAT I MEAN IS... WHAT I WANT TO SAY IS... HOW CAN I PUT IT INTO WORDS? WHAT I'M TRYING TO SAY IS...
POW!
RATS! I WAS HOPING SHE COULD PUT IT INTO WORDS...
SCHULZ
12-4

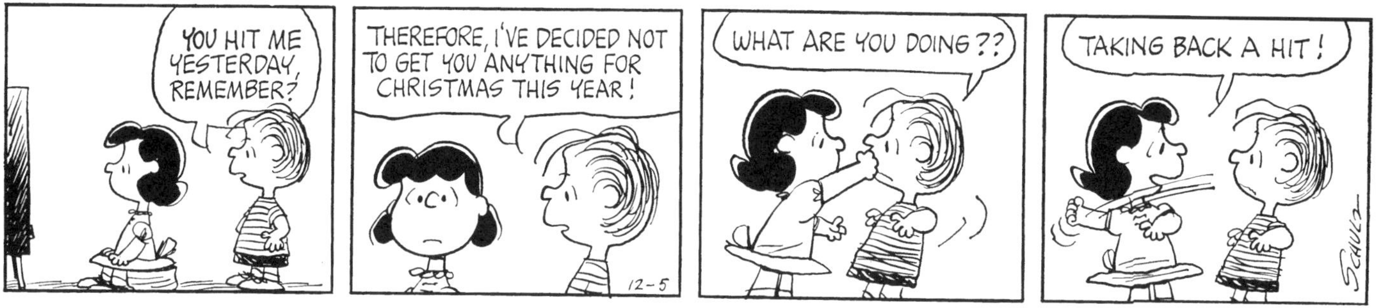
YOU HIT ME YESTERDAY, REMEMBER?
THEREFORE, I'VE DECIDED NOT TO GET YOU ANYTHING FOR CHRISTMAS THIS YEAR!
12-5
WHAT ARE YOU DOING??
TAKING BACK A HIT!
SCHULZ

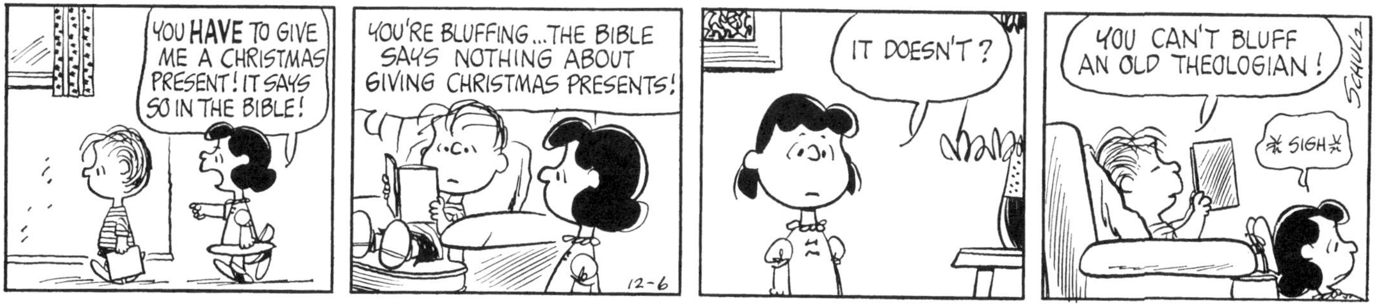
YOU HAVE TO GIVE ME A CHRISTMAS PRESENT! IT SAYS SO IN THE BIBLE!
YOU'RE BLUFFING... THE BIBLE SAYS NOTHING ABOUT GIVING CHRISTMAS PRESENTS!
12-6
IT DOESN'T?
YOU CAN'T BLUFF AN OLD THEOLOGIAN!
SIGH
SCHULZ

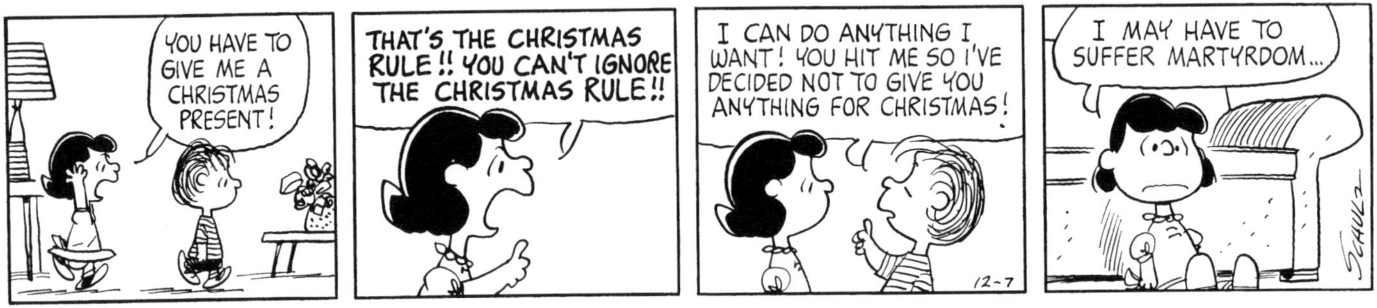
YOU HAVE TO GIVE ME A CHRISTMAS PRESENT!
THAT'S THE CHRISTMAS RULE!! YOU CAN'T IGNORE THE CHRISTMAS RULE!!
I CAN DO ANYTHING I WANT! YOU HIT ME SO I'VE DECIDED NOT TO GIVE YOU ANYTHING FOR CHRISTMAS!
12-7
I MAY HAVE TO SUFFER MARTYRDOM...
SCHULZ

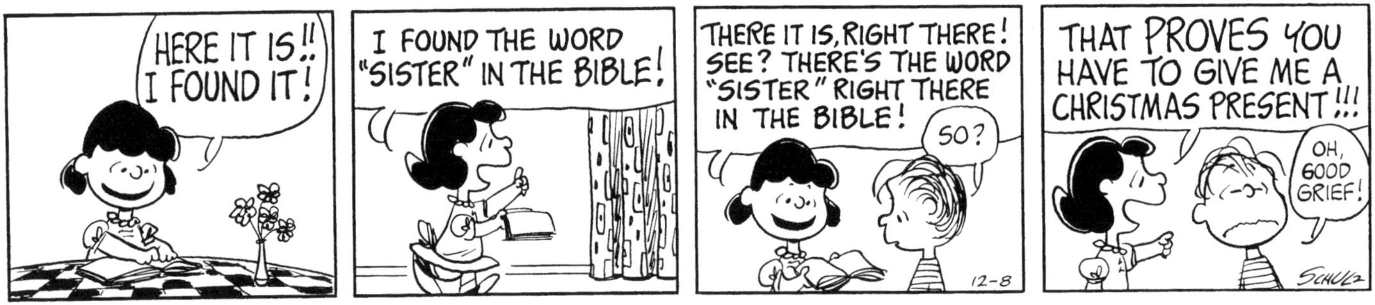
HERE IT IS!! I FOUND IT!
I FOUND THE WORD "SISTER" IN THE BIBLE!
THERE IT IS, RIGHT THERE! SEE? THERE'S THE WORD "SISTER" RIGHT THERE IN THE BIBLE!
SO?
12-8
THAT PROVES YOU HAVE TO GIVE ME A CHRISTMAS PRESENT!!!
OH, GOOD GRIEF!
SCHULZ

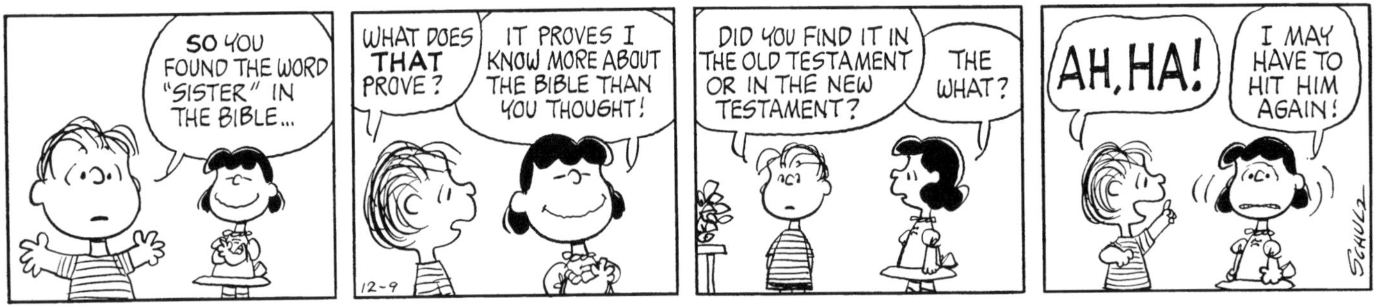
SO YOU FOUND THE WORD "SISTER" IN THE BIBLE...
WHAT DOES THAT PROVE?
IT PROVES I KNOW MORE ABOUT THE BIBLE THAN YOU THOUGHT!
12-9
DID YOU FIND IT IN THE OLD TESTAMENT OR IN THE NEW TESTAMENT?
THE WHAT?
AH, HA!
I MAY HAVE TO HIT HIM AGAIN!
SCHULZ

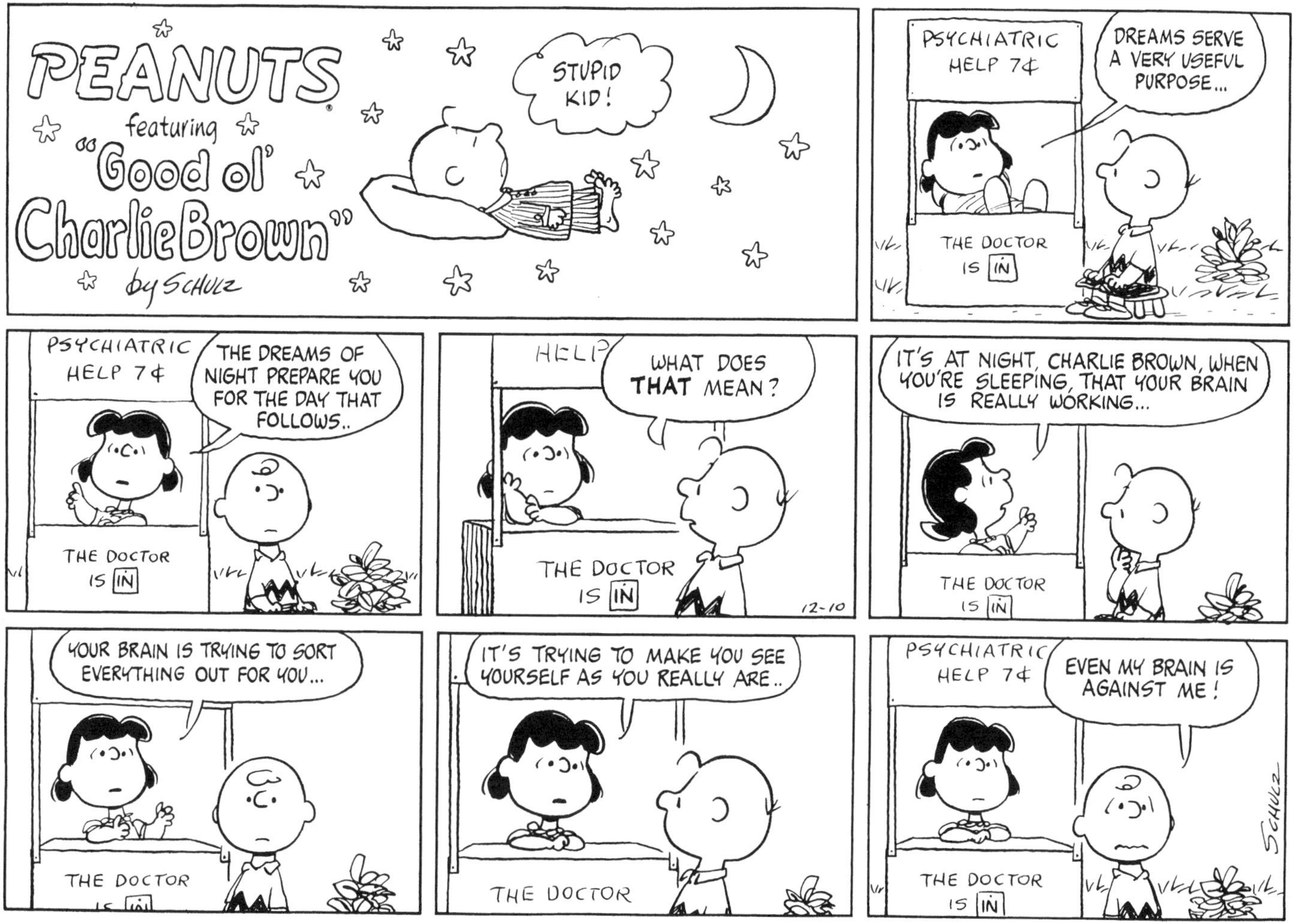
PEANUTS
featuring
"Good ol' Charlie Brown"
by SCHULZ
STUPID KID!
PSYCHIATRIC HELP 7¢
DREAMS SERVE A VERY USEFUL PURPOSE...
THE DOCTOR IS IN
PSYCHIATRIC HELP 7¢
THE DREAMS OF NIGHT PREPARE YOU FOR THE DAY THAT FOLLOWS..
THE DOCTOR IS IN
WHAT DOES THAT MEAN?
THE DOCTOR IS IN
12-10
IT'S AT NIGHT, CHARLIE BROWN, WHEN YOU'RE SLEEPING, THAT YOUR BRAIN IS REALLY WORKING...
THE DOCTOR IS IN
YOUR BRAIN IS TRYING TO SORT EVERYTHING OUT FOR YOU...
THE DOCTOR
IT'S TRYING TO MAKE YOU SEE YOURSELF AS YOU REALLY ARE..
THE DOCTOR
PSYCHIATRIC HELP 7¢
EVEN MY BRAIN IS AGAINST ME!
THE DOCTOR IS IN
SCHULZ

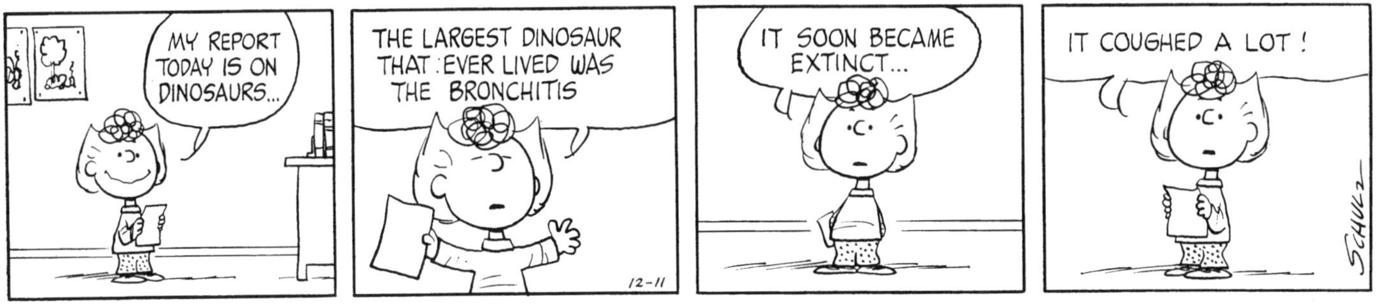
MY REPORT TODAY IS ON DINOSAURS...
THE LARGEST DINOSAUR THAT EVER LIVED WAS THE BRONCHITIS
12-11
IT SOON BECAME EXTINCT...
IT COUGHED A LOT !
SCHULZ

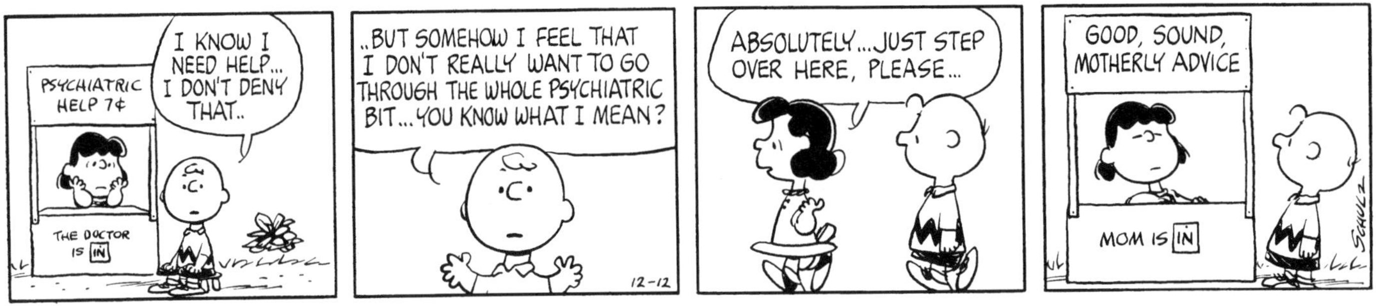
PSYCHIATRIC HELP 7¢
THE DOCTOR IS IN
I KNOW I NEED HELP... I DON'T DENY THAT..
..BUT SOMEHOW I FEEL THAT I DON'T REALLY WANT TO GO THROUGH THE WHOLE PSYCHIATRIC BIT...YOU KNOW WHAT I MEAN?
12-12
ABSOLUTELY...JUST STEP OVER HERE, PLEASE...
GOOD, SOUND, MOTHERLY ADVICE
MOM IS IN
SCHULZ

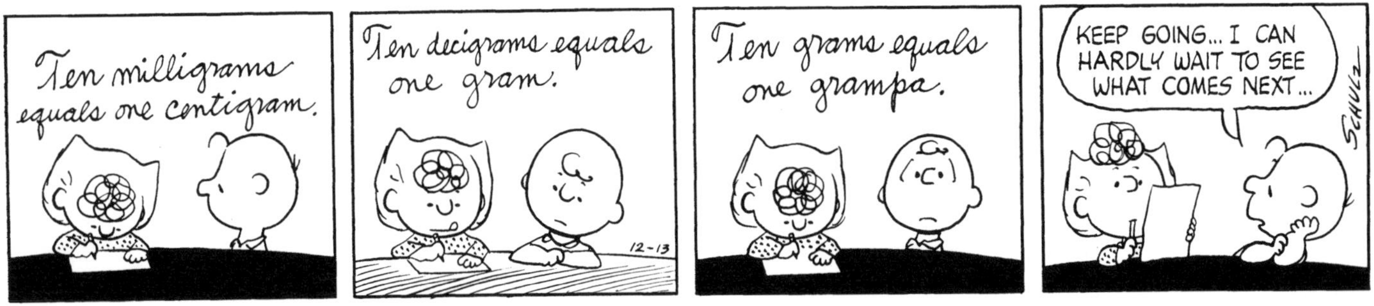
Ten milligrams equals one centigram.
Ten decigrams equals one gram.
12-13
Ten grams equals one grampa.
KEEP GOING... I CAN HARDLY WAIT TO SEE WHAT COMES NEXT...
SCHULZ

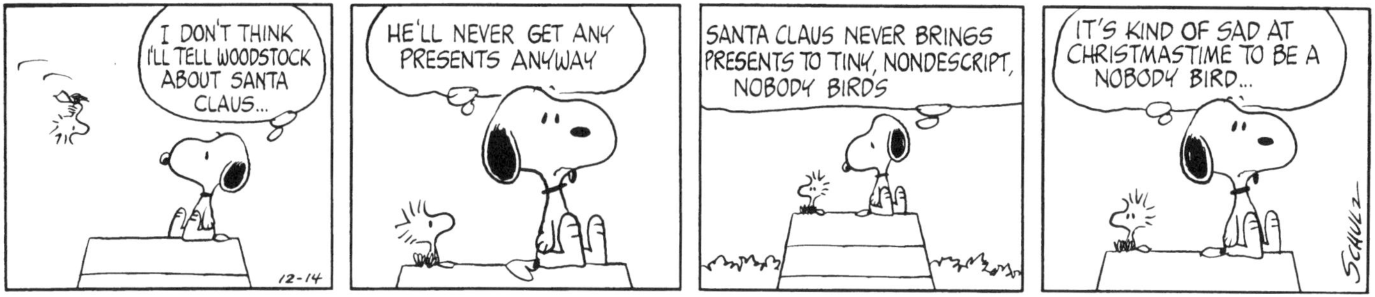
I DON'T THINK I'LL TELL WOODSTOCK ABOUT SANTA CLAUS...
12-14
HE'LL NEVER GET ANY PRESENTS ANYWAY
SANTA CLAUS NEVER BRINGS PRESENTS TO TINY, NONDESCRIPT, NOBODY BIRDS
IT'S KIND OF SAD AT CHRISTMASTIME TO BE A NOBODY BIRD...
SCHULZ

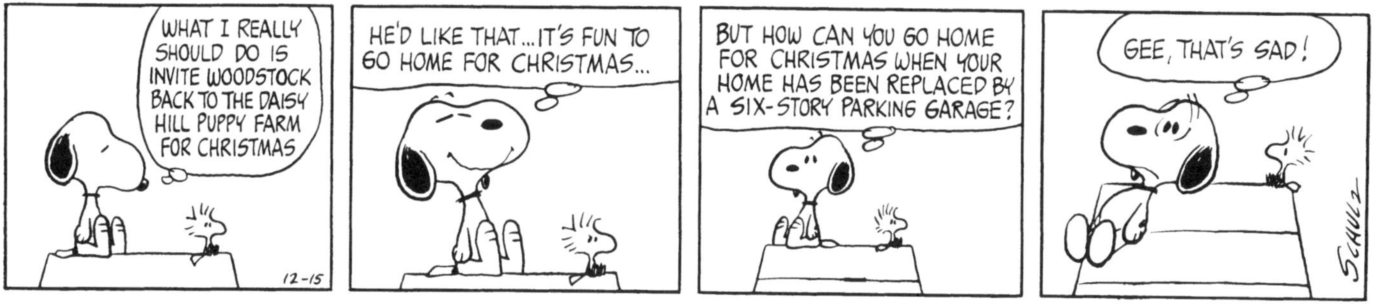
WHAT I REALLY SHOULD DO IS INVITE WOODSTOCK BACK TO THE DAISY HILL PUPPY FARM FOR CHRISTMAS
12-15
HE'D LIKE THAT...IT'S FUN TO GO HOME FOR CHRISTMAS...
BUT HOW CAN YOU GO HOME FOR CHRISTMAS WHEN YOUR HOME HAS BEEN REPLACED BY A SIX-STORY PARKING GARAGE?
GEE, THAT'S SAD!
SCHULZ

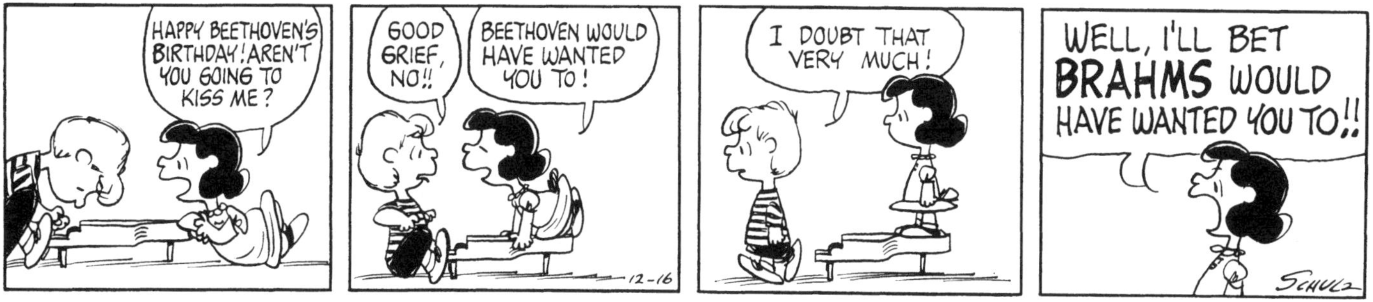
HAPPY BEETHOVEN'S BIRTHDAY! AREN'T YOU GOING TO KISS ME?
GOOD GRIEF, NO!!
BEETHOVEN WOULD HAVE WANTED YOU TO!
12-16
I DOUBT THAT VERY MUCH!
WELL, I'LL BET BRAHMS WOULD HAVE WANTED YOU TO!!
SCHULZ

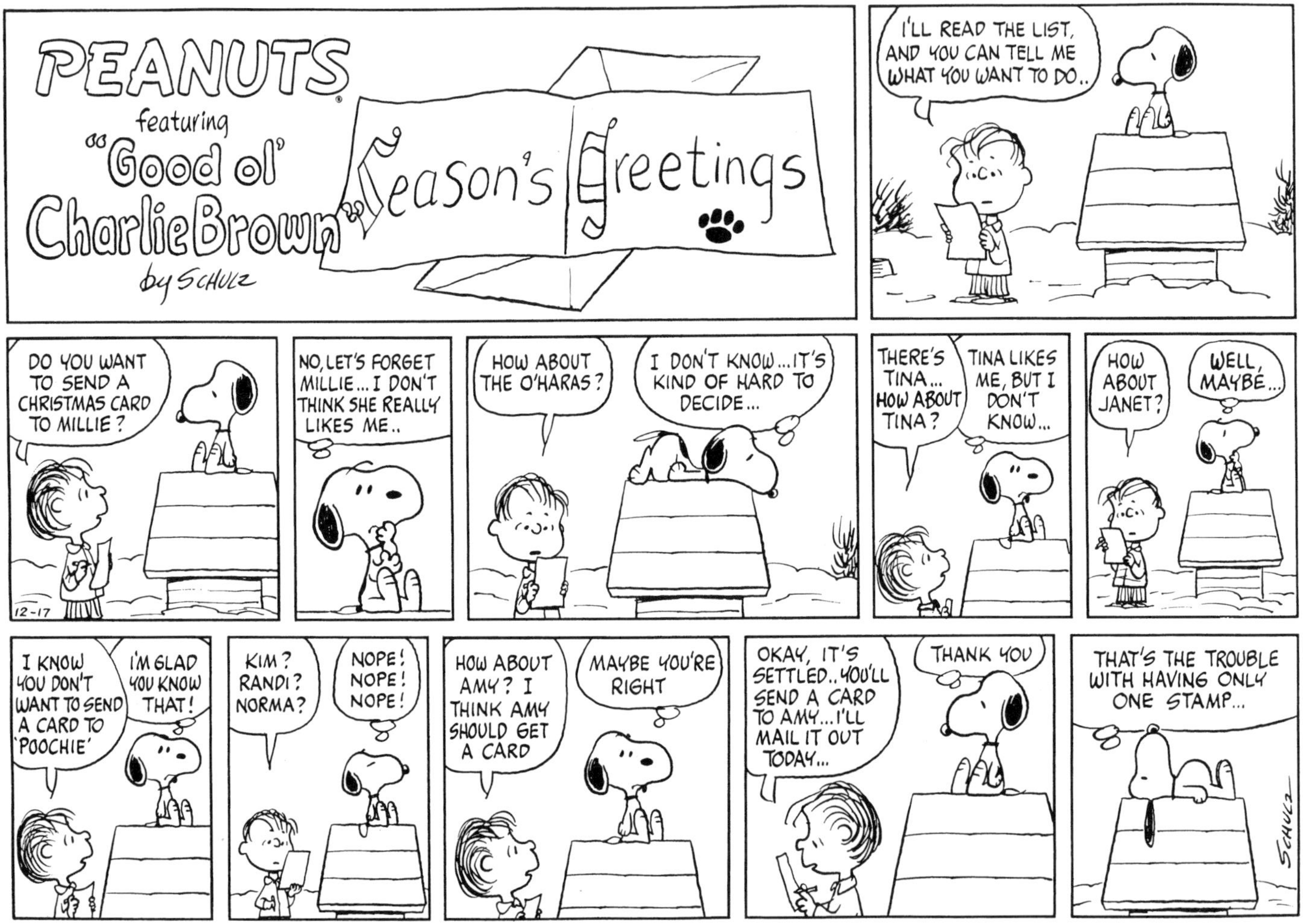

PEANUTS
featuring
"Good ol' Charlie Brown"
by SCHULZ
Season's Greetings
I'LL READ THE LIST, AND YOU CAN TELL ME WHAT YOU WANT TO DO..
DO YOU WANT TO SEND A CHRISTMAS CARD TO MILLIE?
12-17
NO, LET'S FORGET MILLIE... I DON'T THINK SHE REALLY LIKES ME..
HOW ABOUT THE O'HARAS?
I DON'T KNOW... IT'S KIND OF HARD TO DECIDE...
THERE'S TINA... HOW ABOUT TINA?
TINA LIKES ME, BUT I DON'T KNOW...
HOW ABOUT JANET?
WELL, MAYBE...
I KNOW YOU DON'T WANT TO SEND A CARD TO 'POOCHIE'
I'M GLAD YOU KNOW THAT!
KIM? RANDI? NORMA?
NOPE! NOPE! NOPE!
HOW ABOUT AMY? I THINK AMY SHOULD GET A CARD
MAYBE YOU'RE RIGHT
OKAY, IT'S SETTLED.. YOU'LL SEND A CARD TO AMY... I'LL MAIL IT OUT TODAY...
THANK YOU
THAT'S THE TROUBLE WITH HAVING ONLY ONE STAMP...
SCHULZ

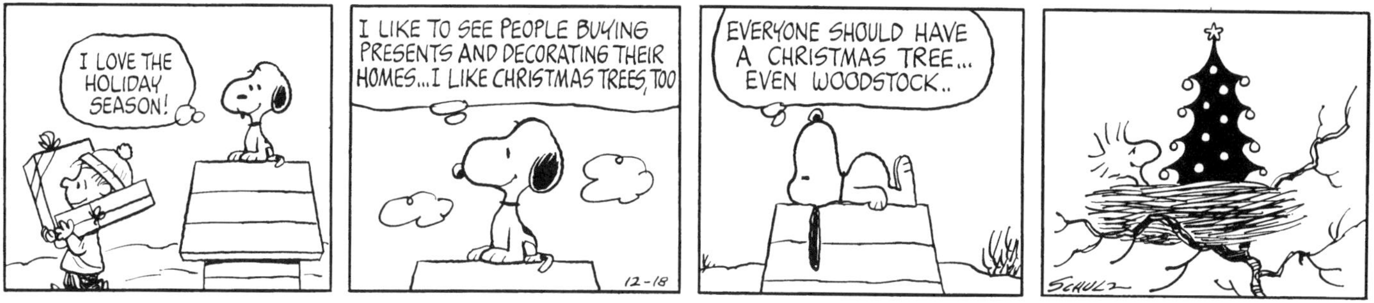
I LOVE THE HOLIDAY SEASON!
I LIKE TO SEE PEOPLE BUYING PRESENTS AND DECORATING THEIR HOMES...I LIKE CHRISTMAS TREES, TOO
12-18
EVERYONE SHOULD HAVE A CHRISTMAS TREE... EVEN WOODSTOCK..
SCHULZ

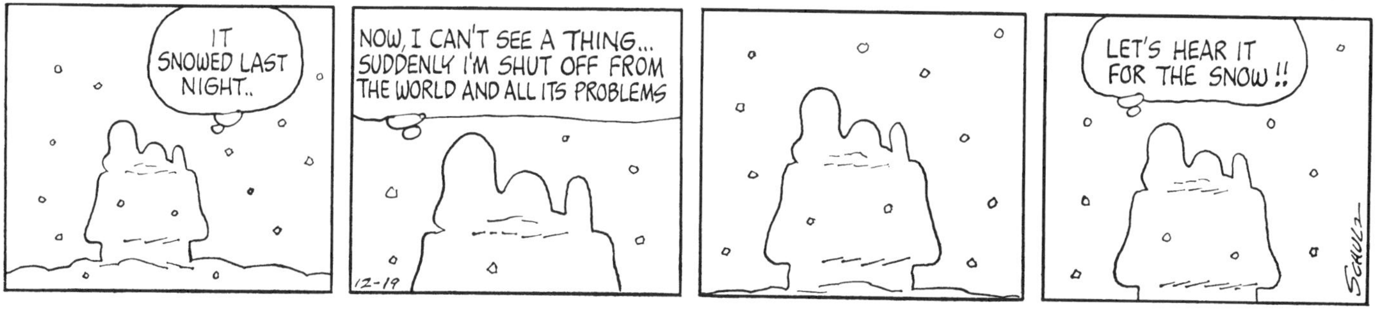
IT SNOWED LAST NIGHT..
NOW, I CAN'T SEE A THING... SUDDENLY I'M SHUT OFF FROM THE WORLD AND ALL ITS PROBLEMS
12-19
LET'S HEAR IT FOR THE SNOW!!
SCHULZ

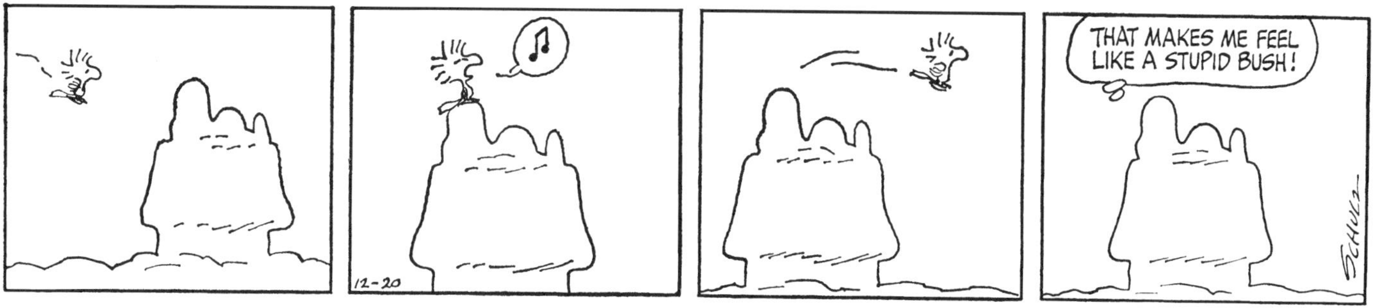
12-20
THAT MAKES ME FEEL LIKE A STUPID BUSH!
SCHULZ

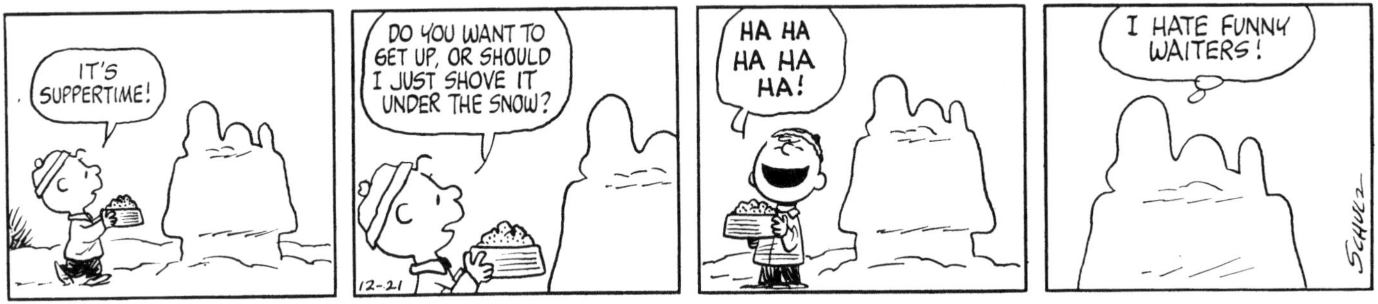
IT'S SUPPERTIME!
DO YOU WANT TO GET UP, OR SHOULD I JUST SHOVE IT UNDER THE SNOW?
12-21
HA HA HA HA HA!
I HATE FUNNY WAITERS!
SCHULZ

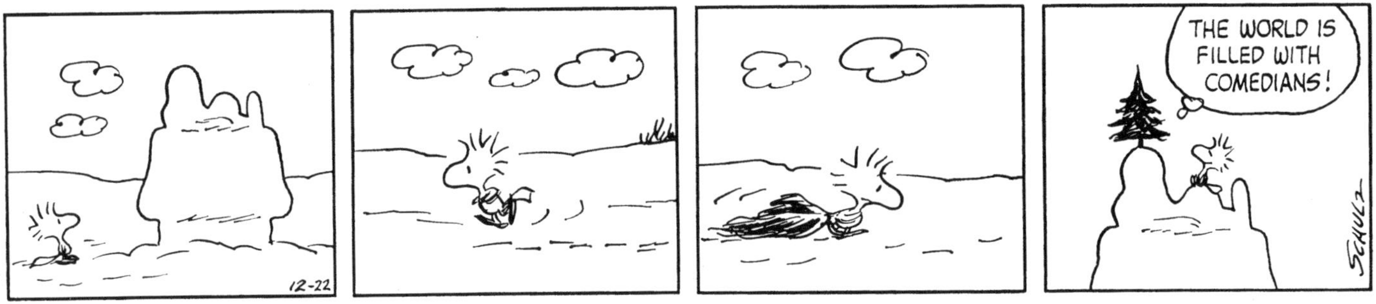
12-22
THE WORLD IS FILLED WITH COMEDIANS!
SCHULZ

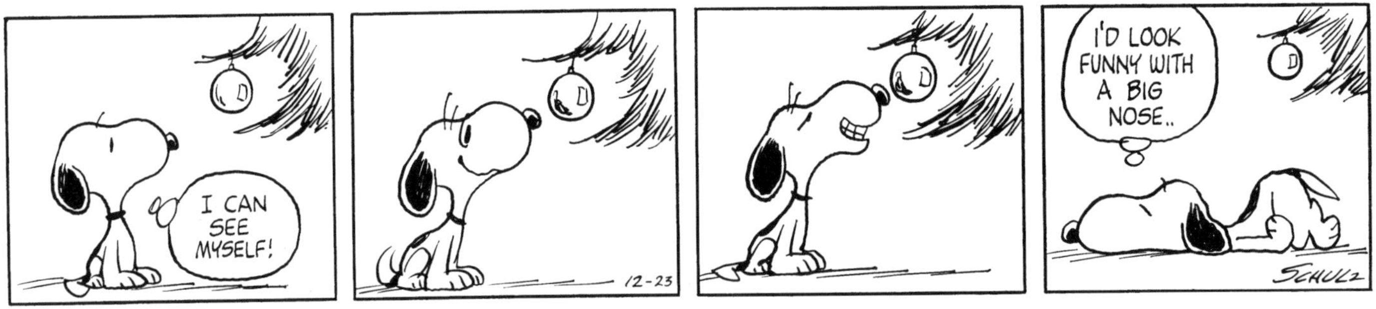
I CAN SEE MYSELF!
12-23
I'D LOOK FUNNY WITH A BIG NOSE..
SCHULZ

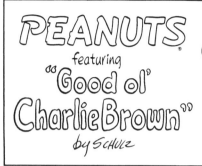
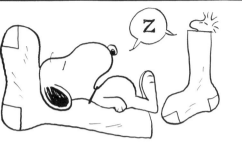

PEANUTS featuring "Good ol' Charlie Brown" by Schulz

Z

POOCHIE?!

GUESS WHAT! YOU GOT A CHRISTMAS CARD FROM POOCHIE!

OH, NO!!

I'LL BET YOU DIDN'T SEND HER ONE, DID YOU?

OF COURSE, I DIDN'T... I WOULDN'T SEND POOCHIE A ROCK!

SHE WROTE A LITTLE NOTE ON THE BACK OF THE CARD...

I DON'T WANT TO HEAR IT!

"DEAR SNOOPY, I HOPE YOU HAVE A NICE CHRISTMAS...I THINK I AM GOING TO BE OUT YOUR WAY SOON...I'LL TRY TO STOP BY...SAY HELLO TO CHARLIE BROWN"

IF SHE COMES WITHIN A THOUSAND MILES OF ME, I'LL SCREAM!

IT'LL BE KIND OF NICE TO SEE POOCHIE AGAIN

SEEING POOCHIE AGAIN WOULD BE LIKE GETTING THE MUMPS TWICE!

YOU'VE NEVER FORGIVEN HER HAVE YOU?

YOU DON'T FORGIVE SOMEONE WHO DOES TO YOU WHAT SHE DID TO ME!

ANYWAY, HERE'S THE CARD..

I'LL BET SHE DOESN'T EVEN REMEMBER WHAT HAPPENED..

THAT WOULD BE JUST LIKE HER NOT TO REMEMBER...SHE'LL COME TO SEE ME, TOO... I KNOW SHE WILL..

JUST WHAT I DIDN'T NEED...A POOCHIE CHRISTMAS!

12-24

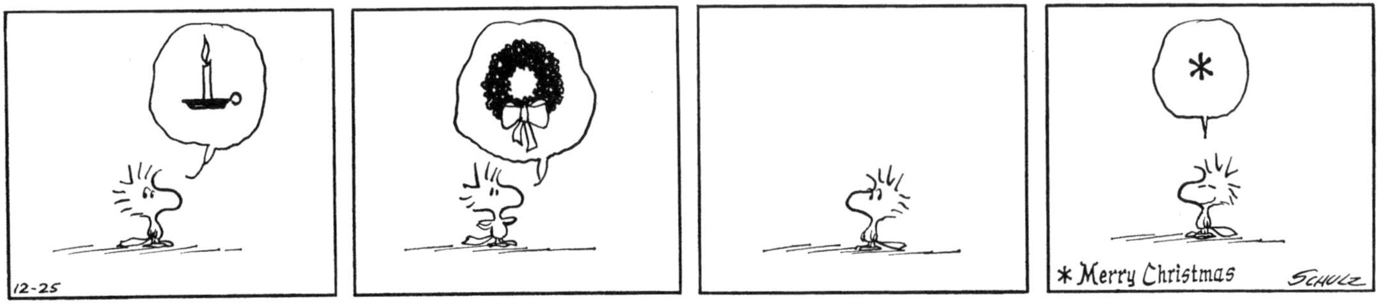
*
12-25
* Merry Christmas
SCHULZ

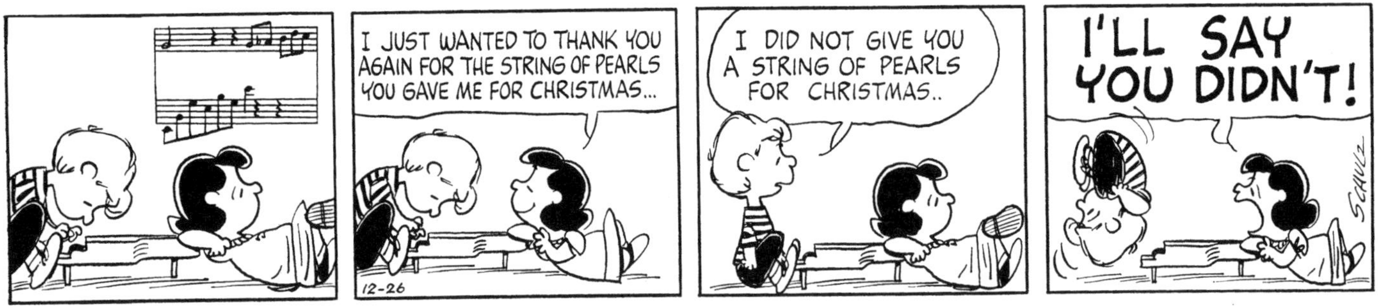
I JUST WANTED TO THANK YOU AGAIN FOR THE STRING OF PEARLS YOU GAVE ME FOR CHRISTMAS...
12-26
I DID NOT GIVE YOU A STRING OF PEARLS FOR CHRISTMAS..
I'LL SAY YOU DIDN'T!
SCHULZ

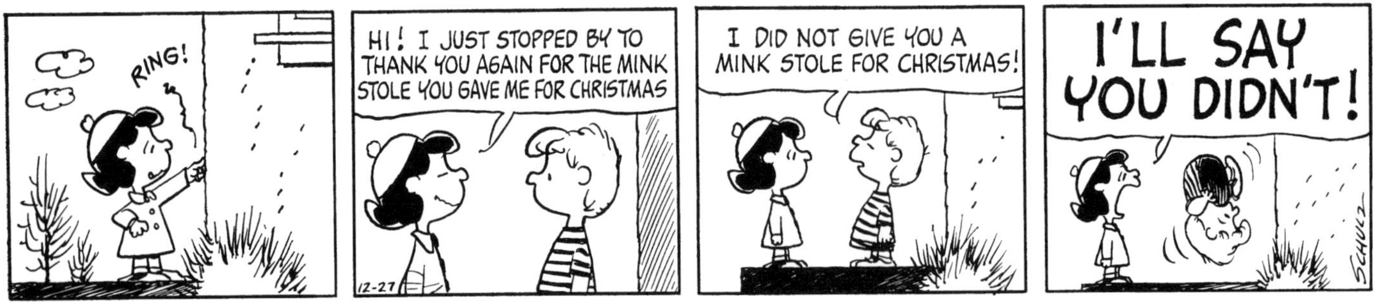
RING!
HI! I JUST STOPPED BY TO THANK YOU AGAIN FOR THE MINK STOLE YOU GAVE ME FOR CHRISTMAS
12-27
I DID NOT GIVE YOU A MINK STOLE FOR CHRISTMAS!
I'LL SAY YOU DIDN'T!
SCHULZ

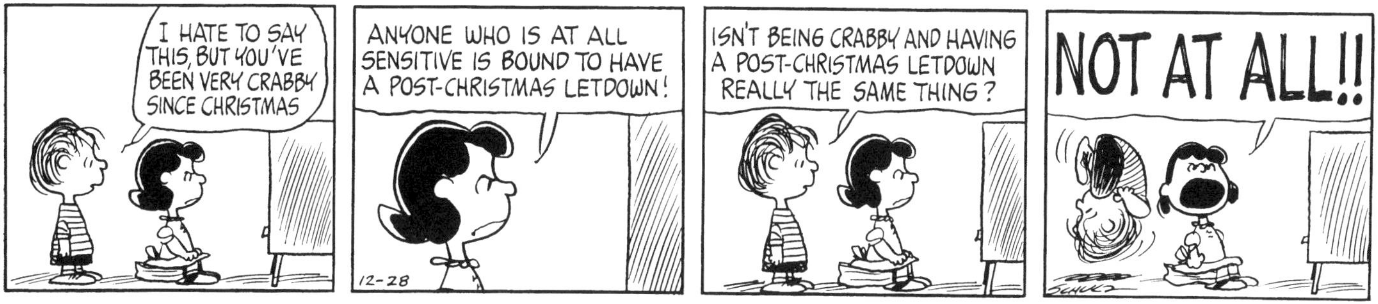
I HATE TO SAY THIS, BUT YOU'VE BEEN VERY CRABBY SINCE CHRISTMAS
ANYONE WHO IS AT ALL SENSITIVE IS BOUND TO HAVE A POST-CHRISTMAS LETDOWN!
12-28
ISN'T BEING CRABBY AND HAVING A POST-CHRISTMAS LETDOWN REALLY THE SAME THING?
NOT AT ALL!!
SCHULZ

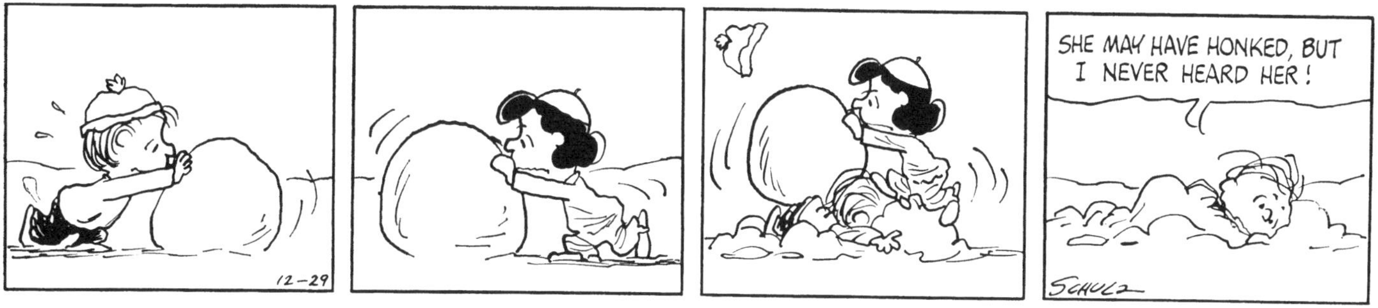
12-29
SHE MAY HAVE HONKED, BUT I NEVER HEARD HER!
SCHULZ

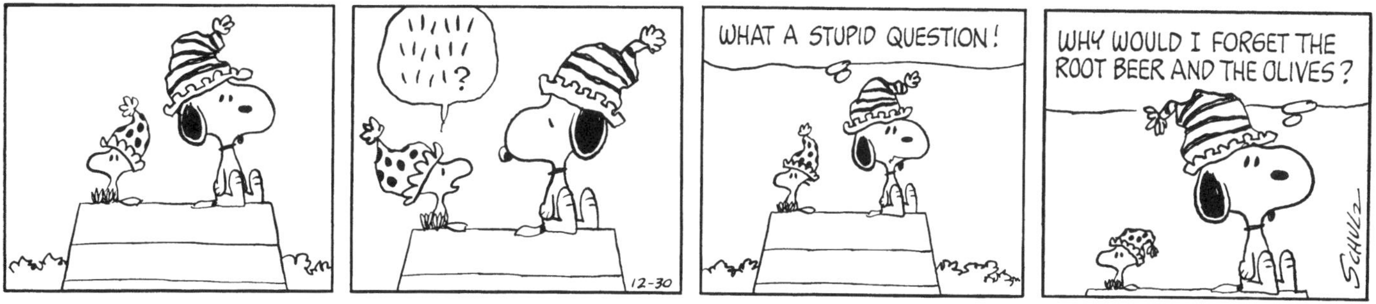
?
12-30
WHAT A STUPID QUESTION!
WHY WOULD I FORGET THE ROOT BEER AND THE OLIVES?
SCHULZ

PEANUTS
featuring
"Good ol' Charlie Brown"
by SCHULZ

POOCHIE'S HERE! SHE WANTS TO SEE YOU

I DON'T WANT TO SEE HER...NOT AFTER WHAT SHE DID TO ME..

THAT WAS A LONG TIME AGO..

I DON'T CARE... WE BEAGLES HAVE MEMORIES LIKE BEAGLES!

"THERE I WAS, AN INNOCENT LITTLE PUPPY, BOUNCING AROUND THE YARD ONE DAY...EAGER TO PLEASE..WILLING TO DO ANYTHING FOR A LITTLE AFFECTION..."

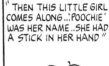

"THEN THIS LITTLE GIRL COMES ALONG...'POOCHIE' WAS HER NAME..SHE HAD A STICK IN HER HAND"

"'HI, CUTE PUPPY!' SHE SAYS. 'DO YOU WANT TO CHASE THE STICK?'"

"SO SHE THROWS THE STICK, AND I, LIKE A FOOL, GO RUNNING AFTER IT..."

"...FALLING ALL OVER MYSELF, BUMPING MY NOSE AND GETTING A MOUTHFUL OF MUD..."

"I GO RUNNING BACK WITH THE STICK, BRIGHT AND EAGER.."

"..JUST IN TIME TO SEE HER WALKING AWAY WITH AN ENGLISH SHEEP DOG!"

I'M AMAZED THAT YOU REMEMBER ALL THAT

HOW COULD I FORGET?

I STILL HAVE THE STICK!

12-31

December

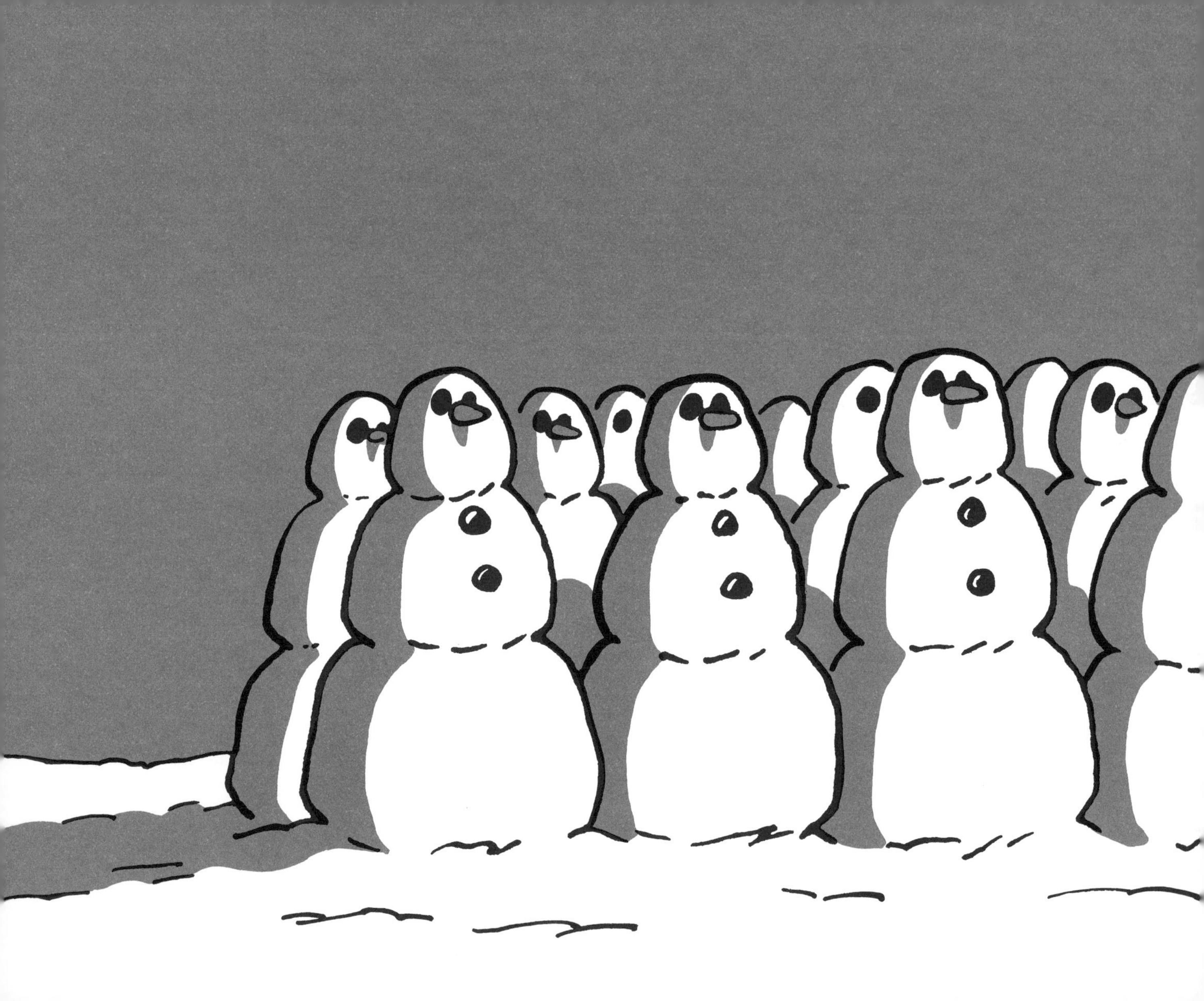

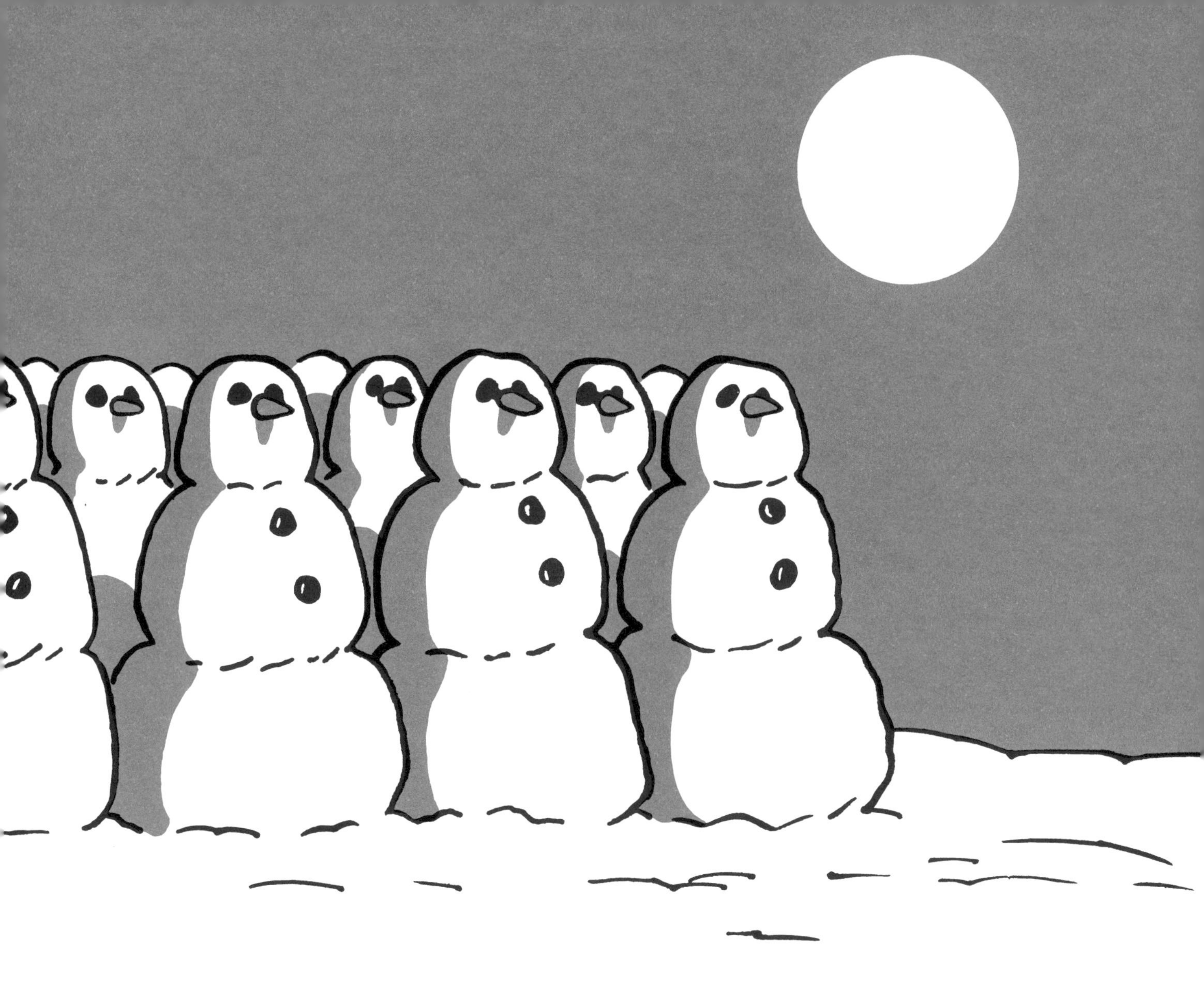

INDEX

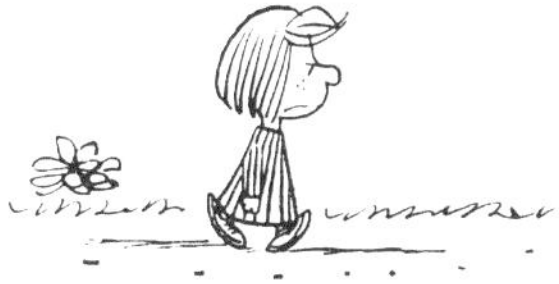

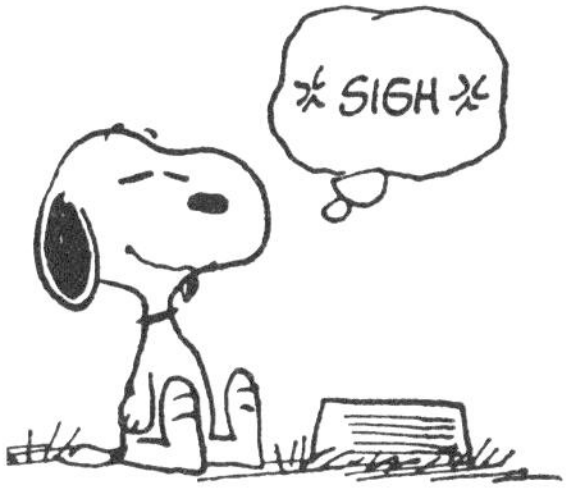
SIGH

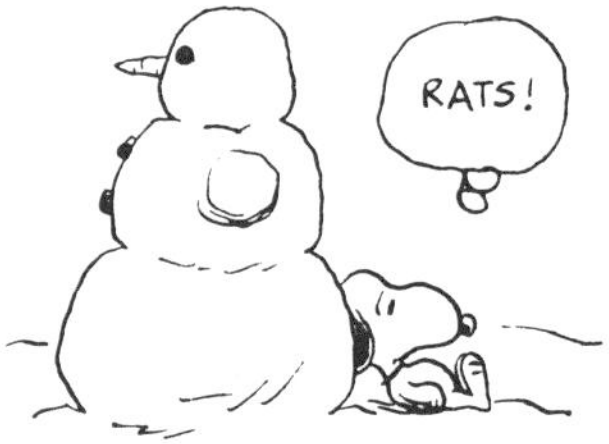
RATS!

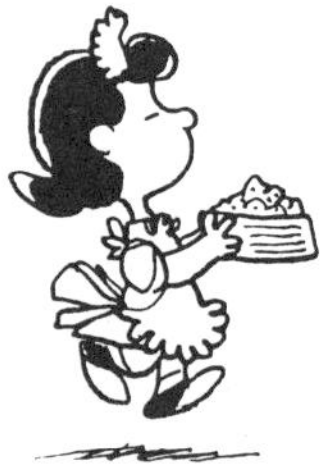

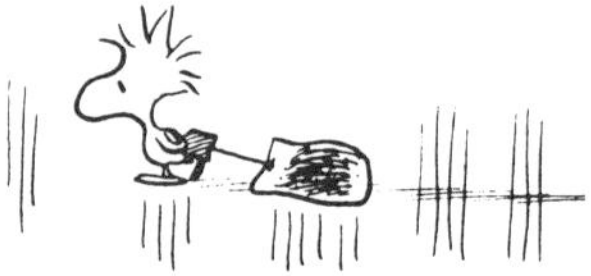

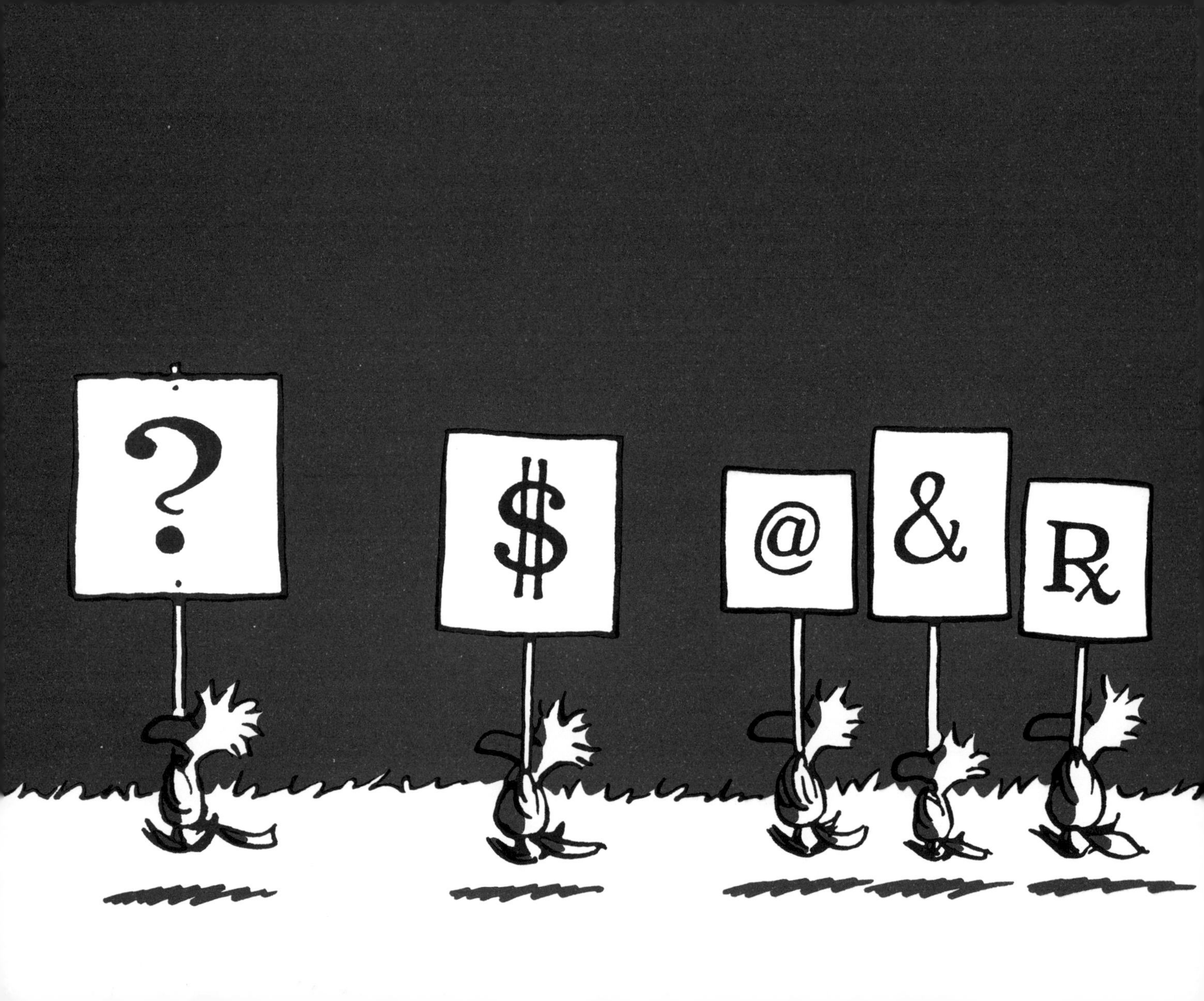
?
$
@
&
Rx

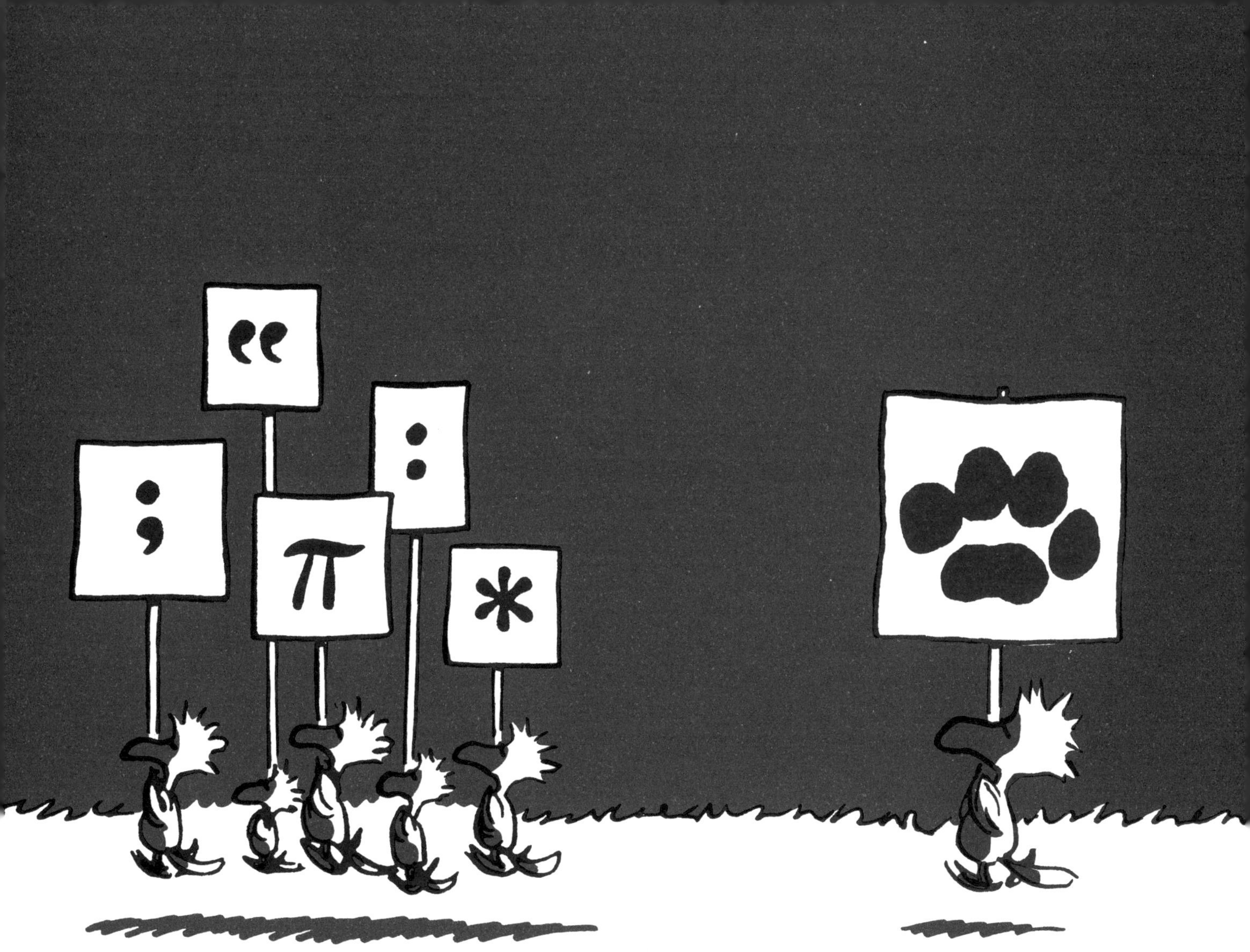

CHARLES M. SCHULZ · 1922 To 2000

Charles M. Schulz was born November 25, 1922 in Minneapolis. His destiny was foreshadowed when an uncle gave him, at the age of two days, the nickname Sparky (after the racehorse Spark Plug in the newspaper strip *Barney Google*).

Schulz grew up in St. Paul. By all accounts, he led an unremarkable, albeit sheltered, childhood. He was an only child, close to both parents, his eventual career path nurtured by his father, who bought four Sunday papers every week — just for the comics.

An outstanding student, he skipped two grades early on, but began to flounder in high school — perhaps not so coincidentally at the same time kids are going through their cruelest, most status-conscious period of socialization. The pain, bitterness, insecurity, and failures chronicled in *Peanuts* appear to have originated from this period of Schulz's life.

Although Schulz enjoyed sports, he also found refuge in solitary activities: reading, drawing, and watching movies. He bought comic books and Big Little Books, pored over the newspaper strips, and copied his favorites — *Buck Rogers*, the Walt Disney characters, *Popeye*, *Tim Tyler's Luck*. He quickly became a connoisseur; his heroes were Milton Caniff, Roy Crane, Hal Foster, and Alex Raymond.

In his senior year in high school, his mother noticed an ad in a local newspaper for a correspondence school, Federal Schools (later called Art

Instruction Schools). Schulz passed the talent test, completed the course and began trying, unsuccessfully, to sell gag cartoons to magazines. (His first published drawing was of his dog, Spike, and appeared in a 1937 *Ripley's Believe It Or Not!* installment.)

After World War II had ended and Schulz was discharged from the army, he started submitting gag cartoons to the various magazines of the time; his first breakthrough, however, came when an editor at *Timeless Topix* hired him to letter adventure comics. Soon after that, he was hired by his alma mater, Art Instruction, to correct student lessons returned by mail.

Between 1948 and 1950, he succeeded in selling 17 cartoons to the *Saturday Evening Post* — as well as, to the local *St. Paul Pioneer Press*, a weekly comic feature called *Li'l Folks*. It was run in the women's section and paid $10 a week. After writing and drawing the feature for two years, Schulz asked for a better location in the paper or for daily exposure, as well as a raise. When he was turned down on all three counts, he quit.

He started submitting strips to the newspaper syndicates. In the Spring of 1950, he received a letter from the United Feature Syndicate, announcing their interest in his submission, *Li'l Folks*. Schulz boarded a train in June for New York City; more interested in doing a strip than a panel, he also brought along the first installments of what would become *Peanuts* — and that was what sold. (The title, which Schulz loathed to his dying day, was imposed by the syndicate). The first *Peanuts* daily appeared October 2, 1950; the first Sunday, January 6, 1952.

Prior to *Peanuts*, the province of the comics page had been that of gags, social and political observation, domestic comedy, soap opera, and various adventure genres. Although *Peanuts* changed, or evolved, during the 50 years Schulz wrote and drew it, it remained, as it began, an anomaly on the comics page — a comic strip about the interior crises of the cartoonist himself. After a painful divorce in 1973 from which he had not yet recovered, Schulz told a reporter, "Strangely, I've drawn better cartoons in the last six months — or as good as I've ever drawn. I don't know how the human mind works." Surely, it was this kind of humility in the face of profoundly irreducible human question that makes *Peanuts* as universally moving as it is.

Diagnosed with cancer, Schulz retired from *Peanuts* at the end of 1999. He died on February 12th 2000, the day before his last strip was published (and two days before Valentine's Day) — having completed 17,897 daily and Sunday strips, each and every one fully written, drawn, and lettered entirely by his own hand — an unmatched achievement in comics.

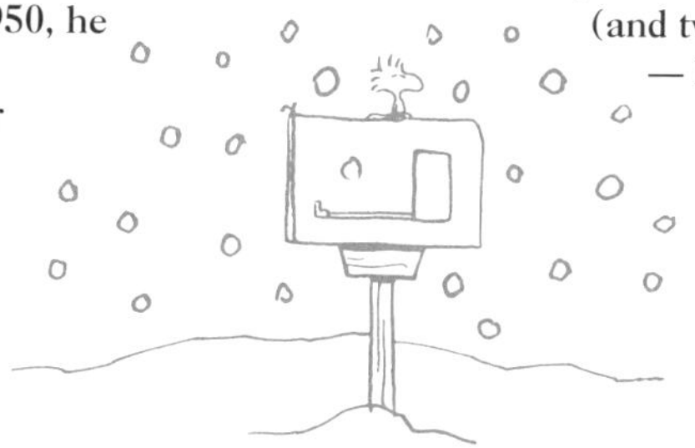

—*Gary Groth*

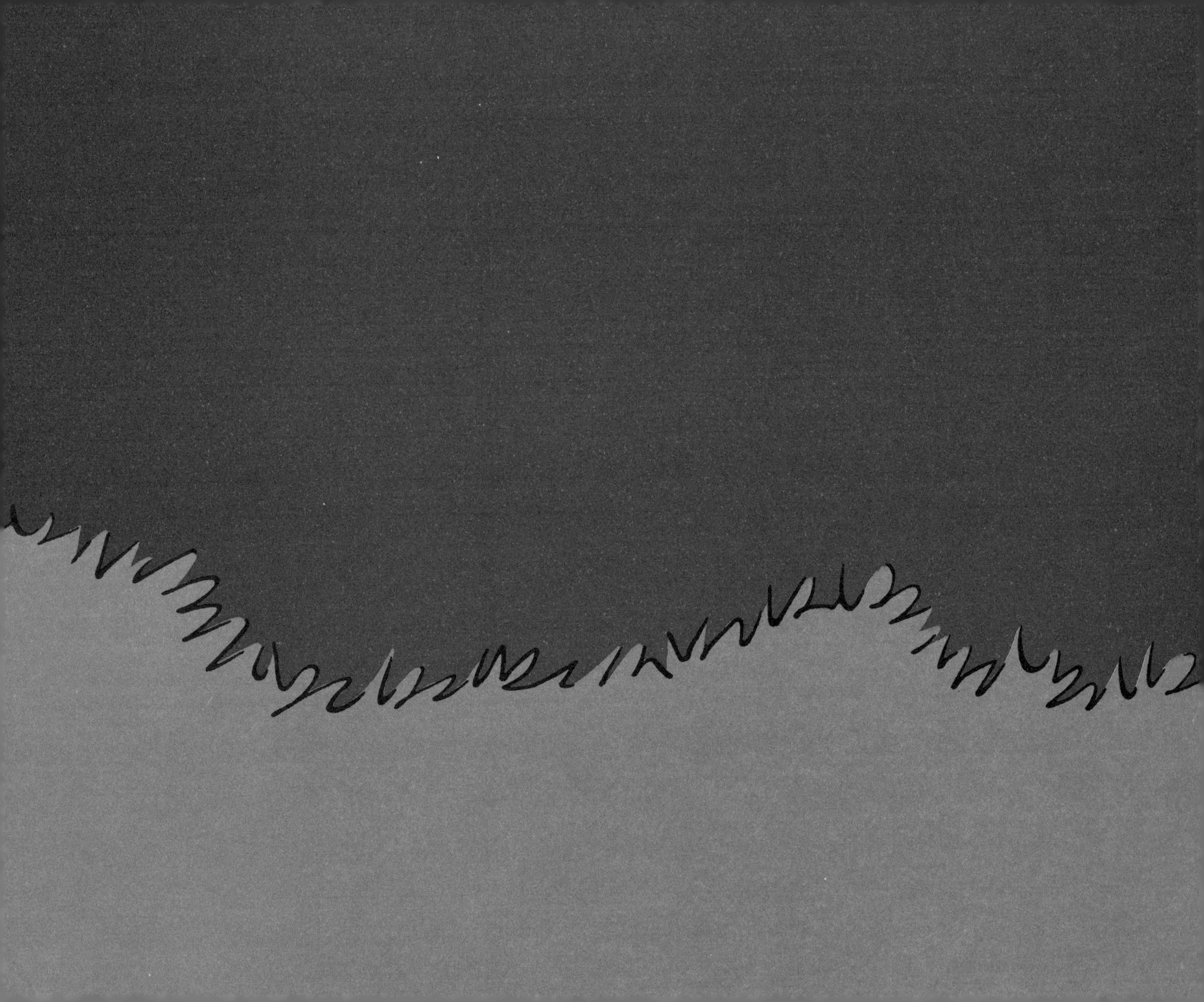

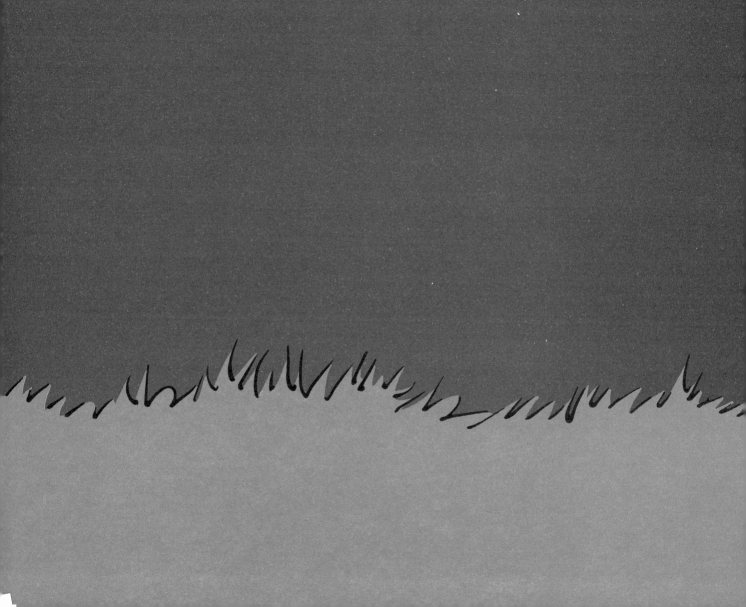

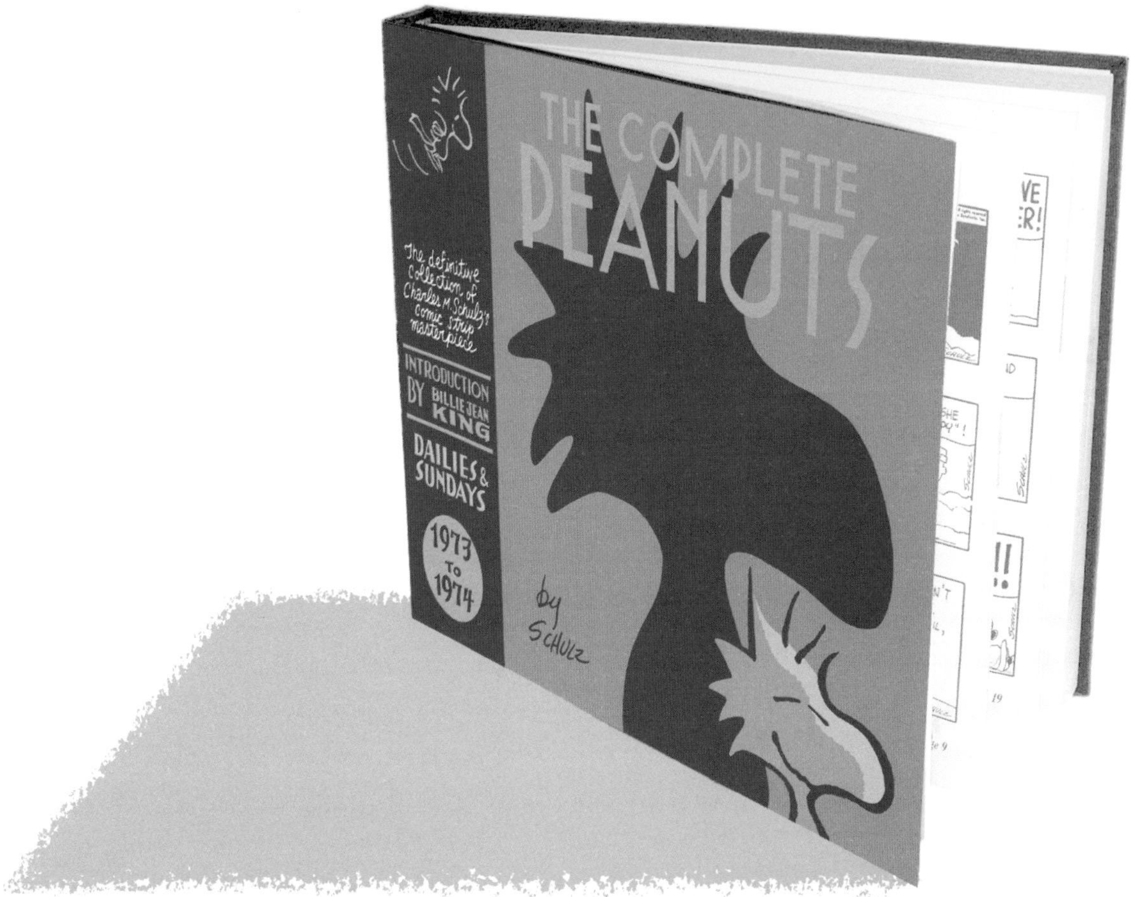
THE COMPLETE PEANUTS
The definitive collection of Charles M. Schulz's comic strip masterpiece
INTRODUCTION BY BILLIE JEAN KING
DAILIES & SUNDAYS
1973 TO 1974
by SCHULZ

Also Available from Canongate: THE COMPLETE PEANUTS: 1973–1974

Lots of tennis, and an introduction by Billie Jean King... readers meet Rerun Van Pelt... and the talking schoolhouse... Snoopy and Woodstock have a New Year's party tiff... a testimonial dinner for Charlie Brown... the "snowman playoffs"... Snoopy becomes a Beagle Scout, a Daisy Hill Puppy Farm Cap finalist, and a one-dog puppet show... all this, and the legendary month-long Charlie-Brown-as-"Mister-Sack" sequence!

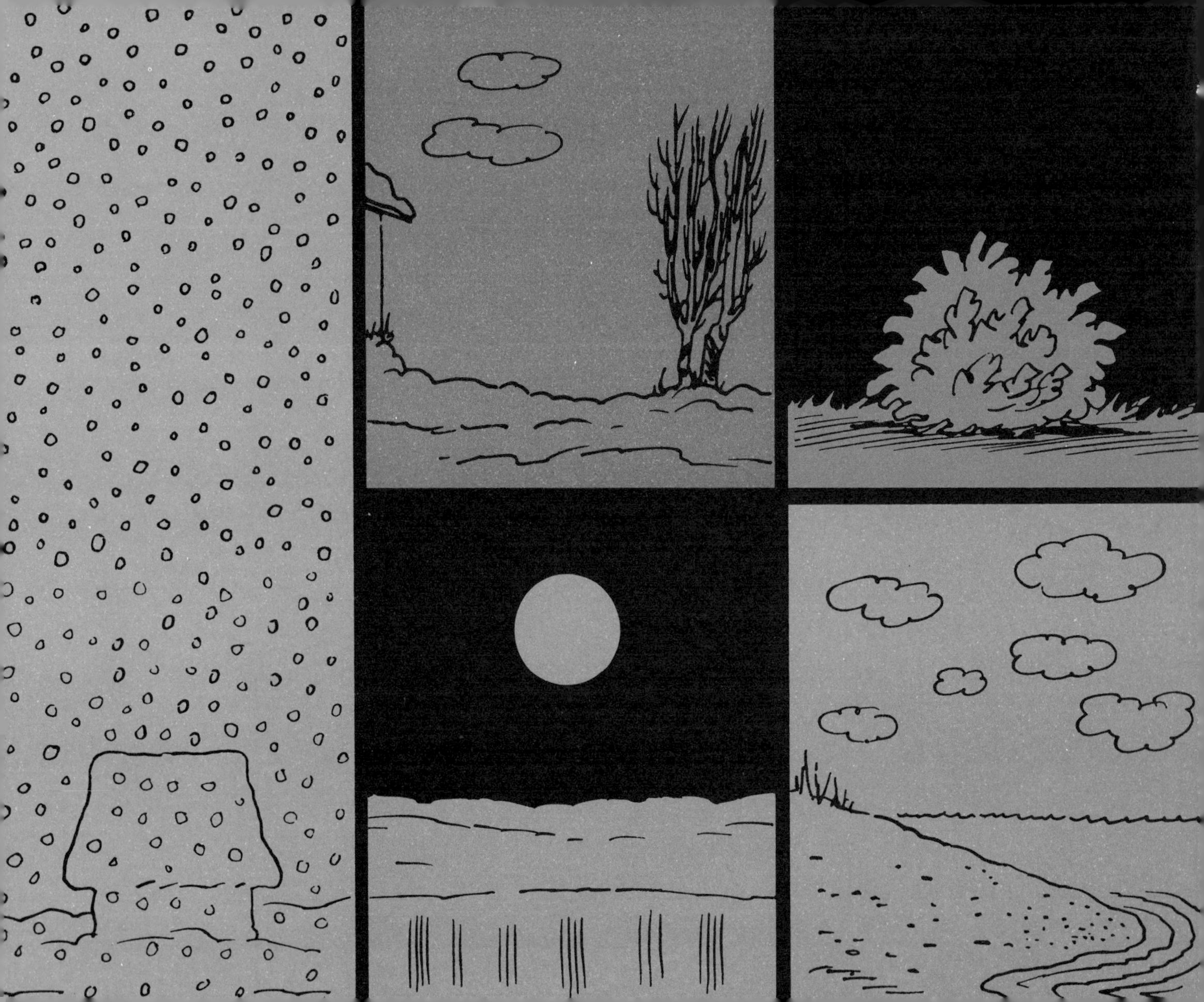